Peter

CATHOLIC SOCIAL TEACHING

Catholic Social Teaching (CST) refers to the corpus of authoritative ecclesiastical teaching, usually in the form of papal encyclicals, on social matters, beginning with Pope Leo XIII's *Rerum Novarum* (1891) and running through Pope Francis. CST is not a social science and its texts are not pragmatic primers for social activists. It is a normative exercise of Church teaching, a kind of comprehensive applied – although far from systematic – social moral theology.

This volume is a scholarly engagement with this 130-year-old documentary tradition. Its twenty-three essays aim to provide a constructive, historically sophisticated, critical exegesis of all the major (and some of the minor) documents of CST. The volume's appeal is not limited to Catholics, or even just to those who embrace, or who are seriously interested in, Christianity. Its appeal is to any scholar interested in the history or content of modern CST.

Gerard V. Bradley is Professor of Law at the University of Notre Dame. He has been a Visiting Professor of Politics at Princeton University, a Fellow of the Hoover Institution at Stanford, and is currently a Senior Fellow of the Witherspoon Institute. At Notre Dame he is Co-Editor-in-Chief of *The American Journal of Jurisprudence* and serves as Co-Director of the Natural Law Institute.

E. Christian Brugger is Professor of Moral Theology at St. Vincent de Paul Regional Seminary in Boynton Beach, Florida. He is author of *Capital Punishment and Roman Catholic Moral Tradition*, 2nd ed. (2014), and more recently, *The Indissolubility of Marriage and the Council of Trent* (2017).

The Law and Christianity series publishes cutting-edge work on Catholic, Protestant, and Orthodox Christian contributions to public, private, penal, and procedural law and legal theory. The series aims to promote deep Christian reflection by leading scholars on the fundamentals of law and politics, to build further ecumenical legal understanding across Christian denominations, and to link and amplify the diverse and sometimes isolated Christian legal voices and visions at work in the academy. Works collected by the series include ground-breaking monographs, historical and thematic anthologies, and translations by leading scholars around the globe.

Books in the Series

Portrait of Leo XIII by August Benziger; drawn during a Vatican Audience on 13 Oct. 1894. From the private collection of the Hon. Joseph Santamaria, Victoria, Australia.

Catholic Social Teaching

A VOLUME OF SCHOLARLY ESSAYS

Edited by

GERARD V. BRADLEY

University of Notre Dame, Indiana

E. CHRISTIAN BRUGGER

St. Vincent de Paul Regional Seminary, Florida

CAMBRIDGE
UNIVERSITY PRESS

CAMBRIDGE
UNIVERSITY PRESS

University Printing House, Cambridge CB2 8BS, United Kingdom

One Liberty Plaza, 20th Floor, New York, NY 10006, USA

477 Williamstown Road, Port Melbourne, VIC 3207, Australia

314-321, 3rd Floor, Plot 3, Splendor Forum, Jasola District Centre, New Delhi - 110025, India

79 Anson Road, #06-04/06, Singapore 079906

Cambridge University Press is part of the University of Cambridge.

It furthers the University's mission by disseminating knowledge in the pursuit of education, learning and research at the highest international levels of excellence.

www.cambridge.org
Information on this title: www.cambridge.org/9781316513606
DOI: 10.1017/9781108630238

© Cambridge University Press 2019

First published 2019

A catalogue record for this publication is available from the British Library

Library of Congress Cataloging in Publication data
NAMES: Bradley, Gerard V., 1954– editor. | Brugger, E. Christian, (Eugene Christian), 1964– editor.
TITLE: Catholic social teaching : a volume of scholarly essays / edited by Gerard V. Bradley, University of Notre Dame, Indiana, E. Christian Brugger, University of Notre Dame, Australia.
DESCRIPTION: New York : Cambridge University Press, [2019] | Series: Law and Christianity
IDENTIFIERS: LCCN 2019001096 | ISBN 9781316513606
SUBJECTS: LCSH: Christian sociology – Catholic Church. | Catholic Church – Doctrines.
CLASSIFICATION: LCC BX1753. C384 2019 | DDC 261.8088/282–dc23
LC record available at https://lccn.loc.gov/2019001096

ISBN 978-1-316-51360-6 Hardback
ISBN 978-1-108-44834-5 Paperback

Germain Grisez (1929–2018)
Joseph Boyle (1942–2016)

Contents

Contributors

Thomas C. Behr is Assistant Professor in Comparative Cultural Studies at the University of Houston.

J. Brian Benestad is the D'Amour Professor in the Catholic Intellectual Tradition at Assumption College.

Joseph Boyle was Professor of Philosophy at the University of Toronto.

Gerard V. Bradley is Professor of Law at the University of Notre Dame.

E. Christian Brugger is Professor of Moral Theology at St. Vincent de Paul Regional Seminary in Boynton Beach, Florida.

Maria Catherine Cahill is Lecturer in Law at University College Cork.

John Finnis is Professor of Law and Legal Philosophy Emeritus at the University of Oxford, and Biolchini Family Professor of Law at the University of Notre Dame.

Kevin L. Flannery, SJ is Professor of the History of Ancient Philosophy at the Pontifical Gregorian University.

Samuel Gregg is the Director of Research at the Acton Institute and a Fellow of the Center for the Study of Law and Religion at Emory University.

Robert G. Kennedy is Professor of Catholic Studies at the University of Saint Thomas (MN).

Patrick Lee is the John N. and Jamie D. McAleer Professor of Bioethics at the Franciscan University of Steubenville.

V. Bradley Lewis is Associate Professor of Philosophy at The Catholic University of America.

Daniel J. Mahoney is Professor of Politics at Assumption College.

Cristóbal Orrego is Professor of Law at the Pontifical Catholic University of Chile.

Catherine Ruth Pakaluk is Assistant Professor of Social Research and Economic Thought at The Catholic University of America.

Ronald J. Rychlak is the Jamie L. Whitten Chair of Law and Government and Professor of Law at the University of Mississippi School of Law.

Martin Schlag is Professor of Catholic Studies and Ethics & Business Law at the University of St. Thomas (MN).

Russell Shaw is a veteran journalist and author.

Christopher Tollefsen is College of Arts and Sciences Distinguished Professor of Philosophy at the University of South Carolina.

Christopher Wolfe is Distinguished Affiliate Professor of Politics at the University of Dallas.

Acknowledgments

The plan to produce this volume originated in a conference held in late October 2013, in Notre Dame Indiana, on (unsurprisingly) Catholic Social Teaching (CST). Several of the papers presented there appear here as chapters; to them we solicited and added the rest. The impetus then and since has been our conviction that, although there is an enormous literature on CST, only a fraction of it is scholarly, and much of that fraction is polemical and often uncritically mortgaged to contemporary ideologies. We believe that a fresh set of rigorously scholarly essays on the key documents and issues, as well as on the thought of popes starting with Leo XIII, will help Catholics and non-Catholics alike understand, and act upon, the perennial moral truths which undergird any just social order.

We are especially grateful to John Berger, Senior Editor for Cambridge University Press, and to John Witte Jr., distinguished Professor of Law and of Religion at Emory University, for including our volume in Cambridge's invaluable Law and Christianity series. We thank also Danielle Mentz for her professional assistance at the early stages of our work with Cambridge University Press; Catherine Smith for her good help on the cover and with the illustration of Leo XIII; and Bret Workman for his efficient final copyediting. Special thanks is also due to the Hon. Joseph Santamaria of Hawthorn Australia for offering us to copy for our front piece the imposing portrait of Pope Leo XIII from the original drawn during a papal audience in 1894 by August Benziger that hangs in the private collection of the Santamarias. Before we sent the manuscript to Cambridge, Pamela Vivolo Bradley scrupulously edited the great bulk of the manuscript and wrangled our authors into timely cooperation on final drafts. Katherine A. Miller, Notre Dame Law School class of 2019, gave the entire manuscript a final proofread, and with Rose L Brugger prepared the tables and indices. We thank each of them.

John M. Finnis, Biolchini Family Professor of Law at Notre Dame and Professor Emeritus of Law, University of Oxford, secured most of the funding and much counsel for the 2013 conference. We are grateful for both, and for his generous contribution (three chapters) to this volume. Professor Finnis has been an irreplaceable mentor to each of us for well over two decades.

Lastly, this book is dedicated to our two dear friends, cherished mentors who were central participants at the conference but did not live to see this volume come to fruition. Germain Grisez and Joseph Boyle exemplified for each of us, as they did for so many others, what it means to be a Catholic scholar. In the words of Saint Pope John Paul II (from his Apostolic Constitution on Catholic Universities, *Ex corde ecclesiae*), they "unite[d] existentially by intellectual effort two orders of reality that too frequently tend to be placed in opposition as though they were antithetical: the search for truth, and the certainty of already knowing the fount of truth."

Abbreviations

Ecclesiastical Documents of Catholic Social Teaching

AAS   *Acta Apostolicae Sedis* (Official Acts of the Holy See)

AP   *Aeterni Patris* (On the Restoration of Christian Philosophy) Leo XIII (1879)

AM   *Africae Munus* (On the Church in Africa) Benedict XVI (2011)

ASS   *Acta Sanctae Sedis* (Official Acts of the Holy See pre-1908)

AV   *Amantissima Voluntatis* (To the English People) Leo XIII (1895)

AL   *Amoris Laetitia* (On Love in the Family) Francis (2016)

AS   *Annum Sacrum* (On Consecration to the Sacred Heart) Leo XIII (1899)

AM   *Quod Apostolici Muneris* (On Socialism) Leo XIII (1878)

AA   *Apostolicam Actuositatem* (Decree on the Apostolate of Laity) Vatican II (1965)

AD   *Arcanum Divinae* (On Christian Marriage) Leo XIII (1880)

AQ   *Auspicia Quaedam* (On Public Prayers for World Peace and Solution of the Problem of Palestine) Pius XII (1948)

CV   *Caritas in Veritate* (On Integral Human Development in Charity & Truth) Benedict XVI (2009)

CC   *Casti Connubii* (On Christian Marriage) Pius XI (1930)

CA   *Centesimus Annus* (On the 100th Anniversary of *Rerum novarum*) John Paul II (1991)

CCC   *Catechism of the Catholic Church, editio typica,* John Paul II (1997)

CL   *Christifideles Laici* (On the Vocation and the Mission of the Lay Faithful in the Church and in the World) John Paul II (1988)

CID   *Communium Interpretes Dolorum* (Appealing for Prayers for Peace During May) Pius XII (1945)

CSDC   *Compendium of the Social Doctrine of the Church*, Pontifical Council for Justice and Peace (2004)

DN   *Datis Nuperrime* (Lamenting the Sorrowful Events in Hungary and Condemning the Ruthless Use of Force) Pius XII (1956)

DF   *Dei Filius* (On the Catholic Faith) Vatican I (1870)

DCE   *Deus Caritas Est* (On Christian Love) Benedict XVI (2005)

DH   *Dignitatis Humanae* (On Religious Liberty) Vatican II (1965)

DP   *Dignitas Personae* (Instruction on Certain Bioethical Questions) Congregation for the Doctrine of the Faith (2008)

DR   *Divini Redemptoris* (On Atheist Communism) Pius XI (1937)

DIM   *Divini Illius Magistri* (On Christian Education) Pius XI (1929)

D   *Diuturnum* (On the Origin of Civil Power) Leo XIII (1881)

DV   *Donum Vitae* (Instruction on Respect for Human Life in Its Origin and on the Dignity of Procreation) Congregation for the Doctrine of the Faith (1987)

DC   *Dominicae Cenae* (On the Mystery and Worship of the Eucharist) John Paul II (1980)

EA   *Ecclesia in America* (On the Encounter with the Living Jesus Christ: The Way to Conversion, Communion and Solidarity in America) John Paul II (1999)

EE   *Ecclesia in Europa* (On Jesus Christ, Alive in His Church, the Source of Hope for Europe) John Paul II (2003)

EJFA   *Economic Justice for All* (U.S. Bishops' Pastoral Letter) (1986)

EG   *Evangelii Gaudium* (On the Proclamation of the Gospel in Today's World) Francis (2013)

EN   *Evangelii Nuntiandi* (On Evangelization in the Modern World) Paul VI (1975)

EV   *Evangelium Vitae* (On the Value and Inviolability of Human Life) John Paul II (1995)

EF   *Exsul Familia* (Apostolic Constitution on Migration) Pius XII (1952)

FC   *Familiaris Consortio* (On the Role of the Christian Family in the Modern World) John Paul II (1981)

FR   *Fides et Ratio* (On the Relationship between Faith and Reason) John Paul II (1998)

FCo   *Firmissimam Constantiam* (On the Religious Situation in Mexico) Pius XI (1937)

GC   *Graves De Communi Re* (On Christian Democracy) Leo XIII (1901)

GE   *Gravissimum Educationis* (Declaration on Christian Education) Paul VI (1965)

GS   *Gaudium et Spes* (Pastoral Constitution on the Church in the Modern World) Vatican II (1965)

HV   *Humanae Vitae* (On the Regulation of Birth) Paul VI (1968)

HG   *Humanum Genus* (On Freemasonry) Leo XIII (1884)

FP   *Il Fermo Proposito* (On Catholic Action in Italy) Pius X (1905)

ID   *Immortale Dei* (On the Christian Constitution of States) Leo XIII (1885)

IDC   *Inscrutabili Dei Consilio* (On the Evils of Society) Leo XIII (1878)

IMC   *In Multiplicibus Curis* (On Prayers for Peace in Palestine) Pius XII (1948)

LA   *Laetamur Admodum* (Renewing Exhortation for Prayers for Peace for Poland, Hungary, and the Middle East) Pius XII (1956)

L   *Libertas* (On the Nature of Human Liberty) Leo XIII (1888)

LC   *Libertatis Conscientia* (Instruction on Christian Freedom and Liberation) Congregation for the Doctrine of the Faith (1986)

LE   *Laborem Exercens* (On Human Work) John Paul II (1981)

LG   *Lumen Gentium* (Dogmatic Constitution on the Church) Paul VI (1964)

LN   *Libertatis Nuntius* (Instruction on Certain Aspects of the "Theology of Liberation") Congregation for the Doctrine of the Faith (1984)

LS   *Laudato Si'* (On Care for Our Common Home) Francis (2015)

LEv   *Luctuosissimi Eventus* (Urging Public Prayers for Peace and Freedom for the People of Hungary) Pius XII (1956)

LF   *Lumen Fidei* (On Faith) Francis (2013)

MCC   *Mystici Corporis Christi* (On the Mystical Body of Christ) Pius XII (1943)

MI   *Mirabile Illud* (On the Crusade of Prayer for Peace) Pius XII (1950)

MBS   *Mit Brennender Sorge* (On the Church and the German Reich) Pius XI (1937)

MM   *Mater et Magistra* (On Christianity and Social Progress) John XXIII (1961)

MP   *Miranda Prorsus* (On Motion Pictures, Radio and Television) Pius XII (1957)

NEN   *Nostis et Nobiscum* (On the Church in the Pontifical States) Pius IX (1849)

NMI   *Novo Millennio Ineunte* (At the Close of the Great Jubilee of the Year 2000) John Paul II (2001)

OA   *Octogesima Adveniens* (On the 80th Anniversary of *Rerum novarum*) Paul VI (1971)

OP	*Optatissima Pax* (On Prescribing Public Prayers for Social and World Peace) Pius XII (1947)
PDMP	*Pacem, Dei Munus Pulcherrimum* (On Peace and Christian Reconciliation) Benedict XV (1920)
PT	*Pacem in Terris* (On Establishing Universal Peace in Truth, Justice, Charity, and Liberty) John XXIII (1963)
PH	*Persona Humana* (Declaration on Certain Questions Concerning Sexual Ethics) Congregation for the Doctrine of the Faith (1975)
PP	*Populorum Progressio* (On the Development of Peoples) Paul VI (1967)
PGP	*Praeclara Gratulationis Publicae* (The Reunion of Christendom) Leo XIII (1894)
QA	*Quadragesimo Anno* (On Reconstruction of the Social Order: 40th Anniversary of *Rerum novarum*) Pius XI (1931)
QC	*Quanta Cura* (Condemning Current Errors) Pius IX (1864)
QAS	*Quarto Abeunte Saeculo* (On the Columbus Quadricentennial) Leo XIII (1892)
QPr	*Quas Primas* (On the Feast of Christ the King) Pius XI (1925)
Qe	*Quemadmodum* (Pleading for the Care of the World's Destitute Children) Pius XII (1946)
QP	*Qui Pluribus* (On Faith and Religion) Pius IX (1846)
QAM	*Quod Apostolici Muneris* (On Socialism) Leo XIII (1878)
QID	*Quod Iam Diu* (On the Future Peace Conference) Benedict XV (1918)
QM	*Quod Multum* (On the Liberty of the Church) Leo XIII (1886)
RP	*Reconciliatio et Paenitentia* (On Reconciliation and Penance in the Mission of the Church Today) John Paul II (1984)
RM	*Redemptoris Mater* (On the Blessed Virgin Mary in the Life of the Pilgrim Church) John Paul II (1987)
RN	*Rerum Novarum* (On the Condition of the Working Classes) Leo XIII (1891)
SC	*Sapientia Christiana* (On Ecclesiastical Universities and Faculties) John Paul II (1979)
SL	*Sertum Laetitae* (On the Hundred and Fiftieth Anniversary of the Establishment of the Hierarchy of the United States) Pius XII (1939)
SQ	*Singulari Quadam* (On Labor Organizations) Pius X (1912)
SRS	*Sollicitudo Rei Socialis* (On Social Concern) John Paul II (1987)
SS	*Spe Salvi* (On Christian Hope) Benedict XVI (2007)
SD	*Studiorum Ducem* (On St. Thomas Aquinas) Pius XI (1923)
SM	*Summi Maeroris* (On Public Prayers for Peace) Pius XII (1950)

SP   *Summi Pontificatus* (On the Unity of Human Society) Pius XII (1939)

TBN   *Testem Benevolentiae Nostrae* (Concerning New Opinions, Virtue, Nature and Grace, With Regard to Americanism) Leo XIII (1899)

UADC *Ubi Arcano Dei Consilio* (On the Peace of Christ in the Kingdom of Christ) Pius XI (1922)

VS   *Veritatis Splendor* (On Fundamental Questions of the Church's Moral Teaching) John Paul II (1993)

VC   *Vita Consecrata* (On the Consecrated Life and Its Mission in the Church and the World) John Paul II (1996)

Introduction

Contingency, Continuity, Development, and Change in Modern Catholic Social Teaching

Gerard V. Bradley and E. Christian Brugger

The impulse (*cupido*) for radical social and political change to which Leo XIII refers in the opening lines of his greatest encyclical had stirred widespread unrest during the pontificate of his predecessor, Pope Pius IX (1846–1878). The abolition of monasteries and convents in France and Spain; *Kulturkampf*s in Germany and Austria, stripping the Church of its remnants of cultural hegemony; and a half-century of acrimonious conflicts with Italian nationalists, including the assassination of the papal minister in 1848 and the pope's daring escape from the Roman mob and subsequent two-year exile in central Italy; a pontificate culminating in 1870 with the military occupation of Rome by King Victor Emmanuel, the historical mega-theft of Church property by the newly formed Kingdom of Italy, and the precipitous end to more than a thousand years of papal temporal rule. Pius's pontificate had been one constant struggle to steady the Church in the face of the more virulent winds set loose by this *cupido* for social change.

Pius's papacy was the last of the dying genre of the prelate-monarchs, popes who not only exercised spiritual rule, but who garrisoned troops, administered secular justice, and governed vast landholdings. Prompted by the historical situation as much as by his own disposition, Leo's was a teaching papacy. The newfound position of the Church in the emerging secular world of nation-states was gradually being clarified. But the winds of social change were no less stormy. The conflict between wageworkers and the "covetous and grasping men"[1] who controlled the means of production produced a powder keg that the early socialists were doing their best to ignite with their goading and powerful social critiques. To the "social question" Leo turned his pen. In doing so, the pope unwittingly inaugurated a potent new tradition of papal

---

[1] Leo XIII, Encyclical Letter *Rerum novarum* (On the Condition of the Working Classes) (1891), no. 3.

engagement with the social and political order, one consistent both with the Church-state relations ushered in by modernity and with Christ's primitive command to preach the Gospel to all nations (cf. Mk. 16:15).

Modern Catholic Social Teaching (CST; 1891–present) can be seen in a sense as the Church's doctrinal pedagogical response to that evolving *cupido* for radical change constantly felt in the world since the Reformation, and at no time greater than the present; a response to its consequences, yes, but also to the desire itself. For it is an alloyed desire, an admixture of good and evil, stemming in the first place from natural inclinations to realize genuine forms of human fulfillment, but marred by a willingness to sacrifice innocence, trample salubrious traditions, and dominate others rather than serve and befriend them. Inasmuch as the desire drives action on behalf of true political liberty and social justice and fair participation in the political order, it needs nurturing and careful guidance. But inasmuch as it drives the destruction or toleration of the destruction of human goods, a reckless resistance to rightful authority, rapacity, and irreligion, it needs confrontation and correction. Modern CST endeavors to offer both. But as Leo makes clear, it concerns itself especially with the way the desire makes itself felt in the economic sphere. For it is in this sphere that earthly subsistence is realized, the toil of work made tolerable, and the leisure necessary to raise one's heart to higher things is bought.

CONTINGENCY, CONTINUITY, DEVELOPMENT AND CHANGE

This text is not a work *of* CST, which – at least as understood by the text's authors – is an exercise of formal ecclesial teaching, usually in the form of encyclicals. Rather it is a scholarly engagement with the 130-year-old documentary tradition. All its authors but one are philosophers, and some are also theologians. All are theologically sophisticated. The combination is important. Although the Catholic Church is a keen observer of human affairs and engages globally at grassroots levels, CST is *not* a social science and its texts are not pragmatic primers for social activists. It is a normative exercise of Church teaching. CST addresses itself above all to moral questions. It reflects upon issues and events *in history* in the light of moral principles and offers guidance for living a Christian life. These principles derive from divine revelation confirmed and assisted by natural reason. Before all else, therefore, CST is an expression – indeed a branch – of moral theology.[2]

[2] Congregation for the Doctrine of the Faith (CDF), *Libertatis conscientia* (Instruction on Christian Freedom and Liberation) (1986), no. 72; John Paul II, Encyclical Letter *Sollicitudo*

If scholarly engagement with the documentary tradition is to avoid the common weaknesses of ideologizing, superficiality, or mere cheerleading, it must engage with four characteristics of that tradition: contingency, continuity, development, and change.

Inasmuch as CST sinks it roots into history, it has a contingent dimension. Social concerns in late nineteenth-century neoindustrialized Europe differ from those of the polarized globe during the Cold War or in the era of biological mastery of the twenty-first-century biotech revolution. Contingency in CST can be acknowledged without fear of ending in a disregard for its enduring contribution to moral reflection.

The enduring dimension – the lenses, as it were, through which the times are assessed – are normative principles. These principles guide deliberation and action to uphold and promote human flourishing, which exists in various forms of harmony within and between persons. The principles of CST, variously expressed and enumerated, are only so many expressions of the requisites of justice. Although these requisites defend and assist innumerable subjects over time, they bear upon a common humanity, a nature that though adaptive in its expressions is in its basic metaphysical capacities *unchanging*. Therefore, CST's principles of justice are unchanging. For example, justice for wage workers threatened by ruthless employers, for members of a community threatened by the global nuclear deterrent, and for embryos threatened by scientists itching for the "greater good" will all share concrete minimum expressions as prescribed by negative norms (e.g., absolute immunity from intentional harm or destruction), as well as positive entitlements prescribed by positive norms (e.g., labor to organize, members of a community to participate in the care for the common good, and new life to be begotten in and through marital intercourse). The expressions of justice vary by time and place; its normative requirements do not.

CST also develops. As new social phenomena evolve (e.g., the rise of the "wage worker") and new threats to human goods appear (e.g., socialism's attack on mediating institutions), the requirements of justice take on greater specificity. For example, Leo's assertion of the importance and rights of associations of mutual support – which he calls "lesser and not independent societies, but, nevertheless, real societies" (*Rerum novarum*, no. 50) – becomes Pius XI's principle of "subsidiary function" (*Quadragesimo anno*, no. 80), and later, more specified still, the "principle of subsidiarity" (*Centisimus annus*, no. 15). Or, again, Leo's insistence in the face of the Marxist doctrine of class

---

rei socialis (On Social Concern) (1987), no. 41; John Paul II, Encyclical Letter *Centesimus annus* (100th Anniversary of *Rerum novarum*) (1991), no. 55.2.

conflict that "capital cannot do without labor, nor labor without capital," that "each needs the other" (*RN*, no. 19), finds more specified expression in the "principle of solidarity" (*Laborem exercens*, no. 8). CST presents multiple instances where, as social reflection matures, a particular requirement of justice at a later stage is seen to be the specification of what was earlier recognized in a less developed form, "differing from itself," as Newman says, "only as what is young differs from what is mature."[3]

Finally, CST is subject to change in at least three ways with regard to its contingent teaching. The first and most obvious is in its objects. For example, the "social question" addressed by both Leo in *Rerum* (1891) and Pius XI in *Quadragesimo anno* (1931) distinctly concerns establishing just conditions in the relations between workers and management. The social question changes after World War II to a global focus concerned with just conditions between nations.[4] Secondly, because reflections in earlier documents are found to have transient value, we do not find them reaffirmed in later texts. For example, the earnest confidence at the time of Vatican II in the fitness of international organizations such as the UN for safeguarding human rights and affirming human dignity is replaced by bitter criticism and calls for reform of the same organizations by John Paul II and Benedict XVI.[5] And thirdly, CST has weaknesses not yet recognized that should be – or so we will argue – altered or dropped; for example, ambiguity about its scope or subject-matter, insufficient attention to the dependence upon empirical and other contingent factors inherent in any justice consideration, inappropriate assumptions about who it is that has primary responsibility for undertaking such considerations, and deciding how to effectuate the resulting moral judgments.

THE TEXT

Our twenty-three chapters are divided over four thematic parts. The two chapters of Part I examine questions that serve as historical background to

---

[3] J. H. Newman, *An Essay on the Development of Christian Doctrine* (South Bend, IN: University of Notre Dame Press, 1994), 163.

[4] See John XXIII, Encyclical Letter *Mater et magistra* (Christianity and Social Progress) (1961), no. 122; Vatican II, Pastoral Constitution *Gaudium et spes* (On the Church in the Modern World) (1965), nos. 6, 8, 29; Paul VI, Encyclical Letter *Populorum progressio* (On the Development of Peoples) (1967), no. 3; Benedict XVI, Encyclical Letter *Caritas in veritate* (On Integral Human Development in Charity and Truth) (2009), no. 13.

[5] See John XXIII, *PT*, nos. 142–145; Vatican II, *GS*, no. 84; John Paul II, *Letter to Nafis Sadik, Executive Director of the United Nations Population Fund, on Preparations for the 1994 Cairo Conference on Population and Development*, no. 10 (March 18, 1994), AAS 87 (1995), pp. 190–196; Benedict XVI, *CV*, no. 67.

modern CST. In Chapter 1 John Finnis asks how the ideas of Aquinas on moral, political, and economic theory are foundational for CST, how Aquinas's ideas – which explicitly take center stage in Pope Leo's harbinger document – can be seen as the most enduring ideas in the modern tradition. Thomas Behr (ch. 2) looks at how the teachings on church, state, and political liberalism of Pius IX (r. 1846–1878) and Leo XIII (r. 1878–1903) as well as the changing sociopolitical situation of the Church in nineteenth-century Europe prepare for *Rerum novarum*.

The seven chapters of Part II examine the most important texts of CST from the pontificates of Leo XIII to Francis. Joseph Boyle (ch. 3) begins with Leo's seminal text. He explicates the main lines of *Rerum's* moral assessments and reasoning, its central conclusions, and the purposes Leo had in writing it.

The following six chapters take a synoptic look at *Rerum's* successors. Samuel Gregg (ch. 4) considers Pius XI's *Quadragesimo anno* (1931); Ronald J. Rychlak (ch. 5) the social teachings of Pius XII (r. 1939–1958); V. Bradley Lewis (ch. 6) four interrelated documents published in close succession, John XXIII's *Mater et magistra* (1961) and *Pacem in terris* (1963), Vatican II's *Gaudium et spes* (1965), and Paul VI's *Populorum progressio* (1967); Patrick Lee (ch. 7) the three great social documents of John Paul II, *Laborem exercens* (1981), *Sollicitudo rei socialis* (1987), and *Centesimus annus* (1991); Brian Benestad (ch. 8) both papal and prepapal writings of Benedict XVI (Joseph Ratzinger), including *Caritas in veritate* (2009) and the CDF Instructions on Liberation Theology, *Libertatis nuntius* (1984) and *Libertatis conscientia* (1986); and Daniel Mahoney (ch. 9) the social teaching of Francis. Each author examines what was new in the texts under consideration, whether newness affects authoritativeness, what if anything seems of transient value, and what from prior texts has been abandoned.

Part III, the largest, is composed of thirteen chapters, each analyzing a key theme in CST. V. Bradley Lewis (ch. 10) tackles the foundational concept of the political common good. He asks how it develops from *Rerum* (1891) to *Laudato si'* (2015); what the strengths and weakness are of that development; and what further developments are needed. Cristóbal Orrego (ch. 11) examines the foundational Christian understanding of goods and ownership referred to as the "principle of the universal destination of the world's resources" and considers why it is complementary and not contradictory to the right to private property. Christopher Tollefsen (ch. 12) questions what has become of Vatican II's important doctrine of the apostolate *of* the laity envisaged in the underread Decree *Actuositatem apostolicam* (1965) and elaborated in John Paul II's extraordinary Apostolic Exhortation *Christifideles laici* (1988). In Chapter 13, John Finnis examines the concepts of the international common good and supra-national authority. He asks what in "globalization" is to be welcomed and promoted, and what resisted (for example, in view of the duty of citizens and public authorities to promote their own familial and civic associations and national culture)? Is Catholic Social Teaching abandoning or substantially modifying its teaching about nations? What is being said – and what should be said – about world government or governance? Christopher Wolfe (ch. 14) assesses whether CST is vulnerable to misuse in the justification of abuse of government power. Is its recognition of the failures of economic systems to achieve their goals – especially unrestricted capitalism – matched by an equal sensitivity to the failure of political systems to achieve their goals? Kevin Flannery, SJ (ch. 15) wades into the turbulent waters of immigration. He examines CST's moral principles governing the development of immigration policies. Does CST balance its treatments of the rights and duties of migrants and the rights and duties of host nations? Robert Kenney (ch. 16) takes up the topic of international finance. He asks what moral principles govern the monetary and macroeconomic relations between nations. How does CST balance its teaching on the rights and duties of developing nations versus the rights and duties of more prosperous nations? What roles should be played by international financial institutions such as the World Bank and the IMF? Maria Cahill (ch. 17) examines the nature and importance of the "principle of subsidiarity," the context for its introduction into the documentary tradition, its antecedents in Catholic theology, and how it can be developed. Catherine Pakulak (ch. 18) considers the important role that the competing economic systems of capitalism and socialism play in CST. In what way is the whole modern tradition a response to these two systems? Has that response been effective? What weaknesses arise in the tradition's treatment of the two because of an inadequate understanding of economics? How could its treatment be improved? Fr. Martin Schlag (ch. 19) looks at the "preferential option for the poor," its antecedents in Catholic tradition, the social conditions giving rise to its introduction into CST, its early and mature formulations, the strengths and weaknesses of those formulations, whether the weaknesses arise because of an inadequate understanding of social conditions or theological principles, and how the option for the poor might be strengthened. The final chapter in Part III (ch. 20), by Russell Shaw, concerns the way CST facilitates people in living a Christian life, especially by promoting the doctrine of personal vocation.

The final three chapters, comprising Part IV, are less analytical and expository and more evaluative and critical. Christian Brugger (ch. 21) provides an account of how and why a spurious conceptual bifurcation exists between the Church's social teaching and its moral teaching on Fifth and Sixth

Commandment issues. He argues that the understanding of CST would be made more coherent, its presentations improved, and its pastoral effect strengthened by an explicit incorporation of other parts of Catholic moral doctrine, especially its exceptionless moral norms about sex and marriage, killing, and lying. Gerard V. Bradley (ch. 22) provides an account of the limited competence of bishops to teach authoritatively on social and political matters, and argues that great good is realized, especially for the Church herself, when pastors respect these limits, *but then fearlessly teach Catholic social doctrine.* He ends by advancing prudential proposals for how bishops should teach CST. In the final chapter (ch. 23), John Finnis undertakes the most ambitious essay of the collection. In what we (the editors) have chosen to refer to as a "radical critique of CST," he identifies three enduring weaknesses in the body of that teaching. He argues that to overcome the enfeebling effects that these weaknesses have upon the Church's primary evangelical mission, a series of "substantial reforms" should be undertaken to the form, delivery, and content of CST.

BALANCING THE SCHOLARSHIP ON CST

Since Vatican II, much secondary literature in CST has assumed theological premises, both ecclesiological and moral, widely held by Catholic theologians who engage in radical theological dissent against the authoritative teaching of the Church. The two most common include the denial of intrinsically evil acts and absolute moral norms and the stubborn assertion that the magisterium is merely one "voice," however important, in the social conversation, but lacks the competency to teach with divine authority on concrete moral matters. Since CST, as we argue, just *is* Catholic moral teaching and so scholarly reflection upon it belongs to moral theology, one's assumptions on the nature of Church authority and morality determine to a very large degree one's scholarship.

This text is meant among other things to offer a corrective to an ideologically lopsided body of literature. Its authors too begin with assumptions. They affirm the divinely assisted authority of the magisterium to teach – usually in non-infallible ways but also, under special conditions, infallibly – on matters of both faith and morals; that its authoritative *moral* teachings are practically reasonable, asserting truths accessible to human reason without the assistance of divine revelation, but set forward by the Church for the sake of assisting reason in securing greater certitude about the truths; that these teachings can and do include the excluding of certain moral objects as always and everywhere wrongful to choose because their choosing always involves a disorder of the will; and that the propositions asserted in these latter teachings are practically prior to matters of prudential judgment that men and women of good faith can and do disagree upon without any fallacy in their thinking or objective disorders in their willing. As stated, these are assumptions. They form a part of a general moral framework brought to bear on everything else set forward in the text's twenty-three chapters.[6]

The text is presented as a piece of Catholic scholarship. But its authors hope that it will be engaged by anyone interested in CST. They especially invite non-Catholic scholars to criticize, correct, and develop its ideas.

---

[6] They are also the unanimous assumptions of the Church's Councils, Fathers, Doctors, scholar-saints, and significant contributors to Catholic moral theology up until the middle of the twentieth century.

PART I

HISTORICAL BACKGROUND

Aquinas as a Primary Source of Catholic
Social Teaching

John Finnis

Aquinas did not speak of "social" teaching. What since *Rerum novarum* has been described as "Catholic Social Teaching" is a set of principles that Aquinas would have regarded as falling within the Church's doctrine on faith and *morality* (*de fide et moribus*), insofar as morality – the living out of that faith which consists in true beliefs about the Creator – embodies the principles, precepts and virtue(s) of *justice*. For among the cardinal virtues, justice is the one bearing on those of our choices that relate to or impact on other persons, persons with whom in one way or another we are associated. And Aquinas's treatment of justice, mainly but not only in his *Summa Theologiae*, is very extensive and very detailed.

With those verbal distinctions and conceptual connections in place, this chapter offers (in Section I) an overview of his significance for Catholic Social Teaching, before examining (in Section II) the appeals to his writings made in *Rerum novarum* and some of its successors, and concludes (in Section III) with his contribution to some leading features of more recent Catholic Social Teaching, including "subsidiarity" and "solidarity."

I

Overview

As an integral part of his wider theological investigations and expositions, and of his ancillary philosophical investigations and commentaries, Aquinas mastered, analyzed, synthesized, and rearticulated the body of Catholic Social Teaching that he found in the prophets of Israel, the Gospels and apostolic Epistles, and the Fathers of the Church. He did so by, or while, taking advantage of the best available philosophy – that is, of the best available thought about these matters developed by thinkers like Plato and Aristotle.

These were open-minded, well-informed, curious, and critical men. But they lacked the inestimable benefit of the divine revelation – the information transmitted first to the people of Israel by the Prophets and then by the other theological sources just listed. The propositional contents of that revelation, as they were appropriated by those prophets and that people, were superior in depth and truth – on the strategic questions of Creation, Providence, human freedom, justice and other key elements of moral truth, and responsibility – to anything attained by the philosophers. And so the recipients and beneficiaries of that revelation, although by comparison to the great classical philosophers unsophisticated in many respects, were able to develop sounder – *truer* – insights into and norms of life in a political community than the philosophers ever did.

Aquinas attended to the observable and inferable facts about human persons (and groups), holding always in view both their particularity as persons (and groups) and their species-specific (generic) character as *kinds* of persons (and of groups) – and as a whole. He attended also to *both* poles of the unresolvable tension between (a) the *wholes* (the groups) that reasonably emerge in service of their *parts* (smaller groups, and families and individuals), and (b) the same *parts* variously subordinated to such wholes. By these refusals to oversimplify and overgeneralize, Aquinas – at least in principle – informed and stabilized *humanism*, if one may use that term to sum up a balanced respect for the freedom, accomplishments, and virtuous fidelities of particular persons (in principle, of each and every human person). He also inoculated that humanism against the intermittent frenzies and constant dreaming of ideologies, not least those that, in the twentieth century, would enjoy the greatest world-historical success: the atheistic socialisms, such as National Socialism and internationalist Marxism. He had indeed begun to see, and show, that the question centrally addressed by any worthwhile "social doctrine" is how a political community, while set up to be sustainable in this world, must nonetheless be dedicated to securing for particular persons (and their subpolitical communities) the opportunity to direct their own lives according to moral truth.

Human fulfillment in the Kingdom of God is, as divine revelation confirmed, the true point of rational seeking and acting.[1] But it cannot and will not be accomplished, so far as concerns the human species as a whole, before the world-ending Second Coming of the Lord in final judgment. So far as the Kingdom concerns each of us, one can reasonably presume that it will not be

---

[1] It is envisaged as a demand of reason in Plato's philosophical myth of judgment and immortality in Plato, *Republic* 614a–621d; see also *Gorgias* 523a–525b.

accomplished before one's own death. By embedding these truths in both the deep structure and the propositional texture of his works, Aquinas inoculated sound Christian thinking against political utopianism, including Liberation Theology and Teilhardist progressivism.[2]

Aquinas's work is characterized by its concern to *transcend, so far as possible, the social and political conditions and questions of his own lifetime,* and to participate in a vast transtemporal conversation ranging back about two millennia. That conversation extends from the pre-Socratic empiricist, materialist, and morally skeptical proto-Machiavellian philosophers to the Greek cultural historians and Roman lawyers, on through the ferment of learned and inspired Christian appropriation and purification, to the dialectical grind of the scholastic and university project of reconciling all these sources of insight, knowledge, and wisdom. The centuries of Israel's fortunes – advances and regressions, fidelities and backsliding – as recorded in the Old Testament presented Aquinas with a special source of empirical material about the vicissitudes of social life. And given his Christian freedom to respectfully reject most of their content as framed, he could find in Mosaic Law and institutions a laboratory for advanced social thinking – a laboratory in which he often worked.

Any outline of Aquinas's social thought[3] must start with his grasp of *human dignity* and *equality* and their objective basis in the reality of each individual's *rational nature.* Having each of us this same nature, which at least by its radical capacities if not also by the flourishing of those capacities in actions and dispositions, we are each an image of the divine nature – above all of its capacity of freely choosing between intelligent alternatives. For that remarkable (and essentially spiritual) capacity puts all human beings, in principle, on a par with each, and each person is superior in essential, radical capacity to every other animal and entity in this world. This reality and responsibility of *free choice* gives salience and solidity to the individual person, by nature not a slave either to subrational instinct or to the instrumentalizing command of another person.

With that base secured, Aquinas can affirm the natural realities of *family and household*, in which instinct and biological dependencies are taken up into rational (and thus truly *human*) commitments, priorities, and loyalties. Along with that, he affirms the complete and fulfilling *equality of man and*

[2] On these deviations and temptations, see "A Radical Critique of Catholic Social Teaching," Chapter 23 in this volume.
[3] For explanation and documentation of the positions summarized in the next four paragraphs, see John Finnis, *Aquinas: Moral, Political, and Legal Theory* (Oxford: Oxford University Press, 1998).

woman as sexual partners in the lifelong mutual commitment of husband and wife, a commitment perfected by children and their nurture and education into responsibility and independence. This extending unit has a natural and chronological priority to the wider communities of neighborhood, of productive avocation in collaborative division of labor, of municipality, and of polity.

Yet the polity has a kind of priority in range and gravity of responsibilities for defense, preservation of just markets, and above all the administration of corrective, restorative, and retributive justice according to law – law critically administered by impartial judges. There emerges thus the distinction, central to Aquinas's political (and much of his social) thought, between *the public* and *the private*, as aspects and spheres of life distinguishable from each other within any one polity, sufficiently to be manageably distinct zones of responsibility and limits of jurisdiction.

For the sake of the common good of individuals, families, and the wider communal wholes, public power legitimately and beneficially appropriates to private owners many of the resources of the world – archetypically land (with what is in it and the empty space above it) – subject only to a condition that wealth beyond the owner's genuine vocational needs is available to persons in genuine need. Public power, for the same generic reasons, justly appropriates portions of the world's surface (together with what is above and below it) as the territory of a nation. All this is then recast by Aquinas into the perspective of a charity that outruns in generosity the demands of justice, while not undermining the principles of justice in contract, restitution, property, and territory – principles that in his view resist being replaced by charity to the extent attempted (as we shall see) by the Catholic Social Teaching launched by Leo XIII.

II

Aquinas in Rerum novarum *and Beyond*

Rerum novarum (1891) is widely taken as initiating Catholic Social Teaching (or Catholic Social Doctrine). But it was also the beginning of a new *phase* in the Church's perennial activity (duty) of evangelizing the world. And among its visible sources was the encyclical in which, nearly twelve years earlier, Leo XIII had urged the whole Church to study the philosophy and theology of Aquinas. In *Aeterni patris* (1878), issued eighteen months after his becoming pope, Leo commends Aquinas for "clearly and fittingly distinguishing reason from faith, while happily associating the one with the other." For by his clarity in distinguishing yet associating the two, Aquinas could "preserve the rights and have regard for the dignity of each; so much so, indeed, that reason, borne on the wings of Thomas to its human height, can scarcely rise higher, while faith could scarcely expect more or stronger aids from reason than those which she has already obtained through Thomas."[4]

In reading these passages, one must bear in mind that the English word "faith" (bare of either article, "a" or "the") is inadequate to translate the Latin of the encyclical (or the Italian in which it was probably first conceived). At each occurrence, the meaning includes both "faith" as the believer's act and disposition of believing and "the faith," the propositional object and content of such belief. That "propositional object" is the set of true propositions that are credible (worthy of belief), and indeed certain because they are conveyed by and in the acts, events, and communications that constitute the historical divine revelation – above all the words and actions of Jesus of Nazareth, the Christ and Word Incarnate, who explicitly and implicitly confirmed and ratified the teachings of the Prophets. *Aeterni patris* does not explain this dual meaning of "faith"; it takes it for granted (as does all theology accepted and presented by bishops generally, until recent decades).

The specific relevance of *Aeterni patris* to Catholic Social Teaching emerges in no. 29:

> For the teachings of Thomas –
> - on the true meaning of liberty, which at this time is running into license;
> - on the divine origin of all authority;
> - on laws and their force;
> - on the paternal and just rule of princes;
> - on obedience to higher authorities;
> - on mutual charity one toward another; and
> - on related subjects –
>
> are teachings that have very great and irresistible force to overcome *those principles of the new politico-legal order* [iuris novi] *which are well known to be dangerous to the peaceful order of things* [pacato rerum ordini] and to public safety.[5]

That sentence in *Aeterni patris* sets out the framework for the first four paragraphs of *Rerum novarum*. They begin and end with references to the conflict and disturbance already created, and now threatened, by the "spirit of

---

[4] Leo XIII, Encyclical Letter *Aeterni patris* (On the Restoration of Christian Philosophy) (1879), no. 18.

[5] Emphasis added. Here and elsewhere I make use of but amend and correct the translation to be found on the Vatican website.

[lust for: *cupidine*] revolutionary change [of lusting for a new order of things: *rerum novarum*]" – a spirit or restless desire that has "long been disturbing the nations of the world" [political communities: *civitates*; peoples: [Italian] *popoli*]. Features of the "new order," besides its context of industrialization and new technologies, include setting aside of the protective workingmen's guilds, the expulsion of the old religion (Catholicism) from "public institutions and laws," and the growth and rapacity of usury – all leading to vast disparities of wealth, concentration of enterprises into the hands of relatively few, and the consequent reducing of "the teeming masses of the laboring poor" to a condition akin to slavery. So, although he had already devoted several encyclicals to the questions of political authority, human freedom, the Christian constitution of states, and related matters, Leo in 1890–1891 judged that he now needed to take up the difficult questions that were emerging from a widespread and growing desire – indeed, an urgent longing, with roots in genuinely pressing problems of poverty and injustice, and accompanying temptations to the false solutions of Socialism – for revolutionary *social* change.[6] As he says near the beginning of *Rerum novarum*, this change was envisioned, both by those who desired it and those who feared it, as more than a political makeover; it would uproot economic arrangements as well, all the way to the abolition of private property in favor of state or municipal ownership of everything. Against such ruinous "solutions," there was, as he put it, need to highlight [make prominent: *emineant*] those *principles* by which, in line with truth and fairness [*aequitas*], the problem can be resolved.

As the sentence in *Aeterni patris*, no. 29 implied, these needed and true principles are articulated in the writings of Aquinas. The list in that paragraph contained only one item bearing on economics as distinct from politics: the reference to mutual charity. And, as we shall see, *Rerum novarum* describes at least one of its key theses as a teaching about charity rather than justice.

Rerum novarum starts its argumentation with a refutation (RN, nos. 5–15) of the radical socialist thesis that property is theft, followed by a sketch of the rational and superior (and Christian) alternative (RN, nos. 16–22). Strikingly, Aquinas's own argument for the *justice* of appropriating the world's resources to private owners is tucked away in a single sentence in no. 15, at the far end of an extended and energetic series of cumulative arguments for the justice of the institution of private property. But even there, Aquinas's argument or set of

---

[6] Urged on eloquently by Cardinal Gibbons of Baltimore and Cardinal Manning of Westminster (London): see Gabriele de Rosa, "L'Enciclica nella Corrispondenza del Vescovi con il Papa," in *L'Enciclica Rerum Novarum e il Suo Tempore*, eds. Giovanni Antonazzi and Gabriele de Rosa (Rome: Edizioni di Storia e Letteratura, 1991), 5–42, esp. 9–21 and 41–42.

arguments for that position is not attributed to him and is said to be *not* an argument or set of arguments or a thesis about justice, but about bad consequences of common as opposed to private possession, management, and disposition of things!

Aquinas is first mentioned in no. 14, but in connection with the supervisory authority that parents, rather than State government, properly have over their children: parental authority is not to be abolished or absorbed by the State.[7] The first explicit and attributed reference to Aquinas in relation to property is later, in no. 22.

> Private ownership, as we have seen, is the natural right of man, and to exercise that right, especially as members of society, is not only lawful, but absolutely necessary. "It is lawful," says St. Thomas Aquinas, "for a man to hold private property; and it is also necessary for the carrying on of human existence." (*ST* II-II 66.2c)

The encyclical says nothing here about the "three reasons" that Aquinas refers to in the very sentence just quoted in truncated form by the encyclical. It had given those three reasons – but not as Aquinas's and not as concerned with *justice*, in no. 15. On this logically prior question whether private persons can justly own property, the main thrust of *Rerum novarum*'s argumentation is not taken from Aquinas's argumentation about the same issue. What, then, is that main thrust, and does Aquinas provide any of its premises?

In answering that question it would be helpful first to glance forward at the version of the argument given summarily and abstractly – too abstractly – nearly 75 years later by Vatican II in *Gaudium et spes*[8] (headed "On Ownership and Private Property; and on Large Estates"):

> Since property and other forms of private ownership of external goods contribute to the *expression of the personality*, and since, moreover, they furnish one an occasion to exercise one's function in society and in the economy, it is very important that the access of both individuals and communities to some ownership of external goods be fostered.
>
> Private property or some ownership of external goods confers on everyone a sphere wholly *necessary for the autonomy of the person and the family*, and it should be regarded as an *extension of human freedom*. Lastly, since it adds

---

[7] Thomas Aquinas, *Summa Theologiae*, II-II 10.12.
[8] Vatican II, Pastoral Constitution *Gaudium et spes* (On the Church in the Modern World) (1965).

incentives for carrying out one's functions and responsibilities, it constitutes one of the conditions for civil liberties. (GS, no. 71; emphasis added)[9]

Compare that with the concreteness of *Rerum novarum*'s first argument against socialist communism, its first argument, that is to say, for the justice of appropriating the world's resources to particular owners. (It is in no. 5, and appeared first in the encyclical's second draft,[10] by Cardinal Zigliara OP, the leading Dominican Thomistic scholar and head of the commission for the editing of the works of Aquinas established by Leo XIII to follow up *Aeterni patris*.)

when a man engages in remunerative labor, the impelling reason and motive of his work is to obtain property, and thereafter to hold it as his very own. If one man hires out to another his strength or skill, he does so for the purpose of receiving in return what is necessary for the satisfaction of his needs; he therefore expressly intends to acquire a right full and real, not only to the remuneration, but also to the disposal of such remuneration, just as he pleases. Thus, if he lives sparingly, saves money, and, for greater security, invests his savings in land, the land, in such case, is only his wages under another form; and, consequently, a workingman's little estate thus purchased should be as completely at his full disposal as are the wages he receives for his labor. But it is precisely in such power of disposal that ownership consists, whether the property consist of land or chattels.

Socialists, therefore, by endeavoring to transfer the possessions of individuals to the community at large, strike at the interests of every wage-earner, since they would deprive him of the liberty of disposing of his wages, and thereby of all hope and possibility of increasing his resources and of bettering his condition in life. (*RN*, no. 5)

Though there are no citations to Aquinas here, the argument in fact takes off from the principles articulated by him in discussing the justice of buying and selling, including buying and selling labor. A just price is one in which sellers are fairly compensated for what they are giving up, and buyers are fairly

[9]   The last nine words of this passage, unlike the preceding words in the same sentence, are also a significant part of the thought of Leo XIII, Encyclical Letter *Rerum novarum* (On the Condition of the Working Classes) (1891). These sentences in *Gaudium et spes*, no. 71 cite to relevant pages in RN, Pius XI's Encyclical Letter *Quadragesimo anno* (On Reconstruction of the Social Order: 40th Anniversary of *Rerum novarum*) (1931), the Christmas Message of 1941 and 1942, and a radio message of Pius XII on September 1, 1944; and John XXIII, Encyclical Letter *Mater et magistra* (On Christianity and Social Progress) (1961).
[10] For all the drafts, and their authorship, see Giovanni Antonazzi, ed., *L'Enciclica* Rerum Novarum: *Testo Autentico e Redazioni Preparatorie dai Documenti Originali* (Rome: Edizioni di Storia e Letteratura, 1991).

compensated for what they are giving up; so there is an equality between buyer and seller. The selling of one's labor is just a specific case of this desirable equality in exchange – exchange of services for wages/salary/fee. Equality here is what a fair-minded person would consider fair when considering the transaction in light of the interests of both employer and employee, the customs of the country, and the nature of the work done.[11] Taking all that for granted, Zigliara's argument in *Rerum novarum*, no. 5 looks then to the disposition *of the worker's savings from his wages*: these savings may rightly be invested in, say, land (or other capital). *Therefore*: "Everyone has by nature the right to hold property as his own" (RN, no. 6).

To some extent, the argument assumes that appropriation of land or other capital goods to private owners is just. So the argument is only a persuasive beginning, not a proof, and it needs supplementation. *Rerum novarum*, nos. 6 to 9 offer the needed supplementation (though this too will need further premises).

> [A]nimal nature, however perfect, is far from representing the human being in its completeness, and is in truth but humanity's humble handmaid, made to serve and to obey. It is the mind, or reason, which is the predominant element in us who are human creatures; it is this which renders us being human, and distinguishes us essentially from the brute. And precisely because man alone among the animal creation is endowed with reason, it must be within one's right to possess things not merely for temporary and momentary use, as other living things do, but to have and to hold them in stable and permanent possession; one must have not only things that perish in the use, but those also which, though they have been reduced into use, continue for further use later. (RN, no. 6)

Aquinas's thought, in its substance, is free from the dualism suggested by *Rerum novarum*'s handmaid metaphor, a metaphor none too happily making the animal aspects of our nature (and the inclinations to preserve one's bodily life, and to propagate) extrinsic as a "humble handmaid" is extrinsic to her mistress. But Aquinas was clear that one's *reason* should govern the other elements in one's nature, and that this governing is appropriately constitutional, not despotic, in character. *Rerum novarum* puts it thus:

> [M]an, fathoming by his faculty of reason matters without number, linking the future with the present, and being *master of his own acts*, guides his ways under the eternal law and the power of God, whose providence governs all things. Wherefore, it is in his power to *exercise his choice* not only as to matters

---

[11] See Aquinas, *Summa Theologiae*, II-II 71.1, 4; Finnis, *Aquinas*, 200–203.

that regard his present welfare, but also about those which he deems may be for his advantage in time yet to come. (Emphasis added) (*RN*, no. 7)

The pivotal idea deployed here is that human persons are masters/owners of their own acts (and thus each is an image of God). This is the idea with which Aquinas chose to open the entire Second Part of his *Summa Theologiae* (see I-II, Prol.). Only left inexplicit in *Rerum novarum*, no. 7 is what Aquinas made explicit: this self-mastery or self-ownership in, by, and through choices is by virtue of the *freedom* we exercise in those choices. *Rerum novarum* here prefers to stress the provident concern to link past, present, and future – a concern that is the mark of *rational* planning and control.

The last of the developed elements in *Rerum novarum*'s arguments for private property owes more to Locke than to Aquinas. But its intended practical conclusions are not in opposition to the moral norms regarding property that are defended by St. Thomas; and the argument itself may perhaps be supportable by going behind Locke and his confused ethical methodology to the moral thinking that was given a juristic form by that somewhat Aristotelian school of Roman jurists which, in opposition to a somewhat Stoic school, explained and delimited the rule of classical Roman law whereby one can unwittingly and honestly become owner of someone else's materials, by pointing to the expending of labor and skill that is involved in transforming those materials into something else.[12] *Rerum novarum* declares:

> [W]hen man thus turns the activity of his mind and the strength of his body toward procuring the fruits of nature, by such act he makes his own that portion of nature's field which he cultivates – that portion on which he leaves, as it were, the impress of his personality – and it is only just that he should possess that portion as his very own, and have a right to hold it without any one being justified in violating that right. (*RN*, no. 9)
> ...As effects follow their cause, so is it just and right that the results of labor should belong to those who have bestowed their labor. (*RN*, no. 10)

Nos. 12–14 of *Rerum novarum* broaden out the argument for private property by showing how essentially bound up that institution is with the maintenance of an even more (indeed supremely) important social institution, the family of husband, wife, and their children.[13] These sections work up to the encyclical's

---

[12] See Gaius, *Institutes* II 79 (on acquisition by *specificatio* in the doctrine of the Proculian jurists rather than the [Stoic-influenced] Sabinian jurists of the first and second centuries AD).

[13] "[I]nasmuch as the domestic household is antecedent, as well in idea as in fact, to people's gathering into a community [*civilis coniunctio*], the family must necessarily have rights and duties which are prior to those of the community, and more natural. If the citizens, if the

first quotation from Aquinas: "'Since the child belongs to its father, it is under the *cura* [authority and responsibility] of its parents until it can make free choices' (*Summa Theologiae* II-II 10.12)." (RN, no. 14)

The encyclical explains:

It is a most sacred law of nature that a father should provide food and all necessaries for those whom he has begotten; and, similarly, it is natural that he should wish that his children, who carry on, so to speak, and continue his personality [*producunt personam*], should be by him provided with all that is needful to enable them to keep themselves decently from want and misery amid the uncertainties of this mortal life. Now, there is no other way a father can effect this save by the ownership [*possessionem*] of productive property, which he can transmit to his children by inheritance.

A family, no less than a state [*civitas*], is, as We have said, a true society [*societas*], governed by an authority appropriate to itself, that is to say, by paternal authority. (RN, no. 13)

Again, though Aquinas is not cited, this is all in line with his thought.[14]

It is only near the end of its argumentation *for* private property that *Rerum novarum* refers (without mentioning that it is so referring) to the ground(s) that Aquinas had treated as primary. As I have already said, it is given in no. 15, and given as an argument, not about justice, but about bad consequences for people, consequences predictably caused by other people's actions. And that is a bifurcation – between (in)justice and (bad) consequences – that Aquinas would have found disconcerting, and one that shows again what a narrow concept of justice *Rerum novarum*'s authors are presupposing. Here then, at long last, is the encyclical's rendering of Aquinas's primary case for private ownership:

And in addition to injustice, it is only too evident what an upset and disturbance there would be in all classes, and to how intolerable and hateful a slavery citizens would be subjected [if private property were abolished]. The door would be thrown open to envy, to mutual invective, and to discord; the sources of wealth themselves would run dry, for no one would have any interest in exerting his talents or his industry; and that ideal equality about which they entertain pleasant dreams would be in reality the levelling down of all to a like condition of misery and degradation. (RN, no. 15)

families on entering into association [*convictus humani*] and fellowship [*societatis*], were to experience hindrance in a commonwealth [*republica*] instead of help [*adiumento*], and were to find their rights attacked instead of being upheld, society [*societas*] would rightly be an object of detestation rather than of desire." (RN, no. 13)

14 On inheritance by children (with priority to sons, since they and their property rights are not lost to the family by marriage), see Aquinas, *Summa Theologiae*, I-II 105.2 ad 2.

Compare that passage with the following paraphrase and synthesis of
Aquinas's whole position on private property:

> [T]he justifications for appropriation of resources to particular owners (or
> holders of lesser property rights) are based on general justice, i.e. on the
> advantages which such appropriation is likely to bring to all members of the
> community. Property rights concern our handling of resources on two basic
> dimensions: (1) their management and distribution [*potestas procurandi et
> dispensandi*]; (2) their use for consumption.
>
> As to (1), appropriation of resources to the ownership (or lesser property
> rights) of particular individuals or groups is appropriate and even necessary,
> for **three reasons** [emphasis added]: where something is held in common, or
> by many people, it tends to be neglected, and the work involved in managing
> it tends to be shirked; its management tends to be relatively confused,
> misdirected, and inefficient; and the whole situation tends to provoke dis-
> cord, quarrelling, and resentment.[15] So the devising of a division and legal
> regulation of possessions brings great benefits to a community.[16]
>
> As to (2), the ultimate use of resources in consumption must remain
> fundamentally "common" (unappropriated). Any appropriation of resources
> to particular owners is always subject to this reservation.[17]

These last two sentences merely introduce the important reservation or
qualification on, or exception to, the absoluteness and *private* character
of just property rights – a reservation on which Aquinas will expend
much care. The substance of his position is outlined in *Rerum novarum*,
no. 22:

> But if the question be asked: How must one's possessions be used? the
> Church replies without hesitation in the words of the same holy Doctor
> [Aquinas]: "Man should not consider his material possessions as his own,
> but as common to all, so as to share them without hesitation when others are
> in need. Whence the Apostle says [1 Tim. 6: 17–18], 'Command the rich of
> this world ... to offer with no stint, to apportion largely'" (*ST* II-II 66.2c).[18]
> True, no one is commanded to distribute to others that which is required for
> his own needs and those of his household; nor even to give away what is
> reasonably required to keep up becomingly his condition in life, "for no one
> ought to live other than becomingly" (*ST* II-II 32.6c). But, when what

[15] Aquinas, *Summa Theologiae*, II-II 66.2c; as to the third reason, see Thomas Aquinas,
Commentary on Aristotle's Politics II.4 nn. 2–3; 5 n. 8.
[16] Aquinas, *Summa Theologiae*, I-II 105.2c and ad 3; limitless accumulation in a few hands is to
be prevented (ad 3).
[17] Aquinas, *Summa Theologiae*, II-II 66.2c. The paraphrase as a whole is quoted from Finnis,
Aquinas, 189–90, where the discussion of consideration (2) runs from 190 to 196.
[18] Sources footnoted in *Rerum novarum* are here introduced into the text, above.

necessity demands has been supplied, and one's standing fairly taken thought for, it becomes a duty to give to the indigent out of what remains over. "Of that which remains, give alms." (Luke 11:41)[19]

Leo XIII immediately adds (still in *RN*, no. 22):

> It is a duty, not of justice (save in extreme cases), but of Christian charity, a duty not enforced by human law. But the laws and judgments of men must yield place to the laws and judgments of Christ the true God, who in many ways urges on His followers the practice of almsgiving.

Now Aquinas certainly treated almsgiving in *ST* II-II 32, in 10 articles (including the one cited by Leo), all under the virtue of charity.[20] But *Rerum novarum* omits to note that the whole analysis of kinds of need, kinds of prior responsibility, and consequently graduated obligations to relieve necessity by charitable alms-giving was repeated (albeit briefly and summarily) by Aquinas under the heading of *justice* and duties of justice in art. 7 of the same *quaestio* the encyclical has just cited.[21] And we should note that Aquinas does not deny that human law could appropriately adopt this moral duty as also a duty of state law, and then enforce it as such – just as reasonable modern laws of redistributive taxation, graduated by taxpayer's wealth, certainly do.

In short, *Rerum novarum* departs significantly, and without articulated or (in my judgment) sufficient warrant, from the teaching of St. Thomas when it presents these responsibilities of owners as if they were only a matter of charity, *not* justice, and therefore (according to Aquinas himself) works not of obligation but of supererogation – counsels of perfection.

Later iterations of Catholic Social Doctrine silently correct this aspect of Leo's teaching. A mature summary is offered by John Paul II in *Sollicitudo rei socialis* (1987):

> It is necessary to state once more the characteristic principle of Christian social doctrine: the goods of this world are originally meant for all.[22] The right to private

---

[19]   For a much more detailed analysis and synthesis of Aquinas's two main treatments of the same set of duties, see Finnis, *Aquinas*, 189–96. When Vatican II cites *Summa Theologiae* II-II 66.2, it immediately cites also a. 7: see *GS*, no. 69 and no. 28 below.

[20]   Aquinas, *Summa Theologiae*, II-II 32.6c.

[21]   Aquinas, *Summa Theologiae*, II-II 66.7c.

[22]   See *GS*, no. 69; Paul VI, Encyclical Letter *Populorum progressio* (The Development of Peoples) (1967), no. 22: loc. cit., p. 268; Congregation for the Doctrine of the Faith, Doctrinal Document *Libertatis conscientia* (Instruction on Christian Freedom and Liberation) (1986), no. 90: *AAS* 79 (1987) 594; Aquinas, *Summa Theologiae*, II-II 66.2.

property is valid and necessary, but it does not nullify the value of this principle. Private property, in fact, is under a "social mortgage,"[23] which means that it has an intrinsically social function, based upon and justified precisely by the principle of the universal destination of goods. (*SRS*, no. 42)

Now, one creates a mortgage on one's property when (usually in the context of securing a loan) one grants to another or others the right, under certain conditions (e.g., in the event of one's failure to repay the loan), to take possession of one's property in whole or in part and dedicate what has been taken to new uses. All this is in the realm not of charity and counsels but of justice and obligations. What is true, and dominates *Rerum novarum*'s treatment of the issue, is that the just social mortgage on private property is in many situations inchoate, uncrystallized, not yet specified by any moral or positive law. But that, I would say, does not render it less real, or less a matter of justice (in a sense of "justice" going wider than already crystallized obligations of commutative justice to specific persons).

In simple terms, Aquinas's teaching about the social mortgage on private property comes to this:

1. For anyone in dire necessity, nothing belongs to anyone in particular; "for anyone in that situation, all resources become *common resources*."[24] That is to say, people who find themselves or their dependents in such life-threatening[25] need are morally entitled to take anything which will relieve that need, and this entitlement overrides anyone else's otherwise legitimate title or property right.[26]

2. In situations where no one confronts extreme necessity, the right of owners and other property-holders to keep their property extends just as far as their ... need to maintain themselves (with their dependents) in the form of life which they have reasonably adopted. All their *further* resources [*residuum; superflua*] are "held in common": all[27] these resources should be made available to those ("the poor") who, though not in extreme necessity, lack the resources to satisfy their ... needs [for resources to fulfill their responsibilities for the support and education

[23] See Address at the Opening of the Third General Conference of the Latin-American Bishops (January 28, 1979): *AAS* 71 (1979) 189–196; Ad Limina Address to Polish Bishops (December 17, 1987), no. 6: *L'Osservatore Romano*, December 18, 1987.
[24] Aquinas, *Summa Theologiae*, II-II 32.7 ad 3, 187.4c.
[25] They need not wait until they are at death's door and incapable of helping themselves: Aquinas, *Commentary on the Sentences* IV 13.2.1 sol. 4 ad 4.
[26] Aquinas, *Summa Theologiae*, II-II 32.7 ad 3; 66.7c and ad 2; 110.3 ad 4.
[27] Aquinas, *Summa Theologiae*, II-II 87.1 ad 4.

of their relatives and household, for maintaining their business[28] ... or other vocation ... and other such genuine responsibilities]. The poor have a natural right that the whole of this *residuum* be distributed[29] in their favor.[30]

This entire Thomist casuistry (application of moral principles to specific kinds of cases, i.e., situations) is presupposed throughout the emerging exposition of Catholic Social Teaching from *Rerum novarum*, through *Gaudium et spes*,[31] down to *Centesimus annus* (1991) and the *Catechism of the Catholic Church* (or the nonmagisterial *Compendium of the Social Doctrine of the Church* (2004)). The important idea summarized in the above passage's reference to "vocation" and "other such responsibilities" is deployed, for example, in the entire, repeated teaching of *Rerum novarum*, that wage-earners may each *save* from their salaries so as to acquire *property* with which to support and educate children (and not merely one or two children, and not merely through grade school and high school, but also – going beyond Leo's words – through college and if appropriate graduate school), and for such legitimate purposes (and indeed, to have something to leave the children as inherited property) can *rightly* make, retain and invest these savings (as in the first instance *capital*) rather than surrender them to the state in excessive taxation or to the neighboring or distant poor who are just getting by. (See, for example, *RN* nos. 13, 46–47.)

III

Subsidiarity, Service, Private Associations, Global Solidarity

With the pillars in place – with the natural and revealed justice of the family and its private property affirmed as requirements of reason and the faith prior to and (albeit in different ways and to a significantly differing extent) independent of state government and law – the *other main elements of Catholic Social Teaching* fall easily into place. They are elements that are rationally interconnected with each other, and they mutually support each other and display the rational strength and soundness of the pillars. These other main features may be summarized as subsidiarity, the service conception of state government and law, the legitimate domain

---

[28] See Aquinas, *Summa Theologiae*, II-II 32.6c; I-II 105.2 ad 6.
[29] Aquinas, *Summa Theologiae*, II-II 66.7c.
[30] Finnis, *Aquinas*, 191–192 (and see the whole casuistry documented over 190–196).
[31] See *GS*, no. 69, citing Aquinas, *Summa Theologiae*, II-II 32, 5 ad 2; 66.2 and a. 7.

of private associations beyond family, and solidarity with the human race beyond the confines of one's own political community. These are all, in differing ways, main teachings of Aquinas, transmitted by him to the whole Church in more or less the way envisaged by Leo XIII in *Aeterni patris.*

Subsidiarity

Aquinas firmly teaches a truth that tends to grate on modern ears: common good is superior to the good of an individual person. One's own good cannot be attained apart from the common good of one's family and *civitas* (or other political community); in many respects, moreover, one is a *part* of a household and a state, and so one's good is *partly* that of being a good husband (wife, daughter, son) and a good citizen. But this is fully compatible with his teaching that, save perhaps in occasional emergencies, the individual members of a community must each be left to fulfill their responsibilities on their own self-directed initiative,[32] in voluntary association with other individuals and associations.[33]

Any adequate account of Aquinas's conception of common good will have to acknowledge that, for him,

> the reasonable pursuit of the "all-inclusive" common good [in and of a political community, a state] is stratified, into three distinct specializations of responsibility. Individual practical reasonableness (*prudentia*, without trace of selfishness), domestic practical reasonableness, and political practical reasonableness are three irreducibly distinct [*diversi*][34] species of *prudentia*, three distinct "parts" of moral practical reasonableness.[35] *Each* of these species of *prudentia* is concerned not

---

[32] Thomas Aquinas, *Summa contra Gentiles* III 71.4; Finnis, *Aquinas*, 120–123.

[33] RN, no. 51 cites Aquinas's early polemical pamphlet *Contra Impugnantes Dei Cultum et Religionem* (1256) II for the simple if not banal proposition that "a private society is one which is formed [within a political community, a *respublica*] for the purpose of carrying out private objects; as for example when two or three enter into partnership with a view to trading in common [i.e., on their joint account]."

[34] Cf. the similar use of *diversi* in respect of the irreducibly distinct types of *ordo* and *scientia* discussed in Thomas Aquinas, *Sententia libri Ethicorum*, I.1 n. 1 [1-2]: "secundum hos diversos ordines ... sunt diversae scientiae" [2].

[35] Aquinas, *Summa Theologiae*, II-II 48.1c; 47.11 ("the good of individuals, the good of families, and the good of *civitas* or realm are different ends [*diversi fines*]; so there are necessarily different species of prudentia corresponding to this difference in their respective ends: (i) *prudentia* without qualification [*simpliciter dicta*], which is directed [*ordinat*[*ur*]] towards one's own good; (ii) domestic prudence directed towards the common good of household or family, and (iii) political prudence directed towards the common good of state or realm"); q. 50 a. 1c (the form of political

(like military prudence)[36] with some special project which can be finished off but with, in a certain sense, "the whole of life [*tota vita*]".[37] The specifically political *prudentia* that is paradigmatically and principally, though not exclusively, the viewpoint of legislators[38] **neither absorbs the other two nor even includes, directly, the whole of their content**. Although rulers are in many respects in charge of their subjects, their direct concern as rulers is only, as we have seen, the promotion of *public good*.

Public good is a part or aspect of the all-inclusive common good. It is the part that provides an indispensable context and support for those parts or aspects of the common good which are private (especially individual and familial good). It thus supplements, subserves, and supervises those private aspects, but without superseding them, and without taking overall charge of, or responsibility for them. "Neither in one's whole being nor in one's belongings is one subordinate to the political community."[39] And here we may add Aquinas's **partial anticipation of the principle of subsidiarity**:[40] "it is contrary to the proper character of the state's government [*contra rationem gubernationis* [*civitatis*]] to impede people from acting according to their responsibilities [*officia*] – except[41] of course in emergencies."[42]

---

prudence, which is proper to state rulers, is the most perfect form of prudence because it extends to more things and attains a further end than the other species of prudence).

[36] Aquinas, *Summa Theologiae*, II-II 48.1c; 50.4. If military prudence deserves its place as a fourth species of *prudentia*, it is because it shares in the open-endedness of political prudence – is, so to speak, the extension of political prudence into the external hazard of war in which the whole life of the *civitas* and its elements is at stake: see II-II 50.4 ad 1 & ad 2.

[37] Aquinas, *Summa Theologiae*, II-II 48.1c; "tota vita" is short for "the common end of the whole of human life" [*communis finis totius humanae vitae*] and "the good of the whole of life" [*bonum totius vitae*]: 47.13c & ad 3.

[38] Aquinas, *Summa Theologiae*, II-II 50.2 (note that in the preamble to this quaestio, the prudence of rulers [*regnativa*] is called the prudence involved in law-making [*legispositiva*]).

[39] Aquinas, *Summa Theologiae*, I-II 21.4 ad 3: homo non ordinatur ad communitatem politicam secundum se totum, et secundum omnia; "and so not all one's acts are meritorious or culpable by virtue of their relationship to that community."

[40] Namely, that it is unjust for more extensive associations to assume functions that can be performed efficiently by individuals or by less-extensive associations, since the proper function of instrumental associations is to help their members help themselves: see John Finnis, *Natural Law & Natural Rights* (Oxford: Oxford University Press, 1980, 2011), 146, 159.

[41] Aquinas, *Summa contra Gentiles* III 71.4. What are these responsibilities? Marriage is one natural responsibility [*officium naturae humana*] with which human law is rightly concerned (*Commentary on the Sentences* IV d. 27 q. 1 a. 3 sol. 1 ad 1; d. 31 q. 1 a. 2c & a. 3 sed contra 2; d. 39 q. 1 a. 2 ad 3) and a community responsibility [*in officium communitatis*] (d. 34 q. 1 a. 1 ad 4).

[42] Finnis, *Aquinas*, 236–237 (bolding added).

In magisterial Catholic Social Teaching, it is only in *Quadragesimo anno*
(1931)[43] that the principle of subsidiarity[44] is finally named and identified as
a principle of justice. But the principle was already intimated in the general
thrust of the second half of *Rerum novarum*, and indeed in the first half's
treatment of the nuclear family as an association that must not be "absorbed":

> Paternal authority can be neither abolished nor absorbed [*absorberi*] by the
> State … (RN, no. 14)
>   We have said that the State must not absorb [*absorber[e]*] the individual or
> the family; both should be allowed free and untrammelled action so far as is
> consistent with common good and the interest of others. … (RN, no. 35)
>   The right to possess private property is derived from nature, not from man;
> and the State has the right to control its use in the interests of the public good
> alone, but by no means to absorb it altogether [*abolere*]. (RN, no. 47)

The principle of subsidiarity can be articulated:

> [T]he principle is one of justice. It affirms that the proper function of
> association is to help the participants in the association to help themselves
> or, more precisely, to constitute themselves through the individual initiatives
> of choosing commitments (including commitments to friendship and other
> forms of association) and of realizing these commitments through personal
> inventiveness and effort in projects (many of which will, of course, be co-
> operative in execution and even communal in purpose). And since in large
> organizations the process of decision-making is more remote from the initia-
> tive of most of those many members who will carry out the decision, the same

[43] *QA*, no. 79:

> just as it is wrong to withdraw from the individual and commit to a group what private
> initiative and effort can accomplish, so too it is a wrong … for a larger and higher association
> to arrogate to itself functions which can be performed efficiently by smaller and lower
> associations. This is a fixed, unchanged and most weighty principle of moral philosophy …
> Of its very nature the true aim of all social activity should be to **help** [*subsidium afferre*]
> members of a social body, and never to destroy or **absorb** them. (bolding added)

[44] John Paul II, Encyclical Letter *Centesimus annus* (On the 100th Anniversary of *Rerum
      novarum*) (1991), no. 48, citing Pius XI's *Quadragesimo anno*, states "the principle of sub-
      sidiarity" thus:

> a community of a higher order should not interfere in the internal life of a community
> of a lower order, depriving the latter of its functions, but rather should support
> [*sustentare*] it in case of need, and help [*adiuvare*] to coordinate its activity with the
> activities of the rest of society, always with a view to the common good.

> One of the two documents of the Second Vatican Council that mention the principle calls
> it, twice, the principle of subsidiary responsibility (*principium subsidiarii officii*): Paul VI,
> Declaration *Gravissimum educationis* (On Christian Education) (1965), no. 3 and 6. This is
> the phrase used in *QA*, no. 80.

principle requires that larger associations should not assume functions which can be performed efficiently by smaller associations.[45]

Service Conception of State Government and Law

Getting its name from *subsidium* (help), subsidiarity as an idea, desideratum, and indeed requirement of justice goes together with, indeed implies, the profoundly Thomist thesis (not invented by St. Thomas!).[46] that political government and state law are *for the sake of* individuals and families, not for the sake of the rulers or of some limited set of individuals and families within the community. To say this is to say that government is justified by, and only by, the standing, indeed permanent need that there be governing for – in service of – common good. Properly understood, making decisions for common good – the common good of one's political community – involves making those decisions all duly respectful of every "part," i.e., of all individual persons and their families within the territory for which one as a ruler (legislator, elector, official) is responsible.

It follows that the content of governing decisions – for example, particular laws enacted – will morally bind those whom they concern if and *only if* they satisfy morally reasonable conditions about their content as well as their motivation, their legal form and compliance with legal conditions of validity, and the fairness of their impact. True, all these conditions should be applied with plenty of allowance for reasonable differences of opinion in view, especially, of differing estimates of the relatively unknowable – risks, side-effects, and other outcomes – and reasonably differing attitudes to keeping faith with past or prior decisions (such as the decision to adopt a certain constitution, or to make an undertaking to a social group as part of some compromise). But allowance is not infinite elasticity, and if the limits are transgressed, the consequence is that the law or other decision leaves its purported subjects morally free to disobey, unless some collateral element in the whole situation makes noncompliance by some class or classes of persons unfair to others (one speaks here, thus, of a moral

---

[45] Finnis, *Natural Law and Natural Rights*, 146. The endnote to this, on 159, having quoted the principle's articulation in Pius XI's encyclical *Quadragesimo anno*, adds: "Later pronouncements of the Roman Catholic authorities have applied the principle to relationships of production in the economy (1961 [*Mater et magistra*], 1967 [*Populorum progressio*]), to world political order (1963 [*Pacem in terris*]) and world economic order (1965 [*Gaudium et spes*]), to the relationships between families, schools, and the state (1965 *Gravissimum educationis*]), to the ecclesiastical community (1969), and to politics at all levels (1971 [*Octogesima adveniens*])."

[46] See the passages from Justinian's *Digest* and *Institutes* discussed in "The Priority of Persons" in *Collected Essays of John Finnis* vol. II, *Intention and Identity* (Oxford University Press, 2011).

obligation to conform or avoid perceptible nonconformity to the norm expressed in an unjust law, rather than to a moral obligation to obey the law).

Aquinas sets out all this with care. *Rerum novarum* takes up his position, albeit in an abbreviated, unnuanced fashion, in no. 52. Speaking of private associations – implicitly of labor or trade unions – *Rerum novarum* says:

> There are occasions, doubtless, when it is fitting that the law should intervene to prevent certain associations, as when men join together for purposes which are evidently bad, unlawful, or dangerous to the State. In such cases, public authority may justly forbid the formation of such associations, and may dissolve them if they already exist. But every precaution should be taken not to violate the rights of individuals and not to impose unreasonable regulations under pretense of public benefit. For laws only bind when they are in accordance with right reason, and, hence, with the eternal law of God. (*RN*, no. 52)

A footnote to this section quotes Aquinas:

> Human law is law only by virtue of its accordance with right reason; and thus it is manifest that it flows from the eternal law. And in so far as it deviates from right reason it is called an unjust law; in such case it is no law at all, but rather a species of violence. (Aquinas, *Summa Theologiae*, I-II 93.3 ad 2)

I say "unnuanced" because, in particular, "unjust law . . . is no law at all" is a slogan in need of careful nuancing, supplied tersely but sufficiently by Aquinas[47] and more amply in recent discussion.[48] In the absence of such nuancing, the slogan both arouses the derision of unbelievers (whole schools of legal theory take its *apparent* defiance of social-fact reality as sufficient reason to consign Catholic legal philosophy to the junk-heap) and, more important, greatly oversimplifies the often differing moral responsibilities of different people in the face of unjust proposals for legislation and in the face of unjust enacted provisions of legislation or judicial orders.

Private Associations beyond Family

Aquinas's discussion of associations intermediate between families and the organs of the state is more implicit than elaborately articulated. The authors of

---

[47] The *locus classicus* is Aquinas, *Summa Theologiae*, I-II 96.4, summarized on p. 29 above.
[48] See citations and discussion in Finnis, *Natural Law & Natural Rights*, ch. 12; Finnis, *Aquinas*, 266–274.

Rerum novarum indicated, without detail, the main locus of his discussion, his pamphlet *Contra Impugnantes* in defense of religious orders and of admitting even children to them. There Aquinas affirms that state laws or arrangements impeding the associating of citizens should be reformed whenever they involve arbitrary restrictions on membership of, for example, universities. Such restrictions create disunity in the political community, he holds. *Rerum novarum* puts this on a more solid basis, that of justice and rights of association, subject always to state oversight that fully respects what *Quadragesimo anno* will call subsidiarity.[49] *Rerum novarum* spells out important implications of that right as it applies to the formation of labor (trade) unions.[50]

Solidarity with the Human Race beyond One's Own Political Community

Aquinas never discussed the question whether there should be a one-world political community and a world government rather than a multiplicity of political communities. This is an aspect of his pervasive silence about the formation of states. He explores in depth what it is for a community to be "complete" (*perfecta*) and thus virtually or actually a political community, a state; and what it needs by way of appropriate institutions, laws, and so forth; but not the question of how many such communities there appropriately are or should be.[51]

What is a "complete community," and which communities are complete? Any answer must be relative. For many purposes, and in many contexts, the "complete community" relevant to one's life of practical reasonableness is the political community within which one lives, with one's family: "complete

---

[49] What this involves – especially abstention (save in emergency) from managerial direction and control – is discussed in reply to Leslie Green in Finnis, "Reflections and Responses" in *Reason, Morality and Law*, eds. John Keown and Robert George (Oxford: Oxford University Press, 2013), 512–515 esp. 514–515.

[50] See the much fuller treatment of this important aspect of *Rerum novarum* in Boyle, ch. 3 of this volume, pp. 69–89.

[51] See "Boundaries" in *Collected Essays of John Finnis* vol. III, *Human Rights and Common Good* (Oxford: Oxford University Press, 2011), 125–132 at 128–132. The discussion begins at 128:

Richard Tuck says that Aquinas, like other Dominicans, "disagreed profoundly with any theory of world authority, preferring instead a vision of a world of independent and equal political communities." I doubt this. To me it seems a cardinal feature of Aquinas's treatment of political matters that he abstracts entirely from all questions about the conditions under which it is proper for political communities to be brought into being or dissolved or otherwise replaced.

community = *civitas* [*perfecta communitas civitas est*]."[52] But a *civitas*, complete in its own way, may be unable to defend itself; so, beyond family and
civitas, there rises a third level of community, communities of *civitates* organized for mutual defence [*compugnatio*]; they may amount to a realm
[*regnum*][53] or a province [*provincia*][54] or simply to a condition of friendship
between states [*amicitia inter civitates*].[55] But the mind's eye cannot rest there;
political philosophy (*politica*) is for the sake of the *civitas*[56] but also for
"human good, that is, the best in human affairs."[57] And *politica*'s primacy
over all other bodies of practical thought and knowledge "comes from the very
nature of its end."

Here is Aquinas, early in his commentary on Aristotle's *Ethics*:

> For ... if the good for one human being is the same good [i.e., human good]
> as the good for a whole *civitas*, still it is evidently a much greater and more
> perfect thing to procure and preserve the state of affairs which is the good of
> a whole *civitas* than the state of affairs which is the good of a single human
> being. For: it belongs to the love which should exist between human persons
> that one should seek and preserve the good of even one single human being;
> but how much better and more godlike that this should be shown for a whole
> people and for a plurality of *civitates*. Or: it is lovable that this be shown for
> one single *civitas*, but much more godlike that it be shown for the whole
> people embracing many *civitates*. ("More godlike" because more in the
> likeness of God who is the universal cause of all goods.) This good, the
> good common to one or many *civitates*, is what the theory, i.e. the "art"
> which is called "civil", has as its point [*intendit*]. And so it is this theory, above
> all – as the most primary [*principalissima*] of all practical theories – that
> considers the ultimate end of human life.[58]

[52]   Aquinas, *Summa Theologiae*, I-II 90.2c.
[53]   *Commentary on Matthew* 12 ad v. 25.
[54]   Thomas Aquinas, *De Regimine Principum* I.2 (I,1) [14] [748].
[55]   Aquinas, *Sententia libri Ethicorum* [*Eth.*] VIII. 4 n. 9. Aristotle's text here was talking about
       friendship between citizens [*cives*], but the translation used by Aquinas read *civitates* in lieu of
       cives. See also IX. 6 n. 7 ("the friendship between diverse states [*civitates*] seems to be the same
       as concord ... for it is a political friendship concerned with matters of advantage [*utilia*] and
       with things needed for human life").
[56]   Aquinas, *Ethicorum*, I.2 n. 11 [29].
[57]   Aquinas, *Ethicorum*, n. 12 [30].
[58]   Aquinas, *Ethicorum*, nn. 11–12 [29–30]. See also *Ethicorum* VI.7 n. 7 [1201]; and *De Veritate* q. 5
       a. 3c, where, having noted that the *paterfamilias* governs the household and the king governs
       the *civitas* or *regnum*, Aquinas immediately adds that what is common to both sorts of
       government is that "common good is higher [*eminentius*] than individual good [*bonum
       singulare*]," and that "as is pointed out in the beginning of the *Ethics*, the good of a people
       [*gentis*] is higher [*divinius*] than the good of a city-state or family or individual person
       [*personae*]."

Is this passage tracking that directiveness of practical reason no further than the flourishing of a nation-state that, like the France of his friend King Louis IX, integrates many formerly independent political communities? We cannot say.

We cannot say, therefore, that the passages in which we find papal expressions of social teaching that favorably envisage world order and world government owe anything definite to Aquinas.

Still, there is a certain openness of his thought that allows the question to be at least raised, even if the appropriate answer for the foreseeable future is that world government would be a breach of subsidiarity, or worse. For one can synthesize or paraphrase relevant strands in Aquinas's thought as follows:

> Who then is my neighbour, my *proximus*? If "people in Ethiopia or India," as Aquinas says,[59] can be benefited by my prayer, they are my neighbours, though he mentions them to his thirteenth-century audience as people so <u>remote</u> that we cannot and therefore morally need not seek to benefit, i.e. to love, them in any other way. As he explains in his discussion of the neighbour-as-oneself principle in *Summa Theologiae*, II-II q. 44 a. 7c, "neighbour" is synonymous here with "brother" (as in "fraternity") or "friend" or any other term which points to the relevant affinity [*affinitas*], which consists in sharing a common human nature [each a natural image of God: *secundum naturalem Dei imaginem*]. "We ought to treat every human being as, so to speak, neighbour and brother [*omnem hominem habere quasi proximum et fratrem*]."[60]

---

59   *De Virtutibus* q. 2 a. 8c. On all this, see Finnis, *Aquinas*, 118–129.
60   Aquinas, *Summa Theologiae*, II-II 78.1 ad 2.

2

The Nineteenth-Century Historical and Intellectual Context of Catholic Social Teaching

Thomas C. Behr

The world today is heir to the "spirit of revolutionary change" that prompted Leo XIII to address the condition of the working classes, directly and in detail, in 1891. Modern Catholic Social Teaching (CST) began with that encyclical, *Rerum novarum* (On the Condition of the Working Classes), issued in the context of dramatic changes involving economy, society, and politics, and of intense Church–state conflict.[1]

In the early nineteenth century, Europe was facing the aftermath of the French Revolution. One of the earliest and most fateful acts of the revolutionary assembly was passage of "The Civil Constitution of the Clergy" (1790) that confiscated Church property, banned monastic orders, subordinated secular clergy to government service, and required an oath of loyalty to the state. Pope Pius VI's resistance to those "reforms" earned him the enmity of all progressive thinkers of the day. There were those among the revolutionaries who considered revealed religion the central obstacle to the triumph of reason and progress, who calculated that Throne and Altar had stood together and needed to fall together. In 1797, the leaders of the coup that brought Napoleon to power sought his assurances that Pius VI would be the last of the Roman pontiffs. The octogenarian pope was arrested, handled roughly, and died in imprisonment in August 1799.

---

[1] General works on this period in Church history: Roger Aubert, et al. *The Church in an Age of Liberalism*, trans. Peter Becker (New York: Crossroad, 1981); Owen Chadwick, *A History of the Popes, 1830–1914* (Oxford: Clarendon Press 1998); Frank J. Coppa, *The Modern Papacy since 1789* (London and NY: Longman, 1998); H. Daniel-Rops, *The Church in an Age of Revolution, 1789–1870*, trans. J. Warrington (London: J. M. Dent & Sons, 1965); Kenneth Scott Latourette, *Christianity in a Revolutionary Age: A History of Christianity in the Nineteenth and Twentieth Centuries. Volume I, The Nineteenth Century in Europe: Background and the Roman Catholic Phase* (New York: Harper & Brothers, 1958).

In the late nineteenth century, Leo XIII's encyclical letter *Rerum novarum* heralded the beginning of a historically unprecedented elevation of papal relevance and teaching authority on a global scale. This *magna carta* of Catholic Social Teaching critiqued the version of modernity proposed by both socialist and *laissez-faire* liberal ideologies. From that time up to today, the voice of the Roman Pontiff on social ethics has only gained in moral authority.

Two major contexts frame this dramatic reversal of fortunes for the Church and the papacy. First, Catholics across Europe had to deal with turbulent conditions often hostile to the faith. Lay Catholic response followed two waves, the first on the "Religious Question" of religious freedom, education, and Church–state relations generally, and the second on the "Social Question" specifically. While some clerics and bishops often played important roles, the nineteenth-century Catholic movement both in its political and social emphasis, in conditions of the expanding electoral franchise and means of social communication, marked a historic change in the role of the laity in the Church and contributed fundamentally to the development of modern CST.[2] The second context, fundamental for CST, was the revival of scholastic philosophy, and in particular of the natural law reasoning of St. Thomas Aquinas.

THE POLITICAL AND SOCIAL CATHOLIC MOVEMENT

In the period before 1848, the attention of the Church and of the lay faithful to the social question was extremely localized according to regional economic and developmental conditions. Across Catholic Europe we find isolated episcopal initiatives in parts of France, Germany, Belgium, and northern Italy.[3]

---

[2] Josef L. Altholz, *The Liberal Catholic Movement in England: The "Rambler" and Its Contributors, 1848–1864* (London: Burns & Oates, 1962); Giorgio Candeloro, *Il movimento cattolico in Italia* (Roma: Edizioni Rinascita, 1953); Gabriele De Rosa, *Il movimento cattolico in Italia. Dalla Restaurazione all'età giolittiana* (Bari: Laterza, 1996); Paul Droulers, SJ, *Cattolicesimo sociale nei secoli XIX e XX. Saggi di storia e sociologia* (Rome: Edizioni di Storia e Letteratura, 1982); Joseph N. Moody, et al. *Church and Society. Catholic Social and Political Thought and Movements, 1789–1950* (New York: Arts, Inc., 1953); Emile Poulat, *Eglise contre bourgeoisie. Introduction au devinir du catholicisme actuel* (Paris: Casterman, 1977); Philip Spencer, *Politics of Belief in Nineteenth-Century France: Lacordaire, Michon, Veuillot* (New York: Grove Press, 1954).

[3] Paul Droulers, "Des évêques parlent de la question ouvrière en France avant 1848," *Revue de l'action populaire* 147 (April 1961): 442–460; Paul Droulers, "L'épiscopat devant la question ouvrière en France sous la Monarchie de Juillet," *Revue Historique* 229 (1963): 335–362; "La

The year 1848 was a watershed for Catholic engagement in political and social questions. There had been a flourishing of Catholic intellectual life during the relatively benign neglect of political-religious issues under Louis Phillippe's reign in France from 1830 to 1848. A Catholic revival included liberals like Hugues-Félicité Robert de Lamennais, Jean-Baptiste Henri Lacordaire, and Charles Forbes René de Montalembert, and an impressive cohort of Catholics in arts and letters, public life, and politics. Catholic objections over state restrictions on religious education formed the basis for consolidating a first wave of political mobilization. The monopoly over education, a tool of ideological indoctrination and also, at the higher levels, a check on access to public and professional careers, had been instituted under the Revolution but was greedily carried over by the restored Bourbon absolutist regimes of Louis XVIII and Charles X. After the fall of the Bourbons in the 1830 Revolution, and their replacement with Louis-Phillippe of the Orléans dynasty, the first wave of the Catholic movement had some early success with the Guizot laws of 1833. These allowed private, religious, elementary schools. The significant aspect of this modern Church and state conflict, over religious freedom in general, and education in particular, is the extent to which Catholic laity mobilized and took the lead. The Catholic movement was primarily a movement of the laity, and the Vatican struggled to direct developments on the ground. Changing conditions of communication and political participation merged with the fact that popes and hierarchy were grappling with unprecedented assaults upon, and an uncertain future for, the global, institutional Church. The days of hurling bulls back and forth across the Alps were long gone!

The second wave of Catholic mobilization developed alongside the first and was in response to the burgeoning social question. Catholics undertook research and proposed policies, making contributions to emerging social sciences, an early example of which is Alban de Villeneuve-Bargemont's *Economie politique chétienne* of 1834.[4] This pioneering and in-depth study, based on research from over a decade of government administration in industrial areas of France, advocated for workers' organizations to resist unequal bargaining power and for state intervention for the health, safety and protection of children.[5] There were considerable social scientific initiatives throughout the pre-1848 period, as well as widespread traditional

presse et les mandements sociaux d'évêques français avant 1848," *Cahiers d'histoire* 9 (1964): 385–397.

4 Alban de Villeneuve-Bargemont, *Economie politique chétienne ou recherches sur la nature et les causes du pauperisme en France et en Europe et sur les moyens de le soulager et de le prévenir*, 3 vols. (Paris: Paulin, Libraire-Éditeur, 1834). Villeneuve-Bargemont's empirical studies were indispensible to the rise of Christian economic thought.

5 Moody, *Church and Society*, 128, 228.

charitable works initiated by lay Catholics at the local level that were influenced by, and influential over, episcopal initiatives. Catholic conservatives, liberals, and socialists were all involved, in various European political contexts.[6] Inadequate living conditions and pauperism in overcrowded cities raised awareness. Conditions of artisanal modes of production became more exploitative in the face of advancing industrial methods. Jean-Baptiste Duroselle dates the beginning of the Social Catholic movement with the foundation in 1822 of the Society of St. Joseph[7] as the first lay association formed to address the new pauperism and other social ills.

Further research and practical initiatives followed. Blessed Frédéric Ozanam founded his Society of St. Vincent de Paul in 1833. Charles de Coux,[8] along with Villeneuve-Bargemont, for example – both of whom had collaborated closely with Lamennais on the *Avenir* journal – began to formulate a Christian approach to political economy in the same period during which that science was forming itself as a discipline in France in the 1830s.[9] The course that Ozanam gave at the University of Lyons in 1838 set much of the agenda for what was to develop as CST over time, including the critique of unrestrained economic liberalism, of the commodification of labor, of the insufficiency of charitable works, of the need for labor associations, and of some state intervention.[10]

The nature of episcopal pronouncements in this early period is significant. Though there are variations in intensity of the critique, the emphasis was on the negative consequences of industrialization, and the basis of the reproach was focused on charitable obligations of Christians to redress the sufferings of workers. The temptation within the sociocultural context of romantic and postrevolutionary Europe to think in nostalgic terms was strong – especially with reference to the dissolution of the Catholic guilds and fraternal aid societies by the revolutionary bourgeoisie. Hope in and even enthusiasm

---

6   Alec R. Vidler, A *Century of Social Catholicism, 1820–1920* (London: S. P. C. K., 1964), 4–5. And see Edgar Alexander, "Church and Society in Germany"; Carlos Castaneda, "Social Developments and Movements in Latin America"; Francis Downing, "American Catholicism and the Socio-Economic Evolution in the U.S.A."; Henry Hague, "The Catholic Movement in Belgium"; Christopher Hollis, "Social Evolution in Modern English Catholicism"; and Joseph N. Moody, "The Time of Resistance (1789–1878)" in Moody, *Church and Society*.

7   Jean-Baptiste Duroselle, *Les Débuts du Catholicisme Social en France (1822–1870)* (Paris: Presses Universitaires de France, 1951), 24, 29–36.

8   *Discours prononcé par M. le Professeur de Coux, le 4 Décembre 1835 à l'ouverture de son Cours d'Économie Politique à l'Université Catholique de Louvain* (Louvain: Chez Vanlinthout et Vandensande, 1835).

9   Duroselle, *Les débuts*, 40–69.

10 Moody, *Church and Society*, 129.

about the beneficent power being unleashed by the advancement of technology stood side by side with fear and outrage over poorly comprehended social side effects.[11] Before 1848, some socially minded Catholics, moved by the sufferings of workers and child labor, levied unmitigated criticism of the profit motive and capitalist greed.

After 1848, Social Catholic voices faced marginalization in the *laissez-faire* liberal versus socialist discourses on the labor question. In the *Manifesto of the Communist Party*, Marx and Engels had already advanced (in 1848) a compelling critique of reformisms and utopian socialisms, including religious socialism. "Scientific" revolutionary socialism, and "dialectical materialism" as a theory of history, human nature, and future communist society offered an energetic paradigm. Socialists viewed Catholic activists as stooges of the bourgeoisie. The *laissez-faire* liberal bourgeoisie, on the other hand, saw social Catholics as dangerous agitators. Confused political and religious allegiances abounded. In his *Democracy in America* (1835), Alexis de Tocqueville regretted the historical trajectory of Church and state association in Europe that had led to unnecessary conflict between the forces of morality and those of social progress.[12] Enlightenment critics of religion had theorized a link between oppression and religion as "the opiate of the masses," as Marx would put it. The vestiges of the Throne and Altar alliance and the absence of an alternative political paradigm of just social order left early social Catholics, churchmen, and lay activists, theoretically and practically, in unchartered territory.

The earliest Catholic congresses were held in 1848 in Germany, Cologne, and then Mainz, when Catholics, concerned about the anti-Catholic orientation of the Frankfurt revolutionary Assembly, formed associations ("Piusvereine") to support Pius IX's leadership. At one of these early meetings, the future Bishop of Mainz, Emmanuel von Ketteler, persuaded participants there to recognize the inseparability of the Social Question from the Religious Question in the Church and state debate. He gave an Advent series of "social sermons on the mount" that set the foundation for the far-reaching influence of the German Social Catholic movement while also exhibiting

[11] Droulers, "L'épiscopat devant la question ouvrière en France," 347.
[12] Alexis de Tocqueville, *Democracy in America*, trans., ed., and with an introduction by Harvey C. Mansfield and Delba Winthrop (Chicago: University of Chicago Press, 2002), 11, "Christianity, which has rendered all men equal before God, will not be loath to see all citizens equal before the law. But by a strange concurrence of events, religion finds itself enlisted for the moment among the powers democracy is overturning, and it is often brought to reject the equality it loves and to curse freedom as an adversary, whereas by taking it by the hand, it could sanctify its efforts."

the lasting problem of his own "ideological dualism." German and Austrian
Catholic activism tended to be torn between liberal reformism and romantic
rejection of capitalist society altogether.[13] The dilemma for Ketteler and for
many Social Catholics was the lack of theoretical principles that could
sustain a middle ground between a *laissez-faire* liberalism that, from their
experience of its worst manifestations, they rejected as dehumanizing, and
the various socialist alternatives that were on the one hand romantic and
unrealistic or, on the other hand, revolutionary and atheistic. Another strain
of the Catholic reform movement can be seen in the work of Ignaz von
Döllinger, who saw in the 1848 revolutions an opportunity for the regeneration of Catholic leadership in the development of modern culture. At the
first meeting of the General Assembly of Catholic Societies in Mainz in 1848
and again in Regensburg (Ratisbon, in English) in 1849, Döllinger gained
widespread attention with his speeches on the "Independence of the
Church" that made the case for a national German Church, with its own
national synod and head.[14]

The emergence of modern Catholic social thought involved research;
charitable efforts; industrial and worker organization experiments; education
of clergy and laity, specifically on the social problem; and, at times, political
mobilization, particularly on issues affecting religious liberty. All of these
facets of the Catholic movement gained momentum in the more advanced
industrial regions of Catholic Europe throughout the 1840s. It is not possible
in this chapter to more than touch on the vast and unprecedented engagement
of the Catholic movement that arose in response to both the legacy of
Revolutionary anti-Catholicism, i.e., the Religious Question, and to the rise
of the Social Question with industrialization. The main facts of nineteenth-
century Catholic political and social thought and action have been identified
for some time now, and yet many topics have been insufficiently explored,
underappreciated, and even misunderstood – this latter case having much to
do with the shifting boundaries and tensions that defy neat ideological cate-
gorization. The German Catholic Congress, for instance, met semiannually
for two years and then annually after 1850 in various German or Austrian cities
and undertook numerous initiatives, and other important congresses took
place in France and Belgium in this early phase of the Catholic movement

---

[13]   Alexander, "Social and Political Movements," 410–417.
[14]   Thomas Albert Howard, *The Pope and the Professor: Pius IX, Ignaz von Döllinger, and the
       Quandary of the Modern Age* (Oxford: Oxford University Press, 2017), 87–89. Döllinger was
       interested above all in restoring historical pride of place to Catholic intellectual life, was
       influenced by Lamennais and his circle from the 1830s, and was close friends with
       Montalembert for instance, and also Lord Acton.

internationally.[15] A vast range of periodicals in the Catholic world, from dailies to quarterlies, covered Catholic culture, controversies, political issues, and also literary and scientific topics, with a range of editorial orientations, from monarchist to liberal.[16] Louis Veuillot remarked, with classic verve, "newspapers have become so dangerous that it is necessary to create many!" Much research remains to be done on the sociocultural and political importance of these Catholic congresses, associations, and press.

By the close of the pontificate of Gregory XVI in 1846, liberal political trends across Europe had been approaching a climax. Gregory's efforts to shore up the Throne and Altar alliance against social revolution, his denunciation of rebellions in Belgium, Poland, and Ireland, his illiberal domestic policies within the Papal States, and his condemnation of Lamennais, taken together conjured an impressive reactionary picture in popular consciousness. At the same time, the Catholic movement had become a genuine political force under the journalistic and political activities of Catholic liberals like Montalembert in France and Vincenzo Gioberti in Italy, although confusion and overlap between liberal Catholics with modernist tendencies and Catholic liberals with Ultramontane beliefs persisted. The same paradigm interregnum that had produced the evolution and confusion of the Abbé de Lamennais's ideas was a fecund period of innovative activism, in thought and practice, between hierarchy and laity, out of which modern CST would emerge.

By the end of Louis Philippe's "July Monarchy" Catholics had been advocating for expanding the voting franchise in their contest over education and religious discrimination, and were found now on both sides of the street fighting of Paris during the June Days in 1848. Archbishop Affre, implored by Ozanam to attempt a peaceful intervention, was killed by a stray bullet on the barricades. Catholic political engagement, allied for a time with the Party of Order, led to the adoption of the Falloux Laws (1850, 1851) enabling Catholic secondary and higher education institutions for the first time since the Revolution. Antidiscrimination committees were instituted. The praxis developed among Catholic laity over the decades from 1830 to 1850

[15] Martin Spahn and Thomas Meehan, "Catholic Congresses," _The Catholic Encyclopedia_, vol. 4 (New York: Robert Appleton Company, 1908). And see also generally by country: Moody, _Church and Society_; for France, Duroselle, _Les débuts_; and for Italy, De Rosa, _Il movimento cattolico_.
[16] Various authors, "Periodical Literature" indexed to articles on Austria, Belgium, Canada, England, France, Germany, Holland, Ireland, Italy, Mexico, Poland, Portugal, Scotland, Spain, Switzerland, and the United States. _The Catholic Encyclopedia_, vol. 11 (New York: Robert Appleton Company, 1911).

diminished the hold of monarchist and Traditionalist conservative paradigms over a broadening of Ultramontane allegiances with moderate liberal political ideas.

In Italy economic and political modernization dictated national integration, perhaps unification. Italian liberal initiatives to modernize their states and Italy as a whole meant confronting not only the political establishments of Piedmont, Austria (Veneto), and Naples, but also the papacy itself with its Papal States, raising the "Roman Question." Italian Catholic liberalism had been slow to develop so long as progressive and nationalistic sentiments were dominated by radical liberal and revolutionary tendencies of secret societies like the Carbonari or Mazzini's "Young Italy" into the 1840s. It took Vincenzo Gioberti's neo-Guelf program, advocated in his *Primato morale e civile degli Italiani* (1843), which imagined papal leadership of an Italian confederation, to bring together moderate liberal and nationalistic sentiments.

PIUS IX (1846–1878)

The young Giovanni Mastai, who took the name of Pius IX, has in the course of time stirred a considerable historiographical debate. What none of the conservative forces of Europe could have expected was that over the altar that they intended to defend their thrones might come to preside a liberal.[17] To contemporaries his policies engendered mad swings of emotion, from early adulation to loathing. The consensus today is that these were the result of exaggerated expectations and an unfortunate lack of statecraft on the part of Pius IX. When Pius issued a general amnesty for political prisoners, which was not unusual, and followed with moderately liberal reforms (such as freedom of association and of the press) he sparked a wave of enthusiasm.[18] Perhaps

---

[17]   Roger Aubert, *Le Pontificat de Pie IX (1846–1878)*, vol. 21 (Paris: Bloud et Gay, 1952), 11–13. And see generally on the papacy of Pius IX: Latourette, *History of Christianity*, 266–293; and Giacomo Martina, "Pius IX," in *Enciclopedia dei Papi* (Roma: Treccani, 2000).

[18]   Cf., for example, the flood of correspondence addressed from both lay and church people to "the zealous reformer of abuses," "the pope of social regeneration," Droulers, *Cattolicesimo sociale*, 171; and the flights of fancy by the social Catholic Ozanam: "[T]his pontiff that one meets on foot in the street ... this courageous reformer of the abuses of temporal government seems truly sent by God to conclude the great affair of the 19th century, the alliance of religion and liberty." Letter to dom Guéranger, early 1847, in Aubert, *Pie IX*, 20, and especially the enthusiasm of a Massimo Taparelli D'Azeglio, recent author of an exposé of corruption in the Papal States, *Degli ultimi casi di Romagna* (1846), and destined to be Prime Minister of the Kingdom of Sardinia (Piedmont, 1849–52): "Here is Pius IX the promoter of the whole liberal movement and the papacy at the head of the century. Who would have said eighteen months ago! ... If Pius IX continues, (and why not?) he will become the moral leader of Europe and he will do what

foreseeably, these liberalizations were among the most important factors leading to the revolution of 1848 in Rome.[19]

There were two crucial obstacles to papal support for unification in Italy along neo-Guelf lines: the first was that while he was opposed to Austrian dominion in Italy, the pope could not possibly favor, let alone preside over, a war between Catholics. Secondly, Pius believed he had no authority, by himself, to relinquish sovereignty over the Papal States, and therefore did not intend to reform his government to the point of doing so.[20]

Precisely because he was a man of his times, full of the concepts of progress and amelioration of society that were then commonplace, Pius had no inherent disagreement with liberalization of institutions in the abstract.[21] Aware of the need for modernization of economy and administration in his own states and beyond, for the combined moral and material progress of humanity, Pius was loath to denounce a movement that he hoped could be turned to the benefit of humanity. He was determined to show that religion was compatible with progress.[22] Pius undoubtedly felt that dangerous principles needing correction in the liberal school of thought had already been adequately condemned by Gregory XVI in the case of Lamennais with *Mirari vos* (1832).[23] When Pius IX revisited errors of unqualified liberalism in *Quanta cura* (1864) it was part of his development of a comprehensive, groundbreaking step to establish the terms on which a Catholic dialogue with modernity could proceed.

Had the public read *Qui pluribus* (1846) at the outset of his pontificate, liberal adulation and exaggerated expectations of Pius IX might have been different. Pius fully reiterated the teachings of his predecessor.[24] There was still lacking in 1846 a sufficient theoretical framework to respond effectively to the intellectual challenges posed by *laissez-faire* liberalism and socialism; however, he took pains to underscore the harmony of faith and reason versus liberal rationalism:[25]

neither Bossuet, nor Leibnitz were able to do, he will reestablish the unity of Christianity," in Aubert, *Pie IX*, 21.

[19] Harry Hearder, *Italy in the Age of the Risorgimento, 1790–1870* (London: Longman, 1983), 109–112.

[20] Moody, *Church and Society*, 37.

[21] Aubert, *Pie IX*, 14–16.

[22] Paul Droulers, "Un Anglican associationniste-chrétien chez Pie IX en 1847," in *Cattolicesimo sociale*, 93.

[23] Droulers, "Un Anglican associationniste," 93.

[24] Cf. Aubert, *Pie IX*, 20.

[25] Pius IX, Encyclical Letter *Qui pluribus* (On Faith and Religion) (November 9, 1846), nos. 5 and 6.

5. In order to easily mislead the people into making errors, deceiving particularly the imprudent and the inexperienced, they pretend that they alone know the ways to prosperity . . . these enemies never stop invoking the power and excellence of human reason; they raise it up against the most holy faith of Christ, and they blather with great foolhardiness that this faith is opposed to human reason.

6. . . . For although faith is above reason, no real disagreement or opposition can ever be found between them; this is because both of them come from the same greatest source of unchanging and eternal truth, God. They give such reciprocal help to each other that true reason shows, maintains and protects the truth of the faith, while faith frees reason from all errors and wondrously enlightens, strengthens and perfects reason with the knowledge of divine matters.

Communism, but not liberalism, is unequivocally repudiated as contrary to natural law, among the "filthy medley of errors" aimed at the corruption of the young:[26]

16. . . . To this goal also tends the unspeakable doctrine of Communism, as it is called, a doctrine most opposed to the very natural law. For if this doctrine were accepted, the complete destruction of everyone's laws, government, property, and even of human society itself would follow.

Pius's modified tone regarding Throne and Altar relations rests on an appeal to mutual support and cooperation on common ends:[27]

34. We hope that Our political leaders will keep in mind, in accordance with their piety and religion, that "the kingly power has been conferred on them not only for ruling the world but especially for the protection of the Church."[27] Sometimes We "act both for the sake of their rule and safety that they may possess their provinces by peaceful right."[28] We hope that with their aid and authority they will support the objects, plans and pursuits which we have in common, and that they will also defend the liberty and safety of the Church, so that "the right hand of Christ may also defend their rule."[29][28]

Therefore, in *Qui Pluribus* there is declared a right of resistance to the exercise of authority violative of religious duties:[29]

---

[26]   *QP*, no. 16.
[27]   *QP*, no. 34.
[28]   Internal footnote references to epistles of St. Leo sent to Emperor Leo and to Emperor Theodosius.
[29]   *QP*, no. 22.

22. . . . Whoever resists authority resists the ordering made by God Himself, consequently achieving his own condemnation; disobeying authority is always sinful except when an order is given which is opposed to the laws of God and the Church.

On a different front, the proclamation of the dogma on the Immaculate Conception in 1854 with *Ineffabilis deus* was a recapitulation of what had long been believed, but not only that. Its enactment reiterated the continuity of tradition, the authority of the pope over declarations of dogma, the honored place of Marian piety, and papal direction of theological study. It also "underlined some essential religious truths denied or left behind by modern thought" including the supernatural order, the adoption of mankind as sons of God, original sin, and the need for redemption.[30]

By the mid-nineteenth century, secular liberal paradigms concerning man and society were being widely taken as grounded on self-evident principles, even by sincere Catholics, though the materialist premises of both *laissez-faire* liberal and socialist ideologies conflicted radically with Catholic conceptions of human nature and human destiny. Meanwhile the proletarian tide was rising fast across Europe. The International Workingmen's Association (the Communist "First International") was formed in 1864. The first volume of Marx's *Das Kapital* was published in 1867. In 1870, the French Second Empire was defeated in the Franco-Prussian war. In 1871, soldiers of the new Third Republic were hard pressed to crush the revolutionary government that took over in Paris, setting up the Commune. Ten thousand *Communards* were killed by the national government, with hundreds summarily executed. Marx (in 1871) wrote *The Civil War in France* in which he described the Paris Commune as a model for the coming "dictatorship of the proletariat."

Bishop Ketteler responded to the challenge of Marxism with his *Labor Question and Christianity* in 1864 condemning capitalist commodification of labor. He proposed Christian "productive associations" with profit sharing. In 1869 he set forth a program of reforms that included Christian trade unions, prohibition of child labor, limiting the workday, disability insurance, and workplace health inspectors.[31]

In response to political instability through the 1850s and 1860s, increasingly authoritarian governments in France, Germany, Austria, and Italy ramped up

[30] Martina, "Pius IX."
[31] Daniel Eissrich, "An Economist's View of the Work of Wilhelm Emmanuel von Ketteler and Its Influence on the Encyclical *Rerum novarum*," in *On the Economic Significance of the Catholic Social Doctrine*, ed. J. Backhaus et al. (Cham, Switzerland: Springer International Publishing, 2017), 15–22.

aggressive centralizing and secularizing initiatives. The culture war (*Kulturkampf*) was not limited to Bismarck's Germany. Restrictions on religious orders and institutions, state control of education, and establishment of civil marriage were common points of attack. Bismarck's domestic political maneuvering reached its apogee with the Falk Laws of 1873–1874. These laws subjected Catholic clergy to state education, examination, and licensure; provided for the imprisonment of objecting bishops; and, in 1875, included the dissolution of contemplative monasteries.

Catholic congresses, particularly in Belgium and Germany, increased in numbers of participants to the tens of thousands in the early 1860s. These brought together research, reports, and proposals from all sorts of associations, in their particular demographic and specialized areas of expertise. International participants included leading laity and churchmen on the social question, including Montalembert, Albert de Broglie, (Blessed) Adolph Kolping, Abbé Gaspard Mermillod, Bishop Ketteler, Cardinals Manning and Wiseman from England, and Bishop Fitzpatrick from Boston, among others. Political differences began to disorient these events. It was at the Catholic Congress of Malines (Mechlin), Belgium, in 1863, that Montalembert gave his famous oration on "a free Church in a free state" that again brought forth the arguments of the *Avenir* group, for which Lamennais had been condemned, and for which people like Döllinger and Acton were on thin ice with the curia. Liberty for the Church required, argued Montalembert, liberty to error, a universal liberty of conscience "without hesitation or qualification."[32] In Munich, at another congress later that summer, Döllinger continued his rise to prominence among German liberal Catholics ("Old Catholics") by insisting on the complete freedom of theologians to speculate on matters not involving dogma, and culminating in 1861 with his argument that the Papal States were of only contingent benefit to the Holy See and, for pragmatic reasons, that the pope would be better off now losing his temporal sovereignty[33] – an argument that had been condemned in *Mirari vos* (1832).

Döllinger could be condemned, but direct condemnation of the widely respected Montalembert had to be avoided, and so the idea was advanced for a comprehensive restatement of modern errors. The encyclical *Quanta cura* (1864), with its appended "Syllabus of Errors," lays out the ideological context of modern confusion in which truth and justice have been replaced by money and might, morality by utility:

---

[32]   Comte de Montalembert, *L'Église libre dans l'état libre, discours prononcés au Congrès Catholique de Malines* (Paris: Ch. Dogniol et Dider et Cie, 1863), 131.

[33]   Howard, *The Pope and the Professor*, 96–98.

4. And, since Religion has been excluded from Civil Society, and the doctrine and authority of divine Revelation, or the true and germane notion of justice and human right have been obscured and lost, and material or brute force substituted in the place of true justice and legitimate right, it is easy to perceive why some persons, forgetting and trampling upon the most certain principles of sound reason, dare cry out together: "that the will of the people, manifested by what they call public opinion, or in any other way, constitutes the supreme law, independent of all divine and human right, and that, in the political order, accomplished facts, by the mere fact of having been accomplished, have the force of right." But who does not see and plainly understand, that the Society of man, freed from the bonds of Religion and of true justice, can certainly have no other purpose than the effort to obtain and accumulate wealth, and that in its actions it follows no other law than that of uncurbed cupidity?[34]

As to the appended list, the famous "Syllabus of the Principal Errors of Our Time, Which Are Stigmatized in the Consistorial Allocutions, Encyclical and other Apostolical Letters of Our Most Holy Lord, Pope Pius IX," a summary list of prior condemnations, a fair criticism is that it is too long, has inadequate context of each error, and mixes essential with secondary matters. The spirit of liberal Catholicism to be condemned, however, is preeminently summed up in the last item of the "Syllabus," Error #80: "The Roman Pontiff can and ought to, reconcile himself, and come to terms with progress, liberalism and modern civilization."[35]

With *Quanta cura* and its "Syllabus of Errors," Pius established the ground rules on which any future dialogue was to be held. This was a necessary step before a theoretical framework could emerge to address the philosophical confusion at the bottom of modern ideological conflict. Predictably, the encyclical revealed cleavages within the Catholic movement. On one side, the more politically conservative and Ultramontanist Catholic liberals welcomed it, while those more politically liberal, and especially theologically liberal, were stunned. Cardinal Manning in England, for instance, saw the battle lines being drawn in a near-apocalyptic fashion between the forces of Ultramontanism, on the side of the papacy as interpreter of the Divine Law, and those of Caesarism on the side of state control over religious belief and practice.[36] The acrimony of

[34] Pius IX, Encyclical Letter *Quanta cura* (Condemning Current Errors) (1864), no. 4 (internal quotation uncited).
[35] QC, "Syllabus of Errors," no. 80.
[36] Edward Norman, *The English Catholic Church in the Nineteenth Century* (Oxford: Clarendon Press, 1984), 263–265.

the debate was dissipated with Bishop Dupanloup's widely read analysis of the encyclical's scholastic Realist hermeneutic.[37] Moderate liberals accepted this reading of the *Syllabus*. Many liberal Catholics, like Acton and Döllinger, insensitive to, or even infuriated by what they considered Dupanloup's "equivocations," moved into open antagonism.[38]

In Pius's encyclical and list, however, natural law reasoning as the basis for a critique of unrestrained liberalism or of socialism is still lacking. This is not to say that Pius did not refer at all to the law of nature or insights from historical experience, but reference to Aquinas's natural law reasoning was not yet a part of the encyclical tradition, and could not become a feature of CST until the formal rehabilitation of scholastic philosophy with Leo XIII in *Aeterni patris* (1879).

A thorough clarification of religious matters, beliefs, and authority, was opportune: there had not been an ecumenical council for 300 years, and much had changed. The Vatican council was called in 1868 and met from December 1869 until it was suspended by the outbreak of the Franco-Prussian war in July 1870, and the subsequent withdrawal of French troops. The document *Dei filius* (*Dogmatic Constitution on the Catholic Faith*, 1870) reaffirmed the deposit of the faith and the mission of the Church, the harmony of faith and reason, and included a canon of beliefs held to be contrary to the faith. Along with rationalism, however, both traditionalism that "routinely devalues reason" and fideism "denying that reason, elevated by grace, prepares man for faith" are equally rejected.[39] As *Dei filius* asserts in Chapter 4, "On Faith and Reason," the Church not only supports but directly advances the cause of reason and of scientific and material progress, when considered in proper subordination to the mysteries of revelation:

> 5. Even though faith is above reason, there can never be any real disagreement between faith and reason, since it is the same God who reveals the mysteries and infuses faith, and who has endowed the human mind with the light of reason.
>
> 6. God cannot deny himself, nor can truth ever be in opposition to truth. The appearance of this kind of specious contradiction is chiefly due to the fact that either the dogmas of faith are not understood and explained in accordance with the mind of the Church, or unsound views are mistaken for the conclusions of reason.
>
> [...]

---

[37] Martina, "Pius IX," and see footnote 59 below on the "scholastic Realist hermeneutic."

[38] Josef Altholz, *The Liberal Catholic Movement in England, the "Rambler" and Its Contributors, 1848–1864* (London: Burns & Oates, 1962), 233–239.

[39] Martina, "Pius IX."

10. Not only can faith and reason never be at odds with one another but they mutually support each other, for on the one hand right reason established the foundations of the faith and, illuminated by its light, develops the science of divine things; on the other hand, faith delivers reason from errors and protects it and furnishes it with knowledge of many kinds.

11. Hence, so far is the Church from hindering the development of human arts and studies, that in fact she assists and promotes them in many ways. For she is neither ignorant nor contemptuous of the advantages which derive from this source for human life . . .

13. For the doctrine of the faith which God has revealed is put forward not as some philosophical discovery capable of being perfected by human intelligence, but as a divine deposit committed to the spouse of Christ to be faithfully protected and infallibly promulgated.[40]

Only the question of ultimate interpretive authority remained, and pressure from Ultramontane Catholics generally to establish papal authority against a whole range of political and cultural enemies made a declaration of papal infallibility inevitable.[41]

Indeed, papal infallibility on matters of faith and morals was a widely held belief historically, and just recently had been exerted with the apostolic constitution *Ineffabilis deus*, on the Immaculate Conception. Establishing infallibility as a dogma itself was also thought opportune by many, but not all. Veuillot and Manning were among those that wanted as powerful a papal voice as possible to confront what they witnessed as the worsening clash of faith and secularization of society in their national contexts. Other prominent leaders of the Catholic movement, like Acton and John Henry Newman in England, Montalembert, Dupanloup in France, and Ketteler in Germany, deemed an official pronouncement counterproductive, particularly in light of what that might mean for the impact of the *Syllabus of Errors* on Catholic political allegiances and social reform efforts underway.[42] Gallican-minded clerics and their followers, as also Döllinger and the various Old Catholic groups stretching from the Netherlands to Hungary, saw the claim as the last

[40] First Vatican Council (1869–1870), Dogmatic Constitution *Dei filius* (July 18, 1870), Chapter 4 "On Faith and Reason," nos. 5, 6, 10, 11, and 13.
[41] Chadwick, *History of the Popes*, 185–186.
[42] Cf. the outrageous politicization by Gladstone, claiming that faithful Catholics could no longer be counted as faithful citizens, W. E. Gladstone, "The Vatican Decrees in Their Bearing on Civil Allegiance," in *A Free Church in a Free State? The Catholic Church, Italy, Germany, France, 1864–1914*, ed. Helmreich (Boston: D. C. Heath and Co., 1964), 29–32. And Cardinal Manning's response, "To the Editor of the Times, 7th November 1874," in *Free Church*, ed. Helmreich, 32–33.

straw of Roman theological imperialism. The second constitution from Vatican I, *Pastor aeternus*, was passed by a large majority of bishops – including also those who left the Council early in protest. *Dei filius* and *Pastor aeternus* are complementary pillars of the position that Pius was reasserting for the Church and for the papal magisterium within the Church, as he prepared her to shepherd the faithful in the new age.

Three successive "wars of Italian independence" had brought all of Italy under Piedmontese rule in a united Kingdom of Italy – only the city of Rome remained in the hands of the pope.[43] *Syllabus* error #76 states: "The abolition of the temporal power of which the Apostolic See is possessed would contribute in the greatest degree to the liberty and prosperity of the Church."[44] As speculative a hypothesis as that was, the course of events put it to the test when French military protection of Rome was withdrawn after Napoleon III's capture by the Prussians. Italian troops took the city of Rome on September 20, 1870. Papal temporal sovereignty was extinguished.[45]

From 1870, as "prisoner of the Vatican," Pius IX was stuck in a policy of intransigence with regard to the Italian state, and was on the defensive on most international fronts. The "Law of Guarantees" (1871) offered by the Italian government would have given the Holy See rights of a sovereign state, to receive and send ambassadors, and to receive an annual indemnity for loss of former territories. Pius refused to accept this potential resolution, and, as he put it, appear as "the king's chaplain."

Bismarck waged a merciless policy of oppression and control against the Church in his *Kulturkampf* as he sought to consolidate the German Imperial state against internal opposition. Nevertheless, the doctrinally, administratively, and educationally strengthened Church under Pius IX, and the voice of morality and justice that the pope exercised in the new conditions of mass communication, were all necessary conditions for the development of CST by his successor. Pius had prepared the terrain in which modern CST could sound above partisan, national, and class interests. Giacomo Martina credits that among Pius's legacies was this broadening of Ultramontane sentiment internationally: "one felt Catholic not because of having been born in this or that country, baptized in this or that parish, but because of fidelity to the pope, to the bishop of Rome, vicar of Christ."[46]

[43] Generally, Frank J. Coppa, *Origins of the Italian Wars of Independence* (New York and Oxon: Routledge, 1992).
[44] Pius IX, "Syllabus of Errors," no. 76.
[45] Chadwick, *History of the Popes*, 213–239.
[46] Martina, "Pius IX."

Across his thirty-one years as pope, Pius witnessed and addressed tremen-
dously complicated and dangerous historical developments. The era of condemning and refuting false doctrines in the age of ideology was winding down,
and the era of propounding a positive social doctrine was ahead. Pius would
have been entitled to say in his last years after Vatican I and the fall of Rome, as
has been attributed to him, that "everything has changed around me, my
approach and my politics have had their day, but I am too old to change
direction."[47]

THE NEO-THOMISTIC REVIVAL

Pius IX cleared the ideological decks in 1864, opening up space, with boundaries, for the development of modern CST and authentic dialogue with the
world. It was against the backdrop of turmoil (political, philosophical, and
theological) that a reconsideration of scholastic natural law reasoning had
begun. The philosophy of St. Thomas Aquinas in particular, which had been
elevated by the Council of Trent at the time of the Reformation as the
preeminent philosophical system of the Church and adopted by the Society
of Jesus as the foundation for formation of their members, had fallen into
neglect and even disrepute in Catholic universities and seminaries. Modernity
can be imagined as having begun with the reversal of classical ideas about the
nature of man and of political society, by thinkers like Hobbes, Locke, and
Rousseau. A distant echo of scholastic natural law reasoning had come down
to eighteenth- and nineteenth-century intellectuals, via inconsistent borrow-
ings among classical liberal economic thinkers. Adam Smith displays influence from a genealogy through Pufendorf and Grotius, to Vittoria and other
late-scholastic thinkers, back to Aquinas.[48] In the political thought of John
Locke the link to Aquinas is more direct, through Richard Hooker.[49] But at the
turn of the nineteenth century, in universities and seminaries alike, Descartes,
Kant, and Hegel were more likely to be the leading lights than any of the
scholastics.

Reform in Catholic higher education and seminary training was a top
priority of all the nineteenth-century popes. A significant locus of reform
was at the Jesuit seminary in Rome. The Collegio Romano had been returned
to the Society of Jesus in 1824 by Pope Leo XII. The first Rector of the restored

[47] Martina, "Pius IX."
[48] Chafuen, *Faith and Liberty: The Economic Thought of the Late Scholastics* (Lanham:
      Lexington Books, 2003).
[49] Peter Munz, *The Place of Hooker in the History of Thought* (London: Routledge & Kegan
      Paul, 1952).

college was Luigi Taparelli D'Azeglio, SJ.[50] He prepared a report in 1827 documenting the intellectual confusion that prevailed, as he argued, due to the abandonment of the Aristotelian-Thomistic philosophical system.[51] He argued for a return to the sound doctrines on which the Society was based since the first "Ratio Studiorum" promulgated in 1586. His proposals for the orientation of studies at the Collegio, submitted at the beginning of the 1827–28 academic year, also argue that to combat the corrosive influence of Cartesian universal doubt on intellectual and moral certainty a return to the metaphysics of the scholastics was necessary.[52]

Taparelli explains the origin of his ideas in what he called a "scientific revolution" that overturned Lockean sensism and enabled a refoundation of metaphysics.[53] It was the very success among Catholics of the eclectic school, led by Victor Cousin, which stimulated the revival of Catholic metaphysical studies aimed at resolving conflicting claims over the relationship between natural reason and supernatural revelation, as these issues were at the heart of a number of doctrinal and political controversies.[54] Taparelli's conversion to Thomism began in the early 1820s and was of far-reaching consequences.[55] In the late 1830s, assigned to teach a course on natural law at the Collegio di Palermo, Taparelli conducted a study of the natural right and natural law literature, from the scholastics to the moderns, and was led to a return to the "sound doctrines" of Aristotle and of the Scholastics. He was acutely sensitive to the relationships between metaphysics, anthropology, political science, and morality.[56] His course materials resulted in his *Saggio teoretico di dritto naturale appoggiato sul fatto* (Theoretical Treatise on Natural Right Based on Fact).

[50]   Robert Jacquin, *Taparelli* (Paris: Lethielleux, 1943). And see Thomas C. Behr, *Social Justice and Subsidiarity. Luigi Taparelli and the Origins of Modern Catholic Social Teaching* (Washington, DC: Catholic University of America Press, due out December 2018).

[51]   "Osservazioni sugli Studii del Collegio Romano" (1827), folder no. 20 "Difesa della Scolastica," box not numbered, Archivio della *Civiltà Cattolica* (ACC).

[52]   "Abbozzo del Progetto d'Ordinazione intorno agli Studii Supp," in folder "Ms. Civ. Cat. (7b1)" [box 8, n.3], ACC.

[53]   *Saggio teoretico di dritto naturale appoggiato sul fatto*, 2 vols. (Rome: Civiltà Cattolica, 1949), 1. Published originally in Palermo between 1840 and 1843, the work underwent numerous subsequent Italian editions and reprintings, including the definitive fourth edition of Rome, updated and reorganized by the author in 1855.

[54]   Spencer, *Politics of Belief*, 50–51. And see also Jean-René Derré, *Lamennais, ses amis et le mouvement des idées a l'époque romantique* (Paris: Librairie C. Klincksieck, 1962).

[55]   Gerald McCool, *Nineteenth-Century Scholasticism* (New York: Fordham University Press, 1989, 25–36, 56–58). See also, generally, Roger Aubert, *Aspects divers du néo-thomisme sous le ponificat de Léon XIII* (Roma: Ed. 5 Lune, 1961); Paolo Dezza, *Alle origini del neo-tomismo* (Milano: Fratelli Bocca, 1940); Amato Masnovo, *Il neo-tomismo in Italia* (Milano: Vita e Pensiero, 1923).

[56]   Taparelli, *Saggio*, 5–8.

Editions of that work were translated rapidly into German, French, and Spanish, and became a standard work in Jesuit seminaries.

The significance of Taparelli's efforts while at the Collegio Romano includes the formation of a clandestine study circle on the works of St. Thomas. There, a student, Vincenzo Gioacchino Pecci, the future Pope Leo XIII, became Taparelli's student assistant. Pecci requested the complete works of St. Thomas from his family in 1828.[57] The personalist social theory that Taparelli elaborates in the *Saggio*, and the concepts of social justice, tantamount to the habit of solidarity in persons and reflected in institutions, and of subsidiary associations that constitute society, exercise fundamental influence over the development of CST.[58]

The political earthquake of 1848, which began in Palermo and spread across the capitals of Europe, awakened Pius IX to certain understandings – even though the revolutions of 1848 generally had no antireligious animus.[59] Even before his safe return to Rome after the Republic of Mazzini and Garibaldi was crushed by French troops, he had contemplated launching some sort of research and journalistic initiative. It was decided that a journal with serious intellectual credentials should be established and Pius IX turned to the Jesuits and to Carlo Maria Curci and to the more experienced Fr. Taparelli, along with his protégé Matteo Liberatore.[60] The energetic Fr. Curci successfully argued that the journal should be of broad appeal, to address the forces of secularism and popular journalism on their own terrain, and he was tasked with directing the enterprise.[61] *Civiltà Cattolica* was born in 1850 with an aggressive mandate and

[57] Jacquin, *Taparelli*, 57, no. 152.
[58] See, Behr, *Social Justice and Subsidiarity*. Besides his personalist social theory, Taparelli's natural law methodology, based on the distinction between abstract/speculative versus concrete/practical reasoning, and between thesis and hypothesis, has been fundamental in CST since Pius IX. The "errors" listed in the "Syllabus" are errors when posited as "theses" claiming either abstract or concrete necessity – this was Dupanloup's "scholastic Realist hermeneutic" in his explanation of the "Syllabus" – it is not clear that Dupaloup had direct knowledge of Taparelli's treatise, although he certainly would have known of Taparelli's work in the *Civiltà Cattolica*. The thesis-hypothesis distinction Taparelli advanced in his *Saggio* for applying natural law abstract reasoning to concrete situations – cf., for example, *Saggio* §95: "Moral duty must therefore arise from a *necessary end*, it must be an absolute duty, in thesis not hypothesis; it must arise from an end towards which each one tends by a true necessity." Indeed as hypotheses the "errors" listed in the "Syllabus" could be examined and tested against the facts, or even tolerated in light of the facts; but this was a line of reasoning that struck many liberal Catholics – like Acton, Döllinger, and Montalembert – as mere obfuscation.
[59] Ross William Collins, *Catholicism and the Second French Republic*, 1848–52 (New York: Columbia University, 1923), chs. 1–3.
[60] Aubert, *Pie IX*, 39.
[61] Carlo Maria Curci, "Il giornalismo moderno ed il nostro programma." *Civiltà Cattolica*, ser. I, vol. I (1850): 8–24. See also Giandomenico Mucci, *Carlo Maria Curci. Fondatore della Civiltà Cattolica* (Rome: Edizioni Studium, 1988).

quickly became identified as the spearhead of Catholic intransigence, and as the "think tank" of the Vatican.[62] These connections are particularly noteworthy in that it was Matteo Liberatore who wrote the first draft and, with Cardinal Zigliara, was coeditor of the final draft of *Rerum novarum*.[63]

Pius IX established a neo-Thomistic armory at the *Civiltà Cattolica*.[64] In the first issue, Fr. Curci reiterated the traditionalist analysis of revolutionary socialism as the direct by-product of "independent reason" and of the rejection of man's supernatural destiny.[65] Fr. Liberatore began with a Thomistic philosophical defense of the personalist *raison d'être* of society and civil government as a means only of guaranteeing the peaceful enjoyment of one's proper rights, never as end in itself.[66]

Taparelli's first article in *Civiltà Cattolica* was "Social Theories on Education," engaging the highly contentious education controversy in opposition to state monopoly, based on his natural law reasoning on the human person and society.[67] He had been in Palermo during the revolutionary outbreak of 1848, and stood up for religious liberty based on freedom of association, essentially voicing arguments in that *de facto* context, in favor of a "free Church in a free State." He explained to the revolutionaries that the Church also is an association and "asks only for liberty," that "right, violated in one case, is violated in all."[68]

Fr. Droulers sees at the *Civiltà Cattolica* already in the early 1850s the bases on which *Rerum novarum* will be built. There is the equal critique of the materialism of individualistic capitalism and collectivist socialism that treats men as mere ciphers. The remedies *Civiltà Cattolica* proposes are restoration of Christian values in social and economic life, limited intervention of the

[62] Francesco Dante, *Storia della "Civiltà Cattolica"(1850–1891), Il laboratorio del Papa* (Roma: Edizioni Studium, 1990).

[63] Giovanni Antonnazi, *L'Encyclica "Rerum Novarum" e il suo tempo* (Roma: Edizioni di Storia e Letteratura, 1991), 63–74; Gabriele de Rosa, "Le Origini della 'Civiltà Cattolica' in *Civiltà Cattolica (1850–1945)*," vol. I (Napoli: Landi, 1971), 94–100, where the author demonstrates the parallels from Liberatore's articles on Christian economy in *Civiltà Cattolica* from 1887 with the text of *Rerum novarum*. Dante, *Storia della Civiltà Cattolica*, chapter "Mateo Liberatore protagonista del 'Rerum Novarum,'" 87–125.

[64] Droulers, "Question sociale, état, église dans la *Civiltà Cattolica* à ses débuts," 95–147.

[65] Carlo Maria Curci, "Il Socialismo plebeo ed il volterianismo borghese," *Civiltà Cattolica*, ser. I, vol. I (1850): 8–24, notes that *Civiltà Cattolica* articles are unsigned, with their authors known only by subsequent cumulative indexes.

[66] Matteo Liberatore, "Razionalismo politico della rivoluzione italiana," *Civiltà Cattolica*, ser. I, vol. I (1850): 553–573.

[67] Luigi Taparelli, "Teorie sociali sull'insegnamento," *Civiltà Cattolica*, ser. I, vol. I (1850): 25–51, 129–157, 257–274, 369–384.

[68] Luigi Taparelli, "Sulla Libertà di Associazione. Ai Siciliani," in De Rosa, *I Gesuiti in Sicilia e la rivoluzione del'48* (Rome: Edizioni di Storia et Letteratura, 1963), 245.

state to assure protection of the rights of all, but especially of the weak, and lastly, the promotion of professional associations found in natural law for the organic and harmonious development of society.[69]

NEW THINGS AND LEO XIII

Vincenzo Gioacchino Pecci's interest in the philosophy of St. Thomas while a student at the *Collegio Romano* in 1828 took second place to his studies in diplomacy and languages. His degree in canon and civil law was completed at the Sapienza Università di Roma in 1835. Pecci gained experience in multiple contexts of administration, diplomacy, and modern social conditions.

After over three decades as Bishop in Perugia, Pecci requested a post in the Vatican that might be less strenuous – never having been in strong health. A sequence of three pastoral letters that he wrote in the last years in Perugia provided his vision for a Catholic modernity as his legacy before retirement. "The Catholic Church and the 19th Century" (1876) reiterated the problem at the base of modern strife, namely the misguided efforts to construct a morality "independently of God and his holy law," rooted in idolatry of the state and unchecked profit motive. The following two letters, one letter in two parts with the same name, "The Church and Civilization" (1877, 1878) began to propound an affirmative program. While repudiating the false premises and promises of radical secularization, Pecci called for an authentic civilizational progress in which Catholics could join with a spirit of collaboration. He paid special attention to labor and social problems that cried out for the attention of Christians and governments.[70] No doubt he had no clue before the papal conclave that his retirement to Rome was going to lead to twenty-five years as Holy Father, and involve him in the production of eighty-five papal encyclicals that would frame the future of the Church across the globe.

As the agenda for his pontificate, Leo XIII laid out in his first encyclical, *Inscrutabili dei consilio* (*On the Evils of Society*, 1878), a catalog of reigning iniquities:

> 2. For, from the very beginning of Our pontificate, the sad sight has presented itself to Us of the evils by which the human race is oppressed on every side: the widespread subversion of the primary truths on which, as on its foundations, human society is based; the obstinacy of mind that will not brook any authority however lawful; the endless sources of

[69] Droulers, "Question sociale," 146, and see also De Rosa, "Le Origini della *Civiltà Cattolica*," 97–100.
[70] Francesco Malgeri, "Leone XIII," in *Enciclopedia dei Papi* (Roma: Treccani, 2000).

disagreement, whence arrive civil strife, and ruthless war and bloodshed; the contempt of law which molds characters and is the shield of right-eousness; the insatiable craving for things perishable, with complete forgetfulness of things eternal, leading up to the desperate madness whereby so many wretched beings, in all directions, scruple not to lay violent hands upon themselves; the reckless mismanagement, waste, and misappropriation of the public funds; the shamelessness of those who, full of treachery, make semblance of being champions of country, of freedom, and every kind of right; in fine, the deadly kind of plague which infects in its inmost recesses, allowing it no respite and forebod-ing ever fresh disturbances and final disaster.[71]

Taking up themes from his pastoral letters in Perugia, Leo asserts that, in fact, civilization worthy of the name has been the product of the care and support of the Church, which stood at the center of nations, supporting their peaceful develop-ment: the Church has been "nurse, mistress, and mother" of authentic progress.[72] The encyclical presents most of the themes that will dominate Leo's voluminous teachings as he aimed to foster positive policies on modern civilization, authentic liberty, marriage, family, and education. In education in particular, and training of youth, Leo emphasized the role of philosophical studies as the foundation of the other sciences, as the handmaid of theology. Leo writes, "Philosophy seeks not the overthrow of divine revelation, but delights rather to prepare its way, and defend it against assailants," and he cites as examples the work of St. Augustine and of the "Angelic Doctor" with "all other teachers of Christian wisdom."[73]

The rise of an anticlerical and considerably antireligious national government and elite culture surrounding the Holy See presented dangers that are not difficult to imagine in the light of subsequent history. Intransigence and the *non expedit*, banning Catholic political participation for Italy (first issued by Pius IX in 1861), remained papal policy. Liberal Catholics continued to hope for conciliation with the new state, and indeed some hoped for a reformation of the Church itself – exposing cleavages again between liberal Catholics, moderate Catholic liberals, and Catholic conservatives that problematized the emergence of any policy of conciliation.[74] Fr. Curci, believing himself to be following Taparellian principles of adaptation to *de facto* concrete circumstances, moved to the conciliationist side and increasingly to the liberal Catholic and socialist side from the early 1870s.[75]

[71]   Leo XIII, Encyclical Letter *Inscrutabili dei consilio* (On the Evils of Society) (1878), no. 2.
[72]   *IDC*, no. 5.
[73]   *IDC*, no. 13; note that St. Thomas is referenced here only by this title.
[74]   Candeloro, *Il Movimento*, 160–164, 192–199, 201–214; and De Rosa, *Il movimento*, 99–118.
[75]   Giacomo Martina, "Curci, Carlo Maria," in *Dizionario Biografico degli Italiani* (Roma: Treccani, 1985).

Leo, conversely, with greater political savvy understood that until the electoral franchise in Italy was expanded, which would not happen until WWI, Catholics were in no position to have a constructive impact on the national level.

Over the course of his long pontificate, Leo demonstrated his diplomatic and real-world experience in other national contexts, displaying the thesis-hypothesis approach to the new things of the modern state and international politics. He was able to reach both a *modus vivendi* with Bismarck and the Kaiser's Germany, recalling the original Investiture controversy,[76] and a *railliement* of French Catholics, majoritarian conservative and monarchist, to join with Catholic liberals against the anticlerical policies of the Third Republic in *Au milieu des sollicitudes* (1892). But Leo's politics in Germany were only a mitigated success, and those in France unleashed a slew of unintended consequences. The effects of a confluence in France of monarchist, Bonapartist-Boulangist, fascistic, progressive, and antisemitic factors into Catholic politics were not anticipated. Since the Paris Commune of 1870, however, the Vatican could no longer stand on the sidelines, and efforts had to be made to reconcile Catholic principles and sound reason with political realities on the ground. The attempted coup d'état of Boulanger in 1889 and the Dreyfus Affair from 1894 to 1906 consolidated the radical Republican grip on the Third Republic and, for Catholics, led to the anticlerical laws of 1905 subordinating clergy and Church to state hegemony unmatched since the Revolution. Leo's efforts in these and other political contexts reveal above all a new thinking about dealing with the modern state, society, and culture, derived in no small part from Taparelli's appropriation and adaptation of his scholastic sources.[77]

In *Quod apostolici muneris* (On Socialism) (1878), published later in that same first year of his pontificate, Leo made it clear that political indifference could not extend to ideologies that were destructive of the common good, or

---

[76] With extremely adept understanding of the German political situation, Leo and his secretary Cardinal Jacobini were able to move Catholic Center party support in return for repeal of most of the effects of the Falk laws with Bismarck's "peace laws" of 1887 – but with considerable "horse trading" and concessions to state authority. Cf. A. J. P. Taylor, excerpt from *Bismarck. The Man and the Statesman* (New York: Knopf, 1955), in Helmreich, ed., *Free Church*, 81–82; Erik Schmidt-Volkmar, excerpt from *Der Kulturkampf in Deutschland 1871–1890*, trans. Ernst and Louise Helmreich, in Helmreich, ed., *Free Church*, 77–78; and Georg Franz, excerpt from *Kulturkampf. Staat und Katholische Kirke in Mitteleuropa von der Säkularisation bis zum Abschluss des Preussischen Kulterkampfes*, trans. Ernst and Louise Helmreich, in Helmreich, ed., *Free Church*, 79–81.

[77] Russell Hittinger, "Introduction to Modern Catholicism," and "Pope Leo XIII (1810–1903). Commentary," chapters in John Witte, Jr. and Frank S. Alexander, *The Teachings of Modern Roman Catholicism on Law, Politics, & Human Nature* (New York: Columbia University Press, 2007), especially 15, 21–22.

more specifically, that embraced a conception of the common good that was contrary to the objective nature of society itself. Socialism violated the natural and divine constitution of society, based as it is on the foundation of the family and private property. Christian principles of charity, true justice, and moral equality were being perverted into claims for equality in material desserts. Leo writes in the second paragraph of *QAM*:

> They leave nothing untouched or whole which by both human and divine laws has been wisely decreed for the health and beauty of life. They refuse obedience to the higher powers, to whom, according to the admonition of the Apostle, every soul ought to be subject, and who derive the right of governing from God; and they proclaim the absolute equality of all men in rights and duties. They debase the natural union of man and woman, which is held sacred even among barbarous peoples; and its bond, by which the family is chiefly held together, they weaken, or even deliver up to lust. Lured, in fine, by the greed of present goods, which is "the root of all evils, which some coveting have erred from the faith," (1 Tim. 6:10) they assail the right of property sanctioned by natural law; and by a scheme of horrible wickedness, while they seem desirous of caring for the needs and satisfying the desires of all men, they strive to seize and hold in common whatever has been acquired either by title of lawful inheritance, or by labor of brain and hands, or by thrift in one's mode of life. These are the startling theories they utter in their meetings, set forth in their pamphlets, and scatter abroad in a cloud of journals and tracts.[78]

In part a restatement and elaboration of Pius IX's condemnation of socialism and communism in *Nostis et nobiscum* (1849), Leo's criticism emphasizes the rejection of divine authority as the starting point of intellectual and moral chaos. He also defends private property, as "sanctioned by natural law" on the basis of inheritance or of labor. With *QAM*, Leo begins to direct his attention to the remedy of the social question. The first step is to recognize the subsidiary structure of society:

> For, He who created and governs all things has, in His wise providence, appointed that the things which are lowest should attain their ends by those which are intermediate, and these again by the highest. Thus, as even in the kingdom of heaven He hath willed that the choirs of angels be distinct and some subject to others, and also in the Church has instituted various orders and a diversity of offices, so that all are not apostles or doctors or pastors, (1 Cor. 12:28) so also has He appointed that there should be various orders in

---

[78] Leo III, Encyclical Letter *Quod apostolici muneris* (On Socialism) (1878), prefatory paragraphs.

civil society, differing in dignity, rights, and power, whereby the State, like the Church, should be one body, consisting of many members, some nobler than others, but all necessary to each other and solicitous for the common good.[79]

Leo contends that the Church, "sustained by the precepts of natural and divine law, provides with especial care for public and private tranquillity in its doctrines and teachings regarding the duty of government and the distribution of the goods which are necessary for life and use."[80] Against false and destructive claims of entitlement to a community of goods, the Church teaches respect for obligations in justice but also promotes provision for the needs of the poor through charitable associations, combined with a reminder of man's eternal destiny. An approach combining natural and divine law is reiterated as the "best way" for solving the social problems of the day. Leo understood the inevitable totalitarian consequence of socialism: "For, as the very evidence of facts and events shows, if this method is rejected or disregarded, one of two things must occur: either the greater portion of the human race will fall back into the vile condition of slavery which so long prevailed among the pagan nations, or human society must continue to be disturbed by constant eruptions, to be disgraced by rapine and strife, as we have had sad witness even in recent times."[81] It was a simple conclusion in theory and verified from history that socialism inevitably leads to anarchy, and that tyranny and slavery follow.

In his first two encyclicals, Leo XIII manifested his understanding that the great conflict of ideologies in industrial society was not between competing political forms with greater or lesser popular participation, or lesser or greater state intervention in the regulation of civil society. Political ideologies, political parties, and policies were surface matters, consequences and derivations from competing visions of the very nature of man and society, of the common good, and of happiness. The challenges of industrial society that the Church had to confront were not merely economic, social, or political, but philosophical and cultural. Leo indicates in his next encyclical, *Aeterni patris* (On the Restoration of Christian Philosophy) (1879), how confused metaphysical and anthropological beliefs were at the root of modern crisis:

> Whoso turns his attention to the bitter strifes of these days and seeks a reason for the troubles that vex public and private life must come to the conclusion that a fruitful cause of the evils which now afflict, as well as those which threaten, us lies in this: that false conclusions concerning divine and human things, which originated in the schools of philosophy, have now crept into all

[79] QAM, no. 6.
[80] QAM, no. 9.
[81] QAM, no. 9.

the orders of the State, and have been accepted by the common consent of the masses. For, since it is in the very nature of man to follow the guide of reason in his actions, if his intellect sins at all his will soon follows; and thus it happens that false opinions, whose seat is in the understanding, influence human actions and pervert them.[82]

In calling for a restoration of "Christian" philosophy in *Aeterni patris*, Leo invokes the example of the early Church Fathers. Philosophy as the product of human reason, implanted in us by God, "if rightly made use of by the wise" has multiple purposes in the divine plan: as *praeparatio evangelica*, in complementing and deepening the understanding of faith, as a preparation for advanced theological thought, and for apologetics in defense of the faith against attacks from philosophical critics.[83] The medieval Scholastic philosophers are singled out for the coherence, clarity, and strength of their reasoning, and St. Thomas is singled out as the most excellent among them in breadth and depth of thought:

> Philosophy has no part which [St. Thomas] did not touch finely at once and thoroughly; on the laws of reasoning, on God and incorporeal substances, on man and other sensible things, on human actions and their principles, he reasoned in such a manner that in him there is wanting neither a full array of questions, nor an apt disposal of the various parts, nor the best method of proceeding, nor soundness of principles or strength of argument, nor clearness and elegance of style, nor a facility for explaining what is abstruse.[84]

Leo XIII, from his earliest education, from his studies with Taparelli at the Collegio Romano, from familiarity with Taparelli's work on "natural right based on fact" and on philosophical, theological, social, political, and economic topics, had deep appreciation for the comprehensive philosophical enterprise of St. Thomas. Liberatore was among the drafters of *Aeterni patris*, and there is a strong reverberation of Taparelli's arguments in favor of a restoration of the philosophy of St. Thomas from the 1820s. Reforming philosophical studies in the universities and high schools was an urgent task, Leo writes:

> 27. Many are the reasons why We are so desirous of this. In the first place, then, since in the tempest that is on us the Christian faith is being constantly assailed by the machinations and craft of a certain false wisdom, all youths,

---

[82] Leo XIII, Encyclical Letter *Aeterni patris* (On the Restoration of Christian Philosophy) (1879), no. 2.

[83] AP, nos. 4–7.

[84] AP, no. 17.

but especially those who are the growing hope of the Church, should be nourished on the strong and robust food of doctrine, that so, mighty in strength and armed at all points, they may become habituated to advance the cause of religion with force and judgment, "being ready always, according to the apostolic counsel, to satisfy every one that asketh you a reason of that hope which is in you,"(1 Peter 3:15) and that they "may be able to exhort in sound doctrine and to convince the gainsayers." (Titus 1:9)

[. . .]

29. For, the teachings of Thomas on the true meaning of liberty, which at this time is running into license, on the divine origin of all authority, on laws and their force, on the paternal and just rule of princes, on obedience to the higher powers, on mutual charity one toward another – on all of these and kindred subjects – have very great and invincible force to overturn those principles of the new order which are well known to be dangerous to the peaceful order of things and to public safety.[85]

As fundamental as *Aeterni patris* is for the formal restoration of scholastic philosophy to Catholic schools, it must be appreciated in context with the rest of Leo's program – his remaining eighty-two encyclicals, administrative reforms, and international activities defending the interests of the Church and faithful in very terrestrial political contexts. What Leo accomplishes for modern CST with *Aeterni patris* is the establishment of a Catholic approach to modernity that advances on the twin pillars of faith and reason, from the wisdom of scripture and tradition to the insights of natural reason, of philosophy and natural law. The institutional component of Leo's program, including the founding in 1879 of the Pontifical Academy of St. Thomas Aquinas, would have a long-lasting impact on the development of Catholic philosophical and theological education well through the first half of the twentieth century.

The sequence and logic of Leo's first encyclicals reveals the forethought he had given to both the cultural and material dimensions of modern crisis. From his time as Nuncio in Belgium he had first-hand experience of the deplorable conditions of industrial workers, and of the flourishing political and social Catholic movement there. As Bishop of Perugia for thirty-two years, and as Apostolic Nuncio to Belgium for three years before that, he experienced all of the political complexities of conflicting factions and parliamentary politics. He dealt firsthand with artisanal and rural impoverishment, ecclesiastical and government corruption, and seminary and university educational deficiencies.[86]

[85]   AP, nos. 27 and 29.
[86]   Malgeri, "Leo XIII."

Although Leo reaffirms in *Immortale dei* (On the Christian Constitution of States, 1885) the Catholic attitude of indifference toward regime form in civil society so long as the regime is oriented to the well-being of its citizens, he underscores that well-being includes the fulfillment of religious duties appertaining to ecclesiastical society of which the Christian is also a citizen.[87] *Immortale dei* includes a broad call for Catholics to become engaged in the political process, beyond local and administrative functions:

> 45. It follows clearly, therefore, that Catholics have just reasons for taking part in the conduct of public affairs. For in so doing they assume not nor should they assume the responsibility of approving what is blameworthy in the actual methods of government, but seek to turn these very methods, so far as is possible, to the genuine and true public good, and to use their best endeavors at the same time to infuse, as it were, into all the veins of the State the healthy sap and blood of Christian wisdom and virtue.[88]

More than reasonable, it is the "duty" of all Catholics "worthy of the name" to become involved in the development of authentic civilization:

> 46. In these Our days it is well to revive these examples of Our forefathers. First and foremost, it is the duty of all Catholics worthy of the name and wishful to be known as most loving children of the Church, to reject without swerving whatever is inconsistent with so fair a title; to make use of popular institutions, so far as can honestly be done, for the advancement of truth and righteousness; to strive that liberty of action shall not transgress the bounds marked out by nature and the law of God; to endeavor to bring back all civil society to the pattern and form of Christianity which We have described. It is barely possible to lay down any fixed method by which such purposes are to be attained, because the means adopted must suit places and times widely differing from one another.[89]

In the years leading up to the publication of *Rerum novarum* (1891) there was a tremendous amount of activity on the Social Question across the Catholic world: study, research, and discussion. The Fribourg Union in Switzerland (*L'Union catholique des études sociales et économique*) had been convoked by Bishop Gaspard Mermillod in 1884 and met each October from 1885 to 1891. Mermillod thought it opportune to summon leaders from all of

---

[87] Leo XIII, Encyclical Letter *Immortale dei* (On the Christian Constitution of States) (November 1, 1885), nos. 4–6.

[88] ID, no. 45.

[89] ID, no. 46.

the various congresses and study circles across Europe to work out a common program in preparation for the social encyclical that was being widely anticipated. With René La Tour du Pin, Mermillod brought together Gaspard Decurtins, Prince Lowenstein, Count Kufstein, Karl von Vogelsang, Albert De Mun, and Charles Perin, among others, with regular visits and presentations to working groups by contributors, including those close to Vatican neo-Thomistic thinking, like Matteo Liberatore.

Bishop Mermillod enjoyed the confidence of Leo XIII and had regular access, being named to an advisory council established in preparation of the social encyclical, and was made a cardinal in 1890. The early meetings were heavily influenced by the work of Ketteler. Position papers often represented compromise resolutions between conservative and moderate liberal arguments.[90] In 1886, during the "just wage" debate, the proposition was approved that wages needed to be evaluated in a double light of economic exchange and negotiated compensation, but also the need to provide for family subsistence. Cardinal Zigliara, one of the main editors of *Rerum novarum* with Liberatore, would later opine that the principles in play in the first instance are of commutative justice, while regard for family subsistence falls under duties of natural honesty and charity.[91] In 1887, on the issue of justice and the social question, Mermillod argued, as Ketteler had, that principles of justice had to be embodied in legislation, assuming the insufficiency of charitable giving.[92] The final resolution on this follows the principle of subsidiarity, that only where *in fact* private charity was insufficient to alleviate the misery of the poor was some state intervention required.[93] Conservatives like Vogelsang advocated for a stronger corporatist vision, but the Fribourg Union resolutions of 1890 largely retained a subsidiarity approach, namely that the state's responsibility was primarily to indirectly assist in the harmonization

---

90 Normand Paulhus, "Social Catholicism and the Fribourg Union," in *Selected Papers from the Annual Meeting (Society of Christian Ethics), 21st Annual Meeting* (Society of Christian Ethics, 1980), 63–88. And see also Guy Bedouelle, "De l'influence réelle de 'Union de Fribourg' sur l'encyclique *Rerum Novarum*," *Publications de l'Ecole Française de Rome* 232 (1997): 241–254.

91 Gabriele De Rosa, "L'Enciclica nella corrispondenza dei vescovi con il Papa," in *L'Enciclica "Rerum Novarum" e il suo tempo* (Roma: Edizioni die Storia e Letteratura, 1991), 20–21.

92 Paulhus, "Fribourg Union."

93 "If society does not manage to give due consideration and influence to [charity] and to say: 'we give to him who gives us nothing in return,' the economic problem will never be solved." Luigi Taparelli, "Critical Analysis of the First Principles of Political Economy," trans. Thomas C. Behr, *Journal of Markets and Morality*, vol. 14, no. 2 (Fall 2011): 630.

of the activities of private interests of individuals and of their various associations with the common good.[94]

A further "think tank" that closely contributed to the teachings in *Rerum novarum* was the *Circolo degli Studi Sociali ed Economici di Roma* that had been founded in 1881 by Papal Secretary Domenico Jacobini. Matteo Liberatore was one of the chief collaborators there as well. When it comes to Liberatore's final edits to the manuscript of *Rerum novarum*, his effort to mitigate the vestiges of conservative anticapitalism and to encourage Catholic moderate liberals is clear from all of the careful studies that have been done on the manuscript under Liberatore's influence. Capitalism is not condemned as a system, but rather abuses driven by greed are.[95] Liberatore had published his *Principii di Economia Politica* in 1889, and had written extensive articles in *Civiltà Cattolica* on Christian economy, worker's associations, and government interventionism in the workplace between 1885 and 1889.

Elevation of private property rights as part of the natural law – not merely artifacts of positive law "sanctioned" by natural law (*QAM*), but now "sacred" and "inviolable" in the encyclical[96] – marks the extent to which the neo-Thomists from Taparelli to Liberatore sought to preserve the advantages of capitalist development, while justifying regulation against capitalist excesses. Leo accepted the Taparellian demonstration that socialism was not a repudiation of laissez-faire liberalism but its logical consequence, both being based on a common materialist worldview, differing only in their proposals for best satisfying bestial needs. Taparelli had sought to baptize Locke's idolatrous conception of property by restoring to it a Catholic understanding of man and society, and of the duties of men toward their creator, themselves, and each other. Individual rights, in this understanding, are the result of the moral recognition of human identity and equality of duties and are what civil government largely exists to defend. This was a thought cherished by Leo XIII.[97]

---

94   Taparelli, *Saggio*, "Chapter VI: Degrees of Subordination Among Diverse Societies, or rather, Hypotactic Right." § 685–720; see "Treatise on Subsidiarity" in Behr, *Social Justice and Subsidiarity*, "Appendix" and Luigi Taparelli, "Ordine sociale e commando diretto," *Civiltà Cattolica*, ser. I, vol. X (1850), 97, 100–104.

95   Gabriele De Rosa, "L'orizzonte e il contesto di un'enciclica," *I tempi della "Rerum Novarum"* in De Rosa, ed. (Roma: Istituto Luigi Sturzo, Rubbettino Editore, 2002), 7.

96   Leo XIII, Encyclical Letter *Rerum novarum* (On the Condition of the Working Classes) (1891), no. 46. RN is also referred to as "Rights and Duties of Capital and Labor" or "On the Condition of Labor" (from the Latin text, *de conditione opificum*), or "On the Condition of the Working Classes."

97   See the essays by Fr. Ernest Fortin on complications that he sees in CST bridging classical and modern worldviews: "'Sacred and Inviolable': *Rerum Novarum* and Natural Rights" and

Rerum novarum was only made possible with the restoration of Thomistic natural law reasoning and was fundamentally shaped by the Taparellian natural law methodology that moved from abstract to the concrete, from thesis to hypothesis, in the comparative analysis of duties and rights in the social order, formulated already since the 1840s. On the other hand, the appearance of *Rerum novarum* at the end of the nineteenth century, when in many places conditions of labor were already improving, was not merely the result of intellectual development but also depended explicitly on the deep and wide-spread experience of Catholic political, economic, social, and charitable praxis.

In this way Cardinal Manning and Cardinal Gibbons influenced the encyclical in its openness to democratic institutions and to the labor movement engaged in the struggle for just treatment. Cardinal Gibbons of Baltimore shared, in an 1887 letter, lessons from the Knights of Labor movement in America.[98] Gibbons pointed out that only an organization capable of defending the interests of workers against the growing strength of monopoly capital interests would be able to counter the rise of masonic and socialist influence among Catholic workers. The Knights of Labor he underlines did not invent the use of the strike, "the nearly universal and perpetual" means by which workers can protest unjust conditions and claim their rights, nor could the occasional eruption of violence be unexpected (though regrettable).[99] The progress of democracy in America had to be regarded with attention for the differences in its character, its "love of order, respect for religion, obedience to authority."[100] Quoting Cardinal Manning, Gibbons writes "In the future era, it is not with princes and parliaments, but with the great masses, with the people, that the Church will have to deal. Whether we wish or not, this is our work, a work for the accomplishment of which we need a new spirit, a new direction of life and activity."[101] Gibbons closed with pointing out that a condemnation of the Knights of Labor on the basis of it being a "simple" union of workmen alone would appear to the American people as "ridiculous as it would be foolish."[102] Leo XIII's endorsement affirming the right of workers to defend their interests by associating with their fellows – "associations of this nature,

"From *Rerum Novarum* to *Centesimus Annus*: Continuity or Discontinuity," in *Human Rights, Virtue, and the Common Good. Untimely Meditations on Religion and Politics, Ernest L. Fortin: Collected Essays*, 3 vols. ed. Brian Benestad (Lanham: Rowman & Littlefield, 1996), Vol. 3, 191–229.

[98] De Rosa, "L'Enciclica nella corrispondenza," 11–14.
[99] De Rosa, 11–14.
[100] De Rosa, 11–14.
[101] De Rosa, 11–14.
[102] De Rosa, 11–14.

consisting either of workmen alone, or of workmen and employers together" (RN, no. 49) – saved the *launch* of modern CST from irrelevance in the eyes of the mass of Catholic working men and of Social Catholic activists. Instead, the natural law principles of social justice and subsidiarity that inform *Rerum novarum* and subsequent CST has shaped the language – between the paradigms of socialist collectivism and *laissez-faire* liberalism – of the universal longing for authentic human progress.

PART II

LEO XIII TO FRANCIS: THE DOCUMENTARY TRADITION

3

Rerum novarum (1891)

Joseph Boyle

This chapter is an analytical summary of the encyclical *Rerum novarum*. My goal is to illuminate the purpose of the encyclical and the main lines of Pope Leo XIII's reasoning – his key premises and central ethical conclusions. I aim to articulate as clearly as I can the teaching that comprises *Rerum novarum*.[1]

I believe that this modest goal is worth pursuing not only because of the great influence this encyclical continues to have on Catholic teaching and thought about economic morality, but also because of its distinctive value as a particularly trenchant and prophetic articulation of Catholic teaching on individual and communal responsibility for proper use of material assets and productive power.

The influence of *Rerum novarum* on Catholic teaching and practice is most manifest in what has been named Catholic Social Teaching, which in various ways identifies this encyclical as its founding statement. This identification is made in the names and citations of some of the most important papal contributions to Catholic Social Teaching: Pius XI's 1931 *Quadragisimo anno*[2] and St. John Paul II's 1991 *Centesimus annus*[3] were named for and issued on anniversaries of the promulgation of *Rerum novarum*. The identification is also pervasive throughout the corpus of Catholic Social Teaching. This is revealed in the ways in which the accepted principles of Catholic Social Teaching are present or anticipated in *Rerum novarum*. These principles are the common good, the universal destination of goods, subsidiarity, and solidarity.[4] Although I will not undertake the large and formidable task of

---

[1] Leo XIII, Encyclical Letter *Rerum novarum* (On the Condition of the Working Classes) (1891).
[2] Pius XI, Encyclical Letter *Quadragesimo anno* (On Reconstruction of the Social Order: 40th Anniversary of *Rerum novarum*) (1931).
[3] John Paul II, Encyclical Letter *Centesimus annus* (On the 100th Anniversary of *Rerum novarum*) (1991).
[4] See *CSDC*, ch. 4.

characterizing Catholic Social Teaching, I will indicate how these principles figure in Pope Leo's analysis. However, I will also underline the extent to which these principles are not the main point of *Rerum novarum* but stand in the service of the moral and religious reform urged by Pope Leo.

The title of the encyclical is a Latin rendition of the idea of revolution or revolutionary change. The title suggests Pope Leo's (hereafter Leo) concern: a new, less focally political but more economic form of social conflict. This arose from the then-new social realities of industrialization, and especially from the economic relationships defined by the fact that workers are paid for labor by owners, who own the facilities for production and employ them. As the pope noted (*RN*, nos. 1–2), the moral and religious questions raised by these relationships did not have ready answers in 1890, even among Catholic authorities.

Nevertheless, Leo found some things to be abundantly clear: immoral behavior by owners, the appeal by social movements to workers' greed and envy, failure by political leaders to satisfactorily address the issues, and violent and otherwise immoral actions by some workers. These are not facts an empiricist would countenance, but moral evaluations of the social reality of his day that Leo understood to be undeniable. They form the central premises for both Leo's diagnosis of and his remedy for the newly emerged social conflict.

Leo's moral condemnation of the behavior of the main participants in the developing industrial revolution obviously brings to bear the general moral norms accepted by the Church, including the precepts of the Decalogue and of the natural law. These universal moral principles are generally taken for granted in *Rerum novarum*, for example, in the condemnation of avarice, envy, and violence. Only those universal principles relevant to clarifying the complexities of the predicament of workers are articulated and defended, the most notable being within the defense of private property. It is in this context that the principles of Catholic Social Teaching play a role in the encyclical. Thus, Leo's use of philosophical and theological analyses is instrumental largely, if not completely, in the service of addressing these very particular social circumstances and of giving content to the moral reform he urges.

Leo addressed his letter to the bishops of the Catholic Church, not to the Catholic faithful, nor to people of good will – groups to whom subsequent social encyclicals have been addressed. Clearly Leo had something to say specifically to his fellow bishops. The three paragraphs introducing the encyclical indicate the rationale for this message to the Catholic bishops; they contain Leo's formulation of the crisis to be remedied and indicate a complex agenda for leaders of the Church.

In the opening paragraph he set out the terms of the revolutionary changes he would address. The disturbing spirit of revolution had spread from politics to the sphere of "practical economics." The elements of the new economic reality are (1) the expansion of industry and science, (2) new relations between employers and workers, (3) the wealth of a few and the poverty of most people, (4) the developing self-reliance and mutual cooperation of workers, and (5) prevailing moral degeneracy.

This social reality was that created by the industrial revolution in Western Europe and North America in the period exemplified by the dominance of the "robber barons" of America's Gilded Age. Owners of factories, mines, and railroads dominated economic life with little political constraint; workers had a difficult existence and struggled, sometimes with socialist support, to create associations such as unions. Leo noted that this state of affairs was a matter of grave concern and was the cause of much unresolved public reflection and debate, which "fills every mind with painful apprehension" (RN, no. 1).

This painful apprehension obviously was not provoked by the elements of the new economic arrangements taken individually but by the overall situation they created. The third element, although not as such an immoral condition, is troubling, particularly in light of the second; the first seems positively beneficial to human welfare; and the fourth, as such, morally good, although in a context of prevailing moral degeneracy it could well be misused. The overall situation, plainly, was a condition to be addressed by moral reform, which social analysis could assist only by clarifying the moral realities involved.

In the second paragraph, Leo indicated explicitly the implications of this state of affairs for his letter to the bishops: he noted that he had written them previously on matters of public concern in order to correct false teaching, "in the interests of the Church and of the common weal." And he declared it opportune to speak in detail with respect to "the condition of the working classes":

> But in the present letter, the responsibility of the apostolic office urges Us to treat the question of set purpose and in detail, in order that no misapprehension may exist as to the principles which truth and justice dictate for its settlement. (RN, no. 2)

Achieving this clarity would be difficult because of the complexities of the mutual rights and duties of capital and labor. These complexities, in turn, made likely the dangerous prospect that agitators would distort people's judgments and stir up revolt. Complexities and possibilities for mischief notwithstanding, a remedy is urgently needed for the "misery and wretchedness" unjustly suffered by people in the working classes (RN, no. 3). He plainly took for granted the immorality of their predicament, but instead indicated some key moral and religious factors generating the immoral state of affairs: the abolition of guilds in the eighteenth century and public rejection of the ancient religion were causes of employers' hardheartedness and unchecked competition, which were increased by usury. The concentration of hiring and trading power in the hands of a relatively few wealthy people allowed them to oppress the laboring poor in a condition hardly better than slavery.

In short, Leo started by pointing to serious and widely recognized wrongs that urgently called out for a remedy. The remainder of the encyclical articulates the elements of a satisfactory remedy. The first step was setting aside the impractical and immoral remedy offered by socialism. In doing this he sought to establish a necessary condition for any satisfactory remedy, that is, respect for private property. He then proceeded to spell out the main lines of an adequate remedy. This remedy had several distinct elements, but his unifying idea was straightforward: that moral and religious commitment by all the parties in society to right the wrongs done to working people alone provided a remedy proportionate to the situation. Leo certainly did not think that actions by the Church or its authorities provided a proportionate remedy, nor that political action did so either, but rather that virtuous living in accord with Christian belief and morality by all members of society was required. I will call this the Catholic Remedy.

My exposition follows what seem to me to be the main topics of Leo's reasoning: first, the rejection of socialism, Section I; then, the articulation of the Catholic Remedy in Section II; then, the detail of the division of labor within that remedy between ecclesial and political action in Section III. Finally, I consider some especially pressing particular matters: strikes, violence and workers' rights in Section IV; just wage and expanding ownership in Section V; and private associations, including unions, in Section VI. I end with some comments on the encyclical's conclusion in Section VII.

I

Socialism and Private Property (RN, nos. 4–15)

Leo began the discussion of socialism with a complex sentence in which he managed both to condemn the strategy of the socialists and to define the position:

> To remedy these wrongs, the socialists, working on the poor man's envy of the
> rich, are striving to do away with private property, and contend that individual

possessions should become the common property of all, to be administered
by the State or by municipal bodies. (RN, no. 4)

The indictment included in attributing to socialists a strategy based on stirring
up envy indicates that Leo objected to socialism not simply because he
believed it a false doctrine of political and economic life, but because its
proponents engage in immoral tactics by seeking to exploit the moral failings
of members of the working class. This indictment repeats a moral concern
already highlighted by Leo in each of the introductory paragraphs: plainly
immoral actions and dispositions, on the part of all the parties to the current
predicament – owners, workers, political leaders, and reformers – are at the
heart of the crisis of the working classes.

The remedy proposed by the socialists is that government ownership of goods
guarantees that all get a fair share of social benefits. But in the opening move of
his refutation, Leo argued that socialist common ownership has just the opposite
effect: workers would be among the first to suffer (RN, no. 4) because they would
be denied the disposal of the wages of their labor – the very reason they have for
working for wages. This motivational consideration plainly applies to labor for
wages and is not reasonably limited to holdings such as land (RN, no. 5).

He proceeded to more substantive moral arguments that the socialist arrangement of economic life is unjust. He argued for two claims: that socialism robs
lawful possessors of what is theirs as a matter of natural right, and that it distorts the
function of the state by interfering with the execution of familial responsibilities.

Leo offered two substantive arguments to support the natural right of private
property. The first of these arguments is that the right to hold goods as one's
own is based on human nature. The aspect of human nature on which he
based this argument is that in which humans are different from animals –
specifically, the ability to conceptualize the future and plan for providing for it
by dealing with things not simply for immediate advantage. Possession of
things, including the land on which they live, alone allows people to provide
for future needs; consequently there is a prepolitical right to provide for one's
basic bodily needs, and so to ownership (RN, nos. 6–7).

The second argument for the natural right of property (RN, no. 9) is based
on the nature of a person's use of the goods of the earth: the earth sustains
human needs because of the labor involved in cultivating it. It follows that the
portion of "nature's field" that a person cultivates bears the imprint of his
personality, and he possesses that portion as his own.[5] On the basis of these

---

[5] Alan Donagan, *The Theory of Morality* (Chicago: University of Chicago Press, 1977), 98, notes
    that this argument is evocative of Locke; Donagan also articulates the obvious worry that this
    sort of argument assimilates property too closely to the moral properties of the human person.

arguments Leo rejected the idea that one cannot own land or an estate but only the fruits of one's labor: the land and estate are precisely what one changes and improves in cultivating it. He thought it obviously unjust for another to hold as theirs what one thus makes one's own and transforms.

Leo turned next to an important objection against the natural right of private ownership, based on the fact that "God has given the earth for the use and enjoyment of the whole human race" (*RN*, no. 8). It is important because God's granting the earth to humankind generally is at its core the principle of the "universal destination of material goods."[6]

Leo's response is to add precession to the Biblical teaching by noting that the objection misconstrues the reality indicated by this statement. Its truth is not that "all without distinction can deal with it as he likes" but rather the conjunction of two points: first, that no part of the earth is assigned to any particular individual; and, second, that the laws of private possession are to be fixed by man's own industry and by the regulations of various communities. Moreover, the goods of the earth, divided into private property, in fact do serve the needs of all. For all depend upon the earth and its cultivation: "there is not one who does not sustain life from what the land produces" (*RN*, no. 8).

The significance of this objection and of Leo's response is highlighted by the final consideration in his defense of the natural right to private property, a further argument, taken by Leo as additional to his defense of property as a matter of justice. This is the argument that the replacement of the right of private ownership with the common ownership advocated by socialism would have very bad moral consequences. Among these is removal of the motivation of people to use their talents or efforts with the further consequence that the goods of the earth will not be well used. Other related consequences are the conflicts between people that include temptations to envy, mutual invective, and discord. This argument is evocative of St. Thomas Aquinas's that individual ownership, though not a matter of natural law, is a way of avoiding a set of difficulties not easily avoided otherwise in the world as it is. St. Thomas is not cited here (*RN*, no. 15), although part of the key text is quoted later in paragraph 22.

This Thomistic argument supposes that earthly things are created by God for the benefit of human beings and is concerned with questions of how that use is to be organized. The division of the things of the world into the property of various individuals and groups is a human invention; it is made to avoid

---

[6]   The vocabulary is Saint John Paul II's: see *CA*, nos. 30–31; *CSDC*, nos. 71–84; Donagan, p. 96, notes that this idea, first articulated in *Genesis*, is the common property of common morality, the Hebrew–Christian moral tradition.

quarrels over things, to provide good order and motivation in dealing with them, in the world as we know it to be. This arrangement facilitates the good use of "exterior things" by limiting the authority of owners to discretion over their property, not over the requirement to use it for human benefit, which must remain common, a distinction also embraced by Leo (RN, no. 22). Thus, although not a requirement of the natural law, and so not a natural right, private property is compatible with moral principle. If the division is carried out so as really to serve these purposes in a fair way, it will be morally justified. This more-Thomistic conception of property, as a device for dealing with some of the results of the fallen human condition, fits very well with Leo's overall moral and religious agenda.[7] Leo accepts the underlying premises of the argument, but seems committed instead to a more robust, Lockean right to private property.

However, even if Leo's arguments for a robust right to private property are philosophically and theologically disputable, what these considerations effectively pointed to is probably sufficient for rejecting the socialist idea of common property managed by public authority. For Leo was most concerned to vindicate the idea that in dealing with the things of the earth and with what people make of them, there are considerations prior to the discretion of political authority. Whatever discretion political authority legitimately has over property regimes, that authority is not over the goods in which human beings find fulfillment. Political authority must, therefore, respect the basic forms of human fulfillment as well as the empowerments to realize them that are served by owners' discretion to dispose of things. This test is not met by a regime of state ownership of the earth and its fruits, where that discretion is taken over by the state. Thus, even if we suppose a more modest justification of private property than Leo mounted, his rejection of socialism seems warranted. For Leo's arguments against state-administered common ownership are credible even if the rationale for private property is pragmatic and qualified.

Leo wrapped up this defense of the natural right of private property (RN, no. 11) by observing the widespread acceptance of private property throughout human history, and by pointing again to its status as a natural right, which is reinforced by the divine law, as indicated in the eighth precept of the Decalogue.

---

[7] The key text of St. Thomas is *Summa Theologiae* II-II q. 66, aa. 1–2. I have interpreted this and developed the ideas in "Natural Law, Ownership and the World's Natural Resources," *The Journal of Value Inquiry* 23 (1989), 191–207; and "Fairness in Holdings: A Natural Law Account of Property and Welfare Rights," *Social Philosophy and Policy* 18 (2001), 206–226.

He then turned to the second argument for the injustice of socialist owner-ship of goods, namely that such ownership distorts the functions of political authority. This distortion happens because socialism implies that political authority should enter into the moral dynamics of family life. Individuals have obligations as members of societies other than political society: in particular, parents have responsibilities within the social unit of the family. Leo was at pains to underline that these responsibilities, and the rights correlative with them, are prepolitical. These responsibilities are not created by the state, but by God, communicated through the natural law.

Leo was careful to allow that political authorities do have some legitimate say in family matters, but only to support a family in distress and needing public help. He held it a great and pernicious error "that the civil government should at its option intrude into and exercise intimate control over the family and the household" (*RN*, no. 14). The intuitive connection between these rights of parents and the injustice of common ownership was affirmed, not argued: "Now in no other way can a father effect this [providing for the necessities of life for his family] except by the ownership of productive property, which he can transmit to his children by inheritance" (*RN*, no. 13). The idea is that if political authority controls the disposal of all the goods in a society it will inevitably interfere with parents' execution of their respon-sibilities, by exercising power over their discretion in carrying out these responsibilities; and that interference is an unjust distortion of the role of political authority. "The socialists, therefore, in setting aside the parent and setting up a State supervision, act against natural justice and destroy the structure of the home" (*RN*, no. 14).

This argument is an application of the principle of subsidiarity, which is not named or formulated in *Rerum novarum* as a general principle but first articulated in *Quadragesimo anno*.[8] The idea is suggested by the Latin word

---

8   Pius XI, Encyclical Letter *Quadragesimo anno* (Reconstruction of the Social Order: 40th Anniversary of *Rerum Novarum*) (1931), 79–80: "As history abundantly proves, it is true that on account of changed conditions many things which were done by small associations in former times cannot be done now save by large associations. Still, that most weighty principle, which cannot be set aside or changed, remains fixed and unshaken in social philosophy: Just as it is gravely wrong to take from individuals what they can accomplish by their own initiative and industry and give it to the community, so also it is an injustice and at the same time a grave evil and disturbance of right order to assign to a greater and higher association what lesser and subordinate organizations can do. For every social activity ought of its very nature to furnish help to the members of the body social, and never destroy and absorb them.
   The supreme authority of the State ought, therefore, to let subordinate groups handle matters and concerns of lesser importance, which would otherwise dissipate its efforts greatly. Thereby the State will more freely, powerfully, and effectively do all those things that belong to it alone because it alone can do them: directing, watching, urging, restraining, as occasion

subsidium, which means help or assistance. The moral meaning of the principle is twofold: (1) assistance to a person or community by a more powerful agent – such as help provided by political society to families or associations – can be morally good and even required depending on the circumstances; but (2) the more powerful agent cannot justly remove the primary agency of those assisted, for that would not be to help them but rather to take over action and its perfective possibilities.[9] In this argument of Leo's the use of this principle is almost entirely to limit the use of state power in respect to the association of families. Its other use in *Rerum novarum*, to constrain state-sponsored welfare assistance (*RN*, no. 30), also seeks to limit state intervention in the initiatives of individuals and associations in providing help to the needy. But the permission of the state to provide such help while honoring the limitation imposed by the prohibitory element of the principle is plainly important and has been invoked in much twentieth-century social teaching.

II

Elements of the Catholic Remedy (Paragraphs 16–25)

With respect for private property established as a necessary condition for any acceptable remedy, Leo set out the central terms of a remedy proportionate to the predicament of workers. He began by stating his authority to address the issue, on the ground of his authority in matters of religion and the Church. He recognized that others also should appropriately address this predicament, explicitly listing them: political authorities, employers, the wealthy, and working people themselves. But Leo insisted that their proper interest does not remove his need and right to speak. He argued that the efforts of others would be in vain if the Church is left out:

> It is the Church that insists, on the authority of the Gospel, upon those teachings whereby the conflict can be brought to an end, or at least rendered less bitter: the Church uses her efforts not only to enlighten the mind but to direct by her precepts the life and conduct of all; the Church improves and betters the condition of the working man by numerous organizations; does her best to enlist the services of all classes in discussing and endeavoring to

requires and necessity demands. Therefore, those in power should be sure that the more perfectly a graduated order is kept among the various associations, in observance of the principle of 'subsidiary function,' the stronger social authority and effectiveness will be the happier and more prosperous the condition of the State."

9 See John Finnis, *Natural Law and Natural Rights: Second Edition* (Oxford: Oxford University Press), 144–147, 159 for commentary.

further in the most practical way, the interests of the working classes; and considers that for this purpose recourse should be had in due measure and degree, to the intervention of law and society. (*RN*, no. 16)

In the immediately subsequent discussion, Leo went on to spell out several of the defining elements in this Catholic Remedy. The first was the rejection of egalitarianism, which reduces society to "one dead level" (*RN*, no. 17). Natural differences among people and groups are inevitable, as are inequalities of fortune. These differences can serve human good because of the different tasks and opportunities that arise in any community. This rejection of egalitarianism is not a rejection of the common human dignity of human beings (*RN*, nos. 20, 33).

The second element was Christian realism about the hardship of bodily labor. Bodily labor is necessary for human life, even without sin, and given the human condition, is a painful necessity. The other hardships of life also endure, because the consequences of sin are bitter and hard to bear. So, there is no device or human plan to banish the ills of human life and it is a fraud to hold out to hard-pressed people the promise of a free, easy life (*RN*, no. 18). Leo invited people to look elsewhere for solace for their troubles. In short, Leo was both anti-egalitarian and anti-utopian.

The third element of Leo's Catholic Remedy was the rejection of the thesis of class war. He rejected this view by first pointing to reasonable grounds for maintaining the complementarity of wealthy employers and workers. There is obvious mutual dependence; and conflict, while possible, causes confusion and "savage barbarity" (*RN*, no. 19). Cooperation and mutual agreement result in good order. Religion, and so the Church, can play an irreducible role in drawing the classes together and in reminding each of its duties toward the other.

Leo went on to list these duties in general terms (*RN*, no. 20). Workers are required (1) to fully perform work equitably agreed upon, (2) to avoid harm to the person or the property of owners, (3) to avoid violence in defending their interests, and (4) to avoid cooperating with "men of evil principles" who make unrealistic promises and instigate foolish hopes.

The fundamental duty of employers is to respect the human dignity of workers, not to treat them as bondsmen. Leo first indicated what the duty did not forbid: an employer may act economically for profit – that as such is honorable. What is shameful, Leo maintained, is the pursuit of profits by treating workers as mere things to be used for their productive utility.

He proceeded to spell out more specific requirements of justice: providing time for workers to carry out religious duties and family responsibilities; seeking to avoid temptations for workers, including that of squandering earnings; and respecting the limitations of workers' capacities, according to age, sex, and strength. Determining fair wages for all workers is complex but is shaped by recognized norms of justice: to avoid exploitation of indigent workers for one's own gain ("condemned by all laws, human and divine"); to avoid defrauding workers of wages ("a crime that cries to the avenging anger of heaven"); and to avoid cutting down wages by fraud, force, or usury (RN, no. 20).

Leo ended this rich and compact paragraph by affirming that fulfillment of these duties by workers and by employers would suffice to end the strife in their relations. Evidently he thought the strife was far from resolved, and that these norms were not being observed – no doubt part of the ground for his earlier moral indictment of owners, and his recurring suggestion that workers might not be wholly innocent either.

This discussion of the mutual rights and duties of capital and labor evokes the principle of solidarity: differences between groups of people are acknowledged, including differences involving clashing interests. The remedy offered mandates overcoming them by just and cooperative action.

A more fundamentally religious element in the Catholic Remedy was then addressed: the horizon provided by Christian hope for eternal life:

> God has not created us for the perishable and transitory things of earth, but for things heavenly and everlasting; He has given us this world as a place of exile, and not as our abiding place. As for riches and the other things men call good and desirable, whether we have them in abundance, or are lacking in them – so far as eternal salvation is concerned – it makes no difference; the only important thing is to use them aright. (RN, no. 21)

Leo went on to spell out the implications of this hope for everlasting life. First, he considered these implications for the wealthy. He began by listing the limitations of wealth to secure happiness here or in heaven, but focused on the obligations of the wealthy to help those in need. Leo used St. Thomas's discussion of property and its necessity as the basis for his reasoning. Thomas distinguished between the power to dispose of something and the right to use it as one wills. In the second respect, "Man should not consider his possessions his own, but as common to all, so as to share them without hesitation when others are in need" (RN, no. 22). Leo immediately went on to interpret this as applying, not to what one needs for one's family or even for living "becomingly" but to one's surplus. Still, Leo's limitation of the doctrine was not the main point; in this context he obviously wished to underline the duties of the wealthy. Thus, Leo stated unequivocally that there is a duty to help the indigent from any property that is extra. The duty in question is not, he asserted, a duty of justice (except in cases of necessity) but of Christian charity, which is a duty not enforced by human law. This, of course, is a developed application and specification of what Catholic Social Teaching calls the universal destination of earthly goods.

Leo next turned to the implications of the Christian conception of human life for those who do not possess the gifts of fortune. Their life of labor is honorable, as Jesus's life and earthly background indicate (RN, no. 23). Moreover, it is virtue that creates the true worth of a person, and that is accessible to all. That virtue is the basis for overcoming the separation between classes, which the pride of the wealthy and the immoderation of the poor together generate (RN, no. 24). When this prospect is located within the brotherly love of those united in the friendship of faith, the prospects for overcoming the strife are excellent (RN, no. 25).

This set of ideas – realism, anti-utopianism, rejection of class struggle as natural, recognition of a set of duties of workers and of owners, the horizon of eternal life and human fellowship – comprises the main elements of the Catholic Remedy. But Leo proposed not only Catholic teaching but also action by the Church to apply the teaching. He turned next to this application.

III

Organized Religious Actions and the Role of Law and Political Action (Paragraphs 26–37)

The central and irreducible action by the Church is teaching people in the way only Christian formation can, that is, by reaching directly into people's hearts and consciences (RN, no. 26). To show the feasibility and importance of Christian formation, Leo sketched a historical lesson concerning the transformation of society by Christian institutions over the centuries. He did not provide specifics, but he did underline the Church's long-standing concern for people's temporal interest. The Church's desire that the poor rise above poverty and wretchedness is his example (RN, no. 27). He linked that effort with the results of living virtuously: the virtuous avoid greed, live frugally, and stay away from the vices of the rich (RN, no. 28). The social effect is economically positive.

Some of the initiatives of the Church and Christian organizations on behalf of the poor, especially associations for their relief, were then noted. These activities created over time a patrimony that the Church has guarded for the poor. Here Leo noted an objection: that the help of the poor provided by the Church should be organized instead by political society. His response was that:

no human expedients will ever make up for the devotedness and self-sacrifice of Christian charity. Charity, as a virtue, pertains to the Church; for virtue it is not, unless it be drawn from the Most Sacred Heart of Jesus Christ; and whoever turns his back on the Church cannot be near to Christ. (*RN*, no. 30)

This seems to disallow virtually any welfare relief for the poor by political society, even by way of a subsidiary political function of assisting people in carrying out a duty they already have. Although it is obviously true that governmental welfare relief could not as such be an exercise of the theological virtue of charity, it is not clear that such assistance to those acting from the motivation of charity must be excluded; accepting such a subsidiary use of political and legal power is not evidently turning one's back on the Church. Moreover, as Leo noted, the duty to use the extra of one's property to help those in need is a general human responsibility, not a specifically Christian duty, which political society can in some circumstances reasonably facilitate, supposing it does not excessively constrain peoples' discretion by high taxes.

Although Leo seems to have been wary of state organized welfare for the needy (perhaps warier than is generally warranted), he did hold that political authority had an irreducible role in the remedy for the condition of working people. He spelled this out in four meaty paragraphs, which complete this section of the encyclical. This is the most explicit discussion of the common good of political society in the encyclical. The common good described here is multifaceted, but the role of political authorities in serving that good is rather limited, particularly in respect to providing welfare to the needy.

Leo began with a brief summary of the role of political leaders as sketched out in his earlier encyclical *On the Christian Constitution of the State*. Rulers should serve the public welfare and private prosperity by directing the laws, institutions, and the administration of the polity to serve this complex common good. They do this most effectively by moral rule, since that promotes virtue and its benefits. This form of rule benefits members of every class, and since it is meant to serve the common good, there is a special ground for providing help to workers, since "the more that is done for the benefit of the working classes by the general laws of the country, the less need will there be to seek for special means to relieve them" (*RN*, no. 32). The reference here to general laws seems to be to the legal enforcement of the duties of employers and to the prevention of discrimination against the working class, not to welfare relief.

Leo turned then to a further and deeper consideration: that the interests of all citizens are equal in political society, and workers are citizens. They are real and functional parts of the body politic. Distributive justice, therefore, requires that the interests of the members of all classes are a matter of concern to rulers. Leo also noted that members of different groups in a society contribute to its common good in different ways, some more directly than others. But those who labor most certainly do contribute to the welfare of the polity. From these considerations Leo concluded:

> Justice, therefore, demands that the interests of the working classes should be carefully watched over by the administration, so that they who contribute so largely to the advantage of the community may themselves share in the benefits which they create – that being housed, clothed, and bodily fit, they may find their life less hard and more endurable. (RN, no. 34)

After noting that the role of rulers is to safeguard the community (RN, no. 35), Leo addressed their responsibility in the face of harm threatened or inflicted on the general interest or on that of any particular class. Peace and good order require state action to defend against such harms. That action is called for by a variety of situations, most of which involve threats to workers' rights in the workplace or to their rights correlative to religious and familial duties. But striking or interrupting work that involves imminent danger to public peace requires that political authority make use of its legal power to stop it. That authority is limited to what the situation demands.

In short, the Catholic Remedy did not exclude political action but included it as an essential part. The role of political authority is primarily legal and administrative, and it consists of setting up the laws in a way that respects the contribution of workers to society and prevents their abuse by the more powerful. Welfare provided by the government is not explicitly excluded but is not emphasized, and strikes can be legally ended if they are violent or otherwise significantly harmful to the community.

IV

Issues of Special Concern: Violence, Strikes, and Legal
Protections for Workers (Paragraphs 38–42)

Leo went on in two meaty paragraphs to spell out his view concerning strikes; he placed this in a wider concern about violence and related threats to public peace. He began with a warning about the widespread passion of greed. This can lead some to steal or to act with violence toward others, including toward owners of productive property. Legal authority should constrain such actions.

He noted that strikes are generally different from these criminal actions, often motivated by legitimate concerns of workers over such things as wages and working conditions. Public action should forestall strikes based on such motivations by addressing in a timely way the causes of such serious conflicts between labor and management. The ground for this kind of preventive intervention by legal authority – by way perhaps (Leo did not get specific) of laws requiring better working conditions or legally binding arbitration for wage disputes – is that strikes inevitably involve harm to the common good:

> for such paralyzing of labor not only affects the masters and their work people alike, but is extremely injurious to trade and to the general interests of the public; moreover, on such occasions, violence and disorder are generally not far distant, and thus it frequently happens that the public peace is imperiled. (RN, no. 39)

At the very least, this verdict sets a stringent standard for legitimacy of strikes; indeed it appears to push in the direction of the complete rejection of their legitimacy, although Leo's acceptance of the contractual nature of the relationship between employer and worker (in RN, nos. 43–45) implies that the worker has a right to withhold his or her labor. The focus is on the organized acts of workers.

But Leo did not address the case in which political society failed to provide a timely intervention to settle a dispute, or cases in which workers act to defend themselves from grave injustices by actions designed to minimize the risk of violence and other public harms. These side-effects of otherwise legitimate strikes do not seem sufficient in all cases for their being impermissible.[10]

It should also be noted that it becomes clear a few paragraphs below (RN, nos. 49–59) that Leo's limiting (perhaps to a nullity) the right of organized workers to strike was not understood as delegitimizing workers' associations, which he endorsed. Leo did not explicitly or precisely discuss trade unions as we now define them, and he clearly preferred other associations as the way to address working people's concerns.

As a counterpoint to his apparent favoring of owners and other public interests as opposed to those of workers in the matter of strikes, Leo also addressed as a special topic some of the interests of working men that require protection through law. The first such interest is the ability to live as the image of God, as a being God himself treats with great reverence. That interest is incompatible with any form of servitude that prevents a person from seeking virtue and living for God. One cannot rightly consent to such servitude, which would defeat the purposes of human life, and indeed violate God's rights. That possibility should

---

[10]   Subsequent social teaching relies on such considerations in justifying strikes; see Jean-Yves Calvez, SJ and Jacques Perrin, SJ, *The Church and Social Justice: The Social Teaching of the Popes from Leo XIII to Pius XII (1878–1958)* (London: Burns and Oates, 1961), 391–394.

be legally prohibited. Evidently Leo was concerned that the essential features of slavery obtained within some of the employment relationships of his day.

Sunday rest and worship was another area of special concern. Here also law should protect a basic human interest of workers. Leo commented that this rest is not for the sake of idleness, spending money, or vicious indulgence, but it is a rest from labor "hallowed by religion" (*RN*, no. 41).

Finally, Leo returned again to his concern that public authority protect workers from the "cruelty of men of greed." Here the focus is on the need to respect the limits of human ability, especially the limits of anyone's physical strength (which requires appropriate rest) and the limits imposed by one's age, especially when physically immature (which excludes factory work for children), and one's sex, particularly that of women (who are not suited for some kinds of work).

V

Just Wage and Expanding Ownership (Paragraphs 43–47)

Leo turned next to the matter of a just wage. Here he developed an argument against the individualist view that wages will be just if they are arrived at by an uncoerced agreement. According to this conception, wages will be unjust only if one of the parties refuses to carry out the agreement; only that injustice should be legally enforced.

Leo's response was to articulate a moral condition on the view that wages are set by mutual agreement. He accepted that agreement is necessary for determining a just wage (see also 45), but argued that another condition also was required. He showed this by way of an analysis of what the labor of an employee involves. It has two components: first, in working on something one is personally involved with it and puts a personal imprint on it; and, second, one does this for a purpose, to achieve certain benefits, starting with self-preservation. Seeking this advantage is integral to the act of laboring. Leo then noted that if one would abstractly consider labor under its personal dimension only, it would be within a workman's rights to accept any wages whatsoever, even none. But the abstraction is falsifying since the two elements of labor are in reality inseparable. The necessity of labor for survival and for the sake of procuring other human goods imposes an obligation that cannot be removed by consent: "The preservation of life is a bounden duty of one and all, and to be wanting therein is a crime" (*RN*, no. 44). He concluded that everybody has a natural right to procure what is needed for life, and the poor can do this only by working for wages.

The overall reasoning of this paragraph seems, then, to be that workers are inevitably motivated in their labor by their interest in self-preservation. Their duty to self-preservation requires that they not exclude this motivation from the terms under which they work. That duty cannot be set aside by the consent of the worker, who would be acting wrongly if he sought to do that. Consequently, that duty generates a right on the part of workers to wages sufficient for survival, which in turn generates a duty of employers to pay such wages.

The subsequent paragraph applies this to the situation where the worker is forced by necessity or fear of worse consequences to accept wages insufficient for survival. In this situation the worker is the victim of force and injustice (RN, no. 45). Leo observed that in this and related matters, such as working conditions, governmental action might not be adequate to the variability of complex situations, and so he instead proposed mediation through boards and associations. Such approaches avoid a general political solution that cannot attend to special conditions and circumstances. Still, he ended this discussion with the acknowledgment that political society must remain ready as needed to safeguard the interests of the workers (RN, no. 46). In short, the moral duty to provide a fair wage is in the first instance that of employers, with a further responsibility on the part of political society to enforce this duty of justice. The mechanism for enforcement is a further matter that should take into account practicalities, and as the reference to boards and associations suggests, workers can have a role to play – but they are not said to have a primary responsibility for enforcing the fair wage.

The topic of a fair wage was closely connected in Leo's understanding with expanding ownership so that property would be more equitably divided. That expansion should be fostered by public action. He linked just wages and ownership by noting that a responsible worker who had enough to survive and support his family would be thrifty, would save something and benefit from that savings. This requires ownership, which the law should favor. Indeed the law should favor ownership by as many as possible (RN, no. 47). That would make the division of property more equitable, and that in turn would have beneficial effects in society: breaking down the classes and their mutual alienation that has been created by the existence of the propertied and the propertyless; increased productivity caused by the willing labor of those who can own its results; and increased patriotism within a community that can prosper.

Leo supposed that addressing the expansion of ownership would require taxation, although he did not explain the precise connection. Instead he focused on a necessary condition for the taxation regime, that it must be one that does not impoverish owners. Taxation is legitimate, but property rights are natural (at least significantly prepolitical), and they amount to nothing if absorbed by the state by harsh taxation. Presumably the criterion for unacceptable harshness in taxing is its tendency to remove an owner's right to dispose of his goods.

VI

Private Associations: Unions and Others (Paragraphs 48–59)

The last of the special topics Leo discussed was the legitimacy of various voluntary associations within a political society. He began by considering a variety of these associations for aiding those in distress, which also have the effect of drawing the two classes together. His examples were societies for mutual help, benevolent foundations, groups set up to provide help in calamities, and institutions for young people and the elderly. He spoke of these as obviously good for all concerned, and he went on later to defend their place within political society and to indicate their vital role within the Catholic Remedy.

He then addressed what he called "workingmen's unions," which he said included all the other associations (*RN*, no. 49). He did not further define this expression, and it does not obviously include modern trade unions, where the association's purpose is to counterbalance the power of owners by negotiating and otherwise acting for workers' interests, in an adversarial way if necessary.

Leo's focus was suggested by his approving references to the artisan's guilds of earlier times, and to their service to the advancement of skill and art as well as the workingman's interest. The modern forms of such associations should be suited to the requirements of modern society, such as the complexity of modern daily life. Leo noted with approval that such unions were on the increase, and also, without evaluative comment, that they were sometimes unions of employers and workers, and sometimes of workers alone.

Leo next turned to the defense of voluntary associations, including workers' unions, as irreducible elements of society. Voluntary associations are an irreducible expression of human sociality, based on the relative weakness of individuals and on the very same impulse to cooperate that binds humans in political society. The differences between voluntary associations and political society are significant but do not imply that voluntary associations are simply creatures of political society, which rulers can suppress at will:

> For to enter into a "society" of this kind is a natural right of man; and the State has for its office to protect natural rights, not to destroy them; and if it forbid

its citizens to form associations, it contradicts the principle of its own existence, for both they and it exist in virtue of a like principle, namely, the
natural tendency of man to dwell in society. (RN, no. 51)

Leo took note immediately of the legitimacy of legal prevention of
associations formed for purposes that are bad, unlawful, or dangerous to
the polity. But that legal power should not become an excuse for
unreasonable regulation of associations (RN, no. 52). That, later popes
might have said, would violate subsidiarity. With this sort of rationaliza-
tion in mind, Leo turned to the defense of associations created by
Church authority or by the piety of Christians. He objected strenuously
to political interference and usurping of the assets of such associations;
the State has no rights in respect to them except to respect and defend
them (RN, no. 53).

Turning back to trade unions, Leo addressed the predicament of Catholic
workers caused by the fact that some of these associations are led by secret
leaders and seem to be based on bad principles. Often workingmen are
coerced into joining such unions. The only alternative is to form their own
Christian unions, since membership in those dubious associations puts the
workers' souls in peril. Leo went on to praise such Catholic organizations
and the many other Catholic associations formed to address the challenges of
working people. Plainly he believed that such associations were a key element in the Church's contribution to the remedy for the plight of
workingmen.

After detailing some of the requirements for the internal organization of
workingmen's associations, Leo provided a summary that focused on the
moral and religious goals they should pursue:

> Working men's associations should be so organized and governed as to
> furnish the best and most suitable means for attaining what is aimed at, ·
> that is to say, for helping each individual member to better his condi-
> tion to the utmost in body, soul and property. It is clear that they must
> pay special and chief attention to the duties of religion and morality . . .
> (RN, no. 57)

Leo then amplified earlier remarks on the internal workings of a good union
and suggested some of the matters such a union would address. Good unions
should be attentive to the rights and duties of employers, not only those of
employees, and would appropriately provide a board for mediating disputes
brought by either party. Leo did not make clear whether he intended such boards
to be set up within workingmen-only associations or within those including
employers or disinterested outsiders. This proposal and others presented, such

as providing welfare for members who become disabled, suggests Leo had in mind not so much a modern trade union as an association, perhaps of workers and others, for the mutual help and relief of workers and their families and for the mediation of disputes between owners and workers.

In short, it is clear that Leo endorsed voluntary associations, and among them associations of workers, and he did not explicitly reject worker-only associations. But he seemed to prefer mixed associations and to emphasize the special role of Catholic associations in addressing the issues of the working classes. After several years of discussion on these points after the publication of the encyclical, Leo clarified his view by allowing that religiously neutral and member-only unions were acceptable.[11]

It remains unclear, however, how far he would accept a modern, adversarial trade union with a recognized right to strike. His pervasive concerns about social peace and the avoidance of conflict, which run through the entire discussion of strikes, associations, and unions, point strongly toward cooperative negotiation and create a presumption against an adversarial understanding of the relationship between labor and capital. The legitimacy of organizing to secure one's rights and so putting oneself in opposition to those violating them does not seem present, and indeed, securing the rights of workers is largely said to be others' responsibility.

VII

Wrap-up (Paragraphs 60–64)

The final paragraphs of the encyclical provide little new content. But they do reinforce the overall religious and moral message of the encyclical:

> . . . and since religion alone, as We said in the beginning, can avail to destroy the evil at its root, all men should rest persuaded that [the] main thing needful is to re-establish Christian morals, apart from which all the plans and devices of the wisest will prove of little avail. (RN, no. 62)

Leo reaffirmed the profound contribution Catholic worker associations would have on remedying the misery of working people. In particular he highlighted an effect of great religious importance: downtrodden workers, demoralized by their mistreatment at the hands of greedy employers, who have given up faith and hope, will be encouraged by a community in

---

[11]   See Calvez, SJ and J. Perrin, SJ, *The Church and Social Justice*, 81.

which their needs are addressed and they are welcomed as brothers (RN, no. 61).

Finally he urged the bishops addressed by the encyclical to use their authority to encourage the clergy to devote their full energy to this issue, to urge on all people of all classes the relevant Gospel teachings, and to arouse in themselves and others the virtue of charity (RN, no. 63).

4

Quadragesimo anno (1931)

Samuel Gregg

1931 was an auspicious year for Pope Pius XI to promulgate the second papal social encyclical. The Great Depression was making its impact felt across the developed economies of North America and Western Europe. Unemployment was soaring in many countries. Politically speaking, Italy was enduring its ninth year of fascist dictatorship, and the National Socialists held the largest number of seats in the German Reichstag. In the Soviet Union, Stalin had established his dominance over the Communist Party and was pursuing his collectivization and industrialization of the Soviet economy. Democratic systems of government were on the brink of faltering in much of Central and Eastern Europe.

In this context, Pius XI reiterated Leo XIII's condemnation of socialism and his critique of aspects of nineteenth-century industrial capitalism. But one of Pius's aims in this document was to outline a program for Catholics to follow in order to address the social and economic upheavals of the time in a lasting and far-reaching manner: hence, the subtitle of *Quadragesimo anno* – "On the Reconstruction of the Social Order."[1]

While *Quadragesimo anno* revisited subjects such as wages and trade unions covered in *Rerum novarum* in seeking to help Catholics, it is perhaps most well-known for two contributions to Catholic Social Doctrine. The first concerned its articulation of two principles of Catholic Social Teaching (CST). The second was the encyclical's articulation of a very substantial prescription for fundamental social change: perhaps *the* most concrete of such proposals ever articulated by the magisterium. As this chapter illustrates, the developments at the level of principle have proved lasting, becoming a set fixture of Catholic Social Doctrine. Yet the particular proposals associated by Pius XI with these principles – most notably, the development of vocational

---

[1] Pius XI, Encyclical Letter *Quadragesimo anno* (On Reconstruction of the Social Order) (1931).

groups and the establishment of a type of corporatist social order – had, by the time of Saint John XXIII, been considerably relativized by the magisterium.

CONTINUITY WITH, AND CHANGE FROM, RERUM NOVARUM

Rerum novarum's subtitle – "On the Condition of Labor" – underscores that Leo XIII's primary attention was directed toward the condition of the emergence of large numbers of employees working for wages in urban settings as industrial capitalism spread across Western Europe and North America in the nineteenth century.[2] Large numbers of these workers had lost or were losing contact with the life of the Church, including in traditionally Catholic countries. The same people were turning to socialist political parties and movements as a vehicle for social change.

In Western Europe, many (if not most) of these socialist groupings were characterized by indifference or even hostility to the Catholic Church and religion more generally. Others were attracted to explicitly Marxist political movements, which, by definition, were marked by deep hostility to the Church. In the Anglo-American world, the situation was somewhat different. The presence in the ranks of the working class of large numbers of immigrant Catholics who remained attached to the Church meant that anti-Catholic and antireligious sentiments were not as widespread in social democrat parties such as the Australian Labor Party.

The Church's reaction to many of these developments helped determine the specific issues addressed by *Rerum novarum*. In some countries, Catholic clergy and laity had established Catholic political parties and movements that involved specific outreach to the industrial working class. The emergence of trade unions in industrial capitalist countries had raised questions about whether the Church regarded such organizations as legitimate and, if so, whether they should be specifically Catholic trade unions, or if Catholics were permitted to join nonconfessional, even quite secular trade unions. At a broader level, there was considerable discussion concerning how Catholic doctrine concerning the nature, ends, and limits of private property could be applied in economies where industrial capitalism meant that increasing numbers of people were deriving their income from wages and capital investment rather than agriculture and other uses of land.

Much of *Quadragesimo anno* essentially involved reaffirming *Rerum novarum*'s responses to all of these issues. Leo XIII's condemnation of socialism, for

---

[2]   Leo XIII, Encyclical Letter *Rerum novarum* (On the Condition of the Working Classes) (1891).

example, was repeated. Although the forty years since *Rerum novarum* had been marked by the emergence of what the encyclical calls "the more moderate section" (*QA*, no. 113) of socialism (understood as stepping back from class war and the proposed extinction of private property), Pius XI stressed that "No one can be at the same time a sincere Catholic and a true socialist" (*QA*, no. 120). The essential problem with socialism, Pius emphasized, including its more moderate expressions, lies in its essentially materialist conception of human nature and human society (*QA*, nos. 118–119). To the extent that any political movement – left, center, or right – accepts such premises, it is irreconcilable with Catholic faith.

Pius XI engaged in significant elaboration of Catholic doctrine concerning the role of the state in the conditions of modern economies. In *Rerum novarum*, Leo XIII outlined very clear boundaries upon the state's economic role. "Man," the pope stressed, "precedes the State" (*RN*, no. 7). This primordial truth, Leo stated, limits the state's role with regard to the creation of wealth and the ownership and use of private property (*RN*, nos. 4, 7) and the family (*RN*, nos. 12, 14). Leo also stated, however, that governments do have responsibilities to fulfill vis-à-vis commutative justice (*RN*, no. 20) and distributive justice (*RN*, no. 33). The latter translates into the state maintaining a particular consideration for the poor (*RN*, nos. 32, 37), regulating working hours (*RN*, no. 42), and facilitating conditions that permit the payment of wages sufficient for someone to maintain a family (*RN*, no. 45). Finally, *Rerum novarum* insisted that the state cannot unreasonably prohibit the growth and activities of what Leo XIII calls "lesser," "particular," and "private" societies (*RN*, nos. 50–51) that in themselves constitute ways in which people fulfill their responsibilities to others and the common good. Significantly, the pope did not just have in mind trade unions but *any* associations that are neither families nor political communities, but which nonetheless help people to support each other. In this connection, Pope Leo noted that it is a "natural right" to join such associations (*RN*, no. 51), which implies that no one can be forced to join any such association – including associations of "working men." This reflects the long-standing Catholic attachment to freedom of association, as well as Leo's recognition that many private associations of his time, including trade unions, were "managed on principles ill-according with Christianity and the public well-being; and that they do their utmost to get within their grasp the whole field of labor, and force working men either to join them or to starve" (*RN*, no. 54).

In *Quadragesimo anno*, Pius XI took many of these positions and integrated them into a general rethinking of the principles that governments ought to follow as part of the wholesale reconstruction of the economic and political order that he believed was rendered necessary by the conditions of the 1930s. This amounted to the magisterium (1) deepening and clarifying two principles of social teaching – specifically, social justice and solidarity – which Catholics are required to reflect upon when considering how to address social questions; and (2) outlining and recommending a set of specific propositions, which might be loosely described as "corporatist," for Catholics to implement in their respective political and economic contexts.[3]

CLARIFYING SOCIAL JUSTICE

The phrase "social justice" appears ten times in *Quadragesimo anno*. Though it is associated twice with the term "social charity,"[4] Pope Pius also links social justice three times to the phrase "the common good."[5] "Commutative justice" is used three times[6] and once associated with "strictest justice."[7] The term "distributive justice" is not used at all, though it is implied in the phrase "just distribution."[8]

By contrast, neither "social charity" nor "social justice" is mentioned in *Rerum novarum*. "Common good," however, is invoked five times. In four of these instances, it is directly associated with "the State," "civil society" (understood as "the political community" rather than intermediate associations that exist between the family and the government or political authority), "rulers," and "the commonwealth." The word "justice" is employed throughout *Rerum novarum*. In one instance, the adjective "distributive" is added to justice, which is described as "strict,"[9] while the phrase "natural justice" is used twice.[10] Justice is also associated four times with the state,[11] and once with "the common good."[12]

---

3   In its 1986 Instruction on Christian Freedom and Liberation, *Libertatis conscientia*, the Congregation for the Doctrine of the Faith refers to what are called "contingent judgments" (*LC*, no. 72). By their nature, such contingent judgments are open to significant changes in content and even emphasis "in accordance with the changing circumstances of history" and the growth of human knowledge and experience (*LC*, no. 72). For this reason, they need to be distinguished from principles of Catholic Social Teaching, which are derived from the Gospel or the natural law.

4   *QA*, nos. 88, 126.

5   *QA*, nos. 58, 101, 110.

6   *QA*, nos. 47, 110, 137.

7   *QA*, no. 110.

8   *QA*, no. 136.

9   *RN*, no. 33.

10 *RN*, nos. 14, 45.

11 *RN*, nos. 33, 34, 36.

12 *RN*, no. 38.

The point of this overview of the different uses of the term "justice" in the two encyclicals is to illustrate a certain lack of clarity in the magisterium's employment of these terms in the first two social encyclicals. *Quadragesimo anno* does not even provide an explicit definition for "social justice," though, as we will see, the phrase "common good" is critical to comprehending its meaning and why Pius XI employed the term.

As an expression, "social justice" had been used by Italian Catholic social thinkers as early as the 1830s. It became more widespread by the 1840s, especially after the publication of Antonio Rosmini's *La Costituzione secondo la giustizia sociale* (1848). In *Quadragesimo anno*, "social justice" was used primarily in the context of showing how justice required a system of property rights, high levels of employment, and the realization of the right to wages that enabled someone to maintain a family, while being attentive to the ability of different businesses to actually pay such wages.[13] In short, social justice is about requiring the state to look beyond the demands of commutative, distributive, and (a narrow conception of) general justice as it seeks to promote the common good.

GENERAL JUSTICE AND THE COMMON GOOD

Pius XI's use of the term "social justice" also needs to be situated in the context of how Aquinas understood the relationship between commutative, distributive, and general justice, and how, as John Finnis and others have illustrated, distorted understandings of this relationship entered Catholic thinking via particular neoscholastic thinkers. *Quadragesimo anno* reflects an effort by Pius XI to restore Aquinas's understanding of general justice to a central place in Catholic political reflection. Generally speaking, "social justice" in *Quadragesimo anno* amounts to the equivalent of what Aquinas understood "general justice" to be.

As a *virtue*, general justice properly understood involves one's general willingness to promote the *common good* of the communities to which one belongs. Here the common good should be understood as the conditions that promote the all-around integral flourishing of individuals and communities. This common good, which is the end of general justice, requires more than simply a broad inclination on the part of individuals and groups to promote the flourishing of others. On one level, as Aquinas specifies, it is a special concern of the rulers since they have a certain responsibility to promote the common good. But Aquinas also notes that it is a concern of every *citizen*: that is, those who participate in some way with the ruling of the community.[14]

[13] QA, nos. 71–85.
[14] See Aquinas, *Summa Theologiae*, II-II, q. 58, a.6c.

There is also the question of general justice's tangible requirements vis-à-vis persons. This is often called "particular justice." Aquinas defined particular justice in the following manner and explained how it produced two species of justice:

> [P]articular justice is directed to the private individual, who is compared to the community as a part to the whole. Now a twofold order may be considered in relation to a part. On the first place there is the order of one part to another, to which corresponds the order of one private individual to another. This order is directed by commutative justice, which is concerned about the mutual dealings between two persons. On the second place there is the order of the whole towards the parts, to which corresponds the order of that which belongs to the community in relation to each single person. This order is directed by distributive justice, which distributes common goods proportionately. Hence there are two species of justice, distributive and commutative.[15]

These two species of justice concern the just resolution of certain coordination problems concerning (1) the relationship between individuals and communities when it comes to the distribution of common resources in a just manner (in accordance with criteria such as merit, desert, function, and need); and (2) relations between individuals and groups engaged in particular exchanges. In the case of distributive justice, there has been considerable attention to its meaning for property arrangements. Commutative justice has been understood as especially applicable to questions such as contracts and the resolution of disputes arising from contractual and other promise-based relationships. In both cases, the state assumes responsibility for coordinating these modes of justice. It provides, for instance, an overall framework that governs the ownership and use of property, and establishes and presides over the arrangements for adjudicating disagreement about the meaning and obligations of contracts.

CONFUSING MODES OF JUSTICE

As illustrated by *Rerum novarum* and *Quadragesimo anno*, the question of the stability of all these terms – legal/general justice, particular justice, commutative justice, distributive justice – vis-à-vis each other has always been the cause of considerable debate and revision in Catholic thought. The distinction between general and particular justice, for instance, can be somewhat obscure. As John Finnis notes, when Aquinas refers to promoting the well-being of the *individuals* in a group, he believes that in doing so one is *also*

---

[15]   Aquinas, *Summa Theologiae*, II-II, q. 61, a.1

acting for the good of that *group*.[16] Likewise, consideration of what commutative justice demands in seeking to determine what two or more people owe each other in a set of mutually agreed-upon arrangements often involves reflection upon the criteria associated with distributive justice.

In Aquinas's thought, all these modes of justice appear to flow from legal/general justice insofar as they are all derived from everyone's responsibility to the common good. It is arguable, however, that efforts to lend stability to these different "parts" of justice caused the tradition, over the long term, to lose sight of this point. This is apparent in the attempt by neoscholastic thinkers such as Cardinal Cajetan and Dominic Soto to clarify the relationship between general, commutative, and distributive justice.[17] Cajetan, for instance, specified that:

> There are three species of justice, as there are three types of relationship between any "whole": the relations of the parts among themselves, the relation of the whole to the parts, and the relations of the part to the whole. And likewise there are three justices: legal, distributive and commutative. For legal justice orientates the parts to the whole, distributive the whole to the parts while commutative orients the parts one to another.[18]

Note how Cajetan essentially places general, distributive, and commutative justice on the same plane. In his schema, general justice is not the foundation of the other modes of justice. The effect of this was to gradually separate commutative and distributive justice from the demands of general justice.[19] This resulted in a narrowing of the scope of something like commutative justice, which came to be seen as strictly limited to dealings between two or more private parties and somehow shielded from the demands of the common good to which general justice points. Likewise, distributive justice came to be defined in terms of relationship between the individual and the state. One finds this schema of justice outlined, for example, in influential mid-twentieth-century books such as Johannes Messner's tome on social and economic ethics as well as Heinrich Rommen's *The Natural Law*.[20]

---

[16] See John Finnis, *Aquinas: Moral, Political and Legal Theory* (Oxford: Oxford University Press, 1998), 217.

[17] On these developments, see John Finnis, *Natural Law and Natural Rights*, 2nd ed. (Oxford: Oxford University Press, 2011), 185.

[18] Thomas de Vio, Cardinal Cajetan, *Commentaria in Secundum Secundae Divi Thomae ad Aquino* (1518), cited in Finnis, *Natural Law and Natural Rights*, 185.

[19] The Cajetan conception of the relationship between general justice, distributive justice, and commutative justice may be found in paragraph 2411 of the *Catechism of the Catholic Church*.

[20] See Johannes Messner, *Social Ethics: Natural Law in the Modern World* (St. Louis: B. Herder Book Co., 1949), 218; Heinrich Rommen, *The Natural Law* (Indianapolis: Liberty Fund [1936] 1998), 67; and Josef Pieper, *Justice* (New York: Pantheon Books, 1955), 125.

WHY "SOCIAL JUSTICE"?

As demonstrated in a series of articles written in the 1960s by the French Dominican Paul Dominique Dognin, one of Pius XI's contributions to Catholic Social Doctrine in the 1930s was to restore the older meaning of general justice to its central place in the tradition's treatment of justice.[21] As observed, *Quadragesimo anno* explicitly associates social justice with the term "common good."[22] But it was not until 1937 when Pius XI spelled out the full meaning of this association in his encyclical condemning communism, *Divini redemptoris*:

> In reality, besides commutative justice, there is also social justice with its own set obligations, from which neither employers nor workingmen can escape. Now it is of the very essence of social justice to demand for each individual all that is necessary for the common good. But just as in the living organism it is impossible to provide for the good of the whole unless each single part and each individual member is given what it needs for the exercise of its proper functions, so it is impossible to care for the social organism and the good of society as a unit unless each single part and each individual member – that is to say, each individual man in the dignity of his human personality – is supplied with all that is necessary for the exercise of his social functions.[23]

Like the bulk of *Quadragesimo anno*'s use of social justice as an expression, the context of these remarks is a discussion of the relationship between employers and employees. They show how *both* groups must go beyond an excessively narrow conception of commutative justice when thinking about what justice requires. Instead they must take into account conditions "outside" this particular relationship that affect the well-being of the wider community. The reference to the common good serves to specify this as the end of social justice, thereby reestablishing general justice as foundational to Catholic Social Teaching about these matters. Thus in *Quadragesimo anno*, the meaning of *social justice* in CST is essentially the same as Aquinas's *general justice*.

The effects of this are several. In the first place, it means that social justice and the common good are not to be confused with either distributive or

[21] See, for example, Paul-Dominique Dognin, OP, "La notion thomiste de justice face aux exigences modernes," *Revue des Sciences Philosophiques et Théologiques* 45 (1961): 601–640.

[22] Jean-Yves Calvez, SJ, and Jacques Perrin, SJ, observe that the association of social justice with the common good may be found in an official letter issued in the name of Cardinal Pietro Gasparri, the Secretary of State, in 1928. See Jean-Yves Calvez, SJ, and Jacques Perrin, SJ, *The Church and Social Justice: The Social Teaching of the Popes from Leo XIII to Pius XII (1878–1958)* (London: Burns and Oates, 1961), 148.

[23] Pius XI, Encyclical Letter *Divini redemptoris* (On Atheist Communism) (1937), no. 55.

commutative justice. Second, it clarifies that the demands of general justice, as understood by both Aquinas and *Quadragesimo anno*, are not limited to the strictly legal/political (as had been implied in the more narrow Cajetan use of the legal/general justice category) but also have implications for the economic realm.

It could be argued, however, that the sheer broadness of the idea of social justice as a general responsibility, particularly of the state, to promote the common good could open up the way for excessive intervention in economic life by the government. For if social justice in the sense that *Quadragesimo anno* uses the term indeed embraces, as Jean-Yves Calvez, SJ, and Jacques Perrin, SJ, claimed in the late 1950s, "all the interrelationships of economic activity,"[24] then the sheer extent of social justice might be seen to create circumstances in which there is no apparent check on its invocation to justify state intervention. Here, however, *Quadragesimo anno*'s very important statements about the principle of subsidiarity serve to repudiate such assumptions.

THE STATE AND SUBSIDIARITY

It is the case that the common good, or at least the political dimension of the common good, has always been understood in Catholic doctrine as a set of conditions for which the state, specifically those charged with political authority in a given political community, has a particular responsibility. In 1891, *Rerum novarum* stated:

> [T]he State must not absorb the individual or the family; both should be allowed free and untrammeled action so far as is consistent with the common good and the interest of others. Rulers should, nevertheless, anxiously safeguard the community and all its members; the community, because the conservation thereof is so emphatically the business of the supreme power, that the safety of the commonwealth is not only the first law, but it is a government's whole reason of existence; and the members, because both philosophy and the Gospel concur in laying down that the object of the government of the State should be, not the advantage of the ruler, but the benefit of those over whom he is placed. (*RN*, no. 35)

Reflecting on *Rerum novarum*'s criticism of liberalism's view of the state, *Quadragesimo anno* made a very similar point:

> Just freedom of action must, of course, be left both to individual citizens and to families, yet only on condition that the common good be preserved and

---

[24] Calvez and Perrin, *The Church and Social Justice*, 150.

wrong to any individual be abolished. The function of the rulers of the State, moreover, is to watch over the community and its parts; but in protecting private individuals in their rights, chief consideration ought to be given to the weak and the poor. (*QA*, no. 25)

As implied in the first sentence, Pius XI, like Leo XIII, was conscious that the state's duties vis-à-vis the common good cannot be a basis for unreasonably constraining the freedom of individuals and families as well as what *Rerum novarum* had called "lesser and not independent societies, but, nevertheless, real societies" (*RN*, no. 50) or, citing Aquinas, "private societies" (*RN*, no. 51). In Pope Leo's words, these private societies "although they exist within the body politic, and are severally part of the commonwealth, cannot nevertheless be absolutely, and as such, prohibited by public authority" (*RN*, no. 51). Though this is preceded by an affirmation of the legitimacy of "workingmen associations," Leo XIII plainly has in mind *any* private association not involved in activities "which are evidently bad, unlawful, or dangerous to the State" (*RN*, no. 52). Examples of legitimate private associations are "confraternities, societies, and religious orders which have arisen by the Church's authority and the piety of Christian men" (*RN*, no. 53).

The question left unclear by *Rerum novarum* was how the relationship between the political authority and the vast swath of private or lesser associations that exist between the state and the family is to be regulated so that the common good is enhanced rather than undermined by either excessive state intervention or a state that does not fulfill its proper responsibilities. In Pius XI's view, this was an especially urgent clarification in light of what he considered to be the necessary "reform of institutions and correction of morals" (*QA*, no. 77).

By "reform of institutions," *Quadragesimo anno* particularly had in mind the state, which, in light of the spread of radical individualism and the subsequent breakdown of associational life, "has been overwhelmed and crushed by almost infinite tasks and duties" (*QA*, no. 78). Certainly this leads to inefficiency. Hence, as Oswald von Nell-Breuning, SJ, stated in his influential book-length commentary on *Quadragesimo anno*, part of Pius XI's purpose here was to rehabilitate state authority precisely by *restricting* its activity.[25]

Pope Pius is, however, concerned with more than efficiency in addressing this question. Though, the encyclical states (*QA*, no. 79), larger associations

---

[25] See Oswald von Breuning, SJ, *Reorganization of Social Economy: The Social Encyclical Developed and Explained* (English edition prepared by Bernard W. Dempsey, SJ) (New York: The Bruce Publishing Company, 1936), 209.

now undertake many activities once undertaken by smaller groups (which may
be viewed as recognition that there is no going back to the numerous small
guilds that once populated the European landscape and acknowledgment that
there are many activities that large organizations do better than smaller
groups), Pope Pius insists that there is a *principle* by which the relationship
between the state and the private and lesser societies identified by *Rerum
novarum* may be *justly* ordered – "the principle of subsidiarity" (*QA*, no. 80):

> [T]hat most weighty principle, which cannot be set aside or changed,
> remains fixed and unshaken in social philosophy: Just as it is gravely wrong
> to take from individuals what they can accomplish by their own initiative and
> industry and give it to the community, so also it is an injustice and at the same
> time a grave evil and disturbance of right order to assign to a greater and
> higher association what lesser and subordinate organizations can do. For
> every social activity ought of its very nature to furnish help to the members of
> the body social, and never destroy and absorb them. (*QA*, no. 79)[26]

The *authoritativeness* with which this statement invests this principle is
underlined by the first sentence, as well as the expression used to describe
violations of the principle: "gravely wrong," "injustice," "grave evil," "disturbance of right order." The evil is derived from two factors. The first is in the
injustice that ensues whenever a government exceeds its authority by unreasonably limiting the liberty of those individuals and groups to help themselves.
Aquinas made a similar point when he stated "it is contrary to the proper
character of the state's government to impede people from acting according to
their responsibilities – except in emergencies."[27]

Violations of subsidiarity are, however, gravely wrong for a second and
deeper reason. The word subsidiarity itself is derived from the Latin *subsidium*, meaning "to assist." And assistance means precisely that: to *help*
a person or a group rather than take over his or the group's activities by making
the choices that fulfill the duties remote from the person or group to whom
those responsibilities properly belong.

---

[26] The authoritative Latin text reads: quae superiore aetate a parvis etiam praebebantur, fixum
tamen immotumque manet in philosophia sociali gravissimum illud principium quod neque
moveri neque mutari potest: sicut quae a singularibus hominibus proprio marte et propria
industria possunt perfici, nefas est eisdem eripere et communitati demandare, ita quae
a minoribus et inferioribus communitatibus effici praestarique possunt, ea ad maiorem
et altiorem societatem avocare iniuria est simulque grave damnum ac recti ordinis perturba-
tio; cum socialis quaevis opera vi naturaque sua subsidium afferre membris corporis socialis
debeat, numquam vero eadem destruere et absorbere.

[27] Aquinas, *Summa contra Gentiles*, III c.71, n.4.

Though the expression "common good" is not deployed in *Quadragesimo anno*'s statements concerning subsidiarity, it seems clear that the interventions of higher communities in the activities of lower bodies should be made with reference to the common good, i.e., the conditions that enable all persons to fulfill themselves. Subsidiarity thus combines axioms *of noninterference* and *assistance*. Thus when a case of assistance proves necessary, as much respect as possible should be accorded to the rightful freedom of the assisted person or community.

Subsidiarity has therefore less to do with the potential efficiency gains it may promote than with the need for us to act and do things for ourselves – as the fruit of our own reflection, choices, and acts – rather than have others do them for us. The point of such forms of assistance cannot be to unduly restrict the sphere of freedom minimally required if people are to make the free choices they need to make if they are to participate in economic life. As Finnis observes regarding subsidiarity, "Being a matter of right (justice), not merely efficiency, it is obviously related to what many people refer to as the right to *liberty*."[28] As formulated by Pius XI, it would still be unjust to remove from persons and communities responsibilities that are properly theirs, even if greater material profit or productivity could be yielded by handing over such responsibilities to a higher community. For the principle of subsidiarity also reminds us of the fact that there are numerous communities that precede the state and that by themselves establish many of the conditions that make up the common good.

These communities thus have a primary responsibility to give others what they are objectively owed in justice, or until it is proved that they are manifestly incapable of doing so. This in turn underscores that one of the points of subsidiarity is to protect and realize the basic good of community life itself by protecting and assisting people and groups in carrying out those tasks they can, not simply for the sake of the fulfillment of the tasks, but for the sake of strengthening and deepening the social bonds to which the sharing of communal tasks contributes. In other words, the primary purpose of the state is to protect and help communities to flourish; when communities work together to fulfill reasonable common tasks, they are more likely to flourish.

Sixty years later, *Centesimus annus* was to further specify that "Such supplementary interventions, which are justified by urgent reasons touching the common good, must be as brief as possible, so as to avoid removing permanently from society and business systems the functions which are properly theirs, and so as to avoid enlarging excessively the sphere of State intervention

---

[28]   Finnis, *Natural Law and Natural Rights*, 159.

to the detriment of both economic and civil freedom" (CA, no. 48). Joseph Boyle makes a similar point when discussing subsidiarity and the welfare state. There is, Boyle states, "a significant limit on the extent to which the polity can provide welfare rights."[29] Part of Boyle's argument is that, first, the political community exists to facilitate, not take over, the flourishing of individuals and communities; and second, that expansive welfare states can undermine opportunities for people to make free choices for themselves by creating conditions in which people expect the state to do many things they are capable of doing for themselves.[30] Subsidiarity thus highlights that maintaining and even promoting the freedom of individuals and private communities vis-à-vis each other and the government is itself part of the common good.

PROPOSING A CORPORATE SOCIAL ORDER

Social justice and subsidiarity – always operating together and never apart – are the two principles that *Quadragesimo anno* clarifies as central to Catholic Social Doctrine. But they are also understood as establishing the foundations for the particular reforms of institutions that Pope Pius plainly believed the multiple social and economic crises of the 1930s called for. Neither liberal individualism nor socialist (or Marxist) collectivism are, the pope maintains, legitimate alternatives. In this regard, Pius XI appears to go further than his predecessor in formally proposing what a social order derived from Catholic Social Teaching should look like.

This development occurs against a background of considerable interest on the part of many Catholic social theorists in the question of how one could build up, or rehabilitate, intermediate associations that exist between the state and the family. At least two decades before the promulgation of *Rerum novarum*, there were considerable discussions between (1) Catholics inclined to support market economies but anxious to limit their potentially corrosive effects upon other forms of social association, and (2) Catholics anxious to see a thorough-going rehabilitation of intermediate associations but who also believed that craft guilds were institutions of the past. Some of the latter, such as the French social Catholic thinker Albert de Mun, argued specifically for legally recognized associations of employees and employers based on professions or industries with legally defined freedoms and responsibilities.[31]

[29] Joseph Boyle, "Fairness in Holdings: A Natural Law Account of Property and Welfare Rights," *Social Philosophy and Policy*, Vol. 18, no. 1 (2001), 218.
[30] Boyle, "Fairness in Holdings," 218.
[31] On this subject, see Calvez and Perrin, *The Church and Social Justice*, 403–406; Paul Misner, *Social Catholicism in Europe: From the Onset of Industrialization to the First World War*

This interest is reflected in *Rerum novarum*'s lamenting the disappearance of "workingmen's guilds" throughout the nineteenth century and the encyclical's claim that, historically speaking, "excellent results were brought about by the artificers' guilds of olden times" (RN, no. 3). For Pope Leo, "They were the means of affording not only many advantages to the workmen, but in no small degree of promoting the advancement of art, as numerous monuments remain to bear witness" (RN, no. 49).

Rerum novarum, as noted, emphasizes the need to develop strong associational life but in forms more suitable to the requirements of "our time." Leo XIII refrains, however, from laying out precise formulae for how this might occur, beyond noting that "there are actually in existence not a few associations of this nature, consisting either of workmen alone, or of workmen and employers together." He adds that "it were greatly to be desired that they should become more numerous and more efficient" (RN, no. 49).

Quadragesimo anno goes far beyond this relatively general schema. In the first place, it speaks of the need for the state not simply to assist "subordinate groups [that will] handle matters and concerns of lesser importance" (QA, no. 80) but to look to ending "the conflict between the hostile classes [*classium oppositarum*]" and promoting the "harmonious cooperation of vocational groups [*concors "ordinum" conspiratio*]" (QA, no. 81), not least by working toward the "reestablishment of the groups [*ordines*]" (QA, no. 82).[32] The establishment of such groups, it is held, will result in people being viewed "not according to the position each has in the labor market but according to the respective social functions which each performs" (QA, no. 84). The point, it seems, is to shift people's focus away from their specific position as employer or employee and toward the fact that they are in fact laboring together in the same group.

Many questions are not answered by Pope Pius's schema. How is one vocational group to be distinguished from each other? Are, for instance, electricians a distinct group, or is their vocational group a larger grouping, such as the building industry? Or by vocational group does the pope have in mind a specific enterprise, or groups that transcend particular enterprises that belong to the same industry? And what would be the place of trade unions in

(London: Darton, Longman and Todd, 1991); and Howard J. Wiarda, *Corporatism and Comparative Politics* (New York: W. E. Sharpe, 1997), 30–46.

[32] The English version of the encyclical on the Vatican website translates the Latin *"ordines"* as "Industries and Professions." A strict English translation, however, of *ordines* is "orders." As Calvez and Perrin note, a more accurate way of understanding this expression in its context is "vocational groups" as this is closer to the sense of Pope Pius's use of *ordines*. Calvez and Perrin, *The Church and Social Justice*, 416–417.

these arrangements? Would their place be effectively subsumed into this broader framework? Or would they maintain a distinct role in this reorganized social order?

It may well be that Pope Pius did not regard these as issues that fell within the magisterium's competence. Pius did nevertheless go to some lengths to distinguish his rather broad, even free-floating vision of vocational groups from what may be called stricter state-directed expressions of corporatism. "Recently," the encyclical states, "there has been inaugurated a special system of syndicates and corporations" (QA, no. 91). There seems little doubt that the encyclical has in mind the corporatist system created by Mussolini's fascist regime.

Quadragesimo anno characterizes this system as one in which the civil authority accords a juridical status to different syndicates of employees or employers. This standing confers upon the syndicate a type of monopoly for negotiating labor agreements for those who belong to specific professions. They also, the pope states, exact dues from all who work in a given profession, regardless of whether they belong to the syndicate (QA, no. 92). Over the syndicates are "corporations" that consist of delegates from employer and employee syndicates that are "true and proper organs and institutions of the State." Their role is to "direct the syndicates and coordinate their activities in matters of common interest toward one and the same end" (QA, no. 93). The same system outlaws strikes and lockouts, and when instances of conflict emerge that appear beyond resolution by the disputing parties, the state intervenes (QA, no. 94).

On one level, the encyclical states, this system has certain advantages. These include the way in which the system outlaws socialism, requires different classes to work together, and places the state in a coordinating role (QA, no. 95). But Pius then immediately states:

> that to Our certain knowledge there are not wanting some who fear that the State, instead of confining itself as it ought to the furnishing of necessary and adequate assistance, is substituting itself for free activity; that the new syndical and corporative order savors too much of an involved and political system of administration; and that (in spite of those more general advantages mentioned above, which are of course fully admitted) it rather serves particular political ends than leads to the reconstruction and promotion of a better social order. (QA, no. 95)

Here Pius XI seems to be arguing that the problem with the fascist version of corporatism is its *fascist* characteristics. This is manifested in its practical workings, which violate subsidiarity. Moreover, the goal of fascist corporatism is not the common good but rather cementing the regime's political control.

The bigger issue, however, is whether *Quadragesimo anno* established its looser, more free-floating vision for vocational groups as *the* model that should, all other things being considered, be pursued by Catholics as they seek to reform the social order. Certainly many Catholics in the wake of *Quadragesimo anno*'s promulgation thought so. In light of subsequent magisterial teaching, however, the answer to the question appears to be no.

Throughout the pontificate that followed Pius XI, Pius XII used expressions such as "corporations," "associations of societies," "associations," "unions," "co-operative societies," "co-operative bodies," and "professional community."[33] The focus of these papal statements on this issue was upon the need for cooperation between employers and employees. Far less attention, however, was given to specific institutional forms through which such cooperation might be realized.[34]

This trend was reinforced by John XXIII in *Mater et magistra*. This encyclical refers extensively to the growth of associational life in general[35] – provided that this growth does not undermine the scope for the exercise of human freedom.[36] *Mater et magistra* makes one reference to "the numerous intermediary bodies and corporate enterprises" that, through their freedom and collaboration, help build up the common good, and which are true communities.[37] John XXIII also underscores the need for these groups to be coordinated and assisted by the state.[38] This is accompanied by a stress upon the need for people working within a business enterprise to find ways to collaborate.[39] Yet the pope additionally specifies that "It is not, of course, possible to lay down hard and fast rules regarding the manner of such participation, for this must depend upon prevailing conditions, which vary from firm to firm and are frequently subject to rapid and substantial alteration."[40]

Overall, this picture is far less prescriptive than what is found in *Quadragesimo anno*. Nell-Breuning himself suggested that *Mater et magistra* represented a deemphasizing of the prescriptions concerning vocational

---

[33] See, for instance, Pius XII, "Speech to Italian Workers," June 13, 1943: in *AAS* 35 (1943), 173; "Message of 1 September 1944," *AAS* 36 (1944), 254; Pius XII, "Speech to ACLI," March 11, 1945: *AAS* 37, 71; Pius XII, "Letter to Charles Flory," July 18, 1947: *AAS* 39 (1947), 444–445.
[34] See, for instance, Pius XII, "Letter to Charles Flory," July 18, 1947: *AAS* 39 (1947), 444–445.
[35] John XXIII, Encyclical Letter *Mater et magistra* (On Christianity and Social Progress) (1961), nos. 59–61.
[36] *MM*, no. 62.
[37] *MM*, nos. 65, 93.
[38] *MM*, no. 65.
[39] *MM*, nos. 91–93.
[40] *MM*, no. 91.

groups laid out in *Quadragesimo anno*.[41] Nor do vocational groups receive significant attention in John XXIII's encyclical *Pacem in terris* (1963), Vatican II's Pastoral Constitution on the Church in the Modern World *Gaudium et spes* (1965), Paul VI's encyclical *Populorum progressio* (1967), his apostolic exhortation *Octogesima adveniens* (1971), or the encyclicals of John Paul II, Benedict XVI, or Francis. In *Laborem exercens*, *Quadragesimo anno*'s prescription is referenced as *one* of many possibilities for realizing this goal.[42] The exhortation in these texts is upon a greater degree of cooperation within enterprises and businesses. On this basis, it is reasonable to conclude that *Quadragesimo anno*'s specific prescriptions for the development of vocational groups are one possible option among many others for encouraging collaboration in the workplace.

CONCLUSION

Many of the ideas expressed in *Quadragesimo anno*, especially its particular vision of a type of corporate social order, may be reasonably assessed as exerting some influence upon the social policies (what might be called "hard corporatism") of authoritarian regimes that were nonetheless close to the Catholic Church, such as Francisco Franco's Spain, António de Oliveira Salazar's Portugal, Vichy France, and Engelbert Dollfuss's Austria. The encyclical's influence can also be seen in the "soft corporatist policies" of Christian Democratic movements and political parties in Western Europe and Latin America after World War II, as well as many institutional features of today's European Union.[43] Some countries such as Austria went so far as to formally co-opt business and trade unions into the setting and implementing of government economic policy.

The roots of corporatism and those who have advocated such policies go beyond the Catholic Church and Catholics. The intellectual roots of this movement varied inasmuch as it drew upon the writings of individuals ranging from the German philosopher G. W. F. Hegel to the French sociologist Emile Durkheim. Corporatist thinkers have included socialists, nationalists, fascists, liberals, and progressives, and have been found on the right and left of modern politics.[44] One should therefore be careful before attributing too much

[41]   See Oswald von Nell-Breuning, SJ, "Some Reflections on *Mater et Magistra*," *Review of Social Economy* 20 (Fall 1962): 97–108.
[42]   John Paul II, Encyclical Letter *Laborem exercens* (On Human Work) (1981), no. 14, fn. 23.
[43]   See Samuel Gregg, *Becoming Europe* (New York, NY: Encounter Books, 2013), 82–86.
[44]   Gregg, *Becoming Europe*, 55–59.

influence to *Quadragesimo anno* when reflecting upon the impact of ideas upon the public square.

Less doubt, however, is obvious with regard to *Quadragesimo anno*'s placing subsidiarity at the very heart of modern Catholic Social Teaching. Subsidiarity is often referred to as the "freedom" principle of Catholic Social Doctrine. In one sense, that is true. Subsidiarity *does* help to limit state power, both by confining its scope and ordering the character of government interventions in a consistent manner. To that extent, it helps to facilitate legitimate spheres of autonomy for individuals and groups. But subsidiarity is not a principle of limited government for the sake of limited government. The *point* of the freedom conferred by subsidiarity is the all-around human flourishing of all persons and communities that can only occur when individuals and communities make free choices for the good. And that good includes the conditions that promote the well-being of others in a given political community, that is, the common good, which is, as Pius XI also made clear, the object of social justice properly understood. To that extent, social justice and subsidiarity are, as *Quadragesimo anno* makes clear, truly inseparable.

5

Pope Pius XII on Social Issues

Ronald J. Rychlak

Pope Pius XII, born Eugenio Maria Giuseppe Giovanni Pacelli, led the Catholic Church through a tumultuous period in world history. Ascending to the papacy just months before the outbreak of World War II, he presided over the Church through that war and much of the Cold War, providing important leadership in both conflicts. This was a time of shift in global leadership of the free world from Catholic Europe to the predominately Protestant United States, and the time of the emergence of a new significant player on the international scene, the United Nations.

At no other point in the modern age was the Catholic Church threatened in the way it was during the papacy of Pius XII. Rome's very existence was under threat of destruction during much of this time, in part because the Church's teachings stood in direct opposition to the ideologies of Fascist Italy, Nazi Germany, and the Communist Soviet Union. Complicating matters, the Church was persecuted, and it was involved in certain clandestine efforts to undermine the totalitarian regimes.[1]

Although Pius issued forty-one encyclicals in his 20 years as pope, he did not author any of the famous encyclicals on social doctrine.[2] He had, however, served as Secretary of State and top adviser to Pope Pius XI when Pius XI released *Quadragesimo anno*, addressing many of the social issues facing the world at that time. That document was still fairly new when Pius XII took the chair of Peter, so there was little immediate need for a new encyclical dedicated specifically to social teachings. Moreover, the threats stemming

---

[1] See Mark Riebling, *Church of Spies: The Pope's Secret War Against Hitler* (Basic Books, 2015); Ronald J. Rychlak, *Righteous Gentiles: How Pius XII and the Catholic Church Saved Half a Million Jews From the Nazis* (Spence Publishing, 2005).

[2] Chief among those that preceded Pius XII's papacy are Leo XIII's Encyclical Letter *Rerum novarum* (On the Condition of the Working Classes) (1891), and Pius XI's Encyclical Letter *Quadragesimo anno* (On Reconstruction of the Social Order) (1931).

from Nazi Germany, Fascist Italy, the Soviet Union, and weapons of unheard-of destructive force consumed much of Pius XII's energy.

While Pius XII did not issue encyclicals directed exclusively to social questions, it "is safe to say that no Roman pontiff has addressed the problems confronting the social order as frequently and as widely outside the formal structure of encyclicals as Pius XII."[3] He taught that man had "a nature which is intrinsically social. He ought to conduct his life according to the demands of nature."[4] Catholic Social Teaching (CST) was absolutely central to his understanding of the Church.[5] As he explained: "[t]he social program of the Catholic Church is based on three powerful moral pillars: truth, justice and Christian charity. To deviate even slightly from the dictates of these principles would be impossible for the Church."[6] Thus, while Pius did not always label his writing as CST, he set forth several new ideas in the field,[7] and he made new connections between existing aspects of CST. As such, he had a huge impact on the magisterium, particularly at the Second Vatican Council, where his writings were highly influential.[8]

---

[3] Rupert J. Ederer, *Pope Pius XII on the Economic Order* (Scarecrow Press, 2011).

[4] Pius XII's "Directive to the 18th Spanish Social Week at Seville" (May 14–20, 1956) quoted in *The Social Teachings of Pope Pius XII: 1956*, 11.

[5] "The social teaching of Pius XII is often an incidental pronouncement, which inevitably suffers from any attempt at systematization." Pietro Pavan, *The Place of Mater et Magistra in Papal Social Teaching*, Christus Rex (1962), 233, quoted in Gerald Darring, *Pope Pius XII, 1939–1958*, www.shc.edu/theolibrary/resources/popes_pius12.htm. Among his most notable statements are his first encyclical, *Summi pontificatus* (On the Unity of Human Society) (1939); his radio address of June 1, 1941, commemorating the 50th anniversary of *Rerum novarum*; and his Christmas radio addresses during the war years. His social teachings were prevalent enough that a small book was devoted to his social teachings from 1956 alone. See *The Social Teachings of Pope Pius XII: 1956*, ed. Cyrill C. Clum (Oxford: The Catholic Social Guild, 1958).

[6] Pius XII, "Radio address to the German Catholic Congress, Bochum" (September 4, 1949), in *Pius XII On Work and Commerce*, eds., Robert Kennedy and Stephanie Rumpza (undated), www.stthomas.edu/media/catholicstudies/center/ryan/publications/publicationpdfs/pius xiipdf/Pius_Section_I_47–50.pdf.

[7] In the Apostolic Constitution *Exsul familia nazarethana* (1952) he addressed the rights of migrants, and in Encyclical Letter *Miranda prorsus* (On Motion Pictures, Radio and Television) (1957) he discussed the moral implications of radio and movies. His writings also contain important developments in magisterial teaching on the subject of democracy and human rights. Anthony G. Percy, "Private Initiative, Entrepreneurship, and Business in the Teaching of Pius XII," *Journal of Markets & Morality* 7, no. 1 (Spring 2004): 7–25.

[8] The annotations to the documents of Vatican II contain over 200 references to Pius XII's works, more than for any source other than the Bible. Michael O. Carroll, *Pius XII: Greatness Dishonored* 182, no. 8 (Laetare Press: Dublin, 1980) (also noting that there are many other quotations from Pius XII's writing that were not attributed to him); Carroll, *Pius XII*, 226, no. 20. See also Jean Chélini and Joël-Benoît d'Onorio, eds., *Pie XII et la Cité: Actes du Colloque de la Faculté de Droit d'Aix-en-Provence* (Presses Universitaires d'Aix-Marseille, 1988); Cardinal

Pope Pius XII has been identified as the final pope of the "Modern" or "Leonine" school of social thought, stemming from the time of Pope Leo XIII.[9] Key components of Leo's vision included support for political democracy, support of workers' rights, support for moderate social welfare policies, and encouragement of lay movements like Catholic Action.[10] These strategies were combined with a philosophical and theological emphasis on natural law, a communitarian vision of the human person, and a hierarchical understanding of church and society. Pope Leo's vision shaped the Church's social teaching for the next four popes, though each of them also made their own contributions to CST.

Pope Pius XII brought these teachings to the laity in an effort to promote human welfare. Through the principle of subsidiarity, he offered resistance to totalitarian governments, and most importantly, he defended the family as society's foundational cell, the "natural nursery and school where the man of tomorrow grows up and is formed."[11] He continued the Vatican practice of forming alliances with democratic nations, but under Pius the Church formed a much closer alliance with the United States. In so doing this, he largely repudiated the so-called "phantom heresy" of Americanism.[12]

Summi pontificatus

Pius XII's first encyclical, *Summi pontificatus* ("On the Unity of Human Society"), was released in 1939, just weeks after the outbreak of World War II. Addressed to "Our Venerable Brethren: The Patriarchs, Primates, Archbishops, Bishops, and Other Ordinaries in Peace and Communion with the Apostolic See," this remarkable document set forth Pius XII's view of current world events,

Fiorenzo Angelini, "The Pope most quoted by Vatican Council II," 30 *Days* 9 (2008) (Cardinal Siri quoted: "If we study the indices of Vatican II, one can easily see that after those taken from Holy Scripture, the most numerous quotations are those derived from the writings of [Pius XII]").

[9] Joe Holland, *Modern Catholic Social Teaching: The Popes Confront the Industrial Age, 1740–1958* (Paulist Press, 2003).

[10] In 1943, Pius XII published *Mystici corporis Christi*, his longest and landmark encyclical on the Catholic Church as the "Mystical Body of Christ." In this encyclical, after summarizing the crisis-oriented social analysis proposed in his inaugural encyclical, Pius XII praised the role of Catholic Action and of lay associations, as well as the centrality of the Christian family.

[11] Pius XII, "Address to the College of Cardinals on the Feast of St. Eugene" (June 2, 1947), in Kennedy and Rumpza, *Pius XII on Work and Commerce*.

[12] Leo XIII, Encyclical Letter *Testem benevolentiae nostrae* (Concerning New Opinions, Virtue, Nature and Grace, With Regard to Americanism) (1899). At the core of this doctrine was endorsement of the separation of church and state of the sort condemned by Pope Pius IX in the Syllabus of Errors in 1864. While its status as a true heresy has been debated, it was seen by many as incompatible with the principle of obedience to authority. See Russell Shaw, "Americanism: Then and Now," *The Catholic World Report* (May 1995).

especially the war and the role of the Church in times of war.[13] Many of the social teachings that Pius XII would later expand upon can be found in *Summi pontificatus*. Moreover, he combined various CST teachings in the context of the world as it was, and he explained how they all worked together.[14]

According to *Summi pontificatus*, the modern age was marked not only by technical progress but also spiritual emptiness and moral disorientation. This, argued Pius, inevitably led to "a drift toward chaos" and "the tempest of war." He attributed this chaos to rejection of the universal moral law, which binds all nations in a common purpose.[15] He explained that the only solution was bringing Christianity into the public sphere and recognizing natural law as the source and foundation for the laws of man, directing him toward perfection.[16]

---

[13] As this author has previously written:

> In his first encyclical, . . . Pope Pius XII set forth his position on Hitler, the war, and the role that he would play. He made reference to "the ever-increasing host of Christ's enemies" (no. 7), and noted that these enemies of Christ "deny or in practice neglect the vivifying truths and the values inherent in belief in God and in Christ" and want to "break the Tables of God's Commandments to substitute other tables and other standards stripped of the ethical content of [Christianity]." In the next paragraph, Pius charged that Christians who fell in with the enemies of Christ suffered from cowardice, weakness, or uncertainty.

> Ronald J. Rychlak, Hitler, the War, and the Pope (Our Sunday Visitor, rev. ed. 2010) (quoting Summi pontificatus), 380.

[14] Pius linked the chaos of a world on the brink of disaster to "abundantly widespread . . . disregard for the law of human solidarity and charity, dictated and imposed both by our common origin and by the equality in rational nature of all men, whatever nation they belong to." Catholic Church. "Social Justice" in the *Catechism of the Catholic Church*, 2nd ed. (Vatican: Libreria Editrice Vaticana, 2012), citing Pius XII, Encyclical Letter *Summi pontificatus* (On the Unity of Human Society) (1939), no. 31.

[15] In 1945, the year of World War II's end, Pius XII issued a brief encyclical on peace, *Communium interpretes dolorum* (Appealing for Prayers for Peace). In it, he again blamed the war on rejection of God and called for a renewal of Christian morals for both private and public life, and for a renewal marked by both justice and peace.

[16] Pius expressed his belief that any structure not founded on the teaching of Christ was destined to perish. Read in context, this was a promise of the ultimate failure of the dictatorships. In fact, he expressly foresaw that Poland, recently overrun by Germany and the Soviet Union, would be resurrected:

> This . . . is in many respects a real "Hour of Darkness," . . . in which the spirit of violence and of discord brings indescribable suffering on mankind . . . . The nations swept into the tragic whirlpool of war are perhaps as yet only at the "beginnings of sorrows," . . . but even now there reigns in thousands of families death and desolation, lamentation and misery. The blood of countless human beings, even noncombatants, raises a piteous dirge over a nation such as Our dear Poland, which, for its fidelity to the Church, for its services in the defense of Christian civilization . . . has a right to the generous and brotherly sympathy of the whole world, while it awaits, relying on the powerful

Pius XII highlighted two errors in understanding as being central to the then-current situation. The first was the denial of the solidarity of humanity as one family.[17] The second was the deification of a state that claimed for itself "that absolute autonomy which belongs exclusively to the Supreme Maker."[18] The combination of these errors led people beyond a healthy patriotism and into dangerous nationalism. As Pius explained, where human solidarity was denied, there could be no social order – international, national, or domestic.[19] Where the state was deified, civil authority had no limits, peace and prosperity were undermined, and the family was victimized.

As he watched the centralization of governmental power, notably in Germany and the Soviet Union, but also in the United States and among the Allies, Pius expressed concern about the impact this would have on international relations.[20] He wrote: "Absolute autonomy for the State stands in open opposition to this natural way that is inherent in man . . . and therefore leaves the stability of international relations at the mercy of the will of rulers, while it destroys the possibility of true union and fruitful collaboration directed to the general good." He stressed the importance of treaties and wrote of an international natural law, which requires that all treaties be honored.[21]

At a time when Jews were being persecuted by a dictatorship just 500 miles north of Rome, Pius vowed that the Church would always be open to all, and he refused to recognize claims that the Nazis made about Jews: "the teaching and the work of the Church can never be other than that which the Apostle of the Gentiles preached: 'putting on the new (man) him who is renewed unto

intercession of Mary, Help of Christians, the hour of a resurrection in harmony with the principles of justice and true peace. (SP, no. 106)

[17] In discussing solidarity, Pius noted that all humans were made in the image of God and came from one original couple. Further, he stressed the equal rights of people of all civilizations. He linked this equality to importance in the global Church of the development of native clergy and national bishops, which he would accomplish during his papacy (SP, no. 36).

[18] SP, no. 53.

[19] Pius XII instructed that formation of the youth should include preparing them with "intelligent understanding and pride in those offices of noble patriotism which give to one's earthly fatherland all due measure of love, self-devotion and service" (SP, no. 67). However, a "person with isolationist or nationalistic leanings will find little of comfort in the writings of Pius XII. More than any other pope in history he emphasized the basic teaching on human solidarity and the implications of this doctrine for the community of nations." R. F. Cour, Review of Politics (1960), 483; quoted in Gerald Darring, "Pope Pius XII, 1939–1958," www.shc.edu/the olibrary/resources/popes_pius12.htm.

[20] Pius responded to the demands for stronger central governments, acknowledging that there may be difficulties that would justify greater powers being concentrated in the state, but he said that the moral law requires that this need be scrutinized with greatest rigor. The state can demand goods and blood, but not the immortal soul. SP, no. 66.

[21] SP, no. 77.

knowledge, according to the image of him that created him. Where there is neither Gentile nor Jew, circumcision nor uncircumcision, barbarian nor Scythian, bond nor free. But Christ is all and in all'."[22] Pius wrote that the goal of society must be development of the individual, not the power of the state.

Pius even provided a direct answer to Hitler's view of the state as set forth in *Mein Kampf*, criticizing the idea of the state as "something ultimate to which everything else should be subordinated and directed," and explaining that such an idea "cannot fail to harm the true and lasting prosperity of nations."[23] Instead of focus on the state, Pius called for a "new international order," standing on the "solid rock of natural law and Divine Revelation."

Pius called the family "the primary and essential cell of society."[24] He noted that "man and the family are by nature anterior to the State, and ... the Creator has given to both of them powers and rights and has assigned them a mission and a charge that correspond to undeniable natural requirements." He bemoaned the reality that the "stress of our times" was borne "so bitterly ... by that noble little cell, the family."[25] The family remained even when other institutions were closed. "When churches are closed, when the Image of the Crucified is taken from the schools," he wrote, then "the family remains the providential and, in a certain sense, impregnable refuge of Christian life."[26]

For Pius, society was never far removed from its spiritual basis.[27] This was particularly evident at times of distress. Speaking of "the ever-increasing host of Christ's enemies," he noted that these enemies of Christ "deny or in

---

[22] SP, no. 48. See David E. Anderson, "The Religious Sources for Modern Human Rights," *Religion & Ethics Newsweekly* (PBS.org: January 3, 2017), reviewing Samuel Moyn, *Christian Human Rights* (in 1937, Pope Pius XI and the future Pius XII began to realize the threat to the moral community presented by totalitarian regimes, fixing that year as "the first critical date for the development of Christian human rights").

[23] SP, no. 60 ("This can happen either when unrestricted dominion comes to be conferred on the State as having a mandate from the nation, people, or even a social order, or when the State arrogates such dominion to itself as absolute master, despotically, without any mandate whatsoever").

[24] SP, no. 61.

[25] SP, no. 63.

[26] SP, no. 91.

[27] SP, nos. 24 to 31 laid out the pope's belief that prayer itself was an important action. He could not contribute political or military strength to the world at that time, but he could bring much-needed faith and prayer. He identified the lack of Christianity as the cause of the "crop of such poignant disasters." SP, nos. 51 to 66 set forth Pius XII's view of a just society. Here he asserted that the first reason for the outbreak of war was that people had forgotten the law of universal charity. The second reason was the failure to put God above civil authority. He argued that when civil authority is placed above the Lord, the government fills that void, and problems develop.

practice neglect the vivifying truths and the values inherent in belief in God and in Christ" and want to "break the Tables of God's Commandments to substitute other tables and other standards stripped of the ethical content of [Christianity]."[28]

In a slap at the racial policies that were spreading across Europe, Pius explained that the Church could not discriminate; all races and nationalities were welcome in the Church and had equal rights as children in the house of the Lord.[29] He put meaning to those antiracist statements by naming new bishops of different races and nationalities.[30]

Pius also saw problems stemming from governmental control over education of the youth.[31] He insisted that education should be aimed at "the balanced and harmonious development of the physical powers and of all the intellectual and moral qualities," not at "a one-sided formation of those civic virtues that are considered necessary for attaining political success." Parents, not the state, were charged by God with the duty of providing "for the material and spiritual good of their offspring and to procure for them a suitable training saturated with the true spirit of religion."[32] He warned about the "crime of high treason against the 'King of kings and Lord of lords' (I Timothy 6:15; cf. Apocalypse xix. 6) perpetrated by an education that is either indifferent or opposed to Christianity."[33]

Throughout his papacy, the focus of Pope Pius XII's ministry was the struggle for peace, and he sought to accomplish it by restoring the Church's

---

[28] SP, no. 7.
[29] SP, nos. 45–50.
[30] SP, no. 48.
[31] SP, no. 62. Later in his papacy, he would elaborate:

> The Church has always insisted on the fact that to establish a lasting social order, there is a need not only of reform in the structure of society, but also of the education of the spirit. It is necessary to form the consciences of men, in keeping with absolute values, and to shape their moral strength in such a manner that they always follow their convictions. The Church affirms, and has herself proved, that she is in a position to form this mentality in men.

> Pius XII, "To the 77th Congress of German Catholics at Cologne" (September 2, 1956), in The Social Teachings of Pope Pius XII: 1956, 17.

[32] SP, no. 66. "The souls of children given to their parents by God and consecrated in Baptism with the royal character of Christ, are a sacred charge over which watches the jealous love of God." SP, no. 68.
[33] SP, no. 68. He asked: "[W]hat scandal is more permanently harmful to generation after generation, than a formation of youth which is misdirected towards a goal that alienates from Christ 'the Way and the Truth and the Life' and leads to open or hidden apostasy from Christ?" (SP, no. 69).

public role in society. Thus, in his first encyclical, he made a plea for peace, and he applied CST in a new and formidable manner.[34]

> What torrents of benefits would be showered on the world: what light, order, what peace would accrue to social life; what unique and precious energies would contribute towards the betterment of mankind, if men would every-where concede to the Church, teacher of justice and love, that liberty of action to which, in virtue of the Divine Mandate, she has a sacred and indisputable right! What calamities could be averted, what happiness and tranquility assured, if the social and international forces working to establish peace would let themselves be permeated by the deep lessons of the Gospel of Love in their struggle against individual and collective egoism.[35]

Expansion on Themes from Summi pontificatus

Summi pontificatus was remarkable for many reasons, not the least of which was Pius XII's application of CST to the existing world situation; but that was certainly not the end of his writings on CST. Many of the themes that Pius introduced in that document were revisited and elaborated upon in his later writings. Pius was often able to see connections between different aspects of CST, for instance, the family, workers' rights (and needs), racial discrimination, migrants, the role of the state, and issues of war and peace.

Work and the Family

The family was always central to Pope Pius XII's vision of CST. In 1942, he wrote that one who would have the "star of peace" shine on society "must defend the indissolubility of marriage, and give to the family the space, light, and air that it needs in order to fulfill its mission." That mission includes perpetrating new life, educating children (including religious education), and "ensuring that the home and place of work are not so distant from each other that the head of the family, the educator of his children, becomes almost a stranger in his own home."[36]

---

[34] See Reginald F. Walker, *Pius of Peace* (M. H. Gill and Son, 1946), 130 (quoting an allocution of December 24, 1939, that set forth a five-point peace plan).

[35] SP, no. 92.

[36] See Walker, *Pius of Peace*, 156 (quoting Pius XII's 1942 Christmas Address). In a 1958 address to the Directors of the Associations for Large Families of Rome and Italy he spoke eloquently of the sacrifice, joy, and generosity so prevalent among families, particularly those that had been abundantly blessed with the gift of children. "Large families are the most splendid flower-beds in the garden of the Church; happiness flowers in them and sanctity ripens in favorable soil. Every family group, even the smallest, was meant by God to be an oasis of spiritual peace."

Along with teachings about family, Pius linked other social teachings. For instance, in *Sertum laetitiae*, the 1939 encyclical on the 150th anniversary of the hierarchy in the United States, Pius XII warned against the dangers of materialism and egoism, particularly regarding the family.[37] He also commended the struggle for social justice, especially for a just wage and a family wage, and he expressed support for workers' unions.[38]

Pius explained his view of the centrality of the family and workers in a 1949 radio address to the German Catholic Conference. "No right-thinking man," said the pope, "will dare to accuse the Church of not having in mind and at heart the problem of the workers and also, in general, the whole of the social question." Harkening back to Leo XIII's encyclical, *Rerum novarum*, Pius pointed out that "few problems have engaged the interest and solicitude of the Supreme Pastors of the Church more than the social question."[39] Pius saw labor as "a way of serving God."[40] He observed that "one's work ought to contribute to the common good; it should testify to the sense of responsibility of each for the well-being of all."[41]

Pius XII's "Address to the Directors of the Associations for Large Families of Rome and Italy" (1958), in *Pius XII on Work and Commerce*.

[37] The rights of workers were, of course, linked to the family. In his 1947 encyclical, *Optatissima pax* (On Prescribing Public Prayers for Social and World Peace), Pius faulted nations for their vast "military expenditures" while warning of "a secret and astute plan" to "embitter and exploit the working man in his distress." He called for prayer and mutual cooperation to overcome the problems. The root cause of all these problems, he explained, was that "the divine religion of Jesus Christ" no longer governed private, domestic, and public life. Restoring the Church's authority, he argued, would replace error with truth and hate with love.

[38] Pius wrote that "it is not possible without injustice to deny or to limit either to the producers or to the laboring and farming classes the free faculty of uniting in association." However, he condemned compulsory unionism in the "free world" as well as in socialist countries in his Christmas Eve Address of 1952. Pius XII, Encyclical Letter *Sertum laetitiae* (On the Hundred and Fiftieth Anniversary of the Establishment of Hierarchy in the United States) (1939), nos. 11–22. He also cautioned that labor "may follow in its turn the mistaken course of capital." Pope Pius, "Address of His Holiness prepared for the delegates to the Catholic International Congresses for Social Study (Fribourg Union) and Social Action (Saint Gall Union)" (June 3, 1950), in *Pius XII on Work and Commerce*. According to Pius, this would "suit a Socialist mentality to perfection" and "prove disturbing to anyone who is aware of the fundamental importance of the right to private property in stimulating initiative and fixing responsibility in economic matters."

[39] Pius XII, "Radio address to the German Catholic Congress, Bochum" (September 4, 1949), in *Pius XII on Work and Commerce*.

[40] Pius XII, "Address to the Personnel of the Bank of Italy" (April 25, 1950), in *Pius XII on Work and Commerce*.

[41] Percy, *Private Initiative*, 10 (discussing Social Function of Banking (April 25, 1950) and Vocation of Businessmen (April 27, 1950)) ("this goal of material well-being is worthwhile precisely because it contributes to the common good.") Addressing about 3,000 employees and directors of the Roman Electrical Society in 1950, the pope spoke of the Church's support for workers:

Pius understood that world economies had not always served families well.[42] He dedicated himself to work so that "the apparent conflict between capital and labor, between the employer and the worker, be transformed into a higher unity, which means to say, into that organic cooperation of both parties which is indicated by their very nature and which consists in the collaboration of both according to their activity in the economic sector and the professions."[43]

In a 1949 address, Pius explained: "To receive one's wage is a prerogative of the personal dignity of anyone who makes his productive contribution in one form or another, as employer or laborer, towards the output of the nation's economy."[44] He noted the material prosperity of the nation and said that "workmen also should be enabled, by the fruit of their savings, to share in the creation of the capital resources of their country."[45] On another occasion Pius, specifically noting the Church's social doctrine, spoke of the need to provide good housing for workers and their families.[46] In fact, he encouraged employees to view their employers like fathers and to see one another as brothers and sisters, thereby becoming "members of the great human family."[47]

Pius encouraged employers to trust employees and to treat them fairly, so that they would become part of the economic venture. When that is done, Pius

> It is always for Us a motive of great satisfaction and joy to receive the testimony of filial love from workers and to seize each opportune occasion to express the esteem and affection which their laborious life inspires in Us. The Church has always protected the worker and his work. Take in your hands, dear Sons, the declarations of the Popes on the social question and the condition of workers. These are not empty words nor vain promises which could not subsequently be realized nor maintained. They constitute rather an effective and just defense of the worker, of his work, and of his well-being.
>
> Pius XII, "Address to the Personnel of the Roman Electrical Society" (July 2, 1950), in *Pius XII on Work and Commerce.*

42 "Modern economics, so boasted, so proud of producing ever more, ever better and cheaper, has not precisely, nonetheless, succeeded in satisfying this real need of man, above all of the family." Pius XII, "Address to the Members of the International Office of Work" (March 25, 1949), in *Pius XII on Work and Commerce.*

43 Pius XII, "Radio address to the German Catholic Congress, Bochum" (September 4, 1949), in *Pius XII on Work and Commerce.* ("Even if, with the years, professional labor should become monotonous, or if, by obedience to the law of God, it should weigh as a constraint, or as a too heavy burden, it should nonetheless always remain for you, Christians, one of the most important means of sanctification, one of the most effective ways of being conformed to the divine will and meriting heaven.")

44 Pius XII, "Address to 400 delegates to the Ninth International Congress of the International Union of Catholic Employers, assembled at the Vatican" (May 7, 1949), in *Pius XII on Work and Commerce.*

45 Pius XII, "Address to 400 delegates" (May 7, 1949), in *Pius XII on Work and Commerce.*

46 Pius XII, "Address to the Members of the International Office of Work" (March 25, 1949), in *Pius XII on Work and Commerce.*

47 Pius XII, *To Domestic Workers of Rome and Italy,* June 3, 1956, *The Social Teachings of Pope Pius XII: 1956,* 36–37.

explained, employees "will readily understand that their superior ... has no intention of profiting unjustly at their expense, or of exploiting their labor excessively."[48] Instead, employees will recognize that they are being afforded "an opportunity to perfect their own individual capacities, to engage in work that is useful and profitable, and to contribute according to their abilities to the service of the community as well as to their own economic and moral improvement."[49]

The relationship of the family to the state was a theme of Pius XII's address at the Feast of Pentecost in 1941. In it, he echoed aspects of Pope Leo's *Rerum novarum*, including labor, the use of material goods, and the family.[50] The following month, July 1941, Pius received in audience Diomedes Aras Scheiber, the Peruvian Ambassador to the Holy See. The pope explained to the ambassador that a united destiny of happiness depended on two things: social justice based upon the teachings of Leo XIII in *Rerum novarum* and the establishment of an international law based on a just and morally sound basis.[51] Referring to Leo's encyclical, Pius said: "The light that diffuses itself from that historic message shines over all men of good will, and proceeds from the eternal hill from which salvation must come to us."[52]

In his 1952 encyclical, *Exsul familia nazarethana*, Pius linked the rights of immigrants and migrants to the family. In that document, he addressed the communities that were experiencing immigration in the wake of World War II. He discussed the importance of recognizing and respecting the rights of migrants and ministering to their spiritual needs, with special concern for the family: "For the same reason that man has a right to private property – so that families can provide for their needs and development – man has a right to migrate in order to provide materially for the family that migrates."[53]

---

[48] Percy, *Private Initiative*, 16.

[49] Percy, 16.

[50] Reprinted in the Tablet of London, June 7, 1941 http://archive.thetablet.co.uk/article/7th-june -1941/7/the-whit-sunday-address-of-pope-pius-xii.

[51] Walker, *Pius of Peace*, 115.

[52] Walker, 115.

[53] Later, Pope John XXIII quoted Pius XII as he tied the right to migrate to the right to private property: "private ownership of material goods has a great part to play in promoting the welfare of family life. It 'secures for the father of a family the healthy liberty he needs in order to fulfill the duties assigned him by the Creator regarding the physical; spiritual, and religious welfare of the family.'" John XXIII, Encyclical Letter *Mater et magistra* (On Christianity and Social Progress) (1961) (quoting Pius XII's Radio Broadcast of Pentecost, June 1, 1941).

Throughout his papacy, Pius encouraged Catholic parents to have children and large families. He spoke about the sacrifices that this imposed on
parents, but he also spoke of the maturity that tended to come to children in
large families and the blessings that came to such families. In doing this, he
did not specifically label his teachings as CST, but he surely shaped
Catholic culture and influenced social teaching for decades after his
earthly life.

On the Economy

Especially after World War II, Pius XII devoted a good deal of attention
to structuring a better society, one that could avoid what he considered
to be tragic results of earlier economic theories. In keeping with traditional Catholic Social Teaching, Pius did not claim to hold all of the
answers to economic questions, but that did not render the Church
silent. He insisted that the Church could not close her eyes "to the
immense social disorder which the age of technology and capitalism has
introduced."[54] Of course, the Church has never claimed that she alone
has the answers to "the social question," but she is entitled "to point
quietly to the values she has forged and which she places at the disposal
of all for the solution of social problems."[55] Among the values identified
by Pius was the Church's "social doctrine, which is entirely directed
towards the Natural Law and the Law of Christ."[56]

Throughout his life, Pius was an extraordinary student, and he understood the importance of economic knowledge and appreciated the intri-
cacies of the market.[57] His writings contain "some of the most positive

---

[54]   Pius XII, "To the 77th Congress of German Catholics at Cologne" (September 2, 1956), in *The
      Social Teachings of Pope Pius XII: 1956*, 17.
[55]   Pius XII, "To the 77th Congress" (1956), in *The Social Teachings of Pope Pius XII: 1956*, 17.
[56]   Pius XII, "To the 77th Congress" (1956), in *The Social Teachings of Pope Pius XII: 1956*, 17.
[57]   Notorious among his intimates for strict documentation in academic presentations, he
      expressed some disdain for those who spoke on economic matters without having sufficiently
      studied the matter.

   Through self-interest, partisan spirit, or considerations more of sentiment than of
   reason, many people, in fact too many people – makeshift economists and politicians –
   approach and treat financial and taxation questions with the more ardor and earn-
   estness, assuredness and airy manner the greater is their incompetence. Sometimes they
   do not seem even to suspect the necessity, in order to solve these problems, of deep
   studies, investigations and numerous observations of comparable experiences. *Pius XII
   on Work and Commerce.*

commentaries on the nature of private initiative, entrepreneurship, and business ever expressed by the Roman Magisterium."[58] In his words: "Every man, as a living being gifted with reason, has in fact from nature the fundamental right to make use of the material goods of the earth, while it is left to the will of man and to the juridical statutes of nations to regulate in greater detail the actuation of this right."[59]

Pius may have been the first pope to address the value of money.[60] He saw it as "a form of productive capital,"[61] and he understood the difference between the productive use of capital and usury (which remained condemned).[62] He spoke of the need for "the free, reciprocal commerce of goods by interchange and gift,"[63] and he directly tied the economy to social well-being: "Economic life means social life – the life of human beings. Hence it cannot be conceived without liberty."[64] For Pius, "the human person represents not only the purpose of the economy, *but is its most important element*."[65]

While Pius cautioned sternly against "the evil rich person who lives but to enjoy, without turning a glance of pity on poor Lazarus who, covered with sores, lies by his door (Luke 16:19)," the pope used scripture to offer "praise and recompense to the good and faithful servant who makes the money he has received bear fruit . . . [by] confiding it to bankers and obtaining from it proper interest (Matthew 25:20–30)."[66] Indeed, Pius had a high regard for the banking profession. "It seems opportune to Us to underline still once more here the high function of the banking system, the great importance which it has always had in the national economy, already in the time of the Ancient Assyrians and Egyptians, and to which the present conditions have only served to give a considerably increased breadth and influence."[67]

Pius recognized the banking system as a tool that could be used for social good,[68] and he explained its important social function: "Does not the social

---

[58] Percy, *Private Initiative*, 8.

[59] Percy, 9.

[60] Percy, 10 (saying that he was the first pope to discuss the value of money).

[61] Percy, 13.

[62] Percy, 13.

[63] Percy, 9.

[64] Robert Kennedy and Stephanie Rumpza, eds., *Christian Principles of International Trade* in *Pius XII on Work and Commerce*.

[65] Percy, *Private Initiative*, 14.

[66] Pius XII, "Address to the Personnel of the Bank of Italy" (April 25, 1950), in *Pius XII on Work and Commerce*.

[67] Pius XII, "Address to the Personnel of the Bank of Rome" (June 18, 1950), in *Pius XII on Work and Commerce*.

[68] For instance, in a 1948 address to the employees of the Bank of Naples, the pontiff noted that much had been asked of that bank during the war and post-war period, and much had been

function of the Bank consist in putting the individual in a position to make capital bear fruit, even slight, instead of dissipating it or letting it lie dormant without any profit either for himself or for others?"[69] Moreover, he noted that bankers make it possible for capital and labor to encounter each other and thus to assist in resolving social problems.[70]

Pius also recognized the special role of the businessman.[71] Not only did he teach that business was indispensable to society, he explained that private initiative reflected man's unique dignity and his transcendent destiny.[72] As such, a businessman was "a stimulating force in the economy."[73] A businessman needed to be "skilled without doubt; he must be a man of affairs, prudent more than sentimental." To these professional qualities "he must add ... a high concept of the ideal of his profession. As a businessman, he must also consider himself a servant of the community."[74] If a merchant "strives to circulate worldly goods, destined by God for the advantage of all, and takes them where they must serve and in a manner to make them serve well – then, indeed, he is a good and true servant of society, a guarantee against misery, a promoter of general prosperity."[75]

As he understood and explained business and businessmen, Pius was also able to explain why socialism and communism were both anti-Christian and doomed to failure.

---

done "to lighten ills and soften sorrows for the material and moral reconstruction" of the community. He went on to praise the bank for its "office of mercy, where you contributed your assistance to healing public and private misfortunes, this glory of holding open the sources of charity will always be for your bank a particularly dear and intelligently maintained title." Pius XII, "Address to the Employees of the Bank of Naples" (June 20, 1948), in *Pius XII on Work and Commerce*.

[69] Pius XII, "Address to the Personnel of the Bank of Italy" (April 25, 1950), in *Pius XII on Work and Commerce*.

[70] Percy, *Private Initiative*, 12.

[71] While the Church had long instructed on business and business ethics, it was not until 1956, when in an address to the First National Congress of Small Industry, Pope Pius XII made "the Roman Magisterium's first explicit reference to the entrepreneur." Percy, *Private Initiative*, 15.

[72] As one commentator has noted:

> Pius XII embraced the whole economic world within the sweep of his teaching, treating of a series of relationships: between employers, directors, furnishers of capital; between enterprise and enterprise; between various professional classes; between producer sectors: agriculture, industry, social services; between private enterprise and state intervention; as well as between national economies themselves on a world plane.

> Pietro Pavan, The Place of Mater et Magistra in Papal Social Teaching, Christus Rex (1962), 233, quoted in Gerald Darring, Pope Pius XII, 1939–1958.

[73] Percy, *Private Initiative*, 16.

[74] Pius XII, "Address of His Holiness to the delegates of the World Congress of Chambers of Commerce" (April 27, 1950), in *Pius XII on Work and Commerce*.

[75] Pius XII, "Address to World Congress" (April 27, 1950), in *Pius XII on Work and Commerce*.

There are even countries where a policy has been adopted, more or less absolute, that places all commerce in the hands of public authority. Let us affirm this clearly: this is a tendency in opposition to the Christian conception of social economy. Commerce is fundamentally an activity of the individual and it is this private activity that gives a man his first impulse and lights the flame of his enthusiasm.[76]

General prosperity required "putting into full effect the individual exercise of commerce for the service of society's material well-being."[77]

In fact, while he expressed general support for various measures like employment-based health and medical insurance for workers, Pius was concerned that welfare programs (which were widespread not only in Communist nations but which also had been the norm under Nazism in the 1930s) were having the effect of reducing personal responsibility.

[T]he anxious desire for security should not prevail over the businessman's readiness to risk his resource to such an extent as to dry up every creative impulse; nor impose on enterprise operating conditions that are too burdensome; nor discourage those who devote their time and energy to commercial transactions. Unhappily, it is an all-too-human tendency to seek out the way of minimum effort, to avoid obligations, and to exempt oneself from the duty of self-reliance in order to fall back upon the support of society and to live at the expense of one's fellows.[78]

Accordingly, the State "ought not to try to take the place of private enterprise, so long as the latter functions usefully and successfully."[79] The "common good *demands* that private enterprise and entrepreneurship enjoy a high degree of freedom in the economic realm."[80] He also cautioned about overtaxation.[81]

In his 1951 encyclical, *Evangelii praecones*, in a section on social justice, Pius called for "social reform" and criticized both communism and other systems that did not protect the worker.[82] Specifically, he worried about

[76] Pius XII, "Address to World Congress."
[77] Pius XII, "Address to World Congress."
[78] Pius XII, *Business and the Common Good*, The Pope Speaks 3, no. 1 (1956), 45, quoted in Percy, *Private Initiative*, 18.
[79] Percy, *Private Initiative*, 18.
[80] Percy, 18.
[81] Percy, 16 (activity of businessmen should "not be barred by too many obstacles" and taxes should not be "too numerous and too heavy").
[82] According to one commentator:

Those who conceived that, because of his frequent castigations of atheistic communism, the pope was thereby an uncritical upholder of capitalism, were disconcerted when he condemned that form of capitalism which was "without any other aim except the enjoyment of ephemeral goods, without any other norm but that of the fait

mechanization that was taking jobs from the workers. "The Church cannot ignore or overlook the fact that the worker, in his efforts to better his lot, is opposed by a machinery which is not in accordance with nature, but is at variance with God's plan and with the purpose He had in creating the goods of the earth."[83] Pius XII envisioned a social order based on cooperation for the common good. He concentrated on the functioning of economic life, with important modifications of structure needed to achieve sound and harmonious action.[84]

In the end, Pius XII's teaching about private property, business, and banking was focused not primarily on economic efficiency but more on Catholic truths related to the human need to act and to develop moral and spiritual virtues.[85] Pius did not provide actual economic or business advice. He instructed on traditional Catholic moral understandings and insisted that they be applied in the workplace and the marketplace.

War and Peace

Elevated to the papacy in the same year that World War II began, it is fair to say that issues of war and peace dominated the papacy of Pope Pius XII. In one of his earliest presentations as pope, Pius made his famous plea for peace:

> accompli" …. He condemned the ruthless ethics of unlimited competition and the social injustices of lingering liberalism as sternly as he condemned communism.

Liam Brophy, Social Justice Review (1958): 263, quoted in Gerald Darring, "Pope Pius XII, 1939–1958," www.shc.edu/theolibrary/resources/popes_pius12.htm. See Pius XII, "Address of His Holiness, Pope Pius XII, prepared for the delegates to the Catholic International Congresses for Social Study (Fribourg Union) and Social Action (Saint Gall Union)" (June 3, 1950), in *Pius XII on Work and Commerce* ("There has been too much experimenting with mass production, with the exploitation, to the point of exhaustion, of every resource of the soil and subsoil. Above all, peasant populations and agrarian economics have been only too cruelly sacrificed to these experiments. Equally blind is the well-nigh superstitious reliance on the mechanism of the world market to restore a balanced economy, and the trust in an Omniprovident State to secure, for each of its subjects and in every emergency of their lives, the right to make demands which must eventually prove to be unattainable.")

[83] Pius XII proclaimed "the dignity of the human person," and "as a natural foundation of life the right to use the goods of the earth." Building on this right, he defended "the fundamental obligation to grant private ownership of property, if possible, to all." For further condemnation of Marxism, see Pius XII, "Radio address to the German Catholic Congress, Bochum" (September 4, 1949), in *Pius XII on Work and Commerce* (he sought "to erect a dam to save not only the workers but all, without exception, from Marxism, which denies God and religion").

[84] John F. Cronin, 686, *Catholic Mind* (1951), quoted in Gerald Darring, "Pope Pius XII, 1939–1958," www.shc.edu/theolibrary/resources/popes_pius12.htm.

[85] Percy, *Private Initiative*, 9 (discussing Pius XII's address on the Fiftieth Anniversary of *Rerum novarum*, June 1, 1941).

"Nothing is lost by peace, but everything may be lost by war."[86] Unfortunately, he could not stop World War II, and it ended with a demand for unconditional surrender and the detonation of two atomic bombs (all of which he opposed).

During the Cold War, the United States and the Soviet Union built up their stockpiles of weapons of mass destruction. That became a serious concern for the rest of Pius XII's life.[87] As other commentators have noted, "Pius XII stands as both a classic expositor of just-war theory and an articulator of major themes to be developed by his successors: the unprecedented danger of modern war, the need to establish a world authority to eliminate the right and need to resort to war, and the reconstruction of the world economic order to ensure mutual prosperity and eliminate the major causes of war."[88]

Three encyclicals issued in 1950 show how the issue of atomic warfare weighed on him. The first encyclical, *Anni sacri*, warned of the new "armaments race," which left "the hearts of all overcome by fear and trepidation." Pius wrote that the "war is over but peace has not yet arrived." He faulted those nations where "the press turns against religion and ridicules religious feelings" as well as those where Christians were being persecuted. According to Pius, public and private atheism undermined morality, and he called for prayer to "quieten human storms."

Later that year came another encyclical, *Summi maeroris*, asking for prayers for peace between the classes and among the nations. Again, Pius warned of the terror of modern weapons that "can destroy not only armies and fleets, not only cities, towns and villages, not only the treasures of religion, of art and culture, but also innocent children with their mothers, those who are sick and the helpless aged."[89] The solution, said Pius, was to be found in religion and "the freedom that is due religion." That freedom of religion, according to Pius, included not only the "primary purpose of leading souls to eternal salvation," but also the purpose of "safeguarding and protecting the very foundations of the State."[90]

Pius issued his third encyclical of the year, *Mirabile illud*, in December 1950. It dealt with his concern about war spreading from Korea to the rest of world. Pius decried as "so terrible" the "mechanical equipment and instruments of modern warfare invented by the genius of man." He linked the

---

[86] Pius XII, "To Those in Power and Their Peoples" (August 24, 1939), in *The Pope Speaks*, 145.

[87] In February 1943 Pius warned about the risks posed by atomic fission. See Walker, *Pius of Peace*, 177 (quoting a pronouncement from February 1943).

[88] William Au. C. J. Reid, Jr., ed., *Peace in a Nuclear Age* (1986), 100.

[89] Pius XII, *Summi maeroris* (On Public Prayers for Peace) (1950), no. 5.

[90] SM, no. 9.

cost of these armaments with economic suffering of the "poorer classes," who were harmed "still more by the further loss of wealth which is a necessary concomitant of war." The pope warned that "new dangers of wars threaten mankind." As before, the papal solution was to follow the moral teachings of the Catholic Church in both public and private life. Only that would guarantee "a peaceful stability, founded on right order and justice." He prayed that "due liberty in all nations" would be granted to "the Catholic religion, which is the most secure foundation of human society and civilized culture."[91]

While Pope Pius XII was unable to stop the carnage, he expended great effort in trying to minimize the suffering. Perhaps his teachings even helped keep the Cold War cold. Certainly, his broadcasts, talks, and writings made important contributions to the proper understanding of CST.

Racial Issues and Solidarity

Throughout his life, but particularly during World War II, Pope Pius XII went out of his way to protect Jewish people and other minorities.[92] In the first year of his papacy, he explained that equal treatment of people of different races was directly tied to the doctrine of solidarity:

> Because of this divine law of human solidarity and charity, and because God loved the whole human race, we are assured, that all men are truly brethren, without excluding the rich variety of persons, cultures and societies, even if they do not belong to the Catholic Church or share the Christian faith. Divine precepts contradict belief in "superiority." Superior and inferior cultures do not exist and different levels of development within and between nations are sources for enrichment and not discrimination of the human race.[93]

That same year, in the encyclical *Sertum laetitiae*, Pius expressed his special affection for "the Negro people."[94] He also set forth a five-point peace plan, point four of which was "Compliance with the needs and just demands of nations, peoples, and ethnic minorities."[95]

[91] Pius XII, Encyclical Letter *Mirabile illud* (On the Crusade of Prayer for Peace) (1950), no. 12.
[92] See Rychlak, *Hitler, the War, and the Pope*; Riebling, *Church of Spies*; Rychlak, *Righteous Gentiles*; Ion M. Pacepa and Ronald J. Rychlak, *Disinformation: Former Spy Chief Reveals Secret Strategies for Undermining Freedom, Attacking Religion, and Promoting Terrorism* (WND Books, 2013).
[93] *Acta Apostolicae Sedis* 31 (1939) 413.
[94] *SL*, no. 9.
[95] See Walker, *Pius of Peace*, 130 (quoting an allocution of December 24, 1939, that set forth a five-point peace plan). He expanded on the importance of the rights of minorities in his Christmas allocution of 1941. Walker, *Pius of Peace*, 137.

In 1944, the *New York Times* reported on how, "fulfilling the instructions of Pope Pius XII," the Catholic University of America had hosted a conference condemning racism in all its manifestations, citing "the great moral or natural law, universal as human nature, before which all men are equal."[96] The following year, *Commonweal* magazine published a ground-breaking article, *The Sin of Segregation,* by Father George Dunne, SJ, in which he called for "an uncompromising repudiation of racism in all its forms," quoting the words of Pope Pius XII: "The only road to salvation is definitely to repudiate all pride of race and blood."[97]

Pius XII also monitored the racial situation around the world.[98] For instance, when word reached him that an American priest in Indianapolis, Indiana, had declared that blacks would not be welcome in his parish, the pope immediately had him removed and disciplined.[99]

During his pontificate, Pius expanded and internationalized the Church by creating 57 new bishoprics, 45 of them in America and Asia. He also replaced colonial bishops with native hierarchies and caused the percentage of Italians in the College of Cardinals to drop to less than half, paving the way for the eventual election of a non-Italian pope. When he passed away, he received enormous praise for all he had done to protect Jewish victims of the Nazis during World War II.[100]

---

[96]   William Doino, "A Civil Rights Hero Remembers a Pope," *First Things* (July 30, 2012) (recounting Roi Ottley's audience with Pope Pius XII).

[97]   Doino, "A Civil Rights Hero Remembers a Pope."

[98]   Recounting an audience that he had with the pope, one African American writer (Roi Ottley) said:

> His Holiness spoke English haltingly. But he asked surprisingly acute questions about Negroes . . .. This statesman, one of the most impressive figures of our time, inspired a remarkable kind of confidence, which led me into describing conditions under which many Negroes live in America. The Pope was manifestly pained by the report. But he brightened perceptibly, when he told me of the reports gathered by parish priests in Italy, which described Negroes stationed in the country as kind, good-humored and winning. He asked me to convey a "special message" to Negroes in the U.S. He sighed and momentarily seemed to be gathering his strength. When he next spoke his words were uttered with great emphasis. He asked that I report the Holy Father's hope for the Negro's happiness, well-being and ultimate triumph over racial obstacles. Thus, by implication, did the Pontiff bring to the Negro's side the moral weight of the Church.

> Quoted in Doino, "A Civil Rights Hero Remembers a Pope."

[99]   Doino, "A Civil Rights Hero Remembers a Pope."

[100] See Rychlak, *Hitler, the War, and the Pope,* 273–74.

On Science

To Pius XII, science and religion were different manifestations of truth, and therefore they could not ultimately contradict each other.[101] Regarding the relationship between faith and science, his close advisor Fr. Robert Leiber wrote that Pius XII "was very careful not to close any doors prematurely."[102] Pius was very firm on this point, and as Leiber explained, he regretted that the Church had made this mistake in the case of Galileo. In fact, in his first speech to the Pontifical Academy of Sciences (1939), Pius included Galileo among the "most audacious heroes of research . . . not afraid of the stumbling blocks and the risks on the way."[103]

Pius XII took a close interest in science and the proceedings of the Pontifical Academy of Sciences. He gave eight papal addresses to the Academy in which he dwelt at length upon major contemporary issues and offered strong doctrinal and moral guidelines, always taking great care to study and understand his topics.[104] At the time Pius XII assumed the papacy, the Academy included, among others, Niels Bohr and Erwin Schrödinger. Among those that Pius himself nominated were Louis de Broglie, Werner Heisenberg, and Max Planck.

Addressing the Academy in 1955, Pius said: "The duty of a scientist is to understand God's design, to interpret the Book of Nature, to explain its contents and to draw from it consequences for the common good." He explained that the scientific method was not to be changed in order to accommodate philosophical assumptions but was to always seek the truth, wherever it was to be found. He defended the autonomy of science and of scientific interpretation.[105]

[101]   *Discorsi e Radiomessaggi di sua Santita Pio XII* (Vatican City, 1940), 407; *Discorsi E Radiomessaggi di sua Santita Pio XII* (Vatican City, 1942), 52; *Discorsi e Radiomessaggi di sua Santita Pio XII* (Vatican City, 1946), 89; *Discorsi e Radiomessaggi di sua Santita Pio XII* (Vatican City, 1951), 28, 221, 413, 574.

[102]   Robert Leiber, "Pius XII," in *Stimmen der Zeit* (November 1958); reprinted in *Pius XII Sagt* (Frankfurt, 1959): 411.

[103]   Pius XII, "Discourse of His Holiness Pope Pius XII given at the Solemn Audience granted to the Plenary Session of the Academy" (December 3, 1939), in *Discourses of the Popes from Pius XI to John Paul II to the Pontifical Academy of the Sciences 1939–1986* (Pontifical Academy of Sciences: Vatican City, 1986), 34.

[104]   These speeches can be found in *Discourses of the Popes from Pius XI to John Paul II*.

[105]   As the Pontifical Academy of Sciences itself has explained:

>   The Pope's statement that the experimental method cannot be influenced by philosophical assumptions and that the autonomy of science and of scientific interpretation is legitimate must be underlined. These words enlightened the Church in a field which had caused misunderstandings in the past that had not yet vanished. Indeed, in his first meeting with the Pontifical Academy of Sciences, Pius XII affirmed the freedom of scientific research: "To you noble champions of human arts and disciplines the Church

Chemist Bernard Pullman devoted part of his book on the history of atomism to Pius XII's interest in quantum mechanics and atomic physics, particularly the scientific and philosophical questions raised by quantum mechanics. Pullman reported that Pius XII's "two speeches to the Pontifical Academy . . . are lengthy and marvelously prepared dissertations that attest to the detailed knowledge the Pontiff had of the subject matter. Reading them is not unlike attending a magisterial lecture, as they constitute genuine updates on the state of knowledge at the time."[106]

Georges Lemaitre, a Catholic priest who was the first to propose the Big Bang scenario for the origin of the universe, was also a member of the Pontifical Academy. Thanks to him, Pius XII was well informed about the rise of modern physical cosmology.[107]

In an address to the World Health Organization, Pius encouraged those who sought to improve human health: "The social doctrine of the Catholic Church allows no doubt to creep in regarding the fact that the health of body and spirit, where reigns also health in social relations, can effectively contribute to the establishing of an atmosphere of the sort most favorable to the interior and mutual peace of peoples."[108] Because health contributes to peace, Pius explained that "the question of health surpasses the framework of biology and medicine; it necessarily has its place in the sphere of morality and religion."[109]

---

acknowledges complete freedom in method and research." This statement expressed a new vision of science, which Pius XII was to reaffirm in all the allocutions given during his Pontificate. Today it can be regarded as the synthesis of an important moment in the history of science and philosophy.

The Pontifical Academy of Sciences, Servant of God Pius XII (1939–1958), www .casinapioiv.va/content/accademia/en/magisterium/piusxii.html.

[106]   Bernard Pullman, *The Atom in the History of Human Thought* (Oxford: Oxford University Press, 1998), 317–321. In February 1943 Pius warned about the risks posed by atomic fission. See Walker, *Pius of Peace*, 177 (quoting a pronouncement from February 1943).

[107]   Commenting on "the state and nature of original matter," Pius acknowledged that science declares this to be an "insoluble enigma" but continued, that "it seems that science of today, by going back in one leap millions of centuries, has succeeded in being witness to that primordial Fiat Lux when, out of nothing, there burst forth with matter a sea of light and radiation, while the particles of chemical elements split and reunited in millions of galaxies." "Discourse of His Holiness Pope Pius XII given on 3 December 1939 at the Solemn Audience granted to the Plenary Session of the Academy," *Discourses of the Popes from Pius XI to John Paul II to the Pontifical Academy of the Sciences 1939–1986*, Vatican City, 82. Pius went on to say that these facts need further investigation, and theories founded upon them need "new developments and proofs in order to offer a secure basis for reasoning."

[108]   Pius XII, "Discourse to the Participants of the World Health Organization" (June 27, 1949), in *Pius XII on Work and Commerce*.

[109]   Ibid.

In 1950, Pius XII promulgated *Humani generis*, which acknowledged that evolution might accurately describe the biological origins of human life, but at the same time criticized those who "imprudently and indiscreetly hold that evolution ... explains the origin of all things." While *Humani generis* was significant as the first occasion on which a pope explicitly addressed the topic of evolution at length, it did not represent a change in doctrine. That encyclical also made an important statement about racism as it rejected polygenism, the theory of human origins positing that the human races are of different origins.[110]

Unlike some other Christians, Pius never feared where science might lead. He, in fact, pleaded for scientific pursuit of the truth, which he knew would necessarily be in harmony with Christianity. That is why, as he explained, "the Church is the mother of many universities and she gathers around her the greatest scientists, the most adventurous searchers into nature's secrets."[111]

Uses of the Media

As Vatican Secretary of State, the future Pope Pius XII played an important role in the installation of the Vatican's radio station. His coronation was the first ever to be broadcast on the radio, and his 1939 encyclical *Sertum laetitiae*, supported the use of the "Marconi Radio, whose voice is heard in an instant round the world – marvelous invention and eloquent image of the Apostolic Faith that embraces all mankind."[112] His first message on Vatican Radio was a pledge to work for unity and a plea for peace throughout the world.[113] He regularly broadcast prayers and messages of peace during World War II. Moreover, as the war went on, Vatican Radio sent out up to 27,000 messages per month trying to locate missing persons.[114]

---

[110] Pius XII, Encyclical Letter *Humani generis* (Concerning Some False Opinions Threatening to Undermine the Foundations of Catholic Doctrine) (1950), no. 37 ("For the faithful cannot embrace that opinion which maintains that either after Adam there existed on this earth true men who did not take their origin through natural generation from him as from the first parent of all, or that Adam represents a certain number of first parents").

[111] Quoted in Walker, *Pius of Peace*, 42.

[112] *SL*, no. 30.

[113] Jan Olav Smit, *Angelic Shepherd: The Life of Pope Pius XII* (Dodd & Mead: New York, Vanderveldt trans., 1950), 238–239. See also Walker, *Pius of Peace*, 114 (quoting Pius XII's statement to General Quintanilla, Bolivian Ambassador to the Holy See, August 1940) ("No true peace is possible for humanity redeemed by Christ outside the principles and norms of justice and charity proclaimed by the Gospel.")

[114] Thomas Bokenkotter, *A Concise History of the Catholic Church* (Crown Publishing Group, 2007), 373.

Pius XII's last major encyclical, *Miranda prorsus*, was published in 1957. In it, Pius discussed the potential of the media to bring about immense good or immense evil and the necessity that those tasked with its supervision ensure that it is used to positively influence the world. He also addressed motion pictures and television. Pius celebrated these technological developments as gifts of God, and he predicted that these new forms of communication would revolutionize how individuals and society as a whole think and act. He saw visual images as particularly congruent with the sacramental approach to God through visible signs. He noted that these new communications media bring people into contact with one another and unite them in their efforts. He celebrated the power of radio and television to reach into the home, where, when used with discretion, it could strengthen the family.

At the same time, Pius warned about the abuse of these media.[115] In the last century with the advent of industrialization, "machines, which ought to serve men when brought into use, rather reduced them to a state of slavery and caused grievous harm." These new media, if used wrongly, could be "the source of countless evils, which appear to be all the more serious, because not only material forces but also the mind are unhappily enslaved, and man's inventions are, to that extent, deprived of those advantages which, in the design of God's Providence, ought to be their primary purpose."[116] Moreover, because of their power to penetrate into the home, these media presented a particular threat to the youth.

Pius well understood the power of technology.[117] He directed bishops to set up special commissions on media, and instructed Church ministries to take full advantage of these technologies.[118] He also established a special commission in the Vatican to deal with new media, and he encouraged the development of Catholic radio stations.

---

[115] Pius cautioned families to take care about what programs were permitted into the home. Pius XII, Encyclical Letter *Miranda prorsus*. Not long after this, experts in the Kremlin were using radio and other media to create a false history about Pius himself. See Pacepa and Rychlak, *Disinformation*.

[116] *MP* (Reasons for this letter).

[117] In 1956, Pius said "economics and technology are useful and even necessary forces so long as they are made subservient to man's higher spiritual needs. They become harmful and dangerous only when they are given undue predominance and the dignity, so to speak, of being ends in themselves." Pius XII, "To Members of the Vatican Diplomatic Corps" (March 4, 1956), in *The Social Teachings of Pope Pius XII: 1956*, 18.

[118] He ordered American radio priest, Fr. Charles Coughlin, off the air due to his political activity and apparent anti-Semitism. Rychlak, *Righteous Gentiles*, 326, n. 9.

On the Roman Patriciate and Nobility

The "preferential option for the poor" is a very well-known aspect of CST, and Pius certainly devoted much effort and many words to the obligation of Christians to help the poor. In fact, during World War II, he went on wartime rations and lived in solidarity with the poor and suffering. At the same time, Pius saw the consequences of class warfare with the rise of communism and oppression of the masses and the Church in the Soviet Union. As such, he also devoted attention to those who were well off, so much so that one author approvingly wrote of Pius XII's preferential option for the nobility.[119]

The Catholic Church has long recognized the hierarchical nature of society, and the obligations that such a structure imposes. In 1943, Pius XII published *Mystici corporis Christi*, his landmark encyclical on the Catholic Church as the "Mystical Body of Christ." In it, he urged the community of the Church to offer supplications on behalf of "kings and princes," as well as of "rulers." In addition, Pius gave annual allocutions to the Roman Patriciate and Nobility from 1940 through 1952 and again in 1958.[120]

In the allocution of January 8, 1940, Pius spoke on the importance of the noble class. He explained that "if it is true that modern society revolts against the idea and the very name of a privileged class, it is no less true that, like ancient societies, this society cannot do without a class of industrious people who, by this very fact, belong to the ruling circles." He therefore encouraged the nobility not to be a leisure class, but to "openly prove that you are and intend to be a willing, active class." In that manner, their children would understand "that no one is allowed to avoid the original and universal law of work, however varied and multiple its intellectual and manual forms."

The following year, Pius spoke of certain duties that fell to the noble class, particularly the duty "not to squander such treasures, to pass them on whole, indeed increased, if possible, to those who will come after you" and the duty "not to reserve these assets for yourselves alone, but to let them generously

---

[119] Plinio Corrêa de Oliveira, *Nobility and Analogous Traditional Elites in the Allocutions of Pius XII* (Hamilton Press, 1993) (introductory material) (noting that the preferential option for the poor and the preferential option for the nobility are "by no means mutually exclusive").

[120] In his allocution of January 16, 1946, Pius pointed out that true nobility was not a right of birth, but a duty that was imposed upon a class of people.

> [I]n a democratic society, which our own wishes to be, the mere title of birth no longer suffices to command authority or esteem; therefore, in order to preserve in worthy fashion your elevated station and social rank, indeed to increase it and raise it, you must truly be an elite, you must meet the conditions and fulfill the indispensable demands of the epoch wherein we live.

benefit those who have been less favored by Providence."[121] He encouraged the nobles to set good examples in their work and in their faith.[122]

The importance of competent people to any society was central to Pius XII's allocution of January 8, 1947. At a time when Italy was in the process of adopting a new constitution, Pius asked: "[W]hat good are the best laws if they are to remain a dead letter?" He explained that "A good constitution is without doubt a thing of great value. What the State is absolutely in need of, however, are men of competence and expertise in political and administrative matters, men wholly dedicated to the greater good of the nation, and guided by clear and sound principles." In the allocution of 1958, he said, "Personal duty requires that you, with your virtue and diligence, endeavor to become leaders in your professions."

The recognition of nobility, of course, suggests possible classism or favoritism. Today, we tend to think of all people as being equal, and nobility suggests a denial of solidarity and human brotherhood. Pius XII addressed that issue. In a speech to a group of parishioners of Marsciano, Perugia, Italy, on June 4, 1953, the pontiff explained:

> It is not a matter of mere appearance; you are truly sons of God, so you are really brothers to one another. Now, brothers are not born equal, nor do they remain equal; some are strong, others weak; some are intelligent, others inept; sometimes one is abnormal or actually becomes a disgrace. A certain material, intellectual, and moral inequality is therefore inevitable even within the same family. To claim absolute equality for all would be like wanting to assign the exact same function to different parts of the same organism.

It would be a misunderstanding of Pope Pius XII's CST to think that in addressing nobility he was in any way diminishing the Church's concern for the poor. It was important, however, that the Church speak to all. Moreover, as Pius made clear, it was important to society that the nobility fill the roles prescribed for them.

---

[121]   Allocution of January 5, 1941. In his allocution of January 15, 1949, Pius explained that "Divine Providence has assigned everyone in human society a specific function; it has therefore also divided and distributed its gifts. These gifts and talents are supposed to bear fruit." Similarly, in his allocution of 1958, he explained: "Social inequalities, even those related to birth, are inevitable: Benign nature and God's blessing to humanity illuminate and protect all cradles, looking on them with love, but does not make them equal."

[122]   In the allocution of January 14, 1952, Pius said: "1) First of all, you must look fearlessly, courageously, at the present reality. 2) Lift your gaze and keep it fixed on the Christian Ideal. 3) Lastly, give your devoted and ready assistance to the common effort." See also Walker, *Pius of Peace*, 124 (audience of January 14, 1945).

CONCLUSION

Catholic Social Teaching runs throughout the writings of Pope Pius XII. Under him and his predecessor Pope Pius XI, the terminology and the concept of "human dignity" began to permeate first the Church, then the rest of society.[123] Pius XII's appeal to the dignity of man among Christians, which came at the beginning of his papacy, was the first step in creating the idea of "human rights," as reflected in the United Nations' Declaration of Universal Human Rights.[124] With the emergence of this concept came an effort to assign "human rights" to individuals.[125]

Just one month into his papacy, Pius XII set forth a modern vision of CST that said that there could be no peace without a more equitable distribution of wealth and an end to social injustices. Treaties had to be honored, justice had to prevail over violence, and of course, justice had to be wedded to "the generous and deep charity of Christ."[126]

Pius XII understood that man had to work out his salvation in society, and his Church was interested in the social order. Pius did not claim that the Church could solve the social question by herself, but he took pride in the fact that the Church nurtured and fostered social virtues, without which no social order could exist.[127] As he understood and taught it, CST was based on the natural law and on the Gospels. During his papacy, CST became an essential part of the training of young Catholic men and women.[128]

Pius understood both economics and science, perhaps better than any of his predecessors. Certainly he understood them well enough to know that unless they properly incorporated Christian teachings, they would bring only disillusionment. He saw the Church's role as bringing Christian values to earthly endeavors like science and economics.

As others have noted, for Pius XII, "the task of the Church was to teach the Gospel and to indicate the principles in the Gospel under which a better social order could be built. These principles comprise the social teaching of the Church, but the task of doing the building belongs to individuals, not to the

---

[123] See David E. Anderson, *The Religious Sources for Modern Human Rights*.

[124] Andrew Evans, *Whatever Happened to Human Rights?*, reviewing Samuel Moyn, *Christian Human Rights*, The Washington Free Beacon (October 11, 2015).

[125] "Forgotten now, the spiritual and often explicitly religious philosophy of the human person was the conceptual means through which continental Europe initially incorporated human rights." Evans, *Whatever Happened to Human Rights?*, quoting Samuel Moyn.

[126] Pius XII, "Easter Sunday homily" (April 9, 1939), in Walker, *Pius of Peace*, 17.

[127] *The Social Teachings of Pope Pius XII: 1956*, 27–28.

[128] Ibid.

Church as such."[129] In other words, the implementation of CST – the actions necessary to transform Christian society – was the job of the laity.[130] Thus he often spoke directly to the people, frequently in radio broadcasts. He explained: "The future belongs to those who love, not to those who hate," and he instructed that the "task confided to you by Providence in this crucial hour is not to conclude a weak and timid peace with the world, but to establish for the world a peace really worthy in the sight of God and man."[131]

Pius wrote on a wide variety of CST topics, but he did not draw a hard line between social teachings and religious, prayerful, or liturgical issues. To him they went hand in hand. In 1947 Pius XII issued *Mediator dei*, in which he canonized the emerging liturgical renewal movement (so central to the later reforms of the Second Vatican Council). According to Pius, liturgical renewal was an importation response to "the needs of our day . . . after a long and cruel war that has rent whole peoples asunder with its rivalry and slaughter." He saw liturgy as aiding the post-war spiritual renewal of Catholic Christians and in turn serving the wider search for world peace. He envisioned that the liturgical movement would serve as an explicit spiritual antidote to the modern rejection of God and denial of human solidarity.

Pius did not author any of the major encyclicals on CST, but he contributed mightily to the doctrine. He instructed Catholics to live their faith in their homes and at their work:

> Do not be content to believe in Jesus Christ or even to practice Christian principles only in your private life. Be Christians in your social and public life also by living the Gospel in the relationship which must exist between those who provide work and those who perform it. All of you are the children of God and all of you are equally necessary to the industrial concern or business enterprise, although in different degrees according to the different functions you perform.[132]

His impact on the Church extended well beyond his own lifetime. Other than Holy Scripture, he was the most-cited authority in the documents of Vatican II.[133] Both Pope John XXIII and Pope Paul VI acknowledged the significant

---

129 Christine E. Gudorf, *Catholic Social Teaching on Liberation Themes* (1981), 76.
130 Pius, in fact, called on Catholics to be inspired by the hatred that is too often directed at the Church. See Pius XII, "Address to the College of Cardinals on the Feast of St. Eugene" (June 2, 1947), in *Pius XII on Work and Commerce*, from *The Catholic Mind* (August 1947), 440–457.
131 "Address to the College of Cardinals on the Feast of St. Eugene."
132 Pius XII, "To Members of the Italian Water Works Society" (April 14, 1956), quoted in *The Social Teachings of Pope Pius XII: 1956*, 19.
133 *Supra* note 8.

impact that he had on their papacies.[134] When Pius died on October 9, 1958, people from around the world recognized his contributions with an over-whelming number of tributes, statements of thanks, and expressions of condolence.[135]

---

[134] Ronald J. Rychlak, *Pius XII, John XXIII, and the Newly-Opened Archives*, Catalyst (March 2007). In 1963, Pope John XXIII passed away and was succeeded by Pope Paul VI (Cardinal Giovanni Battista Montini). In 1965, Paul proposed that "his great model," Pius XII, be considered for sainthood. Pius has been declared "Venerable," and the cause of his beatification is still underway.

[135] Rychlak, *Hitler, the War, and the Pope*, 273–74.

6

Development in Catholic Social Teaching: John XXIII to Paul VI

V. Bradley Lewis

This chapter concerns developments in Catholic Social Teaching during a period of thirteen eventful years that includes John XXIII's *Mater et magistra* (1961), and *Pacem in terris* (1963), The Second Vatican Council's Pastoral Constitution on the Church in the Modern World, *Gaudium et spes* (1965) and Paul VI's *Populorum progressio* (1967). The period was one of great social, political, and economic change and of intellectual ferment in the Church. It is all the more remarkable given that forty years separated the start of the papal social teaching tradition, Leo XIII's *Rerum novarum* (1891) and Pius XI's second installment, *Quadragesimo anno* (1931), itself separated by some thirty years from *Mater et magistra*. These thirteen years are a highly compressed period in which the Church's address of the social, economic, and political phenomena was highly concentrated and intensified by instabilities in the surrounding secular environment. The Church articulated its social doctrine in the face of an especially tense moment in the Cold War connected to the end of colonialism, rapid but uneven economic development, and burgeoning social movements that destabilized the domestic politics of the developed and developing world. The beginning of this period was marked by the optimism of John XXIII about the human possibilities presented by economic modernization tempered by the threat of war among the superpowers. Growing challenges to traditional social order and to the Church were more clearly seen in the deliberations of the Second Vatican Council and manifested powerfully in its contribution to Catholic Social Doctrine, the Pastoral Constitution for the Church in the Modern World, *Gaudium et spes*. In the pontificate of Paul VI one encounters an, at times, seemingly paradoxical combination of anguish over the problems of the modern world and an almost eschatological view of the possibilities of progress.

When considering developments in the pontificates of John XXIII and Paul VI, it is necessary to begin by recalling the rather significant developments made by Pius XI. Indeed, in some respects, Pius XI overshadows Leo XIII. *Quadragesimo anno*, which cannot be read in isolation from Pius's other encyclicals, goes much further in many of its judgments than Leo did and also introduces important innovations. While Pius largely repeated Leo's views about private property and the need for employers to pay workers a living wage, he explained the latter by way of his notion of social justice, which was not defined in his 1931 encyclical, but was in his later encyclical on communism, *Divini redemptoris*, as the "demand for each individual all that is necessary for the common good." He went on:

> But just as in the living organism it is impossible to provide for the good of the whole unless each single part and each individual member is given what it needs for the exercise of its proper functions, so it is impossible to care for the social organism and the good of society as a unit unless each single part and each individual member – that is to say, each individual man in the dignity of his human personality – is supplied with all that is necessary for the exercise of his social functions.[1]

This social justice is in part an equivalent to what Aquinas called "legal" justice, which demands that citizens promote the common good, but goes further in including a concomitant demand that citizens have the resources they need to so contribute. Similarly Pius XI introduced the term and subsequently canonical formulation of the important principle of subsidiarity, although the idea itself can be seen in *Rerum novarum*.[2] In line with both of these principles was his strongly worded condemnation of what he perceived to be an increasingly unfree economy in which a small group of wealthy individuals and corporations dictated terms to everyone else. Less perspicuous was his advocacy of a kind of corporatism, which he took pains to distinguish from fascism, and which did enjoy something of a renaissance in southern Europe and Latin America in the 1970s, but now seems largely irrelevant. The length and detail of *Quadragesimo anno* and the centrality of political as distinct from economic questions in the period dominated by the Second World War probably explains why Pius XII did not write a social

---

[1]   Pius XI, Encyclical Letter *Quadragesimo anno* (On Reconstruction of the Social Order) (1931), no. 57, in *Acta Apostolicae Sedis* 23 (1931) 196; Pius XI, Encyclical Letter *Divini redemptoris* (On Atheistic Communism) (1937), no. 51 in *AAS* 29 (1937), 92.

[2]   *QA*, nos. 79, 203; and see Leo XIII, Encyclical Letter *Rerum novarum* (On the Condition of the Working Classes) (1891), nos. 50–51: *ASS* 23 (1890–91) 664–65, and discussion in Jean-Yves Calvez, SJ, and Jacques Perrin, SJ, *The Church and Social Justice: The Social Teaching of the Popes from Leo XIII to Pius XII*, trans. J. R. Kirwan (Chicago: Henry Regnery Co., 1961), 121–23.

encyclical,[3] although he did contribute to social teaching in a number of influential radio addresses during the war years. When John XXIII took up social questions in 1961 he faced a very different environment and could therefore exercise a relatively free hand in its treatment.

JOHN XXIII

Pope John's two "social" encyclicals are characterized in one sense by a basic division of labor between the mainly social and economic questions treated in *Mater et magistra* (1961) and international affairs treated in *Pacem in terris* (1963). The first has at least part of its context in John's heavy involvement in Catholic action efforts in Italy; the second in both John's experiences as a medical orderly during World War I and the Cuban Missile Crisis of October 1962 (which actually moved him to consider suspending the Second Vatican Council, only just begun). However, while *Pacem in terris* was written later, sparked by the Missile Crisis of the previous year and perhaps also by John's knowledge of his own mortal illness, it is theoretically the more foundational of his two treatments. Much of it is taken up with international questions, but those are discussed within an overarching framework of cosmic and human order understood by reference to divine providence and the natural law. John's authorities, apart from Sacred Scripture, are Popes Leo XIII, Pius XI, and Pius XII, as well as Augustine and Aquinas. This also gives the document a generally more traditional tone than *Mater et magistra*.[4] While building on the work of his immediate predecessors, the character of both of John's encyclicals is also somewhat more positive, one that stresses opportunities for the improvement of human affairs, especially in the economic sphere. Pius XI's worries about the dictatorship of capital and his call for a "reconstruction" of the social order are replaced by a far more optimistic account of the promise of economic growth.

Taking first political life, there are three aspects of *Mater et magistra* and *Pacem in terris* that seem new, at least in emphasis: first, John's discussion of the source of political authority; second, his account of the common good as

---

[3]   This is the customary view; however, the unduly neglected encyclical letter he wrote just after the outbreak of World War II, Pius XII, *Summi pontificatus* (On the Unity of Human Society) (1939): AAS 31 (1939) 413–53, is quite relevant to Catholic Social Teaching.

[4]   On the sources and general character of *Pacem in Terris* see especially Russell Hittinger, "*Quinquagesimo Ante*: Reflections on *Pacem in Terris* Fifty Years Later," in *The Global Quest for Tranquilitas Ordinis: "Pacem in Terris" Fifty Years Later*, The Pontifical Academy of Social Sciences Acta 18, eds., Mary Ann Glendon, Russell Hittinger, and Marcelo Sánchez Sorondo (Vatican City: Pontifical Academy of Social Sciences, 2013), 38–60.

the final cause of political association and practice; and third, a related emphasis on rights as integral to the common good. That political authority is rooted in God's authority is a frequent refrain in the encyclicals of Leo XIII, struck initially in his third encyclical letter, an attack on socialism, among the errors of which he took to be the view that "public authority neither derives its principles, nor its majesty, nor its power of governing from God, but rather from the multitude."[5] Pius XI articulated the same view initially, although later in his pontificate the idea was couched in a political theology that could be interpreted more broadly.[6] In *Quas primas* (1925) he instituted the Feast of Christ the King, mainly it seems, to promote an understanding of the limits on state power within the context of a theology that holds Christ to have been invested with plenary authority over the earth, a power He chose not to exercise, but which He nevertheless retains and that must be acknowledged by faithful Catholics. The authority of earthly princes thus reflects and/or derives from this divine authority.[7] The aim of limiting state power was most forcefully asserted in a tryptich of encyclicals published during a two-week period in 1937: *Mit brennender sorge*, on the situation of the Church in Nazi Germany; *Divini redemptoris*, on communism; and *Fermissimam constantiam*, on the situation of the Church in Mexico.[8] Pius's language is a bit more nuanced here: in *Divini redemptoris*, for example, he argues that if God's authority is not recognized, no earthly authority can be secure, which is a somewhat different claim.[9]

[5] Leo XIII, Encyclical Letter, *Quod apostolici muneris* (On Socialism) (1878), no. 2, ASS 11 (1878), 373. See also, e.g., Leo XIII, Encyclical Letter *Diuturnum* (On the Origin of Civil Power) (1881), no. 5, ASS 14 (1881), 4. In no. 6 of that encyclical Leo seems to endorse the "designation" theory of political authority, the idea that while political authority comes from God, the community can licitly arrange for the people or some group from among the people to designate an official or officials to administer that power. The alternatives are strict divine right, according to which God not only gives the power but delegates it Himself, and transmission theory, according to which God gives political authority to the community, which then transmits it to officials. See Heinrich Rommen, *The State in Catholic Thought* (St. Louis, MO: Herder, 1945), ch. 19; Leo XIII, Encyclical Letter *Immortale dei* (On the Christian Constitution of States) (1885), nos. 3, 18, 30, 35, ASS 18 (1885), 162, 168, 171, 174; Leo XIII, Encyclical Letter *Libertas* (On the Nature of Human Liberty) (1888), no. 13, ASS 20 (1887) 600; Leo XIII, Encyclical Letter *Sapientiae christianae* (On Christians as Citizens) (1890), no. 8, ASS 22 (1889–90), 388.
[6] For the initial view, which seems quite close to that of Leo, see Leo XIII, Encyclical Letter *Ubi arcano dei consilio* (On the Peace of Christ in the Kingdom of Christ) (1922), nos. 28, 39–41, AAS 14 (1922), 683, 687–688. The encyclical concerned the Catholic Action movement.
[7] Pius XI, Encyclical Letter *Quas primas* (On the Feast of Christ the King) (1925), nos. 7, 17, 19, AAS 17 (1925), 595–596, 600–602.
[8] See John Pollard, *The Papacy in the Age of Totalitarianism, 1914–1958* (Oxford: Oxford University Press, 2014), 264–274.
[9] DR, no. 74.

Pius XII writes in a very similar way in *Summi pontificatus*, the encyclical he
wrote at the outbreak of World War II: when God's authority is rejected, the order
of society becomes unstable and vulnerable to tyranny. He cites Leo XIII as his
authority for this view, but clearly interprets Leo's view to mean that God's
authority is manifested more through the moral law than by any direct connection
to any particular government.[10] This leads him to characterize the state (*civitas*) as
a "kind of instrument" (or "like an instrument," *quasi instrumentum*) designed by
the creator for the promotion of the common good of the people.[11] John XXIII's
view is quite similar: while maintaining that authority comes ultimately from
God[12], he tends to stress that authority's mediation through the natural law. This is
most forcefully expressed in *Pacem in terris*, the unifying theme of which is order
understood in a quite comprehensive sense and rooted in the natural law.[13] Order
within and among human beings is a function of "universal, absolute and
immutable" principles that come from God.[14] When discussing the political
community itself, John begins by citing Leo XIII as well as Romans 13:1–6, but
goes on to develop the point by holding that political authority is "permission to
govern in accordance with right reason," and that it "derives its binding force from
the moral order, which in turn has God as its origin and end," a point supported by
appeal to Pius XII.[15] Later he writes that authority "is before all else a moral force,"
which relates it to God's authority.[16] Like his predecessors, he firmly rejects the
idea that political authority is simply the product of popular will.[17]

John, then, maintains the *littera* of Leo XIII (and many previous popes), but
by way of an interpretation, already evident in the writings of Pius XI and Pius
XII, that mediates divine power primarily through the natural moral law. This
is related to two other developments in John's contributions to the social
teaching tradition, his account of the common good and of human rights. In
both these cases, what may seem at first a considerable innovation turns out to
be a stage of developments already underway. In *Mater et magistra*, John
describes the common good of society – he in no way restricts application of

[10] See *SP*, nos. 53–58.
[11] *SP*, no. 59. John Paul II seems to have adopted this interpretation, that is, Pius XII's inter-
      pretation of Leo XIII, in *Centesimus annus* (On the Hundredth Anniversary of *Rerum
      Novarum*) (1991), no. 11, AAS 83 (1991), 806, although he does not mention Pius.
[12] John XXIII, Encyclical Letter *Pacem in terris* (On Establishing Universal Peace in Truth,
      Justice, Charity, and Liberty) (1963) nos. 46, 52.
[13] *PT*, no. 5, where the thesis is initially stated and supported by Rom. 2:15.
[14] *PT*, no. 38, John's authorities here are Pius XII (Christmas Message, 1942) and Thomas
      Aquinas, *Summa Theologica*, I-II, q. 19.4.
[15] *PT*, no. 47.
[16] *PT*, nos. 48–49.
[17] *PT*, no. 78.

the term to the specifically political community – as "the sum total of those conditions of social living, whereby men are enabled more fully and more readily to achieve their own perfection."[18] In *Pacem in terris* the passage is quoted,[19] but also characteristically embedded in a bit more context and, in this case, tied more closely to political authorities. John emphasizes that the common good must be understood by reference to human nature and the human person and that it includes goods of both the body and the soul.

The sense of development is indicated by the fact that the section of the text on the common good is accompanied by ten footnotes, all citing texts from Leo XIII, Pius XI, and Pius XII, especially the two Piuses. In *Mit brennender sorge*, Pius XI had written that "the common good takes its measure from man's nature . . . and from the purpose of society, established for the benefit of human nature." He went on:

> Society was intended by the Creator for the full development of individual possibilities, and for the social benefits, which by a give and take process, everyone can claim for his own sake and that of others. Higher and more general values, which collectivity alone can provide, also derive from the Creator for the good of man, and for the full development, natural and supernatural, and the realization of his perfection.[20]

Similarly, in *Divini redemptoris* he wrote:

> But God has likewise destined man for civil society according to the dictates of his very nature. In the plan of the Creator, society is a natural means which man can and must use to reach his destined end. Society is for man and not vice versa. His must not be understood in the sense of liberal individualism, which subordinates society to the selfish use of the individual; but only in the sense that by means of an organic union and by natural collaboration the attainment of earthly happiness is placed within the reach of all. In a further sense, it is society which affords the opportunities for the development of all the individual and social gifts bestowed on human nature.[21]

[18] MM, no. 65: summam complectitur earum vitae socialis condicionum, quibus homines suam ipsorum perfectionem possint plenius atque expeditius consequi.

[19] PT, no. 58.

[20] Pius XI, Encyclical Letter *Mit brennender sorge* (On the Church and the German Reich) (1937), no. 30, AAS 29 (1937), 160: Die Gemeinschaft ist vom Schöpfer gewollt als Mittel zur vollen Entfaltung der individuellen und sozialen Anlagen, die der Einzelmensch, gebend und nehmend, zu seinem und aller anderen Wohl auszuwerten hat. Auch jene umfassende-ren und höheren Werte, die nicht vom Einzelnen, sondern nur von der Gemeinschaft verwirklicht werden können, sind vom Schöpfer letztes Endes des Menschen halber gewollt, zu seiner natürlichen und übernatürlichen Entfaltung und Vollendung.

[21] DR, no. 29: At Deus pari modo hominem ad civilem consortionem natum conformatumque voluit, quam profecto sua ipsius natura postulat. Societas enim ex divini Creatoris consilio

Even closer to John's formulation is the one given in 1942 by Pius XII:

> All of the political and economic activity of the state is directed to the permanent realization of the common good, which is to say of the external conditions that are necessary to all of the citizens for the development of their qualities and functions, of their material, intellectual, and religious life.[22]

John's formulation, then, is really the culmination of developments already seen in the previous two pontificates.

John adds that "the common good is chiefly guaranteed when personal rights and duties are maintained."[23] *Pacem in terris* includes the most extensive catalogue of rights found in any papal document.[24] It includes rights to life, bodily integrity, means suitable to the proper development of life (food, clothing, shelter, rest, medical care, necessary social services), security in cases of sickness, inability to work, widowhood, old age, and unemployment. There are also rights to respect, a good reputation, freedom in searching for the truth, expressing opinions, the pursuit of art (within the limits of morality and the common good), and information about public affairs. There are rights to basic education and professional training (according to the level of development in one's country), rights to the practice of religion and to choose a state of life. Economic rights include those of opportunity to work and good working conditions, to carry out economic activities according to the degree of responsibility of which one is capable, to a just wage, and to private property (attended by social duties). There are rights to association, to emigrate and

naturale praesidium est, quo quilibet civis possit ac debeat ad propositam sibi metam assequendam uti; quandoquidem Civitas homini, non homo Civitati exsistit. Id tamen non ita intellegendum est, quemadmodum ob suam *individualismi* doctrinam *Liberales*, quos vocant, asseverant; qui quidem communitatem immoderatis singulorum commodis inservire iubent: sed ita potius ut omnes, ex eo quod cum societate composito ordine copulantur, terrenam possint, per mutuam navitatis conspirationem, veri nominis prosperitatem attingere; utque per humanum consortium privatae illae publicaeque animi dotes, hominibus natura insitae floreant ac vigeant, quae temporarias peculiaresque utilitates exsuperant, divinamque praeferunt in civili ordinatione perfectionem; quod quidem in singulis hominibus contingere ullo modo nequit.

22 Pius XII, "Christmas Message (December 24, 1942)": che tutta l'attività dello Stato, politica ed economica serve per l'attuazione duratura del bene comune; cioè, di quelle esterne condizioni, le quali sono necessarie all'insieme dei cittadini per lo sviluppo delle loro qualità e dei loro uffici, della loro vita materiale, intellettuale e religiosa. *AAS* 35 (1943), 13.

23 *PT*, no. 60.

24 In his 1942 Christmas message, Pius XII listed rights to the maintenance and development of physical, intellectual, and moral life, to religious training, to worship God in private and in public, to marriage, to work, to freely choose one's state of life, and to the use of material goods. He also held that human rights were a constituent element of the common good. Moreover, these points had already been made in a somewhat less detailed way by Pius XI. See generally the discussion in Calvez and Perrin, *The Church and Social Justice*, 106–124.

to immigrate (when there are just reasons). Political rights include those to take part in public affairs, and to the juridical protection of one's rights. These rights are described as "natural" and said to be grounded in the natural law.[25] There are also similarly grounded corresponding duties, although these are not spelled out in anything like the detail given for rights.

While John reaffirmed the traditional principle that, beyond the limits imposed by sound morality, Catholic teaching did not specify any particular type of political regime, his call for wide participation in government does move closer to an endorsement of democracy.[26] He goes on to acknowledge with seeming approval what he describes as a kind of contemporary consensus on the need for written constitutions, the upshot of which seems very much in line with the classical ideal of the rule of law.[27]

The most distinctive aspects of John's treatment of economic and social issues are his treatments of what he calls "socialization" and of the agricultural sector of economies, especially those in the developing world. The term "socialization" was used in some previous papal writings, but usually to indicate what would ordinarily be called "nationalization." It means something different in *Mater et magistra*, although the technical term itself gave rise almost immediately to confusion. The encyclical was drafted mostly in Italian, but sections 59 to 67 were drafted in German, mainly (most probably) by Oswald von Nell-Breuning and Gustav Gundlach,[28] who use the term *gesellschaftlicher*. The Italian has *socializzazione*, while the official Latin text avoids a single term, sometimes using *socialium rationum incrementa*, among others.[29] Terminological confusion aside, John's meaning seems clear enough:

[25]   *PT*, no. 28: eademque iura et officia a lege naturae, qua vel tribuuntur vel imperantur, et originem, et alimentum, et firmissimam vim ducunt; 30: Nam quodvis praecipuum hominis ius vim auctoritatemque suam a naturali lege repetit, quae illud tribuit, et conveniens iniungit officium.

[26]   *PT*, nos. 73–74; cf. no. 52. On this question more generally see V. B. Lewis, "Democracy and Catholic Social Teaching: Continuity, Development, and Challenge," in *Studia Gilsoniana* 3 (2014), 167–190.

[27]   *PT*, nos. 75–77.

[28]   Marvin L. Mich, "Commentary on *Mater et Magistra*," in *Modern Catholic Social Teaching*, ed. Kenneth R. Himes, OFM (Washington, DC: Georgetown University Press, 2004), 195–196.

[29]   See Jean-Yves Calvez, SJ, *The Social Thought of John XXIII* (Chicago: Henry Regnery, 1964), 1–4 and 102n13. Calvez also points out that the term was used by Cardinal Tardini, John's Secretary of State, in his letter to the French Social Week that met in Grenoble in 1960 and which was dedicated to the theme of socialization. Several passages from Tardini's letter seem to have made their way into *Mater et magistra* almost verbatim.

Certainly one of the principal characteristics which seem to be typical of our age is an increase in social relationships, in those mutual ties, that is, which grow daily more numerous and which have led to the introduction of many and varied forms of associations in the lives and activities of citizens, and to their acceptance within our legal framework. Scientific and technical progress, greater productive efficiency and a higher standard of living are among the many present-day factors which would seem to have contributed to this trend.[30]

"Interdependence," more commonly used now, captures the sense of this, although it is also related to what is now usually called "globalization" since it has an international aspect. John connects it to the social nature of human beings and elements of modern life like technology and mass communications. Socialization is a source of at least those worries that accompany the expansion of government and possible loss of freedom.[31] This likely explains why the last part of the section on socialization includes the account of the common good discussed above, with its focus on the perfection of the human person.

The third section of the encyclical is devoted to new aspects of the social question. It contains extensive treatments of issues particular to rural workers and of developing countries. John begins by proposing norms understood to require adaptation in their application to particular circumstances.[32] These include the need to improve public services in rural areas; orderly development in different sectors of the economy; taxation that is appropriate to rural conditions, especially to uncertainty about income from year to year; availability of capital at suitable rates of interest (NB that interest as such is not condemned); availability of adequate insurance; price protections; and infrastructure that supports rural life and agriculture.[33] All of this is conditioned by reminders about the superiority – to the extent that it is possible – of the people themselves being and perceiving themselves as responsible for their own improvements,[34] and the necessity to respect the principle of subsidiarity.[35] John's discussion of rural problems begins with an empirical observation about the social problems caused by declining economic conditions in rural areas and the large-scale migration of rural people into cities. He ends it by

---

[30]   MM, no. 59.

[31]   MM, nos. 62–63.

[32]   MM, nos. 126, 142. Some English translations describe these norms as of "permanent validity," but nothing like this phrase is to be found in the Latin, Italian, or French texts.

[33]   MM, nos. 127–40.

[34]   MM, nos. 144, 151, 152.

[35]   MM, no. 152; cf. 5.

praising aspects of rural life because of its connection to traditional values and the family as an institution and because of the close connections between agriculture as a way of life and awareness of Creation. Agriculture, of course, can be organized in different ways and some countries have made policy decisions intended to preserve and support family farms; however, the exodus of many millions from the land is also a reflection of increasingly efficient agricultural productivity. This certainly must be borne in mind in evaluating the continuing relevance of this part of the encyclical.

The treatment of rural life is related to the treatment of international economic development, which was not a theme of previous encyclicals. The basic principle here is an extension of the duty to use superfluous wealth to help the poor.[36] It is again combined with the idea that people should take an active role in their own development.[37] John also holds that aid should respect the cultures of the recipient countries,[38] should be disinterested and rendered without neocolonial ambitions,[39] and with the acknowledgment that scientific and technical achievements are not the highest goods.[40] He also evinces concern about the association among some of development with population control.[41]

Mater et magistra is concerned primarily with economic development and so acknowledges the increasing internationalization of economic affairs and the need for cooperation.[42] *Pacem in terris* goes much further, positing the notion of a "universal common good" (*bonum commune universale*).[43] John did not hesitate to spell out the consequences of this: just as the common good of ordinary nations requires and justifies authority to bring it about, so the universal common good requires and justifies a comparable authority:

> Today the universal common good presents us with problems which are world-wide in their dimensions; problems, therefore, which cannot be solved except by a public authority with power, organization and means co-extensive with these problems, and with a world-wide sphere of activity. Consequently the moral order itself demands the establishment of some such general form of public authority.[44]

---

[36]   *MM*, no. 161.
[37]   *MM*, nos. 168; cf. 73.
[38]   *MM*, nos. 169–70.
[39]   *MM*, no. 172.
[40]   *MM*, no. 175.
[41]   *MM*, nos. 185–99.
[42]   *MM*, nos. 200–202.
[43]   *PT*, no. 133; and see nos. 98, 100, 134–135, 137, 167; and cf. *MM*, no. 80.
[44]   *PT*, no. 137: Cum autem hodie commune omnium gentium bonum quaestiones proponat, omnes contingentes populos; cumque huiusmodi quaestiones nonnisi publica quaedam auctoritas explicare possit, cuius et potestas, et forma, et instrumenta aequa sint amplitudine,

Having crossed this rather consequential bridge, however, John went on to qualify his conclusion in a number of key respects. First, such an authority must not be set up by force, but must be "born" from all peoples (*Quod ex eo nascitur*); like ordinary governments it must respect the human person and her rights; it must respect the principle of subsidiarity; and must not coerce or limit the authority in states.[45] This is followed by a discussion of the United Nations that seems to indicate that the UN has developed in the direction of such an authority, with an expression of desire that the development continue. Many questions present themselves here, and subsequent teaching has not really gone much further in answering them. This is especially important given what are now clearly seen limitations in the effectiveness of UN intervention stemming from the structure and operation of the Security Council. Moreover, the UN and other international organizations have often embraced social policies at odds with other elements of Catholic Social Teaching, especially those concerned with population control.

The overall tone of John's teaching, especially in *Mater et magistra*, is hopeful about the prospects for development and even about capitalism itself, provided that it is understood within the overarching framework of sound morality. At the very start of his discussion of economic questions he states that in economic matters there is always a priority for private initiative.[46] While he also affirms the need for intervention by the state in some circumstances (more circumstances, given the reality of socialization), such calls are almost always immediately accompanied by a restatement of the duty of subsidiarity.[47] He also expresses a generally quite positive view of scientific and technological progress, again, so long as it is always subordinate to morality.[48] What is always crucial is that development never mean only material or economic improvement, but that it contribute to a properly integrated sense of human fulfillment.[49]

VATICAN II: *GAUDIUM ET SPES*

Most of Catholic Social Teaching is contained in an encyclical tradition, one that has developed, in the 125 years since it was initiated, conventions and

---

cuiusque actio tam late pateat quantum terrarum orbis; tum exinde sequitur, ut, ipso morali ordine cogente, publica quaedam generalis auctoritas constituenda sit.
[45] *PT*, nos. 138–141.
[46] *MM*, no. 51.
[47] See, e.g., *MM*, nos. 53, 117, 152.
[48] See, e.g., *MM*, nos. 189, 210, 246.
[49] *MM*, nos. 73–74.

forms of presentation that are well known. Beginning with *Quadragesimo anno*, social encyclicals have typically commemorated previous social encyclicals (usually *Rerum novarum*), begun with interpretations of the original document and then moved to accounts of changed world circumstances and new recommendations or injunctions in light of both the interpreted tradition and present phenomena. The Second Vatican Council's 1965 Pastoral Constitution on the Church in the Modern World, *Gaudium et spes*, is quite different, both from the encyclical tradition and from the other major documents of the Council. The differences concern not only the document's form, but its genesis and content, and all of this in ways that bear on how one reads it. For this reason, it seems important to discuss the drafting of the document.

The origins of *Gaudium et spes* were distinctive and the process of its drafting was perhaps the most vexed of any major document in the modern history of the Church, save perhaps the closely related *Dignitatis humanae*. As one historian of the Council has written, "[n]o other conciliar text was so lacking in coherent preparatory work, and no other conciliar commission was so late in becoming aware of the extent of the problems handed to it."[50] As the final revisions of the text were being completed in November of 1964 some Council fathers asked the pope to put the whole thing off, as some had been urging during the entire drafting process, on the view that the issues dealt with in the Pastoral Constitution were too complex and controversial to be adequately treated in the limited time allowed by the council process. The materials could be saved, they argued, further developed, and then used either by a subsequent synod or by the pope in an encyclical. Paul VI, however, had already taken a keen interest in the document and may have personally ensured that it was finished.[51]

Gaudium et spes had no single ancestor among the schemata prepared for the Council. It was born in the Council itself as a result of a proposal by Cardinal Suenens on December 4, 1962, in response to a speech given in September by John XXIII, in which he called for the Church to address the modern world. On Suenens's recommendation a mixed commission of members of the commissions on doctrine and the laity was formed and began by assembling and reworking discarded parts of the prepared schemata into

---

[50]   Jan Grootaers, "The Drama Continues Between the Acts: The 'Second Preparation' and Its Opponents," in *History of Vatican II*, eds., Giuseppe Alberigo and Joseph Komonchak (Maryknoll, NY: Orbis/Leuven: Peters, 1995–2006), 2: 413.
[51]   See Norman Tanner, "The Church in the World (Ecclesia ad Extra)," in *History of Vatican II*, 4: 275–76; Peter Hünermann, "The Final Weeks of the Council," in *History of Vatican II*, 5: 371, 373, 387, 405.

a draft text with six chapters. During this initial period the document was revised once to make it more pastoral and less scholastic in tone and a second time in light of *Pacem in terris*, which appeared in mid-April 1963. This version, officially called Schema XVII, unofficially later referred to as the "Roman Schema," already gave rise to a worry that would continue through-out the Council and which, eventually, found its way into the text itself. Many members of the commissions were concerned about how detailed the docu-ment should be in its discussions of contemporary economic, social, and political problems and how concrete its recommendations should be. This worry led the Central Commission to accept a proposal that there be two documents, a doctrinal text on the vocation of the human person and a separate text on contemporary problems that would not be considered an authoritative conciliar document.[52] The major concern here was the compe-tence of the Council fathers to pronounce on technical social and economic questions. The second document, therefore, would be composed on the basis of the work of a number of different advisory groups composed of lay experts and advisors.

Suenens himself supervised the production of the new "Malines Text" in the late summer and fall of 1963. This version, on which Yves Congar, among others, seems to have had a major influence, and which made a much greater use of Biblical and patristic sources, fell victim to a sense that it took too many risks theologically and could not meet the expectations of its intended audi-ence. In addition to this there were procedural confusions and disputes among the different commissions with input into the document and a continuing competition between theological and sociological perspectives. This led to an entirely new set of outlines drawn up under the supervision of Bernard Häring and a new draft, the "Zurich Text," discussed in that city for three days in February 1964, revised and redesignated as "Schema XIII." This was the first complete text actually distributed to the Council fathers (in July 1964) and would serve as the real basis for *Gaudium et spes* as it finally appeared.[53] The Zurich Text comprised an introduction and five chapters with five appendices (*adnexa*) to be distributed to the Council, but not considered official texts: they match the chapters of the second part of the final document. It was during the discussion of this text that Karol Wojtyła submitted an entirely new draft to

---

[52]   Grootaers, "The Drama Continues," 420; see also Roberto Tucci, SJ, "Introduction historique et doctrinale a la Constitution pastorale," in *L'Église dans le monde de ce temps: Constitution pastorale "Gaudium et spes,"* eds., Y. M. J. Congar, OP, and M. Peuchmaurd, OP (Paris: Cerf, 1967), 48–50.

[53]   The text, *De ecclesia in mundo huius temporis*, is printed in the *Acta* of the Council: vol. III/5, 116–42.

the commission in the name of the Polish bishops, the content of which was considerably more critical of the modern world. None of the Polish submission was used at this point given the time constraints on the drafters, but Wojtyła did have some input into subsequent versions of the text.[54]

This text was discussed on the floor of the Council between October 20 and November 10, 1964. The *adnexa* continued to be a point of controversy as the discussion began: Archbishop Pericle Felici, the General Secretary of the Council, announced (in reply to a query from Marcel Lefebvre!) that they were to be considered "private" with no official status and intended to expand on the council's thinking. There were then protests from some of the members of the commissions responsible for the document and Felici clarified the status of the *adnexa* as not simply private: they could be discussed by the Council fathers, but would *not* have conciliar status.[55] At this point there were real doubts that Schema XIII could ever be approved given the approaching end of the Council's third session and uncertainty over whether there would be a fourth. Nevertheless, the fathers discussed it. Among the issues debated were the document's discussion of the relationship between the natural and supernatural – here both Karl Rahner and Joseph Ratzinger expressed serious concerns about whether the focus of the text should be more on Christian teaching or on the "signs of the times," a famous phrase that appeared first in the Zurich Text. Some fathers wanted the text to more closely track *Pacem in terris* and Paul VI's recently published *Ecclesiam suam*; others argued for an explicit condemnation of Marxism; and some wanted more attention to the problems of the poor. There was concern that the protection of human dignity had overshadowed God Himself in the document. The most acrimonious discussion concerned the treatment of war and peace, especially whether the document would expressly condemn nuclear weapons.

The desire to complete work on Schema XIII seems to have been an important consideration in the decision to undertake a fourth session, and the floor debate provided a great deal of material for the drafters, who went back to work during the last intersession period. The subcommissions met to discuss the new draft, the "Ariccia Text," in that Roman suburb during the first week of February 1965. While the form and many of the key notions in the Zurich Text remained, the new version's principal draftsman, the French Jesuit, Pierre Haubtmann, wrote from scratch. This itself eventually led to

---

54 Evangelista Vilanova, "The Intersession (1963–1964)," in *History of Vatican II*, 3: 414; and Ricardo Burigana and Giovanni Turbanti, "The Intersession: Preparing the Conclusion of the Council," in *History of Vatican II*, 4: 524–526.

55 Tanner, "The Church in the World (Ecclesia ad Extra)," 274–275.

some controversy as Haubtmann remained the chief draftsman to the end of the process and in the final stages he seems to have introduced changes on his own, changes not recommended by the Council fathers, but perhaps known to the pope, with whom he may well have had a direct line of communication. This is relevant particularly in that Haubtmann seems to have had a fixed and rather negative attitude toward previous Catholic Social Teaching, to the extent that he avoided the phrase itself.[56] This text was sent to the Council fathers in June.[57] It is quite recognizable to anyone who has studied the final text and it now incorporated, evidently without much discussion, the *adnexa* into the official text.

Time pressures were again a major factor, since it was known that this session would be the last. The German bishops and their *periti* were critical of the text for theological reasons; Ratzinger thought it dogmatically weak and that it diluted the Christian message. On the floor of the council some fathers went even further: the Brazilian archbishop, Geraldo Proença Sigaud, called it pagan and argued that all the problems of the modern world had been adequately addressed by Pius XII. Indeed, the debate often reflected differences between those who were most influenced by Pius XII and those most influenced by John XXIII.[58] The most serious debates concerned the document's discussions of marriage and war. On the former subject the controversy concerned how specific the Council should be, given that Paul VI had already reserved to himself the issue of contraception. Some fathers and theologians felt the document did not sufficiently track the teachings of *Casti connubii* and would confuse the faithful. Indeed, this question was behind a final attempt to derail the whole project. The sections on war and peace were discussed under the influence of Paul's speech to the United Nations. Some wanted the text to essentially abandon the notion of just war and embrace, at least functionally, a kind of pacifisim. Cardinal Ottaviani made an impassioned speech on the floor of the Council, calling on it to expressly outlaw war. This was resisted by a group of bishops led by the Americans, Cardinals Spellman and Shahan, and Archbishop Phillip Hannon, which led to a clarifying "interpretation" of the final text that appears to have allayed their doubts. There were also criticisms, especially from German fathers, of the text's treatment of economic questions, which they thought superficial. In the end, the drafters were left all of eight

[56] Hünermann, "The Final Weeks of the Council," 371–372.
[57] It is printed in the *Acta* of the Council, vol. V/1, 435–516.
[58] See Gilles Routhier, "Finishing the Work Begun: The Trying Experience of the Third Period," in *History of Vatican II*, 5: 138–141, 153–154.

days to revise the document so that it could be approved before the close of the Council. The definitive vote occurred on December 7, 1965.

There are a number of remarkable aspects of the document that are related to this context. First, much of the controversy about the Pastoral Constitution emerged from its status as a "pastoral" as distinct from a "doctrinal" constitution and one that, for the first time in the history of the Church, explicitly addressed all mankind.[59] The impetus for this unprecedented effort was Pope John himself, but it introduced a number of complications, e.g., should the document be a "Constitution" at all given that it was addressed *ad extra*? Would it not be more appropriate as a "Declaration" like *Dignitatis humanae*? What is the most appropriate language to use in addressing the whole world: scholastic philosophy, a primarily Biblical idiom, or a rhetoric composed in light of contemporary philosophical currents like phenomenology? Even the name of the document was controversial: in the final voting, the largest number of *non placet* votes was cast against the title.[60] *Gaudium et spes* was also a document developed largely in public, fully in the glare of the modern mass media and by many hands with input from literally hundreds of people over a three-year period. This was not as true even of the other conciliar documents: "no other schema had been drafted so transparently, almost in the public square."[61]

Most problematic was the status of the treatment of contemporary questions involving economics and the other social sciences. In the end, what were originally conceived of as recommendations composed with the advice of experts to be published separately from the Constitution were completely incorporated into it, but with an explicit recognition that they were perhaps to be given lesser weight than the more doctrinal parts of the text and with the admission that they carried with them an implicit expiration date. *Gaudium et spes* is divided into a preface, an introduction, and two parts. The first footnote, which accompanies the document's title, says that the constitution is made up of two parts, "yet it constitutes an organic unity," but that the second part, which considers "various aspects of modern life and human society," is made up of "diverse elements," some of which "have a permanent value; others, only a transitory one." Interpreters are cautioned to bear in mind "the changeable circumstances which the subject matter, by its very nature, involves."

As noted above, the first part of *Gaudium et spes* presents the Council's statement on the human vocation, a statement intended to specifically address

---

[59]   This last point is highlighted by Hünermann, "The Final Weeks of the Council," 424.
[60]   Hunermann, "The Final Weeks of the Council," 420.
[61]   Routhier, "Finishing the Work Begun," 123–124.

the world beyond the Church. The first part of the document is not a social teaching statement per se, although its second chapter treats the theme of "the human community." There are two things that one cannot help noticing about the first part almost immediately if one comes to it from reading the previous documents. One is its self-conscious concern with modernity itself. While it was aspects of modernity that motivated the very initiation of the social teaching tradition by Leo XIII, the phenomenon itself had never before been such a theme, where in *Gaudium et spes* allusions to modernity are ubiquitous, beginning, of course, with the official title, *De ecclesia in mundo huius temporis*.[62] The second distinctive feature – likely related to the first – is the relative paucity of references to the natural law. This is especially striking given the role of the natural law in *Pacem in terris*. The question of the Council's language and the place in that language of traditional scholastic categories as compared to Scripture or more contemporary idioms was a central one throughout the drafting process; the end product refers to the natural law explicitly only three times, all three in the second part.[63] There are other more oblique references, some to moral norms, universal morality, or divine law, but the Council fathers seemed to have intentionally avoided language freighted with traditional associations.[64]

The first part of the document canonizes some of the developments from John XXIII's writings, in particular, the notion of socialization (now Latinized as *socializatio*), a strong emphasis on the human person, and the formulation of the common good as the end of society (discussed above). It takes up a number of topics as particular concerns of modern man, for example, atheism, death, freedom, and concerns about modern science and technology. It also seeks to allay traditional doubts about the place of Christianity in the modern world by emphasizing the rightful autonomy of earthly affairs[65] and the role of the laity.[66] The discussion of the common good is particularly important. Article 26 formulates it thus:

> Every day human interdependence grows more tightly drawn and spreads by degrees over the whole world. As a result the common good, that is, the sum of those conditions of social life which allow social groups and their

[62] See, e.g., nos. 4, 9, 10, 11, 19, 23, 41, and 43. The theme is also prominent in the second part of the document: see, e.g., nos. 46, 47, 51, 54, 63, 75, 79, 88.

[63] See nos. 74 (resistance to political oppression), 79 (the conduct of warfare), 89 (population policies).

[64] See nos. 16, 36, 43, 74, 78, 87. Contrast *PT*, nos. 12, 13, 18, 28, 30, 80, 81, 157, 160; and cf. 5, 6, 85. It should perhaps be noted that natural law does not play much of a role in *Mater et magistra*.

[65] GS, no. 36.

[66] GS, no. 36.

individual members relatively thorough and ready access to their own fulfillment, today takes on an increasingly universal complexion and consequently
involves rights and duties with respect to the whole human race. Every social
group must take account of the needs and legitimate aspirations of other
groups, and even of the general welfare of the entire human family.[67]

In the rest of the article the common good is further described in terms of
rights and duties:

> At the same time, however, there is a growing awareness of the exalted dignity
> proper to the human person, since he stands above all things, and his rights
> and duties are universal and inviolable. Therefore, there must be made
> available to all men everything necessary for leading a life truly human,
> such as food, clothing, and shelter; the right to choose a state of life freely
> and to found a family, the right to education, to employment, to a good
> reputation, to respect, to appropriate information, to activity in accord with
> the upright norm of one's own conscience, to protection of privacy and
> rightful freedom even in matters religious.[68]

As with the discussion above this account seems to emphasize again the aim of
putting political institutions at the service of the good of persons. It avoids
individualism by making the constitutive conditions of the common good
those of both individuals and groups. It has been rightly observed that the
conception of the common good here is both dynamic in the sense that its
norms can be fulfilled in changing ways and circumstances and that it is very
juridical (for example, in its emphasis on the protection of rights) and thus
aimed at disciplining the state.[69] This discussion also incorporates John's
account of the universal common good in *Pacem in terris*.

---

[67] GS, no. 26: Ex interdependentia in dies strictiore et paulatim ad mundum universum diffusa
sequitur bonum commune – seu summam eorum vitae socialis condicionum quae tum
coetibus, tum singulis membris permittunt ut propriam perfectionem plenius atque expeditius consequantur – hodie magis magisque universale evadere, et exinde iura officiaque
implicare, quae totum humanum genus respiciunt. Quilibet coetus necessitatum et legiti-
marum appetitionum aliorum coetuum, immo boni communis totius familiae humanae,
rationem habere debet.
[68] GS: Simul vero conscientia crescit eximiae dignitatis quae personae humanae competit, cum
ipsa rebus omnibus praestet, et eius iura officiaque universalia sint atque inviolabilia. Oportet
ergo ut ea omnia homini pervia reddantur, quibus ad vitam vere humanam gerendam indiget,
ut sunt victus, vestitus, habitatio, ius ad statum vitae libere eligendum et ad familiam
condendam, ad educationem, ad laborem, ad bonam famam, ad reverentiam, ad congruam
informationem, ad agendum iuxta rectam suae conscientiae normam, ad vitae privatae
protectionem atque ad iustam libertatem etiam in re religiosa.
[69] See Roberto Tucci, SJ, "La vie de la communauté politique," in Congar and Peuchmaurd,
L'Église dans le monde de ce temps, 549–553.

The fourth chapter of the second part takes up the common good again, repeating the formulation in the first part,[70] but adding some things. There is a stress on the need for the participation of all citizens (*omnes cives*) that seems awfully close to an outright endorsement of democracy. At the same time, the document also emphasizes the strictures of morality on all political action – indeed, this is one of the rare times when the phrase "natural law" is used.[71] The reality of socialization means that government is more often required to intervene in social and economic affairs; however, in a strong echo of Leo XIII (and, it almost seems, of Tocqueville), citizens are also cautioned against granting government too much authority "and inappropriately seeking from it excessive conveniences and advantages, with a consequent weakening of the sense of responsibility on the part of individuals, families, and social groups."[72]

Explicitly economic matters are treated in the third chapter of the second part. The discussion begins with a warning against the tendency to see everything in narrowly economic terms as against a more fully personalistic perspective.[73] The main governing principle here seems to be the notion that economic life is in the service of complete human development and integrated with the principles of morality; while economics as a discipline has a certain autonomy, as a practical discipline it cannot be separated from the moral order, and economic processes are not automatic or autonomous in the sense of operating apart from human intelligence and agency.[74] Economic growth, therefore, is neither automatic nor simply determined by government authority.[75] Symptomatic of these two errors are imbalances both between the different sectors of the economies of countries and between more and less developed nations. The imbalances lead in turn to inequalities that are unjust and a source of conflict.

The Council proposes (or in some cases, reinterprets traditional) principles regarding economic life. The first asserts a priority for labor in economic life and conceives of it in a way clearly related to the labor theory of value embraced by Leo XIII in *Rerum novarum*. It also refers to labor as both a duty and a right.[76] Whether this conception is overly bound by the characteristics of the classical industrial economy and is adequate to subsequent

[70] GS, no. 74.
[71] GS, no. 74. The same section notes the limits on government power and the limited conditions under which citizens might resist abuses. See also no. 78, where the divine law is mentioned in connection with the common good.
[72] GS, no. 75; cf. no. 69.
[73] GS, no. 63.
[74] GS, no. 64; cf. no. 67.
[75] GS, no. 65.
[76] GS, no. 67.

changes in the nature of labor is worth reflecting on. A second principle calls for increasing worker participation in economic enterprises, something already endorsed by John XXIII. Under this heading is included the traditional right of forming labor unions (and even of, under some conditions, striking).[77] Third, the document repeats the ancient principle of the universal destination of goods and the distinction between ownership and use that follows from it, as well as the duty to aid the poor *even beyond* superfluous wealth. This includes an endorsement of social insurance and other public services with the caution that such assistance should not lead to the kind of individualism that so worried Tocqueville.[78] Moreover, while not using the term, the Council reaffirmed the principle of subsidiarity in this realm as well.[79] Fourth, the distribution of resources should look to full employment and adequate wages, and this not only for the present generation, but for future generations.[80] Fifth, and related to this, is the principle that property should generally be privately held, but that under some circumstances, public ownership is preferable. When private property becomes public, this must really be with an eye to the common good and requires adequate compensation. The principle follows from the social quality of property discussed earlier by Pius XI. The main example the Council fathers seem to have had in mind were the unproductive rural estates (*latifundia*) characteristic of some Latin American countries.[81] In such cases land would be expropriated and then redistributed to those who would make it productive. In one sense this seems a very particular situation; on the other hand, it may be that the root principle could be extended today to capital itself.

The fifth chapter treats international affairs, focusing first on war and peace and then on development. While there was a great deal of talk during the Council of banning war altogether, *Gaudium et spes* does not do this. It does express the desire to outlaw war "by international consent" (*consentientibus nationibus*), but acknowledges that this would require the universal public authority called for by Pope John in *Pacem in terris*.[82] Absent such an authority "governments cannot be denied the right to legitimate defense once every means of peaceful settlement has been exhausted."[83] The Council does

---

[77] GS, no. 68.

[78] GS, no. 69.

[79] GS, no. 75.

[80] GS, no. 70.

[81] GS, no. 71.

[82] GS, no. 82.

[83] GS, no. 79: Quamdiu autem periculum belli aderit, auctoritasque internationalis competens congruisque viribus munita defuerit, tamdiu, exhaustis quidem omnibus pacificae tractationis subsidiis, ius legitimae defensionis guberniis denegari non poterit.

condemn "total war," reaffirming, albeit in a somewhat loose way, the traditional *ius in bello* principles of discrimination and proportionality.[84] It is
similarly critical of the arms race and of deterrence theory itself, cautioning
that the notion of a balance is ill suited to maintaining peace, but it seems to
stop short of a straightforward condemnation.[85]

Socialization and interdependence require cooperation in development. The
Council proposed a series of norms for this cooperation: (a) developing nations
should seek the complete human development of their citizens and should rely
chiefly on their own resources, especially those related to their own qualities and
tradition; (b) advanced nations have an obligation to assist developing nations; (c)
the international community should coordinate and stimulate economic growth,
albeit consistently with the principle of subsidiarity; (d) technical solutions to
development should not operate at the expense of spiritual development.[86]

PAUL VI

Paul VI's social encyclical, *Populorum progressio*, was released on Easter of 1967,
but his general approach was already set in three events that preceded it: his first
encyclical letter, *Ecclesiam suam*, which outlined an agenda for his pontificate;
his August 1974 speech to the United Nations General Assembly; and his role,
already discussed, in the completion of *Gaudium et spes* at the Council.
Ecclesiam suam itself referred repeatedly to the ongoing work of the Council
and Paul's desire not to interfere in its deliberations. One of the three policies
outlined in the document is the Church's "dialogue with the modern world,"
the explicit purpose of *Gaudium et spes*. Another policy, that of "reform" or
"renewal" in the Church, entailed an emphasis on the spirit of poverty that he
hastened to add was "no obstacle to the proper understanding and rightful
application of the important laws of economics." Understanding these laws
was necessary for the Church's "calm and often severe judgment on wealth and
on the luxuries of life," and for it to ensure that wealth "shall be used justly and
equitably for the good of all, and distributed with greater foresight."[87]

The United Nations Address includes "a moral and solemn ratification of this
high institution" the existence of which marks "a stage in the development of
mankind."[88] Paul's praise of the UN went so far as to compare it "in the

---

[84]   GS, no. 80.
[85]   GS, no. 81.
[86]   GS, no. 86.
[87]   Paul VI, Encyclical Letter *Ecclesiam suam* (On the Church) (1964), no. 55, *AAS* 56 (1964), 634–635.
[88]   Pope Paul VI "Address to the General Assembly of the United Nations" (1965), *AAS* 57 (1965),
       878, 879. The address was given in French.

temporal order [to] what our Catholic Church seeks to be in the spiritual order – unique and universal."[89] He went on to suggest that "[n]othing higher [than the UN] can be imagined on the natural level, in the ideological structure of mankind." "Who," he asked, "does not see the need progressively to set up a world authority, able to act effectively on the juridical and political plane?"[90] There were two other noteworthy moments in the speech. The first was the pope's often quoted *cri de coeur*, "Never again war, war never again!"[91] He also repeated a proposal he had made in India in December 1964 that a fund be created to assist developing countries made up "at least in part" of the savings realized by reducing armaments.[92] These points are all indicative of Paul VI's mind and his general approach. It is less clear what one makes of their teaching authority: his endorsement of the UN, which echoes that of John XXIII in *Pacem in terris*, is just that, an endorsement; his call for an end of war was a point of real enthusiasm among the fathers of the Council, who gave the pope something of a hero's welcome on his return to Rome, but it would not seem to change or modify any authoritative teaching; his proposal of a world development fund, repeated in *Populorum progressio*, is a very concrete policy recommendation. The most significant part of this is his seeming (for the phrasing is ambiguous) call for a politically and juridically effective world authority. Such a call had been made by John XXIII, albeit tempered by the need to honor the principle of subsidiarity, a principle that went unmentioned before the UN. The surrounding notions of "stages" in the development of mankind as well as mankind's "ideological structure" only add to the mystery.

Populorum progressio itself is somewhat unusual among social encyclicals in that it does not commemorate any of the earlier documents. Beyond this, it is also somewhat unusual in not much emphasizing the traditional principles of Catholic Social Teaching. There is, for example, no reference to subsidiarity by name, although there is one reference to the substance of the idea.[93] There are quick affirmations of some key traditional principles, e.g., the universal destination of goods and the subordination of property rights to the common good (the usual concomitant emphasis on the right of private ownership is not emphasized),[94] the natural law (mentioned explicitly as such only

---

[89] Pope Paul VI "Address to the General Assembly of the United Nations" (1965), AAS 57 (1965) 880.

[90] AAS 57 (1965), 880.

[91] AAS 57 (1965), 881.

[92] AAS 57 (1965), 882.

[93] Paul VI, Encyclical Letter *Populorum progressio* (On the Development of Peoples) (1967), no. 33, AAS 59 (1967), 273–274; cf. no. 24.

[94] PP, nos. 22–23.

once),[95] the common good (mentioned, but not treated),[96] and social justice, which is mentioned mainly in connection with the inequities needing rectification between international trading partners.[97] Moreover, the general tone of the encyclical is darker than the one to which it is most naturally compared, *Mater et magistra*. John's optimism about economic development is all but gone in Paul's account: "all progress is ambivalent," he writes in the first section, and later, "the world is sick."[98] The notion of solidarity, on the other hand, destined to play a greatly expanded role in the thought of John Paul II, is frequently mentioned, although never defined.[99]

The great theme of the encyclical is development and its two parts treat respectively the regulative idea of development and its various applications in the contemporary world. This was also a theme of *Gaudium et spes* and, one surmises, Paul thought more needed to be said on the matter. The first part of the encyclical dilates on the problems surrounding the notion of development (*progressio*) and aims to explain the notion from a Christian perspective. It includes all the worries about modernity found in *Gaudium et spes*, associating them particularly with material progress.[100] The main principle here is that development should not be identified simply with economic growth, but rather with promotion of "the good of every man and of the whole man." Such growth is described as "integral" and guided by the knowledge that every human being has been given a vocation by God: true development serves the realization of vocation, the end of which is the orientation of the human person toward God as the supreme good.[101] This is later called *ratio humanitatis perfecta*.[102] Paul's main innovation here is the endorsement of the notion that this development is not only individual, but collective: "As the waves of the sea gradually creep farther and farther in along the shoreline, so the

---

[95] PP, no. 59; no. 37 does refer to the "moral law" and no. 81 seems to allude to it.
[96] PP, nos. 23, 31, 38, 76. There is, interestingly, no reference to the *Mater et magistra* formulation ratified in *Gaudium et spes*.
[97] PP, nos. 44, 59, 61.
[98] PP, nos. 19, 66.
[99] PP, nos. 1, 17, 44, 48, 62, 67, 73, 84. Indeed, there is no precise or consistently equivalent Latin term for the notion, although the modern language translations use cognate terms. The Latin tends to refer to human relations and human connectedness and generally constitutes an appeal to the moral relevance of the unity of the human race and its increasingly immediate practical implications in an interconnected world. In this respect it can perhaps best be seen as a moral counterpart to John's sense of "socialization."
[100] See, e.g., no. 19: "all growth is ambivalent" (Quaevis enim progressio ad utramque partem valet); cf. nos. 20, 41.
[101] PP, 14–16.
[102] PP, no. 42; it is accompanied by a footnote to Jacques Maritain's 1936 book, *L'humanisme integral*.

human race inches its way forward through history."[103] Just before this, the text says that "civilizations (*civili cultus formae*) grow up, flourish, and die," setting a contrast between nations, which are transient, and humanity as a whole, which moves on a historical trajectory. Certainly, from an eschatological standpoint, this is true; however, the context here does not seem to be eschatological, but evocative of the similar statement quoted above from the UN address. Moreover, the immediate sequel notes the dangers and temptations of greed and materialism that can accompany progress.[104]

It is in this context that Paul repeats the traditional doctrine of the universal destination of goods and the priority of the common good to private ownership. The pope gave as an example the nonproductive *latifundia*, usually associated with Latin America, and like the Council endorsed, at least under some circumstances, their expropriation.[105] He also condemns "selfish speculation" and transfer of assets overseas. Similarly he rejects liberalism understood as unchecked capitalism, but distinguishes this from industrialism, which is itself necessary for progress. His greatest concern is clearly for poverty in the developing world and the need to promote its alleviation. This includes, almost en passant, the judgment that under some circumstances, revolution (*seditiones et motus*) is licit.[106] The urgency of the situation requires programs of reform planned and initiated by government in cooperation with intermediary bodies.[107] Such programs should give priority to education, support for the family, respect for traditional cultures.

The second section of *Populorum progressio* takes up specific issues in more detail and makes a number of policy recommendations, some more specific than others, under the headings of the duty of solidarity, the duty of social justice, and the duty of universal charity (in fact, all three are also said to follow from solidarity[108]). The duty of solidarity is incumbent on both individuals and peoples. He urges individuals to be prepared to pay higher taxes as well as higher prices for imported goods.[109] The duty of nations is similar: "the superfluous wealth of rich countries should be placed at the service of poor nations."[110] The mechanism for this is the establishment of

---

[103]   *PP*, no. 17: At quemadmodum maris fluctus, aestu crescente, alius alio ulterius litus invadunt, haud secus, in historias cursu, humanum genus procedit.

[104]   *PP*, no. 18.

[105]   *PP*, no. 24. He cites *Gaudium et spes*, no. 71, as calling for the same thing. Where the Council text specifically calls for compensation for land that is expropriated, Paul does not.

[106]   *PP*, no. 31: rebellion could be justified only by "manifest and longstanding tyranny."

[107]   *PP*, no. 33.

[108]   *PP*, nos. 48, 62, 67.

[109]   *PP*, no. 47.

[110]   *PP*, no. 49.

a "World Fund" made up in part from money that would have otherwise been spent on arms, first proposed in Bombay and repeated in the UN speech.[111] This enterprise was clearly important to Paul. The World Bank had been in existence since 1944, but it was not heavily committed to large development loans until after 1968, which perhaps explains Paul's silence about it. While the Bank's policies have not been free of controversy, its current mission (save a connection with disarmament) seems quite close to Paul's vision.[112] In any case, so concrete a recommendation as the establishment of a development fund is necessarily closely tied to the train of events and could not have the status of a principle.

Under the duty of social justice Paul mainly treats trade relations. The actual inequalities between developing nations that mostly supply raw materials and developed nations that manufacture finished products make a regime of purely free trade unacceptable.[113] This is a tenet of "liberalism."[114] Paul applies the principle that consent does not justify the terms of a contract between unequal parties first stated by Leo XIII; free trade is thus only fair if it meets the requirements of social justice.[115] It is never explained just how the norms of international trade are related to social justice as defined by Pius XI. Paul proposes international agreements that would regulate trade relations and guarantee fairness to developing nations.[116] Today's main international forum for trade issues, the World Trade Organization (founded in 1995, although its predecessor, the General Agreement on Tariffs and Trade had existed since 1948), is explicitly committed to extending principles of free trade and so would presumably be open to criticism on the basis of the principles outlined in *Populorum progressio*, although it too is committed to fairness between trading partners as well as legal and financial transparency. At the same time, the broad objective of the encyclical is development itself, especially of the poorest nations. The assessment of specific strategies for development would seem to be driven largely by empirical data and its analysis. The encyclical discusses neither data nor analysis and there are a number of economists – by no means opposed to the pope's broader notion of integrally human development – who have argued for the benefits of free

---

[111] *PP*, no. 51.
[112] Perhaps the most prominent and serious criticisms have been made by Joseph Stiglitz, *Globalization and Its Discontents* (New York: Norton, 2003).
[113] *PP*, no. 58.
[114] *PP*, and cf. nos. 26, 34.
[115] *PP*, no. 59.
[116] *PP*, no. 61.

(which does not mean completely unregulated) trade for developing economies.[117] While the argument for a broad and humane view of development seems important, the policy judgment about free trade is considerably more tenuous and is, in any case, not clearly related to the principle of social justice, which is said to demand it.

Under the third heading the pope remarks on the lack of brotherhood among individuals and peoples and recommends as remedies the establishment of youth hostels and urges international businesspeople to treat workers and all inhabitants of developing countries with respect and justice and to be open to a dialogue between civilizations. It is difficult to see this as anything more than what might go without saying, i.e., that people should behave as Christians in every aspect of their daily lives and work. Following this is a discussion of peace that largely repeats themes in the 1964 UN address, in particular the call for a world authority: "Such international collaboration among the nations of the world certainly calls for institutions that will promote, coordinate and direct it, until a new juridical order is firmly established and fully ratified."[118] The pope goes on to quote the most important passage of the speech. It is perhaps worth noting again that the endorsement of such an authority here is not accompanied, as it was in *Pacem in terris* (leave aside the cost this entailed to coherence), by an injunction to respect the principle of subsidiarity. Moreover, it is followed in a way that evokes passages from the beginning of the encyclical, a seeming identification of progress toward global juridical integration with progress toward God.[119]

One institutional consequence of the Council was the establishment by Paul of the Synod of Bishops as a regular forum for the consideration of important questions in the Church. The second such regular meeting was scheduled to take place in the fall of 1971 and consider two topics: the ministerial priesthood and justice in the world. Paul prepared for that meeting's second topic by issuing an apostolic letter (which has a lower level of authority than an encyclical) in the spring of that year, officially addressed to Cardinal Maurice Roy, who headed the Pontifical Commission for Justice and Peace. The letter, *Octogesima adveniens*, also commemorated the

---

[117] See, e.g., Jagdish Bhagwati, *In Defense of Globalization* (Oxford: Oxford University Press, 2004) and Jay R. Mandle, *Globalization and the Poor* (Cambridge: Cambridge University Press, 2003).

[118] *PP*, no. 78: Haec autem mutua inter nationes opera ad totum pertinens orbem terrarum sane poscit instituta, quae eam praeparent, disponant, regant, donec novus iurium ordo statuatur, quem ratum ac firmum omnes ubique habeant.

[119] *PP*, nos. 79–80.

eightieth anniversary of *Rerum novarum*.[120] Its purpose was to call to the synod's attention certain problems created by the modern economy and set them in the wider context of a "new civilization."[121]

Most of the problems that Paul discussed in detail were related to the global phenomenon of urbanization, itself a function of industrialization and its diffusion throughout the developing world, and to what he took to be the worrisome effects of these processes both on those who were its chief beneficiaries and those who had not yet benefitted from economic development.

> The inordinate growth of these centers accompanies industrial expansion, without being identified with it. Based on technological research and the transformation of nature, industrialization constantly goes forward, giving proof of incessant creativity. While certain enterprises develop and are concentrated, others die or change their location. Thus new social problems are created: professional or regional unemployment, redeployment and mobility of persons, permanent adaptation of workers and disparity of conditions in the different branches of industry. Unlimited competition utilizing the modern means of publicity incessantly launches new products and tries to attract the consumer, while earlier industrial installations which are still capable of functioning become useless. While very large areas of the population are unable to satisfy their primary needs, superfluous needs are ingeniously created. It can thus rightly be asked if, in spite of all his conquests, man is not turning back against himself the results of his activity. Having rationally endeavored to control nature, is he not now becoming the slave of the objects which he makes?[122]

He went on to describe loneliness, anomie, and dehumanizing living conditions, as well as the specific problems of young people, workers, and those groups particularly subject to marginalization in the new economy.

Paul then placed these problems in the context of contemporary political and economic ideas. Modern times reveal two great aspirations that are part of men's sense of their own freedom and dignity: equality and participation. Both of these suggested to Paul a "preferential respect due to the poor" (*praecipuam reverentiam pauperibus*) according to which "the more fortunate should renounce some of their rights so as to place their goods more generously at the service of others."[123] They also suggest the need to promote a more

---

[120] Paul VI, Apostolic Letter *Octogesima adveniens* (On the Occasion of the Eightieth Anniversary of the Encyclical *Rerum novarum*) (1971), AAS 63 (1971), 401–441. The connection to the forthcoming synod was stated in no. 6.

[121] OA, no. 7.

[122] OA, no. 9.

[123] OA, nos. 22–23.

"democratic type of society" (*popularis societatis genus*) and he enjoined Christians to actively take part in the pursuit of new models.[124] At the same time he cautioned against searching for such models through contemporary political ideologies, criticizing both Marxist collectivism and liberal individualism.[125] He also called attention to the development of the social sciences and encouraged Christians to participate in this development while cautioning against the dangers of reductionism and an overly technological understanding of human affairs.[126] This led him to criticize the inherent limitations of economics and emphasize what one might call the primacy of politics in this realm, so long as it was directed to the common good.[127]

Two hundred and ten bishops participated in the Synod that met from late September to early November 1971, devoting roughly half their time to the theme of "justice in the world" and producing a document by that name, which reflected many of the themes of *Octogesima adveniens*, but which also went further than Paul in one crucial and highly controversial respect. After condemning injustices and oppression that the synod perceived as building around the world, the document affirmed that "[a]ction on behalf of justice and participation in the transformation of the world fully appear to us as a constitutive dimension (*ratio constitutiva*) of the preaching of the Gospel, or, in other words, of the Church's mission for the redemption of the human race and its liberation from every oppressive situation."[128] The next ordinary meeting of the synod took place in September and October of 1974 and was dedicated to the single theme of "Evangelization in the Modern World," and the lingering controversy over *De Iustitia in Mundo* carried over into its deliberations, so much so that the 1974 Synod could not agree on a final text and therefore handed over two different drafts with related materials to the

---

[124]   OA, no. 24.

[125]   OA, no. 26.

[126]   OA, nos. 38–40.

[127]   It has been suggested that *Octogesima adveniens* evinces notably less faith in the possibilities of development than *Populorum progressio* and so focuses more on political change, perhaps partly in response to the conference of Latin American bishops that took place in Medellín in 1968 and emphasized liberation over development. See Donal Dorr, *Option for the Poor and for the Earth: Catholic Social Teaching* (Maryknoll, NY: Orbis Books, 2012), ch. 8. As suggested above, it seems to me that Paul expresses ambivalence about development already in *Populorum progressio*, so that the changes of tone in *Octogesima adveniens* are less radical than Dorr argues.

[128]   *De Iustitia in Mundo* (Synod of Bishops on Priestly Ministry and Justice in the World) (1971), AAS 63 (1971), 924. While the document was published in the acta of the Holy See, there is no modern language version on the Vatican website. I quote the translation in *Catholic Social Thought: The Documentary Heritage*, eds., David J. O'Brien and Thomas A. Shannon (Maryknoll, NY: Orbis Books, 2010), 306.

pope for his disposition. With this meeting the practice of the Synod issuing a document of its own was changed: a little more than a year after the Synod concluded, Pope Paul issued an apostolic exhortation summarizing its work under his own name, a practice that has continued ever since. After approvingly noting the previous Synod's affirmation of the Church's duty to proclaim human liberation, *Evangelii nuntiandi* seems to make a kind of corrective adjustment at least to the tone of *De Iustitia in Mundo*, cautioning those who would reduce the Church's mission to a temporal project.[129] Paul went on to write that while the Church is properly concerned with man's temporal well-being, this cannot supplant "the primacy of her spiritual vocation," and to warn against the identification of salvation with liberation. Not every vision of human liberation, he held, is compatible with the Gospel.[130] It is possible to read these statements as a criticism of the 1971 Synod document, although it is also possible to see it more as a kind of theological clarification mainly intended to preclude any instrumentalization of the Gospel in the service of political ideologies.[131] For Paul, human liberation must be understood as an aspect of the Kingdom of God: "Only the kingdom therefore is absolute, and it makes everything else relative."[132]

CONCLUSION

This vexed and intense period of social, economic, and political reflection does seem to contain some important developments, while reaffirming and in some cases more acutely formulating older principles. The papal account of legitimate political power moves further from the sort of sacred notions of authority characteristic of pronouncements in the mid-nineteenth century and earlier, and more toward a cleaner grounding in the natural moral law. Similarly, a view of the temporal common good as a set of conditions emerges into papal teaching in a way consistent with the general view of political authority and also under the influence of the increasing importance of personalism and the ongoing secularization of political institutions and programs in the West. This is partly constituted by a quite extensive embrace of human rights. None of these developments is radical; all have roots in the period

---

[129]   Paul VI, Apostolic Exhortation *Evangelii nuntiandi* (On Evangelization in the Modern World) (1975), no. 32, *AAS* 68 (1976), 27.

[130]   *EN*, no. 34.

[131]   See Charles M. Murphy, "Action for Justice as Constitutive of the Preaching of the Gospel: What Did the 1971 Synod Mean?" *Theological Studies* 44 (1983): 298–311; and discussion in Dorr, *Option for the Poor*, ch. 10.

[132]   *EN*, no. 8.

before John XXIII and none constitutes anything like a decisive break with tradition. They are, precisely, developments, and many of the detailed implications remain subject to prudential evaluation.

The traditional notions of the nature of the universal destination of goods, the distinction between ownership as generally private, but conditioned always by the demands of the common good, is reaffirmed and extended beyond individuals to nations. Similarly, the duty of aid to the poor is extended to nations. The principle of subsidiarity is affirmed and applied especially by John XXIII to international development issues, but its emphasis seems to decline in the period of Paul VI. In general Paul seemed less concerned with the classical principles than with the painful and increasingly challenging exigencies of the day, especially the nexus of economic imbalance and political violence. The related call for an international authority emerged in John's writings and was affirmed by both the Council and by Paul, giving it a certain precedential weight, but its practical implication, especially in light of the duty of subsidiarity, remains somewhat unclear.

One sees in this period a transition from the sort of guarded optimism characteristic of much of the developed world at the start of the 1960s as the immediate postwar era came to a close and new possibilities presented themselves, toward an increasingly wary, indeed agitated sensibility even during the Council, much magnified during the papacy of Paul VI, a period characterized by multiple crises that were global in scale. Perhaps the most significant unresolved problem at the end of this period was the integration of adequate political and economic categories and principles into a presentation of the Christian message tailored to an era of secularization and globalization, and it was just this set of challenges that was squarely faced by John Paul II.

7

Social Teaching in Pope John Paul II

Patrick Lee

Two things above all helped shape Pope St. John Paul II's development of the social teaching of the Church. One was an idea, and the other was a significant political event. The idea was that self-constituting free choice is central to the identity and flourishing of the human person. The political event was the downfall of Communist socialism in Eastern Europe.[1]

Even before he was pope, Karol Wojtyla emphasized that in free choice one constitutes oneself, that free choice involves not just a selection of this or that action, but the building up of a certain kind of self. As Pope John Paul II, he makes this teaching central in the encyclical *Laborem exercens* and applies it to economic issues. In work one fulfills oneself, and this act is inherently good as opposed to being a mere means to the production of an external commodity. This point is important in itself and it will also lead him in his social teaching to emphasize liberty or free initiative, perhaps as much as justice. In deliberating about economic acts or policies, one must ask oneself how they will affect the poor, how they will affect the justice of distribution of material goods. But one must also ask how these acts or policies will affect free initiative by families and individuals.

The second novelty to have an impact on John Paul's social teaching was the downfall of communist socialism in Eastern Europe, the failure of the socialist economies there. In his biography, that downfall was preceded by extensive experience of and interaction with socialist systems, in both their nationalistic and communist forms. Pope John Paul had lived under that regime in Poland, and his actions as pope had a major role in that downfall. It is always perilous to speculate about how events outside shape the logical realm of ideas and arguments, but I think it fair to say that this event, and

---

[1] At the time the encyclical was published, the Communist regimes in East Europe, except for the Soviet Union, had fallen.

prior life experience, enabled John Paul to understand certain points about society and economics that would otherwise have been more difficult to see. Moreover, it seems that this event helped him appreciate the great importance of both the market system and free initiative made possible by a market system.

1 WORK AND THE OWNERSHIP AND USE OF PROPERTY

Social thinkers both on the right and on the left have claimed support for their respective economic views in John Paul's writings. Like his predecessors, John Paul emphasizes two fundamental principles for ethical thinking about economic matters: the right to private ownership of property, on the one hand, and the duty to use these goods for the common good, or the universal destination of material goods, on the other.

These truths, John Paul teaches, are rooted in the book of *Genesis*. *Genesis* teaches that material goods are a gift from God for the good of all humankind, and that God gave humankind dominion over the rest of material creation.

> God gave the earth to the whole human race for the sustenance of all its members, without excluding or favoring anyone. This is *the foundation of the universal destination of the earth's goods*. The earth, by reason of its fruitfulness and its capacity to satisfy human needs, is God's first gift for the sustenance of human life.[2]

This theological argument could be interpreted in various ways, some of which lead to incoherence. It is not as easy to articulate the argument from basic principles as it might first appear. If the natural law understanding of moral norms is correct, then the argument must begin with the truth that God has a plan for his creation, especially for us, and that he has not himself directly assigned properties to any individuals or groups. So, God gives material goods to the human family as a whole, and evidently intends material goods to be used for the fulfillment of his plan – a plan that includes the good of the whole human family. That this is indeed God's intention is revealed in *Genesis* and clearly suggested in Psalm 8. It can also be inferred from the truths that God is the Creator and that material things are not persons, that is, not subjects whose good is worthwhile for its own sake. From these points it

---

[2] John Paul II, Encyclical Letter *Centesimus annus* (100th Anniversary of *Rerum Novarum*) (1991), no. 31. All emphases in quotes from papal texts throughout this essay are in the original texts unless otherwise specified.

follows that making a right use of these material goods is a duty of religion as well as a duty of justice to our neighbor.[3]

Material things were created for the use of all human persons. But the best way of procuring and distributing those material goods, John Paul insists, defending a tradition stemming back to the Church Fathers, is by a private property arrangement. There are two principal reasons for this. First, a private property arrangement, as opposed to a collectivist one, is *most efficient*. He says, for example: "It would appear that, on the level of individual nations and of international relations, the *free market* is the most efficient instrument for utilizing resources and effectively responding to needs" (CA, no. 34).[4] By this he seems to mean that the free market system is the best means of increasing productivity for the nation as a whole. It will not guarantee, just by itself, that the fundamental needs of all are met nor that the cultural ethos is healthy (but neither does he say that a free market system inevitably leads to a depraved ethos).

Second, a private property system allows *scope for free self-constitution*.[5] Having space for self-determined economic activity is important for the development of families as well as for individuals. Families have a right to such scope for self-development. John Paul also affirms other rights that follow upon these fundamental ones, rights that were affirmed by all of the popes from Leo XIII to Paul VI: the right to form private associations (a right that

---

[3]   Daniel Finn offers another way of understanding this type of argument. He endorses what he holds is Aquinas's way of understanding it: "For Thomas, every creaturely thing was created with a purpose from God, and fulfilling that purpose was the essence of that thing's 'natural law.' Thomas's view of private property was based in this analysis." There are problems with this argument. It seems to say that we are morally obliged to act in accord with a finality inscribed within each creature, which is its essence or nature. This would be true of material things, as well as organs or powers within oneself. Now it is true that the natural finality in a material thing is an effect of God, and so in some sense intended by God; but it is not clear that this effect of God's intention, or this particular embodiment of God's intention, is also intended (or prescribed) by God to be followed by us. The argument seems to imply that if I fail to give bread to my neighbor as I should, then it is the nature of bread that I have directly violated, and my neighbor's rights only indirectly. See Daniel Finn, "Commentary on *Centesimus Annus*," in *Modern Social Teaching, Commentaries and Interpretations*, ed. Kenneth Himes, OFM (Washington, DC: Georgetown University Press, 2004), 445.

[4]   He immediately adds, however, that "this is true only for those needs which are 'solvent', insofar as they are endowed with purchasing power, and for those resources which are 'marketable', insofar as they are capable of obtaining a satisfactory price." And he further adds: "It is a strict duty of justice and truth not to allow fundamental human needs to remain unsatisfied, and not to allow those burdened by such needs to perish. It is also necessary to help these needy people to acquire expertise, to enter the circle of exchange, and to develop their skills in order to make the best use of their capacities and resources."

[5]   On these arguments, cf. Leo XIII, Encyclical Letter *Rerum novarum* (On the Condition of the Working Classes) (May 15, 1891), nos. 5–10.

John Paul particularly emphasizes), including to form professional associations and trade unions, to limitation of working hours, of women and children to be treated differently with regard to the type and duration of work, to a just wage, and to discharge freely one's religious duties.

John Paul has made this argument for the right to private ownership more precise by placing it within the context of a developed understanding of the value of work for the worker, or what John Paul terms work in the subjective sense. He first makes this distinction – between the external and the subjective dimensions of work – in *Laborem exercens*, and he presupposes it in later encyclicals.[6]

In *Centesimus annus* he explains that a right to private property is founded fundamentally on the person's and the family's right to free self-determination. Work should not be understood as only a means to producing a commodity, but rather as an activity by which a human person actualizes or fulfills himself, an act of self-realization. Indeed, according to John Paul, when the book of *Genesis*, in its first pages, teaches that man is made in the image of God, this refers in part to the fact that man has been given dominion over the earth and is called to subdue it:

> When man, who had been created "in the image of God . . .. male and female", hears the words: "Be fruitful and *multiply, and fill the earth and subdue* it", even though these words do not refer directly and explicitly to work, beyond any doubt they indirectly indicate it as an activity for man to carry out in the world. Indeed, they show its very deepest essence. Man is the image of God partly through the mandate received from his Creator to subdue, to dominate, the earth. In carrying out this mandate, man, every human being, reflects the very action of the Creator of the universe. (*LE*, no. 4)[7]

John Paul distinguishes between work as a transitive activity – that is, an activity that crosses over from the agent into an external thing – and the immanent dimension of work, that is, the shaping of the will or character of

---

[6] He had philosophically worked out the notion of moral reflexivity in his prepapal writing, *The Acting Person*: Karol Wojtyla, *The Acting Person*, tr. Andrzej Potocki (Dordrecht: D. Reidel, 1979), see esp. 149–153.

[7] The traditional interpretation, of course, was that man is made in the image of God with respect to his intellect and will. Without denying that, John Paul teaches in another context that man is made in God's image also in that man freely subdues the earth, and in that man is male and female and builds a family (see Pope John Paul, *General Audiences*; *Pope John Paul's Theology of the Body*, audiences at September 12, and November 14, 1979; these also can be found in: John Paul II, *Man and Woman He Created Them, a Theology of the Body*, trans., Michael Waldstein (Boston: Pauline Books and Media, 2006), 16, 162.

the agent. For example, if a worker mines coal, the work considered as a transitive act – the act that commences in the worker and terminates in the coal, or in the coal's being in the wheelbarrow – is getting the coal onto the wagon. But the coal miner's work also shapes himself. Since it is a deliberate, rational act – a human act – the coal miner's action involves not just transitive effects on the world outside himself, but also and more importantly shapes what kind of person he will be. Indeed, John Paul asserts that, understood in this way, work has a value in itself (the Latin term is *"vis"* – meaning force or weight, or as it is translated, value).[8]

From this basic point John Paul draws two conclusions. First, work must not be treated as a mere commodity and so, as much as possible, the worker must have an *active share* in the process of production:

> The person who works desires *not only* due *remuneration* for his work; he also wishes that, within the production process, provision be made for him to be able to *know* that in his work, even on something that is owned in common, he is working *"for himself"*. This awareness is extinguished within him in a system of excessive bureaucratic centralization, which makes the worker feel that he is just a cog in a huge machine moved from above, that he is for more reasons than one a mere production instrument rather than a true subject of work with an initiative of his own. (*LE*, no. 15)

The second conclusion he draws from the distinction between the objective and subjective senses of work concerns the value of various types of work. If the central value of work is its immanent dimension, its self-constitutive aspect, then one cannot measure different kinds of work only on the basis of the external products involved. The work of a janitor or a ditch-digger may have in this respect more value in it than the work of a college professor or a philosopher-king. John Paul points out that the ancient world believed in a hierarchy of work. Work that involved the exercise of physical strength was viewed as inferior and unworthy of free human beings. But Christianity "brought about a fundamental change of ideas," for the whole content of the Gospel takes as its point of departure the truth that God became man, and "devoted most of the years of his life on earth to *manual work* at the carpenter's bench" (*LE*, no. 6).

---

[8] "In fact there is no doubt that human work has an ethical value [*vis*] of its own, which clearly and directly remains linked to the fact that the one who carries it out is a person, a conscious and free subject, that is to say a subject that decides about himself." John Paul II, Encyclical Letter *Laborem exercens* (On Human Work) (1981), no 6 (translation amended). The Latin is: Re quidem vera non est dubium quin in labore humano vis ethica insit, quae sine ullis ambagibus proxime cum hoc conectitur quod is qui opus facit, est persona, subiectum conscium et liberum, id est subiectum de se ipso deliberans.

This circumstance constitutes in itself the most eloquent "Gospel of work", showing that the basis for determining the value of human work is not primarily the kind of work being done but the fact that the one who is doing it is a person. The sources of the dignity of work are to be sought primarily in the subjective dimension, not in the objective one. (*LE*, no. 6)

This is because "in the final analysis it is always man who is *the purpose of the work*, whatever work it is that is done by man – even if the common scale of values rates it as the merest 'service', as the most monotonous, or even the most alienating work" (*LE*, no. 6).

2 SOCIALISM

John Paul rejects socialism as inefficient and, more important, as contrary to human dignity and the right of initiative and free self-determination by families and individuals. The central problem with socialism is that it necessarily involves the usurpation by the state of initiative or of the self-determining activity by individuals, families, and other voluntary associations. Like his predecessors, John Paul is opposed to an economic system where there is an absolute predominance of capital (a system in which the owners of capital have inordinate power to control economic policy) on the ground that such power is contrary to the active participation and freedom of those who do not possess capital or power. But he suggests that socialism involves the same type of impairment of economic and personal initiative. As he puts it:

> In the struggle against such a system [that is, a system that upholds the absolute predominance of capital], what is being proposed as an alternative is not the socialist system, which in fact turns out to be State capitalism, but rather *a society of free work, of enterprise and of participation*. (*CA*, no. 35)

The error of socialism is anthropological: "Socialism considers the individual person simply as an element, a molecule within the social organism, so that the good of the individual is completely subordinated to the functioning of the socio-economic mechanism" (*CA*, no. 13). It fails to see that the true good of the individual can be realized only in reference to his free choice, in reference to his free self-constitution: "Man is thus reduced to a series of social relationships, and the concept of the person as the autonomous subject of moral decision disappears, the very subject whose decisions build the social order" (*CA*, no. 13).

The Church also rejects a radical libertarian position. The state should not be viewed as a mere mutual insurance association, having no common goods viewed as valuable in themselves, and – most important here – having no common responsibilities beyond providing protection. The human person is fulfilled not just as an individual, but in communion with others, and so each person has responsibilities toward others, some of which are most effectively fulfilled by acting as parts of the political community. Still, in socialist systems the common good, at least on the economic level, absorbs the personal goods. And so individuals and families are deprived of free self-initiative and are drawn into an unhealthy form of dependency on the state:

> A person who is deprived of something he can call "his own", and of the possibility of earning a living through his own initiative, comes to depend on the social machine and on those who control it. This makes it much more difficult for him to recognize his dignity as a person, and hinders progress towards the building up of an authentic human community. (CA, no. 13)

3 CAPITALISM

Much ink has been spilled about John Paul's teaching on capitalism. Many have argued that John Paul is more favorable to capitalism than his predecessors were,[9] while others have objected that this claim conflicts with his reaffirmation of the universal destination of material goods, and of the state's duties to direct the economy to the common good.[10]

The question, though, is ambiguous – it depends on what one means by "capitalism," whether it is viewed, for example, as a purely economic system or as a cultural ethos. Both Leo XIII and Pius XI taught that the free market should have a significant, though limited, role to play within the distribution of goods and services in society.[11] John Paul repeats this and adds new reasons for a positive evaluation of a market economy. At the same time, he reaffirms that the free market should not be the *only* organizing principle.

---

[9] For example, Michael Novak, *The Catholic Ethic and the Spirit of Capitalism* (New York: Free Press, 1993); Richard Neuhaus, *Doing Well and Doing Good, the Challenge to the Christian Capitalist* (New York: Doubleday, 1992).

[10] For example, David Hollenbach, SJ, "The Pope and Capitalism," *America* 1 (June 1991): 591; John Sniegocki, "The Social Ethics of John Paul II: A Critique of Neo Conservative Interpretations," *Horizons* 33 (2006): 24 ff.; Daniel Finn, "John Paul II and the Moral Ecology of Markets," *Theological Studies* 59 (1998): 669–670. For a general discussion of interpretations of John Paul's encyclical *Centesimus annus*, see Matthew Shadle, "Twenty Years of Interpreting *Centesimus Annus* on the Economy," *Journal of Catholic Social Thought* 9 (2012): 171–191.

[11] RN, no. 6; Pius XI, *Quadragesimo anno* (Reconstruction of the Social Order: 40th Anniversary of *Rerum Novarum*) (May 15, 1931), nos. 88, 110.

It is safe to say that there is a *type of* capitalism that John Paul sees as desirable in a just and free economy. But he also makes it clear that capitalism as it historically developed was deeply flawed – so capitalism *in that sense* is not to be recommended.

John Paul says many positive things about capitalism, which he also refers to as "business economy" or "the free market." The first is that it is the most efficient way of producing wealth: "It would appear that, on the level of individual nations and of international relations, *the free market* is the most efficient instrument for utilizing resources and effectively responding to needs" (CA, no. 34).[12]

It also promotes, or facilitates, free initiative and active self-determination: "The business economy has positive aspects, the fundamental one being the liberty of the person, which is expressed in the economic area just as in all others" (CA, no. 32; translation amended).[13]

John Paul also speaks favorably of the role of profit for the operation of businesses, though he hastens to add that it is not the only measure of the complete success of a business:

> The Church acknowledges the legitimate *role of profit* as an indication that a business is functioning well. When a firm makes a profit, this means that productive factors have been properly employed and corresponding human needs have been duly satisfied. But profitability is not the only indicator of a firm's condition ... Profit is a regulator of the life of a business, but it is not the only one; *other human and moral factors* must also be considered which, in the long term, are at least equally important for the life of a business. (CA, no. 35)[14]

According to John Paul, historically capitalism had both good results and bad. In the West the early phase of capitalism led to grave economic exploitation.

---

[12]   Cf: "Certainly the mechanisms of the market offer secure advantages: they help to utilize resources better; they promote the exchange of products; above all they give central place to the person's desires and preferences, which, in a contract, meet the desires and preferences of another person" (CA, no. 40). Numerous texts explain this point. A seminal essay, showing how the free market uniquely communicates information concerning needs, supply, relative importance, and other facts regarding economic goods, in an indirect way, was Frederick Hayek's "The Use of Knowledge in Society," in *Individualism and the Economic Order* (Chicago: Chicago University Press, 1948), 77–91.

[13]   Hodierna *oeconomia administrationis* utiles admittit aspectus, quorum fundamentum est personae libertas quae in regione oeconomica significatur sicut et in tot aliis. Latin available at: http://w2.vatican.va/content/john-paul-ii/la/encyclicals/documents/hf_jp-ii_en c_01051991_centesimus-annus.html

[14]   This is consistent with criticizing an "all-consuming desire for profit," which John Paul mentions in *Sollicitudo rei socialis* (On Social Concern) (1987), no. 37, though he does not

However, John Paul seems to hold that as it developed some of the policies recommended by Leo XIII were adopted in national economies throughout Europe, and the efficiency of the free market and the creativity it encouraged produced prosperity, so that by the 1990s economic exploitation was not the central problem in advanced countries. It remains, however, a problem to this day in third-world countries and in certain areas even in advanced countries.[15] But the problems in advanced countries with free market economies usually are ethical and cultural rather than strictly economic (CA, nos. 49–50).

In other countries, particularly in the third world, the kind of economic exploitation that characterized the early days of capitalism in the West is still very much a reality. Thus in CA he writes:

> Many other people, while not completely marginalized, live in situations in which the struggle for a bare minimum is uppermost. These are situations in which the rules of the earliest period of capitalism still flourish in conditions of "ruthlessness" in no way inferior to the darkest moments of the first phase of industrialization. (CA, no. 33)

And he goes on to say: "Exploitation, at least in the forms analyzed and described by Karl Marx, has been overcome in Western society" (CA, no. 41).

John Paul distinguishes between old capitalism and new. Old capitalism involved exploitation of workers. New capitalism has different problems:

> Just as in the time of primitive capitalism the State had the duty of defending the basic rights of workers, so now, with the new capitalism, the State and all of society have the duty of *defending those collective goods* which, among others, constitute the essential framework for the legitimate pursuit of personal goals on the part of each individual. (CA, no. 40)

New capitalism has, basically, two problems. First, the advanced capitalist economy has reached the point where knowledge and skill are just as important as capital, just as important as land or material instruments of production. This is not by itself problematic; however, many people suffer from a lack of such knowledge and skills, and so in such economies there is a new type of alienation:

> The fact is that many people, perhaps the majority today, do not have the means which would enable them to take their place in an effective and humanly dignified way within a productive system in which work is truly central. They

in that work say anything positive about the profit motive. It is worth adding that profit motive and "self-interest" do not mean selfishness. See below, text at note 22.

[15] Cf. SRS, no. 13, and the same point is made again by Benedict XVI in 2009, in Encyclical Letter *Caritas in veritate* (On Integral Human Development in Charity & Truth) (2009), no. 27.

have no possibility of acquiring the basic knowledge which would enable them to express their creativity and develop their potential ... Thus, if not actually exploited, they are to a great extent marginalized; economic development takes place over their heads, so to speak, when it does not actually reduce the already narrow scope of their old subsistence economies. (*CA*, no. 33)[16]

This point is important to remember in considering how to correct the deficiencies in those cultures. It does not seem that the solution is simply to provide material goods to people who are marginalized. The goal should be actually to include them as agents in the dynamic economy.[17] After repeating that it is a strict duty of justice not to allow fundamental needs to remain unsatisfied, John Paul adds the following point:

> It is also necessary to help these needy people to acquire expertise, to enter the circle of exchange, and to develop their skills in order to make the best use of their capacities and resources. Even prior to the logic of a fair exchange of goods and the forms of justice appropriate to it, there exists *something which is due to man because he is man,* by reason of his lofty dignity. Inseparable from that required "something" is the possibility to survive and, at the same time, to make an active contribution to the common good of humanity. (*CA*, no. 34)

The operation of the free market is important since it leads to an increase of prosperity or general standard of living, and thus has helped to lift many people out of absolute poverty. Still, this increased productivity also points to the need to develop and regulate the economy so that as many as possible can share not only in the fruits of economic productivity but in the valuable work and responsible participation made possible by that increased productivity.

A second defect of new capitalism is that the culture surrounding it tends toward *consumerism.* The culture tends to place value above all on things as opposed to persons, and enjoyable experiences as opposed to genuine fulfillment. It does not seem that John Paul holds that the capitalist or market economy necessarily leads to such a mentality – which is partly why he does

---

[16] John Paul adds in the next sentence: "They are unable to compete against the goods which are produced in ways which are new and which properly respond to needs, needs which they had previously been accustomed to meeting through traditional forms of organization" (*CA*, no. 33; cf. *SRS*, no. 15).

[17] Richard John Neuhaus provoked the ire of some by remarking that according to John Paul's teaching, "the poor of the world are not oppressed because of capitalism, ... but because of the absence of capitalism." Richard John Neuhaus, "The Pope, Liberty, and Capitalism: Essays on *Centesimus Annus,*" *National Review* 43, no. 11 (June 24, 1991): 8–9, quoted in Finn, "John Paul II and the Moral Ecology of Markets," 664; for a similar analysis, see Samuel Gregg, *Challenging the Modern World, Karol Wojtyla/Pope John Paul II and the Development of Catholic Social Teaching* (New York: Lexington Books, 1999), Chapters 6, 8.

not condemn capitalism as such.[18] But he does point out that the opulence the capitalist economy has made possible has also occasioned the growth of this error.

A different type of alienation has been generated by consumerism:

> The historical experience of the West, for its part, shows that even if the Marxist analysis and its foundation of alienation are false, nevertheless alienation – and the loss of the authentic meaning of life – is a reality in Western societies too. This happens in consumerism, when people are ensnared in a web of false and superficial gratifications rather than being helped to experience their personhood in an authentic and concrete way. (CA, no. 41)[19]

The widespread problems of drug abuse and pornography are results of the spiritual void created by a consumerist mentality or culture. They are the results of the creation of artificial "needs" and focus upon the experiential as opposed to goods that are genuinely fulfilling: "Drugs, as well as pornography and other forms of consumerism which exploit the frailty of the weak, tend to fill the resulting spiritual void" (CA, no. 36).

He also says that these phenomena constitute the destruction of the human environment or human ecology. This consumerist mentality has also led to antifamily and antilife campaigns in advanced countries. In CA and SRS he denounces "anti-childbearing campaigns." These, he says, are based on a distorted view of the demographic realities and involve an "absolute lack of respect for the free choice" of the parties involved, and move toward an intolerable oppression: "These policies are extending their field of action by

---

[18] "A given culture reveals its overall understanding of life through the choices it makes in production and consumption. It is here that *the phenomenon of consumerism* arises. In singling out new needs and new means to meet them, one must be guided by a comprehensive picture of man which respects all the dimensions of his being and which subordinates his material and instinctive dimensions to his interior and spiritual ones. If, on the contrary, a direct appeal is made to his instincts – while ignoring in various ways the reality of the person as intelligent and free – then *consumer attitudes* and *life-styles* can be created which are objectively improper and often damaging to his physical and spiritual health" (CA, no. 36).

[19] Cf.: "Here we find a new limit on the market: there are collective and qualitative needs which cannot be satisfied by market mechanisms. There are important human needs which escape its logic. There are goods which by their very nature cannot and must not be bought or sold. Certainly the mechanisms of the market offer secure advantages: they help to utilize resources better; they promote the exchange of products; above all they give central place to the person's desires and preferences, which, in a contract, meet the desires and preferences of another person. Nevertheless, these mechanisms carry the risk of an 'idolatry' of the market, an idolatry which ignores the existence of goods which by their nature are not and cannot be mere commodities" (CA, no. 40). On consumerism also see SRS, no. 28.

the use of new techniques, to the point of poisoning the lives of millions of defenseless human beings, as if in a form of 'chemical warfare'" (CA, no. 39).

These problems are grave, but they are not strictly defects in the economic systems. Rather, they are defects in the cultural systems surrounding them or providing the framework for them:

> These criticisms are directed not so much against an economic system as against an ethical and cultural system. The economy in fact is only one aspect and one dimension of the whole of human activity. (CA, no. 39)

These problems result, at least in part, from absolutizing the economic part of life, of failing to place the economic system within a larger and personalized framework.[20] Thus, the problem with western liberalism is not that it is based on a free market system but that this free market system is not placed within a larger framework informed by respect for the intrinsic value of the human person, but is enveloped by a culture that holds up mere experience or enjoyment as what alone is of value.

The economic arrangement is one leg of a tripod; the other legs are the political and the cultural aspects of the society. John Paul praises democracy because it promotes active participation or free initiative on the part of families and individuals in the political process (while also reminding that majorities too can violate rights). But freedom can be sustained only if it is also joined to a respect for natural rights:

> Following the collapse of Communist totalitarianism and of many other totalitarian and "national security" regimes, today we are witnessing a predominance, not without signs of opposition, of the democratic ideal, together with lively attention to and concern for human rights. But for this very reason it is necessary for peoples in the process of reforming their systems to give democracy an authentic and solid foundation through the explicit recognition of those rights. (CA, no. 47)

Among these rights is the right to life, including the right of the child to develop within his or her mother's womb. Included also are:

> the right to live in a united family and in a moral environment conducive to the growth of the child's personality; the right to develop one's intelligence and freedom in seeking and knowing the truth; the right to share in the work

---

[20] "If economic life is absolutized, if the production and consumption of goods become the center of social life and society's only value, not subject to any other value, the reason is to be found not so much in the economic system itself as in the fact that the entire socio-cultural system, by ignoring the ethical and religious dimension, has been weakened, and ends by limiting itself to the production of goods and services alone" (CA, no. 39).

which makes wise use of the earth's material resources, and to derive from that work the means to support oneself and one's dependents, and the right freely to establish a family, to have and to rear children through the responsible exercise of one's sexuality. (CA, no. 47)

These different points are brought together when John Paul asks whether capitalism should be recommended to developing countries after the failure of communism, and what advice one should give to third-world countries, that is, what model should be proposed to them? The answer, he says, is complex:

> If by "capitalism" is meant an economic system which recognizes the fundamental and positive role of business, the market, private property and the resulting responsibility for the means of production, as well as free human creativity in the economic sector, then the answer is certainly in the affirmative, even though it would perhaps be more appropriate to speak of a "business economy", "market economy" or simply "free economy". But if by "capitalism" is meant a system in which freedom in the economic sector is not circumscribed within a strong juridical framework which places it at the service of human freedom in its totality, and which sees it as a particular aspect of that freedom, the core of which is ethical and religious, then the reply is certainly negative. (CA, no. 42)

Thus the word "capitalism" can have different meanings. However, if it is interpreted as meaning a free market economic system, then John Paul commends it.

At times the Church's teaching on economic matters has been presented as if it were "a third way" between socialism and capitalism. This is misleading. In John Paul's teaching it is clear that socialism and capitalism are not moral equivalents – socialism is simply false, necessarily diminishes free initiative, and is based on a false anthropology. By contrast, if by capitalism one means a free market economy, it is to be commended, though it needs to be placed within a larger framework, and needs to be understood as a useful principle or tool rather than as the supreme norm.[21]

John Paul reaffirms the teaching that the free market should be an instrument, and not the only principle of organization for the economy. Thus he rejects a system in which capital is made an absolute. Or, more accurately, he teaches that freedom in the market place is not an absolute, it may be restricted for the sake of the common good:

> The Marxist solution has failed, but the realities of marginalization and exploitation remain in the world, especially the Third World, as does the reality of human alienation, especially in the more advanced countries . . .

---

[21] Cf. SRS, no. 42.

Indeed, there is a risk that a radical capitalistic ideology could spread which refuses even to consider these problems, in the *a priori* belief that any attempt to solve them is doomed to failure, and which blindly entrusts their solution to the free development of market forces. (*CA*, no. 42)

Although the goal or ideal is to incorporate marginalized people into the economic process itself as opposed to providing them merely with material goods, it remains equally true that providing such goods is a strict duty in justice. This is true of the third-world economies but is also true in developed economies. Thus, in a paragraph in which he extols the efficiency of the free market and the need to include people in the economic process, John Paul reaffirms the duty to meet basic human needs:

> It is a strict duty of justice and truth not to allow fundamental human needs to remain unsatisfied, and not to allow those burdened by such needs to perish. It is also necessary to help these needy people to acquire expertise, to enter the circle of exchange, and to develop their skills in order to make the best use of their capacities and resources. Even prior to the logic of a fair exchange of goods and the forms of justice appropriate to it, there exists *something which is due to man because he is man,* by reason of his lofty dignity. (*CA*, no. 34)

Thus, John Paul recommends a modified capitalism or free market system; put otherwise, a socioeconomic ethos in which the free market principle has a significant regulatory effect, one that enables individuals and families, rather than a command economy, to shape their economic pursuits.

One might object to this conclusion by arguing that this claim ignores the fact that the capitalist view, that is, the idea that the free market should be such a prominent organizing principle for the distribution of goods and services, logically implies faulty views of the human person and of human freedom. This is a serious objection: If the free market by its very nature involves a denial, say, of the call to each human person to seek first the kingdom, then capitalism is opposed to the Gospel just as much as communism or socialism.

David Schindler has claimed that "liberalism" – by which he seems to mean an ethos emphasizing the free market and not imbued by a Christian notion of love[22] – embodies false notions of the human person and human freedom. By emphasizing profit and self-interest (Schindler argues) capitalism presupposes that selfishness is permissible and even productive. Capitalism embodies a view of the person that is antithetical to the Christian teaching that "man cannot fully find himself except through a sincere gift of himself" (*Gaudium et*

---

[22]   Schindler argues at length that, on the Christian notion of love, receptivity and thus solidarity are understood as prior to creativity or free initiative.

spes, no. 24). In short, capitalism extols self-interest above all, whereas Christianity teaches the primacy of self-gift.[23]

However, in the first place, this objection misinterprets what is meant by "self-interest" when it is said that in a free market economy each agent acts for his "self-interest" and the free market principles – price, supply and demand, etc. – generally lead to an outcome that is economically favorable to the common good. This point does *not* mean – and capitalism does not require – that each person act merely for his own individual good and that he view the other's good as a mere means to his own.[24] The free market system does not presuppose or necessarily encourage any such individualism. Rather, the free market system supposes merely that each economic agent has some end or other, of his own choosing – as opposed to an end selected for him by a central command. That end may be selfish, may be the good of the individual, the good of his family, or the good of a larger group – the point is that the regulation or direction of his activities toward the economic good of the whole society is expected to arise (generally speaking) more surely from the ordering of the price system rather than from central planning (a supposition that leaves some room for tinkering with, or modification of the system by governmental actions). The opposite of "self-interest" is not "other-interest" but, roughly, "shaped by planning for the good of the whole by a central authority." The self-interest by which the economic operations of individuals and groups in a free market system are to be motivated and directed could be the fulfillment of a family, church, or other group. The noted economist Milton Friedman and his wife Rose Friedman made this point particularly clearly:

> Narrow preoccupation with the economic market has led to a narrow interpretation of self-interest as myopic selfishness, as exclusive concern with immediate material rewards ... That is a great mistake. Self-interest is not myopic selfishness. It is whatever it is that interests the participants, whatever they value, whatever goals they pursue. The scientist seeking to advance the

[23] David Schindler, *Heart of the World, Center of the Church*, (Grand Rapids, MI: Wm. B. Eerdmans, 1996), 104–137.
[24] Commenting on Adam Smith's famous discussion of the actions of a baker in *Wealth of Nations*, Schindler writes as follows: "Thus the baker bakes a good loaf of bread because that is the way to ensure profit, and thereby to do good business. The baker intends his own good and in the process creates a good also for the other: namely, a good loaf of bread. The good both of the product and of the other is thus instrumentalized to the baker's own self-interest; but Smith's point is that both the baker and his customer are better off for that self-interest" (Schindler, *Heart of the World*, 122). So Schindler views Smith, and capitalism in general, as advocating individualism as the major organizing principle of the economic order, instead of the common good. But as indicated above, "self-interest" need not be interpreted in this individualist manner.

frontiers of his discipline, the missionary seeking to convert infidels to the true faith, the philanthropist seeking to bring comfort to the needy – all are pursuing their interest, as they see them, as they judge them by their own values.[25]

A second point to make in response to Schindler's objection to capitalism is that it fails to take into account the limited scope and limited goal of the political community. Just as the political community need not itself embrace the true faith, but can be (and should be) limited to providing *the conditions* for individuals and families to discern as best they can the truth about God and then, consistent with the public good, pursue and live in accord with the truth they have discerned, likewise, the political community may, and should, encourage generosity and genuine gift of self, but should recognize the limits on how much it can effectively, and without self-defeat, coercively legislate generosity.

4 CRITIQUE OF THE WELFARE STATE

Having denied that those having capital have absolute rights, John Paul states that the correct alternative is a system that pursues free work, enterprise, and participation: "Such a society is not directed against the market, but demands that the market be appropriately controlled by the forces of society and by the State, so as to guarantee that the basic needs of the whole of society are satisfied" (CA, no. 35). From this as a premise John Paul next criticizes the modern "Welfare State":

> In recent years the range of such interventions has vastly expanded, to the point of creating a new type of State, the so-called "Welfare State". This has happened in some countries in order to respond better to many needs and demands, by remedying forms of poverty and deprivation unworthy of the human person. However, excesses and abuses, especially in recent years, have provoked very harsh criticisms of the Welfare State, dubbed the "Social Assistance State". Malfunctions and defects in the Social Assistance State are the result of an inadequate understanding of the tasks proper to the State. (CA, no. 48)

The first problem with the welfare state is that it too diminishes initiative by individuals and families:

> Here again *the principle of subsidiarity* must be respected: a community of a higher order should not interfere in the internal life of a community of a lower order, depriving the latter of its functions, but rather should support it

---

[25] Milton Friedman and Rose Friedman, *Free to Choose, a Personal Statement* (New York: Harcourt, 1980), 27.

in case of need and help to coordinate its activity with the activities of the rest of society, always with a view to the common good. (CA, no. 48)

In fact, the welfare state is in this respect similar to socialism and a disordered capitalist system. The exact same words John Paul uses to describe its tendencies could also be used to convey his conclusions regarding socialism. Not only does the welfare state lead to a loss of free initiative but, like socialism, it also involves excessive bureaucracy:

> By intervening directly and depriving society of its responsibility, the Social Assistance State leads to a loss of human energies and an inordinate increase of public agencies, which are dominated more by bureaucratic ways of thinking than by concern for serving their clients, and which are accompanied by an enormous increase in spending. In fact, it would appear that needs are best understood and satisfied by people who are closest to them and who act as neighbors to those in need. (CA, no. 48)

This is a significant development. Perhaps this is implicit in previous teaching that the state should function according to the principle of subsidiarity. Still, no previous pope characterized a state as a "welfare state" or a "social assistance state." The criticism suggests that at the time that encyclical was written (early 1990s), becoming a welfare state – given its injustices – was a real danger and not just a theoretical possibility. While the criticism does not, perhaps, preclude any specific program – it does not, for example, preclude pensions or unemployment benefits; indeed, these are commended by John Paul as well as by previous popes – the criticism might apply to the way some welfare programs are administered in contemporary countries.

5 THE PROPER ROLE OF THE STATE IN RELATION TO ECONOMICS

The proper task of the state in relation to economic matters is not itself to organize or plan the economic system, but to set the conditions for its flourishing and to protect those who by accident or disability are in need.[26]

Near the end of *Centesimus annus* John Paul once again emphasizes the principle of subsidiarity. The principal task of the state with respect to the economic field, he teaches, is to provide *a framework for* economic initiative rather than to substitute for self-direction on the part of individuals, families, and other associations:

[26] CA, no. 48.

> Economic activity, especially the activity of a market economy, cannot be conducted in an institutional, juridical or political vacuum. On the contrary, it presupposes sure guarantees of individual freedom and private property, as well as a stable currency and efficient public services. Hence the principal task of the State is to guarantee this security, so that those who work and produce can enjoy the fruits of their labors and thus feel encouraged to work efficiently and honestly. (CA, no. 48)

This emphasis on subsidiarity does not mean, however, that the state should have no positive role in regard to economic matters. John Paul also emphatically rejects an extreme libertarian position.

> Another task of the State is that of overseeing and directing the exercise of human rights in the economic sector. However, primary responsibility in this area belongs not to the State but to individuals and to the various groups and associations which make up society . . . This does not mean, however, that the State has no competence in this domain, as was claimed by those who argued against any rules in the economic sphere. Rather, the State has a duty to sustain business activities by creating conditions which will ensure job opportunities, by stimulating those activities where they are lacking or by supporting them in moments of crisis. (CA, no. 48)

The state has the right and duty actually to intervene where monopolies create delays or other obstacles. And the state may intervene and exercise a substitute function, "when a social sector or business area is too weak or just getting under way" (CA, no. 48). However, significantly, he adds that: "Such supplementary interventions, which are justified by urgent reasons touching the common good, must be as brief as possible" (CA, no. 48).

In a passage where John Paul is commenting on *Rerum novarum*, he notes that Leo teaches that the state has a duty to watch over the common good, including its economic aspect, and then John Paul interprets Leo as holding that the state is really *instrumental* to the good of individuals and families: "On the contrary, he frequently insists on necessary limits to the State's intervention and on its instrumental character, inasmuch as the individual, the family and society are prior to the State, and inasmuch as the State exists in order to protect their rights and not stifle them" (CA, no. 11).[27]

---

[27] Here is the Latin for the last sentence: Ex contrario quin immo saepius ille necessarios terminos inculcat intervenientis Status eiusque indolem uti instrumenti, cum unusquisque homo et familia et societas Statum antegrediantur ipseque eo exsistat ut iura tum illius tum earum defendat neve ea opprimat (CA, no. 37).

The subsidiary role of the state in relation to economics is in harmony with its instrumental role in relation to the good of individuals and families seeking the truth and living in accord with the truth.

John Paul links more closely than was done before economic freedom, political freedom, and religious freedom. He says that:

> The Church values the democratic system inasmuch as it ensures the participation of citizens in making political choices, guarantees to the governed the possibility of both electing and holding accountable those who govern them, and of replacing them through peaceful means when appropriate. (*CA*, no. 46)

On John Paul's view an analogous point could be made about *economic* freedom.

Economic freedom and political freedom, says John Paul, are in fact aspects of the more general freedom to seek the truth and live according to it. These three types of freedom are interrelated: "In a certain sense, the source and synthesis of these rights is religious freedom, understood as the right to live in the truth of one's faith and in conformity with one's transcendent dignity as a person" (*CA*, no. 47). This is a significant point. It adds to the importance of economic freedom: economic freedom is all the more important because it is really a component of that more general freedom which consists in a person's freedom to seek the truth and then organize one's life in accord with the truth one has found.[28] Vatican II had taught that the actual primary basis for the obligation of states to grant its citizens religious freedom is not a relativist view of religion, or an individualist view of fulfillment, but the intrinsic goodness of the good of religion, the fact that an integral part of human flourishing is seeking the truth and freely shaping one's life in accord with the truth one has reached. Every person has a duty to seek the truth about God and one's place in the universe, and to live one's life in accord with the truth one has found. But one can fulfill this duty readily only if one has the space or liberty to do so,

[28] Cf. "All of this can be summed up by repeating once more that economic freedom is only one element of human freedom. When it becomes autonomous, when man is seen more as a producer or consumer of goods than as a subject who produces and consumes in order to live, then economic freedom loses its necessary relationship to the human person and ends up by alienating and oppressing him" (*CA*, no. 39). Also: "The apex of development is the exercise of the right and duty to seek God, to know him and to live in accordance with that knowledge. In the totalitarian and authoritarian regimes, the principle that force predominates over reason was carried to the extreme. Man was compelled to submit to a conception of reality imposed on him by coercion, and not reached by virtue of his own reason and the exercise of his own freedom. This principle must be overturned and total recognition must be given to *the rights of the human conscience*, which is bound only to the truth, both natural and revealed" (*CA*, no. 29).

as well as the liberty to express one's belief to others and unite with others for communal religious activity and mutual support.

The significance of economic freedom, as a component in the multilevel freedom that includes political and religious freedom, lies not primarily in the material prosperity it may facilitate. Rather, economic freedom is important primarily because it provides the space and conditions for individuals and families shaping their lives in accord with the truth about God and their place in the universe. It provides conditions for their self-constitution in accord with the moral truth they have been able to discern.

Thus, free market economies can facilitate economic and political freedom, but also – as mentioned above – can facilitate a consumerist mentality. Particular concrete free market economies will have particular and sometimes grave injustices. But those who emphasize the need for government interventions often speak of the free market or capitalism as if the justice of an economy were an all-or-nothing question, as if the economic system can only be either simply just or simply unjust, ignoring the fact that there are usually a multitude of policies within an economic system. Any given capitalist economy is then treated somewhat like a war. It is presumed to be unjust unless and until certain conditions are met, and when those conditions are not met the system as a whole is judged to be unjust and immoral.[29] By contrast, John Paul looks at economies in advanced countries and instead of condemning them as whole entities approves of some elements and disapproves of others.

As in the social teachings of his predecessors, John Paul's teaching contains various principles that have some tensions with respect to each other. The principle of subsidiarity is often in tension with the principle of solidarity. Free initiative must be protected and promoted – so, less government is better. However, the rights of workers to a job, a just wage, unemployment security, and so on might be interpreted to mean that more government than would

---

[29] For example, in his commentary on *Centesimus annus*, Daniel Finn sets out four conditions for a just economic system and then says: "No one of these can guarantee the morality of an economic system, but the four together come as close to an assurance as is possible . . . But we can say that if all four were indeed resolved in accord with the standard of Catholic social thought, then although individuals would still suffer from misfortune or from mistakes they have made, the ensuing problems would not be evidence of injustice. The economic system could then merit a kind of conditional moral approbation from the perspective of Catholic social thought." Finn, "John Paul II and the Moral Ecology of Markets," 457–458. On this approach – not uncommon, I think – the system as a whole is easily condemned. There is a kind of unity to the economic activities in a system, but there does not seem to be the same kind of moral unity as there is in, say, a war – a communal act, the unity of a decision by a community to do something; and so, the moral assessment will have to be more complex.

otherwise be the case is called for. The balance between these two emphases does not seem to be by way of a clear picture or model. Both principles must be embraced and it seems that, having embraced both, reasonable people may still disagree about particular policies. And so it is difficult to say of a specific policy that it is required, or definitely excluded, by Catholic Social Teaching. Provision of unemployment insurance seems to be clearly desirable – since there do not seem to be any other mechanisms to protect workers in a dynamic economy. But even that could be very difficult to have in an economy just beginning the dynamic phase of growth.

Most governmental economic policies are means toward just ends. They have various side effects, and the ends for which they are adopted could be furthered by alternative means – and those in turn would have a different set of side effects. For example, as we saw above, on the one hand John Paul affirms the right to active participation or free initiative of individuals and families in the economic sphere. On the other hand, he affirms that states have a duty to implement policies aimed at decreasing unemployment. Speaking of just reforms called for by Leo XIII to "restore dignity to work as the free activity of man," he then says the following: "These reforms imply that society and the State will both assume responsibility, especially for protecting the worker from the nightmare of unemployment." But he acknowledges later in that encyclical the tension between these two principles – the emphasis on free initiative, on the one hand, and the duty of the state to intervene for a goal such as full (or near full) employment, on the other. He there says: "The State could not directly ensure the right to work for all its citizens unless it controlled every aspect of economic life and restricted the free initiative of individuals" (CA, no. 48). In what might at first seem to be an attempt to resolve that tension, in the next sentences he adds the following:

> This does not mean, however, that the State has no competence in this domain, as was claimed by those who argued against any rules in the economic sphere. Rather, the State has a duty to sustain business activities by creating conditions which will ensure job opportunities, by stimulating those activities where they are lacking or by supporting them in moments of crisis. (CA, no. 48)

In the first sentence he makes the point that the solution to this tension is not to conclude that the state has no duties with respect to unemployment (or wages, working conditions, etc.), as a radical libertarian would conclude. The next sentence appears to be an attempt to resolve the tension by means of a distinction. It sounds like the assertion that the state should in general act only indirectly. Applied to the full employment issue, that would mean, apparently, that the state (in general) should not try to boost employment considerably by itself being the employer but by creating conditions that will boost employment. But it is not clear where to draw the line between setting conditions for economic activities versus directly regulating them. John Paul is quite aware of this tension, and this tension does not mean the principles are false. It does, however, point to the need for caution in regard to how detailed one expects the guidance to be from Catholic Social Teaching.

CONCLUSION

Throughout his papal writings on social questions, John Paul emphasized – in what seems to be a correction to the scholarly tradition of commentary on Catholic Social Teaching (as distinct from the encyclicals themselves) that he is not proposing a model for the ideal society, but instead an orientation or an affirmation of key principles:

> The Church has no models to present; models that are real and truly effective can only arise within the framework of different historical situations, through the efforts of all those who responsibly confront concrete problems in all their social, economic, political and cultural aspects, as these interact with one another. For such a task the Church offers her social teaching as an *indispensable and ideal orientation*, a teaching which, as already mentioned, recognizes the positive value of the market and of enterprise, but which at the same time points out that these need to be oriented towards the common good. (*CA*, no. 43)[30]

In short, Pope St. John Paul II significantly developed the Church's social teaching. These developments are in the direction of placing more emphasis on free initiative in the economic realm, a recognition of the efficiency of the free market mechanism, and a criticism of the welfare state, while reaffirming the traditional doctrines of the universal destination of material good and the duty in justice to assist the poor.

[30] Cf. *SRS*, no. 41–42.

8

Pope Benedict XVI on the Political and Social Order

J. Brian Benestad

Joseph Ratzinger/Pope Benedict XVI (b. 1927) has extensive reflections on the political and social order dispersed throughout his many writings before and during his papacy (the latter period encompassing April 19, 2005, to February 28, 2013). One chapter would not suffice to present the whole range of his thought, but its essence can be grasped by focusing on selected writings and addresses. Although a prolific writer on political and social matters, Joseph Ratzinger never wrote a magnum opus on Catholic Social Teaching (CST), nor did he write anything that would be the equivalent of his famous *Introduction to Christianity* (1968, German edition; 1969, English edition). Before becoming pope, he just wrote occasional pieces that addressed the issues of the day. He did this kind of writing on a high level primarily under the influence of St. Augustine. He was adept at relating Catholic doctrine and morality, including CST. Ratzinger was nothing short of brilliant in discerning contemporary currents of thought and the influence of modern political philosophy on the Church and the world. In explaining Catholic teaching, he often took into account the criticisms of Christianity made by philosophers such as Nietzsche, Marx, Bacon, Kant, and Sartre. He understood well how some contemporary understandings of social justice could undermine Catholic teaching on faith and morals, but that a sound understanding of CST could immensely benefit secular society, even save it from itself. Ratzinger further understood that faith and reason had to work together to develop an adequate CST, and that they had to correct one another's aberrations in the search for truth. This is becoming ever more important today, because the very survival of this world is at stake. "The absence of God ... [may become] so powerful that man will get into a moral tailspin and that the destruction of the world, apocalypse, ruin lie before Us. We must reckon with that possibility. The apocalyptic diagnosis cannot be ruled out, but even then it remains the case that God protects those who seek him: love is the end, more powerful than hate."[1]

To explore the political and social thought of this most insightful theologian I will first examine insights from Ratzinger's prepapal publications: *The Ratzinger Report* (1985), *Church, Ecumenism and Politics* (1988), *Salt of the Earth* (1997), *God and the World* (2002), *God Is Near Us* (2003), *Truth and Tolerance: Christian Belief and World Religions* (2004), *The Dialectics of Secularization, On Reason and Religion* (2006), *Values in a Time of Upheaval* (2006), *The Essential Pope Benedict XVI: His Essential Writings and Speeches* (2007), and *Joseph Ratzinger in Communio: Volume I. The Unity of the Church* (2010). In the second and longer part of the chapter I will draw from selected papal writings: his three encyclicals, *Deus caritas est* (2005), *Spe salvi* (2007), and *Caritas in veritate* (2009); *Jesus of Nazareth* (2007), a memorable speech in Rome on the four basic principles of Catholic Social Teaching (2008); and, finally, three well-known speeches delivered during his travels outside of Italy in Westminster, England (2010), Berlin (2011), and Regensburg (2006).

PREPAPAL WRITINGS

A Very Brief Comparison between Islam and Christianity

Let us begin by comparing Islam to Christianity in the words of Cardinal Ratzinger: "Islam ... simply does not have the separation of the political and the religious sphere that Christianity has had from the beginning. The Koran is a total religious law, which regulates the whole of political and social life and insists that the whole order of life be Islamic. *Sharia* shapes society from beginning to end."[2] Simply put, Islam is an all-pervasive law; Christianity is a faith with no pretension to dictate what must be done in every area of life. Where faith is silent, reason must provide guidance. That is why Augustine relied on Cicero and Plato, and Aquinas on Aristotle when they addressed political questions. Catholic Social Teaching (CST), properly understood, does not dictate what has to be done in every area in the political and social order, but tries to persuade Catholics and non-Catholics alike to accept certain principles that would provide a solid foundation for law and politics. For example, the fundamental building block of Europe and every healthy

---

[1] Joseph Cardinal Ratzinger, *Salt of the Earth: the Church at the End of the Millennium, An Interview with Peter Seewald* (San Francisco: Ignatius Press, 1997), 221.

[2] Ratzinger, *Salt of the Earth*, 244.

society, Ratzinger argues, is respect for the dignity of the human person, the most solid foundation of which is the conviction that God created man and woman in his image and likeness.[3] A corollary of this fundamental principle is the protection of human rights, especially the right to life.[4] The second crucial element is support for monogamous marriage and the family, coupled with discouragement of divorce, cohabitation before marriage, and same-sex marriage. It is in the family where people most easily learn to receive and give love. The third building block of any society is "reverence for that which is holy to other persons and reverence for the Holy One, God."[5] That is to say, the good in all religions should be respected as should the members of all religions. If the three building blocks are in place, then politics, the realm of moral reason, has a better chance of achieving its goals: justice and peace.

Catholic Social Teaching, of course, counsels the pursuit of justice and peace with moderate expectations of success.[6] Otherwise stated, "Catholic social teaching is not aware of any utopia but rather develops models of the best possible way of shaping human affairs in a given historical situation. For this reason, it rejects the myth of revolution and seeks the way of reform."[7] This is the only thing to do in the face of the fact that freedom will always be more or less misused in every generation, as Augustine taught.[8] That is to say, a utopian political order will never be within reach because not enough citizens will ever practice virtue in every aspect of their lives or even understand what has to be done to establish a good society. With these preliminary remarks on the table let us plunge deeper into the subtle thought of Joseph Ratzinger/Pope Benedict XVI on CST.

The Duty of Individual Christians Toward the State and Society

In *Church, Ecumenism, and Politics*, Cardinal Ratzinger explains the deepest reason for taking great pains to promote the survival and flourishing of every state and society, namely, God's Word. The cardinal quotes what the prophet Jeremiah says to the Jews exiled in Babylon: "Build houses and live in them; plant gardens and eat their produce ... Seek the welfare of the city where

---

[3] Joseph Cardinal Ratzinger, *Values in a Time of Upheaval* (San Francisco: Ignatius Press, 2006), 146, 112, 159.

[4] Ratzinger, *Values in a Time of Upheaval*, 28.

[5] Ratzinger, *Values in a Time of Upheaval*, 148–149.

[6] Joseph Cardinal Ratzinger, *Church, Ecumenism and Politics* (New York: Crossroad, 1988), 148–149.

[7] Ratzinger, *Church, Ecumenism and Politics*, 272.

[8] Ratzinger, *Values in a Time of Upheaval*, 121.

I have sent you into exile. And pray to the Lord on its behalf, for in its welfare you will find your welfare."[9] Clearly, Jeremiah is saying that God wants people to look after the political community in which they live. Commenting on the relevance of Jeremiah's exhortation for Christians and on related texts in the New Testament, Ratzinger writes, "The Christian is always someone who seeks to maintain the state in the sense that he or she does the positive, the good that holds states together. He or she ... is convinced that only strengthening what is good can ever dissolve what is evil and diminish the power both of evil and of evil people."[10] In other words, it is the God-given duty of all Christians to work for the benefit of the temporal society in which they live. Each person "has his particular gift. No one is superfluous, no one is in vain, everyone must try to recognize what his life's call is and how he can best live up to the call that is waiting for him."[11] Ratzinger goes so far as to say that "each person stands in direct relationship with God and each has thus in the great web of world history a significant place and role that have been assigned to him and by means of which he can make an irreplaceable contribution to history as a whole."[12] This is the kind of statement that you would expect Ratzinger to make about only very gifted individuals, but he is talking about everyone. He also maintains that God "speaks [to all individuals] through signs and events, through our fellowmen."[13] In other words, God makes use of family, friends, and neighbors to lead us to salvation and to help us see what role we can play in the public square.

All states "must respect the higher law of God. The refusal to adore the emperor and the refusal in general to worship the state are on the most fundamental level a rejection of the totalitarian state."[14] If the Church is going to stand its ground in the face of a powerful state, bent on tyranny, injustice and the suppression of freedom, enough of the faithful must remain true to their conscience. As Ratzinger says, "The destruction of conscience is the real precondition for totalitarian obedience and domination."[15] The cardinal reinforces his point by quoting a statement of Hitler preserved in *Conversations with Hitler* by Hermann Rauschning. "I liberate man ... from

---

9   Jeremiah 29:5–7, quoted in Cardinal Joseph Ratzinger, *Church, Ecumenism and Politics* (New York: Crossroad, 1988), 149.
10   Ratzinger, *Church, Ecumenism and Politics*, 150. The other New Testament texts are 1 Timothy 2:1–2; 1 Peter 2:12, 2:17, 4:15–16.
11   Ratzinger, *Salt of the Earth*, 42.
12   Joseph Cardinal Ratzinger, *God and the World: A Conversation with Peter Seewald* (San Francisco: Ignatius, 2002), 76.
13   Ratzinger, *Salt of the Earth*, 30.
14   Ratzinger, *Values in a Time of Upheaval*, 20.
15   Ratzinger, *Church, Ecumenism and Politics*, 165.

the filthy and degrading torments inflicted on himself by a chimera called conscience and morality, and from the claims of a freedom and personal autonomy that only a very few can ever be up to." Hermann Goering spoke in a similar vein to Rauschning: "I have no conscience. My conscience is called Adolf Hitler."[16] What every society needs are individuals who are willing to suffer in order to remain true to their conscience. Ultimately, we owe our freedom to the martyrs who willingly accept death to resist the state's usurpation of power and attack on the freedom of its citizens.[17] In sum, the purification of conscience is "the precondition of every social reform, for every improvement in human affairs. For the reform of human relationships rests in the first place on a reinforcement of moral strength."[18] It is gazing upon the Lord Jesus Christ in adoration that purifies the conscience. Benedict goes so far as to say: "Without adoration, there is no transformation of the world," because Eucharistic adoration by fostering love of God provides an effective "'education in active love of one's neighbor'."[19]

Not surprisingly, Ratzinger maintains that very wise and righteous men and women sometimes can accomplish great things by freely following their consciences. "God promised Abraham that he would not destroy the city of Sodom if ten righteous men were found there." The lesson Ratzinger draws from this event is that we "ought to do all we can to ensure that the ten righteous ones who can save a city are never lacking."[20] This is especially a challenge for the family, Church, and educational institutions, because there is no guarantee that faith will necessarily lead to a better world in history. Ratzinger believes that this Augustinian insight is right on the mark.[21] What has to happen is that more than a few individuals come to understand that they have a personal responsibility for the common good of the society in which they live. Ratzinger makes this point by telling the story of Andrei Sakharov, a Soviet physicist, who accepted mistreatment and suffering for arguing before military and government authorities that the use of nuclear weapons had to be guided by ethical considerations. The authorities told Sakharov that he should just improve the weapons and leave decisions as to their use to the government. Ratzinger comments, "Sakharov insisted again and again, with great

---

[16]   *Church, Ecumenism and Politics*, 165.
[17]   *Church, Ecumenism and Politics*, 174.
[18]   Joseph Cardinal Ratzinger, *God Is Near Us: the Eucharist, the Heart of Life* (San Francisco: Ignatius Press, 2003), 98.
[19]   Ratzinger, *God Is Near Us*, 93, 98 [quoting Pope John Paul II, Encyclical Letter *Dominicae cenae* (On the Mystery and Worship of the Eucharist) (1980), no. 6].
[20]   Ratzinger, *Values in a Time of Upheaval*, 121.
[21]   *Values in a Time of Upheaval*, 120.

urgency, on this responsibility that each individual bears for the totality. He perceived his own mission when he perceived the reality of his own responsibility."[22] Ratzinger clearly implies that Sakharov is one of the ten righteous ones so desperately needed by every society.

When great individuals are unable to accomplish great things, such as prevent the outbreak of war, then they and their followers must bring about mutual forgiveness and reconciliation among warring nations, such as happened after World War II. At that time men like Konrad Adenauer, Robert Schuman, Alcide De Gasperi, and Charles DeGaulle insured the victory of a reconciliation policy between Germany and the Allies. People like John Foster Dulles helped make the Japanese Peace Treaty a "treaty of reconciliation" between Japan and the United States. Reconciliation did not happen after World War I. Rather, Ratzinger notes, "the enmity and bitterness remained alive between the warring nations, especially between Germany and France, poisoning people's souls. The Treaty of Versailles deliberately set out to humiliate Germany, imposing burdens that radicalized people and thereby opened the door to Hitler's dictatorship."[23] It stands in sharp contrast, he says, to "the great history of reconciliation" that followed World War II.[24]

The Role of the Church in the Public Square and Its Primary Mission, Salvation

Besides calling on the lay faithful and extraordinary leaders to make their contributions to the society in which they live, Cardinal Ratzinger reflects very carefully on the role of the Church in the public square. In a 1988 lecture appropriately entitled "Peace and Justice in Crisis" Joseph Ratzinger points out what the Church should and should not do to benefit the political and social order. "The task of the Church in this area is … first and foremost 'education,' taking the word in the great sense it had for the Greek philosophers. She must break open the prison of positivism and awaken man's receptivity to the truth and to God, and thus to the power of conscience."[25] The great sense of education for the Greek philosophers means the formation of character and the teaching of wisdom or truth about the most important things, such as the good life and the good society. Escaping from positivism, one of Ratzinger's recurring themes, means the realization that the use of

---

[22] *Values in a Time of Upheaval*, 46.
[23] *Values in a Time of Upheaval*, 124.
[24] *Values in a Time of Upheaval*, 125.
[25] Benedict XVI, "Peace and Justice in Crisis," in *Joseph Ratzinger in Communio, vol. I: The Unity of the Church* (Grand Rapids, MI: W. B. Eerdmans Publishing company, 2010), 114.

reason in the natural sciences is only one valid use of reason, and not the most important, which is the use of reason in the disciplines of philosophy and theology. Catholic education also creates a receptivity or docility in the souls of individuals and thus makes possible the formation of conscience. The well-educated and well-formed laity are ready and disposed to work for justice and peace, and are obligated to work tirelessly for these temporal goals both within and outside the political process.

What the Church should not do is to become "an organization for direct political action." Ratzinger makes this important point because the Church "does not have any specific answers to concrete political questions."[26] The Church does, of course, rightly claim to recognize political evils such as legalized physician-assisted suicide and a healthcare system that doesn't work for a vast number of citizens. However, the church is in no position to propose a just tax code or devise the best health-care system for a particular country. "The leaders of the Church have no authority to take direct political action. They have not received a mandate for it from the faithful, certainly not from the Lord himself."[27] In addition, CST also attempts to persuade the clergy and the laity not to impose debatable policy options on people in the name of Catholicism. As Vatican Council II taught, there are a variety of legitimate ways to apply the fundamental principles of CST in the political arena.[28]

To promote justice and peace effectively, the Church must do what she does best. "Consequently, the Church does less, not more, for peace if she abandons her own sphere of faith, education, witness, counsel, prayer and serving love, and changes into an organization for direct political action ... Only when she respects her limits is she limitless and only then can her ministry of love and witness become a call to all men."[29] The strength of the Church as Church is not to devise political strategies to accomplish political goals, however worthy. That is the role of the Catholic laity.

The Church makes her best contribution to the public square when she seeks the salvation of all people by working to bring about communion between God and human beings and communion among all men and women through their communion with God. In Ratzinger's words, the "starting point of *communion* is ... the encounter with the Son of God, Jesus Christ, who comes to men and women through the Church's proclamation. So there

[26]   Benedict XVI, "Peace and Justice in Crisis," 115.
[27]   "Peace and Justice in Crisis," 116.
[28]   Cf. Vatican II, Pastoral Constitution *Gaudium et spes* (Pastoral Constitution On the Church in the Modern World) (1965), no. 43.
[29]   Pope Benedict XVI, "Peace and Justice in Crisis," 116.

arises communion among human beings, which in turn is based on *communio* with the Triune God."[30] To this end the Church "cannot act according to the motto: What is going to be possible; what is not? She is not there in order to discover the most acceptable form of compromise, but to hold out to people, without distortion, the whole magnitude of God's Word and his will – even if this speaks against herself and against her own spokesmen."[31] The laity needs to be fully informed and formed in order to appreciate and embrace the beauty of *communio* with God and among themselves. Compromise is for the realm of politics, where wisdom has to be reconciled with consent. The Church should not, for example, withhold the fullness of its teaching on marriage and other controversial teachings in homilies and in catechetical programs. Ratzinger does not hesitate to speak against episcopal spokesmen when they withhold the truth: "The words of the Bible and the Church Fathers rang in my ears, those sharp condemnations of shepherds who are like mute dogs; in order to avoid conflict, they let the poison spread. Peace is not the first civic duty, and a bishop whose only concern is not to have any problems and to gloss over as many conflicts as possible is an image I find repulsive."[32] Ratzinger holds the whole Church, not just bishops, to a very high standard even though he knows that the number of active participants in the life of the Church will be greatly reduced. As a minority Church, "she will live in small, vital circles of really convinced believers who live their faith. But precisely in this way she will, biblically speaking, become the salt of the earth again."[33]

The Hostility of the Culture to the Church's Mission and to Its Role in the Public Square

Because of his profound understanding of modern philosophy and modern cultures, Cardinal Ratzinger is at his very best in discerning why the Catholic Church and the Catholic laity struggle to make their contribution to the political and social order. Ratzinger argues that powerful strains of modern culture are not receptive to the influence of the Catholic Church and the Catholic laity in the public square. Among other things, he directs his readers' attention to the dictatorship of relativism, to understandings of autonomy and freedom divorced from truth, to pathologies of reason and religion, and to

[30] John F. Thornton and Susan B. Varenne, eds., *The Essential Pope Benedict XVI: His Central Writings and Speeches* (San Francisco: Harper, 2007), 89.

[31] Ratzinger, *God and the World*, 65.

[32] Ratzinger, *Salt of the Earth*, 82.

[33] *Salt of the Earth*, 222.

blindness regarding the nature of human existence caused by the practice and justification of abortion.

We first turn our attention to the presence of relativism in the culture. In his homily at the mass opening the papal conclave of 2005 Cardinal Joseph Ratzinger made one of his most memorable and insightful statements about the contemporary era: "We are building a dictatorship of relativism that does not recognize anything as definitive and whose ultimate standard consists solely of one's ego and desires."[34] What makes relativism a dictatorship is that opinions are imposed on everyone even though there are no grounds for doing so. Without rational arguments, "forms of behavior and thinking are being presented as the only reasonable ones," as though some kind of truth dictated such a policy.[35] For example, people try to induce the Catholic Church to give up its teaching on marriage in favor of same-sex marriage. Because relativistic opinions are being imposed today, Ratzinger believes that the Church must not only have the courage to proclaim the possibility of arriving at truth, but also the wisdom to teach truths relevant to the public square, which are accessible either to faith or reason. This is, in fact, exactly what Joseph Ratzinger did in his extensive reflections on the political and social order. He did not, however, seek to impose his views, but to persuade people of their truth.

Ratzinger knows that to speak of truth in today's climate is highly problematic because of the widespread tendency to understand freedom apart from truth. In an article entitled "Truth and Freedom" he writes, "The radical cry for freedom demands man's liberation from his very essence as man, so that he may become the 'new man.'" This means liberation from any truth about what it means to be a human being. The goal of "modernity's struggle for freedom is to be at last like a god who depends on nothing and no one, whose own freedom is not restricted by that of another."[36] To bring out the radical nature of modernity's view on freedom Ratzinger indicates what it means for freedom to take its bearings by truth in a brief discussion of the Decalogue. It "is at once the self-presentation and self-exposition of God, the exposition of what man is, the luminous manifestation of his truth ... To live the Decalogue means to live our Godlikeness, to correspond to the truth of our being and thus to do the good." On the other hand, the new man of whom Ratzinger speaks doesn't have a human nature that acts as a guide for his freedom. He chooses his own

---

[34]   Benedict XVI, *Light of the World: A Conversation with Peter Seewald* (San Francisco: Ignatius Press, 2010), 51.

[35]   *Light of the World*, 53.

[36]   Thornton and Varenne, *The Essential Pope Benedict XVI*, 347.

values without guidance from his nature or essence. Ratzinger concludes, "We must also lay to rest once and for all the dream of the absolute autonomy and self-sufficiency of reason. Human reason needs the support of the great religious traditions of humanity."[37]

Not all religious traditions will be of help to reason. In several of his writings Ratzinger warns his readers that there are dangerous pathologies in religion (terrorism based on religious convictions) as well as pathologies of reason (the atomic bomb and cloning). Accordingly, Ratzinger says, "I would speak of a necessary relatedness between reason and faith and between reason and religion, which are called to purify and help one another. They need each other, and they must acknowledge this mutual need."[38] The aberrations of religion can be corrected by reason and the errors of reason by faith. This is a key theme in Ratzinger's thought. Note that in this context Ratzinger uses the terms faith, Christian faith, and religion interchangeably.

The justification and practice of abortion is another aberration of reason, and sometimes of faith. The unborn child is dependent on the mother for his life and when born still depends on the mother or someone else for nurture and care. Dependence is the essential human condition not just for the child, but for all adults as well. "[T]he child in its mother's womb makes us most vividly aware of the nature of human existence as a whole: it is also true of the adult that he can exist only with the other person and from him and thus is forever dependent on this being."[39] All human beings need services from others throughout their lives and are called at various times to provide services. There is no getting around this situation, although, under the influence of the modern fascination with unrestricted autonomy, people unrealistically desire to be free of their need for the services of others and free of their obligations toward others. In other words, humanity "would like to be freed from its own human nature."[40] Such an aspiration is a desire "to be like a god, dependent on nothing and no one." Pope Benedict goes on to say that this is not even the right way to conceive of God. The true God "is, of his own nature, being-for (Father), being-from (Son), and being-with (Holy Spirit). Yet man is in the image of God precisely because the being for, from, and with constitute the basic anthropological shape." To deny this dependence is to deny the truth

---

[37] *The Essential Pope Benedict XVI*, 353.
[38] Jurgen Habermas and Joseph Ratzinger, *The Dialectics of Secularization, On Reason and Religion* (San Francisco: Ignatius Press, 2006), 78.
[39] Joseph Cardinal Ratzinger, *Truth and Tolerance: Christian Belief and World Religions* (San Francisco: Ignatius, 2004), 247.
[40] *Truth and Tolerance*, 247.

about human nature and the human condition; it is "a rebellion against being human in itself."[41]

The practice of abortion conveys a false understanding of human nature, especially human freedom and human dependence, and thereby makes it more difficult to understand the meaning of human existence. "Freedom to destroy oneself or to destroy others is not freedom, but a diabolical parody."[42] Without an accurate grasp of freedom, human beings cannot accurately understand their relationship with God or others. Otherwise stated, the wrong-headed understanding of freedom undermines the teaching of anthropology and ethics. Every abortion is a practical denial of what it means to be a human being.

The Culture Also Causes a Distorted Transformation of the Christian Faith

In addition, there is the skewed understanding of Christianity itself caused by the influence of modern thought and modern culture. Catholics are induced to misunderstand their own faith. Perhaps the most egregious examples of this phenomenon are the influences of Marxist thought and historicist relativism on the understanding of Christian faith. An example of this first phenomenon in various parts of the world is the transformation of the Catholic faith brought about by a Marxist-inspired theology of liberation. (Ratzinger does not deal in *The Ratzinger Report* with theologies of liberation that remain in communion with the Church.) This deviant theology sees itself as "a new way of understanding Christianity as a whole," which requires attempting "to recast the whole Christian reality in the categories of politico-social liberation praxis."[43] It also believes that the Marxist interpretation of history has been "scientifically established," and is therefore normative for Christians. "This means that the world must be interpreted in terms of the class struggle and that the only choice is between capitalism and Marxism."[44] While predominantly in Latin America, Marxist liberation theology has been generated by theologians in Europe and North America and is found in Africa, India, Ceylon, the Philippines, and Taiwan.

The alliance of liberation theology with Marxism decisively affects the interpretation of Scripture and the signs of the times. No longer do the

---

[41] *Truth and Tolerance,* 248.
[42] *Truth and Tolerance,* 248.
[43] Joseph Cardinal Ratzinger with Vittorio Messori, *The Ratzinger Report* (San Francisco: Ignatius Press, 1985), 175, 176.
[44] *The Ratzinger Report,* 180.

hierarchy and the *sensus fidei* of the laity play an important role in the under-standing and interpretation of Scripture. It is the experience of the people or community engaged in the class struggle on behalf of the poor that has the decisive input in clarifying the meaning of Scripture and in determining the best course of action to take in the pursuit of justice. The "community 'interprets' the events on the basis of its 'experience' and thus discovers what its 'praxis' should be." In this perspective "the 'Church of the people' becomes the antagonist of the hierarchical Church." The people no longer need to take their bearings by the teachings of the Church on faith and morals. Their experience in the struggle for justice teaches them how to act effectively. Finally, it is history that takes the place of God and ultimately brings salvation. "History is accordingly a process of progressive liberation; history is the real revelation and hence the real interpreter of the Bible."[45]

The basic premises of liberation theology, of course, lead to a new under-standing of faith, hope, and charity. Faith becomes "'fidelity to history.'" Hope now means "'confidence in the future,'" that is to say, confidence in the successful outcome of the class struggle. "Love consists in the 'option for the poor,' i.e., it coincides with opting for the class struggle." Taking sides in a politically partisan manner is now the new way to fulfill God's command to love your neighbor. Liberation theologians keep the focus on the kingdom of God, "the fundamental concept of the preaching of Jesus," but understand it in partisan terms and with a view to praxis.[46]

Ratzinger's concluding paragraph on liberation theology summarizes its fundamental error:

> It is also painful to be confronted with the illusion, so essentially un-Christian, which is present among priests and theologians, that a new man and a new world can be created, not by calling each individual to conversion, but only by changing the social and economic structures. For it is precisely personal sin that is in reality at the root of unjust social structures. Those who really desire a more human society need to begin with the root, not with the trunk and branches, of the tree of injustice. The issue here is one of funda-mental Christian truths, yet they are deprecatingly dismissed as "alienating" and "spiritualistic."[47]

This emphasis on personal sin as the root of unjust social structures will appear again in Pope Benedict's first encyclical, *Deus caritas est,* and in other writings.

[45]   *The Ratzinger Report,* 181, 182.
[46]   *The Ratzinger Report,* 182, 183.
[47]   *The Ratzinger Report,* 190.

In addition to Marxist-inspired liberation theology, the other great cause of
the distortion of Christianity in the minds of Christians is the pervasive
influence of historicism and dehellenization in contemporary life. This subject will be addressed in my discussion of Pope Benedict's Regensburg speech
at the end of this chapter.

PAPAL WRITINGS

Deus caritas est: *Virtue and the Purification of Reason as the Path to Justice and Charity*

Turning now to Pope Benedict's papal writings, we look at *Deus caritas est*
(December 25, 2005), his first encyclical. Pope Benedict indicates that the very
nature of the Church requires Catholics to take most seriously their obligation
to help those in need. "The Church cannot neglect the service of charity any
more than she can neglect the sacraments and the word."[48] The question
naturally arises whether the Church's love of the poor should lead it to
participate in the political process. *Deus caritas est* begins to answer this
question by reflecting on the roles of the Church and state in promoting
justice. Pope Benedict XVI says, "The just ordering of society and the state is
a central responsibility of politics." This work, always a political battle, is not
the responsibility of the Church. What then is the role of the Church and its
social doctrine with respect to justice?

The aim of that doctrine "is simply to help purify reason and to contribute,
here and now, to the acknowledgment and attainment of what is just."
Because people are blinded by their interests and love of power, they have
difficulty reasoning about justice and seeing what it requires in particular
instances. To be an effective instrument, reason "must undergo constant
purification." As a part of the work of purifying reason the Church forms the
conscience of people, builds their character, and motivates them to act justly.
Still otherwise stated, the Church has a significant role in bringing about
"openness of mind and will to the demands of the common good."[49] In this
perspective the Church *indirectly*, but powerfully, contributes to the realization of justice in society and the state. We will soon see that Pope Benedict's
highly regarded speeches delivered in England and Berlin also demonstrate
the truth of this statement, especially by purifying reason and motivating
people to act.

---

[48] Benedict XVI, Encyclical Letter *Deus caritas est* (On Christian Love) (2005), no. 22.
[49] *DCE*, no. 28.

In a subsequent section of the encyclical Pope Benedict does add that the "*direct* duty to work for a just structuring of society, on the other hand, is proper to the lay faithful" (my emphasis).[50] They have the responsibility to work for policies that will best contribute to the realization of the common good. For example, on the basis of more or less limited knowledge the lay faithful will endorse various positions on health care, taxes, immigration policy, decisions about the wisdom of going to war, and so on. The Church as Church wisely does not endorse debatable policy options as the laity must do to fulfill their responsibilities as citizens. The laity will also contribute to the just structuring of society by practicing the virtues in their family life, at work, and in their relations with neighbors, e.g., by engaging in the spiritual and corporal works of mercy.

The pope explicitly connects what he says about the purification of reason and virtue to the establishment of just structures in society. He argues that "just structures are neither established nor proven effective in the long run" unless the Church helps to purify reason and moves people to act ethically in all areas of their lives.[51] In other words, a just society is not possible unless individuals are just. The corollary is that there will be so much injustice in the structures of society as there is injustice in the souls of individual citizens. This is also the thought of Augustine, Thomas Aquinas, and Thomas More.

Another major point that Benedict XVI makes in his encyclical is about the relation between justice and charity. "Love – *caritas* – will always prove necessary, even in the most just society ... There will always be suffering which cries out for consolation and help. There will always be loneliness. There will always be situations of material need where help in the form of concrete love of neighbor is indispensable."[52] Benedict XVI implies that those arguing for the sufficiency of justice in society do not really understand the nature of a human being, who does not live "by bread alone." Men and women need to give and receive love in order to be happy. A society where people only receive their due would indeed be a cold place. By these remarks the pope is responding to the Marxist objection that with the establishment of a just social order people would "no longer have to depend on charity."

The last point I would like to address in *Deus caritas est* is the encyclical's admonition to avoid two extremes in approaching the reform of the political and social order: inertia in the face of overwhelming tasks and the embrace of some ideology in view of "fully resolving every problem" such as the reliance

---

[50]   DCE, no. 29.
[51]   DCE, no. 29.
[52]   DCE, no. 28.

on Marxism by some liberation theologians.[53] This is the same point that Thomas More makes in Book One of his *Utopia*.

Spe salvi: *Preserving the Moral Treasury of Humanity and Belief in Eternal Life*

Spe salvi (2007) reiterates Pope Benedict's basic argument that the attainment of a just society depends on the practice of virtue by individuals. So he says with emphasis, "Are we not perhaps seeing once again, in the light of current history, that no positive world order can prosper where souls are overgrown?"[54] Just as a garden can be overgrown with weeds, so souls can be overgrown with sins and vices. In the measure that this happens, the prospects for a decent world order diminish.

Pope Benedict then discusses attempts in the modern period to have a reasonably just society as well as comfort and health without overcoming the problems of overgrown souls and the absence of solidarity among people. Originally, "the recovery of what man had lost through the expulsion from Paradise was expected from faith in Jesus Christ: herein lay redemption. Now this Redemption is no longer expected from faith, but from the newly discovered link between science and praxis."[55] Faith is not denied, but is relegated to private affairs and to the other world. Hope for the future is now derived from faith in progress, which results from the Baconian project, the conquest of nature by science in view of man's comfort and health.

Reliance on science and technology for hope, however, proved to be insufficient. So, there was a turn to politics. Benedict explains this turn by summarizing what Marx expected from the political process. "Progress towards the better, towards the definitively good world, no longer comes from science but from politics – from a scientifically conceived politics that recognizes the structure of history and society and thus points out the road towards revolution, towards all-encompassing change."[56] The key change for Marx was, of course, socializing the means of production as the way to bring about the New Jerusalem, a society in which people would no longer be unjust to each other.

Pope Benedict dismisses the exaggerated hopes from science and politics with common-sense observations. He mentions Theodore Adorno's point that progress brought about by science and technology is always ambiguous

---

[53] DCE, no. 36.
[54] Benedict XVI, Encyclical Letter *Spe salvi* (On Christian Hope) (2007), no. 15.
[55] SS, no. 16.
[56] SS, no. 20.

because it can produce both good and evil. "If technical progress is not matched by corresponding progress in man's ethical formation, in man's inner growth (cf. Eph. 3:16; 2 Cor. 4:16), then it is not progress at all, but a threat for man and the world."[57] Think of nuclear weapons, for example, in the hands of terrorists! While we can reasonably expect continuous progress in the areas of science and technology, we cannot reasonably expect similar progress in moral behavior. Why not? Every human being and every generation have the choice either "to draw upon the moral treasury of the whole of humanity" or to reject that treasury. This means that scientific and technological progress will always be a two-edged sword. Some individuals or some generations may lose contact with the moral treasury or may simply choose to ignore it. This is, indeed, happening today in the area of biotechnology.

Because the moral treasury of humanity "is present as an appeal to freedom and a possibility for it ... [t]he right state of human affairs, the moral well-being of the world can never be guaranteed simply through structures alone, however good they are."[58] Not that structures are unimportant: they must, however, be animated by people with wisdom and virtue. Since each generation has to produce enough of those people to make a difference, "the kingdom of good will never be definitively established in the world."[59] Every generation must seek to understand the moral treasury of humanity and make it accessible to more and more people. That is exactly what Catholic Social Doctrine attempts to do for the citizens and nations of the world.

Given Pope Benedict's emphasis on the Church's responsibility for education, it naturally follows that he would dwell on creating and maintaining access to the moral treasury of humanity. The Church must instruct the faithful through catechetical programs and homilies. But that is not all. Catholic universities and seminaries need to preserve the study of theology, philosophy, literature, and the other liberal arts if the moral treasury is really to come alive and have an influence on political and social affairs.

Pope Benedict's response to Marx's reliance on politics to bring about the definitively just society by socializing the means of production logically follows from his understanding of human freedom. Marx's error, the pope argues, is not recognizing that man's freedom to do good or evil remains no matter what shape the structures of society take.

He forgot that man always remains man. He forgot man and he forgot man's freedom. He forgot that freedom always remains also freedom for evil. He

[57] SS, no. 22.
[58] SS, no. 24.
[59] SS, no. 24.

thought that once the economy had been put right, everything would automatically be put right. His real error is materialism: man, in fact, is not merely the product of economic conditions, and it is not possible to redeem him purely from the outside by creating a favorable economic environment.[60]

Pope Benedict's reflection on the potential of freedom for good or ill is both a summons to use freedom well and to recognize that people's bad use of freedom will deny justice and love to many people while they are living on this earth. The only hope for the latter is the Last Judgment, belief in which is fading today. Belief in the Last Judgment moves Christians to love and to work for justice with all their heart and soul, and offers the hope that people not helped by their efforts will receive justice in the afterlife. This is a consoling thought when Christians fail to overcome the injustice in their midst; it sustains them amidst their failures, for example, to protect the life of the unborn from abortion. The victims of injustice especially draw hope from belief in the resurrection of the flesh. Pope Benedict movingly explains:

> There is justice. There is an "undoing" of past suffering, a reparation that sets things aright. For this reason, faith in the Last Judgment is first and foremost hope – the need for which was made abundantly clear in the upheavals of recent centuries. I am convinced that the question of justice constitutes the essential argument, or in any case the strongest argument, in favor of faith in eternal life.[61]

Christ must return as judge if the injustices of this life are not to be the "final word." There would have to be a resurrection of the dead unto eternal life to undo past injustices and sufferings.

Pope Benedict's Memorable Speech on Four Principles of Catholic Social Doctrine

On May 3, 2008, Pope Benedict gave a thought-provoking speech on Catholic Social Teaching to the Pontifical Academy of Social Sciences, which is even more instructive in the light of the pope's first two encyclicals. Relying on philosophical and theological and philosophic reason, Benedict discusses four fundamental principles of Catholic Social Teaching: the dignity of the human person, the common good, subsidiarity, and solidarity.

Dignity refers to the great goodness or worth of the human person, because all people are created in the image and likeness of God. The common good is

[60] *SS*, no. 21.
[61] *SS*, no. 42.

the sum total of the social conditions that enable individuals to strive more effectively, and more easily, for perfection. Solidarity is the virtue inclining individuals "to share fully the treasure of [their] material and spiritual goods" with their fellow citizens, thereby contributing to the common good of their country.[62] Pope Benedict adds a clarifying note: "True solidarity . . . comes to fulfillment only when I willingly place my life at the service of the other (cf. Eph. 6:21)." Making oneself "*less* than another so as to minister to his or her needs" is a way of imitating Jesus's humbling of himself "so as to give men and women a share in his divine life with the Father and the Spirit (cf. Phil 2:8; Mt 23:12)."[63]

Pope Benedict somewhat enigmatically describes subsidiarity as "the coordination of society's activities in a way that supports the internal life of the local communities."[64] More clearly, Benedict says that people act upon the principle of subsidiarity "by promoting family life, voluntary associations, private initiative, and a public order that facilitates the healthy functioning of society's most basic communities."[65] When the public authorities allow and encourage society's little platoons, "they leave space for individual responsibility, and initiative, but most importantly, they leave room for *love*," which itself is an act of love, the most excellent action of every human being.[66] This is a point first made by Pope Benedict in his third encyclical, *Caritas in veritate*. To affirm that respecting the principle of subsidiarity is a way of loving one's neighbor is a brilliant observation that I have not previously found in the body of Catholic Social Doctrine. In other words, people practice charity by observing the principle of subsidiarity, since they show respect for the dignity of others by putting them in a better position to practice charity themselves. Since charity is the "heart of what it means to be a human being," subsidiarity is much more than a principle of government: putting people in a position to love is an eminent contribution to integral development and, thus, to their salvation.[67]

To state in another way what Benedict is getting at, subsidiarity requires participation and community at all levels of society. This means that larger entities should not usurp the role of smaller ones. For example, the federal government should not usurp the role of the states and government itself

---

[62] Benedict XVI, *A Reason Open to God*, edited by John Garvey and J. Steven Brown (Washington, DC: The Catholic University of America Press, 2013), 190.
[63] *A Reason Open to God*, 192.
[64] *A Reason Open to God*, 190.
[65] *A Reason Open to God*, 192.
[66] *A Reason Open to God*, 193.
[67] Benedict XVI, Encyclical Letter *Caritas in veritate* (On Integral Human Development in Charity & Truth) (2009), no. 57.

should not do what families, other mediating institutions, and individuals are able to accomplish on their own. Subsidiarity also means that the larger entities should give aid (*subsidium*) to the smaller ones and to individuals so that they can fulfill their responsibilities more easily, including the practice of charity.

Without much argument Pope Benedict also contends that "the principles of solidarity and subsidiarity are enriched by our belief in the Trinity, but particularly in the sense that these principles have the potential to place men and women on the path of discovering their definitive, supernatural destiny." In other words, the practice of subsidiarity and solidarity in the proper way will help people realize that they are ultimately called to participate in the life of the Trinity by giving and receiving love. That is to say, the supernatural destiny of all human beings is to receive love from God and neighbor and to love them in return. To further clarify his point Pope Benedict says that the Christian vocation to work for justice and peace is "inseparable from their mission to proclaim the gift of eternal life to which God has called every man and woman." As we saw, *Spe salvi* explained how belief in eternal life is necessary to sustain hope in people who do not receive relief from the unjust sufferings in their life.

THREE OF POPE BENEDICT'S SEPTEMBER SPEECHES

The Westminster Speech on the Relation of Religion and Politics

Let us turn to an examination of Pope Benedict's major speeches delivered in Westminster, England on religion and politics and in Berlin on the foundation of law. Among other things these speeches provide further commentary on the four principles of Catholic Social Teaching (without always mentioning them by name) explained by Pope Benedict before the Pontifical Academy of Social Sciences. The September 17 address on the relation of religion and politics is one of the highlights of Pope Benedict's journey to the United Kingdom in the late summer of 2010. The pope first pays tribute to the British Parliament, the worldwide influence of Britain's common law tradition, and the English "vision of the respective rights and duties of the state and the individual, and of the separation of powers,"[68] a vision held in such high regard throughout the world.

---

[68] Marc Guerra, *Liberating Logos: Pope Benedict XVI's September Speeches* (South Bend, Indiana: St. Augustine's Press, 2014), 49.

He then appeals to the figure of St. Thomas More, ever the good servant of the king, who "chose to serve God first."[69] Pope Benedict doesn't mention that More would not take an oath recognizing King Henry VIII as head of the Church in England. The pope does say that More's dilemma of discerning "what is owed to God and what is owed to Caesar" provides a good context for reflecting "on the proper place of religious belief within the political process."[70] By invoking the example of More, Pope Benedict is implying that there are limits to the sovereignty of the government, that Christians have a duty to work for the common good of their country, and that Christian citizens may have to give up their lives rather than violate their consciences by being unfaithful to God.

Pope Benedict next points out the similarity between the British parliamentary tradition and Catholic Social Teaching. The former celebrates "freedom of speech, freedom of political affiliation and respect for the rule of law with a strong sense of the individual's rights and duties, and of the equality of all citizens before the law."[71] The latter says that all people have equal dignity because they are created in the image of God and that every civil authority has the duty to promote the common good. The pope leaves unsaid that human dignity provides a foundation for both rights and duties. All have certain rights because of their God-given dignity, and all must fulfill various duties in order to live in accordance with their dignity. In *Rerum novarum* (no. 37) Pope Leo XIII said that "true dignity and excellence in men and women resides in moral living, that is, in virtue." Such a formulation is most unlikely to be found in the British parliamentary tradition.

The pope spells out what concern for human dignity and the common good requires in the democratic process. It is not just any consensus arrived at by the majority that is sufficient to establish a healthy democracy. Both the economy and the political process need a solid ethical foundation. Benedict gives one example of British legislation that had a firm ethical basis, the abolition of the slave trade. "The campaign that led to this landmark legislation was built upon firm ethical principles, rooted in the natural law, and it has made a contribution to civilization of which this nation may be justly proud."[72] This example suggests that other legislation and British mores could profitably be based on the natural law.

---

[69]   *Liberating Logos*, 50.
[70]   *Liberating Logos*, 50.
[71]   *Liberating Logos*, 50.
[72]   *Liberating Logos*, 51.

Pope Benedict is now at the heart of the matter. After his brief mention of the natural law he looks to reason in general as a reliable guide to discern ethical norms to guide political choices. "The Catholic tradition maintains that the objective norms governing right action are accessible to reason, prescinding from the content of revelation."[73] While reason theoretically has the ability to discern the relevant ethical principles, it can go astray under the influence of culture or various ideologies. It was after all the "misuse of reason" that led to the slave trade and to the totalitarian regimes of the twentieth century. As a remedy for the weakness of reason, Pope Benedict suggests that religion can help "purify" reason (see *Deus caritas est*), making it a more fit instrument of ethical discernment. Here and in other contexts, Pope Benedict makes the point that faith can correct the aberrations of reason, and reason can likewise help faith overcome its errors. "This is why I would suggest that the world of reason and the world of faith . . . need one another and should not be afraid to enter into a profound and ongoing dialogue, for the good of our civilization."[74] Every civilization needs reason and faith working together for the sake of the common good.

The cooperation between faith and religion and politics is not going well these days in various parts of the world. Benedict emphasizes the marginalization of Christianity that is taking place. Many want religious voices silenced or confined to the private sphere, leaving the public square without any religious influence. Some even argue "that Christians in public roles should be required at times to act against their conscience."[75] Benedict doesn't mention in this context that the English king, Henry VIII, tried to force Thomas More to act against his conscience, but intelligent listeners in the audience would naturally think of that fact. Benedict makes a plea for the toleration of religion in the public square and for the encouragement of "dialogue between faith and reason at every level of national life"[76] so that the common good of the nations of the world might more easily be achieved.

After mentioning areas of cooperation between the United Kingdom and the Holy See, Pope Benedict notes "the positive signs of a worldwide growth in solidarity toward the poor," mentioning in particular the contribution of the United Kingdom. He adds that the integral development of the world's peoples is a very important endeavor.

[73] *Liberating Logos*, 52.
[74] *Liberating Logos*, 52.
[75] *Liberating Logos*, 53.
[76] *Liberating Logos*, 53.

Pope Benedict concludes with another plea for an ongoing dialogue between faith and reason and for cooperation between the Church and public authorities. For that cooperation to take place, religious freedom must be protected. Religious bodies – "including institutions linked to the Catholic Church – need to be free to act according to their own principles and specific convictions based upon the faith and the official teaching of the Church."[77] Respecting the freedom of religious institutions to teach and do good deeds is, of course, a respect for the principle of subsidiarity.

Berlin Speech on the Foundation of Law

Pope Benedict XVI reflects on the foundation of law in his speech to the German Parliament (Bundestag) in Berlin on September 22, 2011. He discerns the ultimate foundation of law to be justice. As St. Augustine famously said in his *City of God*, "Without justice – what else is the State but a great band of robbers?" The difficulty lies in coming to know and love what justice requires. Pope Benedict demonstrates the difficulty of this great enterprise by telling a story about King Solomon as portrayed in I Kings. The Biblical story explains that God asks the newly crowned king to make a request. Solomon doesn't ask for wealth or great power, but "he asks for a listening heart so that he may govern God's people, and discern between good and evil."[78] Otherwise stated, Solomon asks for the wisdom to discern and love what is just. Solomon knows that even with a good will it is not easy to know what is right in every circumstance. The acquisition of this knowledge in every age is crucial because, as Benedict says, "to serve right and to fight against the dominion of wrong is and remains the fundamental task of the politician."[79]

The pope next discusses the difficulty of recognizing what is right today. Relying simply on majority opinion is not an option because it may not support true justice. Revelation is of little help in setting up a just government because there is no "juridical order derived from revelation" that Christians can make available to state and society.[80] Through its theologians Christianity, however, does point to "nature and reason as the true sources of law." The pope emeritus briefly explains that Stoic natural law teaching came into contact with Roman law in the second half of the second century. "Through this encounter, the juridical culture of the West was born, which was and is of

---

[77] *Liberating Logos*, 55.
[78] *Liberating Logos*, 40.
[79] *Liberating Logos*, 41.
[80] *Liberating Logos*, 42.

key significance for the juridical culture of mankind."[81] He then adds that this "pre-Christian marriage between law and philosophy" eventually led to the United Nations Declaration of Human Rights and the German Basic Law of 1949. Benedict, of course, leaves out several stages on the way to the mid-twentieth century.

In the second half of the twentieth century the idea of natural law fell into disfavor as a source to recognize what is right in the public square. Positivist understandings of both nature and reason developed and became ascendant. As the object of science, nature came to be understood, "in the words of Hans Kelsen, . . . as an aggregate of objective data linked together in terms of cause and effect."[82] In this perspective, there is no bridge from nature to ethics and law, from an "is" to an "ought." For example, the recent Supreme Court decision declaring a constitutional right to same-sex marriage paid no heed to nature as a source of knowledge about the meaning of marriage. The positivist understanding of reason means that anything not verifiable or falsifiable by the empirical methods of modern science "does not belong to the realm of reason strictly understood."[83]

Pope Benedict acknowledges that the scientific way of using reason yields valuable results that everyone should appreciate. But scientific knowledge is not the only kind of knowledge ascertainable by reason. To regard the positivist use of reason as the only valid way of knowing "diminishes man, indeed it threatens his humanity." This narrow use of reason leaves Europe without a real culture, while "at the same time extremist and radical movements emerge to fill the vacuum."[84]

On numerous occasions Pope Benedict warns educators that universities will fail in their mission if they narrow the scope of their inquiry to that of scientific reason. For example, he writes: "Scientific and technological breakthroughs . . . in a certain way have marginalized the reason that was seeking the ultimate truth of things in order to make room for a reason content with discovering the contingent truths of the laws of nature."[85] Since scientific reason is unable to work out the ethical principles to guide the work of the sciences, it absolutely needs the philosophical and theological reason that deals with the ultimate truths of things. While science and technology have done wonders to increase our standard of living, they can be a great danger when not guided by the ultimate truths discerned by a more expansive reason.

---

[81] *Liberating Logos*, 43.
[82] *Liberating Logos*, 44.
[83] *Liberating Logos*, 44.
[84] *Liberating Logos*, 45.
[85] Benedict XVI, *A Reason Open to God*, 34.

Pope Benedict puts it thisway: scientific "progress puts into the hands of men and women abysmal possibilities for evil and that. nonetheless, it is not science and technology that give our lives meaning and teach us to distinguish good from evil."[86]

The way back to a fuller understanding of nature and reason, Benedict suggests, may be through the ecological movement, which arose in the 1970s in Germany. Young people came to realize that "matter is not just raw material for us to shape at will, but the earth has a dignity of its own and that we must follow its directives ... We must listen to the language of nature."[87] Heeding the earth's directives and respecting nature means not polluting the soil, the sea, or the air, and using the earth in such a way as to ensure its sustainability over time. Genesis put the directive this way: "The Lord God took the man and put him in the Garden of Eden to till it and keep it" (Genesis 1:15). The key word is "keep." When human beings follow God's command to "fill the earth and subdue it (Genesis 1:28), they must do so in such a way that the earth is kept, that is to say, not harmed and preserved in the proper way."

Benedict next draws a parallel between environmental ecology and the ecology of man. "Man has a nature that he must respect and that he cannot manipulate at will. Man is not merely self-creating freedom. Man does not create himself. He is intellect and will, but he is also nature, and his will is rightly ordered if he respects his nature, listens to it and accepts himself for who he is, as one who did not create himself."[88] Benedict is trying to lead people to conclude that just as the human will must respect the nature of the earth, so it must respect its own nature.

To respect human nature means to respect the norms that nature contains. Kelsen argues that if nature contains norms for guidance, then the will of God had to put them there, which, he believes, is something we could never ascertain. Benedict replies that it is not unreasonable to believe that "the objective reason that manifests itself in nature" points to a creator God who created according to reason, aspects of which are visible in nature. In fact, Europe's longstanding belief in a creator God "gave rise to the idea of human rights, the ideal of the equality of all people before the law, the recognition of the inviolability of human dignity in every single person and the awareness of people's responsibility for their actions."[89]

---

86 *A Reason Open to God*, 128.
87 Guerra, *Liberating Logos*, 46.
88 *Liberating Logos*, 46–47.
89 *Liberating Logos*, 47.

In his third encyclical, *Caritas in veritate* (2009), Pope Benedict XVI also addressed the dependence of environmental ecology on human ecology. In order to protect the environment it is not enough to give economic incentives or even to provide an apposite education.

> [T]*he decisive factor is the overall moral tenor of society.* If there is a lack of respect for the right to life and to natural death, if human conception, gestation and birth are made artificial, if human embryos are sacrificed to research, the concept of society ends up losing the concept of human ecology and, along with it, that of environmental ecology.[90]

In other words, if human beings do not respect themselves and one another, if they do not live by some objective standard, they will not respect the environment. In chapter 4 of *Caritas in veritate* Pope Benedict also tries to introduce the theme of objective moral standards by reflecting on the relations between rights and duties. It begins with the countercultural affirmation that unless duties take precedence over rights, the latter can get out of control and become "*mere license.*" When duties are the primary moral counter, they set limits to rights and ensure more respect for the genuine rights of individuals and peoples. If enough people are guided by their duties, they will be moved to do something about "the lack of food, drinkable water, basic instruction and elementary health care in areas of the underdeveloped world and on the outskirts of large metropolitan centers." The priority of duties over rights is not recognized in liberal democracies and has not been consistently emphasized in Catholic Social Teaching.[91]

Benedict concludes his speech by reminding his listeners that the culture of Europe actually came into being from the interaction among Jerusalem, Athens, and Rome, "from the encounter among Israel's monotheism, the philosophical reason of the Greeks and Roman law."[92] Pope Benedict is trying to persuade his listeners that this heritage is much richer than the mere positivism of nature and reason, which is receiving so much emphasis in the West today. Drawing deeper once again from Jerusalem, Athens, and Rome would increase Europe's capacity "to discern between good and evil, and thus to establish true law, to serve justice and peace."[93] Acquiring the wisdom of Solomon through faith and reason would enable Europe to craft better law.

---

[90]   CV, no. 51.
[91]   CV, no. 43.
[92]   Guerra, *Liberating Logos*, 47.
[93]   *Liberating Logos*, 48.

An Alert from the Regensburg Speech about Dehellenization and Historicism

An ever-present temptation is to allow Church teaching to change in order to be in line with the spirit of the age. In the measure that these temptations are not resisted the effective communication and implementation of Catholic Social Doctrine cannot be assured, because it depends on the accurate understanding and practice of the faith. In his speech at the University of Regensburg on September 12, 2006, Pope Benedict alerts his readers to the fact that accommodation to the reigning opinions of the age is carried out in the name of dehellenization and historicism (although Pope Benedict does not use the latter word).

Since the sixteenth century an attempt to "dehellenize" Christianity has occurred in three stages: in Reformation theology, in the liberal theology of the nineteenth century, and in the cultural pluralism of the contemporary period. Reformation theologians thought the Christian faith was falsified by its association with the Greek philosophical heritage and had to be liberated from the grip of philosophy. They introduced the principle of *sola scriptura*, which "sought faith in its pure, primordial form, as originally found in the Biblical Word."[94]

The second stage of dehellenization was especially visible in the theology of Adolph von Harnack. His "central idea was to return simply to the man Jesus and to his simple message, underneath the accretions of theology and indeed of Hellenization ... Jesus was said to have put an end to worship in favor of morality. In the end he was presented as the father of a humanitarian moral message."[95] Harnack's watchword was away from the preached Christ to the preaching Jesus. This led him to reject such philosophical and theological doctrines as the divinity of Christ and the Trinity. He also wanted "to bring Christianity into harmony with modern reason" so that theological scholarship would fit into the modern university by doing historical, and therefore scientific, research, i.e., by applying the historical-critical method to the study of Scripture. Benedict's judgment on Harnack's project is right on target: "Behind this thinking lies the modern self-limitation of reason, classically expressed in Kant's 'Critiques,' but in the meantime further radicalized by the impact of the modern sciences."[96] Otherwise stated, Harnack tried to ensure that Christian theology would always be a reflection of contemporary culture and never an insightful critic of the truncated reason of modernity. Taking its bearings by the reason used in historical and scientific research

---

[94] *Liberating Logos*, 32.
[95] *Liberating Logos*, 33.
[96] *Liberating Logos*, 33.

would not even allow the question of God to be raised, or questions about the origin and destiny of human beings, or any kind of ethical inquiry that would have the "power to create a community."[97] When the scope of reason is reduced the way Harnack recommends, "disturbing pathologies of religion and reason" necessarily arise to fill the void left by a neutered theology.

Pope Benedict, unfortunately, doesn't say much about the third stage of dehellenization, which is with us today. The essence of this stage, according to Benedict, is the conviction "that the synthesis with Hellenism achieved in the early Church ought not to be binding on other cultures." Under the influence of cultural pluralism contemporary scholars reject the view that "the fundamental decisions made about the relationship between faith and the use of reason are part of the faith itself."[98] What they want is the complete freedom to inculturate the faith in every era without being in any way bound by the initial synthesis of faith and the purified Greek heritage. In my judgment, this position amounts to the acceptance of historicism. Its fundamental claim, according to John Paul II, "is that the truth of a philosophy is determined on the basis of its appropriateness to a certain period and a certain historical purpose. At least implicitly, the enduring validity of truth is denied. What was true in one period, historicists claim, may not be true in another" (*Fides et ratio*, no. 87). Benedict clearly thinks that the Church must resist both dehellenization, today as it did in the past, and the contemporary phenomenon of historicism, in order to preserve the permanent truths taught by the Christian faith.

CONCLUSION

The whole Regensburg speech is focused on preserving the integrity of the Christian faith. Ratzinger's "Peace and Justice in Crisis" directed our attention to the danger of subverting the Church and the Christian faith in the work for social justice. I have made reference to Ratzinger's observation that the Church should not become "an organization for direct political action" because it "does not have any specific answers to concrete political questions."

Pope Benedict's reflections on Jesus's third temptation in his *Jesus of Nazareth* shed light on why the Church might be tempted to become an organization focused mainly on political action. In the third temptation the devil offers Jesus kingship over the whole world. How could this be a temptation for the Church today? Pope Benedict comments: "The

---

[97] *Liberating Logos*, 35.
[98] *Liberating Logos*, 35.

Christian empire or the secular power of the papacy is no longer a temptation today, but the interpretation of Christianity as a recipe for progress and the proclamation of universal prosperity as the real goal of all religions, including Christianity – that is the modern form of the same temptation."[99] If the Church were to reinterpret the Messianic hope as universal prosperity, it would make perfect sense for her to become a voluntary organization mainly focused on securing material goods for all, especially the needy, through the political process. If the Church were ever to succumb to this temptation on a wide scale, Catholic Social Teaching would fall apart and lose its potential to have a deep impact on society. Otherwise stated, the preservation of the whole Christian faith in every era is the precondition for establishing, maintaining, and developing an effective Catholic Social Teaching over the centuries. In its threefold work of preaching the Word of God, making the sacraments available, and doing works of charity, the Church remains focused on its primary goal, salvation for all, and thereby has a beneficent impact on the public square with its social doctrine.

At the very beginning of his third encyclical, *Caritas in veritate* (2009), Pope Benedict provides an overarching framework for understanding all that he has said about Catholic Social Doctrine.

> Charity is at the heart of the Church's social doctrine. Indeed every responsibility and every duty spelled out by that doctrine are derived from charity ... but charity in its turn needs to be understood, confirmed, and practiced in the light of truth ... *Only in truth does charity shine forth*, only in truth can charity be authentically lived. Truth is the light that gives meaning and value to charity. That light is both the light of reason and the light of faith, through which the intellect attains to the natural and supernatural truth of charity.[100]

In order to better understand Benedict's stress on truth it is helpful to ponder St. Augustine's statement on the difficulty of being faithful to the commandment to love one's neighbor in everything one does. He wrote, "From this commandment arise the duties pertaining to human society about which it is difficult not to err."[101] In other words, it is easy for human beings to love one another badly, both in personal encounters and in devising proposals for the common good of society. Pope Benedict's presentation of Catholic Social Teaching helps people to know better what love and justice require in the various circumstances of life, knowledge that would escape many without

[99] Benedict XVI, *Jesus of Nazareth* (New York: Doubleday, 2007), 42–43.

[100] CV, nos. 2 and 3.

[101] St. Augustine, *The Catholic and Manichean Ways of Life* (Washington, DC: The Catholic University of America Press, 1966), no. 49.

instruction. His writing on CST has the potential of deepening its influence on the political and social order if it is ever more clearly understood and appreciated by a greater number of Catholics. Pope Benedict's theological corpus and reflections on contemporary culture bring to mind St. Cyril of Jerusalem's memorable instruction to catechumens: "The dragon is at the side of the road watching those who pass. Take care lest he devour you! You are going to the father of souls, but it is necessary to pass by the dragon."[102] Pope Benedict helps his readers to discern the presence and stratagems of the dragon and to be more prudent on their way to the father of souls.

---

[102] I found St. Cyril of Jerusalem's statement about the dragon quoted in Flannery O'Connor, *The Habit of Being* (New York: Farrar, Straus and Giroux, 1979), 126.

9

The Social Teaching of Pope Francis

Daniel J. Mahoney

There is an element of the *bien-pensant* (of fashionable or politically correct thinking) in Francis's papacy. His utterances and self-presentation tend to affirm positions internal to Catholic theology widely held by dissenting Catholic scholars and opinions about politics and the world widely held by left-leaning elites. Francis's frequent ill-disciplined, off-the-cuff remarks are treated with more seriousness than they deserve, and the parts of his thought that are in continuity with Catholic tradition are largely ignored, if not explained away. Among many Catholics there is a growing sense that the pope confuses his personal judgments, largely shaped by his Argentinian experience, with the full weight of Catholic wisdom.

I argue in this essay that what is needed is the deployment of a "hermeneutic of continuity," one that forthrightly reads Francis's continuities and discontinuities within the context of the great tradition of Catholic thought that preceded him. Out of justice, we owe the pope both respect and the full exercise of the arts of intelligence. He is not a despot or Eastern potentate and does not have the authority to redefine Catholic teaching at will. His defenders and his critics need to acknowledge this fact. Loose talk about a Franciscan "revolution" in the Church neither protects the continuity of Catholic teaching nor sustains unity within the Church.[1]

In this chapter, I will closely examine the central themes of the pope's social teaching in such texts as *Caring for Our Common Home*, *The Joy of the Gospel*, *The Church and Europe*, *The Church and America*, *In the Name of Mercy*, *The Family in the Modern World*, and then will conclude with a consideration of *The Other Francis*, the Francis who is prone to troubling off-the-cuff remarks that lack any authoritative status as Catholic teaching or doctrine. I will then

---

[1] For particularly egregious rhetoric about the "Franciscan revolution," see Pope Francis, *Open to God, Open to the World*, with Antonio Spadaro (Bloomsbury Continuum, 2018).

briefly discuss *A Crisis in the Church*, which has arisen from Francis's tendency to question the teachings of his predecessors and to ignore reasonable requests for the clarification of Catholic teaching.[2]

CARING FOR OUR COMMON HOME

Pope Francis's May 2015 encyclical *Laudato si'* (Praise Be to You), and subtitled *On Care for Our Common Home*,[3] repeats Christian wisdom of a decidedly antimodern cast when it laments the project of modern mastery, which reduces human beings to "lords and masters" of nature (*LS*, no. 115–120). It affirms human uniqueness, "which transcends the spheres of physics and biology," and emphasizes our stewardship over the whole of creation (*LS*, no. 81). At the same time, as Father James V. Schall, SJ has argued, *Laudato si'* sets forth more a theology of creation than a theology of redemption and is thus incomplete.[4]

Francis reminds us that technological progress is not coextensive with moral progress. He recounts the central role that technology played in the murderous rampages of communism and Nazism. He counsels "clear-minded self-restraint" and a "setting of limits" (*LS*, no. 105). His critique of a one-dimensional "technological paradigm" that assumes that economics and technology can solve all our problems, without the help of virtue and self-limitation, is salutary and consistent with the best classical and Christian wisdom.

Pope Francis is not wrong when he argues that "modernity has been marked by an excessive anthropocentrism" linked to a "Promethean vision of mastery over the world" (*LS*, no. 116). Man is not God and should eschew all projects of human self-deification. All social progress demands respect for limits and efforts at self-limitation. Yet the pope remains tepid on the contribution that markets and technological innovation can make in addressing a problem such as climate change. His commentaries on markets are invariably negative:

---

[2] This crisis has been exacerbated by explosive charges published in an 11-page letter on August 25, 2018, by Archbishop Carlo Maria Viganò, former papal nuncio to the United States, that Pope Francis "rehabilitated" the disgraced Cardinal Theodore McCarrick and ignored widespread homosexual activity and predation among bishops and priests (see www .lifesitenews.com/news/former-us-nuncio-pope-francis-knew-of-mccarricks-misdeeds-repealed -sanction). Viganò followed it up with a second letter on September 27, 2018, responding to Pope Francis's silence in response to his original charges (see www.lifesitenews.com/news/br eaking-vigano-releases-new-testimony-responding-to-popes-silence-on-mccar).
[3] See Pope Francis, Encyclical Letter *Laudato si'* (On Care for Our Common Home) (2015).
[4] See the lucid and penetrating analysis by James V. Schall, "Concerning the 'Ecological' Path to Salvation," *Catholic World Report*, June 21, 2015.

markets inculcate greed, inequality, economic imperialism, and environmental degradation (see, in particular, *LS*, nos. 48–52, 161). Moreover, he is silent about the horrendous environmental devastation that accompanied and characterized totalitarian socialist systems in the twentieth century.

The pope's social message would be balanced by noting that democratic capitalist systems, whatever their flaws, have remarkable powers of self-correction. As George Will has argued, one has only to compare the levels of pollution in Dickens's London with those in today's London, or look at the remarkable transformation of the Thames over the past fifty years,[5] to question Francis's identification of capitalist "progress" with the accumulation of "debris, desolation and filth" (*LS*, no. 161). Although Francis has indeed noted that "business is a noble vocation" that "is directed to producing wealth and improving the world" (*LS*, no. 129), his texts spend much more time excoriating profit motives and lecturing on the evils of air conditioning and the full array of consumer goods (*LS*, no. 55).

In the summer of 2015, the *Economist* called Pope Francis a "Peronist." That characterization is apt.[6] Peronist populism created a "rancid political culture in Argentina"[7] that emphasized class struggle and redistribution above lawful wealth-creation. As George F. Will has also pointed out, Argentina went from being the fourteenth-richest country in the world in 1900 to the sixty-third today.[8] Sadly, Pope Francis seems to be rather indulgent toward despotic regimes that speak in the name of the poor – his silence about the persecution of mainly Catholic dissidents in Cuba was deafening. During the welcoming ceremony at Jose Marti International Airport in Havana on September 19, 2015, he spoke of his "sentiments of particular respect"[9] for Fidel Castro, a totalitarian tyrant who subjugated the people of Cuba for fifty years and who viciously persecuted the Church.

But the poor need political liberty, too, and the opportunities that come with private property and lawfully regulated markets. It is striking that Pope Francis rarely reiterates the Church's firm defense of private property, a central affirmation of modern Catholic social teaching beginning with *Rerum novarum* and finding continuous voice back to the patristic period.

---

5 See George F. Will, "Pope Francis's fact-free flamboyance," *Washington Post*, September 18, 2015.
6 See *The Economist*, "The Peronist Pope," July 9, 2015.
7 Will, "Pope Francis's fact-free flamboyance."
8 "Concerning the 'Ecological' Path to Salvation."
9 Pope Francis, "Cuba: Point of Encounter" in *Pope Francis Speaks to the United States and Cuba: Speeches, Homilies, and Interviews* (Huntington, IN: Our Sunday Visitor Press, 2015), 9.

The pope should also be more careful about endorsing "a very solid scientific consensus" on the causes and likely results of climate change (*LS*, no. 23). There are reasonable debates about the origins of climate fluctuations, debates that the magisterium of the Catholic Church has no proper authority to settle or attempt to settle; and so, for the good of the unity of the Church and the integrity of its apostolic message, the pope should not preempt the conclusions of these debates by picking winners and losers.

THE JOY OF THE GOSPEL

Pope Francis has emphasized the joy that accompanies the proclamation of – and fidelity to – the Gospel. His 2013 apostolic exhortation *Evangelii gaudium* (*The Joy of the Gospel*) is a call to recover the "good news" in all its amplitude.[10] One must never lose sight of "the delightful and comforting joy of evangelizing," of spreading God's word with the love and hope that are the hallmarks of God's Kingdom (*EG*, no. 7). While not devoted mainly or exclusively to the social teaching of the Church, the document nonetheless touches on fundamental aspects of Christian engagement with the contemporary world.

Yet the document's appropriation of Catholic social thought is rather selective. Gone are the Church's warnings against ideological utopianism, its qualified defense of a market economy rooted in rule of law and sound mores, its defense of private property as necessary for personal dignity and the exercise of the moral virtues, and its forthright condemnation of the socialist confiscation of human freedom. The text claims its fierce condemnations of liberal capitalism are in full continuity with the Church's social teaching (see *EG*, nos. 125–145). Yet its one-sided emphases tend to give a distinctly "progressivist" turn to its social message.

Francis rightly emphasizes that the Christian Gospel cannot "be relegated to the inner sanctum of personal life, without influence on societal and national life, without concern for the soundness of civil institutions, without a right to offer an opinion on events affecting society" (*EG*, no. 183). But rather than identifying Christian engagement in politics with history's greatest Catholic statesmen such as Thomas More in the sixteenth century to Adenauer and de Gaulle in the twentieth, the pope evokes the social witness of Saint Francis of Assisi and Saint Teresa of Calcutta (*EG*, no. 183). Both great souls preach an awe-inspiring eschatological holiness, but they are not

---

[10]   Francis, Apostolic Exhortation *Evangelii gaudium* (On the Proclamation of the Gospel in Today's World) (2013).

remotely statesmen and have little to say about the properly *civic* dimensions of the common good in a sinful and fallen world. Thus, his emphasis on Christian political engagement has a decidedly perfectionist cast. It does not take its bearings sufficiently from Christian realism but rather leaves itself open to appropriation by those who confuse Christian moral and political witness with a thoroughgoing utopian transformation of human nature and society.

The pope speaks about the desire of "authentic faith" to "change the world," to "fight for justice" and to engage in the activity of "building a better world" (*EG*, no. 13). Christians must indeed fight for justice, but as St. Augustine taught in *The City of God*, no political order is simply just and no political order will, or ever can, be.[11] That is to hope for too much in a fallen world. There are better and worse political regimes, and there are limits to justice inherent in the human condition. Christians must indeed work for decency. We must be fearless witnesses to truth and justice. And yet, in a profound sense, the world cannot be "changed." The effects of original sin begin anew in every human heart. Political efforts to establish the kingdom of God on earth invariably lead to misery and tyranny. They place humanitarian, or "revolutionary," concerns above Christian truth and the drama of good and evil in the human soul. Francis's unqualified appeals for us to "change the world" tend to emphasize this worldly amelioration above the supernatural destiny of man. His language, perhaps unintentionally, tends to reinforce the progressivism inherent in a distinctively late-modern sensibility regarding politics.

Pope Francis desires a "Church which is poor and for the poor" (*EG*, no. 198). This affirmation is in the best tradition of Christian wisdom and moral witness. But again the pope rarely emphasizes the tension between "the poor" and the "poor in spirit" which is so central to the Gospel's account of what is today called "the preferential option for the poor." The poor as a sociological category can be selfish, rapacious, and prone to manipulation by demagogues, even as the rich can be oppressive and unjust and confuse their good fortune with moral virtue. To his credit, the pope does note that the option for the poor cannot be reduced to government programs or "unruly activism" and above all suggests a "true concern for the person" (*EG*, no. 199).

Pope Francis's apostolic exhortation has little positive to say about the market economy. Rather than emphasizing social and political measures to ameliorate poverty and to help the poorest of the poor, the pope endorses public action to promote "a better distribution of income" (*EG*, no. 204). This is undoubtedly in some tension with the Catholic Church's long-standing and

---

11   For the *locus classicus* of Christian realism, see Book 19 of St. Augustine's *The City of God*.

tough-minded support of the principle of subsidiarity. A state dedicated to full-scale redistribution will hardly respect decentralization and local initiatives. Francis rather reluctantly acknowledges the legitimacy of private property if it serves larger "social" purposes (*EG*, no. 189). Yet he also insists that solidarity "must be lived as the decision to restore to the poor what belongs to them" (*EG*, no. 189). The pope too easily goes back and forth from theological to questionable sociopolitical affirmations. Redistribution of income or other manifestations of dogmatic egalitarianism have never been central to Catholic social teaching. That oscillation has given rise to ideological interpretations of Francis's thought on the part of many journalists and politicians.

Pope Francis proffers many personal prudential judgments that have a tendency to ignore or underplay the Church's age-old opposition to political utopianism and its concerns about the threat that many versions of socialism pose to human freedom and dignity (*EG*, no. 202–204). However, he rightly strikes a note of modesty regarding the supposed comprehensiveness – and infallibility – of the Church's practical recommendations to the state and civil society: "The Church does not have solutions for every particular issue" (*EG*, no. 241). He thus leaves to thoughtful laymen the task of discerning "those programs which best respond to the dignity of each person and the common good" (*EG*, no. 205).

Yet his own prudential judgments often lack substantiation and pose the risk of being taken as official Church teaching. For example, the pope states that "authentic Islam and the proper reading of the Koran are opposed to every form of violence" (*EG*, no. 253). Yet Mohammed, unlike Christ, murdered many infidels, including the defenseless Jews of Medina. He was a warrior as well as a religious figure. And authentic Islam endorses *jihad of the sword* even if it is not the only or highest meaning of *jihad* or struggle in the Koran or the Islamic tradition.[12] Nothing is gained by obfuscating the troubling fact that "violent fundamentalism" finds some justification in "authentic Islam" and that Islam has never been unqualifiedly a "religion of peace," a fact acknowledged by Pope Benedict XVI in his 2006 Regensburg Address.

THE CHURCH AND EUROPE

The future and destiny of the Christian faith have always been tied to the future and destiny of Europe. Christianity became a truly universal religion when St. Paul crossed over to Macedonia to bring the "good news" to the

---

[12]   *Jihad by the sword* (*jihad bis saif*) refers to holy war as articulated in the Koran and specifically today by Salafist Muslims.

Greeks.[13] Before Pope Francis, the vast majority of those who have held the See of Peter have been Europeans (the Argentinian Bergoglio is himself of Italian descent and speaks Italian as one of his native languages). The Church is inescapably Eurocentric and at the same time inescapably universalistic, in part due to the providential encounter of the Church with Greek philosophy and Roman culture, as Pope John Paul II liked to point out.[14] The Church cannot be indifferent to the fate of European liberty. If Christianity is in the process of losing its European sources of vitality, this would be an immeasurable loss for Europe and for the integrity of the Christian religion. Much is at stake in the Christian religion's continuing ability to inform Europe's practice of liberty and its understanding of human dignity.

Pope Francis's fullest articulation of the relationship between Christianity and Europe can be found in his November 25, 2014, address to the European parliament.[15] He notes that Europe is now whole and free, and that the division into "opposing blocs" is a thing of the past. Like John Paul II, Pope Francis suggests that the defense of the dignity of the human person is unthinkable without Christianity and the multiple ways in which it has helped "shape an awareness of the unique worth of each individual person." Modern Europe must learn not only from "recent events" (the totalitarian denial of human liberty and dignity in the twentieth century) but also from Christianity's "transcendent" affirmation of the human person. The pope argues that there can be no true dignity if human thought and religious liberty are repressed, if the rule of law does not provide a bulwark against tyranny (it might have helped to speak these words in Cuba, too). And he defends the social preconditions of human dignity, rooted as they are in guaranteeing the basic needs of the individual and of employment that makes dignified work possible.

Like his immediate predecessors, Pope Francis defends human rights against the encroachments of a tyrannical state. He also criticizes the "misuse" of the concept of human rights: severed from all notions of a "greater good," appeals to the pure autonomy of human rights can readily give rise to new sources "of conflicts and violence." The human person, so understood, is quite distinct from the "monadic" and willful individual. In one of the best passages in the speech, Pope Francis connects "transcendent human dignity" to an

---

[13] *Acts* 16: 6–10.

[14] See Pope John Paul II, Encyclical Letter *Fides et ratio* (On the Relationship between Faith and Reason) (1998), no. 72 for a discussion of the Church's "providential" encounter with Greek and Roman thought.

[15] Francis, "Address to the European Parliament" (November 25, 2014) in *America* on line (November 25, 2014).

understanding of an enduring human nature that is informed by the "innate" human capacity "to distinguish good from evil." Alluding to St. Paul, he speaks of a "compass" within our hearts, which "God has impressed upon all creation" – thus implicitly appealing to natural law.

The pope emphatically states that human freedom is not "absolute," but always refers to "beings in relation." Today, that understanding of human freedom and dignity is threatened by a technology that escapes moral-political control (Francis habitually refers to a "throwaway culture" which readily disposes of persons and things – see *LS*, no. 22). If Europe is to remain faithful to "the centrality of the human person" it must remain open to "the transcendent." However, one of this address's troubling lacunae is its failure to refer to the European nation as the home of self-government and free and dignified political life. There is no mention in his address of France, Italy, Germany, Poland, or any other European nation. He defends the "diversity proper to each people, cherishing particular traditions, acknowledging its past history and its roots." But he never speaks of the political form that is the nation, the concretized political form that is the home of the very traditions that he rightly says must be safeguarded today.

Churchill memorably argued at Zurich on September 19, 1946, that European unity could only be built on reconciliation and cooperation between a "spiritually great France" and a "spiritually great Germany."[16] There is no Europe, or European Union, without the self-governing nation. As the French Catholic political philosopher Pierre Manent has argued, the European nation allowed one "to govern oneself by the guidance of one's own reason and with attention to grace." It allowed "for the collaboration of human prudence and divine Providence."[17] The Church needs to relearn the language of humane national loyalty, a language that cannot be confused with the kind of toxic and pagan nationalism that abhors the Christian proposition and genuine human universality. It needs to step away from its flirtation with a world state or "world governing authority," one that can hardly be expected to respect human liberty or Christian understanding of the human person.

Francis speaks about "uniform systems of economic power at the service of unseen empires." Some of this is unduly ominous, some of it reflects perfectly legitimate concerns about unchecked globalization. Repeating some of the ecological themes that have been central to his papacy, he emphasizes that

---

[16] See Winston S. Churchill's "Zurich Speech" (September 19, 1946), ("Something that Will Astonish You") in *Blood, Toil, Tears and Sweat: The Great Speeches*, ed. David Cannadine, 309–314, esp. 312.

[17] See Pierre Manent, *Beyond Radical Secularism*, trans. Ralph C. Hancock, introduction by Daniel J. Mahoney (South Bend, IN: St. Augustine's Press, 2016), 63–64.

"each of us has a personal responsibility to care for creation." He reminds us that we are "stewards, but not masters" of nature. Lamentably, however, Pope Francis shows little awareness that increasingly deep ecology has become a "secular religion" shorn of all forms of Christian humanism.[18] Christians are called to enjoy nature and use it properly. They are never called to deify it or make it an idol in place of the transcendent God. Ecological pantheism is hardly Christian in character or inspiration.

The pope also treats "the question of migration" as a strictly humanitarian concern. "We cannot allow the Mediterranean to become a vast cemetery!" That point is undoubtedly true. But it is not enough. Francis does not address legitimate questions of security in an age marked by terrorism, nor does he recognize that the West could be fundamentally transformed by allowing millions of Muslims, mainly young men (and some markedly unfriendly to Western "values"), to enter a Europe that has not wholly left behind its fruitful encounter and engagement with Christianity.

Statesmen, even Catholic statesmen, must weigh and balance the full array of legitimate social and political concerns. Their decisions cannot be ruled by a concern merely for the good of migrants without due consideration of the common good of the nations into which they aspire to migrate. Both perspectives must inform Catholic social teaching if it is to avoid becoming a form of what Alexis de Tocqueville derided as "literary politics" or a barely concealed form of secular humanitarianism.

THE CHURCH AND AMERICA

The United States has a large and vibrant (if declining) Catholic community and it provides a disproportionate share of the resources that are necessary for the Church to carry out its responsibilities in the world. What is more, the United States is increasingly a laboratory for the unfolding of both the best and worst features of liberty in the modern world. The Church therefore cannot remain silent about America or the American proposition that "all men are created equal" (in the memorable words of the Declaration of Independence). The pope's "Address to a Joint Session of the United States Congress" on September 24, 2015,[19] accordingly, is important both as a judgment about the American proposition and as a statement of how the Church understands Christian engagement in the contemporary world.

---

[18] For a good discussion of radical environmentalism and its incompatibility with Christianity, see Schall, "Concerning the 'Ecological' Path to Salvation."
[19] See *Pope Francis Speaks to the United States and Cuba*, 79–88.

Francis states that democracy "is deeply rooted in the mind of the American people."[20] And he invokes the inviolable dignity of the human person and cites the "self-evident truths" of the Declaration of Independence. Pope Francis points out the myriad affinities that exist between what it means to be a Catholic and what it means to be an American.

But he also warns against politics becoming "a slave to the economy and finance."[21] He fashions a vision of the political common good where "particular interests" are sacrificed "in order to share, in justice and peace, its goods, its interests, its social life."[22] What is missing from all of this is a conception of politics that knows how to reconcile individual rights with a substantial conception of a shared or common good – a conception of politics for which the classical and Christian traditions of moral and political reflection provide ample resources.

The pope helpfully acknowledges that business can aid in the fight against poverty and in the creation and distribution of wealth. He states that "the right use of natural resources, the proper application of technology and the harnessing of the spirit of enterprise are essential elements of an economy which seeks to be modern, inclusive and sustainable."[23] In this passage, at least, he is no Luddite: he does not pine for an economic order that escapes the challenges of modernity. Francis's anticapitalist rhetoric, on fiery display in the speeches he delivered in Latin America earlier in 2015, is considerably muted in this address.

Francis also pays eloquent tribute to four exemplary Americans: Abraham Lincoln's defense of liberty and equality and his struggle against slavery and for a "new birth of freedom" in the aftermath of the Civil War; Martin Luther King's struggle for racial justice and "liberty in plurality and non-exclusion"; Dorothy Day's quest for "social justice"; and Thomas Merton's "capacity for dialogue and openness to God."[24] There is much to be recommended in the lives and struggles of these four great Americans (though it must also be noted that Dorothy Day's admirable work for the poor was accompanied by a militant pacifism that denied the legitimacy of self-defense against totalitarian aggression).[25] The pope uses this occasion to denounce "every type of

---

[20]   *Pope Francis Speaks to the United States and Cuba*, 82.
[21]   *Pope Francis Speaks to the United States and Cuba*, 83.
[22]   *Pope Francis Speaks to the United States and Cuba*, 83.
[23]   *Pope Francis Speaks to the United States and Cuba*, 85.
[24]   *Pope Francis Speaks to the United States and Cuba*, 81.
[25]   For a more sympathetic account of Dorothy Day's pacifism, see Terence C. Wright, *Dorothy Day: An Introduction to Her Life and Thought* (San Francisco, CA: Ignatius Press, 2018), 117–136.

fundamentalism" that gives rise to violence and "ideological extremism."[26] But again, he fails, perhaps out of undue ecumenical sensitivity, to mention the Islamist extremism that is the source of so many "brutal atrocities"[27] today. He warns against "simple reductionism which sees only good and evil."[28] He is right to criticize that kind of moral fanaticism, uninformed as it is by charity and a humanizing recognition of the complexity of the soul.

However, he says nothing about the scourge of our time in the prosperous and democratic West, a debilitating moral relativism that denies evil and sin and collaborates with political correctness in all its forms. What Pope Benedict XVI called "the dictatorship of relativism"[29] is a grave threat to American and democratic liberty and to the integrity of souls in the contemporary world. The failure to mention the threat of relativism is a missed opportunity.

IN THE NAME OF MERCY

Pope Francis has placed extraordinary emphasis on the proclamation of God's mercy – he issued an Extraordinary Jubilee Year of Mercy in 2016 and published a book of conversations on this theme with Andrea Tornielli, *The Name of God Is Mercy*.[30] Pope Francis routinely speaks of a humanity that is deeply wounded by the effects of original sin and man's need of the mercy of a gracious God. Yet he rarely speaks of repentance.

As the German Catholic philosopher Robert Spaemann has written, Pope Francis sometimes "gets ahead of God's mercy."[31] For instance, he rightly speaks of the need to treat homosexuals with delicacy and to prevent them from being "marginalized," but there is no talk of abstinence, or the forswearing of sin.[32] Repentance is not emphasized as a precondition for engagement with the life of the Church. There is a larger problem here. The emphasis on the gratuitous love of God seems to crowd out the repentance that is the precondition for the soul's receptivity to divine grace and mercy. In

---

[26] *Pope Francis Speaks to the United States and Cuba*, 81.
[27] *Pope Francis Speaks to the United States and Cuba*, 81.
[28] *Pope Francis Speaks to the United States and Cuba*, 81.
[29] Marc D. Guerra, ed., *Liberating Logos: Pope Benedict's September Speeches* (South Bend, IN: St. Augustine's Press, 2014), 63. The future pope was addressing the papal conclave on April 18, 2005.
[30] See Pope Francis, *The Name of God Is Mercy: A Conversation with Andrea Tornielli* (New York: Random House, 2016).
[31] See Robert Spaemann's interview about *Amoris laetitia* and "getting ahead of God's mercy" at the website of the *Catholic News Agency*, April 29, 2016.
[32] *The Name of God Is Mercy*, 62.

a relativistic age, people are prone to take God's grace for granted, to assume that sin is not truly sinful, that it does not distance the human person from the light of God, that it is not morally and spiritually self-mutilating.[33]

The pope does not explicitly acknowledge the difference between a Christianity that recognizes the legitimate place of punishment and a secular humanitarian ethos that is guided by free-floating compassion. Divine mercy is not humanitarian compassion. It is not a substitute for personal repentance and the firm, if humane, exercise of the rule of law. If one "gets ahead of God's mercy," one risks reinforcing the tragedy of the age: the denial of sin, evil, and personal responsibility. The evocation of divine mercy must never reinforce "the dictatorship of relativism."[34] These are matters that call forth reflection and discernment on the part of all faithful Christians.

THE FAMILY IN THE MODERN WORLD

Released in the spring of 2016, Pope Francis's *Amoris laetitia (The Joy of Love)* is in some respects quite traditional in character.[35] Pope Francis engages in a beautiful exegesis of what Scripture has to say about the family. His reading of St. Paul's famous hymn to love in I Corinthians is one of the highlights of this document. Insightful and lyrical, this discussion prepares the way for a luminous discussion of conjugal love, "the love between husband and wife, a love sanctified, enriched and illuminated by the grace of the sacrament of marriage" (AL, no. 120). Unfortunately, the pope's discussion is routinely marred by a tendency to redefine Christian family life in terms of "values" that the Church presents to the world (see AL, nos. 272–273). The Church's teaching is here presented as a demanding ideal to which fallible men will necessarily fall short.

The pope notes that the Church can "hardly stop advocating marriage simply to avoid countering contemporary sensibilities" (AL, no. 35). But he seems to want to meet the world halfway in the name of "compassion" and human frailty. The work suffers from a latent, and at times not so latent, bifocalism: the Church must not "desist from proposing the full ideal of marriage" (AL, nos. 307–308) in a world marked by moral indifference and relativism and yet, by redefining the Church's teaching on the good life in

---

[33]　See Pope John Paul II's great 1984 encyclical *Reconciliatio et paenitentia* (On Reconciliation and Penance in the Mission of the Church Today) (1984), no. 18 as the most striking feature of the contemporary world.

[34]　Marc D. Guerra, ed., *Liberating Logos: Pope Benedict's September Speeches* (South Bend, IN: St. Augustine's Press, 2014), 63.

[35]　Francis, Apostolic Exhortation *Amoris laetitia* (On Love in the Family) (2016).

terms of amorphous values and ideals, Francis moves far away from the Church's traditional categories of goods and virtues. "Ideals" and "values" are, whatever Francis thinks, not goods and virtues.

Francis assumes an unbridgeable gap between the ideal and reality. He does so quite plainly in a now famous footnote, leaving too much room for pastoral discernment in dealing with cases of adultery and divorce and remarriage (*EG*, chapter 8, no. 351). He again risks getting ahead of God's mercy when he asks the Church to forgive or overlook objectively sinful moral choices and conditions, without repentance or a change in the sinner's behavior. He acknowledges that it is wrong to place the unions of homosexuals "on the same level as marriage" (*EG*, no. 251). But what exactly prevents the same misplaced compassion and mercy that he says we should have for the divorced and remarried from being applied to homosexual unions? Shouldn't humanitarian compassion also be at work here? Francis gives us little principled reason not to think so. His message too readily gives the impression that in the real world the "ideal" has little connection with the "real." This provides a disturbing invitation for accommodating moral relativism at the level of practice or pastoral discernment.

THE OTHER FRANCIS

As this account makes clear, I am troubled by Pope Francis's increasing tendency to conflate Catholic wisdom with a left-leaning secular humanitarianism. So far, I have taken my bearing from the most considered reflections of the pope (his encyclical on ecological matters, his evocations of Divine mercy, his apostolic letters on the joy of the gospel and on human and divine love, as well as his thought-provoking speeches to the European parliament and to the American Congress). I found much in Francis that is in continuity with his great predecessors (more than many of his critics acknowledge). But I also find much that smacks of the *bien-pensant* and politically correct. Still, the balance in these official documents and speeches tilts toward sobriety, thoughtfulness, and fidelity to the great tradition of Catholic wisdom.

The same cannot be said if one pays attention to the interviews and off-the-cuff remarks by the pope that have come to dominate the public impression of his pontificate. He got off to a bad start when he told journalists, on his return from the World Youth Day in Brazil in 2013, "Who am I to judge?" the activities and motives of homosexual Catholics who attempt to remain in communion with Christ and his Church.[36] He should have anticipated that

[36] See John Gehring, *The Francis Effect: A Radical Pope's Challenge to the American Church* (Rowman & Littlefield, 2015), 6.

his remarks would be used at the service of moral relativism and by those who attempt to undermine traditional marriage in the name of open-ended "love" and "marriage equality." Returning from another World Youth Day in Krakow, Poland, the pope made the fantastic and disturbing claim that "Catholic violence" is just as much a problem as "Islamic violence" – and this right after the brutal assassination of Father Jacques Hammel by Islamist terrorists in a church in northern France. The only example of "Catholic violence" that Pope Francis could come up with was that of a baptized young man who had killed his girlfriend for clearly nonreligious reasons or motives.[37] These sorts of comments are shorn of all good sense and smack of an unthinking political correctness.

The pope further insisted that every religion has its "fundamentalists," Islam no more than others.[38] This is at odds with the evidence. And the pope claimed, with no supporting arguments and many clichés, that Islamic terrorists commit heinous acts of violence in response to poverty and social injustice.[39] Capitalism and the "god of money," he said, were the ultimate source of terrorism in the modern world.[40] These sorts of haphazard claims make it harder to respect a pope whose more-considered reflections deserve our attention and respect.

This failure of practical reasoning is typical of Francis's off-the-cuff remarks. He displays a remarkable lack of rhetorical discipline, which can only undermine the integrity of his pontificate and of the papacy more generally. Recently, in an interview with the atheist Italian philosopher and journalist Eugenio Scalfari, he claimed that it is the communists today who "think like Christians."[41] He said nothing about the Church's principled and long-standing opposition to every form of totalitarianism. Communists are said by Francis to have a special Christ-like concern for the poor. The pope is silent about the tens of millions of ordinary workers and peasants who perished at the hands of ideological regimes of the communist type in the twentieth century. In response, Cardinal Zen of Hong Kong wrote in the *Wall Street Journal* (November 4, 2016) that the pope has no understanding of communist theory and practice, that he associates communists exclusively with those activists and intellectuals imprisoned or killed by the military government during the "dirty war" in Argentina during the 1970s. In a word, his vision is remarkably

37 Inés San Martin, "Pope Francis Denies that Islam Is Violent," *Crux*, July 31, 2016.
38 "Pope Francis Denies that Islam Is Violent."
39 "Pope Francis Denies that Islam Is Violent."
40 "Pope Francis Denies that Islam Is Violent."
41 Steve Skojec, "Pope: It Is the Communists Who Think Like Christians," *One Peter 5*, November 11, 2016.

parochial and blind to the greatest evil of the twentieth century, a totalitarianism inspired by viciously anti-Christian ideology.

The pope also freely "psychologizes" those who remain faithful to the Latin Mass. They are said to be "rigid," suffering from some form of Phariseeism.[42] No mercy or understanding is directed at their quarter. These remarks are an implicit assault on his predecessor, Benedict XVI, who aimed during his short pontificate to restore greater dignity and beauty to the Catholic liturgy.

A CRISIS IN THE CHURCH

When Cardinal Burke and three other Cardinals issued "Dubia" requesting clarification on the ambiguities created by the famous footnote in *Amoris laetitia* (does the Church still stand with Christ in affirming the indissolubility of marriage and in repudiating "situational ethics"?), the pope remained silent even as he criticized the "legalism" of those who dared to request doctrinal and moral clarity. Some have gone even further, arguing that the four cardinals should be deprived of the cardinalate, even accusing them of "heresy" and "apostasy" for remaining faithful to age-old Catholic teaching.[43] None of this is good for the unity of the Church and could point to schism down the line. The Argentinean, Maltese, and German Bishops' conferences have already endorsed communion for the divorced and remarried, claiming the authority of the pope's equivocal footnote. But Cardinal Gerhard Muller, former Prefect of the Congregation for the Defense of the Faith, told the Italian magazine *Il Timone* that the traditional teaching of the Church on marriage is still valid and "no power in heaven or on earth, neither an angel, nor the pope, nor a law of the bishops, has the faculty to change it." (See the *Catholic Herald* of February 1, 2017.) Cardinal Muller's emphatic reaffirmation of the Church's teaching regarding marriage did not go unchallenged by an increasingly autocratic pope. His appointment as head of the Congregation for the Defense of the Faith was not renewed in the summer of 2017, even though he was only 69 and nowhere near retirement age. We are clearly in unchartered waters.

Ross Douthat has written in the *New York Times* (September 20, 2017) that the pope's "winks" and "nods" about Communion for the divorced and the remarried have no authoritative status as Catholic teaching. My hope is that

---

[42] Timothy Kirchoff, "Is Pope Francis right about traditionalists who love the Latin Mass?" *America*, September 13, 2017.

[43] Inés San Martin, "Vatican judge says cardinal-critics of pope could lose red hats," *Crux*, November 29, 2016.

the pope learns some rhetorical discipline and ceases to distress faithful Catholics with ill-considered judgments, including those matters that properly belong to the prudence of faithful laymen (citizens and statesman) informed by what Catholic tradition calls "right reason." He must also be careful not to undermine the unity of Christ's Church. With each passing day, Francis demoralizes those who are most faithful and most orthodox. Under the new dispensation, their faith is confused with "rigidity" of one sort or another. Such a situation is unprecedented in the history of the Church.

CONCLUSION

There is wisdom and insight to be found in the writings, speeches, and addresses of Pope Francis. Here the pope is at his most serious. He is at his best when he thinks and writes in continuity with the full weight of Christian wisdom and in continuity with the insights of his immediate predecessors. But when he departs from them, he tends to confuse humanitarian concerns with properly Christian ones. He often gives a one-sided "progressivist" reading of Catholic social teaching. Remarkably, he seems to have learned very little about the gravest evil of the twentieth century, totalitarianism, hence his troubling indulgence toward communist tyranny in Cuba.

Pope Francis could benefit from paying more attention to the reflective experiences of John Paul II with totalitarian communism and Pope Benedict XVI with Nazi barbarism. Was not totalitarianism the fundamental political invention of the twentieth century, and a grave threat to the bodies and souls of human beings? No doubt, if Pope Francis did so (and that would require paying much more sympathetic attention to the lives and thoughts of his immediate predecessors), his thought would resonate more clearly with the timelessness of the best of Catholic social and political thought.[44] At the very least, he would be less apt in his writings and remarks to emphasize private judgments that too easily echo the progressive opinions and prejudices of his most vocal left-leaning admirers.

---

[44] On a hopeful note, Pope Francis spoke clearly and well about the crimes of Nazism and communism during his pastoral visit to Lithuania in September 2018.

PART III

THEMES IN CATHOLIC SOCIAL TEACHING

10

Catholic Social Teaching on the Common Good

V. Bradley Lewis

The idea of the common good has played a central normative role in the history of Western political thought and occupied a signature place in the modern social teaching of the Roman Catholic Church. It is an ancient notion with origins in classical Greek political philosophy,[1] from which it passed into the political writings of the medieval Christian political theologians.[2] When Leo XIII enjoined Catholics to reappropriate the thought of St. Thomas Aquinas in the service of a broader reappropriation of philosophy for the purpose of engaging the modern world in the wake of the revolutionary movements of the eighteenth and nineteenth centuries, the idea of the common good was revived as well.[3] The common good refers most immediately to the end or final cause of political association and of its most characteristic instrument, law. However, in the more strictly speculative regions of metaphysics and theology it refers to the whole order of the universe and its ultimate end in God. These meanings are held together analogically by way of a central notion of what completes and is therefore good for human beings. The common good is a good that is common, sharable by many, indeed, with respect to God and the order of the universe, by all. This analogical character of the common good fits it for use in both speculative and practical reasoning, but has also provided occasion for confusion related to these two modes as well as between philosophical and explicitly theological thinking.

---

[1] See, e.g., Thucydides 4.87.4, 5.90; Plato *Gorgias* 506a; Plato *Laws* 712d-715b; Aristotle *Politics* 1279a17-22; Cicero *Republic* 1.25.39.

[2] M. S. Kempshall, *The Common Good in Late Medieval Political Thought* (Oxford: Clarendon Press, 1999) is an invaluable survey.

[3] See Russell Hittinger, "Pope Leo XIII (1810–1903)," in *The Teachings of Modern Roman Catholicism on Law, Politics, and Human Nature*, ed. John Witte, Jr. and Frank S. Alexander (New York: Columbia University Press, 2007), 39–75.

For purposes of this article two magisterial treatments of the common good will be considered normatively central and decisive: the first is that of the Second Vatican Council's 1965 Pastoral Constitution on the Church in the Modern World, *Gaudium et spes*; the second is that of the *Catechism of the Catholic Church* promulgated by Pope St. John Paul II in 1992 (revised 1997). In *Gaudium et spes* one can see the culmination of a process of development in thinking about the common good and its central place in Catholic Social Doctrine begun in 1891 by Pope Leo XIII in *Rerum novarum*; in the Catechism we see an explication of that notion crystalized in light of the most important subsequent magisterial statements and regularly deployed in interventions in social, economic, and political questions by Vatican bodies, regional and national ecclesiastical conferences, local churches, and many individual Catholic thinkers. These statements reflect not only the Church's thinking about social and political questions, but her reaction to explicitly modern circumstances. In particular they reflect the Church's increasing concentration on the defense of the human person, a defense carried out in conditions dominated by the modern state as a political form, a form that poses stiff challenges to that defense of human dignity and to the freedom and transcendence of the Church.

In this chapter I first look more carefully at the formulation of the common good presented in *Gaudium et spes* and note some particularly salient aspects of the formulation itself and its context. Next I examine the traditional understanding of the common good, especially in the thought of Aristotle and Aquinas as sources of the tradition. Then I discuss the development of the account of the common good in *Gaudium et spes* in the work of neo-Thomist philosophers and theologians and in magisterial statements about the common good in the early twentieth century. Finally I discuss in more detail the application of the idea in the most important magisterial statements about social justice, subsidiarity, and the right to private property. I will argue that one finds in these statements both continuity with earlier Catholic thought, but also distinctively modern elements. With respect to the question of development, there has been extensive discussion of the question whether the account of the common good in contemporary Catholic social teaching has changed so much as to hold that the political common good is merely an instrumental good. It will be argued here that the political common good is complex in that it integrates aspects that are instrumental with aspects that are not. It therefore defeats any classificatory scheme that demands that one choose between honest goods, pleasant goods, and useful goods. Moreover, when thinking about even the political common good one must distinguish between the goods associated with political community as such and those associated with specific features of the modern state as a political form. The institution of the state itself with its characteristically modern features can be described as instrumental.

THE VATICAN II FORMULATION

The Church has employed a particular formulation of the common good in its most important social teaching documents since at least the pontificate of St. John XXIII. The most authoritative and so most frequently cited version of the formulation is given in the Second Vatican Council's Pastoral Constitution on the Church in the Modern World, *Gaudium et spes*: "the sum of those conditions of social life that allow social groups and their individual members relatively thorough and ready access to their own fulfillment."[4] A similar formulation is included in the Council's Declaration on Religious Freedom, *Dignitatis humanae*: "The common good of society consists in the sum total of those conditions of social life which enable people to achieve a fuller measure of perfection with greater ease."[5] The proximate origin of the council's formulation is John's 1961 encyclical letter, *Mater et magistra*, which has this: "the sum total of those conditions of social living, whereby men are enabled more fully and more readily to achieve their own perfection."[6] The formulation was then quoted in the same pope's 1963 encyclical, *Pacem in terris*,[7] and the fact of its place in Pope John's two encyclical letters certainly explains its place in the council documents.

The formulation in *Gaudium et spes* enjoys the highest degree of authority given its place in a document promulgated by an ecumenical council, and it is this formulation that has been either quoted or cited as definitive in every

---

[4] Vatican II, Pastoral Constitution *Gaudium et spes* (Pastoral Constitution on the Church in the Modern World) (1965), no. 26: seu summam eorum vitae socialis condicionum quae tum coetibus, tum singulis membris permittunt ut propriam perfectionem plenius atque expeditus consequantur. The formulation is repeated with only slight variation in no. 74.

[5] Vatican II, Declaration on Religious Liberty *Dignitatis humanae* (On the Right of the Person and of Communities to Social and Civil Freedom) (1965), no. 6: summa earum vitae socialis condicionum, quibus homines suam ipsorum perfectionem possunt plenius atque expeditius consequi.

[6] John XXIII, Encyclical Letter *Mater et magistra* (On Recent Developments of the Social Question in the Light of the Christian Teaching) (May 1961), no. 65: AAS 53 (1961), 417: Sed ad hos optatos exitus quo facilius pervehatur, debent qui publicae rei praesunt compertam habere rectam de communi omnium bono notionem, quae summam complectitur earum vitae socialis condicionum, quibus homines suam ipsorum perfectionem possint plenius atque expeditius consequi.

[7] John XXIII, Encyclical Letter *Pacem in terris* (On Establishing Universal Peace in Truth, Justice, Charity, and Liberty) (1963), no. 58: AAS 55 (1963), 273.

subsequent papacy (save the month-long reign of John Paul I).[8] It is also employed in the authoritative *Catechism of the Catholic Church* promulgated in 1992 by St. John Paul II and in the Pontifical Council for Justice and Peace's 2004 *Compendium of the Social Doctrine of the Church*.[9] It has similarly featured prominently in the statements of national episcopal conferences, often in anticipation of national elections.[10]

We should immediately notice five features of the *Gaudium et spes* formulation: first, the common good is characterized as a sum of conditions. Much of the traditional discussion of the common good characterizes the common good as a kind of final cause, that is, a goal. It is certainly not impossible to see a set of conditions as a goal, but not as a final or ultimate goal: conditions would ordinarily assume some further end or ends made possible by them. In this respect one could call the definition – and some have – an "instrumental" account of the common good. This is an issue to which we will return. In addition to this one must note that the sum here is a sum of conditions, not a sum of personal goods or a sum of the satisfaction or happiness of persons.[11] Many kinds of goods could be described as "conditions," and some of these are presumably the sorts of goods that Charles Taylor has called "irreducibly social."[12] To call something a "condition" does not in itself settle what type of good it is.

The point is reinforced when we notice a second feature of the definition, which is given in terms of "fulfillment." The Latin word used here is *perfectio* in *Gaudium et spes*, as well as in *Mater et magistra*, *Pacem in terris*, *Dignitatis humanae*, and the *Catechism*. While an identification of the common good with conditions seems to thin it out in comparison to other possible conceptions, the notion that it aims at perfection seems to effect just the reverse,

---

[8] See Paul VI, Apostolic Letter *Octogesima adveniens* (A Call to Action) (May 14, 1971), no. 24, 46: AAS 63 (1971), 419, 434; John Paul II, Encyclical Letter *Centesimus annus* (On the Hundredth Anniversary of *Rerum novarum*) (1991), no. 47, in AAS 83 (1991), 852; Benedict XVI, Encyclical Letter *Caritas in veritate* (On Integral Human Development in Charity and Truth) (2009), no. 7: AAS 101 (2009), 645; Francis, Encyclical Letter *Laudato si'* (On Care for Our Common Home), no. 156, AAS 107 (2015), 910.

[9] *Catechism of the Catholic Church*, rev. ed. (1997), no. 1906; Pontifical Council for Justice and Peace, CSDC, no. 160.

[10] See, e.g., Forming Consciences for Faithful Citizenship: A Call to Political Responsibility from the Catholic Bishops of the United States, rev. ed. (Washington, DC: United States Conference of Catholic Bishops, 2015), nos. 49, 63; Bishops Conference of England and Wales, *Choosing the Common Good* (Stokes on Trent: Alive Publishing, 2010), 8.

[11] John Paul II made this point immediately before citing *Gaudium et spes*, no. 26. See CA, no. 47.

[12] Charles Taylor, "Irreducibly Social Goods," in *Philosophical Arguments* (Cambridge: Harvard University Press, 1995), 127–145.

setting the bar rather high. This would seem particularly problematic in the context of modern pluralistic societies with no agreement on what might constitute human perfection. However, one must note that conditions are more capacious than a particular conception of perfection, so that the emphasis on conditions builds in a kind of flexibility that would not automatically be defeated by the empirical fact of pluralism.

A third feature of the definition specifies the perfection as that of both groups and individuals.[13] Thus, while the possible reduction of the notion of the common good to conditions suggests thinning, it is not one that arises from a simple individualism. The social nature of human beings is built into the definition. But it is important that the social aspect here is itself already defined in a pluralistic way. To say that the common good establishes conditions for the perfection of groups indicates that the common good is not simply about political society; it assumes the existence of many subpolitical human associations and relates them to human perfection, thereby precluding any attempt simply to identify the common good with the judgment of the state and its officials, even while underwriting and disciplining their authority.

Fourth, in the second and somewhat fuller treatment of the common good in *Gaudium et spes* the common good is said to "embrace" or "encompass" (*complecti*) the sum total of conditions.[14] Such conditions are included, *but not exhaustive* of the common good. In the Catechism, where the basic formulation is repeated and fleshed out in terms of more specific elements, it is also said that "each human community possesses a common good which permits it to be recognized as such." It goes on to say that it is in the "political community that its most complete realization is found" and that it is "the role of the state to defend and promote the common good of civil society, its citizens, and intermediate bodies."[15] The passage thus distinguishes the state, the political community, and the persons and intermediate bodies that make up civil society. This recalls Pius XI's characterization of the political society (*civitas*) as "a kind of instrument" (discussed below) at the service of the persons and groups that make up the society. These two are related to the common good, that is, have or participate in common goods that cannot be understood as sums of conditions.

Finally, the definition of the common good must not be taken in isolation from its context. In *Gaudium et spes* that context is the document's second

---

[13]   Groups are not mentioned in *Mater et magistra* and *Pacem in terris*, but are a modification of the formulation as found in *Gaudium et spes*, which is the main source for subsequent discussions like the *Catechism*.
[14]   GS, no. 74.
[15]   *Catechism*, no. 1910.

chapter, "On the Human Community." The chapter begins by noting the phenomenon of growing human interdependence and the contribution of Christian revelation in understanding more deeply "the laws of social life which the Creator has written into man's spiritual and moral nature."[16] This is certainly a reference to the natural moral law. The document then discusses "the communitarian character of the human vocation," affirming the brotherhood of all people and their common goal, "God himself."[17] The next article states that the progress of the human person and of society are interrelated since "the subject and the goal of all social institutions is and must be the human person, which for its part and by its very nature stands completely in need of social life."[18] Human social relations are divided into two classes: those most immediately related to man's nature are the family and the political community; others are a result of free decision. These relationships multiply and interrelate in a process called "socialization." The test of such relations is their contribution to the human person's direction toward her destiny. The relationship between the dignity of the person and the social nature of the person is the paramount theme of the chapter. In the immediate sequel to the definition the council fathers emphasize the person's "universal and inviolable rights and duties," and then discuss particular threats to human dignity.[19] The last sections of the chapter all explicitly reject individualism and reemphasize the social virtue of solidarity.[20]

The *Catechism* gives its own summary of the Council's account. After quoting the formulation, it says that the common good consists of "three essential elements": first, respect for persons, which entails respect for "the fundamental and inalienable rights of the human person," privileging in particular freedom of conscience and religion; second, "social *well-being* and *development* of the group itself"; and third, peace, understood as "stability and security of a just social order."[21] The substance of this is that political communities should provide for their members a social context that truly supports their flourishing primarily through the protection of their fundamental rights, facilitation of their integral development, and the maintenance of internal and external peace and security. These are the characteristic tasks of

---

[16] GS, no. 23.

[17] GS, no. 24. The first quote is the title of no. 24.

[18] GS, no. 25: subiectum et finis omnium institutorum socialium est et esse debet humana persona, quippe quae, suapte natura, vita sociali omnino indigeat. This sentence concludes with a note citing Aquinas's commentary on Aristotle's *Nicomachean Ethics* bk. 1, lect. 1.

[19] GS, nos. 26, 27. It bears noting that the document mentions both rights and duties.

[20] GS, nos. 30, 31, 32.

[21] *Catechism*, nos. 1906–1909 (emphasis in the original). The first two aspects are based on the text of *Gaudium et spes* itself, while the third is not.

modern political communities and there is a vast range of specific ways in which such communities can and do promote the common good. Nevertheless, the focus on human rights and development in particular, as well as the whole notion that the common good is about establishing and maintaining a set of conditions has suggested to some that the Council's idea of the common good represents a change from the premodern, particularly Thomistic, understanding that in some sense inspired it. Assessing this contention requires looking at the premodern view and at the development of the *Gaudium et spes* formulation.

THE CLASSICAL VIEW

Aquinas received the idea of the common good from Aristotle by way of his teacher, Albert the Great. However, Thomas's constructive account is somewhat different from that of Aristotle owing in part to the changed political context of the thirteenth century and to its integration into Thomas's larger speculative theological project, influenced both by the content of Christian revelation and by other philosophical currents, notably Neoplatonism. The medieval political theologians focused especially on three Aristotelian texts in their speculative treatments of the common good.[22] The first was his statement from the first pages of the *Nicomachean Ethics* that the good of a city is greater and "more divine" than that of a single individual.[23] The second was Aristotle's treatment of analogy in his criticism of Plato's account of the idea of the good in the sixth chapter of the first book of the *Nicomachean Ethics*.[24] The third was the discussion of the common good in the twelfth book of Aristotle's *Metaphysics*, with its distinction between the intrinsic and extrinsic common good.[25]

These passages are not the ones that would most immediately leap out at one looking to Aristotle's writings on the common good.[26] The actual phrase is used most in the context of his account of the city and its regime or constitutional order. Aristotle famously classifies political regimes across two axes: the first divides those that aim at the common good of the city from those that aim

---

[22] On these three passages see Kempshall, *The Common Good*, 26–38 initially; discussion of them recurs frequently in Kempshall's essential study.

[23] Aristotle *Nicomachean Ethics* 1094b9-10.

[24] *Nicomachean Ethics* 1096a11-b31.

[25] Aristotle, *Metaphysics* 1075a11-15.

[26] The next two paragraphs draw on the more detailed account of these issues I give in "Aristotle, The Common Good, and Us," *Proceedings of the American Catholic Philosophical Association* 87 (2014): 69–88.

only at the good of the ruling class; the second divides those two by the number of rulers: one, few, or many.[27] Monarchy is the rule of one for the common good; tyranny is the rule of one for the good of the tyrant. Aristocracy is the rule of the few (who are the virtuous); oligarchy is the rule of the few (the wealthy) for their own good. A regime in which the many rule for the common good has no distinctive name, but is simply given the name of the genus, "regime," and is a hybrid form comprising a kind of compromise between the few rich and the many poor anchored by a stable middle class. Democracy is the rule of the many poor in their own interest. This is somewhat shocking to modern people who identify democracy with legitimacy, but it is important to recall that democracy for the classical Greeks was different from modern representative democracy in that it meant direct rule of the whole body of citizens physically assembled in open-air meetings. The officials who enforced the law and administered the city in between meetings of the Assembly were chosen by lot for brief terms. All of this was meant to preclude the rise of a permanent ruling class. Aristotle's negative judgment of democracy, as he understood it, is important in his account of the common good.

One of the key differences between the generic regime and democracy is that Aristotle associates the former both with the middle class and with the rule of law. He thought that democracy would lead to confiscation of the property of the wealthy and the nurturing of class conflict that could ultimately destroy the city. A strong middle class, he held, would bridge the distance between rich and poor, and the rule of law would protect everyone in the city from exploitation. These characteristics and his refusal to give the regime a specific name reflect the influence of his teacher, Plato. In his late dialogue, *Laws*, Plato has the main interlocutor condemn the conventional political regimes as merely the rule of factions and argues that the government of a good city would look to the good of the whole rather than that of only the ruling part and says that such a regime would have simply the generic name. Elsewhere he describes such a generic political regime as a mixture of all the principal political claims and holds that in it the law and not the officials would really rule.[28] This is clearly the background of Aristotle's later account.

Plato and Aristotle both advocate a form of government that transcends the narrow partisanship that all too often pushes aside the good of the whole. Interestingly, both associate their alternative not only with law, but with the reason that informs law and even with the divine. This is because they saw human beings motivated by both reason and passion. What the law lacks in

[27] Aristotle *Politics* 1279a22-b11.
[28] Plato *Laws* 689c-693d, 712c-715d.

losing the particular perceptions and judgments of living intellects, it gains in detachment from the subrational motives of actual persons, and this kind of reason detached from passions is like the divine intellect.[29] This connection between the common good and the divine is also a connection to the later medieval accounts that emphasized the three Aristotelian texts mentioned above.

Of those medieval discussions it is that of Aquinas that was most important for the development of Catholic social teaching. One obstacle in understanding Aquinas's view is that he nowhere clearly and systematically explained it; there is no question in the *Summa Theologiae* or any other work explicitly devoted to the common good. To take the bare phrase in its standard Thomistic meaning, a common good is first a type of good, that is, something that is an end because it perfects or fulfills that of which it is an end. Ends are the objects of appetite because they are good, not good because they are the objects of appetite. To say that such a good is common is to say that it can be shared. So a common good is good not just for one person, but for many, and the more common or sharable a good is, the better it is. For Aquinas, goods can be common in three different senses. Some goods are common in the very limited sense that they are actually owned by a group of persons, perhaps by the political community as a whole, and then distributed by that group to its members. These are properly spoken of as "common goods" (note the plural) and constitute an important but peripheral case of the sorts of goods with which we are concerned here.[30] Aquinas holds that other goods are common "by predication," that is, they are conceptually shared in so far as they can be predicated of any number of things, but they do not exist as entities. Health, for example, is a good common by predication since it is good for all persons, but there is no thing in reality called health apart from its instantiation in those persons. Finally, Aquinas holds that some goods are common in a causal sense: they are themselves sharable ends that really do exist and the effects of which reach many persons.[31] His most central example here is the sun, which is one thing with effects that literally radiate to all. As noted above, the more common a good is, the better it is. Thomas discusses three common goods as most superior: God, the order of the created universe, and the political community.

---

[29] Aristotle *Politics* 1287a23-32; Plato *Laws* 712e-714a, 875a-d.
[30] Aquinas, *Summa Theologiae*, II-II, 61.1.
[31] For the distinction between goods common by predication and causally common see, e.g., *Disputed Questions on Truth*, 7.6 ad7; *Summa Theologiae*, I, 39.4 ad 3; and II-II, 90.2 ad2.

God is for Aquinas the universal good, the end that fulfills and perfects every kind of created being. God is the extrinsic end and thus the common good of the entire created universe.[32] The intrinsic end and common good of the universe is its order. The common good of the political community is understood on analogy with these common goods. It is a causal good in so far as it is one end, the effects of which reach the many members who make it up.[33] To speak of the political community in this way, however, raises questions that are uncomfortable from the perspective of modern political philosophy, dominated as it is by the ideas of the social contract and general utility. The social contract tradition begins with individuals and constructs political authority by modeling their (hypothetical) rational agreement. Utilitarianism understands political authority as justified by its facilitation of the highest levels of aggregate or average satisfaction of individuals. Aquinas by contrast often speaks of the relationship of the political community and its members as that between a kind of whole and its parts. This has led some to think of the common good, for better or worse, as a kind of whole with its own interests distinct from and often in tension with the interests of individuals. This was not Aquinas's view.

The correct understanding of Aquinas's language here is related to the senses he gives both to the notion of parts and to the notion of wholes. A part can simply be a piece or appendage in some spatial sense. If this was the way he conceived of human beings in relation to the political community, it would be a disturbing image indeed. But part also indicates incompleteness in a different sense; it indicates a need relative to a thing's perfection. When Aristotle famously wrote that human beings were by nature political animals (and Aquinas follows him explicitly in this) he meant that a human being is a being the good of which simply cannot be achieved alone.[34] To take only the crudest example of this, an infant abandoned immediately after birth cannot survive. But the need for other persons not just in order to survive but to flourish is something that human beings never outgrow. At every stage they seek and require not only goods the achievement of which requires social cooperation, but social activity itself, which is a good for human beings that, in its fullest and most enduring sense, we call friendship. This is true in varying ways related to various kinds and sizes of community. The political community constitutes a kind of limit here in so far as it provides in principle everything that is needed for the natural flourishing of human beings; it encompasses and provides a context for all of the other goods we seek. This

[32] E.g., *Summa Theologiae*, I-II, 19.10; 100.8; 109.3; Aquinas, *Summa contra Gentiles*, 3.17.
[33] Aquinas, *Summa Theologiae*, I-II, 90.2.
[34] Thomas Aquinas, *On Kingship*, 1.1.

is why Aristotle and Aquinas both refer to it as a "complete community."[35] To speak of persons as parts, then, can – and for Aquinas does – indicate their partiality relative to complete communities themselves understood by reference to the flourishing of those very persons. Such communities accordingly constitute a common good, a good that extends to and is shared in by the members.

Understanding what Aquinas meant by the "wholeness" of the political community is the necessary correlate to his account of the "partiality" of persons. The political community has a particular degree of unity: it is more unified than a mere aggregation, but less unified than a substance. Aquinas calls it a "unity of order."[36] This means that a part of the political community retains its own agency apart from that of the group. An army engages in operations, and the individual soldiers who make up the army are parts of such operations, but each individual soldier also operates independently. This is so because, unlike the community, the individual soldier is a substance, an irreducible and independent composite of form and matter. That soldier's arm or leg has no operation independent of the substantial whole that is the soldier. So the community has more unity than a mere aggregation, but less than a substance, and this unity is largely a function of the social body's internal coordination toward the common good of its members.

The common good of the community then is not the good of a kind of super-individual that is opposed to that of the person for two reasons. First, the community is not a substance and therefore not a person in the metaphysical sense (legal personhood or other forms of personification applied to society are another matter), but a unified relation among natural persons effected by their wills and practical reasoning. Second, and just in virtue of this aspect of the community as an object of the practical reasoning of the persons who make it up, the good of the community is not conceived of as separate from, much less as opposed to, the good of those persons. It is an aspect of their proper good as individuals, a necessary condition of their flourishing.

It is also important to see the important respects in which the common good is on Aquinas's account analogical. The most common good and therefore the one that is simply the best is the ultimate good of all human persons: subjectively this is understood as their happiness or flourishing. Objectively, it is the

---

[35]   Aristotle *Politics* 1252b29 and Aristotle *Nicomachean Ethics* 1097b8-11; Thomas Aquinas, *Sententia libri Politicorum*, 1.1 [23]; Thomas Aquinas, *Sententia libri Ethicorum*, 1.1 [4]; and Aquinas, *Summa Theologiae*, I-II, 90.3 ad3; and 91.1c.

[36]   Aquinas, *Sententia libri Ethicorum*, 1.1 [5]; Aquinas, *Summa Theologiae*, 1a2ae, 17.4c; and see John Finnis, *Aquinas: Moral, Political and Legal Theory* (Oxford: Oxford University Press, 1998), 24–25.

thing that most constitutes that happiness, and for Aquinas this is God. After God the most common good is the order of the universe as such.[37] The common good associated with the political community is usually called the temporal common good. But here certain precisions are also necessary. Even from a temporal perspective the common good of human beings is happiness, and the common good of a particular community is the happiness of the persons who make up that community. But this is not necessarily identical to what we might call the political common good, what Aquinas sometimes calls the "public good" of the community and which he identifies with its governing institutions, most centrally its laws. Laws, like the other aspects of specifically political authority, aim at the common good as their final cause. They are, however, limited in what they can accomplish: laws aim neither at the proscription of all vice nor do they command all the acts of the virtues. Rather they aim to prohibit offenses that make living in community difficult or impossible.[38] Aquinas particularly identifies the public good with the law and government's establishment of peace and justice. This is in no sense a denial of the importance of the full range of moral virtues and even their relevance to the good order of the community, but simply a recognition that the law is limited in its ability to secure these goods and that they are best promoted in other ways by other parts of the community, especially in the family and the Church.[39]

For Aquinas then the common good means a number of related things and exists in a number of different but related contexts. At the center of the idea is simply that of the good, the perfection of human life. Since human beings cannot achieve their good alone, they must participate in various unifying relationships like the family, friendships, productive enterprises, particular religious communities as well as the universal religious community that is the Church, political associations, and the form of political association that is complete in the sense that it provides all that is necessary for the flourishing of individual persons as well as these other associations. A crucial part of what the political community provides is overall coordination, some of which is primarily negative, for example, the prohibition of conduct that damages the community and its members, and some of which is more positive, i.e., facilities for the pursuit of goods and the formation of associations for the common pursuit of goods. Such prohibitions and facilities are primarily although not exclusively a function of the political community's legal system. The political

[37]   See, e.g., Aquinas, *Summa Theologiae*, I, 47.1; Aquinas, *Summa contra Gentiles* 2.39 and 3.64.
[38]   Aquinas, *Summa Theologiae*, I-II, 96.2–3.
[39]   See Finnis, *Aquinas*, ch. 7.

community is a common good, one aimed at the further common good that is the perfection of its members, although much of this perfection is beyond the productive capacity of the political community through its legal and other administrative instruments. Moreover, since that community is aimed at the more comprehensive good of persons, it is limited in its authority precisely by that good, which includes most importantly the person's ordination to a flourishing that is constituted by union with God and which transcends every human community.

This Thomistic account of the common good is essential background for the social doctrine of the Church as developed since the pontificate of Leo XIII. Leo's initiation of the modern doctrine was closely related to his initiation of the Thomistic revival and the terms in which social teaching has been expressed are mainly Thomistic. Nevertheless, the context of the development of social doctrine is importantly different from that of Aquinas, separated as it is by six centuries during which political and economic institutions and practices underwent far-reaching changes. It would have been surprising indeed if the manner in which the idea of the common good was understood did not change during this period. The movement from the idea as understood by Aquinas to that of the formulation from *Gaudium et spes* described above is related to these changes.

THE PROXIMATE DERIVATION OF THE VATICAN II FORMULATION

The Vatican II formulation of the common good was worked out mainly by Thomistic moral theologians and social theorists during the late nineteenth and early twentieth centuries as part of the Thomistic revival's attempt to engage the modern world. It reflects the important changes in social, economic, and political life that occurred in the centuries since St. Thomas's own time. Certainly, the centrality of the idea of the common good in the tradition guaranteed it a place in the renewed engagement with social and political questions undertaken by Catholic thinkers in the wake of the revolutions of the eighteenth and nineteenth centuries. The process of thinking through the implications of these changes for the idea and its theoretical context, however, took time. Most references to the common good in the writings of the chief patron of the revival, Leo XIII, are quite generic in character. Nevertheless development had already taken place among some of the principal thinkers of the neo-Thomist movement, which had been underway for more than half a century when Leo wrote his programmatic encyclical, *Aeterni patris*, in 1879.

Among the most consequential of these was the Italian Jesuit, Luigi
Taparelli D'Azeglio (1793–1862). Taparelli was rector of the Collegio
Romano (now the Gregorian University) during the time that Vincenzo
Gioacchino Pecci, the future Leo XIII, was a seminary student and he
aggressively promoted the recovery of the thought of Aquinas as able to supply
the necessary philosophical and theological resources to combat what was bad
in modernity and to appropriate what was good. His own views were developed
in a massive treatise on natural law that he composed in the 1840s, as well as in
the many articles he wrote on social, economic, and political questions for the
important Roman journal that he helped to found, *La Civiltà Cattolica*.[40]
Among the most important ideas in Taparelli's large treatise was the principle
of subsidiarity, which was adopted by Leo in *Rerum novarum* and expounded
in even more detail by Pius XI in *Quadragesimo anno*. Taparelli's treatise on
natural law was aimed at refuting classical liberalism, especially the theory of
the social contract, which Taparelli held to be an abstraction from the obvious
social nature of human beings. In this respect Taparelli was an Aristotelian,
but the facts that provided his account with its content included more contingent realities, most importantly the many respects in which the modern
state was different from the classical polis and the political institutions of
Aquinas's time. This was manifested by some of the interlocutors to be
found in Taparelli's notes, among whom were a number of now largely
forgotten jurisprudential thinkers. What matters most for present purposes is
that Taparelli saw the common good as both the "conformity of social operation with the intentions of the Creator" and in its "realization of *external*
order."[41] Such order is mainly concerned with a "right and duty to aid the
individual in attaining his natural happiness." This aid involves help that
individuals cannot provide for themselves consisting of the provision and
maintenance of "material and conditions" that favor the "perfection of individuals through positive cooperation."[42] In Taparelli, writing in the first half of
the nineteenth century, we can already see the key elements of the *Gaudium et
spes* formulation: the good of society is seen in conditions for the perfection of
the persons who make it up.

[40] On Taparelli see Thomas C. Behr, "Luigi Taparelli D'Azeglio, SJ (1793–1862) and the
      Development of Scholastic Natural-Law Thought as a Science of Society and Politics,"
      Journal of Markets and Morality 6 (2003): 99–115.
[41] P. Luigi Taparelli, *Saggio teoretico di dritto natural appoggiato sul fatto*, 8th ed. (Roma:
      Edizioni "La Civiltà Cattolica," 1949), §734. The book was published originally in four
      volumes, 1840–43.
[42] Taparelli, *Saggio teoretico*, §726, 739.

Taparelli's work was controversial both because of the politics of Italy in the mid-nineteenth century and because of Taparelli's role in internal struggles within his own Society of Jesus. For these reasons Leo XIII proceeded largely without mentioning Taparelli, although one of the principal drafters of *Rerum novarum* was Taparelli's confrere and close collaborator, Matteo Liberatore (1810–92), whose own understanding of the common good was based on Taparelli's.[43] Taparelli's influence was later acknowledged openly by Pius XI as well as by another important Jesuit thinker, Oswald von Nell-Breuning (1890–1991), who was the principal drafter of *Quadragesimo anno*.[44] By then, Taparelli's idea had already been incorporated into at least two generations of manuals authored by Jesuit moral theologians. Particularly noteworthy was that of the Swiss Jesuit, Victor Cathrein (1845–1931), who defined the end of the political community as "an ensemple (*complexus*) of required conditions that enables all members of society to achieve as much as possible their temporal happiness subordinate to their ultimate end."[45] Two things should be noted about Cathrein's formulation, which is the most likely immediate origin of that found in John and the Council. First, it stresses not merely the natural, but what might be called the material aspects of the common good. These conditions are not exclusively or simplistically material – he does note that sound morality is an aspect of the common good – but they are primarily concerned with public prosperity and external order, especially with peace and the protection of rights.[46] Second, Cathrein was a student and colleague of another Jesuit moralist, Theodor Meyer (1821–1913), and cites Meyer's work in his discussion of the common good. Meyer himself was influenced by Taparelli, and both Meyer and Cathrein worked in the Jesuit stadium at Maria Laach, which the Jesuits were forced to leave during the *Kulturkampf*. Both Meyer and Cathrein were therefore quite familiar with the character of the modern state and the abuses that it could perpetrate against the Church and civil society.[47]

[43] See Liberatore's own treatise, *Institutiones Ethicae et Iuris Naturae*, 9th ed. (Prati: Ex officiana Giachetti, filii et soc., 1887), 235; and on his role in drafting *Rerum novarum* see John Molony, *The Worker Question: A New Historical Perspective on "Rerum Novarum"* (Dublin: Gill and Macmillan, 1991), 64–88; Roger Aubert, *Catholic Social Teaching: A Historical Perspective* (Milwaukee, WI: Marquette University Press, 2003), 181–203.

[44] See Oswald von Nell-Breuning, SJ, "The Drafting of *Quadragesimo Anno*," in *Readings in Moral Theology, No. 5: Official Catholic Social Teaching*, eds. Charles E. Curran and Richard A. McCormick, SJ (New York: Paulist Press, 1986), 60–68.

[45] Victor Cathrein, SJ, *Philosophia Moralis in Usum Scholarum*, 5th ed. (Freiburg im Breisgau: Herder, 1905), §516.

[46] Cathrein, *Philosophia Moralis in Usum Scholarum*, §518–19.

[47] On Meyer and Cathrein see Felix Dirsch, *Solidarismus und Sozialethik: Ansätze zur Neuinterpretation einer modernen Strömung der katholischen Sozialphilosophie* (Berlin: Lit Verlag, 2006), 269–80, 287–99.

Cathrein's formulation was slightly modified by Charles Antoine (1848–1921), another Jesuit, originally trained as a chemist, but who later wrote extensively on sociology and economics and whose work influenced many subsequent French Catholic figures as well as Nell-Breuning.[48] Antoine's formulation gets us very close indeed to *Gaudium et spes*: "the end of civil society consists in the temporal public good, that is to say in the ensemble of conditions necessary for citizens to have the possibility of attaining their true temporal happiness."[49]

The most likely source of this line of Jesuit social thought into the modern papal magisterium was another German Jesuit, Gustav Gundlach (1892–1963), who adopted it in his own work, but, more importantly, served as an important advisor to three popes. Gundlach studied sociology and economics before being assigned by his superiors to take over the work of Heinrich Pesch. He was eventually posted to the Gregorian University in Rome, where he helped draft the "lost encyclical" on race for Pius XI. He became a much closer advisor to Pius XII and then very briefly to St. John XXIII.[50] Gundlach played an important role in drafting both encyclicals and speeches for both Piuses and was thoroughly imbued with the Jesuit social thought of the nineteenth and early twentieth centuries.

It seems clear enough, then, that the Vatican II formulation of the common good has its origins in the Jesuit manualists who were themselves indebted to Taparelli's project. The formulation was also accepted and augmented by a line of Dominican thinkers, often with explicit training in law and the social sciences, who were also influential among the drafters of John XXIII's encyclicals as well as of the Vatican II documents. The main artery for their views seems to have been the French and Italian Social Week movements, especially the French, which was founded in 1904 in response to *Rerum novarum*.[51] This Dominican line began in the work of Marie-Benoît Schwalm (1860–1908), who lectured on philosophy, theology, and sociology at the Dominican studium at Corbara and later at Flavigny. Schwalm was inspired by the

---

[48] See Jean-Yves Calvez, SJ and Jacques Perrin, SJ, *The Church and Social Justice: The Social Teaching of the Popes from Leo XIII to Pius XII (1878–1958)*, trans. J. R. Kirwan (Chicago: Henry Regnery Co., 1961), 146–147.

[49] Charles Antoine, *Cours d'Économie Sociale*, 6th ed. (Paris: Alca, 1921), 37.

[50] For Gundlach's life and work, see Johannes Schearte, *Gustav Gundlach S.J. (1892–1963): Maßgeblicher Repräsentant der katholischen Soziallehre wärend der Pontifikate Pius' XI. und Pius' XII* (München: Verlag Ferdinand Schöningh, 1975). For his understanding of the common good, see the encyclopedia article he wrote, "Gemeinwohl," reprinted in his collected essays, *Die Ordnung der menschlichen Gesellschaft* (Köln: Bachem, 1964), 1: 158–61.

[51] See Jean-Yves Calvez, *The Social Thought of John XXIII: "Mater et Magistra,"* trans. George J. M. McKenzie, S.M. (Chicago: Henry Regnery Co., 1964), 4–5, 102n13.

Leonine revival to produce a Thomistically grounded political and social philosophy, which he worked out in a two-volume treatise based on his lectures, posthumously published in 1910.[52] Like the Jesuit manualists, Schwalm's philosophical grounding for social science began by giving an account of society in terms of Aristotle's four forms of causality, the final cause being the common good. However, there was a distinctive element to Schwalm's account: he held that it had a dual character. In one sense the common good was subordinated to the good of each individual and could be seen as a kind of distribution. He denied that this constituted individualism because the individuals had to be understood not simply as singular individuals, but as individuals associated with one another. At the same time one could see the common good as the good of the collectivity, especially of its unity and order. While the individual seeks society as a help to achieving his own good, he must recognize that society has a kind of internal good without which it cannot prove helpful and this makes claims on him. Schwalm also distinguished a "disinterested" common good of society as the perfection of the human species itself.[53]

One of the later Dominicans influenced by Schwalm, Joseph-Thomas Delos (1891–1974), was a lawyer, sociologist, and long-time member of the French diplomatic service. Delos was one of the organizers of the French Social Weeks and contributed some fifteen papers at those meetings between 1925 and 1958. Delos's 1929 treatise on international law describes the common good as "the ensemble of external conditions and objects of human happiness" and as "the complete ensemble of conditions for human development."[54] He gave a similar account four years later in a lecture at the French Social Week in Reims. There are two further relevant elements to Delos's views: first he explicitly placed them in the context of an international situation dominated by the modern state and was especially concerned about the totalitarian states then on the rise.[55] Second, he appealed frequently to Schwalm and adopted his view that the common good is actually distributed to the members of

---

[52] *Leçons de Philosophie sociale*, 2 vols (Paris: Bloud & Cie., 1910). A one-volume abridgment, published as *La Société et l'État* (Paris: Flammarion, 1937) gained even wider circulation. It was cited prominently by, among others, Jacques Maritain and Yves Simon.

[53] *Leçons de Philosophie sociale*, 1:14–28.

[54] Joseph-Thomas Delos, OP, *La société international et les Principes du Droit public* (Paris: A. Pedone, 1929), 134.

[55] See Delos, *Principes du Droit public*, 182–183 with "La sociologie de S. Thomas et le fondement du droit international," *Angelicum* 22 (1945): 5–6; and Joseph-Thomas Delos, OP "La fin proper de la politique: le bien commun temporal," *Semaines sociale de France, 25th session, Reims, 1933, La société politique et la pensée chrétienne* (Paris: J. Gabalda, 1933), 219, where Delos contrasts his view with that of Carl Schmidt.

society, a view also adopted by Maritain. In the notes Delos provided for a volume of the widely used Revue des Jeunes edition of Aquinas's *Summa Theologiae* containing Aquinas's initial questions on justice he presented his view of the common good as "the ensemble of social conditions that permit one to lead a fully human life," and associated the notion with the idea of social justice, which he characterized as having a "mutual overlapping" relationship with distributive justice. He credits the notion to Schwalm and this seems to be precisely the idea – whatever its precise source – that finds its way into Pius XI's discussions of social justice in *Divini redemptoris*.[56]

By the time of *Mater et magistra* this way of thinking about the common good was well established. Just seven years before that encyclical it was elaborated in detail in the great Benedictine medievalist, Dom Odon Lottin's (1880–1965) textbook, *Moral Fondementale*. There he described the common good as "principally the conditions of life favorable to the practice of the virtues, to the repudiation of vices, such that intellectual, moral and physical culture that favors the virtues; secondarily, in the economic order: a wise organization of production, of circulation, and the distribution and use of material goods; in a word it must assure to the citizens all that is useful in view of their temporal happiness.... the common good is nothing other than the ensemble of conditions favorable to the integral development of citizens guaranteed by social authority."[57] The formulation of the common good now associated mainly with *Gaudium et spes* was thus something of a commonplace among moral theologians in the first half of the twentieth century and is found in the works of Jesuit, Dominican, and Benedictine moralists, all of who thought of it as the application of Thomistic ideas to contemporary conditions.

This way of thinking about the common good was clearly adopted by the popes in their own teaching during a period in which the power of ideologically controlled states was threatening not only the peace of Europe but the freedom of the Church. In his 1929 encyclical letter on education, Pius XI reaffirmed the state's responsibility for the temporal common good, which he then went on to characterize as "that peace and security in which families and individual citizens have the free exercise of their rights, and at the same time enjoy the greatest spiritual and temporal prosperity possible in this life, by the mutual union and co-ordination of the work of all."[58] Eight years later, in *Mit*

---

[56] *Somme Théologique, La Justice (2a2ae, Questions 57–62)*, vol. 1, trans. M. S. Gillet, OP with notes and appendices by Joseph-Thomas Delos, OP (Paris: Desclée & Cie, 1932), 209, 222–226.

[57] Dom Odon Lottin, *Morale Fondementale* (Paris: Desclée & Cie., 1954), 1: 132–33.

[58] Pius XI, Encyclical Letter *Divini illius magistri* (On Christian Education) (1929), no. 43: AAS 22 (1930), 63.

brennender sorge, an encyclical treating the increasingly dark situation in Germany, Pius discussed the common good again and tied it to man's nature:

> Society was intended by the Creator for the full development of individual possibilities, and for the social benefits, which by a give and take process, everyone can claim for his own sake and that of others. Higher and more general values, which collectivity alone can provide, also derive from the Creator for the good of man, and for the full development, natural and supernatural, and the realization of his perfection.[59]

In *Divini redemptoris*, published only five days later[60] and directed at totalitarianism from the left, he wrote:

> But God has likewise destined man for civil society according to the dictates of his very nature. In the plan of the Creator, society is a natural means which man can and must use to reach his destined end. Society is for man and not vice versa. This must not be understood in the sense of liberal individualism, which subordinates society to the selfish use of the individual; but only in the sense that by means of an organic union and by natural collaboration the attainment of earthly happiness is placed within the reach of all. In a further sense, it is society which affords the opportunities for the development of all the individual and social gifts bestowed on human nature.[61]

This text is important not least because of its warning that, notwithstanding the common good's direction to human flourishing, it should not be reduced to mere material conditions.

This development went even further under Pius XII. In his most substantial encyclical on social questions, *Summi pontificatus*, written just two years after *Divini redemptoris*, and in the even darker days of the start of World War II, Pius wrote,

> Hence, it is the noble prerogative and function of the State to control, aid and direct the private and individual activities of national life that they converge harmoniously towards the common good. That good can neither be defined according to arbitrary ideas nor can it accept for its standard primarily the

---

[59] Pius XI, Encyclical Letter *Mit brennender sorge* (On the Church in the German Reich) (1937), no. 30: AAS 29 (1937), 160.

[60] *Mit brennender sorge*, *Divini redemptoris*, and *Fermissimam constantiam*, which considered the situation of the Church in Mexico, were all published during an extraordinary two-week period in March 1937 in which Pius XI confronted what he took to be the most serious political threats to the Church. See John Pollard, *The Papacy in the Age of Totalitarianism, 1914–1958* (Oxford: Oxford University Press, 2014), 264–274.

[61] Pius XI, Encyclical Letter *Divini redemptoris* (On Atheistic Communism) (1937), no. 29: AAS 29 (1937), 79.

material prosperity of society, but rather it should be defined according to the harmonious development and the natural perfection of man. It is for this perfection that society is designed by the Creator as a means.[62]

This passage is important in its reiteration of the connection between the state, the common good, and the perfections rooted in human nature. It is also significant for its striking characterization of political society (the Latin term used is *civitas* rather than the more neutral *societas*) as a "kind of instrument" (*quasi instrumentum*). In his 1942 Christmas radio message Pius spoke in a similar way: "All of the political and economic activity of the state is directed to the permanent realization of the common good, which is to say of the external conditions that are necessary to all of the citizens for the development of their qualities and functions, of their material, intellectual, and religious life."[63] For Pius XII the instrumental aspect of the state was a correlate to his personalism, a view that was to become increasingly influential in subsequent papacies. Indeed, these two aspects of Pius XII's thought make him the key figure in the development of the conception of the common good in contemporary Catholic Social Doctrine. The unpacking and development of these ideas continued for the next six decades.

Given both this background in neo-Thomist social thought developing since the mid-nineteenth century, and its increasing adoption by the papal magisterium for over three decades, it is unsurprising to find the formulation of the common good in a major encyclical of John XXIII. In fact the formulation appears twice, almost matter-of-factly, in *Mater et magistra* (nos. 65 and 74) and once in *Pacem in terris* (no. 58). In one crucial respect John was simply following the lead of Pius XII. In addition to this, Pope John had always had a particular interest in social questions. One of the signature features of *Mater et magistra* was the notion of "socialization," which was the main theme of the French Social Week held in Grenoble just one year before the publication of the encyclical. Jean-Yves Calvez pointed out that several passages of *Mater et magistra* were taken verbatim from the letter of Cardinal Tardini addressed to that meeting.[64] Moreover, John's view of socialization is closely connected to personalism. The great challenge in the modern period was to make

---

[62] Pius XII, Encyclical letter *Summi pontificatus* (On the Unity of Human Society) (1939), no. 59: *AAS* 31 (1939), 433. For context see Pollard, *The Papacy in the Age of Totalitarianism*, 308–310.

[63] Pius XI, "Christmas Message" (December 25, 1942): "che tutta l'attività dello Stato, politica ed economica serve per l'attuazione duratura del bene comune; cioè, di quelle esterne condizioni, le quali sono necessarie all'insieme dei cittadini per lo sviluppo delle loro qualità e dei loro uffici, della loro vita materiale, intellettuale e religiosa." *AAS* 35 (1943), 13.

[64] Jean-Yves Calvez, SJ, *The Social Thought of John XXIII*, 4 and 102n13.

socialization serve the development of the person.[65] Given the presence of this conception of the common good in John's two encyclicals, it was virtually inevitable that it would find a place in the documents produced by the Council.

The story of the drafting of *Gaudium et spes* is now well known; it was a fraught process involving hundreds of advisors and many drafters over three years. It was not among the documents projected by the original preparatory commissions. In September 1962 Pope John called for the Council to make some address to the modern world and Cardinal Suenens then proposed a new document to the Council. What became *Gaudium et spes* began as "Schema XVII," and went through at least five substantially distinct drafts.[66] The first version was pieced together from bits of the extant schemata dealing with questions related to the Church in the modern world. It was held to be too scholastic in nature and gave way to the so-called "Roman Schema" of May 1963, which was judged too sociological. The "Malines Text" of September 1963 was far more progressive and theological – too much so for many, and so it yielded to the "Zurich Text" of February 1964 (now called Schema XIII), which provided what became the final basic framework for the document, although heavily rewritten in the "Ariccia Text" drafted during the early months of 1965. It was a version of this last that was eventually approved by Pope Paul VI and debated and revised during the Council's final session and approved on its penultimate day. One can trace the Council's thinking about the common good in some of the drafts introduced during its discussions.

The second or "Roman" schema contained one article devoted to the common good. This brief statement first characterized the common good negatively by denying that it could be understood simply as the sum of the goods of the members; rather it has its own intelligibility (*ratio*). Second, and positively, the common good is said to consist of "all those elements that are required for fruitful social life and in which human beings are able to pursue their proper perfection."[67] This formulation is accompanied by a note that

---

[65] Jean-Yves Calvez, SJ, *The Social Thought of John XXII*, 10, 13, 14, 21–22, 28, 54, 99.

[66] A recent and very accessible account is Michael G. Lawler, Todd A. Salzman, and Eileen Burke-Sullivan, *The Church in the Modern World: "Gaudium et Spes" Then and Now* (Collegeville, MN: The Liturgical Press, 2014), 17–39.

[67] The full passage reads: Bonum commune societatis humanae non est idem ac mere numerica summa bonorum ad eius membra pertinentium. Habet enim bonum illud propriam suam rationem, quae agnoscitur ac definitur respectu habito personae humanae complete cogitate. Constat enim omnibus illis elementis quae requiruntur ad vitam socialem ordinatam ac fecundam, in qua homines suam propriam perfectionem prosequi valeant. *Acta Synodalia Sacrosancti Concilii Oecumenici Vaticani II*, vol. V, pt. 1 (Vatican City: Typis Polyglotis Vaticanis, 1989), 603.

cites Aquinas for the proposition that the common good has its own intelligibility, and for the specific characterization of the common good it cites this
passage from Pius XI's *Mit brennender sorge*: "The real common good ultimately takes its measure from man's nature, which balances personal rights
and social obligations, and from the purpose of society, established for the
benefit of human nature."[68] The July 1964 revision of the "Zurich Text" (now
officially Schema XIII) contained a more extensive treatment of the common
good, although it was contained in one of the five appendices (adnexa) not
originally intended to be part of the official document. The location of the
common good discussion is the same as in the earlier schema, but in place of
the three sentences in the first draft, the second contains about a page of
discussion in which the common good is first given a brief definition and then
elaborated in four sections. Moreover, where the first treatment is grounded in
citations to Aquinas, Pius XI, and Pius XII, the second refers only to one
section of John XXIII's *Pacem in terris*. In this second iteration the document
warned against understanding society in strictly material terms; it is rather
a "spiritual order," one "according to the spiritual vocation of the men who
constitute society, and according to the genuine end of society which is the
common good."[69] The draft then notes the importance of formulating
a notion of the common good in contemporary terms and goes on to give an
account of the idea in four parts. First the common good is ordained to the
complete good of all members of the community and includes social, economic, and political conditions (*condiciones oeconimicas, sociales et politicas*)
that allow all to pursue their vocations. Second, it includes the rights and
obligations in their relations with one another aimed at justice and equity,
peace and concord. Third, the common good includes spiritual goods such as
truth, justice, beauty, mutual love, and liberty. Fourth and finally, the common good is never finished, but always the object of pursuit and development
to which all persons are obligated to contribute according to their capacities
and stations.[70] The last draft introduced on the floor of the Council, a version
of the "Arricia Text," which now incorporated the appendices, was dated
September 21, 1965, and was clearly the basis of the final text. Its formulation
of the common good is explicitly based on the formulation in *Mater et*

[68] *Acta Synodalia Sacrosancti Concilii Oecumenici Vaticani II*, vol. V, pt. 1 (Vatican City: Typis
Polyglotis Vaticanis, 1989), 605. The passage from *Mit brennender sorge* cites the Italian text of
the encyclical in AAS 29 (1937), 181. The note also refers to (without quoting) Pius XII's
Encyclical Letter *Summi pontificatus*, which discusses the natural law.
[69] *Acta Synodalia Sacrosancti Concilii Oecumenici Vaticani II*, vol. III, pt. 5 (Vatican City: Typis
Polyglotis Vaticanis, 1975), 151.
[70] *Acta Synodalia Sacrosancti Concilii Oecumenici Vaticani II*, 151–152.

magistra and is almost identical to what was in the final promulgated document.[71]

THE VATICAN II FORMULATION: ASPECTS AND IMPLICATIONS

The most important general point here is that the formulation of the common good as a sum total of conditions cannot constitute an exhaustive account of the matter. I have already suggested that that formulation, developed by many thinkers and gradually adopted by the magisterium, has an essential context in the character of modern politics, especially the dominance of the modern state with both its extensive technical and material capacities and the dangers posed by the disordered use of those very means, dangers that were fully realized in the mid-twentieth century. Clearly, what I have called the Vatican II formulation is meant to describe the common good in a very important, but restricted sense. It refers most explicitly and clearly to the good that can be reasonably pursued and to an important degree achieved by the means made available by modern political institutions and practices. In this sense it can be called the specifically political common good.[72] It comprises social, economic, and political institutions and practices that are not merely a means, but a constitutive element of the flourishing of the community of persons.

This statement requires two immediate qualifications. First, to call the common good in this sense a means is not simply to reduce it to an instrument in any technical sense. In so far as the ensemble of conditions is for the common good of the people in a broader sense it is always a moral phenomenon, the result of the free deliberate choices of human beings and therefore subject to the natural moral law.[73] It cannot be seen as simply the application of morally neutral techniques. Second, it really is a common good and not

---

[71] *Acta Synodalia Sacrosancti Concilii Oecumenici Vaticani II*, vol. IV, pt. 1 (Vatican City: Typis Polyglotis Vaticanis, 1976), 453. The reduction of the text in the second draft to the much briefer statement in the penultimate draft seems to have been aimed mainly at making the account more precise and succinct. See Peter Hüermann, "The Final Weeks of the Council," in *History of Vatican II*, vol. V, *The Council and the Transition: The Fourth Period and the End of the Council, September 1965–December 1965*, eds. Giuseppe Alberigo and Joseph Komonchak (Maryknoll, NY and Leuven: Orbis and Peters, 2006), 396–397.

[72] As it has by Finnis: see *Aquinas*, 234–239, and "Social Virtues and the Common Good," in *The Truth about God and Its Relevance for a Good Life in Society, Proceedings of the XI Plenary Session of the Pontifical Academy of St. Thomas Aquinas* (Vatican City: Pontifical Academy of St. Thomas Aquinas, 2012), 105–106.

[73] See especially GS, no. 73, 74; *Catechism*, nos. 1807, 1951, 2420; and cf. Francis, Encyclical Letter *Laudato si'* (On Care for Our Common Home) (2015), nos. 54, 105, 107.

simply a means for individuals. *Gaudium et spes* explicitly rejects individualism and the Catechism states that one "essential element" of the common
good is the well-being of "the group itself (*ipsius coetus*)."[74] This must be
understood in light of the documents' references to the social nature of man.[75]

Similarly, the common good is often described or referred to in a way that
indicates something more than a sum of conditions. There are three particularly
important examples of this. First, the common good is sometimes spoken of in an
explicitly ecclesiastical context: charisms in the Church work together for the
common good.[76] One could hardly describe the common good of the Church as
a set of conditions, and this even though the Church has often been described in
the tradition by analogy to the political community, certainly as a society.[77]
Second, "the common good of men is in its basic sense determined by the eternal
law."[78] This is clearly a reference to the good of human beings as such and is
echoed in the Catechism as well, which explicitly appeals to Aquinas's definition
of law as directed to the common good, including the eternal law.[79] Finally, and
related to this last point, the Catechism suggests an analogical understanding of
the common good when stating that the Church has an interest in "the temporal
aspects of the common good" because "they are ordered to the sovereign Good,
our ultimate end."[80] The temporal common good itself contains more than
simply conditions, but beyond this is a transcendent "sovereign" common good
that is the final and complete good for human beings.[81]

Most references to the common good in the Council documents and the
Catechism (and this goes for other magisterial documents as well) are quite
generic in nature. Examples abound: good government "grants recognition . . .
to the demands of the common good,"[82] Catholic citizens who disagree about
social and political questions should engage in "honest discussion, preserving
mutual charity and caring above all for the common good,"[83] cultures should

---

[74] GS, no. 30; *Catechism*, no. 1908.
[75] GS, nos. 12, 25, and cf. 32, 74; *Catechism*, 1879, 1882, 1905.
[76] *Catechism*, nos. 801, 951; cf. 2039.
[77] GS, no. 40; cf. Vatican II, Dogmatic Constitution on the Church *Lumen gentium* (1964),
      no. 8.
[78] GS, no. 78.
[79] *Catechism*, nos. 1951, 1976.
[80] *Catechism*, no. 2420.
[81] See also the suggestion made by Oswald Nell-Breuning in his commentary on *Gaudium et
      spes*, no. 74, *Commentary on the Documents of Vatican II*, vol. 5: *Pastoral Constitution of the
      Church in the Modern World*, ed. Herbert Vorgrimler (New York: Herder and Herder, 1969),
      318. And cf. his article, "Social Movements," in *Sacramentum Mundi: An Encyclopedia of
      Theology*, ed. Karl Rahner, SJ (St. Louis, MO: Herder & Herder, 1970), 110.
[82] GS, no. 42. Cf. also nos. 73–75; CCC, nos. 1880, 1897–1898, 1901, 1910.
[83] GS, no. 43; cf. CCC, no. 2238.

be respected and preserved "within the context of the common good,"[84] education is necessary if people are to "collaborate ... for the sake of the common good,"[85] "information provided by the media is at the service of the common good,"[86] and citizens should vote with a view to the common good.[87] This last is related to a general obligation for citizens to promote the common good.[88] These passages make most sense as referring to the common good in the very general sense that Plato and Aristotle often used at the beginning of the tradition, that is, as an appeal to act for the sake of the whole community rather than for one's own narrow individual, class, or party interest. There are circumstances in which some of these could refer to the "sum total of conditions," but more often they seem to refer to the actual flourishing of the community and its members.

It is this fairly general idea of the common good as that of the whole community pointing toward the flourishing of all of those persons that must be operative in the important notion of social justice (*iustitia socialis*). Social justice increasingly took the place of what Aquinas called "legal justice" during the nineteenth century; this virtue was for St. Thomas concerned with the overall direction of acts to the common good of the society. Despite the name and, while it existed primarily in the ruler as the one directing society to its end, legal justice was not exclusively connected with the state or its laws, but rather served as the very basis of all obligations toward the common good as the end of positive law *and* natural law.[89] The newer term "social justice" was already used by Taparelli in the 1840s and achieved increasing precision in the writings of Heinrich Pesch, Charles Antoine, and Oswald von Nell-Breuning, all influential on the development of social teaching during the period.[90] Pius XI adopted it in *Quadragesimo anno*, where its connection to the common good was explicit:

> Wealth ... must be so distributed among the various individuals and classes of society that the common good of all ... be thereby promoted. In other words, the good of the whole community must be safeguarded. By these principles of social justice one class is forbidden to exclude the other from a share in the profits. This law is violated by an irresponsible wealthy class

---

[84]   GS, no. 59.
[85]   GS, no. 60.
[86]   CCC, no. 2494.
[87]   GS, no. 75.
[88]   CCC, nos. 1913–14, 1916, 2238, 2442.
[89]   See Calvez and Perrin, *The Church and Social Justice*, 144–145, 152; cf. John Finnis, *Natural Law and Natural Rights*, 2nd ed. (Oxford: Oxford University Press, 2011), 184–186, 461–462.
[90]   See Calvez and Perrin, *The Church and Social Justice*, 146–147.

who, in their good fortune, deem it a just state of things that they should receive everything and the laborer nothing. . . .

Each class, then, must receive its due share, and the distribution of created goods must be brought into conformity with the demands of the common good and social justice.[91]

An even more complete formulation was given by Pius six years later in *Divini redemptoris*:

> [T]here is also social justice with its own set obligations, from which neither employers nor workingmen can escape. Now it is of the very essence of social justice to demand for each individual all that is necessary for the common good. But just as in the living organism it is impossible to provide for the good of the whole unless each single part and each individual member is given what it needs for the exercise of its proper functions, so it is impossible to care for the social organism and the good of society as a unit unless each single part and each individual member – that is to say, each individual man in the dignity of his human personality – is supplied with all that is necessary for the exercise of his social functions. If social justice be satisfied, the result will be an intense activity in economic life as a whole, pursued in tranquility and order. This activity will be proof of the health of the social body, just as the health of the human body is recognized in the undisturbed regularity and perfect efficiency of the whole organism.[92]

One should note in these passages that it is the common good that is primary and the norm for judging the character of adequate distribution of resources. That distribution is not simply one of equality; indeed, Pius rejects the notion that those without property could claim for themselves all of the fruits of production.[93] What social justice demands in the name of the common good is that workers receive a wage that allows them to live with dignity and to save. The level of such wages must be consistent with the aim of maximum employment. It also suggests some scheme of social insurance in the event of unemployment or ill health.[94] Note also that the description of a society in which the principle of social justice is operative is in fact a description of the common good.

[91] Pius XI, Encyclical Letter *Quadragesimo anno* (Reconstruction of the Social Order: 40th Anniversary of *Rerum novarum*) (1931), nos. 57–58, 110. That social justice meant to refer to Thomas's "legal justice" was explicitly indicated earlier by Pius XI in his 1923 encyclical letter, *Studiorum ducem* (On the Six-hundredth Anniversary of the Canonization of St. Thomas Aquinas) (1923), no. 27: AAS 15 (1923), 332.

[92] DR, no. 51.

[93] QA, no. 57.

[94] QA, nos. 71, 74.

While Pius held that social justice precluded the economic life of the community being simply the result of free competition and thus requiring regulation by the public authorities who have the most direct care for the common good, it is significant that only a few pages after the discussion of social justice he describes the other notion for which he is most well-known, that of subsidiarity. The general context of Pius's discussion of this principle, one also expounded initially by Taparelli, is the reduction in the pluralism of institutions and communities in modern society that has left the individual face to face with the state. Pius seems to have thought that this was bad for both, since the modern state could pose grave threats to the dignity and well-being of persons, but also that it could scarcely bear the weight of responsibilities now assumed by it.[95] While there is no immediate alternative to this situation, he maintains as "a fundamental principle of social philosophy, fixed and unchangeable," that the community should not take from individuals what they can accomplish for themselves, nor should it take from lesser bodies what they can accomplish.[96] The moral basis of the principle is surely to be found in the fundamental ordering of the person toward her good through acts of free deliberate choice. Such acts can also lead to association with others in the pursuit of common goods, and all of these acts of practical reasoning in themselves constitute participation in a form of good to be found in such deliberation and choice, the restriction or absorption of which must be justified. It is justified where the common good of the complete community requires authoritative choices about means, but such authorities must act in such a way as to respect the participation by persons and groups in the good of practical reasoning.[97] *Gaudium et spes* incorporates the principle both implicitly and explicitly. In the section of the document on the political community:

[95] QA, no. 78.

[96] QA, no. 79: fixum tamen immotumque manet in philosophia sociali gravissimum illud principium quod neque moveri neque mutari potest. For Taparelli's pioneering account see *Saggio teoretico*, dissertation III, §694, 701–704. Taparelli was clearly concerned about the power of specifically modern bureaucratic states and aimed to explain by the principle of subsidiarity the role of the state in protecting rather than absorbing what we now call civil society. See *Saggio teoretico*, dissertation III, §736, and 1148. Leo XIII expressed the principle without the name in Encyclical Letter *Rerum novarum* (On the Condition of the Working Classes) (1891), nos. 50–51.

[97] For philosophical development of this idea see Yves R. Simon, *Philosophy of Democratic Government* (Notre Dame, IN: University of Notre Dame Press, 1993 [1951]), ch. 1, and 127–139; and John Finnis, *Natural Law and Natural Rights*, 144–150; and John Finnis, "Limited Government," in *Human Rights and Common Good, Collected Essays: Volume III* (Oxford: Oxford University Press, 2011), 83–94.

Rulers must be careful not to hamper the development of family, social or
cultural groups, nor that of intermediate bodies or organizations, and not to
deprive them of opportunities for legitimate and constructive activity; they
should willingly seek rather to promote the orderly pursuit of such activity.
Citizens, for their part, either individually or collectively, must be careful not
to attribute excessive power to public authority, not to make exaggerated and
untimely demands upon it in their own interests, lessening in this way the
responsible role of persons, families and social groups.[98]

Similarly, in the section on international politics the document considers the
need for international coordination for the purpose of stimulating economic
growth, but cautions that such coordination should act "with due regard for
the principle of subsidiarity."[99]

A particularly important application of the idea of the common good is seen
in discussions of private property since it is always explained by reference to
the common good understood in several senses. First, the background notion
that has provided the Church's understanding of property with its center since
the patristic era is the principle referred to as the universal destination of
goods. This idea, once again developed in its normative form by Aquinas, is
that the earth was given for the benefit of all human persons. No particular part
of the earth naturally belongs to any particular person; however, the earth and
its fruits cannot benefit human persons without appropriation by them. One
might summarize the principle this way: "things are for people." Given robust
empirical generalizations about human nature and the patterns of human
conduct, the most reasonable scheme for the distribution of things is generally
one of private ownership accompanied by the proviso that the use of property
should always be made with a view to the common good.[100]

The tradition of Catholic social doctrine has adopted this view since its
inauguration by Leo XIII and, over time, its development has been, if anything, more Thomistic.[101] Since Pius XI the teaching has always been explicitly related to the universal destination of goods and attentive to the social

[98] GS, no. 75. See also CCC, nos. 1883, 1885, 2209.
[99] GS, no. 86.
[100] Aquinas, Summa Theologiae, II-II, 66. For discussion see Finnis, Aquinas, 188–96; and
      Joseph Boyle, "Fairness in Holdings: A Natural Law Account of Property and Welfare
      Rights," in Natural Law and Modern Moral Philosophy, ed. Ellen Frankel Paul, Fred
      D. Miller, Jr., and Jeffrey Paul (Cambridge: Cambridge University Press, 2001), 206–226.
      The roots of the idea are in Aristotle Politics, bk. 2, ch. 5.
[101] For Leo see, especially, RN, nos. 6, 22, 46. On Leo's account of property see Ernest
      L. Fortin, "'Sacred and Inviolable': Rerum Novarum and Natural Rights," Theological
      Studies 53 (1992): 209–218, although Fortin's general claims about natural rights are cer-
      tainly overdrawn.

aspects of property rights.[102] This is equally true in *Gaudium et spes* (as well as in the Catechism) where the chapter on economic life first states the principle of universal destination,[103] and then affirms the right to private ownership of property as an expression of personality and as an extension of human freedom.[104] This guarantee itself is quickly followed by a restatement of the common destination principle and accompanied by an affirmation of the propriety of public ownership "according to the demands and within the limits of the common good." Similarly, public authorities can "prevent anyone from abusing his private property to the detriment of the common good." This authority extends even to public expropriation "whenever the common good requires" and with fair compensation. In the teaching on property the goods of the earth in total are seen as a kind of common good for human beings and in this sense the common good is understood as a common stock. The system of laws and institutions that establishes and protects rights to property are part of the common good, as expressed in what I have called the Vatican II formulation of the common good, as an ensemble of conditions according to which individuals and groups can pursue their proper perfection. The authority of government to regulate property for the sake of the common good relies on the most general sense of common good as the flourishing of all the members of the community as well as to the good of the community as such.

That general sense clearly includes more than the security of those conditions. This can be seen in two additional ways. First, as noted in the first section, the common good is said to "encompass" the sum total of conditions required for flourishing persons and groups, but is not limited to those conditions. It includes more. Second, as this passage indicates, but also some others, the common good is often described in such a way as to make it particular to particular societies in ways that seem unlike a set of conditions. *Gaudium et spes* twice describes the common good as "dynamic," suggesting change.[105] Similarly, the common good is related to culture. In the most prominent case this is done in the context of education, and culture can mean simply education. However, this passage refers to the particular qualities of the society and its traditions.[106] The policy implications of this wider notion of common good

---

[102]   See, e.g., *QA*, nos. 45–47, 49. Pius XII, "Radio Message for Pentecost" (On the Fiftieth Anniversary of *Rerum novarum*) (June 1, 1941), 1941: *AAS* 33 (1941) 199; cf. John XXIII, Encyclical Letter *Mater et magistra* (On Christianity and Social Progress) (1961), no. 43.
[103]   GS, no. 69; and see CCC, no. 2401.
[104]   GS, no. 71; and see CCC, nos. 2403, 2406. See also CA, nos. 30–31.
[105]   GS, nos. 74, 78.
[106]   GS, no. 60.

are suggested by the *Catechism*'s discussion of immigration, which explicitly recognizes that public authorities may "for the sake of the common good" subject immigration "to various juridical conditions," and require that immigrants "respect with gratitude the material and spiritual heritage of the country that receives them, to obey its laws and to assist in carrying its civic burdens."[107]

The account I have given of the teaching on the common good is supported by an important set of passages in John Paul II's 1991 encyclical, *Centesimus annus*. In that document's section on state and culture, John Paul discusses the rule of law, democracy, and the protection of fundamental rights. He follows this by some suggestions of how these values are not adequately realized in some developed societies and argues that correcting them requires a sounder understanding of the common good, about which he says this: "The [common good] is not simply the sum total of particular interests; rather it involves an assessment and integration of those interests on the basis of a balanced hierarchy of values; ultimately, it demands a correct understanding of the dignity and the rights of the person."[108] The passage cites *Gaudium et spes*, art. 26, and clearly seems to intend an interpretation of that formulation (i.e., that one should not take the idea of a "sum total of conditions" to be a reduction of the common good to a kind of undifferentiated mass of satisfactions; rather, it must be understood in light of real human goods, those that perfect the human person).[109] The very next paragraph refers to the well-known statement in *Gaudium et spes*, art. 22, that Christ "fully reveals man to man himself and makes his supreme calling clear." The next paragraph begins a new section dealing with regulation of the economy; however, it begins by putting this issue in the context of what has just been said about the common good and then suggests its application by stating that properly ordered economic life

> cannot be conducted in an institutional, juridical or political vacuum. On the contrary, it presupposes sure guarantees of individual freedom and private property, as well as a stable currency and efficient public services. Hence the principal task of the State is to guarantee this security, so that those who work and produce can enjoy the fruits of their labors and thus feel encouraged to work efficiently and honestly.[110]

---

[107] CCC, no. 2241. See also John XXIII, Encyclical Letter *Pacem in terris* (On Establishing Universal Peace in Truth, Justice, Charity, and Liberty) (1963), no. 106.

[108] CA, no. 47.

[109] See also the discussion in the CSDC, nos. 164–165; and see International Theological Commission, "In Search of a Universal Ethic: A New Look at the Natural Law" (2009), no. 85, available at: www.vatican.va/roman_curia/congregations/cfaith/cti_documents/rc_con_c faith_doc_20090520_legge-naturale_en.html.

[110] CA, no. 48.

Taken together I think these passages constitute an important interpretive key to the Vatican II account of the common good, albeit one the basis of which was already available in the writings of previous popes, especially Pius XII: to the extent that the newer understanding is or can be seen as "instrumental," it is a description of the state itself, in particular the modern juridical state. The formulation refers also to aspects of the contemporary economic order, which is, of course, thoroughly connected to the modern state. These things, too, are in many respects instrumental goods, although they are closely connected to and made possible by things that are not simply instrumental good, for example, the sociality and sense of common identity and commitment to a common future that even the functioning of specific political institutions and practices require. But the common good cannot be reduced to even these things, since it also must refer to the ultimate good of all persons.

CONCLUSION

The idea of the common good is a cornerstone of Catholic social teaching as it has developed since Leo XIII's inception of the tradition in 1891. It was drawn from a larger tradition in which it already played a complex role as a component in speculative theology, in which it was related analogically to God Himself and to the order of the universe as causally common goods for human beings, but also for the rest of creation. At the same time it functioned in practical contexts both to justify and limit the power of political authorities and to establish certain moral norms. Its development in the modern social doctrine has been crucially influenced by two developments; first, the increasing emphasis placed on the nature and dignity of the person and the changing character of distinctively modern political institutions and practices. In Catholic social doctrine, the Church came to terms with the distinctive reality of the modern state as a largely secular bureaucratic entity possessed of immense material power. It therefore focused on the need to discipline the state's action by identifying its legitimacy with the provision of the conditions for the flourishing of persons. This development reached its apogee in the documents of the Second Vatican Council, although it had been underway since the mid-nineteenth century.

From a practical point of view the most important point that must be kept in mind is that the common good can never be opposed to the good of persons because it is the good of persons. It is not a good that can exist separately from persons or rival their own good or require that individuals sacrifice their good to it. This is most obvious in those statements that emphasize the place of basic human rights as constitutive elements of the common good. The common good is always also the proper good of those persons for whom it is a good, but it transcends the proper good of individuals in what the medieval theologians called its "communicability," that is, its being sharable by many and in some ways by all. While many elements of the specifically political common good can be characterized as instrumental, this is not true of all such elements even in the political realm, and so one can understand the common good of a specific political community in a much wider sense that is not at all instrumental, since it is characterized by their living well together as a community with a distinct identity constituted over time by their particular free deliberate choices in pursuit of the goods constitutive of human flourishing.

11

The Universal Destination of the World's Resources

Cristóbal Orrego

The Second Vatican Council's *Pastoral Constitution on the Church and the Modern World, Gaudium et spes*, is the first magisterial text that uses the expression "universal destination of earthly goods."[1] The precise term refers back, however, to a concept, or nested set of ideas, worked over by popes since 1891. The Catholic doctrine articulates a complex relationship between private property of goods and the universal destination of the world's resources (and a qualified right to common use). Regardless of the different emphasis on one aspect or the other, the basic idea is always the double requirement of (i) due respect in justice for private property, and (ii) the priority of the universal destination of goods. The root of this teaching is already present in Sacred Scripture and the Apostolic Tradition.

For these reasons, I think that the *universal destination of the world's resources* is foundational to Catholic Social Doctrine. Its most important requirement, and the first one stressed by *Rerum novarum* at the outset of modern Catholic teaching on social matters, is that some form of private property reaches everybody – individuals, families, and social groups – in a just proportion, and according to the requirements of the common good. Misguided interpretations of the texts of the magisterium may induce some to believe that the defence of the universal destination of goods is to the detriment of the right to private property. In what follows I will show that, on the contrary, each development of the teaching of the Catholic Church both reinforced the right to private property for all and extended further the application of the principle of the universal destination (and the right to common use of truly private property) to new issues. The compatibility of private property with the universal destination, and the tension between them,

[1] Vatican II, Pastoral Constitution *Gaudium et spes* (On the Church in the Modern World) (1965), no. 69.

can be grasped in the attempts by the magisterium of the Church to apply them in different circumstances. In my view, the teaching about this principle and its relationship to private property is one of the most stable and consistent doctrines of the social magisterium of the Church, with only minor adjustments of expression, extension to new matters, and differing emphases according to contingent circumstances and the relative force of opposing errors at different times.[2] We do not have here dramatic developments such as those present in the successive teachings on freedom of religion and conscience, capital punishment, usury, the role of women within marriage, collaboration with non-Catholics in social and political organizations, world peace, ecology, and others.

Pope John Paul II underlines the significance of the principle when he declares, in line with some earlier pontiffs, that "the *first* principle of the whole ethical and social order" is "the principle of the common use of goods."[3] In order to better understand in what sense this principle is "the first," one should bear in mind that a single principle is always incomplete and needs to be complemented by other principles, values, requirements of justice, and so on. One must be aware that the texts of the magisterium do not offer a system of thought consistent in every detail, but rather a coherent corpus of fundamental doctrine, expressed in differing ways according to different times, contexts, and problems.[4] For this reason, some isolated expressions may appear to contradict others. For example, in order to stress the importance of some principle or value or fundamental right, sometimes one or the other is called "fundamental" or "first," according to the historical and doctrinal context. But there are many fundamental and first principles, human rights, and values. Taking this into account, even though the principle of universal destination has been called "the first principle of the whole ethical and social order,"[5] something similar has been said about the dignity of the human person,

---

[2] See the philosophical explanation by Manfred Spieker, "The Universal Destination of Goods: The Ethics of Property in the Theory of a Christian Society," *Journal of Markets & Morality* 8, no. 2 (Fall 2005): 333–354. At 334–335, the author refers to some of the thinkers that prepared the intervention by Pope Leo XIII, such as Wilhelm Emmanuel von Ketteler (1811–1877), who "followed Thomas Aquinas entirely," and Luigi Taparelli, Matteo Liberatore, and Tommaso Zigliara, "who prepared the social encyclical *Rerum novarum* for Pope Leo XIII," and apart from Saint Thomas "also relied on John Locke's property theory." See also a wider treatment of the topic by J. Brian Benestad, *Church, State, and Society. An Introduction to Catholic Social Doctrine* (Washington, DC: Catholic University of America Press, 2011), 313–374.

[3] John Paul II, Encyclical Letter *Laborem exercens* (On Human Work) (1981), no. 19 (my italics).

[4] Cf. Benedict XVI, Encyclical Letter *Caritas in veritate* (On Integral Human Development in Charity & Truth) (2009), no. 12.

[5] *LE*, no. 19; see also Francis, Encyclical Letter *Laudato si'* (On Care for Our Common Home) (2015), no. 93.

justice, the common good, and other fundamental principles.[6] Leo XIII includes, for example, the very respect for private property, which is a means to the realization of the universal destination, as itself a first principle: "The *first and most fundamental principle*, therefore, if one would undertake to alleviate the condition of the masses, must be *the inviolability of private property*."[7]

I mention all this in order to stress that there are several first principles and that none of them is an absolute. "The principles of the Church's social doctrine must be appreciated in their unity, interrelatedness and articulation."[8] The inviolability of private property is not an absolute, because it is subordinated to the universal destination of goods; but neither is this latter principle absolute, for it is ordered to the common good, and must be applied in accordance with all the other principles, such as subsidiarity and solidarity, the respect of all human rights (including the right to private property, free enterprise, just wage, etc.) which are requirements of the common good. So when we examine the development of this principle by the magisterium of the Church in the next sections, we must be careful not to use it "only in part or in an erroneous manner."[9] This would be the case if the principle of universal destination of goods "were to be invoked in a disjointed and unconnected way with respect to each of the others."[10] In effect, "[a] deep theoretical understanding and the actual application of *even just one* of these social principles clearly shows the reciprocity, complementarities and interconnectedness that is part of their structure."[11]

Besides, the main difficulty arises precisely from the application of a general idea that is not contested. For it is not difficult to visualize the universal destination in operation in a sort of Edenic community, with a small, fixed number of people to consider. So long as gathering and consuming can meet human needs, where no one is actually a producer and there is no such thing as manufacturing or trade, we could say readily that anyone who picks the apple tree bare and then hoards ten bushels while others starve has cheated them all and defiled God. In the real world, especially in the modern, complex society, one still can and must say that if someone starves (with no fault on his or her part), some others are committing some injustice in some way or

---

[6] See *Compendium of the Social Doctrine of the Church*, nos. 160 and 171.

[7] Leo XIII, Encyclical Letter *Rerum novarum* (On the Condition of the Working Classes) (1891), no. 15.

[8] *CSDC*, no. 162.

[9] *CSDC*, no. 162.

[10] *CSDC*, no. 162.

[11] *CSDC*, no. 162 (my italics).

another. But who? How? When? To what extent? The world presents infinitely more complex economic challenges than those faced in the Garden of Eden, and one could consider the whole development of papal teaching on the universal destination since 1891 as a running series of encounters with that complexity. As John Paul II observes, "at one time the decisive factor of production was the land";[12] later it was capital, and "today the decisive factor is increasingly man himself, that is, his knowledge, especially his scientific knowledge, his capacity for interrelated and compact organization, as well as his ability to perceive the needs of others and to satisfy them."[13]

The magisterium of the Church has articulated with differing emphases this compatibility and equilibrium, somehow in tension, between private property and universal destination of earthly goods. Therefore, the right understanding of the evolution of the doctrine, and of possible new avenues for its renovation and application in the future, requires adopting the hermeneutic of continuity and reform proposed by Pope Benedict XVI.[14] This approach looks for the continuity in the magisterium, even when contingent decisions change according to contingent circumstances; the unity of the magisterium, which does not allow severance of the social doctrines from the whole of Catholic dogma and morals; and, within the social doctrine of the Church itself, the internal consistency of the magisterium, which demands us to consider all principles and values together in their mutual relations. In effect, outside "the Tradition of the apostolic faith,"[15] any isolated text (even a papal encyclical) "would be a document without roots – and issues concerning development would be reduced to merely sociological data."[16] This more general issue about "the coherence of the overall doctrinal corpus"[17] and the correct approach to the social doctrine of the Church is explored elsewhere in this volume.[18] I shall limit myself to presenting the evolution of the formulations of the principle of universal destination before the Second Vatican Council

---

[12]   John Paul II, Encyclical Letter *Centesimus annus* (On the 100th Anniversary of *Rerum novarum*) (1999), no. 32.

[13]   CA, no. 32.

[14]   See Benedict XVI, "Address to the Roman Curia" (December 22, 2005).

[15]   CV, no. 10.

[16]   CV, no. 10. Pope Benedict refers here to Paul VI's Encyclical *Populorum progressio*. In my view, this is also the case with respect to any other magisterial text, if it is read severed from its roots in the whole of the Apostolic Tradition.

[17]   CV, no. 12.

[18]   See especially the three concluding chapters in this volume: "Catholic Social Teaching *Is* Catholic Moral Teaching," by E. Christian Brugger; "How Bishops Should Teach Catholic Social Teaching," by Gerard V. Bradley; and "A Radical Critique of Catholic Social Teaching," by John Finnis.

(following section) and then from Vatican II to Pope Francis (final section). I shall follow a chronological order so that we may better appreciate how the main arguments are present, at least in outline, from the beginning.

BEFORE THE SECOND VATICAN COUNCIL

Pope Leo XIII

Rerum novarum asserts that earthly goods are of relative worth, before any consideration of how and in what measure they may be possessed or allocated. "The things of earth cannot be understood or valued aright without taking into consideration the life to come, the life that will know no death. Exclude the idea of futurity, and forthwith the very notion of what is good and right would perish; nay, the whole scheme of the universe would become a dark and unfathomable mystery."[19] For "God has not created us for the perishable and transitory things of earth, but for things heavenly and everlasting."[20] Therefore, whether we have riches in abundance, or are lacking in them, so far as eternal happiness is concerned, it makes no difference: "the only important thing is *to use them aright*."[21] In relation to this right use of private property, Leo adopts Thomas Aquinas's doctrine on the common use of property.[22] For "riches do not bring freedom from sorrow and are of no avail for eternal happiness, but rather are obstacles."[23] "The chief and most excellent rule for the right use of money ... rests on the principle that it is one thing to have a *right to the possession* of money and another to have a *right to use* money as one wills."[24] Aquinas teaches that it is lawful and necessary to hold private property, and the pope declares this to be a natural right, but as to how one must use one's possessions, Aquinas and the pope reply: "Man should not consider his material possessions as his own, but as common to all, so as to share them without hesitation when others are in need."[25]

This is a recognition of what afterwards will be called *the right to common use* of earthly goods, a moral right that exists even when the corresponding goods have been allocated as personal, private property. It is also recognition of the correlative duty of legitimate owners to make their property available in

---

[19]   RN, no. 21.
[20]   RN, no. 21.
[21]   RN, no. 21 (my italics).
[22]   See the summary by John Finnis, *Aquinas*, 188–196.
[23]   RN, no. 22.
[24]   RN, no. 22 (my italics).
[25]   RN, no. 22.

some way to others, not in the sense that it becomes also the private property of others (which is contrary to the very concept of the right to the private possession of the goods), but rather in that its use is beneficial to all others in many different ways. Both the right to common use and the duty to use one's own goods for the benefit of all (in an ordered way) are grounded in the principle of the common/universal destination of goods. The way in which the three aspects of the question (i.e., private property, common use, universal destination) are articulated shows that the universal destination of goods is not only compatible with private property, but in fact requires it.

Following Aquinas, Leo XIII recalls some principles that were commonly taught by moral theologians. For example, that "no one is commanded to distribute to others that which is required for his own needs and those of his household; nor even to give away what is reasonably required to keep up becomingly his condition in life."[26] But then it is "a duty to give to the indigent out of what remains over."[27] In extreme cases, it is a duty of justice; in all the other cases, it is a duty "of Christian charity," which "certainly the law has no right to demand" [*profecto lege agendo petere ius non est*].[28] The pope appeals, then, above the laws of men to "the laws and judgments of Christ the true God," who will take the service to the poor into account for eternal reward.[29] This declaration that the human law – save in cases of extreme need – has no right to make effective the duty to use riches in favor of the poor will be taught in general by the later magisterium, in defending the right to private property against the overreaching of the socialist state; but it will be subject to qualification by admitting some right of the state to use legal means to redistribute riches as a requirement of the common good.[30] On the other hand, the appeal to the law of Christ, with its eternal reward, might be deemed ridiculous by persons who do not believe in eternal life, or for Christians who believe that all will be saved by God's mercy regardless of how we have used our goods and capacities. But for Catholics it is a most forceful argument.

In my view, neither Pope Leo XIII nor the later magisterium wish to enter into the details about which requirements are a matter of strict commutative justice, that may be enforced directly by law; or of general and distributive justice, which the state may and prudently ought to require by general laws and by distributive policies; or only of Christian charity, which public authority may not enforce, but Christ will demand in the eschatological judgment

---

[26]   RN, no. 22.
[27]   RN, no. 22.
[28]   RN, no. 22.
[29]   Cf. Mt. 25, 40.
[30]   See QA, no. 47.

when He will reward each one according to one's dessert. The magisterium gives only some general orientations. Moral theologians propose different views on the matter, in more detail.[31]

Rerum novarum acknowledges the principle of the universal destination of the world's resources – although in *RN* it has not yet received this developed name – in the context of the socialist proposal to abolish or radically reduce the right to private property. Hence the pope is bent on correcting some erroneous interpretations of the common destination of goods rather than on deducing all of its consequences. It is a "fact that God has given the earth for the use and enjoyment of the whole human race,"[32] but "God has granted the earth to mankind in general, not in the sense that all without distinction can deal with it as they like, but rather that no part of it was assigned to any one in particular, and that the limits of private possession have been left to be fixed by man's own industry, and by the laws of individual races."[33] The principle of universal destination of the goods of the earth continues to be in force and is realized through private property, because "the earth, even though apportioned among private owners, ceases not thereby to minister to the needs of all, inasmuch as there is not one who does not sustain life from what the land produces."[34] Even more, precisely in order to concretize the general destination of goods to all men it is necessary that they be appropriated through the taking of possession of them and the work necessary to make them bear fruit: "Truly, that which is required for the preservation of life, and for life's well-being, is produced in great abundance from the soil, but not until man has brought it into cultivation and expended upon it his solicitude and skill. Now, when man thus turns the activity of his mind and the strength of his body toward procuring the fruits of nature, by such act he makes his own that portion of nature's field which he cultivates, that portion on which he leaves, as it were, the impress of his personality; and it cannot but be just that he should possess that portion as his very own, and have a right to hold it without any one being justified in violating that right."[35]

---

[31] See Dominicus M. Prümmer, OP, *Manuale Theologiae Moralis* (Barcinone: Herder, 1961), nos. 86–87. John Finnis presents Aquinas's response to these issues in *Aquinas*, 188–196.

[32] *RN*, no. 8.

[33] *RN*, no. 8.

[34] *RN*, no. 8.

[35] *RN*, no. 9. It seems to me that Leo XIII is the first pope to adopt the idea that private property is in some measure grounded in the work of the person who somewhat impresses his personality on material things. This doctrine seems to derive from John Locke. See Spieker, "The Universal Destination of Goods," supra note 2, 334. Finnis's careful reading of Aquinas agrees that this sort of argument for private property does not derive from Saint Thomas: "Arguments for founding property rights on alleged 'metaphysical' relationships between persons and the

Leo XIII proposes this doctrine not to protect in a particular way the private property of the rich, but rather in order to promote a realistic solution to the problems of the poor. "The first and most fundamental principle, therefore, if one would undertake to *alleviate the condition of the masses*, must be *the inviolability of private property*."[36] Here we can see one of those instances in which, because of the context, a principle is called "first," although later on the magisterium is going to consider it as secondary and subordinated to another one – to the universal destination of goods. The pope defends "the interests of the working classes,"[37] because "they who contribute so largely to the advantage of the community may themselves share in the benefits which they create – that being housed, clothed, and bodily fit, they may find their life less hard and more endurable."[38]

The "great labor question cannot be solved save by assuming as a principle that private ownership must be held sacred and inviolable. The law, therefore, should favor ownership, and its policy should be *to induce as many as possible of the people to become owners*."[39] Hence it is clear that the common destination has as a requirement the widest possible diffusion of private ownership. Even more, when he speaks about the protection of rights, Leo reiterates the priority to be given to the poor: "when there is question of defending the rights of individuals, the poor and badly off have a claim to especial consideration. The richer class have many ways of shielding themselves, and stand less in need of help from the State; whereas the mass of the poor have no resources of their own to fall back upon, and must chiefly depend upon the assistance of the State. And it is for this reason that wage-earners, since they mostly belong in the mass of the needy, should be specially cared for and protected by the government."[40]

Finally, in *Rerum novarum* we find also the seed of the extension of the principle of universal destination of goods – albeit speaking in terms of common use or benefit – to all kinds of human and divine goods, apart from land and chattel and other material resources. "Whoever has received from the divine bounty a large share of temporal blessings, whether they be external and material, or gifts of the mind, has received them for the purpose of using them for the perfecting of his own nature, and, at the same time, that he may

---

things with which they have 'mixed their labor', or to which craftsmen have 'extended their personality', are foreign to Aquinas" (Finnis, *Aquinas*, 189).

[36]   *RN*, no.15.
[37]   *RN*, no. 34.
[38]   *RN*, no. 34.
[39]   *RN*, no. 46.
[40]   *RN*, no. 37.

employ them, as the steward of God's providence, for the benefit of others. 'He that hath a talent,' said St. Gregory the Great, 'let him see that he hide it not; he that hath abundance, let him quicken himself to mercy and generosity; he that hath art and skill, let him do his best to share the use and the utility hereof with his neighbor.'"[41]

Pope Pius XI

Quadragesimo anno (1931) introduces new language in affirming "the twofold character of ownership, called usually *individual* or *social* according as it regards either separate persons or the common good."[42] For "nature, rather the Creator Himself, has given man the right of private ownership not only that individuals may be able to provide for themselves and their families but also that the goods which the Creator destined for the entire family of mankind may *through this institution* truly serve this purpose."[43] Here is even more forcefully affirmed the fairness of private property as the institution that is the effective means to the realization of the common destination of goods, which is the end or purpose. Since ends are principles in practical matters,[44] it is clear that the universal destination of goods is a principle (end) with priority over private property (means). But since necessary means are obligatory to achieve the respective ends, it is also clear that an appeal to the higher principle may not weaken the right to private property for all. It is important here also to stress that Pius's defense of private property as a means to the realization of the universal destination is made with full consciousness of the unjust social situation both in 1891 and in 1931: "One class, very small in number, was enjoying almost all the advantages which modern inventions so abundantly provided; the other, embracing the huge multitude of working people, oppressed by wretched poverty, was vainly seeking escape from the straits wherein it stood."[45]

Pius XI explains with more detail the distinction between the right of property and its fair use. On the one hand, commutative justice "commands sacred respect for the division of possessions and forbids invasion of others' rights through the exceeding of the limits of one's own property."[46] On the

---

[41] *RN*, no. 22.
[42] *QA*, no. 45 (my italics).
[43] *QA*, no. 45 (my italics).
[44] See Finnis, *Aquinas*, 25–26, 79, and 103.
[45] *QA*, no. 3. Nevertheless, the pope acknowledges that in the intervening years many improvements had come about: see *QA*, nos. 16–39.
[46] *QA*, no. 47.

other hand, "the duty of owners to use their property only in a right way does not come under this type of justice, but under other virtues, obligations of which 'cannot be enforced by legal action.'"[47] "Therefore," the pope continues, "they are in error who assert that ownership and its right use are limited by the same boundaries; and it is much farther still from the truth to hold that a right to property is destroyed or lost by reason of abuse or non-use."[48]

Notwithstanding this confirmation of the Leonine doctrine in general terms, Pius XI introduces a nuance that seems to go in the contrary direction by allowing enforcement of the fair use of property rights by means of the law, based precisely upon the teaching that the exact contours of private property as an institution are a matter not of natural law but for determination by positive law. Due to "the individual and at the same time social character of ownership[49] . . . men must consider in this matter not only their own advantage but also the common good."[50] It "is the function of those in charge of the State" precisely "to define these duties in detail when necessity requires and the natural law has not done so."[51] "Therefore, public authority, under the guiding light always of the natural and divine law, can determine more accurately upon consideration of the true requirements of the common good, what is permitted and what is not permitted to owners in the use of their property."[52] The State, however, "is not permitted to discharge its duty arbitrarily."[53] "The natural right itself both of owning goods privately and of passing them on by inheritance ought always to remain intact and inviolate," and "it is grossly unjust for a State to exhaust private wealth through the weight of imposts and taxes."[54]

---

[47] QA, no. 47. The internal quotation, despite the different English translation, is from *Rerum novarum*, no. 22, as we have seen: "certainly the law has no right to demand" [*profecto lege agendo petere ius non est*].

[48] QA, no. 47.

[49] QA, no. 49.

[50] QA, no. 49.

[51] QA, no. 49.

[52] QA, no. 49.

[53] QA, no. 49.

[54] QA, no. 49. Inheritance is an institution that follows both from one component of the right to private property, namely the right of disposition (which can be *inter vivos* or *mortis causa*), and from the social character of property, which is destined not only for the good of the individual person but also of others, and in the first place for the good of his or her own family. This aspect of the topic, albeit not central, and many times just taken for granted, has been present in modern social doctrine since *Rerum novarum*. A father cannot provide for his family, says Leo XIII, "except by the ownership of productive property, which he can transmit to his children by inheritance" (no. 13). It has more to do with the defense of the family against the intrusion of the state than with the exact relationship between private property and universal destination of earthly goods.

There is no contradiction, however, between the teaching that the law *must not* enforce the duties of using property in the right way according to virtues other than justice (*Rerum novarum*, no. 22; *Quadragesimo anno*, no. 49) and the other teaching that the law may and must protect the common good against the unjust use of property, and even enforce some duties of owners toward the common good. In fact, Leo XIII had already stated: "For since the right of possessing goods privately has been conferred not by man's law, but by nature, public authority cannot abolish it, but can only *control its exercise and bring it into conformity with the common weal.*"[55] The longer text in *Rerum novarum*, however, stresses the *limitation* of the state: "The right to possess private property is derived from nature, not from man; and the State has the right to control its use in the interests of the public good alone, *but by no means to absorb it altogether. The State would therefore be unjust and cruel if under the name of taxation it were to deprive the private owner of more than is fair.*"[56] By omitting the last part of the quotation, which I have emphasized, Pius XI stressed instead the authority of the state to regulate property for the common good. To which the pope adds an explicit declaration that the lawful protection of the common good – this kind of legal enforcement of the duties of owners – is at the same time a protection of private property. For "when the State brings private ownership into harmony with the needs of the common good, it does not commit a hostile act against private owners but rather does them a friendly service; for it thereby effectively prevents the private possession of goods, which the Author of nature in His most wise providence ordained for the support of human life, from causing intolerable evils and thus rushing to its own destruction; it does not destroy private possessions, but safeguards them; and it does not weaken private property rights, but strengthens them."[57]

The context of oppositions between social classes, widely exploited by communist class struggle and widely disregarded by individualistic and unrestricted forms of capitalism, helps to understand how the pope is at pains both to reassert the right to private property and to reinforce its universal destination to aid the needs of all human beings. Pius XI recalls Pope Leo XIII's formulation of the principle: "However the earth may be apportioned among private owners, *it does not cease to serve the common interests of all.*"[58] Here again the emphasis by Leo XIII was in the *fact* that the earthly goods do serve the

---

[55] RN, no. 47, quoted by QA, no. 49 (my italics). Note that QA refers to RN, no. 67 because it uses a previous numeration than the one that is now being used.

[56] RN, no. 47 (my italics). This is the same passage, but longer, and I have kept the different translations.

[57] QA, no. 49.

[58] QA, no. 56, quoting RN, no. 8 (my italics).

common interests of all: "Moreover, the earth, even though apportioned among private owners, ceases not thereby to minister to the needs of all, inasmuch as there is not one who does not sustain life from what the land produces. Those who do not possess the soil contribute their labor; hence, it may truly be said that all human subsistence is derived either from labor on one's own land, or from some toil, some calling, which is paid for either in the produce of the land itself, or in that which is exchanged for what the land brings forth."[59] Pius XI, on the other hand and without contradiction, stresses the *norm* that this should be the case for all, that is to say, the principle of universal destination: "the division of goods which results from private ownership was established by nature itself *in order that* created things may serve the needs of mankind in fixed and stable order."[60] Therefore the same need for a fixed and stable order requires both private property and its subordination to the common good, so that private property "may serve the needs of mankind."[61] *Quadragesimo anno* gives a special tone to the formulation of the principle of universal destination by defending the pairing of universal destination/private ownership in the midst of the then too-sharp opposition between two socioeconomic classes:

> But not every distribution among human beings of property and wealth is of a character to attain either completely or to a satisfactory degree of perfection the end which God intends. Therefore, the riches that economic-social developments constantly increase ought to be so distributed among individual persons and classes that the common advantage of all ... will be safeguarded; in other words, that the common good of all society will be kept inviolate. By this law of social justice, one class is forbidden to exclude the other from sharing in the benefits. Hence the class of the wealthy violates this law no less, when, as if free from care on account of its wealth, it thinks it the right order of things for it to get everything and the worker nothing, than does the non-owning working class when, angered deeply at outraged justice and too ready to assert wrongly the one right it is conscious of, it demands for itself everything as

59 RN, no. 8. The original "earthly good" that was the main point of reference for stating the doctrine on private property, common use, and universal destination was land, soil. This is not strange because for the bulk of human history, and well into the twentieth century, the possession of land was the main source of both riches and work. Besides, land is in the most immediate manner that "created resource" entrusted to all persons by God. From the beginning of social doctrine, however, there were allusions to other forms of material and spiritual resources that should also benefit all human beings, as we have already noted referring to RN, no. 22, and as we shall see more clearly in subsequent developments of the social doctrine of the Church.

60 QA, no. 56 (my italics).

61 QA, no. 56.

if produced by its own hands, and attacks and seeks to abolish, therefore, all property and returns or incomes, of whatever kind they are or whatever the function they perform in human society, that have not been obtained by labor, and for no other reason save that they are of such a nature.[62]

Leaving aside those requirements of Christian charity, already mentioned, which exceed what is due to others according to natural law, the fair coordination between the right of legitimate owners and their duties toward others – or also, between the obligation of everybody toward the inviolable private property of others, and the right to common use – is a matter of both distributive justice and of social justice. The exact point of equilibrium depends on the requirements of the common good. The frontiers among "charity," "commutative justice," "distributive justice" and "general justice," and the precise meaning of "social justice" are not clear or stable. They have been a matter of too many debates among Catholic theologians and philosophers.[63] Even the magisterium of the Church does not adopt a single criterion of demarcation among these virtues, and does not seem to care much about it. The point of Pius XI's teaching, however, seems simply to assert that the excessive distance between the rich and the poor, and the obvious deficiencies in the distribution of earthly goods, constitute a kind of injustice (not only a lack of Christian charity) because it affects the common good, and not only the good or well-being of the poor or the private relations between rich and poor. "To each, therefore, must be given his own share of goods, and the distribution of created goods, which, as every discerning person knows, is laboring today under the gravest evils due to the huge disparity between the few exceedingly rich and the unnumbered propertyless, must be effectively called back to and brought into conformity with the norms of the common good, that is, social justice."[64] In this way, no one can any longer interpret *Rerum novarum* as if any action in favor of the poor, beyond the assistance to meet their bare necessities, were just a matter of private charity, and not of justice, law, and public action by those in charge of the temporal common good of society.

Pope Pius XII

Sertum laetitiae (1939), *On the Hundred and Fiftieth Anniversary of the Establishment of the Hierarchy in The United States*, was Pius XII's second

---

[62] *QA*, no. 57.
[63] John Finnis discusses the "instability in Aquinas's classification of justice," and to what extent the several distinctions of kinds of justice are useful, in *Aquinas*, 215–217.
[64] *QA*, no. 58.

encyclical. After deploring the *agitation*, the *acrimonies*, the *disorders* that the unresolved "social question" provoked at the time in the world, and in the United States of America in particular, the pope states: "The fundamental point of the social question is this, that *the goods created by God for all men should in the same way reach all, justice guiding and charity helping.*"[65] The principle is used here to explain another aspect of the question, namely the necessary differences between rich and poor, which ought not to be extreme or too wide. On the one hand, there is the historical fact "that there were always rich and poor,"[66] and the reasonable expectation "that it will always be so,"[67] which "we may gather from the unchanging tenor of human destinies."[68] On the other hand, the pope sheds light on the mission of rich people: "Worthy of honor are the poor who fear God because theirs is the Kingdom of Heaven and because they readily abound in spiritual graces. But the rich, if they are upright and honest, are God's dispensers and providers of this world's goods; as ministers of Divine Providence they assist the indigent through whom they often receive gifts for the soul and whose hand – so they may hope – will lead them into the eternal tabernacles."[69]

From this point of departure, the Supreme Pontiff goes on to show that these differences are a part of God's plan, provided there is moderation regarding both riches and hardships: "God, Who provides for all with counsels of supreme bounty, has ordained that for the exercise of virtues and for the testing of one's worth there be in the world rich and poor; but He does not wish that some have exaggerated riches while others are in such straits that they lack the bare necessities of life. But a kindly mother of virtue is honest poverty which gains its living by daily labor in accordance with the scriptural saying: 'Give me neither beggary, nor riches: give me only the necessaries of life' (Proverbs XXX: 8)."[70] Some obligation of the rich toward the poor stems out of mercy and charity, but "their obligation is all the greater to do them justice,"[71] especially by providing jobs and paying fair wages.[72] It seems to me that in this way the pope is harmonizing previous popes' references to charity and justice regarding the moral duties of owners, while at the same time affirming that the

---

[65]   Pius XII, Encyclical Letter *Sertum laetitiae* (On the Hundred and Fiftieth Anniversary of the Establishment of the Hierarchy in the United States) (1939), no. 34 (my italics). GS takes from here its formulation of the principle at no. 69.

[66]   SL, no. 34.

[67]   SL, no. 34.

[68]   SL, no. 34.

[69]   SL, no. 34.

[70]   SL, no. 35.

[71]   SL, no. 36.

[72]   SL, nos. 36–38.

fulfillment of these duties of justice is not to be reduced to following the directives of the state. The rich must assume their own calling to be ministers of Divine Providence and realize the universal destination of goods not simply by paying taxes or distributing their riches, but mainly through creating well-paid jobs, as John Paul II will stress later on.

On the 50th anniversary of *Rerum novarum*, Pius XII gave his Radio Message *La Solennità* (1941). The Roman Pontiff repeats the formulation of *Sertum laetitiae* and calls the principle both fundamental point and non-derogable requirement.[73] But now the pope presents the principle that later will be called universal destination as a natural right of every human person. There is no distinction here between the principle of universal destination and the right to common use of goods, which are naturally closely connected. "Every man, as a living being endowed with reason, has by nature the *fundamental right to use the material goods of the earth*, although it is left to the human will and the juridical forms of the peoples to control the details of its practical implementation."[74] Pius XII is talking here of an individual right, which "cannot be in any way suppressed, even by other clear and undisputed rights over material goods."[75] He presents this right alongside the right to private property as two institutions that are in need of regulation by public authority: "No doubt the natural order, deriving from God, demands also private property and the free reciprocal commerce of goods by interchange and gift, as well as the regulatory function of the public authorities regarding both of these institutions."[76] The universal use and destination is, however, of primary importance. For "all this" (i.e., private property, free commerce and gifts, legal regulations by public authority) "remains subordinated to the natural end of material goods, and may not be made independent from the first and fundamental right that grants the use to everyone; but rather it should serve to make possible the implementation in accordance with its end."[77] The distinction between *ownership* and *use* is now recalled in order to stress the subordination of private ownership as a means to common use as its end. For "only in this way it will be possible and due to achieve that the property and use of material goods bring to society a fruitful peace and a live stability, instead of precarious conditions that give rise to struggles and envy, left at the mercy of the blind interplay of force and weakness."[78]

---

[73] Pius XII, Radio Message *La Solennità* (1941), no. 12.
[74] *La Solennità*, no. 13.
[75] *La Solennità*, no. 13.
[76] *La Solennità*, no. 13.
[77] *La Solennità*, no. 13.
[78] *La Solennità*, no. 13.

Then the pope declares this "original right to the use of material goods" to be "in intimate connection with the dignity and with the other rights of the human person."[79] For this reason, it offers to the human person "a secure material base" for "the fulfilment of his or her moral duties."[80] "The protection of this right will secure the personal dignity of man, and will facilitate to attend and to fulfil with just freedom that sum of stable obligations and commitments regarding which he is directly responsible before his Creator."[81]

From here, Pius XII draws several conclusions or applications. One of them refers to the true nature of the economy and of economic progress. "The national economy . . . only aims at securing without interruption the material conditions under which the individual life of the citizens can develop."[82] It can be said, then, that a people is truly economically rich when these conditions are met, because "the general well-being and, accordingly, the personal right of all to the use of worldly goods is thus brought to fruition in conformity with the plans of the Creator."[83] In other words, "the economic riches of a people do not properly consist in the abundance of goods, measured according to a purely and strictly material calculation of their value, but rather in that such an abundance amount to and actually and effectively constitute the material foundation sufficient for the due personal development of its members."[84] This is a matter of distributive justice, of the fair participation of all in the common good. Without such a "just distribution of goods," the true end of the economy would not be achieved, "because even if such a fortunate abundance of goods were available, the people, not called upon to share in it, would not be economically rich, but poor."[85] On the contrary, if such a fair distribution is effectively realized, and in a permanent way, "you will see a people that, even when having fewer goods, will become and remain economically sound."[86]

At this point of the development of the principle of common use, its foundational character makes it clear that it can be applied to every field of social doctrine. Leo XIII and Pius XI had implicitly done so when applying the same equilibrium between private rights of property and the common use/common good to issues such as the right to work and just wages, because most

---

79   *La Solennità*, no. 14.
80   *La Solennità*, no. 14.
81   *La Solennità*, no. 14.
82   *La Solennità*, no. 16.
83   *La Solennità*, no. 16.
84   *La Solennità*, no. 17.
85   *La Solennità*, no. 17.
86   *La Solennità*, no. 17.

people acquire property through work, and thereby earn the fruits of the earth meant by God for the benefit of all persons. In the same way, the principle is applied to the defence of the rights of both work and capital, with the primacy given to work over capital. Pius XII, in *La Solennità*, reaffirms some of these ideas related to work[87] and the family,[88] and then extends them to the common destination of the land to all families of the world, and therefore to the issue of migrations. The pope says:

> Our planet, with all its extent of oceans and seas and lakes, with mountains and hills covered by eternal ice and snow, with great deserts and inhospitable and barren lands, is not want of regions and vital places abandoned to the vegetative caprice of nature, and well suited to be cultivated by man, to serve his needs and his civil obligations; and more than once it is inevitable that some families migrating from one spot here, look for a new home elsewhere.[89]

When this happens, "the right of the family to a vital space is recognized."[90] Then "emigration attains its natural purpose," which is "the more favorable distribution of man on the earth's surface . . . which God created and prepared for use by all."[91]

It is clear to me that the Church is applying the same principles, and the same dynamic of equilibrium and tension between private property and universal destination, by analogy to the distribution of the whole earth among all the peoples and among all human beings and families. Here again there must be some sort of equilibrium between countries:

> If the two parties, the one that agrees to leave its native land and the one that admits the newcomers, are solicitous to eliminate as far as possible all obstacles to the birth and growth of a real confidence between the country of emigration and the country of immigration, all participants in these changes of places and people will profit: the families will receive land that will be native land for them in the true sense of the word; the thickly inhabited countries will be relieved, and their peoples will acquire new friends in foreign countries; and states which receive the emigrants will acquire industrious citizens. So the nations who give and those who receive, on the same will both contribute to human welfare and progress of human culture.[92]

---

[87] *La Solennità*, nos. 19–21.
[88] *La Solennità*, nos. 22–25.
[89] *La Solennità*, no. 25.
[90] *La Solennità*, no. 25.
[91] *La Solennità*, no. 25.
[92] *La Solennità*, no. 25.

Hence it seems clear that, as the Church will teach in more detail in years to come, the issue of migrations also implies some sort of common destination of the earth to all human beings, alongside some kind of legally regulated private property over the land as a true right of individuals, families, and countries. The analogy implies, in my view, that the respect of legal boundaries between countries, and of the regulations of movements of migrants, corresponds to the collective right to private property of the state community over their territory. Without these private territories of each nation, the universal destination of the earth would not be realized. On the other hand, the same universal destination implies that, in the case of extreme need, everybody has the right to immigrate to a better or safer place. The distinction must be made, as in the case of material needs, between extreme need, relative need, urgent need, and so on. The recipient country has the right to limit immigration according to the needs of the common good. Since the topic is discussed in another chapter of this volume,[93] it suffices now to recall the summary of the Catechism of the Catholic Church:

> The more prosperous nations are obliged, to the extent they are able, to welcome the foreigner in search of the security and the means of livelihood which he cannot find in his country of origin. Public authorities should see to it that the natural right is respected that places a guest under the protection of those who receive him.
>
> Political authorities, for the sake of the common good for which they are responsible, may make the exercise of the right to immigrate subject to various juridical conditions, especially with regard to the immigrants' duties toward their country of adoption. Immigrants are obliged to respect with gratitude the material and spiritual heritage of the country that receives them, to obey its laws and to assist in carrying civic burdens.[94]

The principles on immigration that as far as I am aware have been confirmed by Popes Benedict XVI and Francis can be summed up thus: the priority of not being forced to migrate, and to be able to live in one's own country; the duty to welcome migrants, according to just laws that guarantee the human rights of migrants and refugees, and at the same time protect the common good of the recipient country and the rights of its citizens; the equilibrium between the generosity to receive newcomers, and the political prudence to accept them only in such numbers and qualities as can be reasonably accommodated, aided, and integrated; and the several obligations

---

[93]   See chapter 15 in this volume: Kevin Flannery, SJ, "The Moral Principles Governing the Immigration Policies of Polities."
[94]   *Catechism of the Catholic Church*, no. 2241.

of the immigrants, such as to obey the laws of the new country, including those on immigration itself in the measure in which they are morally obligatory (which is the general rule but allows for exceptions). The ideology of no borders, or open borders, is against natural law, against the common good of the nation. I have not read anything close to it in official Catholic social doctrine.

Pope John XXIII

Mater et magistra (1961) states that "private ownership of property, including that of productive goods, is a natural right which the State cannot suppress. But it naturally entails a social obligation as well. It is a right which must be exercised not only for one's own personal benefit but also for the benefit of others."[95] And again: "With regard to private property, Our Predecessor reaffirmed its origin in natural law, and enlarged upon its social aspect and the obligations of ownership."[96] Then John XXIII recalls Pius XII's teaching on the priority of the right to common use over "every other economic right, even that of private property,"[97] because "in the objective order established by God, the right to property cannot stand in the way of the axiomatic principle that 'the goods which were created by God for all men should flow to all alike, according to the principles of justice and charity.'"[98]

John XXIII teaches again the ordination of private property to its universal destination (without using this denomination yet): "it is not enough to assert that the right to own private property and the means of production is inherent in human nature. We must also insist on the extension of this right in practice to all classes of citizens."[99] According to the changing circumstances, the pope says: "Now, if ever, is the time to insist on a more widespread distribution of property, in view of the rapid economic development of an increasing number of States."[100] He favors an economic and social policy of the state "which facilitates the widest possible distribution of private property in terms of durable consumer goods, houses, land, tools and equipment (in the case of craftsmen and owners of family farms), and shares in medium and large

---

[95] John XXIII, Encyclical Letter *Mater et magistra* (On Christianity and Social Progress) (1961), no. 19.
[96] MM, no. 30.
[97] MM, no. 30.
[98] MM, no. 30. The internal quotation is from Pius XII's *La Solennità*, which repeats the formulation of *Sertum laetitiae*.
[99] MM, no. 113.
[100] MM, no. 115.

business concerns."[101] At this point of history, it is already clear that the possession of land is not the only nor the most common form of earthly resources that are universally destined to all.

In his Encyclical *Pacem in terris* (1963), John XXIII simply reiterates the basic idea that there is a natural right to private property that "entails a social obligation as well."[102] He also applies this principle to the right to emigrate and immigrate "when there are just reasons in favor of it";[103] but giving the priority to the right to remain in one's own country: "We advocate in such cases [i.e., where there is some imbalance between land, workers, and resources] the policy of bringing the work to the workers, wherever possible, rather than bringing workers to the scene of the work. In this way many people will be afforded an opportunity of increasing their resources without being exposed to the painful necessity of uprooting themselves from their own homes, settling in a strange environment, and forming new social contacts."[104] For this reason, I think that the universal destination of earthly goods, when applied to immigration, is to be realized primarily by the movement of goods (i.e., resources, jobs, capital, etc.), and secondarily by the movement of people (i.e., immigrants). The excessive movement of people, either immigrants or refugees, is a sign precisely that the material wealth has not been fairly distributed among the countries of the world, or even more a sign that the spiritual goods that are the basis for material development have not reached the poorest countries (e.g., an acceptable level of respect and protection of natural rights, the rule of law, public honesty, science and technology, increased levels of education, religious and moral instruction).

Finally, it is worth mentioning that Pope John XXIII, in *Mater and magistra* and in *Pacem in terris*, applies to the relations among states the principle that the wealth of the rich is to be used for the good of all. He appeals "to the more wealthy nations to render every kind of assistance to those States which are still in the process of economic development."[105] For "the solidarity which binds all men together as members of a common family makes it impossible for wealthy nations to look with indifference upon the hunger, misery and poverty of other nations whose citizens are unable to enjoy even elementary human rights."[106]

---

[101]   *MM*, no. 115.
[102]   *PT*, no. 22.
[103]   *PT*, no. 25.
[104]   *PT*, no. 102.
[105]   *PT*, no. 121, and *MM*, nos. 157–158.
[106]   *MM*, no. 157.

FROM VATICAN II TO POPE FRANCIS

The Second Vatican Council is not original in its teaching about private property and the right to common use of goods, but it applies it to differing circumstances, building upon previous papal teaching. As we saw in the introduction, *Gaudium et spes* is the first magisterial text that uses the formula "universal destination of earthly goods."[107] The ground of the principle is in the doctrine of creation: "God intended the earth with everything contained in it for the use of all human beings and peoples."[108] The formulation is close to that by Pope Pius XII: "Thus, under the leadership of justice and in the company of charity, created goods should be in abundance for all in like manner."[109] Private property is to be compatible with this origin and aim: "Whatever the forms of property may be, as adapted to the legitimate institutions of peoples, according to diverse and changeable circumstances, attention must always be paid to this universal destination of earthly goods."[110]

The main consequence of this principle is the duty of the owners correlative to the right of all to common use, based upon the distinction, that we have seen, between the *right* to property and the *use* of it: "In using them, therefore, man should regard the external things that he legitimately possesses not only as his own but also as common *in the sense that they should be able to benefit not only him but also others*."[111] I stress here that the universal destination and the so-called right to common use do not imply that some persons, for example the poor, are also owners of the private property of others, e.g., the rich. This interpretation would annul the very concept of private, which means the *exclusion of others from* ... possessing and disposing of something (private property), knowing (private life or information), etc. In fact, the very word private comes from the Latin "privare," which means "deprive": one has something in or as private precisely because one may exclude others from it. Hence the Council explains that one same thing is not regarded as one's own and also as common *in the same sense*: it is one's own in the sense that one legitimately possesses it, and benefits oneself in that specific way, namely by exercising the faculties proper of the private owner; but it is *regarded* as common only in the sense that it "should be able to benefit ... also others." (This is the classical position of Aquinas, repeated in *Rerum novarum*, no. 22.)

---

[107] GS, no. 69.
[108] GS, no. 69.
[109] GS, no. 69.
[110] GS, no. 69.
[111] GS, no. 69 (my italics).

Gaudium et spes states that "the right of having a share of earthly goods sufficient for oneself and one's family belongs to everyone."[112] For this reason, the Fathers and Doctors of the Church taught "that men are obliged to come to the relief of the poor and to do so not merely out of their superfluous goods."[113] This is also the traditional doctrine:[114] one must relieve the poor using superfluous goods, at least; but also, in emergency situations (extreme need), one must use in the service of others those resources relatively necessary, that is, needed not for the bare necessities of life (which one is almost never obliged to forgo) but for the satisfaction of those reasonable needs of one's social position, family well-being, profession, legitimate life options, prudent provision for the future, etc. For example, I have no obligation to receive at my home a homeless person, and to accommodate him or her indefinitely; in the midst of a hurricane, however, if my house is strong enough and to the extent of my possibilities, I must receive in it whoever is looking for refuge close by, for the time of the emergency.

After recalling the classical and most clear consequence of the right to common use, namely that "if one is in extreme necessity, he has the right to procure for himself what he needs out of the riches of others,"[115] the Council applies this principle of universal destination to individuals and peoples alike:

> Since there are so many people prostrate with hunger in the world, this sacred council urges all, both individuals and governments, to remember the aphorism of the Fathers, "Feed the man dying of hunger, because if you have not fed him, you have killed him," and really to share and employ their earthly goods, according to the ability of each, especially by supporting individuals or peoples with the aid by which they may be able to help and develop themselves.[116]

Gaudium et spes reminds us also about the plurality of ways in which the principle may be realized according to different circumstances of time and place. "In economically less advanced societies the common destination of earthly goods is partly satisfied by means of the customs and traditions proper to the community, by which the absolutely necessary things are furnished to

---

[112] GS, no. 69.
[113] GS, no. 69.
[114] See Finnis, *Aquinas*, 191–192.
[115] GS, no. 69.
[116] GS, no. 69. As we have seen, John XXIII also applied the principle to international relations. This requirement to aid other peoples is the other side of the coin of immigration, as we have seen, because it is better to move jobs to where the poor live before immigration becomes necessary or even urgent.

each member."[117] "Similarly, in highly developed nations a body of social institutions dealing with protection and security can, for its own part, bring to reality the common destination of earthly goods."[118] The fact, however, that society as a whole provides for the effective concretization of the universal destination and common use of earthly goods should go along with vigilance, which "is necessary to prevent the citizens from being led into a certain inactivity *vis-a-vis* society or from rejecting the burden of taking up office or from refusing to serve."[119] All these suggestions about how to make effective the universal destination, without giving too much power to the state and with no hindrance of the responsibility of persons and peoples, shows that there is no real ownership of the poor over the goods of the rich, but rather a title in justice to be helped with those goods that are from the beginning ordered to the well-being of all. Only in cases of extreme need, as we have seen, may the poor help themselves with whatever they may have at hand to alleviate that need.

Then the Council applies the principle to investments, which, among other things, "must be directed toward procuring employment and sufficient income for the people both now and in the future."[120]

After defending again the institution of private property,[121] *Gaudium et spes* declares it to be compatible with public property, and recalls that "it is the right of public authority to prevent anyone from abusing his private property to the detriment of the common good."[122] For "by its very nature private property has a social quality which is based on the law of the common destination of earthly goods. If this social quality is overlooked, property often becomes an occasion of passionate desires for wealth and serious disturbances, so that a pretext is given to the attackers for calling the right itself into question."[123]

The Council observes: "In many underdeveloped regions there are large or even extensive rural estates which are only slightly cultivated or lie completely idle for the sake of profit, while the majority of the people either are without land or have only very small fields, and, on the other hand, it is evidently urgent to increase the productivity of the fields."[124] Therefore, apart from improving the situation of the workers on many respects, the Council affirms

[117] GS, no. 69.
[118] GS, no. 69.
[119] GS, no. 69.
[120] GS, no. 70.
[121] GS, no. 71.
[122] GS, no. 71.
[123] GS, no. 71.
[124] GS, no. 71.

that "insufficiently cultivated estates should be distributed to those who can make these lands fruitful; in this case, the necessary things and means, especially educational aids and the right facilities for cooperative organization, must be supplied. Whenever, nevertheless, the common good requires expropriation, compensation must be reckoned in equity after all the circumstances have been weighed."[125]

Pope Paul VI

After the Council, *Populorum progressio* (1967) repeated that the grounds of the principles related to property and the universal destination of goods are in the doctrine of creation: "In the very first pages of Scripture we read these words: 'Fill the earth and subdue it.' (*Gen.* 1, 28) This teaches us that the whole of creation is for man, that he has been charged to give it meaning by his intelligent activity, to complete and perfect it by his own efforts and to his own advantage."[126] From this "it follows that every man has the right to glean what he needs from the earth."[127] Here the pope quotes the Council's formulation of the principle of universal destination (*Gaudium et spes*, no. 69) and draws the consequence: "All other rights, whatever they may be, including the rights of property and free trade, are to be subordinated to this principle."[128] The other rights "should in no way hinder" the principle, but rather "actively facilitate its implementation."[129] "Redirecting these rights back to their original purpose must be regarded as an important and urgent social duty."[130]

From here, again, Paul VI affirms the primacy of common use over private property, based on the New Testament and the Fathers of the Church:

> "He who has the goods of this world and sees his brother in need and closes his heart to him, how does the love of God abide in him?" (1 John 3,17) Everyone knows that the Fathers of the Church laid down the duty of the rich toward the poor in no uncertain terms. As St. Ambrose put it: "You are not making a gift of what is yours to the poor man, but you are giving him back what is his. You have been appropriating things that are meant to be for the common use of everyone. The earth belongs to everyone, not to the rich." (*De*

---

[125] GS, no. 71.
[126] Paul VI, Encyclical Letter *Populorum progressio* (On the Development of Peoples) (1967), no. 22.
[127] *PP*, no. 22.
[128] *PP*, no. 22.
[129] *PP*, no. 22.
[130] *PP*, no. 22.

Nabute, c. 12, n. 53: PL 14.74722) These words indicate that the right to private property is not absolute and unconditional.[131]

The pope is using here prophetic language to assert a very mild and traditional conclusion: the right to private property is not absolute and unconditional. But he is not actually defending that the poor have immediate right of ownership over the superfluous goods of the rich. This is made clear in what follows. Since "no one may appropriate surplus goods solely for his own private use when others lack the bare necessities of life," and "the right of private property may never be exercised to the detriment of the common good," then "when 'private gain and basic community needs conflict with one another,' it is for the public authorities 'to seek a solution to these questions, with the active involvement of individual citizens and social groups.'"[132]

In several previous teachings, the Church had already extended the interplay between private property and common use/universal destination of earthly resources to all sorts of human goods, even spiritual goods and anything that may be considered a God-given talent for the benefit of oneself and neighbor.[133] Vatican II and Paul VI, however, explicitly extended the application of the principle of universal destination and the right to private property to almost every field of social ethics: culture and education,[134] investments,[135] future generations,[136] the relations between rich and poor countries,[137] social funds, rights, and services provided by society.[138] "This is true not only of material property but also of immaterial things such as professional capacities."[139] The wider the application of the principle, the clearer – in my view – the analogy: *everything* is a gift from God the Creator and the Redeemer for all his children; each good (from a piece of land to a special supernatural grace) is possessed, and administered, in some private way only by the person so endowed, and thereafter is to be used for the benefit also of everybody else in an ordered manner. In so far as one does not use well the gift, one abuses it, but does not forfeit it (*abusus non tollit usum*); but if that abuse constitutes a serious injustice against the common good, the competent

---

[131] *PP*, no. 23.
[132] *PP*, no. 23. The internal quotation is from Paul VI's *Letter to the 52nd Social Week at Brest*, in *L'homme et la révolution urbaine*, Lyon: *Chronique sociale* (1965), 8–9.
[133] *RN*, no. 22.
[134] *GS*, no. 69.
[135] *GS*, no. 70.
[136] *GS*, no. 70.
[137] *GS*, no. 70.
[138] *GS*, no. 71.
[139] *GS*, no. 71.

authority can, and even must, intervene to secure justice for all. Similarly, the complementarity between private ownership of any good and the universal destination of them all is a matter for prudent regulation by the laws of the respective order, and for different ways of realization according to different circumstances of time and place.

Pope John Paul II

John Paul II addressed the topic of private property and universal destination/ common use of earthly goods in many of his documents on social matters, mainly in his three social encyclicals: *Laborem exercens* (1981), *Sollicitudo rei socialis* (1987), and *Centesimus annus* (1991).[140]

Laborem exercens articulates "the principle of the priority of labor over capital."[141] This principle is based upon the fact that "all the resources contained in the visible world and placed at man's disposal . . . can serve man only through work."[142] But then we need ownership, among other reasons, because "the only means that man has for causing the resources hidden in nature to serve himself and others is his work. And to be able through his work to make these resources bear fruit, man takes over ownership of small parts of the various riches of nature."[143] Now, behind both labor and capital "there are people, living, actual people: on the one side are those who do the work without being the owners of the means of production, and on the other side those who act as entrepreneurs and who own these means or represent the owners."[144] The Church defends all persons, the owners of the capital and the workers. Private property of the means of production may not be abolished, but the Christian tradition "has never upheld this right as absolute and untouchable."[145] The Church "has always understood this right within the broader context of the right common to all to use the goods of the whole of creation: the right to private property is subordinated to the right to common use, to the fact that goods are meant for everyone."[146] For this reason,

---

[140]   Under his pontificate, moreover, two important documents were published: The CSDC (2004) and the CCC (1992). The *Compendium of the Catechism* was published under Pope Benedict XVI. These three documents present in a more organized and summary manner the magisterium of the Church.

[141]   John Paul II, Encyclical Letter *Laborem exercens* (On Human Work) (September 14, 1981), no. 12.

[142]   *LE*, no. 12.

[143]   *LE*, no. 12.

[144]   *LE*, no. 14.

[145]   *LE*, no. 14.

[146]   *LE*, no. 14.

a consequence of the right to common use is that isolating the means of production "as a separate property in order to set it up in the form of 'capital' in opposition to 'labor' – and even to practise exploitation of labor – is contrary to the very nature of these means and their possession."[147] According to John Paul II, "the only legitimate title to their possession – whether in the form of private ownership or in the form of public or collective ownership – is that they should serve labor, and thus, by serving labor, that they should make possible the achievement of *the first principle of this order,* namely, *the universal destination of goods and the right to common use of them.*"[148]

From here the pope proposes "various adaptations in the sphere of the right to ownership of the means of production"[149] so that

> on the basis of his work each person is fully entitled to consider himself a part-owner of the great workbench at which he is working with everyone else. A way towards that goal could be found by associating labor with the ownership of capital, as far as possible, and by producing a wide range of intermediate bodies with economic, social and cultural purposes; they would be bodies enjoying real autonomy with regard to the public powers, pursuing their specific aims in honest collaboration with each other and in subordination to the demands of the common good, and they would be living communities both in form and in substance, in the sense that the members of each body would be looked upon and treated as persons and encouraged to take an active part in the life of the body.[150]

In this encyclical John Paul II says that "the first principle of the whole ethical and social order" is "the principle of the common use of goods."[151] But now he uses the principle to ground the thesis that "the justice of a socioeconomic system and, in each case, its just functioning, deserve in the final analysis to be evaluated by the way in which man's work is properly remunerated in the system."[152] For "wages, that is to say remuneration for work, are still a practical means whereby the vast majority of people can have access to those goods which are intended for common use: both the goods of nature and manufactured goods."[153] This observation by Pope John Paul II is,

---

[147]   *LE,* no. 14.
[148]   *LE,* no. 14 (my italics). *Laborem exercens* refers this doctrine, again, to the classical teachings of Aquinas on the right to property: Thomas Aquinas, *Summa Theologiae,* II-II, q. 66, arts. 2 and 6; *De Regimine Principum,* book 1, chapters 15 and 17, and, on the social function of property, Aquinas, *Summa Theologiae,* II-II, q. 134, art. 1, ad 3.
[149]   *LE,* no. 14.
[150]   *LE,* no. 14.
[151]   *LE,* no. 19. The formulation is slightly different, but it is the same idea as in no. 14.
[152]   *LE,* no. 19.
[153]   *LE,* no. 19.

in my view, a confirmation that the universal destination of goods does not imply any direct entitlement of those who have fewer goods over the resources privately owned by those who have more, but rather the right to the most effective means to have access, on their turn, to acquire private property. At some point in history, this may have meant to own a piece of land under one's feet; today, for the great majority of people, it means to have an honest job with a fair wage; in the future, it might amount to some other, more convenient way for all to share in the benefits of common life and work, in an ordered society.

Sollicitudo rei socialis explains that "the option or love of preference for the poor,"[154] "given the worldwide dimension which the social question has assumed,"[155] "cannot but embrace the immense multitudes of the hungry, the needy, the homeless, those without medical care and, above all, those without hope of a better future."[156] In this context, the pope reaffirms briefly the principle of universal destination and its relation to the right to private property:

> It is necessary to state once more the characteristic principle of Christian social doctrine: the goods of this world are originally meant for all. The right to private property is valid and necessary, but it does not nullify the value of this principle. Private property, in fact, is under a "social mortgage," which means that it has an intrinsically social function, based upon and justified precisely by the principle of the universal destination of goods.[157]

Centesimus annus realizes that the amount of space devoted by *Rerum novarum* to the right to private property shows the importance attached to it.[158] In spite of the changes in forms of private property, however, "the reasons adduced to safeguard" it are not less valid today.[159] Furthermore, "this is something which must be affirmed once more in the face of the changes we are witnessing in systems formerly dominated by collective ownership of the means of production, as well as in the face of the increasing instances of poverty or, more precisely, of hindrances to private ownership in many parts of the world, including those where systems predominate which are based on an affirmation of the right to private property."[160] The pope recalls, however, that Pope Leo XIII (whose encyclical *Rerum novarum* reached its one-hundredth

---

[154]   John Paul II, Encyclical Letter *Sollicitudo rei socialis* (On Social Concern) (1987), no. 42.
[155]   *SRS*, no. 42.
[156]   *SRS*, no. 42.
[157]   *SRS*, no. 42. Internal references are omitted.
[158]   *CA*, no. 6.
[159]   *CA*, no. 6.
[160]   *CA*, no. 6.

anniversary just after the fall of communism in Europe around 1989) "is well aware that private property is not an absolute value, nor does he fail to proclaim the necessary complementary principles, such as the universal destination of the earth's goods."[161]

The whole of Chapter IV of *Centesimus annus* is entitled *Private Property and the Universal Destination of Material Goods*.[162] After referring to the teachings of the previous magisterium on the matter,[163] John Paul II elaborates further: "Re-reading this teaching on the right to property and the common destination of material wealth as it applies to the present time, the question can be raised concerning the origin of the material goods which sustain human life, satisfy people's needs and are an object of their rights."[164] On the one hand, "the foundation of the universal destination of the earth's goods"[165] is that "the original source of all that is good is the very act of God, who created both the earth and man, and who gave the earth to man so that he might have dominion over it by his work and enjoy its fruits (Gen 1:28). God gave the earth to the whole human race for the sustenance of all its members, without excluding or favoring anyone."[166] On the other hand, however, "the earth does not yield its fruits without a particular human response to God's gift, that is to say, without work."[167] Through work, man "makes part of the earth his own, precisely the part which he has acquired through work; this is the origin of individual property. Obviously, he also has the responsibility not to hinder others from having their own part of God's gift; indeed, he must cooperate with others so that together all can dominate the earth."[168] In this way, work and land are combined, in different relationships throughout history, to realize the universal destination of earthly goods.

The pope applies this idea of the fruitfulness of work to nonmaterial and material wealth.[169] He extends the relationship between property and work, and between private property and universal destination/common use, to "another form of ownership which is becoming no less important than land: the possession of know-how, technology and skill."[170] In effect, "the

---

[161] CA, no. 6. As we have seen, the expression was not in *RN*, but the fundamental idea and principle was clear.
[162] Cf. CA, nos. 30–43.
[163] Cf. CA, no. 30.
[164] CA, no. 31.
[165] CA, no. 31.
[166] CA, no. 31.
[167] CA, no. 31.
[168] CA, no. 31.
[169] CA, no. 31.
[170] CA, no. 32.

wealth of the industrialized nations is based much more on this kind of ownership than on natural resources."[171] The fruitfulness of human work leads to an extension of the meaning of the principle of universal destination even farther than material goods, for "besides the earth, man's principal resource is man himself."[172] "His intelligence enables him to discover the earth's productive potential and the many different ways in which human needs can be satisfied."[173] The application of the principle of universal destination shifts according to which is, or becomes, "the decisive factor of production,"[174] whether land, capital, knowledge, human capacities, or work. Correspondingly, there are new forms of marginalization of people from the enjoyment of these new resources that have become decisive, and that ought to benefit all. In fact, "for the poor, to the lack of material goods has been added a lack of knowledge and training which prevents them from escaping their state of humiliating subjection."[175]

Among many other applications of the principle, John Paul II extends it to "the ecological question which accompanies the problem of consumerism and which is closely connected to it."[176] "In his desire to have and to enjoy rather than to be and to grow, man consumes the resources of the earth and his own life in an excessive and disordered way."[177] The pope denounces "an anthropological error,"[178] namely, that "man, who discovers his capacity to transform and in a certain sense create the world through his own work, forgets that this is always based on God's prior and original gift of the things that are."[179]

POPE BENEDICT XVI AND POPE FRANCIS

Pope Benedict XVI did not develop in a specific way the topic of the universal destination of the world's resources in his major magisterial documents, and when he mentioned it, in some messages and addresses, he did this only to recall previous pontifical teachings.

Pope Francis has followed the steps of his predecessors on the matter we have been examining. Chapter II, section VI of his social Encyclical *Laudato*

---

[171] CA, no. 32.
[172] CA, no. 32.
[173] CA, no. 32.
[174] CA, no. 32.
[175] CA, no. 33.
[176] CA, no. 37.
[177] CA, no. 37.
[178] CA, no. 37.
[179] CA, no. 37.

si' (2015) is entitled *The Common Destination of Goods.*[180] He applies the principle to ecological issues, but he explains it in very general terms. Although "for believers"[181] the principle "becomes a question of fidelity to the Creator, since God created the world for everyone,"[182] the pope enlists nonbelievers in defending it: "Whether believers or not, we are agreed today that the earth is essentially a shared inheritance, whose fruits are meant to benefit everyone."[183] "The principle of the subordination of private property to the universal destination of goods, and thus the right of everyone to their use," says the pope, "is a golden rule of social conduct and 'the first principle of the whole ethical and social order.'"[184] Therefore, "every ecological approach needs to incorporate a social perspective which takes into account the fundamental rights of the poor and the underprivileged."[185] After recalling the main formulations of the principle by John Paul II, and in particular that it is against God's plan that the gift of creation "be used in such a way that its benefits favor only a few,"[186] Francis concludes that "this calls into serious question the unjust habits of a part of humanity."[187] A consequence or application of the principle is that "the natural environment is a collective good, the patrimony of all humanity and the responsibility of everyone. If we make something our own, it is only to administer it for the good of all. If we do not, we burden our consciences with the weight of having denied the existence of others."[188] Then he echoes the bishops of New Zealand, who "asked what the commandment 'Thou shall not kill' means when 'twenty per cent of the world's population consumes resources at a rate that robs the poor nations and future generations of what they need to survive.'"[189] This is not a statement on economics or a prediction of fact, as if the pope knew a direct and monocausal connection between consumerism of the wealthy and the poverty of some peoples, often due more to lack of sound policies, and to corruption, than to what other people do in rich countries; or as if the pope could know that the resources that we use today are depriving future generations of their own share in earthly goods (as prophets of doom have said with no scientific evidence for decades). The pope and the New Zealand bishops utter a moral calling – in prophetic

[180] LS, nos. 93–95.
[181] LS, no. 93.
[182] LS, no. 93.
[183] LS, no. 93.
[184] LS, no. 93, quoting LE, no. 19.
[185] LS, no. 93.
[186] LS, no. 93.
[187] LS, no. 93.
[188] LS, no. 95.
[189] LS, no. 95.

tone – for all of us to stop styles of life that consume, for selfish enjoyment, the resources that we ought to use, here and now, to help the poor.

Pope Francis has also based part of his teaching on evangelization upon the principle of universal destination: "Solidarity is a spontaneous reaction by those who recognize that the social function of property and the universal destination of goods are realities which come before private property."[190] The pope even gives as a justification of private property – without negating all the other arguments proposed by previous social teaching – the very principle of universal destination, so that earthly goods better serve the common good, and specially the needs of the poor: "The private ownership of goods is justified by the need to protect and increase them, so that they can better serve the common good; for this reason, solidarity must be lived as the decision to restore to the poor what belongs to them."[191] Francis applies this conviction, apart from material goods and its fair distribution, to spiritual goods as well: "the worst discrimination which the poor suffer is the lack of spiritual care. The great majority of the poor have a special openness to the faith; they need God and we must not fail to offer them his friendship, his blessing, his word, the celebration of the sacraments and a journey of growth and maturity in the faith. Our preferential option for the poor must mainly translate into a privileged and preferential religious care."[192]

CONCLUSION

My purpose in this exposition has been to furnish the reader with the main texts of the social doctrine of the Church about the principle of universal destination of earthly resources, so that the stability of the teaching on this matter may appear as self-evident. If one attends only to the principal pronouncements of the magisterium and not to minor documents or other forms of teaching (or even private opinions of the bishops and popes), it seems to me that the main thesis is always the same: priority of universal destination as an end, and its compatibility with a strong right to private property as a means. This tenet is always reasserted, and then expanded to new issues.

Since this is a matter of principles, I think that the new social realities will call for new applications of the principles. The specific configuration of the right to private property over things which are incorporeal – that therefore can be enjoyed at the same time by innumerable persons – should be moderated

---

[190] Francis, Apostolic Exhortation *Evangelii Gaudium* (2013), no. 189.
[191] EG, no. 189.
[192] EG, no. 200.

even further, or relativized when vital goods are at stake, especially regarding the poor who cannot pay for them. This should be accomplished with due respect to the right to a fair reward for the original inventors or discoverers, so that the reasonable incentives to produce those goods are duly preserved. I refer here, among other things, to scientific and technological discoveries, especially in the fields of health and education; to the benefits of computer machines and sophisticated software, artificial intelligence, and so on.

The expansion of the principle to even more fields depends, however, on the contours of a future that cannot be predicted. I wish that it could be applied to the mission of the Church herself: that the gifts of faith, hope, and charity, and of eternal salvation, that we have received explicitly from Jesus Christ, and all the spiritual riches of the Catholic Church – her doctrine, her sacraments, her liturgy – should no longer be kept from reaching all persons under the false pretext that all will be saved anyway in some mysterious manner known only to God.

In any case, the basic requirement of any new development of the universal destination, in relation either to material or to spiritual goods, will always be the complementariness between the good of those who have the first and direct control of the resources (normally in the form of private ownership) and the requirement that all goods and services benefit everybody in a just social order.

12

The Apostolate of the Laity

Christopher Tollefsen

The absence of awareness of an "apostolate of the laity" is a manifest feature of life in the post–Vatican II Church. This is in sharp contrast to the role of "ministry" as an all-purpose term used to designate the activities of lay persons inside and outside the parish.[1] In this essay, I argue that this replacement is in fact a loss. First, though, I discuss the approach to the laity that preceded the Second Vatican Council; then I look at what *Lumen gentium* (LG), and *Apostolicam actuositatem* (AA), *The Decree on the Apostolate of the Laity* have to say, and also at John Paul II's discussion in *Christifideles laici* (CL). Penultimately, I discuss the shift from apostolate to ministry; and finally, I say something about what is lost in this shift, and what would be gained by returning to the concept of a lay apostolate. My discussion is neither exhaustive nor definitive, but rather somewhat programmatic; indeed, I think far more work should be done on this topic than I am here in a position to do.

APOSTOLATE AND LAITY PRIOR TO THE COUNCIL

There are at least three aspects of Catholic thought and history that need discussion to understand the pre-conciliar context of thought and practice concerning lay people. The first concerns the barriers, prior to the late nineteenth and twentieth centuries, to fully helpful thinking about the laity, their role in the Church, and their apostolate. I'll mention four such barriers, all of which are discussed by a number of thinkers, from Yves Congar, to Russell Shaw and Germain Grisez.

---

[1] The eclipse of apostolate by ministry has been documented by Russell Shaw in *Ministry or Apostolate? What Should the Catholic Laity Be Doing?* (Huntington, IN: Our Sunday Visitor, 2002). I will discuss his work later in this chapter.

The first was the phenomenon of Christendom. Several writers on the topic of the laity note, in John Sheerin's words, the "close cooperation that existed between St. Paul and his lay co-workers."[2] Shaw notes too that the *Epistle to Diognetus* presents a picture of the laity as active in the world yet visibly not of it. But the close cooperation between Church and State in the post-Constantinian Church diminished the cooperation between the hierarchy and the laity. Again, Sheerin: "Churchmen felt no need to enlist the help of the great mass of the laity when kings and princes were taking it upon themselves to achieve the goals of the Church in human society." Aspects of feudal society also contributed, since, as Grisez and Shaw point out, it "offered most people few options and required that they make comparatively few vocational judgments."[3]

A second factor arises in the Counter-Reformation context, in the need for the Church to emphasize its institutional and hierarchical nature contrary to the congregational aspects of Protestant thought. Fr. Congar argues that Reformation thought failed to recognize that the institutional Church precedes the fellowship of Christians, and held instead that the Church is *made* by the faithful. In opposition to this, the Catholic Church "elaborated rather one-sidedly" a "theology only of her institutional and hierarchical powers of mediation."[4] Congar notes that this process proceeded apace with increasing secularism, and writes that "While Protestantism was making the Church a people without a priesthood and Catholic apologists were replying by establishing the rightfulness of priesthood and institution, the Church in more than one place was finding herself reduced to the state of a priestly system without a Christian people."[5]

A consequence of this overemphasis is the first of a number of dichotomies that make a proper appreciation of the laity's role in the Church difficult, namely, the contrast between the clergy as active, and the laity as passive recipients of the clergy's action. An example of this can be seen in the entry for "Laity" in the 1910 *Catholic Encyclopedia*. There, the author writes:

> The Church is a perfect society, though all therein are not equal; it is composed of two kinds of members (see can. "Duo sunt," vii, Caus. 12, Q. i, of uncertain origin): in the first place, those who are the depositaries

---

[2] "Decree of the Apostolate of the Laity of Vatican Council II, with Commentary by John B. Sheerin, C.S.P." (Glenn Rock, NJ: Paulist Press, 1966), 9.

[3] Germain Grisez and Russell Shaw, *Personal Vocation: God Calls Everyone by Name* (Huntington, IN: Our Sunday Visitor, 2003), 47.

[4] Yves M. J. Congar, OP, *Lay People in the Church*, tr. Donald Attwater (Westminster, MD: Newman Press, 1962).

[5] Congar, *Lay People in the Church*, 41.

of sacred or spiritual authority under its triple aspect, government, teaching, and worship, i.e. the clergy, the sacred hierarchy established by Divine law (Conc. Trid., Sess. XXIII, can. vi); in the second place, those over whom this power is exercised, who are governed, taught, and sanctified, the Christian people, the laity.[6]

A more dramatic statement of the role of the laity is the well-known remark of Msgr. Talbot: "What is the province of the laity? To hunt, to shoot, to entertain."[7]

A third obstacle may be found in the inattention to or occasional deprecation of marriage. The view that marriage is unqualifiedly inferior to the state of celibacy or to religious life puts in jeopardy the possibility of a positive theology of lay life. Even if it is acknowledged, as it was, that individual married laypersons could be holier than individual clerics or religious, there is still a problem. As John D. Gerken, in his *Toward a Theology of the Layman*, puts it, "It is traditional to say that the lay state is inferior to the religious state or to the state of celibacy. [So] when one deliberately chooses to be a layman, he is at least apparently choosing something inferior. His choice, therefore ... can be considered as marking him as an inferior Christian. Is this true?"[8]

The fourth barrier is related to the previous two. Christians have always asked: what is the relationship between the goods of this world, and the good of the heavenly kingdom? And what is the relationship between those moral norms that are constitutive of an uprightly lived Christian life and entrance into that kingdom? An overly dualistic, neo-Platonist approach, not fully embraced, but certainly deeply influential for many Christians, holds that the value of morality is primarily instrumental, and that a large part of morality consists in the renunciation of the temptations of the world, which are, at best, necessary evils. Accordingly, even for the laity, spirituality has been "often modeled on monastic," and contemplative spirituality.[9] Such an approach has made it difficult to say what a properly Christian task is for the Christian *in* the world; "in but not of," we could say, has lacked an adequate interpretation.

These are some of the barriers to a fully developed theology of the laity and the lay apostolate. This brings us to the second, and contrasting, aspect of the immediately pre-conciliar context, which is the work of Church theologians in

---

[6] A. Boudinhon, "Laity," in *The Catholic Encyclopedia* (New York: Robert Appleton Company, 1910).

[7] Quoted in John Coulson, "Introduction," in *On Consulting the Faithful in Matters of Doctrine* (New York: Sheed and Ward, 1961), 41–42.

[8] John D. Gerken, SJ, *Toward a Theology of the Layman* (New York, NY: Herder and Herder, 1962), 41–42.

[9] Sheerin, "Decree of the Apostolate of the Laity," 16.

the decades leading up to the Second Vatican Council who were trying to rethink the nature of the laity and their role in the Church. Yves Congar is perhaps the most important; Karl Rahner and others also wrote on the topic.

To say something very briefly about Congar, it is notable, among other aspects of his *Lay People and the Church*, that he denies, as was asserted by the *Catholic Encyclopedia*, that the role of the clergy *exhausts* the three roles of king, prophet, and priest; he denies that lay life is to be characterized by its passivity relative to the activity of the clergy; and he argues that the fellowship and life of the faithful is the *actualization* of the institutional Church; the Church could exist without such activity, but it would not in some sense be fully actualized or realized. These ideas play a role in the development of thought about the laity that characterizes the Second Vatican Council.

The third aspect of the standing of the laity prior to the Council concerns the idea of the apostolate of the laity as it is understood, at least semiofficially, in the hierarchical thinking of the Church in the decades of the twentieth century prior to the Council. That there should even be such an understanding is progress, but it is progress shaped by what came before, and specifically by the existence of Catholic Action.

"Catholic Action" was, from the late nineteenth century until the middle of the twentieth, a somewhat loosely organized movement of Catholic lay groups and associations, generally operating under the authority and supervision of the local bishop. Russell Shaw suggests that there was, and perhaps is, a conflation of the lay apostolate *with* Catholic Action, a conflation apparent in Pope Pius XI's definition of Catholic Action as "the participation of the laity in the apostolate of the hierarchy."[10] On this approach, there is one "apostolate," that of the ordained clergy; it is the task of the laity to assist in this. But there is no sense of an apostolate proper to the laity. Moreover, the laity's performance of that task is associated somewhat exclusively with the work of Catholic Action.[11]

There are examples of popes struggling against this conflation. In an address of Pope Pius XII in 1957 to the Second World Congress of the Lay Apostolate, Pius anticipates the Second Vatican Council by speaking of the need for the laity to make "the Christian spirit penetrate all family, social, and political life." Nevertheless, this account of the task of the laity is described as continuous with the laity's taking part in the task of the priest. So described, "Not all

[10] Shaw even quotes Joseph Cardinal Ratzinger as saying that Pius XI "founded the lay apostolate"! Russell Shaw, "Laity in the Mission of the Church," *The Newman Rambler* 7 (2003): 3.
[11] And at times, perhaps, the task is viewed in reductively political terms; see Tom Truman, *Catholic Action and Politics* (Melbourne: The Merlin Press, 1959; second edition, 1960); but note: Truman is no friend of the Catholic Church, and is occasionally quite tendentious.

Christians are called to engage in the lay apostolate in its strict sense." And Pius goes on to describe the "classic example" of the lay apostolate as that of catechist, in part because "he makes up for the shortage of priests."[12]

So the preconciliar "official" understanding of the lay apostolate was shaped partly in relation to Catholic Action. But that term is itself somewhat ambiguous. On the one hand it served, as just noted, as an umbrella term for a number of Catholic lay organizations. Pius XII complains, in the address just mentioned, that there is a sense that Catholic Action has a monopoly on the lay apostolate. Organizations that exist outside the framework of Catholic Action are seen as lesser, or not part of, the lay apostolate. But the motivation for Pius's complaint seems not to be that the lay apostolate should not be seen as an extension of the hierarchy, as Catholic Action was, but rather that lay organizations *can* be such extensions even if *not* within the specific framework of Catholic Action. Groups within Catholic Action in the stricter sense of the term typically obtained a mandate from their bishop, and thus were "cooperators" in a fairly close and delegated way. But obviously Catholic lay people outside the official parameters of Catholic Action could also cooperate with the hierarchy.

The term Catholic Action was also used in a broader way to indicate the action specifically appropriate to Catholic laity. Any such action *is* "Catholic Action." In this broad sense, the term "Catholic Action" points to a more adequate understanding of the apostolate of the laity than that which associates it with the stricter sense. But the pointing requires an account of what the apostolate of the laity *is* in the first place.

The stricter sense of Catholic Action, particularly when identified with the apostolate of the laity, is at least concerned with the right problem: what is the role of the laity in the Church? Nevertheless it is too beholden to the active/passive contrast, and to the superior/inferior claim and to clericalism more generally. Pius XI's understanding of the lay apostolate and the idea that priestly life is superior to lay life are easily linked: if priestly life is better, then the best that might be available to the laity is to help the priests. Putting any pressure on the unqualified claim to superiority would require finding some proper role for the laity in the life of the Church that was not simply as an extension of the hierarchy. The same could be said of the active/passive distinction.

[12] Pius XII, "Address on Guiding Principles of the Lay Apostolate to the Second World Congress of the Law Apostolate" (October 5, 1957).

VATICAN II

What, then, of the Second Vatican Council? The two most important documents for our discussion are *Lumen gentium*[13] and *Apostolicam actuositatem,
The Decree on the Apostolate of the Laity*.[14] The former, which was approved
about a year before the latter, begins by endorsing Congar's claim that the
faithful, because they are one body with Christ through baptism, are "in their
own way made sharers in the priestly, prophetical, and kingly functions of
Christ" (*LG*, no. 31); moreover, they "carry out for their own part the mission
of the whole Christian people in the Church and in the world" (*LG*, no. 31).
The participation of the laity in this mission just is the lay apostolate.

What is the mission, and what is the laity's part in carrying it out? *The Decree
on the Apostolate of the Laity* identifies the mission of the Church as "the
spreading of the kingdom of Christ throughout the earth for the glory of God
the Father, to enable all men to share in His saving redemption ... that
through them the whole world might enter into a relationship with the
Christ" (*AA*, no. 2). This activity is the apostolate of the Church. The
Council's argument for the claim that the laity shares in this apostolate
seems unimpeachable: *the mission is Christ's mission, which He assigns to
His body the Church; and the laity are, through baptism, incorporated into that
Body; they are then strengthened by the power of the Holy Spirit so as to be able
to carry out the mission that is theirs from their union with Christ.*

In Chapter II, "Objectives," the *Decree* identifies the specific apostolate of
the laity, by holding that "Christ's redemptive work, while essentially concerned with the salvation of men, includes also the renewal of the whole
temporal order" (*AA*, no. 5). Immediately, the Council asserts that the mission
of the Church has two aspects; one is bringing the word and grace of Christ to
men, the other is the perfecting of the temporal order. While both apostolates,
that of the clergy, and that of the laity, share in the two aspects, the share is not
equal: word and grace are communicated "mainly through the ministry of the
Word and the sacraments" (*AA*, no. 6), which is the mission of the clergy. By
contrast, the laity, living as they do in the world, are charged with the renewal
of the world. The *Decree* describes the relationship therefore as "complementary," which seems a considerable distance from the active/passive approach of
the Catholic Encyclopedia.

---

[13] Vatican II, Dogmatic Constitution *Lumen gentium* (1964).
[14] Vatican II, Decree on the Apostolate of the Laity *Apostolicam actuositatem* (Apostolic Activity)
(1965).

The crucial development here is that the laity now are said to have their own apostolate, a part of the mission that is appropriately considered special to them, without which the mission of the Church as a whole could not be adequately pursued. This corrects the emphasis on the passivity of the laity, and demands, instead, activity; it is also indirectly ecumenical, acknowledging in a certain sense the priesthood of all believers and, as Sheerin puts it, the "priestly dignity of every baptized Christian."[15]

The *Decree* goes on to at least indirectly address the other two barriers to a fuller understanding of the laity's role in the Church, namely, the unqualified assertion of the superiority of clerical or religious life over lay life, and the deprecation of the world's goods in favor of heavenly fulfillment. On this last point, the *Decree* should be read in light of *Gaudium et spes*, which offers an important corrective to this deprecation.

Where is the apostolate of the laity to be exercised? The *Decree* first gives a general answer: "All those things which make up the temporal order, namely, the good things of life and the prosperity of the family, culture, economic matters, the arts and professions, the laws of the political community, international relations, and other matters" (*AA*, no. 7). And then later, the *Decree* addresses, in order, lay apostolate in the parish and diocese, then in marriage and the family, among youth, in the social milieu, encompassing customs, laws, and structures of community, and then on the international stage.

Two points are important here. The first is that these domains are the domains of "good things of life." While it is true that the *use* of temporal things has "been marred by serious vices" and "affected by original sin," the Church sees temporal things as a domain that can be perfected, and in which the works of the apostolate can "by their very nature . . . become vivid expressions of charity" (*AA*, nos. 7, 8). The renewal of the temporal order calls for "Christian social action" and creates obligations to provide for the needs of those without "food, drink, clothing, housing, medicine, employment, [or] education" (*AA*, no. 8). The renewal of the temporal order is to be accomplished through engagement with and promotion of that which is *good* for human beings, respecting as well their freedom and dignity. A central end of the apostolate of the laity is concern for human flourishing, which is not here seen as incompatible with a rightly ordered will to friendship with God. The *Decree* emphasizes this: the goods sought *both* "aid in the attainment of man's ultimate goal but also possess their own intrinsic value" (*AA*, no. 7). And again,

---

[15] Sheerin, "Decree of the Apostolate of the Laity," 25.

"the natural goodness of theirs takes on a special dignity as a result of their relation to the human person, for whose service they were created" (AA, no. 7).

The second point concerns the emphasis on marriage and family, and the centrality of these to the lay apostolate: conjugal society is the "beginning and basis of human society," as well as a sacrament for the Church, and thus "the apostolate of married persons and families is of unique importance for the Church and civil society" (AA, no. 11). The family is both one of the goods to be protected by the apostolate of the laity, but also the source from which comes the activity dedicated to that protection, and an agent of that activity. The basic mission of the family is to be "the first and vital cell of society" (AA, no. 11), and the decree enumerates a variety of ways that the family can fulfill this task.

With regard to both the goods of the world and the specific good of marriage, the *Decree* converges on a point made by Congar, learned, he says, from St. Thomas and others, that "the work of the world is not the last end, [but] neither is it *solely a means*; subordinate to the absolute end, it partakes of the character of means, but also of *intermediate end*, having its *own* value in its order."[16] This thought is extended in *Gaudium et spes*. The work of the apostolate of the laity in renewing the temporal order is so far from being merely instrumental that nothing good that is done will be lost to the Kingdom. Rather, as stated in one of that document's most significant passages,

> For after we have obeyed the Lord, and in His Spirit nurtured on earth the values of human dignity, brotherhood and freedom, and indeed all the good fruits of our nature and enterprise, we will find them again, but freed of stain, burnished and transfigured, when Christ hands over to the Father: "a king-dom eternal and universal, a kingdom of truth and life, of holiness and grace, of justice, love and peace." On this earth that Kingdom is already present in mystery. When the Lord returns it will be brought into full flower. (GS, no. 39)

The *Decree* makes a number of further claims. The apostolate can be carried out by individuals, or in groups, as is natural and fitting. Some of those groups, insofar as they meet four criteria, deserve the title "Catholic Action," one mark of which is a closer form of cooperation with the hierarchy than is normative for everyone. The section titled "External Relationships" articulates the relationship that should exist between laity engaged in aposto-late and clergy. Some of these relationships are given "explicit recognition by

---

[16] Congar, *Lay People in the Church*, 400.

the hierarchy," and among them are the entrusting to the laity of "certain functions which are more closely connected with pastoral duties, such as the teaching of Christian doctrine, certain liturgical actions, and the care of souls" (AA, no. 24). I will return to this later. Finally, the *Decree* ends by stressing the importance of sound formation for the apostolate. I will return to this as well.

First, however, I will turn to Pope John Paul II's Post-Synodal Apostolic Exhortation *Christifideles laici*,[17] which could be considered in some ways an updating of *Apostolicam actuositatem*, or perhaps an updating on where the mission marked out in that *Decree* has ended up. *Christifideles laici* is a long document, to that point in John Paul's pontificate, at least, his longest, and it contains much more than can be discussed here. I'll mention just a few passages as of special interest.

The first occurs quite early and is negative in tone. John Paul begins the exhortation by acknowledging that in the wake of the Council, the Church has inspired "new aspirations towards holiness and the participation of . . . [the] lay faithful" (CL, no. 2). But John Paul immediately cites the synod's concerns that the "post-conciliar path" has experienced two temptations in particular, that of being "so strongly interested in Church services and tasks that some fail to become actively engaged in their responsibilities in the professional, social, cultural and political world"; and the second that of an "unwarranted separation of faith from life" (CL, no. 2).

The crux of the worry is that increased lay participation in the apostolate of the Church risks becoming exclusively inward-looking: the laity, in order to be active, have looked too much toward becoming active in the way of the internal life of the Church, and too little in the field of what John Paul throughout the document calls "culture." Having done so, laity can feel that they have fulfilled their obligations as Catholics, thus effecting the division between faith and life that John Paul speaks of. Put another way, the laity may think that, because they participate actively as, say, extraordinary ministers, lectors, members of the parish council, and so on, they have no further obligations *as lay persons* outside the doors of the Church.

John Paul extends this claim in section 23. Following the Council, the laity have become more involved in the liturgy and its preparation, and have taken on many of the tasks previously reserved to those in ordained ministry. Many of these tasks, and numerous other functions as well, now themselves go by the name of ministry, and the Synod is concerned, John Paul writes, "about a too-indiscriminate use of the word 'ministry,' the confusion and equating of the

[17] John Paul II, Post-Synodal Apostolic Exhortation *Christifideles laici* (On the Vocation and the Mission of the Lay Faithful) (1988).

common priesthood and the ministerial priesthood, the lack of observance of ecclesiastical laws and norms, the arbitrary interpretation of the concept of 'supply,' the tendency toward a 'clericalization' of the lay faithful and the risk of creating, in reality, an ecclesial structure of parallel service to that founded on the Sacrament of Order" (*CL*, no. 23).

I will return to these developments in the next two sections of this paper, but for now I will suggest that it is in light of these concerns that an important feature of the Apostolic Exhortation is to be understood, namely, for want of a better word, its outward-lookingness. The document works with the model of Church as communion, but a considerable part of its emphasis is on the need for the Church, especially in the persons of the laity, to be looking outward toward the world, the temporal order, and particularly toward what John Paul calls "culture." The outward stance is to be one of protecting the individual, in his or her dignity; and it is to be one of service to society. Both of these, John Paul writes, are "expressed" and find "fulfillment through the creation and transmission of culture, which especially in our time constitutes one of the more serious tasks of living together as a human family and of social evolution" (*CL*, no. 44).

This leads to the final two, complementary, aspects of the document that I want to mention: its concluding focus on the need for formation, and its invocation not just of apostolate but also of vocation. The complementary nature of the two ideas is shown in *CL* no. 58: "The fundamental objective of the formation of the lay faithful is an ever-clearer discovery of one's vocation and the ever-greater willingness to live it so as to fulfill one's mission." Formation is to be formation for vocation; but this formation is thereby the solution to the problems mentioned by the pope earlier. The pope writes:

> In discovering and living their proper vocation and mission, the lay faithful must be formed according to the union which exists from their being members of the Church and citizens of human society. There cannot be two parallel lives in their existence: on the one hand, the so-called "spiritual" life, with its values and demands; and on the other, the so-called "secular" life, that is, life in a family, at work, in social relationships, in the responsibilities of public life and culture. (*CL*, no. 59)

In other words, proper formation will orient laity toward fulfilling their responsibilities in the world, thereby renewing the face of the earth; but this life in the world, with all that goes along with it, must be informed by the spirit of faith. Activity in the world shaped by Christian faith is the recipe here for what John Paul calls, hearkening back to the earlier negative point, a "unified life."

John Paul makes an additional point of interest. For those who have "responsibilities in various fields of society and public life," the specific need, in terms of formation, is for them to have "a more exact knowledge … of the Church's social doctrine" (*CL*, no. 60). They cannot simply be encouraged to be good, or even to be faithful: they must be provided the guiding moral and social principles, which they are then to apply in service of the good and dignity of the human person. There appears here a division of labor: pastors must propose moral principles, the laity must apply them. That pastors have, to various extents, overstepped their bounds and gone from the proposal of principles to judgments of prudence, better left to the laity, and that the laity have too frequently neglected principles in favor of a more worldly kind of prudence, are, from the standpoint of *Christifidelis laici*, clearly failures in the Church's implementation of *Apostolicam actuositatem's* teaching.

Before turning to the next two, briefer, sections, I will close this one by making a few remarks about the relationship between apostolate and vocation. In *CL* no. 56, the pope says that there are within the lay state "diverse 'vocations' … given, that is, there are different paths in the spiritual life and the apostolate which are taken by individual members of the lay faithful." This is helpful, but we can start at an even higher level of generality, and say: there is a general apostolate of the Church. This apostolate is spoken of in *AA*, in a passage I have already quoted, and which is cited repeatedly in the relevant documents: "the spreading of the kingdom of Christ throughout the earth for the glory of God the Father, to enable all men to share in His saving redemption, … that through them the whole world might enter into a relationship with the Christ" (*AA*, no. 2). For the laity, that apostolate is specified as the lay apostolate, which is carried out in the temporal order, and includes, as its special charge, the renewal of that order. This specification of the Church's apostolate for the laity can be called generally the "lay vocation," to be contrasted with the general vocation to priestly or celibate life.

But then, the general lay apostolate can itself be specified in an individual's life. Accordingly, as Grisez writes, "Personal vocation is the personal specification of faith to one's own life. Thus, personal vocation is the medium by which confirmation shapes the whole of one's life as an apostolate."[18] Grisez adds here reference to the sacrament of confirmation, and I will return to this later. An additional question to which I will return in the final section is this: why is it necessary to hold on to the two notions, personal vocation *and* lay apostolate, and what happens if only one of these is retained?

---

[18]   Germain Grisez, *The Way of the Lord Jesus, Vol. 1, Christian Moral Principles* (Chicago, IL: Franciscan Herald Press, 1983), 754.

MINISTRY

I am not competent, either historically or theologically, to do all that could be done to detail the process by which the notion of "ministry" came to displace the notion of lay apostolate in the practical life of the Church, and to identify fully both the difference and the relationship between apostolate and ministry. These tasks are made difficult by occasional language, even in documents such as *CL*, that seems to blur the distinction: *CL* no. 55, for example, speaks of "every one of us possessing charisms and ministries, diverse yet complementary."

In what follows, I rely heavily upon Russell Shaw's book, *Ministry or Apostolate*. Shaw addresses both the historical and the theological question. The basic theological ideas are two. First, ministry is "something people do within the framework of the Church and on its behalf – it is building up the Body of Christ, service rendered to the People of God themselves."[19] On the other hand, apostolate "is something done *outside* the confines of the Church – it is service rendered to the world and its people; it is evangelization, especially perhaps what these days is called the evangelization of culture."[20] Second, "ministry," when used to refer to the tasks and functions of those who have not received the Sacrament of Order, "has an essentially analogical meaning."[21] The primary referent of the term is the work of priests, bishops, and deacons.

Shaw also distinguishes between Lay Ecclesial Ministry, which is paid work for the Church, and the larger body of lay people who serve the Church in a variety of voluntary capacities, many of which are referred to, in any Sunday Church Bulletin you might pick up, as "ministries."

As regards the history, Shaw identifies a number of factors and landmarks. Some of the displacement, he thinks, is attributable to the influence of Edward Schillebeeckx. More popularly, Thomas O'Meara's book *Theology of Ministry* became a source text for those wishing to increase the number and visibility of Church ministries. The document "Called and Gifted," issued by the National Conference of Catholic Bishops, also is cited; that document discusses a call to ministry as among the calls to be heard by the laity, but it does not talk about a call to the apostolate. As Shaw says, "the overall message was clear: Ministry was in, apostolate was out."[22]

One consequence of this is that even tasks that are obviously of the lay apostolate are increasingly spoken of as tasks of "lay ministry"; so a key

[19] Shaw, *Ministry or Apostolate?*, 9.
[20] *Ministry or Apostolate?*, 10.
[21] *Ministry or Apostolate?*, 17.
[22] *Ministry or Apostolate?*, 32.

theological distinction is missing when we look at a lot of what is said about the laity. A second consequence is the profusion of graduate programs for those wishing to enter lay ministry. Graduates of those programs have Lay Ecclesial Ministry in mind rather than voluntary ministry, and Shaw thinks that LEMs clearly get more attention from the hierarchy when they are thinking of lay ministry. There are no graduate programs for formation into the lay apostolate. Shaw summarizes the situation:

> for the two decades during which the bishops' conference of the United States devoted substantial time and resources to lay ministry . . ., it said and did virtually nothing to encourage and promote lay apostolate. The Catholic laity's participation in the mission of the Church in and to the secular world largely disappeared from the agenda of the bishops' national organization, as it did from the agendas of many dioceses, parishes, and Church institutions and groups.[23]

In fact, and this is not a point Shaw makes, when lay apostolate is mentioned, it is clearly sometimes simply being assumed that apostolate and ministry mean the same thing. So, for instance, an essay in the *National Catholic Reporter* titled "The Lay Apostolate in a Clerical Church" speaks immediately of the "calling to ministry by virtue of baptism," and then goes on to speak exclusively of the need for more ministry positions and "power sharing" between lay and clergy.[24]

One final point needs to be made about the sociology of this change by way of transition to the final section of this chapter. Shaw thinks, and cites others who think – and this point can be verified on many a Sunday morning – that one result of this has been encouragement of the idea that "'ministry' within the parish setting is what really *good* Catholics do."[25] In support of this, I can report by way of anecdote a recent declaration by my own parish priest that he wanted everyone to get involved in some sort of parish ministry so that no one would just be "ordinary."

PROBLEMS

What, then, are the problems that result from the eclipse of apostolate with ministry? In what follows, I briefly mention some; the complete work of identifying what has gone wrong, and to what extent, will, however, remain.

---

[23] *Ministry or Apostolate?*, 37.
[24] Theresa Malcolm, "The Lay Apostolate in a Clerical Church," *National Catholic Reporter*, September 17, 2004.
[25] Shaw, *Ministry or Apostolate?*, 37.

One paradoxical problem is that the overemphasis on ministry feeds clericalism while simultaneously, in some cases, warring against it in a fairly ideological way. The *National Catholic Reporter* article just mentioned and an accompanying article think of clericalism in the following way: the clerics have the power, and that is wrong and bad; the solution is to wrest as much as possible from them. Lay ministry is the path to doing just that, with a view to more just power sharing (or not sharing). But this is surely a simple-minded understanding of clericalism, which seems more to do with the automatic elevation of clerics, in virtue of their state of life, to the status of being worthy of the authority they exercise, which authority is to be exercised actively by contrast with the largely passive role of the laity. As Shaw puts it, clericalism "fosters an ecclesiastical caste system in which clerics comprise the dominant elite, with lay people serving as a passive, inert mass of spear-carriers tasked with receiving clerical tutelage and doing what they're told."[26] Power sharing might be one part of an answer to this, but only one. And if it is seen as *the* answer, then what you get, seemingly, is simply an expansion of the clerical caste.

It is a caricature, but one with which many will be familiar, to say that some of those in lay ministry, and especially lay ecclesial ministry, now themselves bustle around with self-importance, make high-handed decisions, and in general lord it over the rest of the parish. This does not describe the whole of lay ministers and probably not a majority: but it is the end result of the kind of thinking on display in the *National Catholic Reporter*.

A related problem is that with all the focus on ministry, the concrete need for apostolate goes unmet. Not that there are not apostolates – surely there are many. But there are many who are not contributing to the mission of the Church because they have not in any way been formed to believe that they have a part in that mission, if they are not engaged in ministry. And even those who do think of themselves in apostolic terms as regards their relation to the world are often not given adequate support within the parish.

In this context, too, there are various points to be made about the phenomenon of "separation of faith from life" of which John Paul spoke. There can be a danger that those engaged in ministry use that engagement as a substitute for some other essential part of the Christian life. Here are three examples of "substitution" (or worse). First, ministry, as Shaw points out, is *overwhelmingly* female; in 1997, 82 percent of lay parish ministers were women. Shaw speculates that for some – certainly not all or even a majority – "lay ecclesial ministry is meant to substitute for priestly ordination" (for others, Shaw

[26] Russell Shaw, "On Clericalism," *Catholicity*, May 6, 2008.

believes that it is "intended as an interim stage on the way"). Second, for whatever reason or reasons, members of some ministries, including teaching ministries, are very ill-catechized, or perhaps simply not interested in knowing what the Church teaches. Yet they are engaged in ministry and thus see the need for no corrective formation for themselves. Finally, I have recently heard a priest friend speak of the problem – he was using the example as representative – of an extraordinary Eucharistic minister having a "fling" while on a work trip and arriving back home in time to distribute Holy Communion on Sunday. This person was, in this priest's telling, unaware of any discrepancy. Again, perhaps this is a case in which participation in a form of ministry was allowed to substitute for the need to know, or follow, the Church's *moral* teaching. These are problems with the replacement of apostolate with ministry, or the overshadowing of one by the other.

A different problem is that without the apostolate of the laity, the sacrament of confirmation lacks its fullest possible intelligibility, to the detriment of those receiving the sacrament. Recall the earlier quotation from Grisez: "personal vocation is the medium by which confirmation shapes the whole of one's life as an apostolate." On Grisez's account, baptism initiates but does not organize Christian life; it is, relatively, passive. What is the shape of a life that is actively organized as a Christian's life should be? It is a life whose shape is that of apostolate, a life carrying out the Church's mission, witnessing in word and deed to the Good News. But what organizes a Christian's life into that shape sacramentally? It is confirmation, which gives to Christians the power to share in Christ's mission "as it communicates or hands on divine truth and love." Grisez writes, "The point here is simply that, if one understands what the apostolate is and how confirmation is a principle of Christian life, it follows necessarily that confirmation is the sacrament which assigns and strengthens Christians to live their entire lives as their share in the Church's apostolate."[27]

Speaking again anecdotally, I can say that in neither of the two parishes, otherwise as different as could be, in which my children have been confirmed, nor in the parish in which I was confirmed, is anything like this understanding on display – hardly a surprise since the notion of the apostolate is or was completely absent in each of these contexts. For many confirmands the sacrament of confirmation seems an odd man out, with no well-explained purpose or role in the sacramental economy. Restoring emphasis on the apostolate of laity would be an aid here.

Following in the same line, without the apostolate of the laity, it is difficult to see how we can have an appropriate understanding of the idea of personal

[27] Grisez, *Christian Moral Principles*, 753.

vocation, if we have one at all. The general lay apostolate requires specification: how am *I* to share in Christ's mission, and renew the face of the earth? It
points in the direction of personal vocation. But suppose we had the latter idea
without the former somehow. Then it would be unclear how one's personal
vocation was related to one's life in Christ, how it could be more than simply
the plan by which one would lead what seemed to be the most satisfactory life,
getting what one wanted and being a person of accomplishment. Without
being seen in its relation to the apostolate, personal vocation is not much more
than a rational life plan.

Here, in closing, is a final point on a more or less optimistic note. A recent
and popular book among Catholic laity and clergy who are excited about their
faith and want to grow in it is Sherry A. Weddell's *Forming Intentional
Disciples*. Weddell's overarching point in this book is that

> there is a chasm the size of the Grand Canyon between the Church's
> sophisticated theology of the lay apostolate and the *lived* spiritual experience
> of the majority of our people. And this chasm has a name: *discipleship*. We
> learned that the majority of even "active" American Catholics are still at an
> early, essentially passive stage of spiritual development. We learned that our
> first need at the parish level isn't catechetical. Rather, our fundamental
> problem is that most of our people are not yet disciples. They will never be
> apostles until they have begun to follow Jesus Christ in the midst of his
> Church.[28]

There is in Weddell's book perhaps a touch of overemphasis on what it means
to be "active" in ministry, but her point seems sound: apostleship and discipleship must go together. That is the path toward the unified Christian life that
John Paul II was pointing to. This path would require taking advantage of the
momentum in favor of "discipleship" that has come about as a result of her
book, to also make this a moment of "apostleship." Such a development would
be greatly to the good of the Church and Her people.

---

[28] Sherry A. Weddell, *Forming Intentional Disciples: The Path to Knowing and Following Jesus
Christ* (Huntington, IN: Our Sunday Visitor, 2012), 11.

13

Globalization

John Finnis

"Globalization" denotes at least three different matters that should be considered quite distinctly:

1. *the fact of growing interconnections*, interactions between people all over the world: economic, financial, military, touristic, educational, migratory, and so on; and consequent *interdependencies*, reinforcing other interdependencies such as availability and exhaustion of natural resources, ease and rapidity of transfer of resources, money, means of destruction, and people, susceptibility to pollution and environmental degradation, and so on;
2. *proposals* to respond to all that (and to "dangerous anthropogenic global warming") by establishing global law and, before very long, global legal authorities with legislative, executive, and enforcement powers, a form of *world government*, or at least an assembling of international authorities ever more nearly amounting to such a world government;
3. *proposals to widen the opportunities for migration* from poorer countries to richer for the sake of a better life for the migrants; and even to bring about an at least *de facto* right of any poor person to be granted entry to another, richer country of their choice; a policy of substantially open borders and even a duty to open them to all who wish for a better life for themselves (and their relatives or other dependents).

This essay outlines the evolution of CST on these matters. At no time has it been doubted that states and their peoples have a responsibility to respect other states and peoples and the common good of human persons worldwide; or that individuals and groups have, in dire necessity, rights to seek and find refuge in nearby safe states for at least the duration of that danger and necessity. But beyond these sometimes unarticulated basics of Christian morality and CST, there have been developments, in a variety of directions. This chapter traces some main developments over the past 125 years.

LEO XIII

Three years after *Rerum novarum*, Leo XIII addressed "to all rulers and peoples" a review of the world situation, political as well as "social." Trains and ships, he noted, now traverse immense tracts of land and sea "with incredible rapidity," giving promise of great benefits not only for commerce and scientific research but also through the spreading of the word of God "from dawn to dusk." "Indeed, in so far as human reason is able to interpret events, it seems that the mission entrusted by God to Europe is: to spread through all the world the Christian civilization [*civiltà cristiana*]." This "sacred mission," he said, was going well until, in the sixteenth century, religious dispute and wars broke out in Europe itself. That discord so persisted that, unsurprisingly, a large part of humanity remains even now subject to inhuman customs or ways of life and irrational religions [*soggiogata da disumani costume e da riti insani*].[1] Europe itself remains now (in the 1890s) fearful of war, subject to anarchist outrages, its young men subjected to all the moral dangers and wasted opportunities involved in being conscripted into national armed forces; and Europe's treasuries and resources are dissipated on preparations for war – on an armed peace that cannot last much longer. "Is this the natural condition of civil society?"

But this train of thought did not lead Leo to postulate, let alone propose, any international order of cooperation or law more definite than "preserving the

---

[1] Leo XIII, Apostolic Letter *Praeclara gratulationis publicae* (The Reunion of Christendom) (1894). See also Leo XIII, Encyclical Letter *Quarto abrupto saeculo* (On the 400th Anniversary of Columbus' Discovery of America) (1892):

> By his toil another world emerged from the unsearched bosom of the ocean: hundreds of thousands of mortals have, from a state of blindness, been raised to the common level of the human race, reclaimed from savagery to gentleness and humanity; and, greatest of all, by the acquisition of those blessings of which Jesus Christ is the author, they have been recalled from destruction to eternal life. Europe, indeed, overpowered at the time by the novelty and strangeness of the discovery, presently came to recognize what was due to Columbus, when, through the numerous colonies [established in] America, through the constant intercourse and interchange of business and the ocean-trade, an incredible addition was made to our knowledge of nature, and to the commonwealth; whilst at the same time the prestige of the European name was marvellously increased.

> Explorers before and after Columbus have "advanced the ends of knowledge and humanity, and increased the common prosperity of the [human] race," but he outdid them all by his aim "to open a way for the Gospel over new lands and men." Seventy-one years later, in John XXIII's Encyclical Letter *Mater et magistra* (On Christianity and Social Progress) (1961), no. 172, the pope warns against "a new form of colonialism, cleverly disguised, no doubt, but actually reflecting that older, outdated type from which many nations have recently emerged."

rights of nations and respect for treaties, as well as the bonds of fraternity
[between nations and peoples]."² Still, in the previous year he had welcomed
proposals for a negotiated creation of international rules and standards for
labor laws (especially in relation to labor by children and women of child-
bearing age), proposals that by 1900 had helped generate an International
Association for Labour Laws and in 1919 the International Labour
Organization. As Leo XIII wrote to the author of such a proposal, doubtless
adopting and ratifying the recipient's own argumentation:

> Obviously the protection given to the workmen's labor would be very imper-
> fect if it were protection only by the different laws elaborated by each people
> [nation] on its own account. For the differing merchandises come from the
> several countries and confront one another in the same market, and the
> regulation of labor imposed here and there would lead to the produce of
> the industry of one nation gaining to the detriment of another.³

But this direct concern with the international or global as such remained for
Leo XIII exceptional. What most concerned him, looking at the world as
a whole, was the prospect of "the overthrow of that whole religious and
political order of the world that Christian teaching has produced" and the
replacement of that order by what he called Naturalism.

That worldview's opposition to Christian civilization he summarized in 1884:
all religions are alike, there is no true religion, and religions should have no
place in public life; the masses should be satiated with boundless liberty of vice
and so made more amenable to power; marriage should be converted into such
changeable and uncertain unions as fancy first puts together and then breaks
apart; no religion should have any place in the educating of the young; rulers
may be deposed at the mere will of the people; and the Catholic Church is
especially to be despised, defamed, and opposed (if not dissolved) because it
opposes these theses.⁴ And what moved Leo in this and in later encyclicals and
letters was his judgment that these ideas were being pursued and disseminated

---

² "Rimanere integri sia i diritti delle nazioni e il rispetto dei trattati, sia i vincoli di fratellanza";
   PG, 8.
³ Leo XIII, Letter to Gaspar Decurtins *Nihil nobis optatus* (We have nothing to do) (1893): *Acta
   Sanctae Sedis* 26 (1893–1894), 74–76.
⁴ Leo XIII, Encyclical Letter *Humanum genus* (On Freemasonry) (1884). In his Apostolic Letter
   to the bishops of the world, *Vigesimo quinto anno* (1902), Leo elaborated extensively on the
   error, and bad consequences, of the rationalism, pantheism, naturalism, and materialism
   becoming ever more dominant, and separately on the character of Freemasonry as a kind of
   conspiracy (of global reach) to propagate these errors, foster hatred of Catholic Christianity,
   and bring it under the power of these ideas: see *The Great Encyclical Letters of Pope Leo XIII*
   (Rockford: Tan Books, 1995 [1903]), 554–580 at 560–564, 572–575; likewise his Apostolic Letter
   Praeclara gratulationis publicae (The Reunion of Christendom) (1894).

not so much by the many academic teachings and writings proposing them, as rather by a network (also international) of *associations* dedicated – not without much secrecy and many pressures on hesitant adherents – to spreading the ideas and putting them into effect everywhere. One of the concerns that moved him to dedicate an encyclical to the Church in the United States in 1895 was to remind the bishops that freedom of association, not least the right and freedom he had proclaimed in *Rerum novarum* to form and join labor unions ("working men's associations"), carries with it severe dangers of being caught up in the projects of persons unfriendly to religion and willing to use unjust means.[5]

In that encyclical to and about the Church in America, *Longinqua oceani* ("Traversing in spirit and thought the wide expanse of ocean … "), written as a follow-up to his letter on Christopher Columbus, and expressing the intent to help make America great,[6] Leo emphasized the social preconditions of any national greatness, indeed of any enduring human polity at all. First and foremost: morality (for the preservation of which – along with the defence of religion – the Church was founded by the will and ordinance of Christ); and first among moral concerns: the unity and indissolubility of marriage, and the truth that nothing tends so effectually to undermine the strength and prosperity of nations as the corruption of morals[7] and the ruin of families. Secondly, integrity, self-restraint, and conscientiousness in public life and conduct of public duties, which are subject to the same rules of probity as private business.[8] Thirdly, the virtue of temperance (rule over one's passions), and the observance of the just laws and institutions of the Republic. Fourthly, as mentioned above, care in associating with others – Catholics should prefer to

[5] Leo XIII, Encyclical Letter *Longinqua oceani* (On Catholicism in the United States) (January 6, 1895):

> [W]hilst it is proper and desirable to assert and secure the rights of the many, yet this is not to be done by a violation of duty; and that these are very important duties; not to touch what belongs to another; to allow everyone to be free in the management of his own affairs; not to hinder any one to dispose of his services when he please and where he please. The scenes of violence and riot which you witnessed last year in your own country sufficiently admonish you that America too is threatened with the audacity and ferocity of the enemies of public order. The state of the times, therefore, bids Catholics to labor for the tranquillity of the commonwealth, and for this purpose to obey the laws, abhor violence, and seek no more than equity or justice permits.

[6] "All reasonable people agree … that America seems destined for greater things [*reservatam ad maiora Americam videri*], and it is Our wish that the Catholic Church should … help bring about this prospective greatness [*magnitudinem*]."

[7] Three months later, in an Apostolic Letter, *Amantissimae voluntatis* (To the English People) (1895), Leo XIII makes particular mention of the vicious double standard in popular *mores* allowing men looser sexual conduct than women.

[8] See further nn. 28–29 below.

join Catholic associations. Fifthly, the influence for good and evil of the media ("writings … journals …"). With a closing call to evangelize Indians and African-Americans still in the darkness of superstition, Leo's thought circled back to the blessings, individual, familial, private, and social, that Columbus brought to so many peoples previously unknown to the Catholic faith's globalizers – "making disciples of all nations" (*Matthew* 28:19).

PIUS X[9]

One of the earliest and initially most successful forms of Catholic Action[10] arising in the wake of *Rerum novarum* was the French movement *Le Sillon* (the Furrow). Founded in 1894 as a journal dedicated to reconciliation between working men and Christianity, and to superseding the equations French Catholic = monarchist, republican = "anti-clerical" (anti-Catholic), *Le Sillon* by 1900 was a vast and spreading educational and social movement that at its height had a thousand "circles." Initially welcomed by Pius X in 1903 and 1904, it opened its ranks to non-Catholics and unbelievers in 1905, and in August 1910 Pius condemned it in a letter to French bishops, *Notre Charge Apostolique*,[11] and called upon it to reconstitute itself as Catholic Action of the standard form, that is, action under episcopal direction. *Le Sillon* had, he

---

[9] In his allocution at the beatification of Pius X on June 3,1951 in *AAS* 43 (1951), 475–476, Pius XII said:

> What meaning, We asked ourselves at the outset, was the name of Pius X to convey to us? Now, it seems, we see it clearly. In his person and through his work, God would prepare the Church for new and sterner duties of the future years. God wishes to prepare in due season a Church united [*concorde*] in doctrine, solid in discipline, effective in its pastors; a generous laity, a well instructed people; a youth made holy from its earliest years; a Christian conscience alert to the problems of social life.

[10] In his encyclical to Italian bishops *Il Fermo Proposito* (1905), Pius X said:

> Our predecessor, Leo XIII, has pointed out, especially in … *Rerum Novarum* and later documents, the object to which Catholic Action should be particularly devoted, namely, the practical solution of the social question according to Christian principles [principles that foster better than all others the true economic interests of the people]. We also, following such inspiring norms, have by Our Motu Proprio of 18 December 1903 [*Fin dalla Prima*] concerning Popular Christian Action – which itself embraces the whole Catholic social movement – have given fundamental principles which should serve as a practical rule.

> The 19 principles or "fundamental regulations" of CST/Catholic Action that Pius X ordered in *Fin dalla Prima* to be posted in all relevant meeting rooms make no reference to matters outside the national domain.

[11] *AAS* 2 (1910), 607–633. The current Vatican website collection of papal documents happens to omit this very substantial document (one that has evident bearing on the situation of the Church itself since 2013).

wrote, defied Leo XIII's prescriptions by locating sovereign authority in the people rather than in God, by seeking the leveling out of "diversity of [social] classes," by an unhealthy utopianism, and by sidelining the necessarily Christian and Catholic basis for a true restoration of society and healing of its wounds. Founding its ideas on dignity, the movement understood this truth in a philosophically mistaken [scil. Kantian] way, grounded in autonomy, liberation (*émancipation*), and equality. It wanted the employer–employee relationship to be superseded by a system of cooperatives. Guiding everything in *Sillon*ism was a moral ideal of love, beyond self and family, love of one's profession, one's compatriots, of all human persons: Liberty, Equality, Fraternity.

This, wrote Pius X, was more dream than theory; if theory, it was theory opposed point by point to Catholic teaching about social relationships in human societies. The cooperative ideal presented every employee as his own employer, and the democratic ideal was understood as making every citizen a king, a free comrade of free comrades, such that every order he received would be for him an attack on his liberty, every subordination a diminution of his person, all obedience a deprivation. All this (wrote Pius) generates jealousy and injustice, and subverts social order. Its fundamental error is a misunderstanding of human dignity, a dignity that in truth the humble of this world do not *lack* when they modestly plough the furrow that Providence has assigned them, fulfilling their duties in humility, obedience, and Christian patience – these persons "the Savior will one day raise from their obscure condition to place them in heaven among the princes of his people."

And at bottom, *Le Sillon* conceived itself (wrote Pius) as preparing for a future (earthly) City, a religion more universal than the Catholic Church, reuniting all persons now become brethren and comrades in "the reign of God." Thus its original pure stream had been captured by the Church's modern enemies in the great movement of apostasy, "organized, in all countries, for the establishment of a universal Church without dogmas or hierarchy, and without rule for the mind or bridle for the passions – one that under pretext of liberty and human dignity would spread throughout the world (if it triumphed) *the legal reign* of deception and force, and oppression of the weak, who suffer and work."[12]

"We know only too well the dark workshops in which these poisonous doctrines are prepared"; clear minds would not have been seduced, but *Le Sillon* was left defenseless by its exalted sentiments, its blind good-heartedness, and philosophic mysticism mixed with "enlightenment" [*illuminisme*], all

[12] AAS 2 (1910), 628 (emphasis added).

enticing it to a new gospel in which it thought it saw the true Gospel of the
Savior (whom they dare treat with supremely disrespectful familiarity).[13]

BENEDICT XV

Elected as World War II began, Benedict XV responded to its end and to the
opening of the Peace Conference at Versailles with a brief encyclical promising to "exert all the influence of Our Apostolic Ministry that the decisions
which are to be taken to ensure forever in the world the tranquillity of order
and concord be willingly accepted and faithfully carried out by Catholics
everywhere."[14] His encyclical, eighteen months later, nearly a year after the
establishment of the League of Nations in June 1919, expressed approval of the
League (albeit without naming or identifying it as such).[15]

PIUS XI

As soon as December 1923, the new pope's first encyclical wrote off the League
of Nations (indirectly but very clearly identified) as an attempt at peaceful
solution of international problems that was having "almost negligible results"
especially in serious disputes between nations.[16] Pius XI contrasted it unfavor-
ably with medieval Christendom ("that true League of Nations")[17] and
devoted much of the encyclical to the kingship of Christ, which he held out
as a necessary condition of that respect for divine law and the obligation of

---

[13] AAS 2 (1910), 628.
[14] Benedict XV, Encyclical Letter *Quod iam diu* (On the Future Peace Conference) (1918).
[15] Benedict XV, Encyclical Letter *Pacem, Dei munus pulcherrimum* (On Peace and Christian
reconciliation) (1920), no. 17:

> Things being thus restored, the order required by justice and charity reestablished, and
> the nations reconciled, it is much to be desired, Venerable Brethren [sovereigns and
> peoples of the world], that all States, putting aside mutual suspicion, should unite in
> one league [*consociatio*], or rather a sort of family of peoples, calculated both to
> maintain their own independence [*libertas*] and safeguard the order of human society.
> What specially, amongst other reasons, calls for such an association of nations [*gentium
> consociatio*], is the need generally recognized of making every effort to abolish or reduce
> the enormous burden of the military expenditure which States can no longer bear, in
> order to prevent these disastrous wars or at least to remove the danger of them as far as
> possible. *So would each nation [populus] be assured not only of its independence but also
> of the integrity of its territory within its just frontiers.* [Emphasis added]

AAS 12 (1920), 209.
[16] Pius XI, Encyclical Letter *Ubi arcano dei consilio* (On the Peace of Christ in the Kingdom of
Christ) (1923), no. 45.
[17] UADC, no. 45.

promises, and that trust in peaceful solutions, without which international peace is impossible. *Ubi arcano* seems to propose for the Catholic Church, as the "living interpreter" of Christ and "infallible teacher of his doctrines," "a supremely important role" in "providing a remedy for the ills which afflict the world today and in leading mankind towards a universal peace." The encyclical incautiously – as if forgetful of recalcitrance of wills – seems to say that, if only individuals, families, and nations were conscientiously "apprised" of their personal and civic duties and aware of the Church's "demands" for conformity to God's law, "in a short time" 'Christ would be all, and in all.'"[18]

The companion encyclical *Quas primas*,[19] two years later, establishing the liturgical feast of Christ the King, presents this kingship (and its celebration) as "an excellent remedy for the plague which now infects society": of anticlericalism, which "denies the right" which "the Church has from Christ himself, to teach mankind, to make laws, to govern peoples in all that pertains to their eternal salvation." "Then gradually the religion of Christ came to be likened to false religions and to be placed ignominiously on the same level with them."[20] It is "the duty of Catholics to do all they can to bring about the return of society to our loving Savior." Those who "bear the lamp of truth" ought to have a station and authority in society such as will enable them to "engage in conflict" with "the enemies of the Church" and "ever to fight courageously under the banner of Christ the King," striving "to win over to their Lord those hearts which are bitter and estranged from him," and to "valiantly defend his rights."[21] The ambiguities of this rhetoric were cruelly exposed when, in some of the Church's heartlands, anticlericalism reached revolutionary frenzy and was met with armed rebellion by Catholics (sometimes, in some cases, deploying actual banners of "Christ the King"); in Spain the bitter civil war was also by proxy an international war between rival anti-Catholic, ideological state powers, foreshadowing imminently a renewed World War.

The inherent disadvantage of framing CST in terms of Christ's Kingship is this. Kings (and other supreme lords) have not only the legislative,[22] judicial,

[18] UADC, nos. 21, 41, 43.
[19] Pius XI, Encyclical Letter *Quas primas* (On the Feast of Christ the King) (1925).
[20] QP, no. 24. The surrounding passage in effect conveys (without referring to it) the general line of Pius X's critique (after n. 11 above) of *Le Sillon* and its (quasi-) masonic universalism (in the sense of cosmopolitanism) (cf. Francis, Encyclical Letter *Laudato si'* (On Care for Our Common Home) (2015), nos. 62–63, 199–201).
[21] QP, no. 24.
[22] Another disadvantage is that portraying Christ as legislator – though true because as the Word incarnate he is source of nature and reason – tends to obscure the accessibility (in principle) of natural moral law to reason unaided by revelation and even in the absence of any ratification or supplementation by revealed divine law.

and executive (law-applying and judgment-enforcing) functions rightly
pointed to in *Ubi arcano*[23] as pertaining also to Christ; kings *also* must make
on behalf of their people many prudential judgments about what is possible
and suitable in the circumstances of the moment, and about what risks to take
in ever-changing situations of often profound danger and uncertainty. So:
presenting Christ as King and the Church as his appointed agent inevitably –
despite protestations that this is a purely spiritual kingship "concerned with
spiritual things"[24] – foreshadowed ecclesiastical involvement in the conduct of
secular affairs and vast clerical overreach under the banner of promoting "a
lasting world peace."[25] That is doubtless why Vatican II placed Christ's
Kingship in the frame of the Last Judgment, beyond this world;[26] and why
the theme (with its accompanying ungainly discourse about "the social rights
of Jesus Christ") has substantially disappeared from CST.[27]

But reflection on the implications of this Kingship encouraged Pius XI to
give new prominence to the permanently important observation[28] that moral
standards – and essentially the same moral standards (though this is implied

---

[23] *QP*, no. 14.
[24] *QP*, no. 15. Cf. *QP*, no. 17: "It would be a grave error, on the other hand, to say that Christ has
      no authority whatever in civil affairs."
[25] See *UA*, no. 49.
[26] See Vatican II, Pastoral Constitution *Gaudium et spes* (On the Church in the Modern World)
      (1965), no. 39. Contrast this with John XXIII, Encyclical Letter *Mater et magistra* (On
      Christianity and Social Progress) (1961), no. 261: courageous cooperation with the principles
      and directives of CST and the encyclical

> will surely help to bring about the realization of Christ's Kingdom in this world, "a
> kingdom of truth and life; a kingdom of holiness and grace; a kingdom of justice, of love
> and of peace," ... which assures the enjoyment of those heavenly blessings for which we
> were created.

      The quotation both here and in GS, no. 39 is from the Preface in the Feast of Christ the
      King, instituted by *Quas primas*.
[27] *Catechism of the Catholic Church*, no. 2105 ends with the *Catechism*'s one and only sentence
      about "the kingship of Christ over all creation and in particular over human societies" [citing
      Quas primas, nos. 8, 20, Leo XIII, Encyclical Letter *Immortale dei* (On the Christian
      Constitution of States) (1885) and Vatican II's decree on the laity]; the theme of no. 2105 is
      the duty to worship God and the "social duty of Christians to respect and awaken in each man
      the love of the true and the good" including Catholic worship – to infuse their communities'
      institutions with "the Christian spirit" by evangelizing. CST is here virtually invisible.
[28] *QP*, no. 18:

> "[T]ruly the whole of mankind is subject to the power of Jesus Christ." [Leo XIII,
> Encyclical Letter *Annum sacrum* (On Consecration to the Sacred Heart) (1899), no. 3]
> Nor is there any difference in this matter between the individual and the family or the
> State; for all men, whether collectively or individually, are under the dominion of
> Christ.

more than expressed) – apply to states and their rulers as they apply to individuals in their private affairs.[29]

As to globalization as such, the discussion of it in *Quadragesimo anno* (1931) was terse. No. 88 states that neither free competition nor "the economic supremacy[30] which within recent times has taken the place of free competition"

---

[29] In face of National Socialism (and in the background Marxist Communism), Pius XI sharpens this articulation in his encyclical *Mit brennender sorge* (On the Church and the German Reich) (1937), no. 10:

> God, this Sovereign Master, has issued commandments whose value is independent of time and space, country and race. As God's sun shines on every human face so His law knows neither privilege nor exception. Rulers and subjects, crowned and uncrowned, rich and poor are equally subject to His word.

This is taken up again by John XXIII in *PT*, nos. 80–81:

> The same law of nature that governs the life and conduct of individuals must also regulate the relations of political communities with one another … it is quite impossible for political leaders to lay aside their natural dignity while acting in their country's name and in its interests. They are still bound by the natural law, which is the rule that governs all moral conduct, and they have no authority to depart from its slightest precepts.

Nos. 82–84 then give three arguments for this thesis, none of which envisages let alone answers the objection that the tradition, exemplified by Aquinas, considered that public office confers moral responsibilities toward the common good, such that what is morally always forbidden for private persons (e.g., killing with intent to kill) is morally licit for bearers of relevant public responsibilities, e.g., in the suppression or punishment of serious crime. (Neither Aquinas nor the tradition recognized any exemption for bearers of public duty from the exceptionless moral norms against adultery and lying: see John Finnis, Aquinas, ch. 5 secs 2, 3, 4.) John Paul II says in *VS*, nos. 96–97 (emphases in original):

> When it is a matter of the moral norms prohibiting intrinsic evil, there are no privileges or exceptions for anyone. It makes no difference whether one is the master of the world or the "poorest of the poor" on the face of the earth. Before the demands of morality we are all absolutely equal … The fundamental moral rules of social life thus entail specific demands to which both public authorities and citizens are required to pay heed. Even though intentions may sometimes be good, and circumstances frequently difficult, civil authorities and particular individuals never have authority to violate the fundamental and inalienable rights of the human person. In the end, only a morality which acknowledges certain norms as valid always and for everyone, with no exception, can guarantee the ethical foundation of social coexistence, both on the national and international levels.

To this he adds in *CCC* a treatment of killing in legitimate defense and war in which the grounds of the permissibility of the acts of public authorities are substantially equated to the grounds for comparable acts of private persons, and exclude intention precisely to kill: nos. 2263–2268.

[30] One might think that this refers to the state, but *QA*'s principal draftsman says that it refers to "concentrated capitalism," scil., the dominance of oligopolistic corporations and their allies: Oswald Nell-Breuning, SJ, *Reorganization of Social Economy: The Social Encyclical Developed and Explained* (NY: Bruce, 1935), 249; the securing of social justice is the work of "the supreme authority in society," the State.

can be allowed save within the stern and uncompromising rule of "social justice and social charity" – the latter as "the soul of" the former, which itself must be "operative to build up a juridical and social order able to pervade all economic activity." No. 89 then says:

> Further, it would be well if the various nations, in common counsel and endeavor, strove to promote a healthy economic co-operation by prudent pacts and institutions, since in economic matters they are largely dependent upon one another, and need each other's help.

The contemporaneous commentary by QA's principal draftsman says:

> *World Economy.* The Pope even goes beyond national boundaries and the domain of national economies, and considers the establishment of proper *world economic order.* Here, too, he addresses himself to the several national states. A world economy comprising directly the whole population of the world is unknown to the Pope. Neither does he consider a world state or superstate in which individual states would figure as member-states. In accordance with Christian social tradition, the Pope considers the state as the highest society of this world, and, therefore, *the national economy [die Volkswirtschaft] the supreme economic unit;* contrasted with it the world economy is not a uniform structure, but merely a relationship constituted by the dealings between national economies.[31]

NATIONAL PATRIOTISM v. (EXAGGERATED) NATIONALISM

It seems to be with Pius XI, and certainly in the period of his pontificate, that CST develops a terminology distinguishing "patriotism" (or "national patriotism") – legitimate – from "nationalism" (or "exaggerated nationalism") – a vice and error in political thought.[32]

---

[31] Nell-Breuning, *Reorganization of Social Economy,* 251–252 (translation adjusted; emphases in original), Oswald Nell-Breuning, SJ, *Die Soziale Enzyklika* (Cologne: Katholische-Tat Verlag Köln, 1932), 171. John J. Wright [Bishop of Worcester, later Cardinal], *National Patriotism in Papal Teaching* (Westminster, MD: Newman Bookshop, 1943), 232–233, quotes other statements made by Fr. Nell-Breuning in 1931, acknowledging more plainly the reality of international or global interdependencies and connections, and the error of seeking any sort of absolute national autarky.

[32] Thus in *Ubi arcano:*

> 24. The inordinate desire for pleasure, concupiscence of the flesh, sows the fatal seeds of division not only among families but likewise among states; the inordinate desire for possessions, concupiscence of the eyes, inevitably turns into class warfare and into social egotism; the inordinate desire to rule or to domineer over others, pride of life, soon

PIUS XII
MIGRATION

Speaking by radio on June 1, 1941 (Pentecost; one year and one week after France's surrender; three weeks before the German invasion of the Soviet Union; six months before Pearl Harbor), and commemorating the just passed 50th anniversary of *Rerum novarum*, Pius XII undertook "to give some further directive moral principles on three fundamental values of social and economic life ... values which are closely connected one with the other, mutually complementary and dependent ...: The use of material goods, labor and the family."[33] In the course of discussing family, and linking it back to *RN*'s argument for private property as a source of a family's just independence (and linking it also to labor as source of paternal support for children), Pius XII said:

> as a rule only that stability which is rooted in one's own holding makes of the family the most vital and most perfect and fecund cell of society, joining up in a brilliant manner in its progressive cohesion the present and future generations.
>
> If today the concept of the creation of vital spaces is at the center of social and political aims should, not one, before all else, think of the vital space of

> becomes mere party or factional rivalries, manifesting itself in constant displays of conflicting ambitions and ending in open rebellion, in the crime of *lese majesté*, and **even in national parricide**.
>
> 25. These unsuppressed desires, this inordinate love of the things of the world, are precisely the source of all international misunderstandings and rivalries, despite the fact that oftentimes men dare to maintain that acts prompted by such motives are excusable and even justifiable because, forsooth, they were performed for reasons of state or of the public good, or out of love for country.
>
> **Patriotism, the stimulus of so many virtues and of so many noble acts of heroism when kept within the bounds of the law of Christ**, becomes merely an occasion, an added incentive to grave injustice when true love of country is **debased to the condition of an extreme nationalism**, when we forget that all men are our brothers and members of the same great human family, that **other nations have an equal right with us both to life and to prosperity, that it is never lawful, nor even wise, to dissociate morality from the affairs of practical life**, that in the last analysis, it is "justice which exalteth a nation: but sin maketh nations miserable." (Proverbs 14:34) (emphases added)

> See Wright, *National Patriotism in Papal Teaching* 21–72. In his *Memory & Identity* (London: Weidenfeld, 2005), Karol Wojtyla/John Paul II says at 77–78 that the right way of avoiding unhealthy nationalism is

> through patriotism. Whereas nationalism involves recognizing and pursuing the good of one's own nation alone, without regard to the rights of others, patriotism ... is a love of one's native land that accords rights to all other nations equal to those claimed for one's own.

> See John Finnis, *Intention and Identity* (Oxford: Oxford University Press, 2011), 123.

[33] Pius XII, "Radio Message *La Solennità della Pentecoste*" (1969).

the family, and free it of the fetters of conditions which do not permit even the idea of forming a homestead of one's own.

Pivoting thus on the idea of a "vital space," the message opened it out to the globe's still uninhabited or underpopulated regions:

> Our planet ... [is not] without habitable regions and vital spaces now abandoned to wild natural vegetation and well suited to be cultivated by man to satisfy his needs and civil activities; and more than once it is inevitable that some families, migrating from one spot to another, should go elsewhere in search of a new homeland [*patria*]. Then, according to the teaching of *Rerum novarum*, the right of the family to a vital space must be recognized [*va rispettato*].
>
> When this happens, emigration attains its natural purpose, as experience often shows; we mean the more favorable distribution of men on the earth's surface suitable to colonies of agricultural workers; that surface which God created and prepared for the use of all. If the two parties, those who agree to leave their native land and those who agree to admit the newcomers, remain loyally careful to eliminate as far as possible all obstacles to the birth and growth of real confidence between the country of emigration and that of immigration, all those affected by such a changing of places will be advantaged: families will receive a plot of ground [*un terreno*] which will be native land [*terra patria*] for them in the true sense of the word; densely populated countries [*le terre di densi abitanti*] will be relieved, and their people will acquire new friends in foreign countries; and the States which receive the emigrants will acquire industrious citizens. In this way the nations which give and those which receive will each contribute to increased human wellbeing and the progress of human culture.

Migration is thus identified as a right under conditions identified as win-win – what might be called the vanishingly easy case. Not that it was an imaginary case; migration in the subsequent two decades from southern Italy to Australia, Argentina, and some other parts of South America was of the kind postulated by Pius XII. In his allocution to the cardinals on July 1, 1946, he again

> called upon the nations with more extensive territory and less numerous populations to open their borders to people from over-crowded countries. Of the latter, as is well known, Japan today happens to be the most overpopulated one.[34]

Foundational for modern CST on migration is Pius XII's Apostolic Constitution *Exsul Familia* on the Spiritual Care of Emigrants (August 1,

---

[34] This is the summary given by Pius XII in his Apostolic Constitution *Exsul familia nazarethana* (1952), so "today" presumably means 1952, seven years after Japan's devastating defeat. Six million Japanese persons were returned to Japan in and after 1945, and emigration from Japan remained slight during the rest of the twentieth century.

1952). Though largely devoted to the history of and future arrangements for the Church's care for migrants, it includes a brief section on rights to emigrate and immigrate. It was written in a period when restrictions on *emigration* (from the USSR and its satellite European states, for example) were somewhat more prominent than restrictions on immigration; and when an international Convention on the Status of Refugees had recently been adopted, dealing with the rights of refugees within what may be called broadly the European space.[35]

Recalling his 1941 radio message, Pius XII said that "the right of people to migrate ... is founded in the very nature of land." Quoting what he had written to the bishops of the United States in 1948, he defined a category: "those who have been forced by revolutions in their own countries, or by unemployment or hunger to leave their homes and live in foreign lands."

> The natural law itself, no less than devotion to humanity, urges that ways of migration be opened to these people. For the Creator of the universe made all good things primarily for the good of all. Since land everywhere offers the possibility of supporting a large number of people, the sovereignty of the State, although it must be respected, cannot be exaggerated to the point that access to this land is, for inadequate or unjustified reasons, denied to needy and decent [*honestis moribus*: of sound morals] people from other nations, provided of course that this [access] is not contrary to the public weal [*publicae utilitati*], assessed with even scales[36] [*vera libra ponderandae*].

[35] When founding the European Convention on Human Rights 1950 [ECHR] and at the same time the Geneva Convention on the Status of Refugees 1951 (extended to signatory countries beyond the European space as from 1967), the European states involved specified in many different ways that states have no obligation to let in refugees arriving at their borders *en masse*; indeed, have no legal or treaty obligation to accept refugees at all; and have no absolute obligation to continue to provide asylum for refugees who are a danger to the community. The Universal Declaration of Human Rights (UDHR) (December, 10 1948) proclaims that everyone has the right to a nationality (art. 15), that everyone has the right to *leave* any country, including his own, and to return to *his* country (art. 13(2)), and that everyone has the right to *seek* and to *enjoy* in other countries asylum from persecution (art. 14). At the insistence of Britain (among other nations), article 14 abstained from saying that a persecuted person has a human *right to be granted* asylum. All that is affirmed is the right to apply for asylum and then, *if asylum is granted*, the right not to be disturbed by, for example, the persecuting state's threats of reprisals if it is not revoked. And even the right to *apply* is unavailable "in the case of prosecutions genuinely arising from nonpolitical crimes or from acts contrary to the purposes and principles of the United Nations" (art. 14(2)).

Equally deliberately, the proclaimed UDHR rights to emigrate (art. 13(2)) and to change one's nationality (art. 15(2)) are not "matched" by any right to be admitted into or enter a country whether as tourist, visitor, or immigrant, or to be granted its nationality. No such right was stated, admitted, or in any way implied.

[36] Cf. at n. 54 below.

The opening sentences of *Exsul familia* define the persons similarly:

> every migrant, alien and refugee of whatever kind who, whether compelled
> by fear of persecution or by want, is forced to leave his native land, his beloved
> parents and relatives, his close friends, and to seek a foreign soil.

And a later sentence verbally distinguishes those migrating "in the hope of
becoming prosperous" from "others driven by want."

JOHN XXIII
MIGRATION

John XXIII removed the question from the lingering framework of agricultural
colonists welcomed into (or at least entitled to be welcomed into) underpopulated and undeveloped wilderness regions, but not altogether from the
framework of compulsion by persecution or poverty. In *Pacem in terris* (1963),
the first papal document to be couched expressly, resolutely, and extensively in
terms of human *rights*, we find (tacked onto the end of a discussion of refugees)
the basic proposition:

> 106. And among man's personal rights we must include his right to enter
> a country [*nationem*] in which he hopes to be able to provide more fittingly
> for himself and his dependents. It is therefore the duty of a political commu-
> nity's officials to accept such immigrants[37] and – so far as the good (rightly
> understood) [*non fucatum bonum*: real not feigned good] of their own com-
> munity permits – to accede to the proposal of those who may wish to become
> new members of it.

Even if this does implicitly exclude from the entitlement those who wish to
immigrate in order to enjoy high levels of state-funded or charitable welfare,
and does implicitly authorize states of immigration to insist upon valid and
lawful applications and quotas, it nonetheless articulates no distinction
between entering by permission and entering without permission but claiming a natural "personal right." Nor does it begin to consider how the country of
immigration is to assess, rightly, its "good (rightly understood)." Is that country

---

[37] In summarizing the 1941 message, John XXIII's *Mater et magistra*, no. 45 takes for granted that
this means "the right of families to migrate" (as distinct from a right to enter for a period as
a guest-worker without dependents or an expectation of eventual "family reunion," but with
a right to make remittances to the family – one element in Japan's immigration policy since
World War II, a policy designed to avoid the bad side effects of multiethnicity and multiculturalism). Cf. John Finnis, "Migration Rights" in *Human Rights and Common Good*
(Oxford: Oxford University Press, 2011), 119; John Finnis, "Cosmopolis, Nation States, and
Families," in *Intention and Identity* (Oxford: Oxford University Press, 2011).

entitled (or indeed required) to consider the wellbeing of the poorer, less able, and more vulnerable members of its indigenous (that is, existing, national) population, many of whom will be in competition with immigrants for scarce resources? Its medium-term civil peace?[38]

GLOBAL GOVERNANCE

Mater et magistra, for the 70th anniversary of *RN*, made much of the expansion and diversifying of social relationships in every domain including the global. But its response to such changes on the global plane was muted:

> 200. The progress of science and technology in every aspect of life has led, particularly today, to increased relationships between nations, and made the nations more and more dependent on one another.
>
> 201. As a rule no single commonwealth has sufficient resources at its command to solve the more important scientific, technical, economic, social, political and cultural problems which confront it at the present time. These problems are necessarily the concern of a whole group of nations, and possibly of the whole world [*plures atque aliquando omnes terrarum nationes ex necessitate quadam contingent* = with some degree of necessity concern many and sometimes all the nations of the world].

But *Pacem in terris*, two years later, marks a significant shift in CST, in this as in several other respects:

> 137. Today the universal common good presents us with problems which are worldwide in their dimensions; problems, therefore, which cannot be solved except by a public authority *with power, organization and means coextensive with these problems,* and with a worldwide sphere of *activity.* Consequently the moral order itself demands the establishment of some such general form of public authority. (emphasis added) … [140] … The special function of this universal authority must be to evaluate and find a solution to economic, social, political and cultural problems which affect the universal common good. These are problems which, because of their extreme gravity, vastness and urgency, must be considered too difficult for the rulers of individual States to solve with any degree of success.[39]

What *Pacem in terris* thus seemingly gives with one hand it seems to take away with the other:

---

[38] See at n. 44 below.
[39] John XXIII, Encyclical Letter *Pacem in terris* (On Establishing Universal Peace in Truth, Justice, Charity, and Liberty) (1963).

138. But this general authority *equipped with worldwide power and adequate means for achieving the universal common good* cannot be imposed by force. It must be set up with the consent of all nations. If its work is to be effective, it must operate with fairness, absolute impartiality, and with dedication to the common good of all peoples. The forcible imposition by the more powerful nations of a universal authority of this kind would inevitably arouse fears of its being used as an instrument to serve the interests of the few or to take the side of a single nation, and thus the influence and effectiveness of its activity would be undermined. For even though nations may differ widely in material progress and military strength, they are very sensitive as regards their juridical equality and the excellence of their own way of life. They are right, therefore, in their reluctance to submit to an authority imposed by force, established without their cooperation, or not accepted of their own accord . . . (emphasis added)

140. The same principle of subsidiarity which governs the relations between public authorities and individuals, families and intermediate socie-ties in a single State, must also apply to the relations between the public authority of the world community and the public authorities of each political community.

141. . . . it is no part of the duty of universal authority to limit the sphere of action of the public authority of individual States, or to *arrogate any of their functions* to itself. On the contrary, its essential purpose is to create world conditions in which the public authorities of each nation, its citizens and intermediate groups, can carry out their tasks, fullfill their duties and claim their rights with greater security. [Emphasis added]

The last sentence preserves or reinstates the ambiguity of the whole treatment.[40] For the idea of creating conditions in which persons and groups can fulfill responsibilities and advance their rights with greater security is essentially the idea of the political common good which Vatican II will use to define the function and authority of state government and law. And the authority of state government and law is such that it is often a crime, and can even be the crime of treason, to defy its directives. So, in sum, it remains unclear whether, and if so how far, John XXIII was envisaging and promoting a world government and a legal order that would be essentially not interna-tional – between states – but global. Such a global regime would reduce the plethora of independent states and nations to provinces and subgroups of the worldwide *imperium*, subject only to their initial consent, a consent that, like

---

[40] Here *PT* cites Pius XII's "Address to Young Members of Italian Catholic Action" (September 12, 1948): *AAS* 40 (1948) 412.

consent to federate in the United States of America or the Commonwealth of Australia, once given would doubtless be treated as irrevocable.

SECOND VATICAN COUNCIL

The Council, with its hundreds of bishops from scores of newly or imminently independent national states, did not entertain any notion of a world federation. In *Gaudium et spes* (1965) it says no more than:

> 84. In view of the increasingly close ties of mutual dependence today between all the inhabitants and peoples of the earth, the apt pursuit and efficacious attainment of the universal common good now require of the community of nations that it organize itself in a manner suited to its present responsibilities, especially toward the many parts of the world which are still suffering from unbearable want ... Already existing international and regional organizations are ... the first efforts at laying the foundations on an international level for a community of everyone, to work for the solution to the serious problems of our times, to encourage progress everywhere, and to obviate wars of whatever kind.[41]

PAUL VI
GLOBAL GOVERNANCE

Paul VI's encyclical *Populorum progressio* on the Development of Peoples says, almost at its end, in three consecutive sections:

> 77. Nations are the architects of their own development, and they must bear the burden of this work; but they cannot accomplish it if they live in isolation from others. Regional mutual aid agreements among the poorer nations, broader based programs of support for these nations, major alliances between nations to coordinate these activities – these are the road signs that point the way to national development and world peace.
>
> 78. *Toward an Effective World Authority.* Such international collaboration among the nations of the world certainly calls for institutions that will promote, coordinate and direct it, until a new juridical order is firmly established and fully ratified. We [Paul VI] give willing and wholehearted support to those public organizations that have already joined in promoting

---

[41] *The Instruction of the Pontifical Council for Pastoral Care of Migrants and Itinerant People* (2004), no. 21 says that GS, no. 87, "recognized the right of the public authorities, in a particular context, to regulate the flow of migration." But GS, no. 87 refers specifically only to migration from rural to urban areas.

the development of nations, and We ardently hope that they will enjoy ever growing authority. As We told the United Nations General Assembly in New York: "Your vocation is to bring not just some peoples but all peoples together as brothers... Who can fail to see the need and importance of thus gradually coming to the establishment of a world authority capable of taking effective action on the juridical and political planes?"

The reference in no. 78 to a "gradually" established "world authority" is relatively cautious. What follows it is not.

> 79. *Hope for the Future*. Some would regard these hopes as vain flights of fancy. It may be that these people are not realistic enough, and that they have not noticed that the world is moving rapidly in a certain direction. Men are growing more anxious to establish closer ties of brotherhood; despite their ignorance, their mistakes, their offenses, and even their lapses into barbarism and their wanderings from the path of salvation, they are slowly making their way to the Creator, even without adverting to it.

Thus the pope's hope commingles that global unity (and the path he envisages toward *that*) with the Church's hope for and path to *salvation* (and with the way to our Creator). Such commingling is theologically and philosophically most questionable. Perhaps the apparent link between nos. 78 and 79 was an accident of flawed composition or editing.

MIGRATION

Populorum progressio (1967) envisages migrant workers leaving their families behind. But *Octogesima adveniens* (1971), in a section juxtaposed with the section against racial discrimination, denounces "a narrowly nationalist attitude in their regard" and calls for "a charter which will assure them a right to emigrate, favor their integration, facilitate their professional advancement and give them access to decent housing where, if such is the case, their families can join them."[42]

JOHN PAUL II
MIGRATION

In *Laborem exercens* (1981), emigration in search of work is treated as a source of loss and harm for the country of emigration, but though "in some aspects an evil, in certain circumstances it is, as the phrase goes, a necessary evil." The encyclical's consideration of the impact on the country of immigration is less

---

[42] Paul VI, Apostolic Letter *Octogesima adveniens* (A Call to Action) (1971), no. 17.

careful. The downward pressure on the wages of the least well-off indigenous (national, citizen) inhabitants is not directly considered, though the document teaches that foreign workers (seasonal or would-be permanent) should have the same working conditions, rights, and remuneration as nationals. The objection is not confronted that, where there is more or less full employment of nationals, remuneration of foreign workers at lower wages can be just if (as is often the case) it enables them to support their dependents abroad as well or better than they would otherwise be supported (given the different costs in their native country). Doing so may be an opportunity for unjust, exploitative profiteering by employers, but may also, in other cases, make possible production and employment that would otherwise be unfeasible, with fair benefit therefore to all concerned.

The treatment of migration in the CCC, no. 2241 has a weight comparable to its treatment in *PT*. Rightly understood, it answers some if not all of the questions left unanswered[43] by *PT*:

> 2241. The more prosperous nations are obliged, to the extent they are able, to welcome the foreigner in search of the security and the means of livelihood which he cannot find in his country of origin. Public authorities should see to it that the natural right is respected that places a guest under the protection of those who receive him.
>
> Political authorities, for the sake of the common good for which they are responsible, may make the exercise of the right to immigrate subject to various juridical conditions, especially with regard to the immigrants' duties toward their country of adoption. Immigrants are obliged to respect with gratitude the material and spiritual heritage of the country that receives them, to obey its laws and to assist in carrying civic burdens.

This seems compatible with – perhaps even to require – an immigration policy that, for the sake of the poorer and more vulnerable among the indigenous (national) population, restricts entry to persons of high and needed qualifications, and refuses entry to or deports those who have entered unlawfully ("without documentation"), or who have attempted fraud on the immigration system; and those who adhere to religions or ideologies opposed to morally permissible elements of the country's constitutional laws and conventions, political ethos, and so forth; and those who on a plea of multiculturalism (whether advanced by them or by their indigenous supporters) enter without real resolve to assimilate to and adopt the language, the morality (when sound), and the political conventions of the indigenous population.

[43] See at n. 38 above.

In every year but one from 1985 to 2005, John Paul II signed a message for World Migration Day. Though not of very high magisterial weight, these messages cannot be ignored. A primary characteristic of them is their lack of clarity about whether the duties they proclaim are duties of the Church and its pastors and members as such, or are said to be also duties of state government and law (and of citizens as indirectly participants in law-making). One moment of clarity about this appears in the Message for 1996, entitled in Italian, French, Spanish, and Portuguese "Irregular Migrants," and in German "Migrants without Stay-status," but in English "Undocumented Migrants." In any case, the reference is to persons who enter clandestinely, not to seek asylum on grounds of persecution, but to evade the processes of applying for permission. (The body of the document more reasonably calls them "illegal migrants" or persons engaged in "illegal immigration.") The document's fundamental proposition is that illegal immigration should be prevented:

> *Illegal immigration should be prevented*, but it is also essential to combat vigorously the criminal activities which exploit illegal immigrants. The most appropriate choice, which will yield consistent and long-lasting results, is that of international co-operation which aims to foster political stability and to eliminate underdevelopment.[44]

A duty of the state authorities to prevent illegal immigration can only be fulfilled by systems of border surveillance and deportation, if not also by a system of inspecting identity in employment and perhaps elsewhere. The document articulates none of those entailments, but rightly observes that:

> His irregular legal status cannot allow the migrant to lose his dignity, since he is endowed with inalienable rights, which can neither be violated nor ignored.[45]

It is not asserted that these inalienable rights include the right to enter without permission sought before or at the border or as soon as possible after crossing it. All the grounds that make private property normally just, and make violation of property rights normally unjust and unlawful (as carefully analyzed in *RN* and all subsequent CST discussions of property), are grounds that also normally hold good, by analogy, in relation to the rights that particular peoples and political communities can assert to treat defined territory as their sovereign territory, to be entered only by permission.

---

[44] John Paul II, *Undocumented Migrants* (Message of Pope John Paul II for World Migration Day, 1996) (July 25, 1995), no. 2 (emphasis added).

[45] *Undocumented Migrants*, no. 2.

The treatment of migration in the *Compendium of the Social Doctrine of the Church,* near the end of John Paul's pontificate, gives consideration only to economic effects of migration. Much of the brief treatment in nos. 297–8 ("Immigration and work") says – as nations tend to notice without ecclesiastical guidance – that immigration can bring economic benefit when the local workforce is insufficient, and so on. It denounces the "frequent perception" that immigration is "a threat to the high levels of well-being." It does not address the more frequent perception that immigration may threaten to impair the already low relative levels of well-being of citizens who are unemployed or employed on low wages that are very likely to be lowered (or prevented from rising) by the supply of immigrant labor from regions of the world with lower standards (and costs) of living. Longer-term consequences for civil life,[46] political order, the discriminatory impact of antidiscrimination (and perhaps pro-quota, "affirmative action") law, and so forth are not really on the *Compendium*'s horizon.

BENEDICT XVI
MIGRATION

In view of the increasingly unfocussed statements on migration issued over John Paul II's name in the late years of his pontificate, it is not surprising that Benedict XVI took a fairly early opportunity to rearticulate one or two fundamentals:

> single [i.e., individual] believers are called to open their arms and their hearts to every person, from whatever nation they come, allowing the Authorities responsible for public life to enforce the relevant laws held to be appropriate for a healthy co-existence.[47]

---

[46] Consider *MM*, no. 181:

> "The Church of Jesus Christ," as Our Predecessor Pius XII observed with such penetration, "is ... certainly too wise to discourage or belittle those peculiarities and differences which mark out one nation from another. It is quite legitimate for nations to treat those differences as a sacred inheritance and guard them at all costs ... Every nation has its own genius, its own qualities, springing from the hidden roots of its being. The wise development, the encouragement within limits, of that genius, those qualities, does no harm; and if a nation cares to take precautions, to lay down rules, for that end, it has the Church's approval."

[47] Benedict XVI, "Address to Pontifical Council for Pastoral Care of Migrants and Itinerant People" (May 15, 2006).

Even this essential statement was accompanied, however, by remarks that left unelaborated the duty of state authorities and their electorates to consider accurately the preconditions for "healthy coexistence":

> The theme chosen for this Session – *Migration and Itinerancy from and towards Islamic Majority Countries* – concerns a social reality that is becoming ever more present. Therefore, human mobility with regard to Muslim countries calls for a specific reflection, not only because of the extent of the phenomenon, but above all because the *Islamic identity is both religious and cultural*. The Catholic Church realizes with increasing awareness that interreligious dialogue is part of her commitment to the service of humanity in the contemporary world.

The sentence here italicized states in a low-key way the problem confronting authorities and peoples subject to migration and itinerancy *from* Muslim countries; but what follows that sentence swings immediately away to the very different responsibilities of the Church and its members, and stays away. CST on migration remains radically underdeveloped.

GLOBALIZATION

Projecting encyclicals on charity, hope, and faith respectively, Benedict XVI signed *Caritas in veritate*, "On Integral Human Development in Charity and Truth," devoted in large measure to CST, in June 2009. It includes in no. 42 a good many words on globalization. The clearest statement is the following:

> The processes of globalization, suitably understood and directed, open up the unprecedented possibility of large-scale redistribution of wealth on a worldwide scale; if badly directed, however, they can lead to an increase in poverty and inequality, and could even trigger a global crisis. It is necessary to *correct the malfunctions*, some of them serious, that cause new divisions between peoples and within peoples, and also to ensure that the redistribution of wealth does not come about through the redistribution or increase of poverty: a real danger if the present situation were to be badly managed.

To "manage" the "situation" or "crisis" "*in terms of communion and the sharing of goods*" (emphasis in the original), the encyclical speaks first of subsidiarity:

> In order not to produce a dangerous universal power of a tyrannical nature, the governance of globalization must be marked by subsidiarity, articulated into several layers and involving different levels that can work together. Globalization certainly requires authority, insofar as it poses the problem of

a global common good that needs to be pursued. This authority, however, must be organized in a subsidiary and stratified way [citation to *PT*], if it is not to infringe upon freedom and if it is to yield effective results in practice.[48]

The main proposition is advanced ten sections later, where no. 67 articulates a series of circumstance-relative judgments or *aestimationes* ("one also senses ... "):

> 67. In the face of the unrelenting growth of global interdependence, there is a strongly felt need, even in the midst of a global recession, for a reform of the United Nations Organization, and likewise of economic institutions and international finance, so that the concept of the family of nations can acquire real teeth. One also senses the urgent need to find innovative ways of implementing the principle of the responsibility to protect and of giving poorer nations an effective voice in shared decision-making. This seems necessary in order to arrive at a political, juridical and economic order which can increase and give direction to international cooperation for the development of all peoples in solidarity. To manage the global economy; to revive economies hit by the [global financial] crisis [of 2008]; to avoid any deterioration of the present crisis and the greater imbalances that would result; to bring about integral and timely disarmament, food security and peace; to guarantee the protection of the environment and to regulate migration: for all this, there is urgent need of a true world political authority, as my predecessor Blessed John XXIII indicated some years ago [scil. in *Pacem in terris*].[49]

There follows a list of preconditions:

> Such an authority would need to be regulated by law, to observe consistently the principles of subsidiarity and solidarity, to seek to establish the common good,[50] and to make a commitment to securing authentic integral human development inspired by the values of charity in truth. Furthermore, such an

[48] Benedict XVI, Encyclical Letter *Caritas in veritate* (On Integral Human Development in Charity and Truth) (2009), no. 57.

[49] The last sentence here will be quoted in *Laudato si'* (2015), no. 175.

[50] Here a citation is made to *CSDC*, no. 441 and to *PT* as cited in *CSDC*, no. 441. At the end of the next sentence is a citation to *GS*, no. 82 (meaning 84; the miscitation derives from *CSDC*, no. 441 fn 993). *CSDC*, no. 441 goes on to say "it is essential that such an authority arise from mutual agreement and that it not be imposed, nor must it be understood as a kind of 'global super-State'." The citation offered for this in turn is to John Paul II, "Message for World Day of Peace" (2003), "*Pacem in terris*: a Permanent Commitment," no. 6; the relevant sentences are:

> Is this not the time for all to *work together for a new constitutional organization of the human family*, truly capable of ensuring peace and harmony between peoples, as well as their integral development? But let there be no misunderstanding. This does not mean writing the constitution of a global super-State. Rather, it means continuing and

authority would need to be universally recognized and to be vested with the effective power to ensure security for all, regard for justice, and respect for rights. Obviously it would have to have the authority to ensure compliance with its decisions from all parties, and also with the coordinated measures adopted in various international forums.

This affirms less than it may seem to. For the main citation it makes is to a section of the *Compendium of the Social Doctrine of the Church*, insisting that the projected "authority" is not to be understood as a "kind of 'global super-State'," and citing John Paul II insisting that any *"new constitutional organization of the human family"* would not

> mean writing the constitution of a global super-State. Rather, it means continuing and deepening processes already in place to meet the almost universal *demand for participatory ways of exercising political authority.*

Were it not for these obliquely indicated qualifications, the preconditions stated in the first sentence and a half of *Caritas in veritate*, no. 67 would seem so unlikely ever to be satisfied that it would seem unreasonable to incur any risks or costs to meet the "urgent need" asserted. For an institution of a global "authority" that amounted to the government of a global political community (state) "with teeth" (i.e., with police and military forces of sufficient size and strength to "ensure security for *all*") but without genuine commitment (how secured against default?) to the preconditions would entail very bad consequences from which there could be little or no escape without war – war that would thus, as if by constitutional design, be *civil* war and therefore most likely to be of outstanding fury and grimness.

Meanwhile, in the years immediately following *Caritas in veritate*, the economies "hit" by the Financial Crisis of 2008 substantially "revived" without benefit of any global authority of the kind the encyclical said was "urgently needed." To anticipate chapter 23, later in this volume: no. 67 of the encyclical, if taken at face value, could reasonably be considered a paradigm of clerical overreach, that is, of intrusion of the Church's prelates – reaching far beyond the Church's authentic responsibility to articulate moral principles and norms – into the domain of fact-contingent secular *aestimatio* and decision-making about causes and effects, risks and likelihoods.

> deepening processes already in place to meet the almost universal *demand for participatory ways of exercising political authority, even international political authority, and for transparency and accountability at every level of public life.* [Emphases in original]

FRANCIS
GLOBAL GOVERNANCE

Pope Francis's encyclical on care of the environment, *Laudato si'* (2015), perhaps surprisingly leaves matters of global governance much where they stood with his predecessor. No. 175 leads up thus to a quotation from *Caritas in veritate*, no. 67:

> Given this situation [of environmental degradation and threat, and poverty], it is essential to devise stronger and more efficiently organized international institutions, with functionaries who are appointed fairly by agreement among national governments, and empowered to impose sanctions. As Benedict XVI has affirmed in continuity with the social teaching of the Church: "To manage the global economy . . . [etc.]"[51]

More significant in the encyclical is its almost wholesale adoption of the perspectives and programs of, and theses and language promoted by, an international ideological, plutocrat-bureaucrat secularist movement that can reasonably be thought of as in continuity with the views and currents of thought warned against in Pius X's critique of *Le Sillon*.[52]

MIGRATION

Pope Francis's teachings on immigration come less than 125 years after Leo XIII's celebration of European colonies and of past and prospective European missionary efforts. The new teachings address instead a Church that in most places has declined to a quarter or less (or much less) of the numbers, institutions, and resources it had in the times of Pius XII and John XXIII, a Church that now in many places in Europe is maintained by missionaries from lands that were mission territories for European countries. The Holy See under Francis addresses in their own languages peoples who foresee as probable that in their own lifetime immigration will have reduced them to minorities in their own country and may well have caused their social and political order to be set aside in favor of one that their own highest courts have recently declared incompatible with the rights acknowledged by *Pacem in terris* and *Gaudium et spes*.[53] This pope nonetheless has proclaimed, and proclaims, a teaching about migrants (whether lawful or unlawful, refugees, seekers for a better life, or zealots of an Arabian religion with society-

---

[51] See sentence quoted at n. 50 above.
[52] See pp. 321–322 and n. 20 above.
[53] The European Court of Human Rights (Grand Chamber) held unanimously in 2003:

transforming ambitions) that is unilateral – free from pretense of assessing with "even scales."[54] It is most plainly expressed in his Message dated August 15, 2017, for the World Day of Migrants 2018.

Rarely if ever articulated now is the distinction between the responsibilities of the Church (and its members) as such and the moral responsibilities of states (and citizens) as such. Every migrant is to be identified with "Jesus Christ knocking at our door." Processes for granting humanitarian visas and for "reuniting" families must be increased and simplified. "The principle of the centrality of the human person ... obliges us to always prioritize personal safety over national security." Those who enter without authorization should not be detained: "we must strive to find alternative solutions." Unauthorized migrants, like the authorized, should be allowed bank accounts, freedom of movement, employment and "enough to live on," education if under-age, "family reunification" even if the grandparents, siblings, and grandchildren will all live on social welfare at the expense of citizen taxpayers; their integration should be promoted with no requirement of assimilation; citizenship should be granted without linguistic or financial prerequisites. These and other responsibilities of states and citizens to cooperate in their own submersion the pope summarizes as "to welcome, to protect, to promote and to integrate," the object of these infinitive, quasi-imperative verbs being migrants of every kind.

Absent from such statements is any identification of limits; of reciprocal responsibilities; of the moral and legal duty of very many of the relevant migrants to stay in – or return to – their home country rather than attempt by fraud and stealth to secure a new life at the expense of both their law-abiding fellow-citizens and the citizens of the countries whose generally just laws they plan to violate or have violated; or of the probable very bad outcome of such nonvoluntary mixing of ethnicities and of culturally and politically

> [T]he Court considers that sharia, *which faithfully reflects the dogmas and divine rules laid down by religion, is stable and invariable*. Principles such as pluralism in the political sphere or the constant evolution of public freedoms have no place in it ... a regime based on sharia ... clearly diverges from Convention values, particularly with regard to its criminal law and criminal procedure, its rules on the legal status of women and the way it intervenes in all spheres of private and public life in accordance with religious precepts ... [A] political party whose actions seem to be aimed at introducing sharia ... can hardly be regarded as an association complying with the democratic ideal that underlies the whole of the Convention.
>
> *Refah Partisi (No. 2) v. Turkey* 37, European Human Rights Reports 1 (2003) at sec. 123 (emphasis added). On the significance of this judgment and its implicit adoption in the highest court of the United Kingdom, see John Finnis, "Discrimination between Faiths: A Case of Extreme Speech?" in *Extreme Speech and Democracy*, eds. Ivan Hare and James Weinstein (Oxford: Oxford University Press, 2010), 430–444.

[54] Cf. n. 36 above.

opposing religions. Pope Francis acknowledges that the Church communities in Europe have a "deep unease about the massive influx of migrants and refugees." He ascribes the unease to "an economic crisis [of 2008] that has left deep wounds" (and was caused by the profit motive and plutocracy), to "the general unpreparedness of the countries that receive them, and by often inadequate national and community policies," and to "the limits of the process of European unification"; and he points up the "obstacles hindering the concrete application of universal human rights and the expression of that integral humanism which is among the finest fruits of European civilization," and the "factors [to] be interpreted, in opposition to a self-enclosed and secularist mentality, in the light of the unique, God-given dignity of each human person." Immigration of Muslims, for example, "represents a fertile ground for the growth of open and enriching . . . interreligious dialogue," to be engaged in by Catholics because of "profound esteem for other [i.e., non-Christian] religious communities."[55]

Thus, while the grounding of CST about immigration (and about globalization in general) on the doctrine of conditionally just appropriation of resources to owners (persons with a just though not unlimited right to exclude nonowners) remains undisputed, the presuppositions that determine the doctrine's application to globalization – presuppositions about facts, motivations, and causal trajectories, and about fidelity to antecedents – have been radically reversed between Leo XIII, Pius X, or Pius XI (and the faithful of their times) and, on the other hand, Francis and the many Catholic prelates and secular powers for whom he speaks.

CONCLUSION

As the twentieth century dawned, globalization in the sense of factual **interdependencies** between peoples and nations worldwide was neither overlooked nor focused upon by the Holy See and other leaders of Catholic Social Teaching. Globalization in the sense of cosmopolitan responses was, however, clearly envisaged and firmly disapproved by the Holy See. Globalization in the form of society-transforming migration was not a topic of teaching by the Holy See, and bishops tended to concur in national responses even as these moved toward restrictive and ethnically selective

---

[55] Quotations in this and the preceding paragraph are from Francis's Address on September 22, 2017, to National Directors of Pastoral Care for Migrants of the Catholic Bishops' Conferences of Europe, *AAS* 109 (2017) 995–998; see also 1294–1296, 1327–1332.

policies such as those that culturally and economically stabilized the United States between 1924 and 1965.

In the latter part of the twentieth century and increasingly in recent years, the Holy See has actively involved Catholic Social Teaching in the promotion of generalized favor for the idea of *world government*, and for the idea that *religion*, as distinct from faith in Christ, is a cosmopolitan good. *Migration* is likewise treated as if it were a good to be firmly promoted without authoritatively encouraged attention to the harms and injustices it can create, not least for the Christian faithful and mission, and for societies hitherto respectful, in some measure, of Christian believers and their faith. These reversals and developments exemplify acutely the issues discussed later, in chapter 23, "A Radical Critique of Catholic Social Teaching."

14

Are Some Men Angels? Modern Catholic Social Thought and Trust in Government

Christopher Wolfe

"It may be a reflection on human nature, that such devices should be necessary to control the abuses of government. But what is government itself, but the greatest of all reflections on human nature? If men were angels, no government would be necessary. If angels were to govern men, neither external nor internal controls on government would be necessary. In framing a government which is to be administered by men over men, the great difficulty lies in this: you must first enable the government to control the governed; and in the next place oblige it to control itself."

James Madison, *Federalist* No. 51[1]

The premise of Madison's famous dictum from *The Federalist* is wrong. Yves Simon's classic discussion of authority takes up the issue of whether political authority would be necessary in a community of men who were the moral equivalents of (good) angels, and shows convincingly that it would be.[2]

But that doesn't make any less important the necessity of coming to grips with the issue Madison poses: given that the men who govern are, in fact, far from angels, what do we do about this? The matter is more urgent because, at least since the Second Vatican Council, Catholic Social Teaching has not only recognized and accepted, but also called for and promoted, much greater government action for the common good. There are various possible reasons for this. One is that modern circumstances (population growth, new means of transportation and communication, etc.) have led to an increasingly interdependent world, which undoubtedly requires more government intervention to

---

[1] James Madison, "The Structure of Government Must Furnish the Proper Checks and Balances Between the Different Departments," *New York Packet*, February 8, 1788, http://avalon .law.yale.edu/18th_century/fed51.asp (*Federalist*, no. 51).

[2] Yves Simon, "General Theory of Government," in *The Philosophy of Democratic Government* (Chicago: University of Chicago Press, 1951).

coordinate activities to attain the common good (e.g., in economic matters) than in earlier times.

At the same time recent popes – especially John Paul II and Benedict XVI – have expressed worries about the influence of original sin upon those who exercise this enormous power. The *Catechism of the Catholic Church* explains:

> The doctrine of original sin, closely connected with that of redemption by Christ, provides lucid discernment of man's situation and activity in the world. By our first parents' sin, the devil has acquired a certain domination over man, even though man remains free. Original sin entails "captivity under the power of him who thenceforth had the power of death, that is, the devil." Ignorance of the fact that man has a wounded nature inclined to evil gives rise to serious errors in the areas of education, politics, social action, and morals. (CCC, no. 407)

Original sin affects not only personal morality, but also politics and social action. In *Centesimus annus*,[3] John Paul II says

> Moreover, man, who was created for freedom, bears within himself the wound of original sin, which constantly draws him towards evil and puts him in need of redemption. Not only is this doctrine an integral part of Christian revelation; it also has great hermeneutical value insofar as it helps one to understand human reality. Man tends towards good, but he is also capable of evil. He can transcend his immediate interest and still remain bound to it. The social order will be all the more stable, the more it takes this fact into account and does not place in opposition personal interest and the interests of society as a whole, but rather seeks ways to bring them into fruitful harmony. In fact, where self-interest is violently suppressed, it is replaced by a burdensome system of bureaucratic control which dries up the wellsprings of initiative and creativity. (CA, no. 25)

Not only is original sin a reality that must be taken into consideration to understand the social order, but it should help shape our awareness of the possible remedies for social problems, in light of the permanent weaknesses of men rooted in our fallen nature.

Likewise, Benedict XVI points out in *Caritas in veritate*:[4]

---

[3] John Paul II, Encyclical Letter *Centesimus annus* (On the 110th Anniversary of *Rerum novarum*) (1991).

[4] Benedict XVI, Encyclical Letter *Caritas in veritate* (On Integral Human Development in Charity and Truth) (2009).

Sometimes modern man is wrongly convinced that he is the sole author of himself, his life and society. This is a presumption that follows from being selfishly closed in upon himself, and it is a consequence – to express it in faith terms – of original sin. The Church's wisdom has always pointed to the presence of original sin in social conditions and in the structure of society: "Ignorance of the fact that man has a wounded nature inclined to evil gives rise to serious errors in the areas of education, politics, social action and morals." In the list of areas where the pernicious effects of sin are evident, the economy has been included for some time now. (*CV*, no. 34)

The weaknesses implicit in original sin affect not just personal actions but also social structures. John Paul II devotes an important section of *Sollicitudo rei socialis* to "structures of sin," which "are rooted in personal sin, and thus always linked to the concrete acts of individuals."[5] An awareness of the moral dimensions of social problems is essential, especially one based on faith in God and on his law. Particular manifestations of sin at the root of structures of sin are the all-consuming desire for profit and the thirst for power, which lead to imposing one's will upon others, at any price.

In this chapter I want to explore what Catholic Social Teaching (CST) has to say about how to build structures of government that provide reasonable assurances that human defects and sin will not conspire to corrupt government and thereby harm the common good. As CST has embraced the idea of more active government, it has always qualified that embrace with important limits, some of which I will discuss below. I want to ask two questions: first, to what extent has CST considered the possibility of government abusing its expanded powers to regulate economic affairs?; second, what, if any, suggestions does CST offer for dealing with such abuses? The answer to both questions is, I think, "Not enough."

I

Catholic Social Teaching in the modern era is generally said to date from Leo XIII's 1891 encyclical *Rerum novarum*, and includes a variety of encyclicals and apostolic exhortations, as well as some documents of the Second Vatican Council.[6] This teaching provides broad principles for understanding politics and economics, as well as somewhat more specific commentary on modern social conditions, events, ideologies, issues, and policies.

---

[5] John Paul II, Encyclical Letter *Sollicitudo rei socialis* (On Social Concern) (1987), nos. 35–37.

[6] Leo XIII, Encyclical Letter *Rerum novarum* (On the Condition of the Working Classes) (1891).

More recent influences on CST have been trends in modern secular thought and political practice that have placed a greater emphasis on government solutions to social problems (and are less inclined toward other, especially free-market, solutions).[7] The reasons for these secular trends might include not only objective requirements of the common good, but also the possibility that increased government intervention benefits certain interests more than others, and people tied to those interests may therefore be more likely – not only due to cynical self-interest, but also out of sincere but skewed perceptions of the common good – to be overly inclined toward government solutions.[8]

CST starts with the common good, rooted in the even more fundamental principle of the dignity of the human person. The common good is defined as "the sum of those conditions of social life which allow social groups and their individual members to reach their perfection more fully and more easily."[9] The aim of political authority is precisely to secure the common good: political authority has responsibility for the common good. The securing of different elements of the common good can occur in many ways. These include action of the state or government itself, or the action of intermediary bodies, or voluntary associations, or the family, or by individuals and groups cooperating in free markets. But even if action in markets, or by families, or by voluntary associations (rather than action directly by government) is the best way to secure some aspect of the common good, it is still true that the political authority is making the ultimate judgment that, in this instance, the best way to attain the common good is to leave action to those lower levels of community.[10]

7 On the influence of modern thought, see Ernest L. Fortin, "The Trouble with Catholic Social Thought," chapter 25 in *Human Rights, Virtue, and the Common Good*, ed. J. Brian Benestad (Rowman and Littlefield, 1996). See also Robert G. Kennedy, "Social Justice, Charity, and Catholic Social Doctrine" in *The Concept of Social Justice*, ed. C. Wolfe (forthcoming, St. Augustine's Press).

8 For example, some neoconservative commentators and scholars, turning Marxist analysis on its head, offer an account of a "new class," the standing and interests of which are tied to growing government. See Irving Kristol, "About Equality," *Commentary* (November 1, 1972) and John McAdams, *The New Class in Post-Industrial Society* (New York: Palgrave and Macmillan, 2015).

9 Vatican II, Pastoral Constitution *Gaudium et spes* (On the Church in the Modern World) (1965), no. 26 (quoting MM). Whether this "instrumental" conception of the common good is an adequate definition is subject to some scholarly dispute. See contrasting views in John Finnis, "Is Natural Law Theory Compatible with Limited Government?" in *Natural Law, Liberalism, and Morality*, ed. R. George (New York: Oxford University Press, 1996), and Michael Pakaluk "Is the Common Good of Political Society Limited and Instrumental?" *The Review of Metaphysics* 55 (September 2001): 57–94.

10 Some political conservatives are mistaken, therefore, when they seem to think that limits on government mean that political authority doesn't have responsibility for the entire common good. The political authority in a community always has that responsibility. Even when

However, even though there is no getting away from the need for political authority to make decisions regarding the best way to secure the common good, in all its diverse aspects, CST also contains important elements that often militate against direct governmental or state action to secure the common good. CST has, in fact, rejected a kind of "statism" that looks to government to solve all the problems of the common good.[11]

A primary example of these limits on government is subsidiarity. Originally stated in Pius XI's *Quadragesimo anno*[12] (but implicit earlier in Leo XIII's *Rerum novarum*), the principle of subsidiarity says:

> Still, that most weighty principle, which cannot be set aside or changed, remains fixed and unshaken in social philosophy: Just as it is gravely wrong to take from individuals what they can accomplish by their own initiative and industry and give it to the community, so also it is an injustice and at the same time a grave evil and disturbance of right order to assign to a greater and higher association what lesser and subordinate organizations can do. For every social activity ought of its very nature to furnish help [*subsidium*] to the members of the body social, and never destroy and absorb them. (*QA*, no. 79)

This principle is cited in many CST magisterial documents.[13] Even where the word "subsidiarity" is not used, there are typically clear statements in CST documents on the importance of government not displacing the initiative of those whom it is trying to help.[14] Moreover, there are other limits on

a political community decides to adopt a free market as the best way to achieve a multitude of economic goods, that free market is itself founded on a political decision of the nation.

[11] "Statism" is explicitly rejected by John Paul II in his 1994 *Letter to Italian Bishops*: "A profound social and political renewal is certainly necessary today. Alongside those who, aspiring to Christian values, have contributed to governing Italy for almost half a century, obtaining undeniable benefits for the country and its development, there are persons who have been unable to escape grave accusations as well: people, in particular, who have not always been able to withstand the strong pressures leading to excessive statism or seeking to promote personal interests over the common good" (no. 6).

[12] Pius XI, Encyclical Letter *Quadragesimo anno* (On Reconstruction of the Social Order: 40th Anniversary of *Rerum novarum*) (1931).

[13] For example, see John XXIII, Encyclical Letter *Mater et magistra* (On Christianity and Social Progress) (1961), nos. 53, 117, John XXIII, Encyclical Letter *Pacem in terris* (On Establishing Universal Peace in Truth, Justice, Charity, and Liberty) (1963), no. 140, *Centesimus annus*, nos. 15, 48, and *Caritas in veritate*, nos. 47, 57–58, 60, 67. See also *Gaudium et spes*, no. 86, and *Catechism of the Catholic Church*, no. 1883).

[14] E.g., Paul VI, Encyclical Letter *Populorum progressio* (On the Development of Peoples) (1967), no. 34, Paul VI, Encylical Letter *Octogesima adveniens* (A Call to Action on the 80th Anniversary of *Rerum novarum*) (1971), no. 46, Vatican II, *Gaudium et spes*, no. 75, John Paul II, Encyclical Letter *Laborem exercens* (On Human Work) (1981), no. 18, *Sollicitudo rei socialis*, no. 44.

government as well, such as objective moral principles that government, no less than individuals, should not transgress.

There are various ways in which government can be limited. The ultimate political authority might decide that government should be excluded from regulating a given area – as when a constitution, adopted by the people acting as the ultimate political authority (under God) in a modern democracy, guarantees religious liberty. Certain issues might be constitutionally reserved to lower levels of political community (e.g., states in the US constitutional system). Or, even where government has constitutional authority to act in a specific area, political authorities might decide that it is prudent not to exercise a power that they have, because some good can be attained more effectually by a nongovernmental actor (e.g., voluntary associations or free exchange in markets). In each of these cases, the securing of the common good requires a decision by political authority – whether constitutionally or legislatively or in some other way – as to how it is best achieved. But, whether it is best achieved by the action of government or by the action of other groups and individuals in society is a matter of political prudence.

It would therefore be a mistake to think that CST does not adopt a strong position emphasizing the need for limited government. The argument of this article is *not* that CST does not recognize the importance of limits on government. I want to focus, rather, on the kinds of concerns that give rise to the need for limits, and on different kinds of limits. More specifically, I want to ask: to what extent does CST advocate limits on government because of the potential likelihood of government abuse of its power? Should the possible abuse of a power affect the form in which and the extent to which the power is granted?

To give a simple analogy: imagine a small business that has a rudimentary accounting system, including a simple process for writing checks to support the business's activities. Such a business might adopt a policy or process whereby all checks written for the business must have at least two signatures by officers of the company. This would be inconvenient in some ways, because it might slow down necessary disbursements of money. But it would also make embezzlement, or even simply thoughtless and imprudent expenditures, more difficult. Such a company might accept the inconvenience in order to achieve greater security against abuses by company employees: an awareness of human malice and fallibility would lead it to accept a certain inconvenience, or to pay a certain price, to protect the company.

Of course, on a much grander scale, government involves extreme complexity and almost limitless opportunities to abuse power for personal benefit or to use power very imprudently, at the expense of the common good. How much should that lead us to impose limits on government, and, if so, what kinds of limits?

Limits on Government

It is important to distinguish three sorts of limits on government. The first kind of limit is a *norm* or moral principle that says, in effect, "this particular kind of action should not be done." This first kind of limit is predominant in classical political philosophy (e.g., Aristotle), in which the emphasis was on the need for good rulers in order to achieve the common good. No set of institutions was considered adequate to guarantee the common good, because the goal of politics (the common good) is so broad and necessarily involves so much discretion in the hands of rulers. What is most needed for good government is virtuous (especially prudent) rulers who understand and apply appropriate norms – whose actions are limited because they recognize and follow good moral principles.

This first kind of limit on government is especially appropriate when an action of government is wrong but is the operation of an undoubted and legitimate power. Congress undoubtedly has (and must have) broad discretionary power to declare war, for example, but it would be wrong for it to declare war unjustly. And the response to a valid criticism about the improper exercise of this kind of power would not be taking away from Congress the discretionary power to declare war, but rather trying to ensure in the ordinary operations of political life that the power not be abused, appealing to norms for the proper exercise of the power, such as just war theory.[15]

A second kind of limit on the power of government is a denial or complete withholding from government of some power – where the power itself is illegitimate. These kinds of limits most often take the form of constitutional prohibitions. One example is the US Constitution's prohibition of Congressional laws respecting an establishment of religion.[16] In this case, the very power itself is considered to be improper, and so the limit consists in a denial of the power.

---

[15]   The focus here on norms as a limit does not preclude other kinds of "internal" limits on the exercise of the power, such as the separation of powers described below.

[16]   Whether CST, even today, shares the idea that establishment of religion should always be beyond the power of government is a difficult question, with a long and complex historical background. But it is at least clear that, under some circumstances, including modern religious pluralism, such constitutional prohibitions of establishment are legitimate (and guarantees of free exercise of religion are always required).

A third kind of limit is more complicated. It involves cases in which the power of government is, in principle, legitimate, but where it is susceptible to abuse, and in which there is some institutional way of limiting the exercise of the power that can help to prevent its abuse.

The second and third kinds of limits on government are emphasized in modern political philosophy, which, due to a pessimism as to whether good rulers can be consistently secured, and also a narrower conception of the goal of politics,[17] has emphasized the need for good institutions that can either prohibit or channel the action of less-than-good rulers. For example, the text just prior to the quotation at the start of this chapter is:

> But the great security against a gradual concentration of the several powers in the same department, consists in giving to those who administer each department the necessary constitutional means and personal motives to resist encroachments of the others. The provision for defense must in this, as in all other cases, be made commensurate to the danger of attack. Ambition must be made to counteract ambition. The interest of the man must be connected with the constitutional rights of the place. It may be a reflection on human nature, that such devices should be necessary to control the abuses of government.[18]

Institutions that channel self-interest (such as personal ambition) are a more reliable guarantee of good government – at least a good approximation of justice – than good and prudent rulers, who will very often not be available.

Even modern liberal political philosophy is not able to dispense with all concern for the character of rulers (and, in a democracy, this includes the people). A system of good institutions itself requires a certain public-spiritedness, both in those who establish the system and in those who operate it. For example, Madison says in *Federalist* No. 55:

> As there is a degree of depravity in mankind which requires a certain degree of circumspection and distrust, so there are other qualities in human nature, which justify a certain portion of esteem and confidence. Republican government presupposes the existence of these qualities in a higher degree than any other form. Were the pictures which have been drawn by the political jealousy of some among us, faithful likenesses of the human character, the inference would be that there is not sufficient virtue among men for self-

---

[17] On the effect of narrowing the goal of politics, see Martin Diamond, "Ethics and Politics: The American Way," in *The Moral Foundations of the American Republic*, ed. R. Horwitz (Charlottesville: University Press of Virginia, 1977).

[18] James Madison, *Federalist* no. 55.

government; and that nothing less than the chains of despotism can restrain them from destroying and devouring one another.

Still, modern liberal political philosophy emphasizes the inadequacy of simply relying on virtuous rulers and the importance of relying on good institutions that channel the often selfish passions of mankind.

These institutional limits include first, "external controls," such as government responsibility to citizens through elections;[19] and second, "internal controls," which are of two, overlapping sorts: (1) constitutional limits on powers, such as bills of rights, and (2) structural configurations of government, such as (in the US Constitution) federalism, separation of powers with checks and balances, and the extended republic.[20]

It is important to note that these institutional limits can be obstacles not only to the abuse of power, but also to its good use. That is, they involve a certain trade-off: in exchange for preventing the misuse of power in important ways, they also can make it difficult to accomplish good objectives in political life. For example, being successful in elections typically requires a good deal of compromise in a free and pluralistic society – compromise not only regarding secondary or unimportant or even unattractive goals, but also very good ones. And institutional mechanisms such as federalism, separation of powers, and the extended republic have the effect of diffusing power among many groups in society, making it necessary to compromise to achieve action and often creating "choke-points" that make it difficult to act at all (whether for good or for ill).

It should be clear that all three kinds of limits on government – moral norms, constitutional prohibitions, and institutional arrangements – are legitimate, important, and necessary in appropriate circumstances. It is not a question of relying exclusively on one or the other of them.

---

[19] Madison in *Federalist* no. 51: "A dependence on the people is, no doubt, the primary control on the government."

[20] The extended republic is discussed in *Federalist* No. 10 (and in the second half of No. 51). These two sorts of internal controls are overlapping, due to the fact that enforcement of constitutional limits on government power ordinarily implicates separation of powers, because it usually requires some part of the government being able to enforce these limits against other parts, e.g., judicial review in the US Constitution.

It is noteworthy that constitutional limits on power, such as bills of right, are probably the first sort of limits on government power that people think about today, but they were less important in the minds of the leading founders of American government than the structural limits. (The founders did not, after all, include a bill of rights in the original Constitution, although, under pressure from anti-federalists, they quickly amended the Constitution to include one.)

Complicating the issue of limits on government is the fact that some limits include government's positive responsibility not to omit or fail to perform certain duties. Here, paradoxically, the limit on government is that it should not *fail* to act, it is obligated to *do* something. These positive-obligation limits can, in turn, be subdivided into two kinds. First, government should not fail to prohibit and punish certain acts, such as attacks on innocent persons, as it does when it authorizes or simply permits acts such as abortion, euthanasia, or lynching.[21] Second, government should do what is necessary and possible to ensure that all people have access to the basic resources (food, clothing, shelter, medical care, education, etc.) that they need in order to live a good life.[22] This sort of limit is more complex because it is conditioned by questions of practicality and the trade-offs entailed by different ways of achieving often incompatible ways of achieving the goal.[23]

CST and Limits on Government

CST recognizes the importance of the various kinds of limits on government. First, it recognizes that there are some things government should not do and

---

[21] I think the original understanding of the equal protection clause of the Fourteenth Amendment was focused primarily on this sort of failure: for example, local criminal enforcement ignoring the lynching of blacks and their sympathizers in the South after Reconstruction.

[22] Note that this moral obligation of government to ensure access to the necessities of life does not itself speak to the question of what is the best way to achieve that end, whether by government programs, voluntary associations, free markets, or other methods – that is a question of prudence, depending on the particular circumstances of various political communities.

[23] Certain practical questions enter into the first category of positive-obligation limits as well, but they are different sorts of practical questions (what might be called extrinsic practical constraints). The government has an absolute obligation to protect all innocent life from direct assaults (e.g., prohibiting direct procured abortion), but, at a given time and place, there may be insufficient political support for a full achievement of that goal, which may require temporary compromises and a policy of gradualism until the full right can be protected [as John Paul II's Encyclical Letter *Evangelium vitae* (On the Value and Inviolability of Human Life) (1995) noted].

   With respect to positive government obligations to ensure all people access to the material conditions of a good life, the practical limits derive not just from insufficient political support to do something that is practicable, but from questions of inherent or intrinsic practicality in given circumstances, and especially trade-offs among various goods. For example, money invested to research and develop future drugs is unavailable to provide access to current drugs (or other desirable resources).

   Positive government obligations to provide access to resources are also heavily conditioned by the historical circumstances of a given political community (and of mankind) at a given time. Modern economic affluence, for example, has made possible, or even imperative rights, many things unthinkable even for the richest people in earlier societies, such as a right of access to decent medical care.

that these things should simply be prohibited. In *Dignitatis humanae*, for example, Vatican II declared:

> The demand is likewise made that constitutional limits should be set to the powers of government, in order that there may be no encroachment on the rightful freedom of the person and of associations. This demand for freedom in human society chiefly regards the quest for the values proper to the human spirit. It regards, in the first place, the free exercise of religion in society. This Vatican Council takes careful note of these desires in the minds of men. It proposes to declare them to be greatly in accord with truth and justice. (*DH*, no. 1)

Another example would be the prohibitions of genocide and torture in international law.

Second, CST establishes many norms for the exercise of political and economic power. For example, in *Centesimus annus*, John Paul II clearly states that respect for the dignity of a firm's employees – e.g., not humiliating them – is an essential moral norm for businesses, which cannot be subordinated to the goal of making a profit (*CA*, no. 35). I think it is doubtful that any merely legal (constitutional or statutory) provision could guarantee that people never be humiliated and their dignity offended. Although certain forms of humiliation could be prohibited and certain actions to reflect dignity could be commanded, in the final analysis, a lively and effective respect for human dignity requires people to embrace that moral norm and act on it conscientiously.

With respect to limits on government in the form of not omitting its positive obligations, there are many examples in CST. One example of such limitations is that government *not* refuse to protect the lives of innocent persons, as it does when it permits abortion and euthanasia. Another would be the duty of government to intervene to protect workers' rights, when necessary. *Quadragesimo anno*, for example, says that *Rerum novarum* stimulated civil authority to protect workers:

> A new branch of law, wholly unknown to the earlier time, has arisen from this continuous and unwearied labor to protect vigorously the sacred rights of the workers that flow from their dignity as men and as Christians. These laws undertake the protection of life, health, strength, family, homes, workshops, wages and labor hazards, in fine, everything which pertains to the condition of wage workers, with special concern for women and children. (*QA*, no. 28)

Modern CST (that is, especially since 1960) has recognized an expanding list of particular positive obligations of government – especially regarding economic life and material necessities – as necessary ways to foster the common good.

CST and Institutional Limits

Among the different kinds of limits we have discussed, what is *not* notably present in CST is significant concern for *institutional* limits on government. The emphasis in modern CST on expanding powers of government to meet certain obligations required by the common good has not been matched by a corresponding concern for institutional limits to prevent possible abuse of such expanded powers.

There has been a lively and prudent awareness throughout CST of the possibility of concentrated economic power exercising undue political power. For example, in *Quadragesimo anno*, Pius XI said:

> This concentration of power and might, the characteristic mark, as it were, of contemporary economic life, is the fruit that the unlimited freedom of struggle among competitors has of its own nature produced, and which lets only the strongest survive; and this is often the same as saying, those who fight the most violently, those who give least heed to their conscience.
>
> This accumulation of might and of power generates in turn three kinds of conflict. First, there is the struggle for economic supremacy itself; then there is the bitter fight to gain supremacy over the State in order to use in economic struggles its resources and authority; finally there is conflict between States themselves, not only because countries employ their power and shape their policies to promote every economic advantage of their citizens, but also because they seek to decide political controversies that arise among nations through the use of their economic supremacy and strength. (QA, nos. 107–108)

Talking of the evils of contemporary society, Pius XI goes on to say, with respect to government itself:

> To these are to be added the grave evils that have resulted from an intermingling and shameful confusion of the functions and duties of public authority with those of the economic sphere – such as, one of the worst, the virtual degradation of the majesty of the State, which although it ought to sit on high like a queen and supreme arbitress, free from all partiality and intent upon the one common good and justice, is become a slave, surrendered and delivered to the passions and greed of men. (QA, no. 109)

Likewise, in *Centesimus annus*, John Paul II notes that "Certain demands which arise within society are sometimes not examined in accordance with criteria of justice and morality, but rather on the basis of the electoral or financial power of the groups promoting them" (CA, no. 47).

This concern has spread beyond states in the contemporary world, as international economic combinations can exercise great power beyond political boundaries. Benedict XVI in *Caritas in veritate* points out that, at the time of *Populorum progressio*:

> [p]roduction took place predominantly within national boundaries, and financial investments had somewhat limited circulation outside the country, so that the politics of many States could still determine the priorities of the economy and to some degree govern its performance using the instruments at their disposal. Hence *Populorum progressio* assigned a central, albeit not exclusive, role to "public authorities."
>
> In our own day, the State finds itself having to address the limitations to its sovereignty imposed by the new context of international trade and finance, which is characterized by increasing mobility both of financial capital and means of production, material and immaterial. This new context has altered the political power of States.
>
> Today, as we take to heart the lessons of the current economic crisis, which sees the State's public authorities directly involved in correcting errors and malfunctions, it seems more realistic to re-evaluate their role and their powers, which need to be prudently reviewed and remodeled so as to enable them, perhaps through new forms of engagement, to address the challenges of today's world. (CV, no. 24)[24]

But, despite the recognition that concentrations of economic power can exercise excessive control over government, CST generally does not raise the question of institutional limits on government, to prevent abuse. It enjoins us all to prevent abuses, without suggesting (at least in a general way) that institutional limits might be one way to prevent or limit them.

A rare instance in which modern CST has recognized the need for institutional limits on political power occurs in *Centesimus annus*:

> Pope Leo XIII was aware of the need for a sound theory of the State in order to ensure the normal development of man's spiritual and temporal activities, both of which are indispensable. For this reason, in one passage of *Rerum novarum* he presents the organization of society according to the three powers – legislative, executive and judicial – something which at the time represented a novelty in Church teaching. Such an ordering reflects

---

[24] While there is a strong reaffirmation of subsidiarity in this same document, with respect to international governance ("In order not to produce a dangerous universal power of a tyrannical nature, the governance of globalization must be marked by subsidiarity" [CV, no. 57]), there is no discussion of institutional limits on government.

a realistic vision of man's social nature, which calls for legislation capable of protecting the freedom of all. To that end, it is preferable that each power be balanced by other powers and by other spheres of responsibility which keep it within proper bounds. This is the principle of the "rule of law", in which the law is sovereign, and not the arbitrary will of individuals. (CA, no. 44)

This observation on the necessity of balancing powers of government in order to keep them within proper bounds is also repeated in the *Compendium*.[25] But there is little or no other discussion of institutional limits on government in CST.

In the rest of this chapter, I would like to give reasons why a more prominent consideration of the need for institutional limits on government in CST would be appropriate.

Regulation in the Service of the Regulated

CST has been very emphatic in its recognition of what is sometimes referred to (though not in CST itself) as market failure. This is strongly supported by a well-developed literature in economics on that subject. There is little discussion, however, of government failure.[26] Let me briefly point out two notable instances of government failure.

The first example is the oft-noted phenomenon in the modern regulatory state of regulatory capture. A classic expression of this theory is found in Nobel laureate George Stigler's classic 1971 article "The Theory of Economic Regulation."[27] Regulatory capture occurs when groups that have a significant interest in regulation that affects them – one that is much greater than the relatively limited interest private individuals have or perceive – exert their

---

[25]   Pontifical Council for Justice and Peace, *Compendium of the Social Doctrine of the Church* (2004), no. 408. There is also a reference in John XXIII's *PT*, no. 68, to the separation of different governmental powers – but without associating this idea with checks and balances.

[26]   One early use of the term "government failure" was by Ronald Coase: "It is no accident that in the literature (and for that matter in Professor Caves's paper) we find a category 'market failure' but no category 'government failure.' Until we realize that we are choosing between social arrangements which are all more or less failures, we are not likely to make much headway." See "The Regulated Industries: Discussion," *American Economic Review* 54, no. 2 (March 1964): 195.

   In principle, it should be noted, government failure includes not only government intervention in economic matters that makes things worse than they would have been without the intervention, but also government failure to intervene to rectify market failures of various sorts.

[27]   *The Bell Journal of Economics and Management Science* 2, no. 1 (Spring 1971): 3–21. An article by a more politically liberal Nobel Laureate, Joseph Stiglitz, draws on this theory as well. See Joseph Stiglitz, "The Private Uses of Public Interests: Incentives and Institutions," *Journal of Economic Perspectives* 12, no. 2 (Spring 1998): 3–22.

influence and power to control the regulator, so that the regulation ends up advancing their own self-interest. The classic example of regulatory capture in the United States is the Interstate Commerce Commission, which was established in the late nineteenth century in order to regulate large transportation interests, especially railroads, but ended up by generally regulating on behalf of precisely those interests.[28]

Regulatory capture in the United States was often historically associated with the so-called "iron triangle" of particular economic interests, congressional committees whose jurisdiction encompassed those interests, and bureaucratic agencies that had regulatory power regarding those interests. The interests of each part of the triangle, including the so-called regulators, could often be advanced by supporting the interests that were supposedly the object of the regulation. Note that the idea of regulatory capture is not simply that once in a while some regulatory agency happens to fall under the political sway of the interests it was intended to regulate. Rather, it is that the structure of incentives – especially (1) the intense interests of the entities to be regulated, as compared to the relatively diffuse "public interests" in regulating them, and (2) the personal interests of the regulators, often in the form of current political and financial support, and future job opportunities – makes it *likely* that such "capture" will be a common phenomenon, at least in free democratic societies.

A second, related example of government failure is the now widely used term "crony capitalism."[29] The basic idea here is: "an economy that is nominally free-market, but allows for preferential regulation and other favorable government intervention based on personal relationships. In such a system, the false appearance of 'pure' capitalism is publicly maintained to preserve the exclusive influence of well-connected individuals."[30] There are various forms of the idea, some more associated with the left (arguing that capitalism inherently offers opportunity to the rich and powerful to advance their interests, often through government action), others with the right arguing that it is the fact of government involvement that makes possible distortions in the free market). In either case, however, the idea is that government becomes a servant of particular economic interests rather than seeking the common good. More generally, this can be viewed as a kind of political capture of the

---

[28] See, for example, Timothy B. Lee, "Entangling the Web," *New York Times*, August 3, 2006.

[29] For an interesting discussion of this term, see William Safire, "On Language; Crony Capitalism," *New York Times*, February 1, 1998.

[30] *Business Dictionary.com*, "Crony Capitalism," www.businessdictionary.com/definition/crony-capitalism.html.

regulatory state.[31] Under these circumstances, government can become an instrument of injustice.[32]

CST AND RESPONDING TO GOVERNMENT ABUSE OF POWER

The key question with respect to abuses such as these is how to respond to them. It is possible (and desirable) to articulate general norms that say essentially "don't let these abuses happen." But to make such a norm effective requires more. Returning again to Madison's discussion, we see that in *Federalist* No. 47 he points out that there is widespread agreement on the need for separation of powers: "The accumulation of all powers, legislative, executive, and judiciary, in the same hands, whether of one, a few, or many, and whether hereditary, self-appointed, or elective, may justly be pronounced the very definition of tyranny." After identifying the different powers, "the next and most difficult task is to provide some practical security for each, against the invasion of the others." But, he warns, experience shows that "parchment barriers" – simply writing into a constitution that the separation of powers shall be respected – are inadequate, because of the "encroaching spirit of power." What then can be done?

In *Federalist* No. 51, Madison suggests that the separation of powers should be maintained by "so contriving the interior structure of the government as that its several constituent parts may, by their mutual relations, be the means of keeping each other in their proper places." This is the familiar American idea of checks and balances:

[31] "Regulation is also subject to 'political capture'; indeed, political capture may be a much greater threat than capture by producer groups outside of the political system. Where political capture occurs, the regulatory goals are distorted to pursue political ends. Under political capture, regulation becomes a tool of self-interest within government or the ruling elite." See J. Jalilian, C. Kirkpatrick, and D. Parker, "The Impact of Regulation on Economic Growth in Developing Countries: A Cross Country Analysis," in *Regulating Development: Evidence from Africa and Latin America*, ed. E. Amann (Edward Elgar Publishing, 2006).

[32] In this section, I have focused especially on the potential for government capture by private economic interests, because there is common ground on both sides of the political spectrum in opposition to this kind of abuse. This is not the only possible form of government abuse of power. Government can also be in the service of ideologies (think of Marxist-Leninism, for example) or in the service of a majoritarian coalition of the "have-nots" in society that use their power to transfer wealth unfairly from those who have earned it justly to those who have not (Aristotle's original description of "democracy" as one of the corrupt forms of government that serve private interests rather than the common good). The former example would have been controversial before 1989 (less so now), and the latter example would be highly controversial today.

> But the great security against a gradual concentration of the several powers in the same department, consists in giving to those who administer each department the necessary constitutional means and personal motives to resist encroachments of the others... This policy of supplying, by opposite and rival interests, the defect of better motives, might be traced through the whole system of human affairs, private as well as public. We see it particularly displayed in all the subordinate distributions of power, where the constant aim is to divide and arrange the several offices in such a manner as that each may be a check on the other that the private interest of every individual may be a sentinel over the public rights.[33]

The need for checks and balances is premised on the acknowledgment that among human beings there is a "defect of better motives," which is a reflection of human weakness and malice (and, from the perspective of faith, sin). The capacity of men to abuse power requires that power be checked.

There is one particular implication of the system of checks and balances, however, that has to be emphasized. If checks work to prevent, or at least minimize the possibility of, abuses of government power, they can also work to prevent, or minimize, good action by government as well. So the question becomes: does the value of checks that prevent, or limit the possibility of, government abuse outweigh the lost opportunities for valuable government action? Are the safeguards of the system worth the price that must be paid?

I would argue that, given original sin (by definition universal) and human experience with the abuse of government power, prudence will always counsel providing for effective institutional limits on the power of government – checks built into the structure of government in order to limit the possibility of abuses. The particular form and scope of these checks will inevitably vary with the particular form of government and with the circumstances (history, social structure, political culture) of a given nation or people.

There is no guarantee, of course, that checks and balances will prevent "rent seeking" – and, in fact, those who seek to advance their self-interest at the expense of the common good will certainly try to use the checks to advance their self-interest (e.g., by preventing the adoption of reasonable government regulation of private interests). But government has a potential for monopoly power that exceeds the reach of even powerful private combinations, because it has the exclusive power to make and enforce law.

---

[33]   James Madison, *Federalist* no. 51.

Government and Economic Regulation

What are the implications of this analysis for CST and its teaching on government regulation of economic affairs?

The possibility of the abuse of regulatory power does not lead to the conclusion that there should be no government power to regulate economic affairs. Since any power can be abused, that logic would lead to a denial of any government power at all. Perhaps even more importantly, an absence of government action doesn't mean that there is no abuse of power – it just means that power will be in (unregulated) private hands, especially those with economic and other kinds of private power. As Madison argues in *Federalist* No. 51: "In framing a government which is to be administered by men over men, the great difficulty lies in this: you must first enable the government to control the governed; and in the next place oblige it to control itself."[34] A recognition of the second half of that principle (the need to control government to prevent abuse of its power) cannot lead to ignoring the first half of the principle (the need for government to control the governed). Why do we have government, after all? Governments are instituted among men to secure the rights with which men are endowed by their Creator. In a world with no, or excessively weak, government, the weak and the poor – the most vulnerable – are left at the mercy of the strong, the rich, and the powerful.

Government must have the necessary power to control the governed, to protect the rights of all. But government is no magic talisman, whereby the people invariably use government justly, to protect against abuse of private power. As John Paul II powerfully described in *Evangelium vitae*, and again in *Centesimus annus*, democratic nations can fall prey to the temptation to do injustice: "a democracy without values easily turns into open or thinly disguised totalitarianism."[35] This can occur, not only in the area of life issues (the focus of *Evangelium vitae*), but also in other areas, including the realm of economic regulation, wherein government can be captured by private interests to accomplish their own unjust purposes. How, then, to provide for necessary limits on abuse?

One approach would be to identify the ways in which the regulatory state can be configured in order to reduce the likelihood, or at least the extent, of such self-serving practices. There is an economics literature that offers valuable observations on how to do this.[36] At the same time, it must be observed

[34] James Madison, *Federalist* no. 51.
[35] CA, no. 46, quoted in the CSDC, no. 407. See also *Evangelium vitae*, no. 20.
[36] See, for example, H. Jalilian, C. Kirkpatrick, and D. Parker, "The Impact of Regulation on Economic Growth in Developing Countries: A Cross-Country Analysis," in *World*

that the same forces that lead to abuses may forestall the adoption of institutions and practices that would limit those abuses.

There is also a literature – especially in public choice economics – that raises the question whether the forces leading to abuse of government regulatory power might counsel against vesting too much regulatory power in government.[37] For example, lawmakers might choose to establish, instead of a broad regulatory regime that requires frequent or great government action, a legal framework that ensures effective competition in the marketplace, in order to prevent the concentration of economic power in a few enterprises and provide nongovernmental checks on economic power.

Competition – especially unbridled or completely unregulated competition – has come in for a great deal of criticism in CST, but there is one positive discussion of it in recent CST. Pius XI's condemnation in *Quadragesimo anno* of competition as a directive principle of economic life acknowledged that competition can be an effective instrument or tool:

> Just as the unity of human society cannot be founded on an opposition of classes, so also the right ordering of economic life cannot be left to a free competition of forces. For from this source, as from a poisoned spring, have originated and spread all the errors of individualistic economic competition. Destroying through forgetfulness or ignorance the social and moral character of economic life, this teaching held that economic life must be considered and treated as altogether free from and independent of public authority, because in the market, i.e., in the free struggle of competitors, economic life would have a principle of self-direction which would govern it much more perfectly than would the intervention of any created intellect. But free competition, while *justified and certainly useful provided it is kept*

Development 35, no. 1 (January 2007): "Economic development is seen not simply as a matter of amassing economic resources in the form of physical and human capital, but as a matter of 'institution building' so as to reduce information imperfections, maximise economic incentives and reduce transaction costs. Included in this institution building are the laws and political and social rules and conventions that are the basis for successful market production and exchange. In particular, relevant modes of conduct in the context of the regulatory state might include probity in public administration, independence of the courts, low corruption and cronyism, and traditions of civic responsibility. 'Institution building' including building a 'good' regulatory regime is one of the most difficult problems facing developing countries and the transition economies at the present time (Kirkpatrick and Parker, 2004)."

[37] "Likelihood of regulatory capture is a risk to which an agency is exposed by its very nature. This suggests that a regulatory agency should be protected from outside influence as much as possible. Alternatively, it may be better to not create a given agency at all lest the agency become victim, in which case it may serve its regulated subjects rather than those whom the agency was designed to protect. A captured regulatory agency is often worse than no regulation, because it wields the authority of government." *Wikipedia*, s.v. "Regulatory Capture," https://en.wikipedia.org/wiki/Regulatory_capture.

within certain limits, clearly cannot direct economic life – a truth which the application of this evil individualistic spirit has more than sufficiently demonstrated. (*QA*, no. 88, emphasis added)

The *Compendium* observes, more positively, that

A truly competitive market is an effective instrument for attaining important objectives of justice: moderating the excessive profits of individual businesses, responding to consumers' demands, bringing about a more efficient use and conservation of resources, rewarding entrepreneurship and innovation, making information available so that it is really possible to compare and purchase products in an atmosphere of healthy competition.[38]

Although "the market cannot find in itself the principles of its legitimization," it can be a useful instrument. It can achieve things – such as moderating excessive profits – that might otherwise be attempted by direct government regulation.

Conclusion

The primary point of this chapter is not that CST ought to adopt a particular stance regarding the specific institutional limits on government that should be employed, or how much government power ought to be limited in order to prevent the bad consequences of its likely abuse. These are questions of prudence, and involve factual judgments that are best left to free discussion among conscientious Catholics and other men of good will – especially those who have detailed professional knowledge of the particular context and circumstances.

My point, rather, is that it is a significant gap in CST that it barely considers the issue of government abuse of power at all, that it hardly shows an awareness of its existence. And, just as CST is right to advocate the use of government power to secure the common good in various ways, it should also consider (as an important element of the common good) the need for institutional limitations on government power, in light of the ways that government often, in predictable ways, damages the common good by its interventions.

[38] CSDC, no. 347. Interestingly, the previous paragraph on the benefits a free market can offer is able to cite *Centesimus annus* on several points, but this paragraph on the benefits of competition is unfootnoted – suggesting that the point has not been made in the social encyclicals.

15

The Moral Principles Governing the Immigration Policies of Polities

Kevin L. Flannery, SJ

The present essay is an attempt to make philosophical – and ultimately theological – sense of Catholic Social Teaching (CST) regarding immigration. Set out first (in section 1) are the major ideas of the relevant Church teaching and then (in section 2) the philosophical basis of this teaching. Section 1 is itself divided into two subsections: the first (1.1) on Church teaching up to and including the pontificate of Pius XII; the second (1.2) on some more recent statements coming out of the Holy See. Section 2 is divided into three subsections (2.1 to 2.3). The first is on Aristotle, the second on Thomas Aquinas, and the third on Francisco de Vitoria. Section 3 returns to questions left open in section 1.2, offering some answers to those questions in the light of the philosophical ideas set out in section 2, plus others to be found primarily in the writings of Thomas Aquinas.

1 CHURCH TEACHING

The sheer vastness of the Church's teaching on immigration is an obstacle to its comprehensive grasp. Fortunately, however, Pope Pius XII, surely aware of this obstacle, promulgated in August of 1952 the apostolic constitution *Exsul familia*, in which he summarizes the history of the Church's expressed care for those who, for one grave reason or another, find themselves outside their homeland.[1] Offered in subsection 1.1 are some of the main points of Pius XII's summary of this tradition. Subsequent to the pontificate of Pius XII, neither the problem of immigration nor the amount of Church teaching has

---

[1] Pius XII, Apostolic Constitution *Exsul familia* (Apostolic Constitution on Migration) (1952): AAS 44 (1952) 649–704. Traditionally, Vatican documents, especially papal documents, are known by their incipit, in this case the words "Exsul familia." The document appears on the Vatican's website in Latin; there is no official English translation.

diminished. And so – with even less pretension of being comprehensive – considered in subsection 1.2 are a number of official statements that supplement that which is found in *Exsul familia*.

1.1 *Exsul familia*

Pius XII's *Exsul familia* has often been called the *magna charta* of the pastoral care of migrants and refugees.[2] The incipit ("Exiled family") refers to the Holy Family, described in the document's first sentence as "emigrating into Egypt and, exiled in Egypt, taking refuge from the fury of an evil king." The pope, who had sheltered Jews throughout Rome during the World War II, says that that family is

> the archetype, exemplar, and the protection of emigrants, foreign residents, and refugees of every origin and of whatever time and place, who, constrained by either fear of persecution or by want, are forced to abandon their native land, their beloved relatives and dear neighbors and friends, and to make for foreign lands.[3]

In its official title, *Exsul familia* is described as "An Apostolic Constitution on the spiritual care of emigrants," which might suggest that its main concern is with Christians; but the words just quoted, "refugees of every origin and of whatever time and place," as well as other remarks in the document make it apparent that its concern is not so limited. Its main concern is to demonstrate that the care of migrants *in general* is a constant throughout the Church's history. Mentioned first in this regard is St. Ambrose (d. 397), who, following the defeat of the Emperor Valentine by the Goths in the battle of Adrianopolis (today Edirne in northwestern Turkey), advocated the selling of sacred vessels in order to help refugees. "Who is so hard-hearted, severe, and unyielding," writes Ambrose, "as to be displeased that a man is saved from death, a woman from the impurities of the barbarians (which are worse than death) – or that adolescents or children or infants be saved from contact with idols, by which, out of fear of death, they would be defiled."[4]

[2] Pontifical Council for the Pastoral Care of Migrants and Itinerant People and Pontifical Council Cor Unum, *Welcoming Christ in Refugees and Forcibly Displaced Persons: Pastoral guidelines* (Vatican City: Vatican Press, 2013), no. 16; also Pontifical Council for the Pastoral Care of Migrants and Itinerant People, *Erga migrantes caritas Christi: AAS* 96 (2004) 772. *Exsul familia* is spoken of as the *magna carta* also by Velasio De Paolis, created a Cardinal by Benedict XVI [Graziano Tassello and Luigi Favero, eds., *Chiesa e Mobilità Umana: Documenti della Santa Sede dal 1883 al 1983* (Rome: Centro Studi Emigrazione, 1985), xxxii].
[3] *AAS* 44 (1952), 649.
[4] Ambrose of Milan, *De officiis*, ed. Maurith Testard (Turnhout: Brepols, 2000), 146 [*Patrologia Latina* 16, col. 140].

The document praises those Christians who "labored to relieve from their abject condition those Negroes nefariously borne away from their homeland and subject to impious trafficking in the ports of America and Europe, and to gain them for Christ."[5] Pius XII also mentions his two namesakes, Pius VI (d. 1799) and Pius VII (d. 1823), whose efforts on behalf of those fleeing the French Revolution and taking refuge "within the confines of the Pontifical Dominion and especially in Rome" are commemorated in the fifty volumes published by the Vatican under the title *De charitate Sedis Apostolicae erga Gallos*.[6]

Pius XII mentions too his own efforts in this regard during and after the 1948 war in Palestine, today's Israel:

> Innumerable refugees, having undergone unspeakable sufferings, were forced to abandon what was their own and to wander elsewhere, here and there, throughout Libya, Syria, Jordan, Egypt and the region of Gaza. These individuals, having in common only shared calamities, rich and poor, the faithful and those yet without the light of faith, presented a horrendous and mournful spectacle.[7]

These efforts included the erection of the Pontifical Mission for Palestine, which, with funds supplied especially by the Catholic Near East Welfare Association, set up by the bishops of United States, "even now relieves the dire needs of Arab refugees." The latter statement remains true today.[8]

So, this *magna carta* of the pastoral care for migrants is clear indication that active concern for migrants is deeply embedded in what it means to be Christian: it is part of Christianity's very essence. But Pius XII exhorts not only Christians. He notes that he himself has "insistently appealed to the governors of polities and the heads of institutions, as many as are upright and willing men, with earnest attention to consider and to resolve the most serious situation of refugees and migrants."[9] He quotes his own letter, dated December 24, 1948, to the Bishops of the United States:

> You know with what anxious thoughts and concern we have followed the plight of those who, pressed by revolutions in their fatherland or by

---

[5] AAS 44 (1952), 652. A lengthy note then quotes documents from the pontificates of Benedict XV (d. 1922) and Leo XIII (d. 1903) regarding such trafficking.

[6] AAS 44 (1952), 654–656. Another lengthy note, this one of over four pages, details the contents of these volumes. Not insignificant is the fact that the Papal State is referred to (656) as the Pontifical Dominion or Sovereignty (*Pontificia Ditio*).

[7] AAS 44 (1952), 677.

[8] AAS 44 (1952), 678. The Pontifical Mission for Palestine has offices in Jerusalem, Amman, and Beirut. It has been operated since its inception by the Catholic Near East Welfare Association, whose headquarters are in New York.

[9] AAS 44 (1952), 681.

dearth of employment and sustenance, have been compelled to leave
their native environs and transfer their premises to foreign nations. Not
only compassion for the human race but also the law of nature itself
demands that ways of migrating be opened up to these people. For the
creator of all things provided all good things in the first place for the good
of all.[10]

1.2 *More Recent CST*

In years subsequent to Pius XII's pontificate, what Mary Ann Glendon has
identified as "rights language" began to appear more and more frequently in
Church teaching regarding migration.[11] This could have unfortunate consequences in so far as the term "right" in most contemporary languages signifies
something that morally cannot be denied a person in any situation whatsoever.
Sometimes the term is quite appropriate, as when reference is made to
innocent persons' right to life. But sometimes the rights referred to, if understood in the strong sense as absolutely inviolable, would be logically incompatible with other genuine obligations and duties binding upon other
individuals. Such apparent incompatibility makes the task of giving
a convincing account of the teaching more difficult – unless (as shall be
argued below) the teaching is interpreted in accordance with the tradition
from which it has emerged.

Even some recent documents, however, employ a qualified understanding
of rights. See the 2013 document *Welcoming Christ* (§26):[12]

> The encyclical letter *Pacem in terris* stated that "every man has the right to
> life, to bodily integrity, and to the means which are suitable for the proper
> development of life; these are primarily food, clothing, shelter, rest, medical

---

[10] AAS 44 (1952), 683. The letter to which Pius XII refers can be found at AAS 41 (1948), 69–71.
Immediately after the just quoted remarks, Pius XII however adds: "And so, since the land, no
matter where, provides abundantly for the nourishment of many, and although the dominion
of individual polities [*singularum Civitatum dominium*] is to be revered, this ought not to
bring it about that, for scarcely sufficient and equitable reasons, access is denied to the needy
born elsewhere and provided with sound morals – when this does not impede public utility,
which is to be weighed in the proper balance."

[11] See Mary Ann Glendon, *Rights Talk: The Impoverishment of Political Discourse* (New York:
Free Press, 1991). See also John Finnis, "Migration Rights," in *Human Rights and Common
Good: Collected Essays, Volume III* (Oxford: Oxford University Press, 2011), 116–124 and
John Finnis, "Absolute Rights: Some Problems Illustrated," *American Journal of
Jurisprudence* 61, no. 2 (2016): 195–215. To be considered below is the meaning of the word
jus – often translated "right" – in authors such as Thomas Aquinas and Francisco de Vitoria.

[12] See above, note 2. *Welcoming Christ* bears the signatures of Antonio Maria Cardinal Vegliò
and Robert Cardinal Sarah, the presidents of the two councils responsible for the document.

care, and finally the necessary social services."[13] It can be deduced that if a person does not enjoy a humane life in his/her country, he or she has the right, under certain circumstances, to move elsewhere, since every human person has an inherent dignity which should not be threatened.

At first glance, this passage could be read as saying that a person's inviolable right to emigrate corresponds to a reciprocal inviolable right to immigrate into the country of that person's choice. Fortunately, however, the second sentence includes the phrase "under certain circumstances." It is also worth noting that into the same sentence the document inserts a note that quotes a passage in the 2004 document entitled *Erga migrantes caritas Christi*, which in turn cites and summarizes a number of passages in Vatican II's *Gaudium et spes*. The passage in *Erga migrantes caritas Christi* recognizes that at no. 65 "the Council reaffirmed the right to emigrate" but also says that at no. 87 it "recognized the right of the public authorities, in a particular context, to regulate the flow of migration."[14]

Similarly, a few sections later, *Erga migrantes caritas Christi* cites Paul VI and John Paul II affirming (as the document puts it) "the fundamental rights of the person, in particular the right to emigrate so that the individual can turn his abilities, aspirations and projects to better account," adding immediately however (in parentheses) that this is affirmed "in the same context with the right of every country to pursue an immigration policy that promotes the common good."[15]

Other sections of *Welcoming Christ* speak more straightforwardly than the one quoted just above (§26) about the complex moral issues presented by

---

[13]   John XXIII, Encyclical Letter *Pacem in terris* (On Establishing Universal Peace in Truth, Justice, Charity, and Liberty) (1963): *AAS* 55 (1963), 257–304. The passage quoted is found at no. 11. No. 9 also speaks of rights (and duties), saying that they "flow as a direct consequence from [man's] nature." "These rights and duties," it says, "are universal and inviolable, and therefore altogether inalienable." The encyclical refers here to Pius XII's radio message on Christmas Eve, 1942 [*AAS* 35 (1943), 9–24] and to John XXIII's own sermon of January 4, 1963 [*AAS* 55 (1963), 89–91]. In the former, the word "right" [*diritto*] is occasionally used; but there is no talk of rights in the sense of inviolable human rights belonging to each individual. Pius XII speaks rather of the *tranquillitas ordinis*, as understood by Saints Thomas Aquinas and Augustine [*AAS* 35 (1943), 10]. Near the beginning of the message, he says that the Church "does not intend to take sides with respect to the one or other of the particular and concrete forms with which individual peoples and states attempt to resolve the enormous problems of the internal order and international cooperation, when these forms respect the divine law" [*AAS* 35 (1943), 9–10].

[14]   Pontifical Council for the Pastoral Care of Migrants and Itinerant People and Pontifical Council Cor Unum, *Welcoming Christ*, no. 26 (p. 18, n. 24); Pontifical Council for the Pastoral Care of Migrants and Itinerant People, *Erga migrantes caritas Christi*, no. 21 (773).

[15]   Pontifical Council for the Pastoral Care of Migrants and Itinerant People, *Erga migrantes caritas Christi*, no. 29 (777). The *Catechism of the Catholic Church* makes much the same point in the second paragraph of no. 2241.

migrants. In its opening remarks, for example, it speaks interestingly of a right *not* to emigrate, and then immediately acknowledges that some are forced to emigrate because of persecution or natural calamities. It then continues:

> Others decide to leave their homeland because they can no longer afford to live with dignity there, while there are those who simply want to find better life opportunities abroad. There is, therefore, a difference between migrants and refugees or asylum seekers. This must be maintained notwithstanding the fact that there are "mixed" migration flows, in which it becomes difficult to distinguish between classically-defined asylum seekers, those in need of other kinds of protection or aid, and those who simply take advantage of the migration flow. (no. 1)

We shall come back to these distinctions below.

2 THE PHILOSOPHICAL BASIS OF THE TRADITIONAL TEACHING

Since the expression of recent teaching on immigration proves sometimes to be less than satisfactory from a theoretical perspective, it makes sense to delve into the philosophical basis of its previous expression. In the present context, it is impossible to survey all of the major thinkers who, in a more philosophical mode, have contributed to the Church's traditional teaching on the migration of peoples. One does, however, attain some understanding of that basis by considering the relevant writings of Thomas Aquinas, whose thought informs the Church's moral teaching in general, and those of the Spanish renaissance philosopher and theologian, Francisco de Vitoria, a truly prophetic voice in these matters, often described as one of the fathers of international law. Vitoria's influence upon Christian thought and teaching regarding international relations – including the teaching reviewed by Pius XII in *Exsul familia* – has been profound.[16] Since, however, both Aquinas and Vitoria frequently invoke Aristotle, especially his *Politics*, in support of their own ideas related to the migration of peoples, it makes sense to begin with Aristotle and proceed then to consider, in order, Aquinas and then Vitoria.

[16] See Quentin Skinner, *The Foundations of Modern Political Thought* (Cambridge; New York: Cambridge University Press, 1978), 135–173; and Anthony Pagden, *The Fall of Natural Man: The American Indian and the Origins of Comparative Ethnology*, Cambridge Iberian and Latin American Studies (Cambridge: Cambridge University Press, 1982), 60, but also passim.

2.1 Aristotle

One of the two major philosophical issues connected with immigration – the other being the basis of the sovereignty of polities – is the basis of the right to be accepted into a polity as a citizen. In a way, the thought of Aristotle is not the most obvious place to go to in order to establish such a basis since, as is well known, Aristotle accepts the idea of "natural slaves," such as would, by their very nature, be excluded from citizenship. But, setting that problem aside, Aristotle also maintains that "man is by nature a political animal."[17] This idea – this principle – would be used by subsequent authors to argue that to leave a person (a refugee) and/or his family without at least the prospect of citizenship in some polity is to deprive that person of something that is part of human nature itself. If a citizen of the polity being asked to take in a refugee (or refugees) were later to find himself similarly without a polity, his nature too – and not just he as an individual – would cry out for citizenship.

This principle is connected with Aristotle's metaphysical ideas regarding the unity of material substances. Aristotle holds that the parts of such a substance get their very sense from the substantial unity of which they are a part. A hand is a hand because it is part of a living human body; if it is cut away from that body, or if the body dies, the hand is no longer a hand except in an equivocal sense. A polity, as Aristotle insists against Plato, has not the same, strong unity that a living human body has; but it has a unity of sorts and one that emerges from human nature (or natures) as such.[18] And so, to deprive a person of the prospect of citizenship is something like amputating a hand from the body: the "hand" is no longer really a hand; the human being without a polity is less of a human being.

Aristotle presupposes such an analysis in the very passage in which he says that "man is by nature a political animal."

---

[17]   Aristotle *Politics* 1.2.1253a2–3. Employed in this chapter is the Revised Oxford Translation [*ROT*], adjusted occasionally for the sake of consistency with the present argument. For instance, *ROT* translates the word *polis* as "state"; this is changed here to "polity" in order not to exclude any entity with a claim to sovereignty, whether, for instance, an ancient *polis* (the notably small city-state) or a country as large as the United States.

[18]   Wolfgang Kullmann discusses the "biological origin of the idea that man is a political animal" at Wolfgang Kullmann, "Man as a Political Animal in Aristotle," in *A Companion to Aristotle's "Politics,"* eds. David Keyt and Fred D. Miller Jr. (Oxford/Cambridge, MA: Blackwell, 1991), 108–114. In the concluding remarks of his essay, Kullmann mentions Aristotle's personal experience of frequent – if irregular – political catastrophes. "If states reappear immediately after such catastrophes, that is only a confirmation of the biological constancy of the political character of man" [Kullmann, "Man as a Political Animal in Aristotle," 116–117].

Hence it is evident that the polity is a creation of nature, and that man is by nature a political animal. And he who by nature and not by mere accident is without a polity [ἄπολις], is either a bad man or above humanity; he is like the "tribeless, lawless, hearthless one," whom Homer denounces. The natural outcast is forthwith a lover of war; he may be compared to an isolated piece at draughts.[19]

Aristotle associates the man described here as "by *nature* and not by mere accident" without a polity, not with godliness (such as would be "above humanity"), but with the man whom Homer denounces and who really has lost something of his humanity. The refugee finds himself, although "by accident," in that same situation of exile from humanity. Just as any human being, by virtue of his reason and language capacities, is owed the truth – or, more precisely, not to be lied to – so any human being, by virtue of his political nature, is owed citizenship.[20] Only in the latter case, the "owing" is more imperative since the alternative deprivation concerns not just individual linguistic exchanges but the threat of permanent – or at least long-term – exile.

Connected with the issue of a right to be accepted into a polity as a citizen is the question, just what does it mean to be a citizen? For, if a citizen is defined, for instance, as one who is accepted by a ruler (or rulers) as a citizen, then there can be no natural right to become a citizen – not even for refugees. A cursory acquaintance with Aristotle's political theory might suggest that he was inclined toward such an approach since – not without a good deal of to-ing and fro-ing – in his evaluation of various types of regimes, he does in the end maintain that the best is monarchy.[21] Even this position, however, is severely qualified since he also holds that

---

[19] *Pol.* 1.2.1253a1-7. Within a few lines, Aristotle speaks about the relationship between being-without-a-polity and armed violence. "For man, when perfected, is the best of animals, but, when separated from law and justice, he is the worst of all; since armed injustice [ἀδικία ἔχουσα ὅπλα] is the more dangerous, and he is equipped at birth with arms [ὅπλα], meant to be used by intelligence and excellence, which he may use for the worst ends" [*Pol.* 1.2.1253a31-35]. The word ὅπλα, usually signifying the arms used in battles, can also signify the limbs of any animal used in self-defense; see Aristotle's *De partibus animalium* 4.10.687a26. That man has arms Aristotle associates with his nature as an intelligent being [687a8-12]. A nonhuman animal might have "arms" but it can just use *them* to defend itself; by contrast, man's hand "is spear, and sword, and whatever other weapon or instrument you please" [687b3-4]. That same rational nature allows man to use his arms to, for instance, play the flute [687a10-16].

[20] Cf. *Nicomachean Ethics* [=EN] 4.7.1127a28-29 and *Pol.* 1.2.1253a10-15.

[21] See *Pol.* 3.18.1288a33-36, where he says that the best form of government is one which is administered by "one man, or a whole family, or many persons, excelling all the others in excellence"; but at *EN* 8.10.1160a35-36 he says that the best regime is a monarchy.

governments which have a regard to the common interest are constituted in accordance with strict principles of justice, and are therefore true forms; but those which regard only the interest of the rulers are all defective and perverted forms, for they are despotic, whereas a polity is a community of freemen [*Pol.* 3.6.1279a17-21].

In the end, Aristotle acknowledges – one might even say "concedes" – that his definition of the term "citizen" is "best adapted to the citizen of a democracy" [*Pol.* 3.1.1275b5-6]. A polity is a composite of citizens, he says, and this composite is distinct from the government – that is to say, from the statesman and the lawgiver [*Pol.* 3.1.1274b36-38]. He goes on immediately to say that, "He who has the power to take part in the deliberative or judicial administration of any polity is said by us to be a citizen of that polity; and, speaking generally, a polity is a body of citizens sufficing for the purposes of life" [*Pol.* 3.1.1275b18-21].[22] This is not to say, however, that the existence of a polity depends upon the consent of the citizens (or prospective citizens): besides going against the idea that monarchy is the best regime, that would contradict the idea that the existence of polities is natural. The core idea is rather that of providing that which suffices "for the purposes of life."

2.2 *Thomas Aquinas*

St. Thomas makes a number of remarks – unfortunately not contained in a single treatise but scattered about in a number of works – in which it becomes clear nonetheless that he regards as basic the Aristotelian principle that "man is by nature a political animal." At *Summa Theologiae* 1.96.4,[23] for instance, where the question is whether even in the state of innocence a man would have been subject to another, he replies that yes, he would have been, "because man is naturally a social animal, and so in the state of innocence men lived socially."[24] Thus, the inclination to be part of a polity is not, as, for

---

[22]   Terence Irwin [Terence Irwin, "The Good of Political Activity," in *Aristoteles' "Politik": Akten Des XI Symposium Aristotelicum*, ed. Günther Patzig (Göttingen: Vandenhoeck & Ruprecht, 1990),82] translates the opening words of this passage as "the one who has the opportunity to share," translating ἐξουσία in 1275b18 as "opportunity" instead of "power." Irwin's translation probably comes closer to Aristotle's point. This article by Irwin considers in some detail Aristotle's thesis that the political life is an intrinsic part of human happiness: see especially 73–84.

[23]   The abbreviation for this work is *ST*. The abbreviation for the first part is *ST* 1 followed by the question number and the article number, as in *ST* 1.96.4 (*Summa Theologiae* part one, question 96, article 4). The second part of *ST* is divided into two subparts: they are abbreviated *ST* 1-2 and *ST* 2-2 respectively; part three is abbreviated *ST* 3.

[24]   Thomas is following here William of Moerbeke's translation of *Pol.* 1.2.1253a1-3: *ex his igitur manifestum, ... quod homo natura civile animal est.*

instance, in Cicero, a desire to be free from the threats of others that prevail in the state of nature; we have that inclination even in that state in which all are sinless and nonthreatening.[25]

In *ST* 1–2.95.4, Thomas says that to the "law of nations" [*ius gentium*] pertain such things as "just buyings and sellings"; without these, he says, "men cannot live in the company of others – which is of the law of nature since man is naturally a social animal, as is proved in the first book of the *Politics*." Noteworthy here are two things: first, that Thomas connects the idea that man is a social or political animal with the law of nations, which means that it is authoritative not just within individual polities but also among them; secondly, that he associates the same idea explicitly with commerce. We shall see below that this aspect of our political nature is pivotal also for Vitoria in his argument that the native inhabitants of the Americas were deserving of full recognition as humans and also that the Spanish (or at least their descendants) quite reasonably might have become citizens of polities they found in the Americas.[26]

Nor does Thomas shy away from invoking Aristotle's principle even while giving a positive account of those who seek perfection in the solitary religious life. He says, first of all, that solitude is not the essence of the perfection sought but rather a means to it. He says too that solitude is fitting to the contemplative who has already achieved perfect self-sufficiency.[27] In order to achieve this state, one of two things is necessary: either a special grace from God (as in the

---

[25] As Quentin Skinner points out [Skinner, *The Foundations of Modern Political Thought*, vol. 2, 157], both Robert Bellarmine and Francisco Suárez also strongly opposed the positing of a savage state of nature. Bellarmine, arguing explicitly against Cicero, says that it is false, indeed impossible, that "there was a time in which men wandered about in the manner of beasts, only to be persuaded by a certain wise and eloquent man, by the power of his eloquence, to convene and to live together" [Robert Bellarmine, *Opera omnia*, ed. Justinus Févre (Paris: Vivès, 1870–74), vol. 3, 10]. Bellarmine is referring to Cicero's *De inventione* 1.2: *Nam fuit quoddam tempus, cum in agris homines passim bestiarum more vagabantur* ... (and so on). Interestingly, in this passage, Cicero says that in that primitive state there were no "legitimate marriages."

[26] Thomas, however, following Aristotle, is somewhat wary of merchants (see *Pol.* 7.6.1327a11-40); see *De regno* 2.7.38–49, 80–88 (see also below, note 33).

[27] See *EN* 10.7.1177a27-b1, where Aristotle discusses the self-sufficiency of the (philosophical) contemplative. This man, says Aristotle, "even when by himself, can contemplate truth, and the better the wiser he is; he can perhaps do so better if he has fellow-workers, but still he is the most self-sufficient" [1177a32-b1]. The concept of self-sufficiency is a constitutive part of the idea that membership in a polity is natural for man. Aristotle also holds that men naturally divide up into families; this natural character has to do, however, with the survival of the species: the family is not self-sufficient (see *Pol.* 1.2, in particular 1253a18-19). On the strained relationship between man as political animal, friendship, and self-sufficiency, see Irwin, "The good of political activity," 84–95.

case of John the Baptist, who went to the desert even as a boy) or "the exercise of virtuous action" such as requires society. The article (*ST* 2–2.188.8) finishes with this remark:

> A man can lead a solitary life in two ways: first, as one who, on account of his savage character, cannot bear human society – and this is bestial; secondly, in order to adhere totally to divine things – and this is above the human. And so the Philosopher says in the first book of the *Politics* that "he who has no contact with others is either a beast or a god – that is, a godly man."

In his commentary on the *Politics*, Thomas also discusses Aristotle's stipulation (seen above) that that man becomes a "bad man" [φαῦλος] who is without a polity "by nature and not by mere accident" (or "not through bad fortune").[28] Thomas gives as examples of those who are without a polity by accident "those who are not citizens on account of fortune, because, for instance, they have been expelled from a polity, or on account of poverty must cultivate fields or tend animals." He compares such an individual to one whose hand is amputated or who is deprived of food.[29] Thomas's position on immigration, especially of political refugees but also of what are sometimes called "economic refugees," is based upon the conviction he shares with Aristotle that man is by nature a political animal. A good and holy man might *choose* a solitary life, having once achieved the perfection of his social nature; but no man should be forced to live in a situation in which such socialization – possibly the prelude to a contemplative life in solitude – is rendered impossible for either him or for his family.[30]

Thomas also makes a number of pertinent remarks in his *De regno ad regem Cypri* ("On rule, to the king of Cyprus").[31] In the first chapter of *De regno*,

[28] ὁ ἄπολις διὰ φύσιν καὶ οὐ διὰ τύχην [*Pol.* 1.2.1253a3-4]. The word τύχη is often translated "chance" or "fortune."

[29] Thomas Aquinas, *Sententia libri Politicorum*, vol. 48, *Opera Omnia* (Rome: Commissio Leonina, 1971), 1.1b.83–92. As indicated above, in as much as it is essential to human nature to be part of a polity, Aristotle would possibly compare such a person rather to the severed "hand" no longer properly called a hand. The Marietti edition [Thomas Aquinas, *In libros Politicorum Aristotelis expositio*, trans. R. M. Spiazzi (Turin/Rome: Marietti, 1951), no. 35] has *vel cum privatur oculo* instead of *vel cum privatur cibo*. Under the former reading ("or when someone is deprived of an eye"), it might be possible to read the remark in the more Aristotelian way. Thomas's speaking of the one who tends fields, etc., as outside the polity presupposes Aristotle's definition of the citizen as one who "has the power to take part in the deliberative or judicial administration" [*Pol.* 3.1.1275b18-19]. See above, note 22.

[30] Here (and elsewhere in this essay) I use the term "man" in its inclusive sense to include both males and females.

[31] The work is also sometimes called *De regimine principum*; here I shall refer to it simply as *De regno*. In the present essay, reference is made to the text as established in the Leonine edition of Thomas's works [Thomas Aquinas, *De regno ad regem Cypri*, vol. XLII, *Opera Omnia*, Cura et

which is about the meaning of the term "king," Thomas cites Aristotle's principle ("It is natural to man to be a social and political animal, living within a multitude") and contrasts man's situation with that of other animals ("to whom it is proper to live singly"), speaking then immediately (as does Aristotle at *Pol.* 1.2.1253a31-35) of man's hands (in Aristotle, "arms"), such as must be guided by reason.[32] Mere animals have in a way an advantage over men, he says, for they know by nature and as individuals that certain single things are necessary for – or inimical to – their well-being and survival: they might know, for instance, that the wolf is dangerous or even that this particular herb is hygienic. But man knows such matters "only in general" [*solum in communi*], that is, by his intellect – which means that he is dependent for his very survival upon a society that will teach him, for instance, as part of medicine, which particular things are healthful and which not [*De regno* 1.1.39–55].

But, although Thomas certainly recognizes that our shared human nature imposes a strong obligation with respect to those who have been forced to leave behind their native polities, he also recognizes that the same natural need of common protection that imposes that obligation also imposes upon sovereign polities the obligation to be prudent in its dealings with nonnatives and in accepting immigrants. In *De regno*, for instance, while discussing the self-sufficiency required of a polity, he remarks:

> Dealings [*conversatio*] with foreigners, according to Aristotle's teaching in his *Politics*, corrupts the morals of many citizens, for it necessarily happens that foreigners, nurtured under other laws and customs, in many regards behave in a manner that differs from the morals of the citizens and so, when citizens are led by their example to behave similarly, civic life [*civilis conversatio*] is disturbed.[33]

And in *ST* 1–2.105.3 (on the judicial precepts of the old law regarding foreigners), where he again cites Aristotle (*Pol.* 3.2.1275b22-24), he warns that some foreigners, "not yet having the public good firmly at heart," could attempt something contrary to that good. He notes that the Jews of the Old Testament admitted Egyptians, after the third generation, into the "fellowship [*consortium*] of the people." The reason was that Egyptians had "a certain affinity"

studio Fratrum Praedicatorum (Rome: Editori di San Tommaso (Leonine Commission), 1979), 417–471].

32 *De regno* 1.1.20–38; see also above, note 19.
33 *De regno* 2.7.41–49. Thomas is thinking of *Pol.* 5.3.1303a25-28 and 7.6.1327a11-15. In this passage in *De regno*, Thomas is speaking primarily about dealings with foreign traders; the passage in *Pol.* 5.3, however, is about "the reception of strangers in colonies, either at the time of their foundation or afterwards" [1303a27-28].

toward the Jews. But he notes too that the Ammonites and Moabites, with whom the Jews were constantly at war, were never admitted.

There are other principles in Thomas's writings that are useful in confronting the issues connected with immigration – a couple of important ones will be utilized below – but again, the key principle having to do specifically with immigration is the principle he derives from Aristotle's remark that man is by nature a political animal.

2.3 Francisco de Vitoria

Francisco de Vitoria, like Thomas Aquinas, was a Dominican friar. He was born in the year Columbus (from a European perspective) "discovered" America; he died in 1546. Of his writings, most pertinent to present concerns are *De potestate civili* ("On civil power") and (especially) *De Indis* ("On Indians").[34]

Near the beginning of *De potestate civili*, Vitoria speaks of Aristotle's cardinal idea that "man is a social animal" [*De potestate civili*, 7]. He also speaks of Aristotle's idea that the man who cuts himself off from human society becomes beastly, mentioning in this regard Timon of Athens, a philanthrope turned misanthrope a generation or two before Aristotle.[35] "The family," he

---

[34] The two works mentioned are called *relectiones theologicae: Relectio de potestate civili* and *Relectio de Indis*; used here, however, will be the simpler titles. The term "Indians" refers to the native populations of the Americas; in what follows, the term refers to these same peoples. As Anthony Pagden and Jeremy Lawrance explain in their "Critical note on texts and translations" [Francisco de Vitoria, *Vitoria: Political Writings*, ed. and trans. Anthony Pagden and Jeremy Lawrance, Cambridge Texts in the History of Political Thought (Cambridge: Cambridge University Press, 1991), xxxiii–xxxviii], the manuscript tradition for Vitoria's works is extremely complicated. In the present chapter, all translations of Vitoria are taken from the Pagden/Lawrance volume. The latter does not contain a Latin text, although the two scholars have consulted the available manuscripts and made choices regarding the best readings; in effect, their volume is an English translation of a critical edition that does not (yet?) exist. This is particularly true of their translation of *De potestate civili*, for which, as they say, "there is still no satisfactory critical edition." They do, however, speak highly of the Pereña/Pérez Prendes edition of *De Indis*: Francisco de Vitoria, *Relectio de Indis: o Libertad de los Indios*, eds. and trans. Luciano Pereña and José M. Pérez Prendes, Corpus Hispanorum de Pace (Madrid: Consejo Superior de Investigaciones Científicas, 1967) – although, even there, they do not always follow the published text.

[35] "For that reason I regard Timon of Athens, who was prompted by his inhuman and perverse nature to cut himself off from the companionship of men, as having led a miserable existence; in the opinion of Aristotle such men should be counted as beasts [*Pol.* 1.2.1253a1-7, 31–37]" [*De potestate civili*, 8]. John Jowett, referring to this section in the *Politics*, maintains that Shakespeare, who wrote (or collaborated on) the play *The Life of Timon of Athens*, where the self-exiled Timon is portrayed as truly beastly, "may have known a translation of Aristotle's *Politics* published in 1598" [William Shakespeare and Thomas Middleton, *The Life of Timon of Athens*, ed. John Jowett, The Oxford Shakespeare (Oxford: Oxford University Press, 2004), 29].

says, "provides its members with the mutual services which they need, but that does not make it whole and self-sufficient (*una sibi sufficiens*), especially in defense against violent attack" [*De potestate civili*, 9]. This dependence upon a polity puts man at a certain disadvantage with respect to animals, "for, whereas they are able to understand the things that are necessary for them on their own, men cannot do so" [*De potestate civili*, 8]. "The clear conclusion," says Vitoria, "is that the primitive origin of human cities and commonwealths was not a human invention or contrivance to be numbered among the artefacts of craft, but a device implanted by nature in man for his own safety and survival" [*De potestate civili*, 9].

As in Aristotle and Aquinas, therefore, the idea is that to be without – or to be deprived of – a polity is to lack something of one's very nature or essence. Vitoria would distinguish such membership not only from membership in a family, which is natural in another sense, but also – and more emphatically – from any membership that depends upon human decision (a "social contract"):

> To be sure, if men or commonwealths did not derive their power from God, but formed an agreement to set up a power over themselves for the public good, then this would be a [human] power, such as the power which members of a religious order ascribe to their abbot. But it is not so.[36]

"Civil societies," he goes on to say, "which have no sovereign and are ruled by a popular administration often boast of their liberty, accusing other civil societies of being the servile bondsmen of sovereigns." He calls this a "stupid and ignorant idea" and cites Aristotle's remarks [*Pol.* 3.7.1279a32-39] on the various types of government (monarchy, aristocracy, and popular rule). "I say that there is no greater liberty in one than in another of these" [*De potestate civili*, 19].[37] It was apparently Vitoria's understanding of sovereignty, as deriving not from consent but from divine law as manifest in the natural human desire for safety and survival in community, that led Pope Benedict XVI to

---

[36]   *De potestate civili*, 17. Corresponding to the word "commonwealths" is the word *respublica* [Francisco de Vitoria, *Obras de Francisco de Vitoria: Relecciones teologicas*, ed. and trans. Teofilo Urdanoz (Madrid: Biblioteca de Autores Cristianos, 1960),164]. In this quotation, "this" refers to royal power, although Vitoria's general argument in this section is that "we must say about royal power exactly what we have asserted about the power of the commonwealth, namely that it is set up by God and by natural law [*a Dio et a iure naturali*]" [*De potestate civili*, 17]. Also, given this context, when he speaks in the quotation of power deriving from God, he understands that power as deriving more immediately from natural law.

[37]   Pagden and Lawrance connect these remarks with the fact that Vitoria, "in common with most scholastics refused to accept the republican claim that virtue derives from participation and not protection" [*De potestate civili*, 21].

associate him with the concept of sovereignty as "the responsibility to protect."³⁸

Vitoria brings these same ideas to his analysis in *De Indis* of the ethical factors pertinent to his native polity's entrance into South America and its treatment there of the local peoples. Unlike many of his academic contemporaries, he makes strong arguments to the effect that these "Indians" should be treated as citizens of their own polities and not as beasts or as (Aristotelian) natural slaves.³⁹

De Indis consists of three questions, each comprised, in Thomistic fashion, of several articles. The first asks, "whether these barbarians" – that is, the Indians – "before the arrival of the Spaniards, had true dominion, public and private"⁴⁰ The second considers "by what unjust titles the barbarians of the New World passed under the rule of the Spaniards"; the third, "the just titles by which the barbarians of the New World passed under the rule of the Spaniards."⁴¹ In order to understand Vitoria's position on both the respect due to the Indians and on immigration, it is important to note that arguments he makes in distinct questions – especially the first and the third – intersect in so far as they depend upon the same principles.

In concluding the first question, article six, Vitoria argues against those who say that the Indians do not have dominion because they are like madmen or because they are irrational.

---

³⁸ AAS 100 (2008) 333. Benedict XVI made the remark in his 2008 address to the General Assembly of the United Nations; the text contains no specific reference to a work by Vitoria. The same idea, with reference to Benedict's address, is mentioned at *Welcoming Christ* no. 69 (Pontifical Council for the Pastoral Care of Migrants and Itinerant People and Pontifical Council *Cor Unum*).

³⁹ Pagden, in a book that appeared in 1982, argued that Vitoria's ultimate position in *De Indis* was that the Indians were not natural slaves but rather "nature's children," which would be to stop short of granting them full exercise of dominion or territorial sovereignty [Pagden, *The Fall of Natural Man: The American Indian and the origins of comparative ethnology*, 57–108]. In their 1991 book, Pagden and Lawrance are not quite so assertive: "Vitoria conceded, therefore, that the Castilian crown might (but only might) be able to claim a right to hold the Indians and their lands in tutelage until they reached the age of reason" [Vitoria, *Vitoria: Political Writings*, 36]. To the present author it appears that Vitoria is not at all inclined to think of the Indians as children, although Vitoria is also aware that he does not have logically or empirically compelling arguments against that position.

⁴⁰ "Dominion" [*dominium*] in Vitoria's vocabulary refers to one's ownership or being master [*dominus*] of property, private or public. In the latter sense, it is equivalent to sovereignty.

⁴¹ Immediately after this third title, we read: "I shall now discuss the legitimate and relevant titles by which the barbarians could have come under the control of the Spaniards" [*De Indis*, 277]. The conditional phrasing used here, "could have come," [*venire potuerunt*] is significant. See Francisco de Vitoria, "*De indis et De iure belli relectiones*": *Being parts of the "Relectiones theologicae XII*," ed. Ernest Nys, Classics of International Law (Washington: The Carnegie Institution of Washington, 1917), 257.

The proof of this is that they are not in point of fact madmen, but have judgment like other men. This is self-evident, because they have some order [*ordo*] in their affairs: they have properly organized cities, proper marriages, magistrates and overlords [*domini*], laws, industries, and commerce, all of which require the use of reason. They likewise have a form [*species*] of religion, and they correctly apprehend things which are evident to other men, which indicates the use of reason [*De Indis*, 250].

Vitoria is drawing here upon Aristotle's *Pol.* 7.8.1328b4-15, which lists six things that are indispensable for the existence of a polity (a *polis*): food, crafts, arms ("for the members of a community have need of them, and in their own hands, too, in order to maintain authority both against disobedient subjects and against external assailants"), "a certain amount of revenue," religion, and "sixthly, and most necessary of all, there must be a power of deciding what is for the public interest, and what is just in men's dealings with one another."

Vitoria's mention of commerce [*commutationes*], which corresponds to Aristotle's revenue and "men's dealings with one another," is particularly important since it is also the basis of his argument, in question 3, that "the Spaniards have the right [*jus*] to travel and dwell in those countries [in the Americas], so long as they do no harm to the barbarians, and cannot be prevented by them from doing so" [*De Indis*, 278].[42] This "right to travel and to dwell" is also a right to immigrate. Vitoria offers a number of proofs for the existence of the right, citing first of all "the law of nations" (*ius gentium*), which "either is or derives from natural law," and mentioning too that, "in the beginning of the world, when all things were held in

[42] Vitoria's understanding of the term *jus* ("right") is discussed below. Vitoria's remark here about the "right to travel" is an indication of the seriousness – indeed, the severity – with which the justice of entering foreign lands was regarded by Vitoria and others of his day and prior. The right [*jus*] falls under the title of question 3, article 1, "First just title: of natural partnership and communication [*naturalis societatis et communicationis*]." St. Augustine regarded the denial of the "right of passage" grounds for war. At *Quaestiones in Heptateuchum* book 4, no. 44, Augustine considers the Israelites' conquering and then settling in the cities of the Amorites, as recorded at Numbers 21–25. He says: "It is reasonable to mention the sense in which they waged just wars, for innocent transit had been denied, which, by virtue of the most equitable law of human society [*iure humanae societatis aequissimo*], ought to have been granted." This passage is cited by Pagden and Lawrance [*De Indis*, 278 (no. 75)], together with part 2 of Gratian's *Decretum*, 23.2.3 (*Innoxius transitus . . .*) [Aemilius Ludovicus Richter and Aemilius Friedberg, eds., *Decretum Magistri Gratiani*, vol. 1, *Corpus Iuris Canonici* (Leipzig: B. Tauchnitz, 1879), 895]; the latter is in fact a quotation of the remark by Augustine. See also Jonathan Barnes, "The just war," in *The Cambridge History of Later Medieval Philosophy: From the Rediscovery of Aristotle to the Disintegration of Scholasticism*, 1100–1600, eds. Norman Kretzmann, Anthony Kenny, and Jan Pinborg (Cambridge: Cambridge University Press, 1982), 781.

common, anyone was allowed to visit and travel through any land he wished." Although the law of nations permitted the division of property, he says, "it was never the intention of nations to prevent men's free mutual intercourse [*invicem communicationem*] with one another by this division" [*De Indis*, 278].

And then, after a couple of other proofs, he offers three more:

> Fifth, exile is counted amongst the punishments for capital crimes, and therefore it is not lawful to banish visitors who are innocent of any crime.
>
> Sixth, it is an act of war to bar those considered as enemies from entering a city or country, or to expel them if they are already in it. But since the barbarians have no just war against the Spaniards, assuming they are doing no harm, it is not lawful for them [the Indians] to bar them [the Spaniards] from their homeland
>
> A seventh proof is provided by Virgil's verses:
> > What men, what monsters, what inhuman race,
> > What laws, what barbarous customs of the place,
> > Shut up a desert shore to drowning men,
> > And drive us to the cruel seas again![43]

One thinks immediately of Lampedusa, the island off the coast of Sicily, approaching which in recent times a number of ships carrying migrants have sunk.[44]

With explicit reference to Aristotle, Vitoria goes on to maintain that

> ... if children born in the Indies of a Spanish father wish to become citizens (*cives*) of that community, they cannot be barred from citizenship or from the advantages enjoyed by the native citizens born of parents domiciled in that community. The proof is that the law of nations (*ius gentium*) clearly defines a "citizen" (*civis*) as a man born in a community (*civitas*).[45] The confirmation is that man is a civil animal (*animal civile*), but a man born in one community is not a citizen of another community; therefore, if he is not a citizen of the first community, he will not be a citizen of any community, and this would be inequitable by the law of nature and of nations (*ius naturale et gentium*). [*De Indis*, 281]

---

[43]   *De Indis*, 278; Pagden and Lawrance give Dryden's translation of *Aeneid* 1.539–40: *Quod genus hoc hominum? quaeve hunc tam barbara morem / Permittit patria? hospitio prohibemur arenae!* A less poetic translation would be: "What race of men is this? What barbarous nation permits such a custom? To prohibit the hospitality of the sea shore!"

[44]   See, for instance, Deborah Ball, "Hundreds of migrants believed dead in shipwreck off Libya," *Wall Street Journal*, April 19, 2015.

[45]   Pagden and Lawrance cite the *Codex Iustinianus* 10.40.7 [Paulus Krueger and Theodorus Mommsen, eds., *Corpus Iuris Civilis* (Berlin: Weidmann, 1900–1905)].

3 PRINCIPLES, COMMON AND PROPER, AND DEFEASIBLE *JUS*

That brings us back to the problem raised initially in section 1.2 above: that CST often seems to posit an absolute and even universal human right to immigrate and yet also suggests that this right can, in certain circumstances, justifiably not be honored. And it might now also appear that the same problem is present in Thomas Aquinas and Francisco de Vitoria. In both these authors, a very strong "right" to immigrate finds expression; and yet, according to the same authors, this right is not incompatible with the sovereignty of nations and *their* right – indeed, their duty – to control immigration.

In Thomas, however, we find an explanation of how principles or precepts of the natural law (although not all the principles or precepts of the natural law) might in certain circumstances not apply. In *ST* 1–2.94.4 he draws a distinction between the common principles and the proper principles of the natural law.[46] "Although," he says, "in the common principles there is a certain necessity, the more one descends to the proper principles, the more one encounters defect," that is, failure to apply. As an example of a common principle, he mentions the principle that one should conduct oneself according to reason. As an example of a proper principle, he mentions the principle that "deposits are to be returned" – that is to say, if someone leaves with another an item of personal property, the person holding the item is obliged to return it to its owner when the latter requests it.

But, says Thomas, it could happen that the item in question is a lethal weapon and the person requesting its return does so "for the purpose of fighting against the fatherland." In this case, it would be "injurious and so irrational" to return the item when it is requested; and so the proper precept fails to apply. What in other circumstances would be the rational thing to do, in these circumstances is not rational. It is not as if, in those circumstances, there is present an act having the characteristics mentioned in the proper principle, which characteristics are simply ignored; in the "intention of the legislator," such a case never fell under the proper principle, even if such

---

[46] The words "common" and "proper" correspond to Aristotle's τὰ κοινά (common things) and τὰ ἴδια (proper things) in his *Posterior Analytics* 1.10. Thomas described the proper principles as "quasi conclusions" of the common principles. (Emphasis should be placed upon the word "quasi" since, in the syllogistic, conclusions follow necessarily from their premises.) *ST* 1–2.94.4 is cited in Pope Francis's apostolic exhortation *Amoris laetitia* (On Love in the Family) (2016), no. 304. For a criticism of that document's use of *ST* 1–2.94.4, see Thomas V. Berg and Kevin L. Flannery, "*Amoris Laetitia*, Pastoral Discernment, and Thomas Aquinas," in *Nova et Vetera* (English) 16 (2018): 95–101.

exclusions were (or are) never mentioned.[47] The proper precept that deposits are to be returned depends upon the common precept requiring one to conduct oneself according to reason. To return the weapon to the person intent on harming the fatherland would be irrational.

This explanation of how certain principles of the natural law work is useful – even essential – in dealing with immigration. We might formulate the relevant common principle in the following way: "Polities should recognize rights." The proper principle would be: "The right to immigrate is to be recognized." The common principle applies to polities as a consequence of their "responsibility to protect," which in turn depends upon the same natural propensity to associate in polities that confers upon individuals the right to immigrate. The term "right" (or *jus*), as used in authors such as Thomas and Vitoria, is like the term "rational" in the common principle of *ST* 1–2.94.4: in certain circumstances, the term is simply inapplicable, for that particular right does not exist. As we have seen, in certain circumstances, it is irrational to return a deposit (e.g., a weapon): such an act of returning never really fell under the common or the proper principle. Similarly, in certain circumstances, there is no *jus* (that is, "just thing to do") *to be* recognized as pertaining to the prospective immigrant, for accepting the immigrant would go contrary to "right" – contrary, that is, to *jus*. Indeed, if accepting an immigrant goes contrary to what is just, there is a "duty" – another translation for the word *jus* – not to accept him.

Thomas discusses the meaning (or meanings) of the term *jus* in the very first article of his very long treatise on justice (*ST* 2–2.57–79). Justice is unusual among the moral virtues in as much as the other moral virtues "perfect a man solely in those things that benefit him with respect to himself." Thus, "the fitting" [*rectum*] for the other virtues, which serves as their proper object, is not to be understood "except in relation to the agent." In the case of justice, however, the fitting, "even independently of relation to the agent," has to do with others. It is a matter of establishing "a certain equality with the other," which is to say that there is present justice only when no one is receiving more than what is due to him. "And so," Thomas concludes, "it is peculiar to justice that, unlike the other virtues, it is determined by its object, which is called 'the just' [*iustum*]. And this indeed is 'the right' [*jus*]. Clearly then the right [*jus*] is the object of justice" [*ST* 2–2.57.1].

A right in Thomas, at least in the primary meaning of the term, is not something that a person *has* (as in "my right to immigrate"); it has to do rather with a person's situation in justice in relation to the rights of others. Pius XII,

---

47   See Thomas Aquinas, *Sententia libri Ethicorum*, vol. 47, *Opera Omnia* (Rome: Commissio Leonina, 1969), 5.16.83–151 (§§1083–86).

following both Thomas and Augustine, would speak in this connection of the
"tranquility of order."[48] To say that a person's relation to the rights of others is
not in order is to say that the *jus* is simply not there. As in the case, mentioned
in *ST* 1–2.94.4, of the return of a lethal weapon to a determined enemy of the
polity, in certain instances a supposed right to immigrate was never included
in the common principle ("polities should recognize rights") or the proper
principle ("the right to immigrate is to be recognized"). It is not a matter of
there being a right which in this instance is not respected; "right" in Thomas
(and others) implies that the person's relation in justice *is* in order.

The argument of the present chapter is not that "rights language" (in the
negative sense)[49] cannot be found even in pre–twentieth-century works and/or
Church teaching. John Finnis, having first described the way in which Thomas
understands *jus* in *ST* 2–2.57.1, notes that one finds in Francisco Suárez
(1548–1617) a more individualistic understanding of the term. "Here," says
Finnis, "the 'true, strict and proper meaning' of *jus* is said to be: 'a kind of
moral power [*facultas*] which every man has, either over his own property or
with respect to that which is due to him'."[50] Nonetheless, Thomas's influence
upon traditional CST has been profound, rendering it therefore perfectly capable
of providing answers, when needed, to questions posed by "rights" that ought not
be respected. In earlier teaching, talk of rights was more restrained than is the case
today, for then it was embedded in a more Thomistic understanding of right (*jus*).

Presupposing then this more Thomistic understanding of right, it is possible
to sketch out a few principles in terms of which prudent authorities of
sovereign polities might establish policies regarding the various classes of
potential immigrants mentioned even in more recent CST. As we have
seen, the 2013 document *Welcoming Christ* recognizes a distinction between
refugees (or asylum seekers) and economic migrants. The latter "decide to
leave their homeland because they can no longer afford to live with dignity
there"; the former are *forced* to leave their homelands. It would be remiss not
to mention that some – most likely very few – potential immigrants attempt to
enter another polity in order to harm it; others are quite likely to harm it

---

48 See above, note 13.
49 See above, note 11.
50 John Finnis, *Natural Law and Natural Rights* (Oxford: Oxford University Press, 2011),
    206–207. Francisco de Vitoria, writing some years before Suárez, is insistently on Thomas's
    side in this matter. In his commentary on *ST* 2–2.57.1 he reaffirms the idea that, unlike the
    other moral virtues, the object of justice is "others" and not oneself: *"Differentia ergo est quia
    objectum justitiae dicit ad alios; objecta autem aliarum virtutum solum ad se"* [Francisco de
    Vitoria, *De Justitia (Qq. 57–66)*, vol. 3, *Comentarios a la secunda secundae de Santo Tomas*,
    ed. Vicente Beltran de Heredia (Salamanca: Consejo Superior de Investigaciones Científicas,
    1934), 2].

(given, for instance, previous criminal activity). And so, it is possible to posit (in a very rough manner) three categories of immigrants: refugees, economic immigrants, and dangerous elements. No attempt will be made here to define with any precision the bounds of these categories.[51]

A prudent authority of a sovereign polity would be obliged by natural law in the strongest manner – if not absolutely – to admit genuine refugees. At the beginning of his account in the *Nicomachean Ethics* of the virtue of prudence (or φρόνησις), Aristotle says: "Now it is thought to be a mark of a man of [φρόνησις] to be able to deliberate well about what is good and expedient for himself, not in some particular respect, e.g. about what sorts of thing conduce to health or to strength, but about what sorts of thing conduce to the good life in general" [*EN*, 6.5.1140a25-28]. He goes on to speak of "Pericles and men like him" – that is, men involved in politics – as being able to see "what is good for themselves and what is good for men in general" [1140b5-10]. One is not forcing an interpretation upon Aristotle to say that this coincidence of the individual and the common good – see also *EN* 1.2.1094b7-10 – is connected with his principle that man is a political animal. But we have also seen that this principle is the basis not only of the sovereignty of polities but also of the right [*jus*] to immigrate. A political authority who refuses to admit genuine refugees would be acting against his own nature.

With respect to the second category of immigrant, we can also speak of a right [*jus*], in the sense that it would be a just thing to accept an economic immigrant into a polity, provided it is likely that the person's (or the family's) acceptance will contribute to the good of the polity itself. It should also be presupposed that this outcome is indeed likely since it is natural for men to enter into what Vitoria calls "mutual intercourse" and to find in the common their individual good. On the other hand, it would be imprudent of a civil authority to accept into a polity members of the third category. Refusing entrance – or setting up screening procedures with the purpose of excluding such dangerous elements – does not contradict the proper principle that "the right to immigrate is to be recognized" since, in accordance with Thomas's *ST* 1–2.94.4, accepting such persons is not to be recognized as falling under that principle. To accept such persons would be to fall short of the "responsibility" – that is, the duty or *jus* – "to protect."

---

[51] On the issue of distinguishing refugees and economic migrants, see Cristopher Llanos, "Refugees or Economic Migrants: Catholic Thought on the Moral Roots of the Distinction," in *Driven from Home: Protecting the Rights of Forced Migrants*, ed. David Hollenbach (Washington, DC: Georgetown University Press, 2010), 249–269, and William R. O'Neill and William C. Spohn, "Rights of Passage: The Ethics of Immigration and Refugee Policy," *Theological Studies* 59, no. 1 (1998): 84–106.

CONCLUSION

As is made overwhelmingly clear in Pius XII's *Exsul familia*, the Church has always called upon Christians and non-Christians alike to be open to immigrants and, especially, to refugees. But it also teaches that responsibility for such decisions rests with those in positions of political – and not ecclesiastical – authority. Speaking of the autonomy of, among other strictly human activities, the governance of polities, the Second Vatican Council document *Gaudium et spes* asserts: "If by the autonomy of earthly affairs we mean that created things and societies themselves enjoy their own laws and values which must be gradually deciphered, put to use, and regulated by men, then it is entirely right to demand that autonomy." Natural law itself, therefore, which falls under divine law, acknowledges that polities have the right – and, indeed, the duty – to make decisions regarding immigration. But the same section of *Gaudium et spes* goes on to say: "But if the expression, 'the autonomy of temporal affairs,' is taken to mean that created things do not depend on God, and that man can use them without any reference to their Creator, anyone who acknowledges God will see how false such a meaning is" [no. 36].

16

International Finance and Catholic Social Teaching

Robert G. Kennedy

It is a common misperception that the Catholic social tradition, or at least its modern version, begins with the publication of *Rerum novarum* in 1891. On the contrary, as Pope Leo XIII acknowledges in the opening paragraphs of the encyclical, he had published no fewer than six encyclicals on political issues (which are indeed social) before turning his attention to the "new things" of the commercial/industrial economy of late nineteenth-century Europe. The social teaching of the Church, in fact, is as old as the Church itself, though it has taken different shapes in response to the challenges of time and place. Through much of the Middle Ages, for example, from the time of Pope Gregory I (early seventh century) into the fourteenth century, the social teaching of the Church was preoccupied with political questions, specifically the tensions between civil and ecclesiastical authorities.

This changed gradually as trade and economic activity was reanimated in Europe beginning in the twelfth century. The Church began then to turn its attention to economic issues, led by scholars of law who had rediscovered the model and importance of Roman civil law. They explored questions of contract, sale, lending, and price, which explorations came eventually to influence moral theologians such as St Thomas Aquinas. Still later, in the sixteenth and seventeenth centuries, prompted by growing trade with the East and the European discovery of the New World, Italian and Spanish Scholastics offered remarkably sophisticated reflections on money and banking, government finance, and (again) the morality of lending at interest.[1] Their work rightly belongs to the Church's social tradition.

---

[1] A useful introduction to the Spanish Scholastics is Alejandro Antonio Chafuen, *Faith and Liberty: The Economic Thought of the Late Scholastics*, 2nd ed. (Lanham, MD: Lexington Books, 2003). Two more comprehensive studies, by Marjorie Grice-Hutchinson, are *The School of Salamanca* (Oxford: Clarendon Press, 1952) and *Early Economic Thought in Spain 1177–1740* (London: George Allen & Unwin, 1978). See also Joseph A. Schumpeter, *History of*

At the same time that the universities were developing their economic theories, the shock of the Reformation, followed by a series of political revolutions, prompted the Church's pastors to focus their attention once again on pressing political questions. The expansion of trade had affected urban populations, especially those tied to the sea, but rural populations (who remained the majority) were slow to change, both politically and economically. A cascade of "new things," beginning with the French Revolution in the final decade of the eighteenth century, brought dramatic changes to Europe, first in the political arena and then more slowly but no less profoundly in the economic arena. The political changes posed existential threats to the Church and could not be ignored. It was not until 1891, after some stability had returned to the Church's situation, that Pope Leo XIII felt that it was appropriate, and indeed urgent, to turn the Church's attention to economics once more. In doing so, he drew implicitly on centuries of canonical and theological reflection that preceded him.

One of the characteristics of the Church's magisterium regarding social issues is that it is shaped and elicited by challenges of the day.[2] That is to say, it is topical and not at all a systematic, comprehensive reflection on principles. It is not surprising, then, that in the 128 years since the publication of *Rerum novarum*, popes and bishops have had a great deal to say about the situation of workers and the poor but very little of substance to say about systems of finance. Yet systems of finance, to say nothing of trade and markets, have

---

Economic Analysis (London: Allen & Unwin, 1954), who devotes a long chapter to Scholastic theologians.

[2] For example, in the decades following the French Revolution (1789), when the Church faced the first deliberately secular society in Europe, the popes sought to articulate a rationale for the Church's role and independence in such a culture. In the final decades of the nineteenth century, following many other revolutions and the loss of the Papal States, Pope Leo XIII addressed the rise of democratic forms of government and the role of Catholic citizens in such states. Later, he and his successors turned their attention to the emergence of both industrial economies and, eventually, the phenomenon of globalization, brought on by dramatic changes in transportation and communication. More recently, Pope Francis has spoken to issues of human and natural ecology [Encyclical Letter *Laudato si'* (On Care for Our Common Home) (2015)]. In this large collection of papal literature, principles belonging to a more fundamental and comprehensive social doctrine can often be discerned [e.g., the principle of subsidiarity in Pope Pius XI, Encyclical Letter *Quadragesimo anno* (On Reconstruction of the Social Order: 40th Anniversary of *Rerum novarum*) (1931), nos. 79–80] but only on rare occasions do the popes step back and offer foundational reflections on their own. Pope John Paul II's early encyclical, *Laborem exercens* (On Human Work) (1981), is one example of the exception, as are parts of Pope Benedict XVI's encyclical letter *Deus caritas est* (On Christian Love) (2005) and encyclical letter *Caritas in veritate* (On Integral Human Development in Charity and Truth) (2009). Both men were university professors early in their lives.

much to do with the creation and distribution of wealth and the prosperity of communities – all of which condition the lives of workers and the poor.

It is worth noting that profound social changes are often difficult to perceive as they occur and almost always are best understood at some distance in time. In our own era, technical advances in communication, information management, and transportation have made a genuine globalization possible, with all its benefits and flaws. However, in all humility, we must say that we do not adequately understand the implications and consequences of these changes, or even their trajectory or end state. The medievals and the Scholastics, like Pope Leo, were able to offer guiding principles for addressing the new things of their times, in spite of the limitations of their knowledge. Similarly, despite the uncertainty we acknowledge concerning the economic arena, the Church's social teaching does have resources to bring to bear on the analysis and design of systems of finance, both on the domestic and international levels (which are increasingly interconnected).

In this regard, it has not only a critique to offer (which it does more often than not) but also principles for reform. It is not the purpose of this chapter to highlight the usual defects of human behavior related to money – greed, selfishness, deceit, anxiety, indulgence, theft, cheating, and exploitation. These are well known, and no reasonable person defends them nor is there much real benefit derived from broad exhortations to avoid these tendencies. Instead, the intention here is to suggest how the concepts and principles of Catholic Social Teaching might promote a healthier and more effective structuring of financial systems, with special attention given to the particular problems of international operations and relationships.

These concepts and principles are distinctive though not for the most part unique to the Catholic social tradition. Taken as a coherent whole, however, they probably do represent a moral tradition unique to Catholicism, though most of the concepts and principles are not rooted in revelation or in uniquely Catholic understandings of the Gospel. They therefore are accessible, in principle, to citizens who do not share the Christian faith. As a consequence, they do form a perspective, as Catholic leaders have long insisted, that deserves a place in public discussions of social issues. Even so, a modern criticism of the social tradition complains that it has not been sufficiently grounded in biblical theology, and efforts have been made to remedy this defect.[3]

---

[3] A prominent example of this is the US Bishops' pastoral letter, *Economic Justice for All* (1986), which includes an extended reflection on biblical foundations.

The task of identifying and applying concepts and principles is not as straightforward as it might seem. By and large, the pastors of the contemporary Church, in venues such as papal and curial documents, tend to offer either very general principles or merely to make observations about states of affairs. The general principles offer little practical guidance, and the descriptive observations are often problematic and subject to debate. By its own admission, the Church has no technical solutions to offer in the economic arena, even if it frequently offers some in any event.[4] Furthermore, the struggles the Church has endured in recent decades to bring its own financial house in order – to reform its own accounting practices, for example, to bring them into line with modern standards – clearly indicate that it is itself not yet a practical model for the secular order.

This should not be distressing. As the Second Vatican Council emphasizes so powerfully, the role of the clergy is to teach, govern, and sanctify the Church. By contrast, the vocation of the lay faithful – who are no less members of the Church than the clergy – is to internalize the teaching of the Gospel and on this basis to work to renew and to perfect the temporal order.[5] To put it another way, it is not the role of the clergy to devise technical solutions for secular challenges but rather it is their charge to be faithful witnesses to the Gospel and to nurture and encourage lay men and women, whose work is in the secular order, to devise these solutions. And there is no irony in observing that where this is successful, the laity in turn become the teachers, instructing the clergy about the best practices for managing the operations of the Church (e.g., accounting, investments, and risk management) that mirror secular activities.

This work of penetrating the temporal order with the spirit of the Gospel effectively begins with the acceptance by individuals of the invitation to make their occupations authentic Christian vocations. That is, the occupation

---

4   The Church consistently affirms the proper autonomy of the political order but nevertheless insists on its freedom to call attention to the moral order and the demands this makes on political action. See, for example, Second Vatican Council, Pastoral Constitution *Gaudium et spes* (On the Church in the Modern World) (1965), no. 36; Pope Paul VI, Encyclical Letter *Populorum progressio* (On the Development of Peoples) (1967), no. 13; Pope Paul VI, Encyclical Letter *Octogesima adveniens* (A Call to Action on the 80th Anniversary of *Rerum novarum*) (1971), no. 4; Pope John Paul II, Encyclical Letter *Sollicitudo rei socialis* (1987), no. 41; Pope John Paul II, Encyclical Letter *Centesimus annus* (On the 100th Anniversary of *Rerum novarum*) (1991), nos. 43, 47; Pontifical Council for Justice and Peace, *Compendium of the Social Doctrine of the Church* (Vatican City: Libreria Editrice Vaticana, 2004), no. 424; *Caritas in veritate* (2009), no. 9.
5   Second Vatican Council, Decree *Apostolicam actuositatem* (On the Apostolate of Laity) (1965), no. 2.

becomes a genuine path to holiness as well as an avenue for charity and beneficence, which enables persons to put their gifts, resources, and talents at the service of the common good and the building of the Kingdom.[6] This is no less true of the occupations associated with finance, each of which can be embraced and transformed as a vocation, whether on the local, national, or international level. Just as grace builds on nature, each occupation so transformed builds upon professional competence (which is indispensable) to elevate both the ends pursued and the means employed.

What, then, does Catholic Social Teaching have to offer to finance? Even if the Church does not have a model to offer in its own activities, it does propose a vision of human fulfillment and the common good as well as a set of moral norms oriented to this vision. To be sure, much of what the Church proposes is in tension with the convictions of contemporary secular society about the human person, about the nature of a good human life, and about the proper functioning of the economic sector. But the functional areas of a system of finance, within the overall economy, for the most part represent means rather than ends in themselves. The ends are supplied by a source outside the system. Even in modern Western society, it is not too late to ask whether these ends will emerge from a Christian vision or a secular one.[7]

If we wish to offer a Christian vision and propose Christian ends to a system of finance, we need to be clear about the ordinary operations of the system and how these operations might be refocused in the light of the Catholic tradition.

MONEY AND THE SYSTEM OF FINANCE

When people speak of someone as a "financier" or learn that an individual works in "finance," they probably think of Wall Street, the City of London, or a stock exchange in general. In fact, "finance" is a complex system concerned with the management of objects that can be valued in money. Some of these objects are tangible (such as real estate, precious metals, livestock, and works of art) while others are intangible (such as

[6] Second Vatican Council, Dogmatic Constitution *Lumen gentium* (On the Church) (1964) nos. 31, 33, 39–40. Pontifical Council for Justice and Peace, "The Vocation of the Business Leader: A Reflection" (2012), no. 6.

[7] One might also add that much of the world, in contrast with the West, is still shaped by religious convictions and commitments. To the extent that a global system of finance demands in practice a commitment to a secular world view, it may encounter cultural and even legal resistance, especially in emerging economies.

the right to receive cash flows, equities, bonds and debt obligations, and contracts of various sorts).

In very broad terms, at its best the system of finance serves the common good insofar as it facilitates the effective and efficient management of money (and objects that can be valued in money) to serve the flourishing of human beings. When it functions well, whether locally, nationally, or globally, it serves a number of instrumental purposes: it manages money directly, it makes possible the sharing of risk, and it promotes the accumulation, allocation, and productivity of capital.

We might also note that the God of Jews and Christians is a God of abundance, not scarcity. The resources of the earth are more than sufficient to supply the needs of the entire human family but these resources are unevenly distributed. Many can only be accessed through hard work and ingenuity, which typically also require assembling financial resources. As a consequence, human well-being requires a high degree of interaction and cooperation. Many factors have to be successfully managed, including law and politics, technology, and finance.

Consequently, the system of finance involves a number of functional areas and participants, principal among which are banking, insurance, investments, and government.[8] What unites them into a system, at least loosely, is the focus on money and its management.

FINANCE AS A CHRISTIAN VOCATION-

One of the great strengths of Christianity is its capacity to recognize the good and the true in the many forms in which they arise in different cultures and systems. And once recognizing the good and the true, Christians have had considerable success in accommodation. They have been able to shape customs and practices and professions according to the Gospel and its vision of human fulfillment but at the same time they have also been shaped by the pagan or secular visions they encounter.

Foundational to the Christian approach to professional work, and indeed to all social action, are the virtues of justice and charity. The natural virtue of justice firmly inclines a person to give to others what they need and deserve to have. More profoundly, it aims at sustaining the radical equality (in dignity) of

---

[8]   It is worth noting that these divisions are somewhat porous. Insurance companies engage in some activities that are very like banking, investment firms often seek to manage and distribute risk, while governments may be both consumers and regulators of the services offered by participants in the markets.

human persons and of making viable the civic friendship that makes social life possible.[9] Thus justice and the civic friendship it promotes require individuals in a community to regard one another as equals in dignity, to respect this equality in their relationships with one another, and to repair it whenever circumstances or actions create practical inequalities. Even so, justice may not require individuals, or states, actively to seek the well-being of others to whom they are not formally obligated. The theological virtue of charity, however, supplements the requirements of justice. Charity enables and inclines a person to love God as well as to love and to serve the image of God apparent in other human persons.[10] Animated by these virtues, Christian professionals exhibit a lively sense of the practical good they can do for others and a determination not to achieve goods for themselves by committing or tolerating injustices.

The particular challenge to Christians working in finance is to bring their vision of the purpose of business activity, a vision inspired by the Gospel and the social teaching of the Church, to their work without diluting that vision to conform to the ordinary practices of the profession.[11] To be sure, Christians must acknowledge and master the technical requirements of professional practice – piety is not a substitute for competence – and the many elements of the good and the true that they encounter. (There is, for example, no distinctly Christian method of calculating the time-value of money.) But professional techniques are usually morally neutral and can be employed in the pursuit of many ends, both good and bad. The task facing the Christian is to employ sound techniques in an excellent manner in pursuit of genuine human well-being.

As the tradition reminds us, to embrace one's work as a genuine vocation often requires a change of heart and mind. The Christian soldier may need to go to war but he does so to defend the common good and to restore peace, not

9   To be sure, in most societies throughout history, some groups of individuals – slaves, women, outcasts, foreigners – were not considered persons in the political sense and therefore did not deserve all of the benefits of just treatment. Nor were they properly eligible to participate in civic friendship. Nevertheless, the concept of justice was honored, even if its benefits were not extended to everyone.

10 In this regard, the Christian understanding of charity goes well beyond the classical notion of justice. The Greeks considered friendship to be possible only among equals and therefore denied that human and divine persons could be friends. Charity makes possible friendship with God, and it enhances the possibilities for friendship, and therefore benevolence, among all persons.

11 "Catholic social thought does not just challenge economic outcomes, but even more significantly, it challenges the philosophical preconceptions upon which economic and financial theories are constructed." Charles M. A. Clark and David A. Zalewski, "Rethinking Finance in Light of Catholic Social Thought," *Journal of Catholic Social Thought* 12 (2015): 19–44, esp. 32.

to dominate and to conquer. The Christian lawyer must be an advocate for truth and justice and must at times turn away clients who have other objectives. The Christian physician can never be content to see patients merely as technical problems to be solved nor may she permit her technical skills to serve patient wants in opposition to real human goods.

Similarly, Christians in finance must bring a clear vision of the goods to be served in the functional area in which they practice and must be ready, to the extent that they can, to shape their day-to-day operations according to this vision. This vision is concretely informed by three basic concepts drawn from the social tradition: the logic of gift, the virtue of solidarity, and the concept of integral human fulfillment.[12]

THE LOGIC OF GIFT

To be a Christian disciple is to accept the fact that human persons are dependent upon the Creator for their very being. And more than this, everything that we have, from our lives, our families, and our friends to our talents, opportunities, and material possessions, are gifts. The world itself and the very order we discover in the universe must be taken as given; they are not the products of human creativity even if they may be the instruments of human work.

We are therefore born in debt and dependency, and ought to live our lives in gratitude.[13] As Christians, we realize that we are the beneficiaries of the merciful love of God and that the love and mercy we have been shown should be the model for our relationship with other persons. Pope Benedict XVI made this notion of gift and gratitude a central theme in his encyclical *Caritas in veritate*, and in so doing added a new element to Catholic Social Teaching that has particular relevance to finance.[14]

Pope Benedict drew a contrast between "the logic of gift" and other "logics" that are dominant in social life.[15] These other logics are principally the logic of the market (which he also calls "commercial logic" or "economic logic") and

[12] We will assume here, without extended discussion, that the demands of justice must everywhere be observed in all dimensions of a system of finance.
[13] *CSDC*, no. 195.
[14] *CV*, no. 34. Pope Benedict XVI's treatment of gift and gratuity is an innovation in social doctrine, though it reflects in important respects the classic idea of beneficence as a specification of the virtue of charity. See Thomas Aquinas, *Summa Theologiae*, secunda secundae, question 31.
[15] *CV*, no. 39. By "logic" here is meant a set of convictions about the world and society as well as practical principles drawn from these convictions that direct action and define what is rational in a given sphere of life.

the logic of the state. Each tells us what we must do, what we must give, in order to participate successfully in the economy and in civic life. But each is incomplete because neither acknowledges the full truth about the human condition and human fulfillment. Both need to be supplemented by "the principle of gratuitousness as an expression of fraternity" in order to be open to the fullness of human development.[16]

The suggestion here is that both the logic of the market and the logic of the state focus too narrowly on material aspects of human well-being and therefore fail to address integral human development or the development of the whole person.[17] Pope Benedict proposes that creating space for enterprises that deliberately move beyond the logic of the market to embrace the logic of gift can enrich the economic arena.[18] By this he means that investors and other constituents might evaluate the success of a business by recognizing values other than (but not apart from) profitability, that maximizing shareholder wealth might not be the only criterion employed.[19]

This, by the way, is not offered as a criticism of markets in principle. Despite the claims of some advocates of social justice, the Church is itself a defender of markets.[20] Nevertheless, Pope Benedict observed:

> the market does not exist in a pure state. It is shaped by the cultural config-urations which define it and give it direction. Economy and finance, as instruments, can be used badly when those at the helm are motivated by purely selfish ends. Instruments that are good in themselves can thereby be transformed into harmful ones. But it is man's darkened reason that produces these consequences, not the instrument *per se*.[21]

---

[16] CV, no. 34.

[17] "Authentic development is not merely economic development. It is integral human develop-ment, which entails the development of each man and of the whole man." Pope Paul VI, Encyclical Letter *Populorum progressio* (On the Development of Peoples) (1967), no. 14.

[18] "Space also needs to be created within the market for economic activity carried out by subjects who freely choose to act according to principles other than those of pure profit, without sacrificing the production of economic value in the process." CV, no. 37.

[19] This same spirit may have moved Pope Pius XI to encourage the wealthy to invest their resources in ways that would create employment for others, calling such action "an out-standing exemplification of the virtue of munificence and one particularly suited to the needs of the times." See *Quadragesimo anno* (1931), no. 51. We might also take note of a very short encyclical letter this same pope published in late 1931 urging a "crusade of charity" in response to the economic crisis of the day, a crusade that would aim at creating work for those who needed it. See Pope Pius XI, Encyclical Letter *Nova impendet* (On the Economic Crisis) (1931).

[20] "The Church has always held that economic action is not to be regarded as something opposed to society ... the market can be a negative force, not because it is so by nature, but because a certain ideology can make it so." CV, no. 36.

[21] CV, no. 36.

"Therefore," he continued, "it is not the instrument that must be called to account, but individuals, their moral conscience and their personal and social responsibility." To accept personal responsibility, on this account, would be to embrace the logic of gift as part of one's vocation in a system of finance.

What does the logic of gift require? Perhaps, first of all, it requires a different approach to professional activities. Where the logic of the market asks, "What must I give in order to receive?" and the logic of the state asks, "What does the law demand of me?" the logic of gift asks, "How best can I use what I have been given to address the needs of others?" The logic of gift understands resources as gifts given with a purpose, to be used for the benefit of the recipient, to be sure, but also for much more than that. The gifts and the recipient are both instruments in service of persons and the common good.

More specifically, the first question on the mind of the Christian professional in finance would not be "How can I use this resource to make a profit?" or "What does the law permit me to do with this resource?" but rather "How can I best use this resource to serve others?" Note that this is not a question of whether a profit can or should be earned; business activities can and should be profitable. It is a question instead of how one determines which practical possibilities to pursue and perhaps at times a question of what priorities to honor. The logic of the market, to say nothing of the very real pressures that follow upon this logic, gives priority to maximizing profit, while the logic of gift would insist that increasing profit might sometimes, perhaps often, be balanced against the very real good that some courses of action would produce for real persons.[22] Benedict's proposal is that professionals who accept their work in finance as a genuine Christian vocation seek ways in which they can create space for the logic of gift to shape their particular markets. In so doing, they would act on their commission to penetrate the secular order with the spirit of the Gospel.

In another way, too, the logic of gift would encourage professionals in finance, especially those working in investments, to focus on opportunities for resources to be allocated to productive purposes and not merely to trading. While holding and trading securities for profit is not immoral in principle, an excessive emphasis on trading can reflect the difference between the logic of

---

[22] Mary L. Hirschfeld explores this theme and distinguishes between a real economy, in which concrete goods and services provide benefits to particular people, and an artificial economy, "which deals entirely in transactions involving the abstraction of money." See her eloquent article "Reflection on the Financial Crisis: Aquinas on the Proper Role of Finance," *Journal of the Society of Christian Ethics*, vol. 35.1 (2015): 73–74. In the classical moral tradition of Aristotle and Aquinas the pursuit of money in abstraction from concrete goods leads to avarice since there is no natural limit to the amount of money one might possess.

gift and the logic of the market, where the former is concerned with creating wealth by promoting real goods, while the latter may be satisfied with the accumulation of wealth without any real goods promoted at all.[23]

SOLIDARITY AND THE COMMON GOOD

The second basic concept relevant to the system of finance is the virtue of solidarity. In the classical moral tradition, a virtue is a sort of personal excellence. It is a settled trait of character that enables a person consistently to choose and to do the good. Where the logic of gift focuses on the good that one might do for others, the virtue of solidarity is defined in connection with the common goods of the communities to which one belongs.

"Common good" is an equivocal phrase. It has a number of legitimate meanings in the Catholic moral tradition and many more in the larger history of ethics.[24] The relevant context for our considerations is the instrumental common good of a civil community, which, depending on the focus of attention, could be the common good of a village or a town, or of a nation, or of humankind as a whole. It received its classic definition in the Catholic tradition from Pope John XXIII: "the sum total of those conditions of social living whereby men are enabled more fully and more readily to achieve their own perfection."[25] The *Compendium of the Social Doctrine of the Church* adds: "The [instrumental] common good of society is not an end in itself; it has value only in reference to attaining the ultimate ends of the person."[26]

The instrumental common good, then, embraces all of the conditions – material, social, intellectual, cultural, and spiritual – that enable human persons to flourish. As a practical matter, this common good is never fully instantiated in any human community, much less the world as a whole. Every society, however small or large, is tainted by human sinfulness and as a consequence falls short of establishing the conditions that would permit every member of the community,

[23] John Kay laments "the rise of the trader" in his book, *Other People's Money: The Real Business of Finance* (New York: Public Affairs, 2015), 16–23, and elsewhere throughout the book. Robert J. Shiller offers a somewhat less critical assessment in his chapter, "Traders and Market Makers," in *Finance and the Good Society* (Princeton, NJ: Princeton University Press, 2012).

[24] In the teaching of the Church, beatitude (the share in divine life enjoyed by the saints), is a good common to all human persons as the supernatural end of a human life. Civic friendship, or active participation in a society, is another sort of *substantive* common good and one of the natural goals of a life well lived. Our concern here is with the instrumental common good that is the goal of state action in society.

[25] *MM*, no. 65. He repeated this definition two years later in his encyclical *PT*, no. 58, and it was adopted in 1965 by the Second Vatican Council in *GS*, no. 74.

[26] *CSDC*, no. 170.

without exception, to flourish. Nevertheless, it should be the aspiration of every
society, and is the particular responsibility of every government, to do its best to
establish, sustain, and defend this common good.

Solidarity, as a human virtue, is a personal orientation to support the
common good. Pope John Paul II famously defined it:

> When interdependence [of peoples] becomes recognized ... the correlative
> response as a moral and social attitude, as a "virtue," is solidarity. This then is
> not a feeling of vague compassion or shallow distress at the misfortunes of so
> many people, both near and far. On the contrary, it is a firm and persevering
> determination to commit oneself to the common good; that is to say to the good
> of all and of each individual, because we are all really responsible for all.[27]

To possess the virtue of solidarity, or to approach one's work in a system of
finance from the posture of solidarity, is to be alert to and actively concerned
about the common good and the impact of one's choices and actions upon it.
To put it another way, in solidarity we recognize other members of the society,
and indeed the human community, as friends in principle, not merely as
"cordial strangers."[28] In solidarity, we are prepared to treat others, even those
whom we do not and cannot know personally, as if they were friends in fact.
This entails a willingness to recognize the needs of others and actively to seek
their well-being where it is practical for us to do so. It also requires us not only
to strive to avoid harm to others but also to resist giving unreasonable priority to
our own needs and wants. Since Christians acknowledge God as a God of
abundance, we also acknowledge that the resources of the earth (which is
God's gift to humanity) are adequate to address the needs of the whole human
community. The human experience of poverty and deprivation throughout
history is not a denial of this conviction but instead points us to the pervasive
effects of sin. Lingering scarcity is always a function of greed and disordered
appetites, which the virtue of solidarity can overcome.[29] If properly ordered,

---

[27] SRS, no. 38.
[28] This phrase is employed by Lewis Hyde in speaking of Jean Calvin's analysis of commercial society.
See *The Gift: Imagination and the Erotic Life of Property* (New York: Vintage Books, 1979), 135.
[29] This is not to claim that shortages of important resources cannot arise or that poverty is simply
a matter of sinful or poor judgments. Certainly history is replete with shortages and famines
created by natural disasters, wars, and other events. But these are what we might call "acute"
shortages, not "chronic" or lingering shortages. Acute shortages can cause immense human
suffering, but I suggest that they persist as a consequence of human sin and error; sometimes
where the sins and errors of some are inflicted on innocent others. But these events, however
common they may have been, are not signs of the inadequacy of the created order to supply
genuine human needs. I submit that poverty, as a condition of human life rather than
a temporary experience, is a result of human behavior, not a consequence of the fundamental
insufficiency of the resources of creation. There may indeed be good reasons to be quite

a system of finance, for its part (especially in its banking and investment functions), can serve the universal destination of resources that faith in a God of abundance promises.

Furthermore, the concept of solidarity focuses our attention on the well-being of the community and not principally, in contrast with the logic of gift, on the good that might be done for particular individuals or groups. As a further contrast, solidarity often demands that we attend to the harms that our choices may visit on communities. It requires that we consider how the goals we pursue and the means we choose may impose unnecessary costs on others and that we take responsibility for the consequences of our actions. For example, over the past couple of decades a number of companies have failed very publicly to take responsibility for the working conditions under which their products are manufactured in less developed countries. Even where this failure (and the public embarrassment that accompanies it) was not con-sciously chosen, it is still a result of a narrow vision that does not consider, or take responsibility for, all of the elements of a production process.[30]

Analogous examples could be found in finance as well, in areas such as lending practices, currency arbitrage, and investment decisions. In many cases, the issue may indeed not be one of studied indifference to the harms caused by a business decision but rather a failure to consider the possibility of harm and to accept responsibility for choices made.

INTEGRAL HUMAN DEVELOPMENT

Regardless of the intentions and ambitions of individual participants, the contribution that a system of finance should make to the common good is to facilitate the efficient management of money in support of the exchange of goods and services (including the management of risk) as well as the creation

---

sparing, in certain times and places, in the use of particular resources but there is good reason to acknowledge the abundance of nature in principle.

[30] Pope John Paul II addresses this in *LE*, no. 17. He distinguishes between "direct employers," who are immediately responsible for a production process, and "indirect employers," "who determine one or other facet of the labor relationship, thus conditioning the conduct of the direct employer when the latter determines in concrete terms the actual work contract." In other words, an American company contracting with a foreign manufacturer is an indirect employer of the workers making the product. The prices and other terms demanded by the American company materially shape the conditions under which the workers in that factory labor. If the terms can only be met by paying workers poorly, by ignoring safety procedures, or by requiring excessively long hours of work to meet production schedules, the American company bears some responsibility for these effects – as do the consumers of the products.

of wealth and prosperity for the community. All of this, in turn, serves the flourishing of individuals when it is well ordered.

A consistent theme in modern papal teaching about social issues, however, has been a warning about the dangers of ordering social life around a false or incomplete understanding of the nature and situation of the human person.[31] These mistaken understandings take many forms but each involves neglecting or denying some element of the truth about human beings. The Church's concern to encourage the flourishing of humanity has in recent decades focused on the idea of development.[32]

In a world corrupted by sin, the flourishing of persons is impeded by factors both external and internal to the individual and to the community. The work of overcoming these obstacles in order to permit and to realize the potential for human flourishing is what the tradition means by development. This work takes many forms as the resources, conditions, and obstacles vary greatly from community to community.

As material creatures and embodied spirits, human beings require a variety of resources to enable their flourishing, from food, clothing, and shelter to education, ordered society, and culture. At the same time, it is abundantly clear that the material resources of creation, to say nothing of the particular talents and responsibilities of individuals, are unequally distributed. As Pope Leo XIII noted in his encyclical *Rerum novarum*:

> There naturally exist among mankind manifold differences of the most important kind; people differ in capacity, skill, health, strength; and unequal fortune is a necessary result of unequal condition. Such inequality is far from being disadvantageous either to individuals or to the community. Social and public life can only be maintained by means of various kinds of capacity for business and the playing of many parts; and each man, as a rule, chooses the part which suits his own peculiar domestic condition.[33]

Pope Leo categorically rejected the view that this inequality was an evil that required a remedy in the form of forcibly leveling out the differences in society, through the violent conflict of classes, if necessary. On the contrary, his view was that the differences were in fact an occasion and incentive for

---

[31]   See Pope John Paul II, *Centesimus annus*, nos. 11, 13, 29.

[32]   Pope John Paul II remarked that the Church had deliberately chosen the word "development" over the word "progress" because development implies an intentional and personal effort to secure a more profound improvement in the well-being of people, where progress implies an impersonal process leading "rapidly towards an undefined perfection of some kind." See SRS, no. 27.

[33]   Pope Leo XIII, Encyclical Letter *Rerum novarum* (On the Condition of the Working Classes) (1891), no. 17.

cooperation between members of a community (which later could be under-stood to mean the entire human community) and, in the case of those with greater gifts, skills, resources, and opportunities, the differences imposed solemn responsibilities.[34]

Such differences, of course, are evident not merely at the level of individuals but also at the level of nations, where various resources are widely and unevenly dispersed. These differences have often been the occasion of conflict between nations but they would be better understood, on Pope Leo's account, as an occasion for cooperation and mutual aid. The international system of finance has played a role in this, especially since the end of World War II.

In order to prosper, nations need a variety of resources: material, intellectual, cultural, and financial, to name a few. In some sense, the mere distribution of material resources has been the most tempting factor to address and it is the one that has occupied the bulk of international postwar efforts in support of Less Developed Countries (LDCs). It is tangible and measurable. It often has immediate, beneficial effects – even if the longer-term effects may be less beneficial or even harmful. But these efforts have often failed to produce a sustainable improvement in the lives of the people they were intended to help.[35] We now see that there are a variety of reasons for these failures, many of which have to do with the neglect of the immaterial (i.e., spiritual, cultural, social, personal) factors of human flourishing.

As long ago as 1967, Pope Paul VI, in his encyclical *Populorum progressio*, warned of the consequences of an excessively narrow vision of the person and of human flourishing.[36] While he was strongly in favor of development aid contributed by developed nations to LDCs, he was also concerned that the aid would endorse and encourage the sort of materialist and consumerist anthro-pologies that, to one degree or another, characterized both the Western and

---

[34]   One of these responsibilities was to ensure fair compensation for all workers. In many cases, this would be ensuring that compensation (cash plus benefits) would be in fact a "living wage," that is, an income that would permit a full-time worker to support a modest family in a minimally decent lifestyle. For a further discussion of this question see my article: "The Practice of Just Compensation," *Journal of Religion and Business Ethics* 1 (2010), http://via .library.depaul.edu/jrbe/vol1/iss1/1.

[35]   See, for example, William Easterly, *The White Man's Burden* (New York: Penguin, 2006); Dambisa Mayo, *Dead Aid: Why Aid Is Not Working and How There Is a Better Way for Africa* (New York: Farrar, Straus and Giroux, 2009); and Abhijit V. Banerjee and Esther Duflo, *Poor Economics* (New York: Public Affairs, 2011).

[36]   *PP*, nos. 14–21: "Authentic human development is not merely economic development. It is integral human development, which entails the development of each man and of the whole man" (no. 14).

socialist blocs.[37] The alternate vision that he proposed, and named "integral human development," emphasized the unity and integrity of the person as more than just a consumer of material resources. Each and every human person is also an image of God, with a transcendent destiny and a capacity for growth and fulfillment in many dimensions: spiritual, intellectual, moral, cultural, social, and more. Part of the soundness of Pope Paul's insight into development was his observation that human development, whether personal or national, was something that others could assist but it was not something that could be done by these others *to* or *for* the persons or nations seeking to develop.[38]

Pope John Paul II carried this concern one step further. He warned:

> There is a better understanding today that the mere accumulation of goods and services, even for the benefit of the majority, is not enough for the realization of human happiness . . . On the contrary, the experience of recent years shows that unless all the considerable body of resources and potential at man's disposal is guided by a moral understanding and by an orientation towards the true good of the human race, it easily turns against man to oppress him. A disconcerting conclusion about the most recent period should serve to enlighten us: side-by-side with the miseries of underdevelopment, themselves unacceptable, we find ourselves up against a form of super-development, equally inadmissible, because like the former it is contrary to what is good and to true happiness. This super-development, which consists in an excessive availability of every kind of material goods for the benefit of certain social groups, easily makes people slaves of "possession" and of immediate gratification.[39]

The pope concluded:

> This then is the picture: there are some people – the few who possess much – who do not really succeed in "being" because, through a reversal of the hierarchy of values, they are hindered by the cult of "having"; and there are others – the many who have little or nothing – who do not succeed in realizing their basic human vocation because they are deprived of essential goods.[40]

Christians working in a well-ordered system of finance, a system ordered to the authentic and integral development of the whole person and of each

---

[37] See *PP*, no. 54.
[38] See *PP*, no. 77: "Nations are the architects of their development and they must bear the burden [onus munusque] of this work." See also nos. 15, 34, and 65.
[39] *SRS*, no. 28.
[40] *SRS*, no. 28.

person, can contribute in powerful and indispensable ways to the common good. To do so, they must remain mindful of the goods and services that genuinely support human well-being and committed to serving them in their work. They must also avoid, on the one hand, the pursuit of riches detached from, and therefore not limited by, real benefits acquired by real persons. And on the other hand, they must remain alert to the real needs, especially of the poor and the vulnerable, that are so easily and so often overlooked in a materialistic world.

THE CATHOLIC PROFESSIONAL AND INTERNATIONAL FINANCE

Despite the fact that the Church at various levels has not hesitated to offer or endorse specific policy proposals, the Catholic social tradition does not really lend itself to fine-grained judgments about what ought to be done in particular circumstances. The circumstances surrounding real social problems are usually complicated and quite often, in their totality, specific to a particular time and place. Practical policy choices, then, are not simply deductions from general principles, even if some would prefer to make them so, but rather are prudential judgments, shaped by moral norms that function as general guidelines and sometimes as firm prohibitions. Catholics charged with making and implementing policy should seek to inform their judgment by drawing upon the teaching of the Church but must, in the end, rely on their own capacity for prudence. As a result, men and women of good will may often disagree about what policies and practices are best and, indeed, may judge that in particular circumstances there may be limits to the extent to which they may be implemented.[41]

The Catholic professional, pursuing work in a system of finance and accepting this work as a genuine Christian vocation, will certainly face limitations. Reducing these limitations and creating greater opportunities to act according to the logic of gift (in contrast with the logic of the market) and solidarity is what Pope Benedict XVI meant by creating space in an economic system.[42] How does a Catholic professional do this? A starting point is to

---

[41] This is not to suggest that there are occasions on which one must choose a moral evil but rather that one's pursuit of the good might be limited by constraints and impediments. Furthermore, as the Second Vatican Council reminds us (GS, no. 43), no one is authorized to appropriate the social teaching of the Church to support his judgment on prudential matters in order to dismiss or to suppress the judgment of others inspired by that same teaching.

[42] It is worth noting here that our objective in this discussion is not to highlight and warn against ethical lapses in the system of finance. With so much money involved, there are certainly many opportunities for fraud, exploitation, theft, and other crimes and misbehaviors. We will assume that all such ethical failures are absolutely to be avoided and never to be justified. Our

acknowledge the degree of freedom one has in a particular occupation and position. The president of a bank has greater freedom, obviously, than a branch manager or a personal banker. All of them, however, in their own way may bring a different mode of thinking to their work.

This requires the courage to lead and to question the prevailing logic of business. It may even require the courage to change one's employment in preference for a position that is more consistent with Catholic values. More fundamentally, it requires calling into question the maximization of shareholder/owner wealth as the immutable logic of the market and the objective of business decision making.[43] Instead, embracing the logic of gift in a system of finance would move one toward the objective of creating value not only for shareholders and owners (whose interests cannot justly be ignored) but also for others affected by a business decision. It could mean, for example, creating a financial product or service that benefits the poor and provides a return to owners, even if that return *might* be less than other business opportunities would provide.[44]

---

objective, however, is to consider what effect there might be on the work of a Catholic professional in finance if that person were to take seriously the concepts and principles discussed above. Furthermore, these comments are intended to be general and suggestive rather than prescriptive. Professionals in finance will have a better sense of what is possible and prudent in the contexts in which they operate but they should also be encouraged to think in new ways about addressing real human needs.

[43] "For every Christian there is a special call of the Spirit to become committed decisively and generously so that the many dynamics under way will be channeled towards prospects of fraternity and the common good." Pontifical Council for Justice and Peace, "Towards Reforming the International Financial and Monetary Systems in the Context of Global Public Authority" (2011), 13.

[44] Maximizing shareholder wealth is a convenient theoretical concept but it is impossible to employ as a practical management tool. At the end of any accounting period, it is not possible for managers to know that the decisions they made maximized returns to shareholders. In principle, some other decision might have marginally increased returns. (And a measurement that can be made only after decisions have been implemented is not a useful management tool.) Instead, as a practical matter, managers typically aim at operating objectives intended to achieve a reasonable return to shareholders and owners. But, to take Pope Benedict's point, these objectives could just as well be generated by the logic of gift as the logic of the market. The logic of gift, in this example, could easily include the pursuit of other values that sustain the common good, in addition to a return on investment. These values might include increased opportunities for employment, greater participation in the economy by those on the margins, and so on. It should be noted that achievement of such objectives also benefits owners in indirect ways, by supporting a safer and more productive society. At the very least, embracing the logic of gift, and rejecting the maximization of shareholder wealth as the overarching purpose of business, would direct social energies away from the indefinite pursuit of wealth, which is toxic in itself.

THE ROLE OF GOVERNMENT

Before considering specific roles for Catholic professionals in a system of finance, especially at the international level, a few words about the role of government are in order. In a very general way, civil authorities have a duty in justice to set in place the conditions in a society that promote and support morally sound economic choices.[45] Laws and regulations ought to ensure as far as possible that participants in markets act honestly and responsibly. The weak and the vulnerable, whether persons, groups, or nations, must be protected against the excesses of the strong and the aggressive. Authorities must eliminate corruption and resist the efforts of lobbyists and special interests to promote laws and practices that favor them over the common good. Indeed, promotion and protection of the common good, national and international, must be the guiding star for politicians and civil servants.

Moreover, they ought to recognize that fundamentally we participate in an economy of families, not individuals (as Pope Leo XIII argued so eloquently in *Rerum novarum*). In the majority of cases, men and women work to provide for their families, not merely for themselves. They grow businesses and accumulate wealth in hopes of leaving something for their children. Decisions about employment, for example, do not affect individuals alone, but families as a whole (to say nothing of communities). Policies that attend only to impacts on individuals fail to grapple with the reality of the economic arena.

In a system of finance, civil governments are unique actors. In some ways, they act within the system while in other ways they create the conditions within which the system operates. In the latter case, they establish the constraints and opportunities, the obstacles and the incentives, with which professionals working in the system must contend. The Catholic social tradition offers reflections on the role of government with regard to the economy, as discussed above, though these reflections are for the most part neither uniquely nor distinctively Catholic. On the international level, however, there are some additional considerations that have an impact on systems of finance.

One such consideration is the management of trade. While the Church recognizes the value of free markets on the international level, it is also mindful of some difficulties.[46] Free trade does not mean unregulated trade nor does it mean a situation in which stronger nations are able to take

---

[45] See Pope John Paul II, CA, no. 48, where he insists that the principal task of the state is to guarantee the foundations of economic activity.

[46] See CA, nos. 33–34; CV, no. 35–36.

advantage of weaker ones. In principle, it means participation in markets in which different nations, with different capacities and advantages, may nevertheless engage with one another more or less as equals. While generally in favor of reducing barriers to trade, the Church still has concerns that vulnerable industries in less developed countries not be severely disadvantaged by trade agreements. And so at times it has looked favorably on temporary protections for these industries. In this context, it is worth noting that protective barriers often arise in a climate of distrust between nations (prompted by past injustices and sustained inequalities), even though the barriers may work to the disadvantage of all concerned.[47] In effect, distrust creates economic friction and increases costs. An identification of and commitment to the common good of all can help to reduce this friction.

A second consideration has been the management of currency exchange rates, especially where the exchange rates of dominant currencies (e.g., the dollar, the Euro) move in directions unfavorable to the trade and debt service of LDCs. Central banks need to consider not only the impact of monetary policies on their domestic economies but also the sometimes severe impact of changes in exchange value on weaker nations. By the same token, the governments of LDCs must be fiscally prudent so as to avoid forced devaluations. Needless to say, systems of finance can be at the mercy of these factors.[48]

A third area of attention concerns the regulation of multinational businesses and partnerships. This has to do with rules that permit and facilitate investment, the purchase of assets and the formation of partnerships, taxation and remittances, and the adjudication of disputes. While the Church has said relatively little about this in any formal way, it does have concerns about the sharing of knowledge and technology[49] as well as the collection of tax receipts from multinationals. Work remains to be done to craft a fair and prudent set of rules and policies in addition to creating trusted venues for resolving conflicts. Financial professionals have a role to play in this but, once again, ought to focus on the common good and not merely on how they can craft, or exploit, rules to their benefit.

---

[47] See *MM*, nos. 203–204; *CV*, no. 32.

[48] In developed nations, not least the United States, private firms have come to spend a great deal of money in lobbying governments for legislation and policies, and perhaps even judicial and regulatory judgments, that favor their businesses. In such lobbying, Catholic professionals should be mindful of the requirements of the common good, not merely the good of their corporations.

[49] See *CA*, nos. 31–32.

THE CATHOLIC PROFESSIONAL IN BANKING

The banking function in a system of finance provides services that are indispensable to those seeking to participate in the economy, at any level.[50] As presently constituted, the banking function does a great deal that is commendable, and much of the world's trade and prosperity is made possible by the services it provides. Even so, many people exist on the margins of the economy and are impeded from participating more fully because of inadequate banking services available to them. These are people who may be poor but who would benefit from access to ordinary banking services – secure deposits, return on savings, modest loans – but who collectively would generate less attractive profits for banks. The logic of gift and the virtue of solidarity would turn attention to the possibility of serving these people and perhaps unleash the creativity required to devise modes of service that would meet their needs while generating adequate profits for the banks.[51]

In particular, on both the domestic and international levels, banks could offer services that would provide more effective access to interest-bearing deposit accounts and more convenient forms of payment services, to say nothing of short-term credit arrangements. The need for such services is particularly acute in less developed countries but it also exists in developed economies.[52] No doubt there are also possibilities for banks to craft new international partnerships that would facilitate payments and receipts across national borders even for small businesses.[53]

There are also, of course, possibilities for lending in the international market, as the climate for business development improves in various parts

---

[50] As a persistent theme, the Catholic social tradition strongly endorses the right of individuals and nations to participate in work and in the economy. See *CSDC*, no. 333.

[51] See Banerjee and Duflo, *Poor Economics*, 183–204, for a discussion of the problems and possibilities. Note particularly their observations about the assumptions that are sometimes made about the inability of the poor to manage their own lives.

[52] The continued existence of payday loan services and nonbank financial service agencies specializing in services to poor communities, as well as certain forms of retail operations offering to finance purchases (e.g., rent-to-own) at relatively high rates of interest suggest that there may be a market for more traditional banking services if the right products can be devised. The risks associated with this, as well as regulatory challenges, must be acknowledged but may it not also be the case that many banks simply do not see these markets as sufficiently attractive? Could a stronger sense of solidarity and perhaps a more positive assessment of the poor as potential customers revise this calculation?

[53] Here again we may see nontraditional entities devising ways to employ new technologies to facilitate trade, as such things as more sophisticated versions of PayPal and Bitcoin emerge. It would be unwise to predict what these might be, but they may begin with the recognition that there is a market for such services among communities on the margin, markets that more traditional banking enterprises may overlook.

of the world. The Catholic professional, in a spirit of solidarity, should be inclined to more careful discernment about the real value of projects to be financed; that is to say, about the contribution to human well-being and the common good of the projects, not merely the profit potential. This also might entail deliberate decisions to make a greater share of assets available for lending in less developed countries. If this were done, Christian professionals would also be concerned about establishing and sustaining the creditworthiness of borrower nations. This could mean defining measurements of success in employing borrowed funds and efforts to resist various forms of corruption. Above all, it may mean taking steps to ensure that in the future citizens are not burdened with the obligation to repay loans made to regimes that did not use the money to benefit their populations.[54]

BANKING AND THE DEBT OF LDCS

Undoubtedly the topic that has most engaged the formal attention of the Church in recent decades has been the issue of the debt obligations of LDCs. While the problem of nations and monarchs failing to repay debts as promised is hardly new, the issue took on a new urgency in the 1970s. Dozens of LDCs had taken on large debt obligations, and the combination of high oil costs, high inflation, and high interest made these obligations unsustainable. As a consequence, domestic budgets were overwhelmed and economic progress was often halted or even reversed.

The problem as a whole was very complicated and might be best characterized as a set of dozens of individual problems, each with its own peculiar history and details, but united with the others by the specter of default and crushing poverty for innocent citizens. Corruption was often a factor, as was the competition between Western and communist powers. Money borrowed was too often not used for economic growth but rather for the purchase of armaments or for projects serving the whims of governing elites. Frequently the regime that borrowed the money was no longer in power when the crisis arose and could not be held accountable.

---

[54] See CV, nos. 58–60 for reflections on the proper objectives of aid programs. This is not to suggest that default on sovereign debt is an appropriate solution, or that governments of creditor nations guarantee loans made by banks in their countries to less developed nations. Rather, it is an encouragement to craft programs and agreements in the beginning that genuinely seek and serve the well-being of the citizens of less developed nations *and* do not lead to unsustainable indebtedness.

One of the best analyses of this set of problems offered by the Church was published by the Pontifical Commission for Justice and Peace in 1986.[55] The Commission took note of the range of miscalculations, corruptions, bad behaviors, and unforeseen events that precipitated the crisis and recognized that it was a modern tragedy with no painless solutions. In the end, it advocated a sharing of responsibility and sacrifice aimed at freeing LDCs trapped by their debt obligations and permitting them to return to a path promising growth and a better future. In the last decade or so, further steps have been taken to relieve the situation of highly indebted poor countries (HIPCs) and to avoid similar problems in the future.[56]

THE CATHOLIC PROFESSIONAL IN INSURANCE

On the commercial level, the insurance industry, like the banking industry, is quite sophisticated in the international arena, providing a variety of products to protect persons and property. On the retail level, however, much remains to be developed in LDCs to protect farmers and small businesspeople. Local regulations may make it difficult for nondomestic firms to operate in these markets, but there may be other ways in which experienced firms could encourage the development of insurance products for the poor, such as through sharing data and experience.[57]

THE CATHOLIC INVESTOR AND THE PROFESSIONAL IN FINANCE

"Investment" is an equivocal term. In broad outline, it refers to the purchase of a security or some other asset with a view to obtaining a future profit from the ownership of that asset. There are different general forms of investment (investment proper, speculation, and trade), a variety of objectives for investing, and at least two principal actors engaged in most investments (owners of

---

[55] Pontifical Commission, "Iustitia et pax," "At the Service of the Human Community: An Ethical Approach to the International Debt Question" (Vatican City: Vatican Polyglot Press, 1986).

[56] A recent fact sheet from the International Monetary Fund about efforts at debt relief can be found here: www.imf.org/About/Factsheets/Sheets/2016/08/01/16/11/Debt-Relief-Under-the-Heavily-Indebted-Poor-Countries-Initiative?pdf=1. The United States Conference of Catholic Bishops has been active in promoting the quest for solutions. A summary of their statements can be found here: www.usccb.org/issues-and-action/human-life-and-dignity/debt-relief/index.cfm.

[57] See Banerjee and Duflo, *Poor Economics*, 147–155.

capital and financial professionals). The consideration before us is how a Catholic perspective might shape investment decisions.

One justification for the investment function in a system of finance is that it allocates resources to enterprises that most need it and most want it. But this is an ideal, and one can reasonably wonder how often the ideal is realized. Is it not the case that resources are more often allocated where they can receive the highest return, not where there is greatest need (however that might be defined)? Or are resources allocated where there is a preferred balance of risk and reward, regardless of the needs that might be served? Might it be that investment opportunities in LDCs are neglected because technical reasons (estimates of risk and return) outweigh judgments about goods to be served?

The Catholic investor or finance professional, inspired by the logic of gift, the virtue of solidarity, and a vision of integral human development, might offer different answers to these questions from those prompted by the logic of the market.[58]

A starting point for Catholic investors and their counselors is the question of what God wants them to do with the resources at their disposal.[59] (In some cases, the answer might be that the resources ought to be used to address some immediate need and not invested at all.) This is less a question about what one is obligated to do or to avoid than it is a deliberate effort to discern the possibilities to benefit individuals and groups (even nations) that have been illuminated by the key principles of the social tradition.

Trading and speculation, while not immoral in principle, seek to profit from holding an asset or commodity, without regard to the underlying benefit that might be offered or withheld. That is to say, it is not part of the trader's intention that some real benefit be offered to (or withheld from, for that matter) a particular individual. His or her intention is simply to derive

---

[58] By some estimates, the majority of "investment" activity, on both the domestic and international levels, is constituted by trading and speculation, which provide no direct support to real economic activities.

[59] For the moment, we will treat investors and finance professionals as if they were in the same situation. It is certainly true, though, that finance professionals often have a much more limited freedom of action than the owners of capital. Sometimes finance professionals merely counsel investors, at other times they actively manage on behalf of investors (and may have strict fiduciary responsibilities), or they may have direct decision-making authority for Catholic institutions (such as universities and religious communities). Nevertheless, the questions facing investors may also be questions that finance professionals must address even if they are constrained in their ability to act on the answers.

a profit by holding the asset for a period of time, however short or long, and selling it to someone at a higher price. No other result is pertinent.[60]

There may be many sound reasons for trading or speculating in financial markets (as well as abusive practices). Individuals or nonprofit organizations may require an income stream, and trade or speculation may be a reasonable and prudent way to obtain this. But investors, properly considered, may be called to do something else.

The logic of gift calls us to regard our possessions, including our investable assets, as gifts from a loving Creator, entrusted to us and to be used for the Creator's purposes. These purposes include not only our own welfare but also benefits that we can offer to others. As discussed above, embracing this logic of gift moves us to a lively awareness of the needs and possibilities around us, both locally and globally. Just as some might be moved to make charitable donations, to contribute professional expertise, or even to prepare for a lifetime of service, Catholic investors should be moved to consider carefully how their investments can obtain a reasonable return (which may not be a hypothetical maximum) *and* provide some real benefits to individuals and groups.

Investors may be passive or active. Passive investors hold an asset (stocks or bonds, for example) in anticipation that the success of an organization's activities will generate a cash flow (dividends) or directly increase the value of the asset. In purchasing the asset, they are assumed to intend the success of the organization but generally have little or no influence on its operations. As noted above, in most cases passive investors contribute nothing directly to the organization itself, having purchased the asset from a previous owner. At times passive investors seek to influence the governance or strategic direction of the organization but hardly ever have an effect on day-to-day operations.[61]

Active investing (sometimes called "impact investing"), which is much less common than passive investing, seeks to do more.[62] Animated by the logic of

---

[60] "A transaction will clearly be labeled as speculative when an agent is not only neglecting the secondary effects of his action on the underlying asset but is also attempting to reap some direct benefit through the market without any other motive than greed." Jef Van Gerwan, SJ, "Global Markets and Global Justice? Catholic Social Teaching and Finance Ethics," in *Catholic Social Thought: Twilight or Renaissance?* eds. J. S. Boswell, F. P. McHugh, and J. Verstraeten (Leuven: University Press, 2000), 201–219, esp. 209. Van Gerwen criticizes speculation too strongly but acknowledges the difference from investment.

[61] This sort of activist investing plays a role in the portfolios of a number of Catholic religious communities.

[62] "Active investing" should be distinguished from "actively managed" funds, which seek higher than average (market) returns through active buying and selling of securities.

gift and a spirit of solidarity, it seeks to identify real activities and enterprises that would benefit from financial support. The vision of integral human development provides the criteria for discerning which activities deserve support, and the spirit of solidarity prompts active investors to remain open to supporting sound enterprises in more remote parts of the world.[63]

None of this implies that active investors must be self-sacrificing or imprudent about choosing investments. Many otherwise worthwhile opportunities may be found in countries where unwise government policies and practices make investment difficult or excessively risky. The active investor must evaluate these situations wisely and may often decide to contribute to a less worthy but also less risky venture. Even so, it may also be the case that active investors should be content to accept a return on their investments that, while still reasonable, might be a bit lower than other opportunities. In doing so, they recognize that other goods are worth serving, and worth including in a calculation of returns, beyond those that are purely monetary.

So, Catholic investors, and the finance professionals who advise them, should be open to seeing their activities as part of an authentic Christian vocation, shaped by key principles of Catholic Social Teaching.[64]

SUMMARY

Modern Catholic Social Teaching, especially as articulated by the popes, the curia, and the bishops, has said little directly and formally about systems of finance. Where these voices have spoken, they have encouraged sound practices in broad outline and criticized obviously unsound and immoral behaviors. Unfortunately, their own financial management practices have not offered good models for what might be done. Nevertheless, key principles

---

[63] "There is a wealth of deserving investment projects, especially in LDCs, which are impossible to implement both because local saving is inadequate and often diverted towards alternative skewed forms of financial investment, and because the world financial markets are busy elsewhere and do not spot those investments. In other words, the missing line in the contemporary debate about financial markets is marginalization of poor regions from the credit circuit." Simona Beretta, "Ordering Global Finance: Back to Basics," in *Catholic Social Thought: Twilight or Renaissance?*, eds. J. S. Boswell, F. P. McHugh, and J. Verstraeten (Leuven: University Press, 2000), 221–238, esp. 229.

[64] It would be a mistake to conflate the vocation of the Catholic in finance with the Christian duty of almsgiving. Catholic professionals are bound to use their skills to serve the common good by creating wealth and encouraging its wise and productive use. Individuals and organizations engage in almsgiving when they employ money and property to address particular needs, without expectation of return. Both activities can effectively meet real needs in the community but they do so in different ways.

like the logic of gift, the idea of solidarity and the common good, and the vision of integral human development, coupled with the competence and integrity of Catholics working in systems of finance, can imagine possibilities and generate inspiring models of professional conduct. The key to making this work well is to understand and embrace the possibility of pursuing work in the system of finance as a genuine Christian vocation that in its own way helps to build the Kingdom of God.

In service of this, the pastors of the Church at every level can and should affirm this profession as a vocation, encourage Catholics to bring their faith to their work, avoid unnecessary criticism, and assist them to see the challenges they face more clearly.

17

Subsidiarity

Maria Catherine Cahill

The principle of subsidiarity is one element of the social doctrine of the Catholic Church that is self-consciously embraced by politicians in the context of globalization, increasingly included in international legal texts, and willingly acclaimed by scholars of transnational governance. To take a case in point, the project of European integration embraces the principle of subsidiarity with enthusiasm even as the European Union becomes the most developed example of supranational governance. Subsidiarity is celebrated as the protector of the position of the nation-states[1] and championed as the last defense against the bureaucratic overreach of the European institutions.[2] The principle of subsidiarity has been enshrined both in the Treaty on European Union[3] and in the European Convention on Human Rights and Fundamental Freedoms,[4] and has been interpreted both by the Court of Justice of the European Union and the European Court of Human Rights.

[1]   Former President of the European Commission Jacques Delors famously remarked that the subsidiarity principle entails that one "never … entrust to a bigger structure what can be implemented by a smaller one." Address given October 17, 1989.
[2]   Current President of the European Commission Jean-Claude Juncker exhorted that "applying the principle of subsidiarity … [we must] ensure that the European Commission – and the European Union – concerns itself with the really major European issues instead of interfering from all angles in every detail of people's lives." Speech before the European Parliament, July 15, 2014.
[3]   Article 5.3 of the "Treaty on European Union (as amended by the Treaty of Lisbon)," signed February 7, 1992, states that "in areas which do not fall within its exclusive competence, the Union shall act only if and in so far as the objectives of the proposed action cannot be sufficiently achieved by the Member States, either at central level or at regional and local level, but can rather, by reason of the scale or effects of the proposed action, be better achieved at Union level."
[4]   Protocol No. 15 of the "European Convention on Human Rights," signed on November 4, 1950, inserts a new recital into the Preamble, which states that: "Affirming that the High Contracting Parties, in accordance with the principle of subsidiarity, have the primary responsibility to secure the rights and freedoms defined in this Convention and the Protocols thereto,

Academic commentaries broadly welcome the notion of subsidiarity,[5] register the intention that the principle of subsidiarity would bolster the position of the nation-states,[6] and then describe how its interpretation and implementation are systematically skewed in favor of the European institutions,[7] thereby failing to fulfill its original purpose and even exacerbating the problem of centralization.[8]

I have argued elsewhere that the root of this impasse lies in the fact that political and legal discussions about subsidiarity tend not to be fully cognizant of the philosophical commitments that the principle entails and, as a result, tend to latch on, in a rather dogmatic way, to the idea that decision making at so-called lower levels is presumptively preferable, without articulating a reason as to why this might be the case and without having a reason to rebut that presumption.[9] Presented in such an unintelligible way, subsidiarity becomes a shallow, feeble principle that is particularly vulnerable to being overborne by the drive for efficiency. The solution, I posited, is to theorize subsidiarity.[10] Recourse to Catholic social thought on the concept of subsidiarity is one way – the concept predates the encyclicals by about two thousand years – to more fully explore subsidiarity's intellectual weightiness.

This chapter will draw out the specifically Catholic perspective on the nature, purpose, and operationalization of subsidiarity as part of that broader

and that in doing so they enjoy a margin of appreciation, subject to the supervisory jurisdiction of the European Court of Human Rights established by this Convention."

5   Deborah Cass, "The Word that Saves Maastricht? The Principle of Subsidiarity and the Division of Powers within the European Community," *Common Market Law Review* 29, no. 6 (1992): 1170; Andreas Føllesdal, "Survey Article: Subsidiarity," *Journal of Political Philosophy* 6 (1998): 190.

6   Antonio Estrella, *The EU Principle of Subsidiarity and Its Critique* (2003); Kees van Kersbergen and Bertjan Verbeek, "The Politics of Subsidiarity in the European Union," *Journal of Common Market Studies* 32 (1994): 215; Paul Marquardt, "Subsidiarity and Sovereignty in the European Union," *Fordham International Law Journal* 18 (1994): 616; Ingolf Pernice, "The Framework Revisited: Constitutional, Federal and Subsidiarity Issues," *Columbia Journal of European Law* 2 (1996): 403.

7   Gareth Davies, "Subsidiarity: The Wrong Idea, in the Wrong Place, at the Wrong Time," *Common Market Law Review* 43 (2006): 63; see also Gráinne de Búrca, "The Principle of Subsidiarity and the Court of Justice as an Institutional Actor," *Journal of Common Market Studies* 36 (1998): 214; Christoph Henkel, "The Allocation of Powers in the European Union: A Closer Look at the Principle of Subsidiarity," *Berkeley Journal of International Law* 20 (2002): 359; Theodor Schilling, "Subsidiarity as a Rule and a Principle, or: Taking Subsidiarity Seriously," *Harvard Jean Monnet Working Paper* 10/95 (1995).

8   Gareth Davies, "Subsidiarity as a Method of Policy Centralisation," *Hebrew University International Law Research Paper* 11/06 (2006).

9   Maria Cahill, "Theorizing Subsidiarity: Towards an Ontology-Sensitive Approach," *International Journal of Constitutional Law* 15(1) (2017): 201, 202–207.

10 Cahill, "Theory Subsidiarity," 201, 202–207.

endeavor to theorize subsidiarity. In doing so, of course, it has in mind not only the problems of European integration and globalization but also the imperative of vindicating associational freedom within the state. Legislative agendas may compromise associational freedom either by illegitimately interfering with the internal governing structures of associations or by shirking the responsibility of bolstering those associations through the provision of necessary assistance. Government regulation of private enterprises, charities, sporting organizations, schools and universities, and so on may breach the principle of subsidiarity and thereby damage the viability of these associations. Legal disputes in which associational freedom is at stake (i.e., those concerning businesses, charities, schools, and so on) cannot be adjudicated upon as if they only concerned clashes between individual rights holders.

We cannot arrive at greater lucidity about subsidiarity without first acknowledging the paradox that the principle of subsidiarity seems to mandate contradictory things: on the one hand, it exhorts that the state should not interfere in the associational life of its citizens and, on the other hand, its *raison d'être* is to permit and encourage the state to grant assistance to those very associations. Although it seems, at first, to defend the immunity of families, universities, small businesses, charities, and so on from the action of the state, at the same time, it prescribes that that immunity should, at times, be pierced in the name of those self-same associations. As a result of this paradox, it is difficult for those in the process of drafting a constitution, supposing they were committed to enshrining subsidiarity as a fundamental constitutional principle, to know exactly what they should include in its specific provisions. Similarly, it is not obvious how a newly elected legislator, determined to support associational freedom without reneging the responsibilities invested in him or her as a member of the legislature, could devise a legislative agenda that would both support associational autonomy and provide appropriate state assistance to associations. The paradox also impacts on those of us who will never be called upon for such awesome undertakings, because it means that when we criticize a policy position or legislative agenda or judicial decision or constitutional amendment for failure to respect the principle of subsidiarity (in whatever professional or social settings we do that), that criticism is blunted by its own opacity and ambiguity and, as a result, it does not pack the same punch as a criticism based, for example, on concerns about human rights or equality, or even concerns about democracy, the separation of powers, or the rule of law.

The initial temptation, faced with this seemingly contradictory mandate, is to dichotomize subsidiarity itself, referring to positive subsidiarity (the state's obligation to give assistance) and negative subsidiarity (the state's obligation to refrain from interference). This approach seems, at first blush, to offer some of the much-needed clarity, and it accurately describes what subsidiarity entails from the perspective of state agency, using the state as the fulcrum on which subsidiarity turns. On deeper reflection, though, this approach can be found to be unhelpful because it perpetuates the idea of the state as the locus of all authority within society, whereas subsidiarity's main contribution is to say that associations exist independently of the state and prior to the state, and that the state should vindicate associational freedom out of respect for their prior claims to self-government. According to the principle of subsidiarity, the fulcrum is not the state but the associations themselves, and the state pivots in order to accommodate their needs rather than having them bend to its will. Thus, this chapter will eschew the terminology of positive and negative subsidiarity both because of its state-centric perspective and because it accentuates, rather than overcomes, the sense that subsidiarity is intellectually incoherent and ambiguous, and, having no settled content, that it is ripe for political manipulation.

Instead, hypothesizing that the paradox may resolve itself if we understand the principle of subsidiarity at a deeper level, this chapter seeks to arrive at greater clarity about (1) the nature, (2) the purpose, and (3) the operationalization of the principle of subsidiarity through a close examination of the social encyclicals of the Catholic Church, in which the neologism "subsidiarity" was first proposed (although, importantly, the encyclicals themselves make clear that the origin of the concept of subsidiarity is significantly older (QA, no. 79)). It is well to begin with a warning: if we approach the social teaching of the Catholic Church expecting to find therein an abstract, academic, and systematic treatment of the principle of subsidiarity that consciously grapples with this paradox (explicating why these contradictions are only apparent and teaching us how to strike the right balance between associational autonomy and state intervention); or, if we expect the encyclicals to identify a single political purpose that subsidiarity will conduce toward (efficiency or decentralization or legitimate decision making or so on); or, if we expect to find a list of practical guidelines on how to craft laws or legislative agendas so as to create associations and associational freedom, we will, for the most part, be disappointed. Perhaps that is an indication that greater attention could be given to the nature, purpose, and operationalization of subsidiarity in future encyclicals, but my suggestion is that the current corpus of statements on subsidiarity, precisely in its failure to meet these three expectations, is both intelligible and revelatory. In the first place, the encyclicals do not include a treatise on subsidiarity as a freestanding concept because subsidiarity does not exist in isolation from the other principles of Catholic social thought. They do not outline how it should work in the abstract because it cannot be understood apart from the particular associations whose existence it protects. Secondly, while subsidiarity certainly assists in the achievement of political goals such as those noted above, its ultimate purpose is altogether more ambitious. Thirdly, while the role of law is vital in the defense of associational freedom, it is also a modest one, since law cannot *generate* associations without breaching the principle of subsidiarity and violating associational freedom. In essence, the encyclicals are not paralyzed by this paradox because what they reveal about the nature, purpose, and operationalization of subsidiarity transcends the state-centric assumptions that give rise to the sense of contradiction in the first place.

THE NATURE OF SUBSIDIARITY: NEITHER FREESTANDING NOR ABSTRACT

The principle of subsidiarity, referred to in the Compendium of the Social Doctrine of the Catholic Church as *"among the most constant and characteristic directives of the Church's social doctrine"*[11] enjoys extensive references in numerous papal encyclicals, exhortations, and apostolic letters written by popes since the nineteenth century. Certain of these passages have been extracted from the encyclicals and presented in a decontextualized way as the soundbite definitions of the principle of subsidiarity, most famously the following two quotes, which are taken from *Rerum novarum*[12] and *Quadragesimo anno*[13] respectively:

> The State should watch over these societies of citizens banded together in accordance with their rights, but it should not thrust itself into their peculiar concerns and their organization, for things move and live by the spirit inspiring them, and may be killed by the rough grasp of a hand from without. (*RN*, no. 55)

> [T]hat most weighty principle, which cannot be set aside or changed, remains fixed and unshaken in social philosophy: Just as it is gravely wrong to take from individuals what they can accomplish by their own initiative and industry and give it to the community, so also it is an injustice and at the same time a grave evil and disturbance of right order to assign to a greater and

[11] Pontifical Council for Justice and Peace, *Compendium of the Social Doctrine of the Church*, no. 185, emphasis in original.
[12] Leo XIII, Encyclical Letter *Rerum novarum* (On the Condition of the Working Classes) (1891).
[13] Pius XI, Encyclical Letter *Quadragesimo anno* (On Reconstruction of the Social Order: 40th Anniversary of *Rerum novarum*) (1931).

higher association what lesser and subordinate organizations can do. For every social activity ought of its very nature to furnish help to the members of the body social, and never destroy and absorb them. (*QA*, no. 79)

If we reify these decontextualized passages in order to define subsidiarity as a rebuttable presumption in favor of decision making at lower levels rather than higher levels (the standard formula), then we set ourselves on a course that dogmatizes that definition because it strips from subsidiarity its philosophical basis in the nature of the associations, their prior claim to authority, and the good that they promote.[14] The encyclicals, precisely in their failure to speak about subsidiarity as a freestanding and abstract concept, are thereby indicating that this is the wrong path.

First, subsidiarity is not freestanding because it is only one of the four "permanent principles of the Church's social doctrine,"[15] and therefore cannot be fully appreciated except by reference to the other three, namely, the dignity of the human person, the common good, and solidarity. Pope Benedict XVI drew out these connections in a 2008 address to the Pontifical Academy of Social Sciences:

> *Human dignity* is the intrinsic value of a person created in the image and likeness of God and redeemed by Christ. The totality of social conditions allowing persons to achieve their communal and individual fulfilment is known as the *common good*. *Solidarity* refers to the virtue of enabling the human family to share fully the treasure of material and spiritual goods, and *subsidiarity* is the coordination of society's activities in a way that supports the internal life of the local communities.[16]

Going further, he wrote that subsidiarity is intrinsically connected to human dignity because it "liberates people … to engage with one another in the spheres of commerce, politics, and culture,"[17] allied to solidarity because while solidarity "binds the human family" together, subsidiarity "reinforce[s] it from within,"[18] and is necessary for the achievement of the common good because this achievement is no monolithic exercise but the accumulated efforts of groups bound together to respond to each other's needs through personal service. The link between subsidiarity and human dignity, specifically "the creative subjectivity of the citizen" (*SRS*, no. 15), is particularly emphasized, and understandably so

---

[14] Cahill, "Theory Subsidiarity," note 8.
[15] *CSDC*, no. 160.
[16] Pope Benedict XVI, *A Reason Open to God: On Universities, Education and Culture* (J. Steven Brown ed. 2013), 189, 190.
[17] Benedict, *A Reason Open to God*, 193.
[18] Benedict, *A Reason Open to God*, 191.

since the "family, groups, associations, local territorial realities" that subsidiarity is concerned to protect are the "original expressions of social life."[19] *Rerum novarum* affirms that it is a "natural impulse which binds men together in civil society; and it is likewise this which leads them to join together in associations" (RN, no. 50) while *Caritas in veritate* describes subsidiarity as "a form of assistance to the human person via the autonomy of intermediate bodies," thus honoring human dignity both in the fact that assistance is given to groups for the sake of the individual and in the fact that that assistance "is always designed to achieve their (individuals') emancipation, because it fosters freedom and participation through assumption of responsibility" (CV, no. 57).

Secondly, Catholic Social Teaching does not treat subsidiarity as an abstract principle capable of being understood or discussed without reference to the nature of the organic associations that it protects, for the same reason that it does not treat of human dignity without reference to the nature of men and women made in the image of God. Just as the principle of human dignity is premised upon a thorough understanding of the human person, so the principle of subsidiarity is premised upon a thorough understanding of those associations. The indissoluble connection between subsidiarity and the associations it defends is made clear from the fact that discussion of the meaning and implications of subsidiarity takes place almost exclusively in the context of particular associations and their specific needs. Even the celebrated quotes from *Rerum novarum* and *Quadragesimo anno* recorded earlier are to be found in the midst of long discussions of the need for and place of workers' unions.

Although the principle of subsidiarity first came to prominence in the context of the need for trade unions and the protection of workers' rights, it has always been the family that has been held up as the most fundamental of all forms of associations. From *Rerum novarum* to *Laudato si'*, the family has been heralded as "the most basic cell of society" and "outstanding" by comparison to other associations (LS, no. 157). As a result, the state, duty bound to recognize the antecedence and "social priority of the family,"[20] has a "grave obligation" to defend and protect this unit, never taking away from families "the functions that they can just as well perform on their own or in free associations" (FC, no. 45) or absorbing or substituting "the social dimension of the family,"[21] but instead:

> [i]n the conviction that the good of the family is an indispensable and essential value of the civil community, the public authorities must do

[19]   CSDC, nos. 185, 186.
[20]   CSDC, no. 252.
[21]   CSDC, no. 252. Cf. Vatican II, Declaration *Gravissimum educationis* (On Christian Education) (October 28, 1965) on the priority of the parental role in education.

everything possible to ensure that families have all those aids – economic, social, educational, political and cultural assistance – that they need in order to face all their responsibilities in a human way. (FC, no. 45)

The role of the state is to be found therefore in the sustaining and honoring of families through the provision of necessary assistance.[22] Reflecting on these passages, we understand that subsidiarity is not about finding a balance between underregulation and overregulation by reference to the bureaucratic capacities of the state or on the basis of the ambition or languor of state agencies. Moreover, we realize that subsidiarity is not about finding an exact midpoint or a perfect compromise between noninterference and interference. Instead, everything is focused on and ordered toward the vitality of the family: the state should conscientiously refrain from interfering in family life when that promotes the health and vitality of the family unit and the state should conscientiously interfere in family life when that promotes the health and vitality of the family unit.[23] When the family (or other relevant association) takes center stage, and the principle of subsidiarity is understood as a tool to promote the welfare of the family, rather than an abstract political principle to gauge the activity of the state, then the sense of contraction we began with simply melts away.

Although the family is the gold standard association as far as subsidiarity is concerned, our understanding of subsidiarity is further developed by reading how it applies to private enterprises. The state should encourage and sustain private enterprise, "avoiding any interference which would unduly condition business forces,"[24] and at the same time intervening when moments of economic crisis or particular monopolies obfuscate that development[25] in order to ensure "the continuation of economic development" and therefore the

---

[22] CSDC, no. 214. Cf. Letter of John Paul II to Mrs. Gertrude Mongella, Secretary-General of the Fourth World Conference on Women of the United Nations, in which he stated that:

> The challenge facing most societies is that of upholding, indeed strengthening, woman's role in the family while at the same time making it possible for her to use all her talents and exercise all her rights in building up society. However, women's greater presence in the work force, in public life, and generally in the decision making processes guiding society, on an equal basis with men, will continue to be problematic as long as the costs continue to burden the private sector. In this area the State has a duty of subsidiarity, to be exercised through suitable legislative and social security initiatives. In the perspective of uncontrolled free-market policies there is little hope that women will be able to overcome the obstacles on their path.

[23] Maria Cahill, "The Origin of Anti-Subsidiarity Trends in the Regulation of the Family," *International Journal of the Jurisprudence of the Family* 4 (2013): 85.

[24] CSDC, no. 354.

[25] CSDC, no. 351.

promotion of the common good (*MM*, no. 152). While guarding against corruption, the state should also respect charities out of a realization that the suffering person needs not only material help but also "loving personal concern," which can only be provided by those initiatives that arise as a result of "closeness to those in need" (*DCE*, no. 28).[26] The principle of subsidiarity also applies in the context of the development of social welfare programs: the state should avoid degenerating into a welfare state and at the same time ensure that it does not fail to provide for the poor because both extremes fail to honor human dignity (*CV*, no. 60).[27] Through these examples, we can see again that subsidiarity requires that the state should avoid both errors of omission and errors of commission. The true course for the state involves "neither neglecting nor exaggerating its responsibilities."[28] Yet, in each context, the state should avoid seeking a middle ground between overinterference and underinterference driven only on its own capacity, budget, or agenda but rather strive to best serve the associations in question by reference to their needs and the good that they seek to achieve.

The need for subsidiarity in the context of globalization is also addressed with some frequency in the encyclicals: *Caritas in veritate* notes that subsidiarity "is particularly well suited to managing globalization and directing it towards authentic human development" (*CV*, no. 57). Acknowledging, as *Pacem in terris* does, that there are some problems "which, because of their extreme gravity, vastness and urgency, must be considered too difficult for the rulers of individual States to resolve with any degree of success" (*PT*, no. 140), while guarding against the emergence of a "dangerous universal power of a tyrannical nature" (*CV*, no. 57), subsidiarity's role is to establish "a greater degree of international ordering ... for the management of globalization" (*CV*, no. 67). The encyclicals insist that "it is no part of the duty of a universal authority to limit the sphere of action of the public authority of individual States" (*PT*, no. 141; *GS*, no. 86), and "much less to take its place,"[29] if for no other reason than the practical one noted by Pope John Paul II in an address to the United Nations, that "there are many groups and peoples who can solve their own problems better at a local or intermediate level."[30]

Subsidiarity, then, is neither a freestanding nor an abstract concept, and it cannot best be conceived of as requiring that the state should strike the

[26]   CSDC, no. 357.
[27]   CSDC, no. 351.
[28]   Peter Cardinal Turkson, "Subsidiarity in a Company" (Speech, Venite Roundtable of Entrepreneurs, Bratislava, December 1, 2014).
[29]   CSDC, no. 441.
[30]   Message of John Paul II to the General Assembly of the United Nations, August 22, 1980.

right balance or find a middle ground between a hands-off approach and a very domineering approach to associations. Rather, the common thread in these passages is that subsidiarity can best be defined as the effort to articulate the right relationship between the state and particular associations, each with its own function to fulfill, and that that should be done by focusing on the nature of the associations themselves, ensuring that they are both free to pursue the goods for which they exist and that they are fully supported, when necessary, in that endeavor. Subsidiarity requires both the granting of assistance as much and as often as is necessary to support the particular associations in question and, at the same time, holding back as much and as far as possible from interfering in their internal life in order to allow those associations to grow and to succeed in achieving their good. In this way, we transcend the language of higher and lower levels and the terminology of positive and negative subsidiarity, resolving the paradox through heightened appreciation of the meaning of subsidiarity. None of this means, of course, that it is impossible to theorize subsidiarity in a more systematic way, merely that as we do so we need to pay homage to the philosophical commitments that subsidiarity entails. Taparelli himself,[31] Chantal Delsol,[32] John Finnis,[33] Russell Hittinger,[34] and many others,[35] have already contributed their efforts to bringing the principle of subsidiarity "into the full light ... of life" (QA, no. 20).

---

[31] Luigi Taparelli d'Azeglio, *Saggio Teoretico di Dritto Naturale Appogiato Sul Fatto* (2011).

[32] Chantal Delsol, *Le principe de subsidiarité* (1993); Chantal Delsol, *L'état subsidiare* (1992).

[33] Finnis considers subsidiarity as a "principle ... of justice [which] affirms that the proper function of an association is to help the participants in the association to help themselves or, more precisely, to constitute themselves through the individual initiatives of choosing commitments (including commitments to friendship and other forms of association) and of realising these commitments." John Finnis, *Natural Law and Natural Rights* (2nd ed., 2012), 146.

[34] Russell Hittinger, "The Coherence of the Four Basic Principles of Catholic Social Doctrine: An Interpretation," in *Pursuing the Common Good: How Solidarity and Subsidiarity Can Work Together,* eds. Margaret S. Archer and Pierpaolo Donati (2008), 75.

[35] An incomplete list of whom includes: Nicholas Aroney, "Subsidiarity, Federalism and the Best Constitution: Thomas Aquinas on City, Province and Empire," *Law & Phil.* 26 (2007): 161; Thomas Behr, "Luigi Taparelli D'Azeglio, SJ (1793–1862) and the Development of Scholastic Natural-Law Thought as a Science of Society and Politics," *Journal of Markets & Morality* 6 (2003): 99; Patrick McKinley Brennan, "Subsidiarity in the Tradition of Catholic Social Doctrine," in *Global Perspectives on Subsidiarity* (Michelle Evans and Augusto Zimmermann eds., 2014): 29; Paolo Carozza, "Subsidiarity as a Structural Principle of International Human Rights Law," *American Journal of International Law* 97 (2003): 38; Jonathan Chaplin, "Subsidiarity and Social Pluralism," in *Global Perspectives on Subsidiarity* (Michelle Evans and Augusto Zimmermann, eds., 2014): 65; Franz H. Meuller, "The Principle of Subsidiarity in the Christian Tradition," The *American Catholic Sociological*

The Political, Moral and Final Purposes of Subsidiarity

While a state-centric definition of subsidiarity, focusing only on whether or not the state should intervene, leads us to believe that the principle of subsidiarity is only useful insofar as it helps to achieve particular political purposes (decentralization, increased legitimacy, etc.), the vision of subsidiarity presented in Catholic social thought, in which the associations are the fulcrum on which the activities of the state turn, allows us to realize that subsidiarity's purposes are much broader, including but transcending political goals.

Political Purposes

Since the principle of subsidiarity is the antidote to pure theories of sovereignty, and since the liberal framework that many of our nations have adopted inherits its conception of authority from these theories of sovereignty,[36] the political purposes and advantages of subsidiarity are articulated with the image of a highly centralized state in mind. (If we were consider the topic at a different point in history, in which our political systems were less influenced by a disembedded theory of authority, the list of political advantages of subsidiarity might have a different emphasis.) Five political purposes of subsidiarity can be identified from the social teaching of the Catholic Church: increased participation, more proximate decision making, better outcomes, more efficient decision making, and the alleviation of the state's administrative burden.

The first is that subsidiarity necessarily promotes participation, to be understood as "*a series of activities by means of which the citizen, either as an individual or in association with others, whether directly or through representation, contributes to the cultural, economic, political and social life of the civil community to which he belongs.*"[37] Addressing the United Nations, Pope John Paul II noted that practical involvement in society "gives [people] a direct sense of participation in their own destinies,"[38] and *Caritas in veritate* underscores how subsidiarity "fosters ... participation through assumption of responsibility" (CV, no. 57). The second political purpose of the principle of subsidiarity, and a corollary of increased participation, is that it results in increasingly proximate decision making because it ensures that, as much as

---

Review 4 (1943): 144; Robert K. Vischer, "Subsidiarity as a Principle of Governance: Beyond Devolution," *Indiana Law Review* 35 (2001): 103.

[36] Maria Cahill, "Sovereignty, Liberalism and the Intelligibility of Attraction to Subsidiarity," *American Journal of Jurisprudence* 61 (2016): 109.

[37] *CSDC*, no. 189, emphasis in original.

[38] Message of John Paul II to the General Assembly of the United Nations, August 22, 1980.

possible, decisions having an impact on a person's life are made by those "who are closest to them and who act as neighbors to those in need" (*CA*, no. 48). A third great purpose and advantage of subsidiarity, which again builds on the second one, is that when decisions are made proximately to the needs to be addressed, those needs are more intimately understood and more fully satisfied (*CA*, no. 48) and subsidiarity thereby promotes better outcomes.[39] This has been a consistent message of the encyclicals since *Rerum novarum* (*RN*, no. 57): respecting the decision-making autonomy of associations means that they can propose more holistic and more "effective" solutions (*CV*, no. 57) by addressing the needs of the whole person and not only those that can be solved materially or mechanically, through bureaucratic initiative (*DCE*, no. 28).

A fourth purpose of subsidiarity is that it ensures that decision making is more efficient, because if the state has to assume responsibility for decision making within associations, it must develop the expertise and capacity to do so, which in turn "leads to a loss of human energies and an inordinate increase of public agencies, which are dominated more by bureaucratic ways of thinking than by concern for serving their clients, and which are accompanied by an enormous increase in spending" (*CA*, no. 48). A corollary of this is the fifth political purpose of subsidiarity, which is the protection of the role of the state: trusting associations to secure the good they seek through their own efforts (aside from the exceptional circumstances in which the state must intervene) will mean that the state will "more freely, powerfully, and effectively do all those things that belong to it alone because it alone can do them" (*QA*, no. 80). This point, as developed in *Quadragesimo anno*, draws attention to the fact that it is not only associational freedom that is compromised when the state interferes in the life of civil associations to such an extent that it subsumes their activities as its own: "great harm" is done to the state, too, because, having taken over "the burdens which the wrecked associations once bore the State [is] overwhelmed and crushed by almost infinite tasks and duties" (*QA*, no. 78). To the contrary, honoring the principle of subsidiarity will ensure that "the happier and more prosperous [is] the condition of the State" (*QA*, no. 80).

Moral Purposes
The principle of subsidiarity does not just supply political benefits to a community that takes it seriously. There are also significant moral benefits: the vindication of social freedom, the protection of unity and harmony within associations, the flourishing of associations and civil society, and the prevention of state tyranny. These four moral purposes will be considered in turn.

---

[39] Message of John Paul II to the General Assembly of the United Nations, August 22, 1980.

Firstly, as explained by *Caritas in veritate*, the principle of subsidiarity in fact constitutes "an expression of inalienable human freedom" because of its support for associations and because it exhorts the state to assist, without overbearing, those associations, remembering that subsidiarity is "always designed to achieve ... emancipation, because it fosters freedom and participation" (*CV*, no. 57). *Octogesima adveniens* had previously referred to the need that each person should recognize "the concrete reality and the value of the freedom of choice" that is offered to him or her for the sake of engaging in politics at different levels and thereby seeking "to bring about the good of the city and of the nation and of mankind" (*OA*, no. 46), while *Laudato si'* similarly notes that the principle of subsidiarity "grants freedom to develop the capabilities present at every level of society" (*LS*, no. 196). In his speech before the PASS, Pope Benedict remarked that:

> A society that honors the principle of subsidiarity liberates people from a sense of despondency and hopelessness, granting them the freedom to engage with one another in the spheres of commerce, politics, and culture.[40]

Secondly, the principle of subsidiarity promotes "unity of purpose and harmony of action" by allowing civil associations to establish the internal rules and organizational structures that "best conduct to the attainment of their respective objects" (*RN*, no. 56). As Hittinger explains, if an association is denied the capacity to self-govern according to its internal rules, then, within that association "common action will depend entirely on spontaneous unanimity,"[41] and since spontaneous unanimity is impracticable, the association will likely disintegrate as a result of internal divisions. By honoring the right of an association to organize itself, the principle of subsidiarity promotes both the good purpose that the association seeks and the peaceful achievement of that purpose.

Thirdly, and very much linked to the first two purposes, the principle of subsidiarity, by creating the conditions where associations can thrive and flourish, forecloses the possibility that civil society groups become extinct, leaving a situation where there "remain virtually only individuals and the state" (*QA*, no. 78). Although the principle of subsidiarity does not mandate the creation of groups by the state (as will be seen in the next section), it does mandate the establishment of the conditions in which groups can constitute themselves and be successful in the achievement of their aims; it retains the

---

[40]   Pope Benedict XVI, *A Reason Open to God*, 189, 193.
[41]   Russell Hittinger, "The Coherence of the Four Basic Principles of Catholic Social Doctrine,"
75, 109.

idea and "structure of social governance" as opposed to state governance (*QA*, no. 78). The fourth moral purpose of subsidiarity is that adherence to the principle of subsidiarity forecloses the possibility of state tyranny, because it ensures that the state "acts within the limits of its competence" by taking final responsibility for the achievement of the common good without denying that the primary and presumptive responsibility for this achievement rests with the associations due to their superior capacity to honor personal dignity and social freedom (*OA*, no. 46). Addressing a group of lawyers in 1978, Pope John Paul II insisted that freedom would not properly be respected "if the tendency prevailed to attribute to the State and to the other territorial expressions of the public authority a centralizing and exclusive function of organization and direct management of the service or of rigid control."[42] In practical terms, the principle of subsidiarity has been described as "the most effective antidote against any form of all-encompassing welfare state" as well as a guard against the establishment of "a dangerous universal power of a tyrannical nature" (*CV*, no. 57). Moreover, it means that state agencies "must not extend their ownership beyond what is clearly required by considerations of the common good properly understood, and even then there must be safeguards" (*MM*, no. 117). Summing up this final moral purpose, *Evangelii gaudium* very aptly describes the role of the state, though "fundamental," as one that "calls for profound social humility" (*EG*, no. 240).

Final Purpose

Until relatively recently, discussion of the purposes of subsidiarity might have stopped here. However, the encyclicals given during the pontificates of Pope John Paul II, Pope Benedict XVI, and Pope Francis reveal a deeper dimension that had not previously been made apparent. In the same passage that highlights the need to respect the principle of subsidiarity, *Centesimus annus* added that "certain kinds of demands often call for a response which is not simply material but which is capable of perceiving the deeper human need," and specifically lists the needs of refugees, immigrants, the elderly, the sick, drug addicts, and others in circumstances that demand assistance (*CA*, no. 48). The encyclical holds that "all these people can be helped effectively only by those who offer them genuine fraternal support, in addition to the necessary care," the clear implication being that associations that spontaneously and personally respond to these deeply personal needs are to be preferred over government programs designed to secure maximum return on investment (*CA*, no. 48). Building on this idea, *Deus caritas est* (*DCE*) makes explicit

---

[42] John Paul II, "Address to Catholic Jurists, Rome" (November 25, 1978).

that "[t]here is no ordering of the State so just that it can eliminate the need for a service of love," and that the purpose of the principle of subsidiarity is to avoid the prospect of state tyranny but, at the same time, to avoid the prospect that the state becomes "a mere bureaucracy incapable of guaranteeing the very thing which the suffering person – every person – needs: namely, loving personal concern" (*DCE*, no. 28).

In adhering to the principle of subsidiarity, the state should gratefully acknowledge and foster initiatives and associations that emerge as a result of a combination of spontaneity and "closeness to those in need" in order to offer to those who suffer not only the material help that they need but also "refreshment and care for their souls . . . which often is even more necessary" (*DCE*, no. 28). *Caritas in veritate* goes on to describe the principle of subsidiarity as "[a] particular manifestation of charity and a guiding criterion for fraternal cooperation," which recognizes in each person "a subject who is always capable of giving something to others" (*CV*, no. 57) because of its elevated understanding of human dignity. By conceiving of "reciprocity as the heart of what it is to be a human being," subsidiarity ensures that assistance offered and received by associations does not injure the already fragile self-image of those in need (*CV*, no. 57). Furthermore, Pope Benedict XVI developed these ideas further in his PASS speech, when he noted that subsidiarity "encourages men and women to enter freely into life-giving relationships with those to whom they are most closely connected and upon whom they most immediately depend and demands of higher authorities respect for those relationships."[43] From the perspective of those public authorities, then, as they respect the principle of subsidiarity they not only promote participation, ensure better outcomes, or reduce the administrative burden of the state, they also "leave space for individual responsibility and initiative, but most importantly, they leave space for *love*,"[44] subsidiarity's ultimate purpose.

Finally, in *Laudato si'*, Pope Francis urged that we avoid a "mindset which . . . lacks concern for the inclusion of the most vulnerable members of society" and emphasizes "success and self-reliance" and does not seem to "favor an investment in efforts to help the slow, the weak or the less talented to find opportunities in life," by keeping the final purpose of the principle of subsidiarity in mind (*LS*, no. 196).

---

[43] Pope Benedict XVI, *A Reason Open to God* (Vatican City: Libreria Editrice Vaticana, 2013), 189, 192–193.
[44] *A Reason Open to God*, 193.

OPERATIONALIZING SUBSIDIARITY: THE NECESSARY BUT LIMITED ROLE OF LAW

The social teaching of the Catholic Church clearly contemplates a role for law in defending the principle of subsidiarity, as most succinctly expressed by *Pacem in terris* when it states that:

> The good order of society also requires that individuals and subsidiary groups within the State be effectively protected by law in the affirmation of their rights and the performance of their duties, both in their relations with each other and with government officials. (*PT*, no. 69)

Specifically referring to the emergence of labor law following the publication of *Rerum novarum*, *Quadragesimo anno* endorsed this expansion of the legislative mandate in defense of workers' rights (*QA*, no. 28). The International Theological Commission in its 2009 report entitled "In Search of a Universal Ethic: A New Look at Natural Law" meanwhile seems to envisage that the principle of subsidiarity should operate not only at legislative but also at constitutional levels when it states that "[n]atural law contains the idea of the state, based on law, structured according to the principle of subsidiarity, respecting persons and inter-mediate bodies, and regulating their interactions."[45] Indeed, part of the motivation for law in upholding associational freedom and the right of associations to be self-governing could be to defend the principle of constitutional self-determination at the level of the nation state, as *Rerum novarum* explains:

> Private societies ... cannot nevertheless be absolutely, and as such, prohibited by public authority. For, to enter into a "society" of this kind is the natural right of man; and the State has for its office to protect natural rights, not to destroy them; and, if it forbids its citizens to form associations, it contradicts the very principle of its own existence, for both they and it exist in virtue of the like principle, namely, the natural tendency of man to dwell in society. (*RN*, no. 51)

The Compendium notes, at the other end of the scale, that the judiciary should be involved in the provision of practical assistance to individual associations.[46] Other tasks that seem to fit with juridical competence would be those of determining whether or not exceptional circumstances exist to

---

[45] International Theological Commission, "In Search of a Universal Ethic: A New Look at Natural Law" (Vatican City, 2009), no. 99.

[46] *CSDC*, no. 419; no. 186.

justify an intervention by state agencies[47] and monitoring the assistance given to ensure that it does not overstep its proper bounds and is withdrawn as soon as possible. Although law could never ban associations as such, without undercutting the legitimacy of its own mandate (*RN*, no. 51), nevertheless, it will occasionally be "fitting that the law should intervene to prevent certain associations, as when men join together for purposes which are evidently bad, unlawful, or dangerous" and to dissolve such associations that already exist (*RN*, no. 52).

Despite having many good reasons to honor the principle of subsidiarity, the encyclicals note that there have been many occasions when law has followed "a very different course," when state authorities have "laid violent hands" on communities that were "perfectly blameless" and, rather than fulfilling its duty "to respect and cherish them and, if need be, to defend them from attack," has instead "placed them under control of civil law, taken away their rights as corporate bodies, and despoiled them of their property" (*RN*, no. 53). This antisubsidiarity tendency jeopardizes the political, moral, and final purposes of subsidiarity and ultimately conduces to a situation where there exist only individuals and the state, civil society associations having been eradicated.

Aside from the danger that law may be used as an antisubsidiarity tool in its tendency to precipitate the extinction of associations, there is another danger, which is less well recognized, and that is that law may be used as an antisubsidiarity tool in its tendency to take upon itself the authority to establish associations. A state that "decentralizes" power by creating smaller agencies and delegating its own power to them or by creating relationships between people and conferring mutual duties on them does not vindicate associational freedom; it infringes it. Catholic Social Teaching presents this idea when it underscores the necessity of allowing social groups to emerge spontaneously and "through informal means," without the involvement of the state.[48] Law should therefore avoid the temptation to initiative a program of social engineering by assuming the responsibility of creating families, companies, charities, and so on. Instead, in the exercise of "profound social humility" that the principle of subsidiarity conditions (*EG*, no. 240), law must confine itself to recognizing and honoring associations that already exist, and then pursuing objectives that make it more likely that new associations will emerge. These objectives include:

> [R]espect and effective promotion of the human person and the family; ever greater appreciation of associations and intermediate organizations ...; the

---

[47]   *CSDC*, no. 188.
[48]   *CSDC*, no. 419; cf. *RN*, no. 53, *QA*, no. 24, *DCE*, no. 28.

encouragement of private initiative ...; the presence of pluralism in society and due representation of its vital components; safeguarding human rights and the rights of minorities; bringing about bureaucratic and administrative decentralization; striking a balance between the public and private spheres, with the resulting recognition of the *social* function of the private sphere; appropriate methods for making citizens more responsible in actively "being a part" of the political and social reality of their country.[49]

This discussion of the operationalization of the principle of subsidiarity reveals a noteworthy asymmetry: while law can respect civil society through its adherence to the principle of subsidiarity and law can destroy civil society through its failure to respect the principle of subsidiarity, law cannot create civil society because law cannot create associations except in violation of associational freedom and the principle of subsidiarity. This insight was present in Taparelli's original theory of society and social justice, in which he held, as Burke describes, that:

> The large society is built, not from the top down but from the bottom up out of the small one. Therefore, the large society is in an important sense *subordinate to* the small ones. Each of these smaller societies has its own end, its own authority, its own principles of action, and its own rights ... Each lesser society must preserve its own inner unity without threatening that of the whole; and every larger society must maintain its unity without destroying the unity of the lesser societies.[50]

This asymmetry further confirms that the state-centric understanding of subsidiarity is inadequate to capture its true nature.

If the state cannot create civil society because it cannot create associations, and if we live, as many of us do, in a polity in which there is a need to revitalize civil society,[51] to what or whom can we turn in hopes of such a renaissance? To the irrepressibly creative and social human spirit and the ever-fruitful mutual engagement between persons, to the goods that are achieved when children play soccer and young people run a soup kitchen and colleagues work as a team, and even to the Church herself, who through her parishes, voluntary organizations, and outreach programs is particularly suited to the formation of associations that serve the needs of others, thereby reenergizing civil society,

---

[49] CSDC, no. 187.
[50] Thomas Patrick Burke, "The Origins of Social Justice: Taparelli d'Azeglio," *Modern Age* 52 (Spring 2010), 97, emphasis added.
[51] Paolo Carozza, "The Problematic Applicability of Subsidiarity to International Law," *American Journal of Jurisprudence* 61 (2016): 51.

protected by the fact that she cannot replace the state by assuming responsibility for building a just legal system and constitutional order (*DCE*, no. 28).

CONCLUSION

Having canvassed the social teaching of the Catholic Church to discover the
nature, purposes, and operationalization of the principle of subsidiarity, it
becomes plain that the principle of subsidiarity must not be conceived of in
a state-centric way because the associations that it protects are the fulcrum on
which it rests, because its purposes transcend the political advantages that it
offers, and because associations cannot be generated by state action but must
freely emerge spontaneously in response to some particular need and in the
service of some particular good. In essence, the paradox that subsidiarity
seemingly requires contradictory things is resolved when we reach the more
perfect understanding that the principle of subsidiarity reorients the state away
from itself and toward service to associations and the vindication of
associational freedom.

18

Socialism and Capitalism in Catholic Social Thought

Catherine Ruth Pakaluk

One cannot easily overstate the place of socialism in the development of
Catholic social thought. Dubbed "pernicious fictions" by Pius IX,[1] socialism
and communism are the founding heresies of the formal tradition of the social
teaching of the Church.[2] Between the advent of Marxism and the close of
World War II – nearly a full century – the papacy devoted at least eight major
encyclicals[3] to socialism, communism, or questions of social, political, and
economic life bearing directly upon socialism or communism. Among these
are *Nostis et nobiscum* (On the Church in the Pontifical States) written by Pius
IX in 1849, attributing to "the wicked theories of this Socialism and
Communism" the goal of "turning the spirits of the Italian people away
from the Catholic faith" and plotting for the "overthrow the entire order of
human affairs" through the haze of "perverted teachings."[4] The major documents also include letters that bookend Leo XIII's papacy, *Quod apostolici
muneris* (On Socialism) in 1878, the second letter issued by Leo, in the very
first year of his pontificate, declaring socialism a "deadly plague" leading
society to the "verge of destruction," and *Graves de communi re* (On

---

[1] Pius IX, Encyclical Letter *Nostis et nobiscum* (On the Church in the Pontifical States) (1849),
    no. 18.
[2] Socialism and communism have a variety of historical, political, and ideological expressions.
    Unless otherwise noted, this chapter refers to the socialism of the late eighteenth and early
    nineteenth centuries with a primary political embodiment in continental Europe and roots in
    the Saint-Simonians. Also, when speaking of communism, this chapter refers principally to the
    political expressions of Marxian communism, especially in the twentieth century in Soviet
    Russia after the pair of revolutions of 1917 and in Mexico beginning in 1910 through 1920. These
    political movements grew out of the work of Karl Marx and Frederick Engels in the mid-
    nineteenth century. Early communist agitation was often placed under the heading of "soci-
    alism" in general – though into the twentieth century papal thought begins to address com-
    munism more specifically.
[3] See Table 1.
[4] *NEN*, nos. 6 and 3, respectively.

Christian Democracy) in 1901, in which the consequences of socialism are likened to a "harvest of misery," nearly a half-century before F. A. Hayek published *Road to Serfdom*.[5] Finally, to these major documents pertaining to socialism belong *Rerum novarum* (On Capital and Labor) presented in 1891 by Leo XIII, *Quadragesimo anno* (On the Reconstruction of the Social Order) in 1931 by Pius XI, and the letter that represented the final statement of Pius XI on socialism, *Divini redemptoris* (On Atheistic Communism) released in 1937, on the Feast of St. Joseph, in which communism is denounced as "intrinsically wrong," or *cum intrinsecus sit pravus* according to the original Latin text.[6] In that dramatic statement, the pope pleads with the bishops to guide the faithful away from any form of collaboration with the "satanic scourge."[7]

A careful examination of the other social texts of the Leonine era (from roughly 1850 to 1950)[8] reveals, moreover, explicit references to the influence of socialism in areas of social life distinct from, or more accurately *prior to*, economic and political life. These include the family, in *Arcanum* (On Christian Marriage) in 1880, in which Leo XIII lists the "Communists" among those whose efforts are "aimed at the destruction of Christian marriage,"[9] and in *Casti connubii* (On Christian Marriage) in 1930, in which Pius XI describes the "the wicked aim of Socialists and Communists" to cause "not only private families, but all public society" to be "miserably driven into that general confusion and overthrow of order."[10] These also include education, as belonging to the family and to the Church before it belongs to the state, in *Divini illius magistri* (On Christian Education) in 1929, in which Pius XI credits the "theories of advanced Socialism" with the "present-day lamentable decline in family education" where "children are actually being torn from the bosom of the family, to be formed (or, to speak more accurately, to be deformed and depraved) in godless schools and associations, to irreligion and hatred";[11] and the Church, in *Quod multum* (On the Liberty of the Church) in 1886, in which Leo XIII explicitly refers to the "danger of

---

[5]   Leo XIII, Encyclical Letter *Quod apostolici muneris* (On Socialism) (1878), no. 1; Leo XIII, Encyclical Letter *Graves de communi re* (On Christian Democracy) (1901), no. 21; c.f. F. A. Hayek, *The Road to Serfdom* (Chicago: University of Chicago Press, 1944).

[6]   Pius XI, Encyclical Letter *Divini redemptoris* (On Atheist Communism) (1937), no. 58. *Cum intrinsecus sit pravus* could be more literally translated as "fatally flawed from within."

[7]   DR, no. 7.

[8]   The papacy of Leo XIII spans from 1878 to 1903. I include under the Leonine era also the preceding papacy of Pius IX beginning in 1846, as well as the papacies following Leo XIII through Pius XII.

[9]   Leo XIII, Encyclical Letter *Arcanum divinae* (On Christian Marriage) (1880), no. 13.

[10] Pius XI, Encyclical Letter *Casti connubii* (On Christian Marriage) (1930), no. 92.

[11] Pius XI, Encyclical Letter *Divini illius magistri* (On Christian Education) (1929), no. 73.

Socialism" for the Church.[12] One may additionally find direct mention of socialism and communism in the major encyclicals related to the innovations in political life, taking hold in Europe and the United States in the late nineteenth and early twentieth centuries. Among these, written by Leo XIII, are *Diuturnum* (On the Origin of Civil Power) in 1881, where Leo boldly condemns communism and socialism (together with nihilism) as a "false philosophy" that has "already produced great ills amongst men," has "reached the limit of horrors," and "will cause the very greatest disasters to posterity";[13] *Libertas* (On the Nature of Human Liberty) in 1888, in which Leo equates "Socialists and members of other seditious societies" with "a road leading straight to tyranny"; and *Graves de communi re* (On Christian Democracy) in 1901, where he describes the Church's "duty to warn Catholics, in unmistakable language, how great the error was which was lurking in the utterances of Socialism, and how great the danger was that threatened not only their temporal possessions, but also their morality and religion."[14]

To all of the above, one may add a number of major and minor texts, especially of Pius XI, which address national threats from communism in various countries. For instance, *Divini redemptoris* (On Atheistic Communism) in 1937 points out the "conspiracy of silence on the part of a large section of the non-Catholic press of the world"; this conspiracy reveals a blatant contradiction:

> [I]t is impossible otherwise to explain how a press usually so eager to exploit even the little daily incidents of life has been able to remain silent for so long about the horrors perpetrated in Russia, in Mexico and even in a great part of Spain; and that it should have relatively so little to say concerning a world organization as vast as Russian Communism.[15]

In addition, *Acerba animi* (On the Persecution of the Church in Mexico) acknowledges the presence of "communistic propaganda" existing in Mexico.[16] Lastly, one must not fail to mention the major (and minor) decadal reaffirmations of the teachings of *Rerum novarum* in 1891, each of which deals in its own way with the tenets of socialism or communism, or with the legacy of these errors: *Quadragesimo anno* on the 40th anniversary in 1931, *Radio*

---

[12]   Leo XIII, Encyclical Letter *Quod multum* (On the Liberty of the Church) (1886), no. 4.
[13]   Leo XIII, Encyclical Letter *Diuturnum* (On the Origin of Civil Power) (1881), no. 23.
[14]   Leo XIII, Encyclical Letter *Libertas* (On the Nature of Human Liberty) (1888), no. 16; GC, no. 2.
[15]   DR, no. 18.
[16]   Pius XI, Encyclical Letter *Acerba animi* (On Persecution of the Church in Mexico) (1932), no. 9.

Message of Pius XII on the 50th in 1941, *Mater et magistra* (On Christianity and Social Progress) on the 70th in 1961, *Octogesima adveniens* on the 80th in 1971, and *Centesimus annus* on the 100th in 1991. Altogether, socialism and communism appear so often in the papal texts of the Leonine era, and with such importance, that they might be described as central foils over and against which the doctrine of the Church is defined and refined over time. No other heresy addressed by the social magisterium can claim such prominence in the Leonine era, nor in the era which follows, the John Pauline era, which includes the papacies of John XXIII, Paul VI, John Paul II, and Benedict XVI.

In contrast, the place and role of capitalism in Catholic social thought is significantly subtler and more nuanced, since it does not constitute an "opposite" heresy, and therefore bears no *analogous* treatment to that of socialism. According to Pius XI's gloss on *Rerum novarum*, the capitalist economic regime "is not to be condemned in itself. And surely it is not of its own nature vicious."[17] Understood principally in the industrial expression that dominated the Leonine era, both Leo XIII and Pius XI affirm of capitalism that "capital can [not] do without labor, nor labor without capital"[18] and envision the possibility of a harmonious relation between owners and nonowning workers if "norms of right order"[19] are respected. *Quadragesimo anno* provides the fullest and most detailed treatment of a capitalist system *per se* in the entire formal tradition of social thought; as such, it assists retrospectively in a complete interpretation of *Rerum novarum* and also sets the tone for the magisterial treatment of capitalism prospectively. This tone is characterized by two primary tensions: first is the need to situate the mind of the Church somewhat decisively with respect to an economic system that is itself *emerging and developing*. The nascent capitalist system was then, and is still now, struggling to understand itself, and admits of no single, authoritative definition; therefore, the magisterial documents exhibit an uneasiness in the use of the term capitalism (or capitalist system) that is not at all similar to the contemporaneous uses of the term socialism (or communism).[20] The difficulty I highlight here is illustrated memorably in the John Pauline era, with the "if by Capitalism" statement in *Centesimus annus*, in which the Pontiff

[17] Pius XI, Encyclical Letter *Quadragesimo anno* (On Reconstruction of the Social Order: 40th Anniversary of *Rerum novarum*) (1931), no. 101.
[18] Leo XIII, Encyclical Letter *Rerum novarum* (On the Condition of the Working Classes) (1891), no. 19; QA, nos. 53 and 100.
[19] QA, no. 101.
[20] A complete treatment of the historical development of the understanding of capitalism could not be sustained in a chapter of this length. It suffices to attempt to point out the complexity of the problem to highlight the work that still remains for scholars of political economy and Catholic social thought.

predicates affirmation of capitalism on a definition of the same that corresponds to an authentically Christian social and economic order.[21]

The second tension arises from the need to differentiate between capitalism *per se*, a particular economic regime that has both advantages and disadvantages, and that set of principles of "right order" that are affirmed by the Church, such as the right to private property. The difficulty arises since many of the principles of right order affirmed by the Church are present to a greater or lesser degree in specific instantiations of capitalist economies, and yet "The Church has no models to present."[22]

In the remainder of this chapter, I will first aim to provide an account of socialism and communism as founding heresies of the social doctrine of the Church, aiming to distill the essence of the Church's condemnation. In the second section, I will argue that capitalism does not constitute a similar (but, say, opposite) heresy, since capitalism is not *in essence* an error about human nature and man's relation to created goods. Finally, I will attempt to provide a schema for thinking about the axis of philosophical mistakes related to socialism and capitalism. This axis derives from the famous "twin rocks" treatment in *Quadragesimo anno*, a passage which emerges not only as a key for unlocking the problems with socialism and communism, but also presents a paradigm that allows for a correct understanding of the conditions under which capitalism best serves the common good of human society. For the sake of tractability, the treatment in this chapter focuses primarily on the development of the social magisterium in the Leonine era.

I SOCIALISM

A Three Primary Doctrines on the "Community of Goods"

The teaching on socialism has many expressions in the century-long Leonine period, but the classic and clearest treatment remains the one articulated in

---

[21] "If by 'capitalism' is meant an economic system which recognizes the fundamental and positive role of business, the market, private property and the resulting responsibility for the means of production, as well as free human creativity in the economic sector, then the answer is certainly in the affirmative, even though it would perhaps be more appropriate to speak of a 'business economy,' 'market economy' or simply 'free economy.' But if by 'capitalism' is meant a system in which freedom in the economic sector is not circumscribed within a strong juridical framework which places it at the service of human freedom in its totality, and which sees it as a particular aspect of that freedom, the core of which is ethical and religious, then the reply is certainly negative," John Paul II, Encyclical Letter *Centesimus annus* (On the 110th Anniversary of *Rerum novarum*) (1991), no. 42.

[22] CA, no. 43.

the first fifteen paragraphs of *Rerum novarum*. Three primary propositions (or doctrines) about private property, the abolition of which was "the main tenet of Socialism," may be taken as the distillation of Leo's teaching on the "community of goods."[23]

The first of these propositions is that remunerative labor is the basic right and duty of man, and that labor for wages is oriented to the accumulation of property, where a man "intends to acquire a right full and real" (*ius verum perfectumque sibi quaerit*, more literally, "true and complete") including both use and disposal of that property. It is explicit that this right of disposal of property is "as he pleases" (*uti velit*) in no. 5 and extends to accumulated wealth beyond what "is necessary for the satisfaction of his needs." *Rerum novarum*, no. 5 additionally makes the strong claim that the "liberty of disposing of wages" through, for instance, savings or acquisition of land is itself directed to "the hope and possibility" of bettering of one's condition in life.[24] Leo sees the right to wage labor and private property as the path by which the poor can be encouraged to labor diligently (virtuously) in pursuit of a better life. The complete Leonine position, elaborated throughout *Rerum novarum*, is already explicit in no. 5: that the working classes should not be captured by envy, nor greed, nor stealing – all ascribed to socialists – but neither should they be consigned to hopelessness if economic life follows right principles.

The second proposition is stated explicitly at the beginning of no. 13: "That right to private property, therefore, which has been proved to belong naturally to individual persons, must in like wise belong to a man in his capacity of head of a family; nay, that right is all the stronger in proportion as the human person receives a wider extension in the family group."[25] Thus Leo expands but also strengthens his claim about the inviolability of private property, offering a new foundation for the same proposition. Whatever it is we think we know about society, he says, this at least holds true: that "the family must necessarily have rights and duties which are prior to those of the community, and founded more immediately in nature" since the "domestic household is antecedent, as well in idea as in fact, to the gathering of men into a community."[26] From this, Leo asserts that there is "no other way" for a father to fulfill his "sacred" duty according to the "law of Nature," which is "to provide food and all necessaries for those whom he has begotten." He adds that a man must be able "to transmit to his children by inheritance" the "ownership of productive property," which he

---

[23]   RN, no. 15.
[24]   RN, no. 5.
[25]   RN, no. 13.
[26]   RN, no. 13.

has acquired through his labor. The duty of parents to provide for their children, Leo maintains, must not be "abolished nor absorbed by the State."[27] The socialist assault on private property would certainly "destroy the structure of the home." This second doctrine therefore attaches an inviolable right to property *to individuals*, but *for the sake of those* who are naturally (and rightly) dependent upon them, both now and in the future. This proposition is advanced as a strong, nonindividualist basis for private property, and at the same time, a normative principle of right order and a safeguard of intergenerational justice.

The third primary doctrine advanced by Leo at the outset of *Rerum novarum* ascribes to private property a *nonaccidental* role in the wealth and prosperity of nations in general, and, a fortiori, in the welfare of the working classes. Without private property, Leo says, "the sources of wealth themselves would run dry, for no one would have any interest in exerting his talents or his industry."[28] Taking a position very close to Adam Smith's in *Wealth of Nations*, Leo sees private property as the fulcrum by which individual efforts are leveraged for the benefit of society. The lever is the incentive for personal gain, and can only be safeguarded when there is a tight and close connection between the efforts of a man on the one side, and that which he is able to reap for himself on the other. Thus, like the butcher, brewer, and baker in Smith's famous passage[29] and without intending it directly, men who labor for their own gain – even merely to earn wages which they may keep – lift the general welfare and play a role in the cultivation of creation.

Leo's final pronouncement on the community of goods in *Rerum novarum*, no. 15 goes beyond the positive principles listed above: in the absence of private property, the "ideal equality about which [the socialists] maintain pleasant dreams would be in reality the levelling down of all to a like condition of misery and degradation."[30] There cannot be equality in prosperity, Leo warns, but only equality in poverty.

B Doctrine of Natural Difference and Two Correlates

This warning gives way to a fourth primary doctrine, laid out in *Rerum novarum*, no. 17, so important as to warrant attention both to its existence, its

---

[27] RN, no. 14.

[28] RN, no. 15.

[29] "It is not from the benevolence of the butcher, the brewer, or the baker that we expect our dinner, but from their regard to their own interest," Adam Smith, "Of the Principle Which Gives Occasion to the Division of Labour," in *An Inquiry into the Nature and Causes of the Wealth of Nations* (1776).

[30] RN, no. 15.

meaning, and a particular historical precedent. The principle might be called the "doctrine of natural difference," and pertains to social order in general rather than to the question of private property. It is worth rendering *Rerum novarum*, no. 17 in its entirety:

> It must be first of all recognized that the condition of things inherent in human affairs must be borne with, for it is impossible to reduce civil society to one dead level. Socialists may in that intent do their utmost, but all striving against nature is in vain. There naturally exist among mankind manifold differences of the most important kind; people differ in capacity, skill, health, strength; and unequal fortune is a necessary result of unequal condition. Such unequality is far from being disadvantageous either to individuals or to the community. Social and public life can only be maintained by means of various kinds of capacity for business and the playing of many parts; and each man, as a rule, chooses the part which suits his own peculiar domestic condition. As regards bodily labor, even had man never fallen from the state of innocence, he would not have remained wholly idle; but that which would then have been his free choice and his delight became afterwards compulsory, and the painful expiation for his disobedience. "Cursed be the earth in thy work; in thy labor thou shalt eat of it all the days of thy life."[31]

The doctrine advanced here contains three subpropositions. The first is that civil society is organically colored by contours derived from natural differences in the human condition and unequal fortunes in life.

The second, related to the first, is that these differences are not, in themselves, bad for society. On the contrary, they are necessary, since they lead to a special kind of good: the good of depending upon each other for the satisfaction of material and spiritual needs. This good is special because it is the "glue" of social order, and the basis for solidarity, best defined as the "the Christian virtue of unity among friends,"[32] where friendship is understood as constituted and perfected by gifts from one to the other. By definition, giving requires the offering or exchanging of what the other lacks. One cannot receive as a gift what one already possesses. Thus, the unity arising from friendship – what the magisterium calls solidarity – is predicated on differences in material and spiritual endowments. Notably, we find a compelling historical precedent for the notion of difference as constitutive of friendship

---

[31] *RN*, no. 17.
[32] Catherine Ruth Pakaluk, Joseph Anthony Burke, and Andreas Widmer, "Solidarity and Job Creation: Substitutes or Complements?" in *The Challenge of Charity: Freedom and Charity Working Together*, ed. M. Schlag, J. A. Mercado, and J. E. Miller (Rome: MCE Books, 2015), 243–256.

(love) in the thought of the medieval mystic Catherine of Siena, particularly in her *Dialogue*:

> All these I have given indifferently, and I have not placed them all in one soul, in order that man should, perforce, have material for love of his fellow. I could easily have created men possessed of all that they should need both for body and soul, but I wish that one should have need of the other, and that they should be My ministers to administer the graces and the gifts that they have received from Me. Whether man will or no, he cannot help making an act of love.[33]

From these considerations, we can attest that: "Factual inequality is required [for social unity] ... not because we have to be respected for being different, but because without it we lack reason to be responsible for anyone,"[34] where responsibility is understood as – in essence – the moral obligation to give to one another, in the context of familial or communal relations, as well as in the formal economy, where purchase and exchange in a Christian culture has more than an arms-length meaning, but a personalist one as well.

The third subproposition in *Rerum novarum*, no. 17 is simple: bodily work and labor is not itself an evil. What is evil is rather the suffering we experience in work which is a consequence of sin.[35] Labor would still be the occupation of humanity even without the fall. Thus, striving against the burden – or necessity – of labor is in vain, and is part and parcel with a romanticized vision of human life, which is inconsistent with Christianity. "Nothing is more useful than to look upon the world as it really is," Leo says, "and at the same time to seek elsewhere, as We have said, for the solace to its troubles."[36] The doctrine of natural difference therefore operates as a kind of Christian realism – a realism which rejects ambition for equality of condition, while providing the basis for equality of dignity, which is brotherhood in Christ and the universal call to holiness.

From this doctrine of natural difference, two correlates follow, held steadily by Leo and all the popes in the Leonine era. First, socialism is *unnatural*: a heresy against nature and "the world as it really is."[37] For Leo, the core truth about man and his relation to creation is that he is made to cultivate the garden

---

[33]   Catherine of Siena, A Treatise on Divine Providence, in Late Medieval Mysticism, ed. Ray C. Petry, The Library of Christian Classics, vol. 13 (Philadelphia: Westminster Press, 1957), 282.

[34]   Catherine Ruth Pakaluk, "Dependence on God and Man: Toward a Catholic Constitution of Liberty," *Journal of Markets and Morality* 19, no. 2 (Fall 2016): 227–252.

[35]   "Yet no one can escape the experience of suffering or the evils in nature which seem to be linked to the limitations proper to creatures: and above all to the question of moral evil," *Catechism of the Catholic Church*, no. 385.

[36]   RN, no. 18.

[37]   RN, no. 18.

through (unavoidable) hard work and care (by the sweat of his brow); to accumulate the fruits of this labor and make use of this property to sustain those who
are naturally dependent upon him. He is further to pass on what is left at the end
of his laboring (estate). The abolition of private property attacks this core reality
about man and creation, and puts in its place a fictional account of man in
relation to the goods of the earth, in which romantic dreams are encouraged and
base passions stirred up. The fiction is ultimately "pernicious"[38] since it "only
injures those whom it would seem most to benefit."[39]

The second correlate, which follows from the first, is that socialism is
inherently *technocratic*. To see this, begin with the Aristotelian notion of
violence as that which arrests the natural motion or tendency of
something.[40] Since socialism is unnatural, to impose it must be violent,
achieved by dint of force and not reason. By "technocratic" we understand
therefore the violent (or forced, or tyrannical) application of science – or
a scientific "mechanism of human design" – for practical ends that are
contrary to faith and reason, since together these enlighten our understanding
of what is properly natural.[41] Commensurate with these points, Pius XI,
building on the insights of Leo XIII and Pius IX, asserts that socialism and
communism are bound up with the errors of the Machine Age:

> [T]he immortal Leo XIII, in his Encyclical *Quod Apostolici Muneris*, defined
> Communism as "the fatal plague which insinuates itself into the very marrow
> of human society only to bring about its ruin."[2] With clear intuition he
> pointed out that the atheistic movements existing among the masses of the
> Machine Age had their origin in that school of philosophy which for

---

[38] *RN*, no. 14.
[39] *RN*, no. 15.
[40] "So when fire or earth is moved by something the motion is violent when it is unnatural, and
natural when it brings to actuality the proper activities that they potentially possess" (Bekker,
255a 28–30). And, also, "If then the motion of all things that are in motion is either natural or
unnatural and violent, and all things whose motion is violent and unnatural are moved by
something, and something other than themselves, and again all things whose motion is natural
are moved by something – both those that are moved by themselves and those that are not
moved by themselves (e.g., light things and heavy things, which are moved either by that
which brought the thing into existence as such and made it light and heavy, or by that which
released what was hindering and preventing it); then all things that are in motion must be
moved by something" (Bekker, 255b 31-256a3). Aristotle *Physics*, trans. R. P. Hardie and
R. K. Gaye. In *The Complete Works of Aristotle: The Revised Oxford Translation*, edited by
Jonathan Barnes. 2 vols. (Princeton, NJ: Princeton University Press, 1984).
[41] For classic treatments in the John Pauline era, see especially Paul VI, Encyclical Letter
Populorum progressio (On the Development of Peoples) (1967), no. 34, and Benedict XVI,
Caritas in veritate (On Integral Human Development in Charity and Truth) (2009), no. 6, esp.
nos. 69–72.

centuries had sought to divorce science from the life of the Faith and of the Church.[42]

Necessary to the development of the social magisterium with respect to socialism is the understanding of persons as naturally – organically – connected by fixed relations of dependence, which form the basis for human rights. For instance, rights vis-à-vis property arise from duties owed to God (to the cultivation of creation),[43] to self (sustenance),[44] and to family (care, support, inheritance).[45] It is not accidental that the socialist-communist proposal starts from a mistake about property, and moves to a mistake about the family. The collectivism of socialism implied by the "community of goods" requires that men and women owe nothing more – and nothing less – to their offspring or to their parents than they owe to the most distant members of the community. As there are, in this schema, no special relations between any persons or groups of persons, the community of goods implies the atomization of individuals – typically achieved, always imperfectly, through coercive mechanisms of the state that may be aptly called technocratic. People do not give up the affections or the obligations of family life naturally or easily.

C Negative versus Positive Principles, and the Development of Social "Doctrine"

The teaching on socialism is both negative and positive; negatives abound, and many of the colorful ones are cited in the introduction to this chapter. However, the most important part of the teaching takes the form of the naming of positive principles, or "norms of right order."[46] These principles *affirm* what is correct rather than merely *reject* what is incorrect. The three doctrines on property are examples, as is the doctrine on natural difference.

The process by which the popes of the Leonine era identify such principles of "right order" in social life as "social doctrine" is analogous to the way that the Church tends to define doctrine in general. That is, the Church takes a conservative position first, waiting to state what is affirmatively true – the positive teaching – until she has rejected what isn't true, the negative teaching; this process can look defensive since it involves responding *ex post* to a growing, possibly entrenched heresy, which is not understood fully as such

---

[42] *DR*, no. 4.
[43] *RN*, nos. 7–8.
[44] *RN*, no. 44.
[45] *RN*, nos. 12–14.
[46] *QA*, no. 101.

until the declaration of the contrary (correct) teaching. For instance, while the Arian heresies about the nature of the Trinity arose during the time of the teaching of Arius (who lived from 256 to 336 AD), it took the better part of a century to finally put the heresies aside *after the death of Arius*, beginning with the First Council of Nicaea, which condemned the teaching of Arius and provided the original Nicene Creed of 325 AD, and ending with the First Council in Constantinople in 381 AD, including the revised Nicene Creed of the same year, at which time the doctrines on the Trinity are generally accepted to have been settled.[47]

Analogously, it is rightful to understand socialism as the *founding heresy of the social magisterium*; the positive principles of social doctrine arise *ex post*, in response to, a unified set of heresies related to socialism and communism. The need to argue that socialism was an unnatural, vicious system gave rise to the Church's interest in articulating the principles of right order. Once articulated, however, the principles are available to the Church across time, place, and circumstance. Therefore, the positive doctrines related to private property, labor, and capital, and the role of religion in society, developed in response to socialism and communism, aided the primary development of the teachings on capitalism.

II CAPITALISM

A Quadragesimo anno *and the Social Question*

Quadragesimo anno (On the Reconstruction of the Social Order) takes pride of place among encyclical letters for its clarity of teaching on matters related to capitalism. Written in 1931, between the two great wars and on the 40th anniversary of *Rerum novarum*, Pius XI enjoyed a closer vantage point than more recent letters written in anniversary of *Rerum novarum* – such as *Centesimus annus* – but also had the benefit of an intervening forty years to refine and restate Leo XIII's initial contribution. Pius XI, ordained a priest in 1879 and studying at the Gregorian University and the Academy of St. Thomas Aquinas in Rome under the direction of teachers who collaborated and influenced the papacy of Leo XIII,[48] can be trusted as a particularly faithful interpreter of the Leonine magisterium, and his own pontificate develops and enlarges many of the themes and notes of Leo's.

---

[47] *The Catholic Encyclopedia*, "Arianism."
[48] Zsolt Aradi, *Pius XI: The Pope and the Man* (Literary Licensing, LLC, 2012).

The questions about capitalism are taken up in *Quadragesimo anno* in light of the charges leveled against it by "its most bitter accuser, socialism."[49] Following Leo XIII, Pius XI hoped to propose the "surest rules to solve aright that most difficult problem of human relations called 'the social question.'"[50] By "the social question" Pius XI meant the division of society into "two classes," one smaller enjoying the advantages of economic development, while the other, "the huge multitude of working people" (also called the "non-owning working class"[51]), lived "oppressed by wretched poverty."[52] Pius XI believed that this chasm of inequality posed a grave danger to the stability and harmony of society, through temptations to socialism among the poor, but also through an unwarranted confidence that liberalism, without the aid of "religion and the Church,"[53] could solve the social problem. Interestingly, Pius XI makes it clear that capitalism is not "the only economic system in force everywhere," and mentions agriculture as a separate kind of economic arrangement, an older one, whose members are also "being crushed by hardships and difficulties."[54] Thus, while primarily directed to a development of the teachings on socialism and capitalism, *Quadragesimo anno* spreads its concern to all of those who "live undeservedly in miserable and wretched conditions."[55]

B Primary Teachings on Capitalism

What did Pius XI mean when he used the term capitalism? Roughly, the answer can be found in no. 100 of *Quadragesimo anno* where, referring to *Rerum novarum*, Pius XI says that Leo XIII had in mind "that economic system, wherein, generally, some provide capital while others provide labor for a joint economic activity."[56] In no. 103 he further applies the phrase "modern industry" to refer to capitalist economic life, and so we have at least a fair idea that Pius XI understands capitalism to be the transformations in economic life often attached to the Industrial Revolution, but having roots generally in the British Isles, especially Northern England and Scotland. This is admittedly an embryonic sense of capitalism, divergent from contemporary manifestations of capitalism primarily in its emphasis on material capital and physical labor, as distinct from

---

[49] QA, no. 98.
[50] QA, no. 2.
[51] QA, no. 101.
[52] QA, no. 3.
[53] QA, no. 11.
[54] QA, no. 102.
[55] QA, no. 10; RN, no. 15.
[56] QA, no. 100.

intellectual capital – the understanding of which moderates and develops many of the earlier concerns about entrepreneurship, and from human capital – the understanding of which moderates and develops many of the earlier concerns about exploitation and the vulnerability of labor. Note that the notions of intellectual capital and human capital each tend to blur that older, sharp distinction between capital and labor; they also separately point to the need for a discussion about the legal and institutional framework for a capitalist economy that goes well beyond the tired comparison of *laissez-faire* "capitalism" to a more regulatory state. In reality, no form of capitalism can exist *laissez-faire* since the legal apparatus required to establish and protect property rights – intellectual and otherwise – already implies a fairly sophisticated set of protections and regulations. Given these distinctions between earlier and later forms of capitalism, it is especially valuable that the social magisterium develops via general principles of social order, rather than through the promotion of specific models for political economy.

Quadragesimo anno, following *Rerum novarum*, promulgated two primary teachings about capitalism. The first is that capitalism, understood in its most basic form, "that economic system, wherein, generally, some provide capital while others provide labor for a joint economic activity" is not to be rejected outright, since it is not – like every form of socialism – intrinsically wrong. "[I]t is evident," wrote Pius XI, "that [capitalism] is not to be condemned in itself. And surely it is not of its own nature vicious."[57] The second teaching, related to the first, is that capitalism – as an organic, and "natural" organizing structure, natural because springing from the inviolable right to private property – ought to be routinely scrutinized as to its correspondence to the aforementioned principles. Thus, we have Pius XI's praise of *Rerum novarum* as Leo's effort "to adjust this economic system according to the norms of right order."[58] Together these two teachings provide the basis for the claim, stated in the introduction to this chapter, that capitalism has not been treated *analogously* to socialism, as say, an opposite but equally grave error. On the contrary, in every explicit mention of capitalism (or capitalist economy) in the Leonine and John Pauline eras, capitalism is treated in a contingent way: as an acceptable, and even praiseworthy institution so long as, in the words of John Paul II, it "recognizes the fundamental and positive role of business, the market, private property and the resulting responsibility for the means of production, as well as free human creativity in the economic sector" while at the same time, circumscribing economic freedom "within a strong juridical framework which places

[57] QA, no. 101.
[58] QA, no. 101.

it at the service of human freedom in its totality, and which sees it as a particular aspect of that freedom, the core of which is ethical and religious."[59] This is absolutely distinct from every treatment of socialism in the social magisterium, and particularly in *Quadragesimo*: there are no special circumstances or qualifications which can render it even plausibly acceptable, since it begins – unlike capitalism – with an error about human nature in relation to created goods, to other persons, and ultimately in relation to God. On this point, Pius XI says memorably:

> If Socialism, like all errors, contains some truth (which, moreover, the Supreme Pontiffs have never denied), it is based nevertheless on a theory of human society peculiar to itself and irreconcilable with true Christianity. Religious socialism, Christian socialism, are contradictory terms; no one can be at the same time a good Catholic and a true socialist.[60]

At least two conclusions are warranted here. First, the essence of capitalism as understood by the social magisterium is not, fundamentally, an error about human nature – as is socialism. Rather, it is an economic arrangement that *may or may not be* oriented to a complete expression of the common good.[61] Second, since capitalism typically springs from principles that are consistent with right order, it is acceptable to work to revise and improve a specific capitalist economy – even if such an economy falls desperately short of the conditions that are needed for the common good. Practically speaking, this means that Christians need not refuse to work within a flawed capitalist economic order; for instance, one that does not regularly make allowances for the religious obligations of workers on the Lord's Day. Rather, Christians are urged to make use of prudence and professional expertise to "adjust" the economic order to reflect greater and greater correspondence with "the norms of right order," what I have previously called the "positive" principles of the social doctrine.

C *Just Wages, and Some Preliminaries*

Since capitalism is understood as "that economic system, wherein, generally, some provide capital while others provide labor for a joint economic

---

[59] CA, no. 42.
[60] QA, no. 120.
[61] I say "oriented" here because the Church never thinks of structures or institutional forms as guaranteeing a complete expression of the common good. Structures can only be oriented to or consistent with such an expression. The realization of the common good depends in practice more heavily on the degree of virtue present in the members of society and their collective progress toward virtue.

activity,"[62] the teachings related to wages form an essential part of the teachings on capitalism. However, since wages fall under the broader class of things owed by employers to workers, some preliminaries are required for the exposition of the teaching on fair wages. To begin, Pope Leo reminds employers in *Rerum novarum* that "according to natural reason and Christian philosophy, working for gain is creditable, not shameful, to a man, since it enables him to earn an honorable livelihood."[63] To this he adds that owners must not "look upon their work people as their bondsmen, but [instead] respect in every man his dignity as a person ennobled by Christian character," further admonishing that "to misuse men as though they were things in pursuit of gain, or to value them solely for their physical powers – that is truly shameful and inhuman." Owed to laborers, foremost, is a relationship grounded in respect. Therefore, when wages are *merely* fair, the duties of owners and employers toward workers have not yet been acquitted: such a view would reduce the relationship between employers and employees to an opportunistic exchange governed by arms-length considerations and a defective view of human solidarity.

The Leonine pontiffs insist instead that principles of right order call for employers to cultivate – in an appropriate manner – the full good of workers. Consequently:

> justice demands that, in dealing with the working man, religion and the good of his soul must be kept in mind. Hence, the employer is bound to see that the worker has time for his religious duties; that he be not exposed to corrupting influences and dangerous occasions; and that he be not led away to neglect his home and family, or to squander his earnings. Furthermore, the employer must never tax his work people beyond their strength, or employ them in work unsuited to their sex and age.[64]

Pius XI, for his part, mentions the importance of a "new branch of law" that has developed to protect the "sacred rights of the workers" including considerations for "life, health, strength, family, homes, workshops, wages and labor hazards ... with special concern for women and children."[65] These various categories, which include also respect for the Lord's Day and the religious duties of workers, outline a more complete picture of what is owed to workers above and beyond "fair" pay. They also raise difficult questions about the vulnerability of workers who are employed by non-Christian enterprises or entities that do not have the spiritual good of employees in view. There is at

---

[62] *QA*, no. 100.
[63] *RN*, no. 20.
[64] *RN*, no. 20.
[65] *QA*, no. 28.

least an implicit recognition that the "new branch of law" include religious liberty protections for workers whose (self-declared) duties to God in conscience are at odds with the interests of their employers, or even with prevailing notions of the common good.

The reason for establishing these additional, metaphysical, obligations of employers toward workers is to avoid an obvious *misuse* of the notion of fair wages, which is the idea that the agreed-upon price of labor should reflect *all the parts of justice* that are demanded by the magisterium. Indeed, a consistent difficulty in the interpretation of the social doctrine is that what is meant broadly to fall under the heading of "social justice" clearly extends *in principle and in practice* beyond what can be adequately, or even appropriately, covered by legal justice – or what can be required or protected in law. The tension comes into view on the matter of wages as much as on the matter of property. For instance, in Pope Leo's most extensive elaboration of the subject of fair wages, found in *Rerum novarum*, nos. 43–46, the Pontiff clearly regards justice as including not only what has been agreed upon, but also the suitability and rightness of what has been agreed upon. He writes: "Wages, as we are told, are regulated by free consent, and therefore the employer, when he pays what was agreed upon, has done his part and *seemingly is not called upon to do anything beyond*" [emphasis mine]. Leo rejects the notion that public enforcement of private contracts ensures justice in labor relations; the wage-level itself, in addition to the obligations considered above, including spiritual and human goods, are rightly subject to evaluation by norms of justice, even "natural justice" as Leo calls it in *Rerum novarum*, no. 45. But what is less clear is how the pontiffs envision the intervention of public authorities – such as the state or local municipalities – when circumstances are apprised to be "unjust."

A brief answer is that Leo XIII and Pius XI see the role of public authorities as primarily corrective – a measure of last resort – rather than primarily preventive, or even proscriptive. This may be seen most clearly in the language of *Rerum novarum*, no. 45, where the pope urges the formation of intermediary associations, "societies" or "boards," to safeguard "the interests of the wage-earners; the State being appealed to, should circumstances require, for its sanction and protection."[66] Leo also remarks that such associations are desirable *precisely* to "supersede undue interference on the part of the State" in view of the fact that "circumstances, times, and localities differ so widely."[67]

---

[66] *RN*, no. 45.
[67] *RN*, no. 45.

One notes in this *corrective role* for the public authority in matters of labor relations an application of the principle of subsidiarity, articulated exactly in this regard in *Quadragesimo anno*, no. 80:

> The supreme authority of the State ought, therefore, to let subordinate groups handle matters and concerns of lesser importance, which would otherwise dissipate its efforts greatly. Thereby the State will more freely, powerfully, and effectively do all those things that belong to it alone because it alone can do them: directing, watching, urging, restraining, as occasion requires and necessity demands. Therefore, those in power should be sure that the more perfectly a graduated order is kept among the various associations, in observance of the principle of "subsidiary function," the stronger social authority and effectiveness will be the happier and more prosperous the condition of the State.[68]

Importantly, while the principle of subsidiarity is often thought to be a matter of restraining the state, Pius XI advances subsidiarity not as antagonist, but as medicinal to the health of the state. As he says in no. 78:

> following upon the overthrow and near extinction of that rich social life which was once highly developed through associations of various kinds, there remain virtually only individuals and the State. This is to the great harm of the State itself; for, with a structure of social governance lost, and *with the taking over of all the burdens which the wrecked associations once bore, the State has been overwhelmed and crushed by almost infinite tasks and duties.*[69] [Emphasis mine]

From the foregoing at least two additional preliminaries arise in relation to the discussion of wages in capitalism. The first is that injustices in labor relations having to do with the wage level, or indeed any other human or spiritual good, are referred principally (though admittedly not solely) by the magisterium to intermediary associations to be addressed through cultural and moral suasion, habits and traditions, rather than by the state which can address the same only through the arm of legal justice. "Hard cases make poor law," it is said, and the magisterium appears to have had this in mind throughout the early development of the social doctrine. The role of public authorities, and especially that of the highest public authority, the state, is described minimally, even where it is admitted that broad matters of justice are in play.

The second preliminary is that the "rich social life" marked by associations, societies and boards, described in both *Rerum novarum* and *Quadragesimo*

---

[68]   QA, no. 80.
[69]   QA, no. 78.

anno, is exactly where the remedy is supposed to lie for the various "disadvantages and vices"[70] inherent in a capitalist system. In other words, a robust civil society is not marked out as an alternative to capitalism, but rather as a necessity of any humane economy, and a prophylactic against the ruin of the state – a danger that arises especially when individualism props up collectivism through the destruction of intermediary associations.

With these preliminaries in mind, and having made clear that *merely fair* wages is not the whole of what is owed to the worker, I will outline in the remainder of this section three primary teachings, or doctrines, concerning "just" wages. In the first place, and of no small importance, the Leonine pontiffs assert that what is "fair" or "just" as regards wages is a manifestly complex matter. Pius XI, building on *Rerum novarum*, no. 20, says in *Quadragesimo anno*, no. 66:

> The just amount of pay, however, must be calculated not on a single basis but on several, as Leo XIII already wisely declared in these words: "To establish a rule of pay in accord with justice, *many factors must be taken into account.*" [Emphasis mine]

Interpreting Leo XIII, Pius XI condemns "the shallowness of those who think this most difficult matter is easily solved by the application of a single rule or measure – and one quite false."[71] He is referring here to the idea that laborers are owed the entire surplus value of the products they produce – an idea derived in part from the "labor theory of value," which was popular with nineteenth-century Marxian thinkers. But the rejection of a simplistic rule for the determination of a fair wage runs up against other propositions over the years, including, as I note later, the ideal of the "family wage," which, however important, doesn't rise to the level of a binding norm for the simple reason that it must be given weight in the context of competing economic realities, some of which may completely supersede the realization of the ideal. In view of the economic debates of the nineteenth and early twentieth centuries, and even in view of those continuing today, the declaration of complexity in the determination of just wages evidences a fairly sophisticated magisterial teaching for its day.

The second doctrine – and a principle of right order – is that work, like property, has both an individual and a social character. Pope Pius XI says:

> It is obvious that, as in the case of ownership, so in the case of work, especially work hired out to others, there is a social aspect also to be considered in

[70] *QA*, no. 103.
[71] *QA*, no. 67.

addition to the personal or individual aspect. For a man's productive effort cannot yield its fruits unless a truly social and organic body exists, unless a social and juridical order watches over the exercise of work.[72]

This principle is aimed at a *just division of the real value created in economic activity*; the principle cannot mark the division precisely, but it excludes resolutely the extreme positions in which labor, or capital, take all the jointly created value for themselves. For instance, Pius XI says, "it is wholly false to ascribe to property alone or to labor alone whatever has been obtained through the combined effort of both, and it is wholly unjust for either, denying the efficacy of the other, to arrogate to itself whatever has been produced."[73] Interestingly, this principle effectively *bounds* the amount of fair pay: wages *too low* injure the individual, robbing from him a portion of the value that is rightly his; but wages *too high* injure the business enterprise, or the immediate entity that employs the laborer, overlooking the fact that the individual contribution depends upon "the social and juridical order" as well as the cooperation and mutual complementarity of the "various occupations" that "combine and form a single [interdependent] whole."[74] Therefore, Pius XI insists that "It will be impossible to evaluate work justly and pay it according to justice," says Pius XI, "where the social and individual nature of work is neglected."[75]

The "boundedness" of just wages implied by the twofold character of work deserves some elaboration, as at least two important doctrinal propositions on wages follow from it. First, the pontiffs clearly mean wages ought not be *unduly low*. To "exercise pressure upon the indigent and the destitute for the sake of gain, and to gather one's profit out of the need of another, is condemned by all laws, human and divine."[76] It hardly needs stating in this context that the popes are united in their invocation of Scripture to censure those who withhold wages. "To defraud any one of wages that are his due is a great crime which cries to the avenging anger of Heaven."[77]

But it is also in this *lower-boundedness* that the call for a "family wage" emerges. "In the first place," Pius XI says, "the worker must be paid a wage sufficient to support him and his family."[78] Since the natural structure of human dependence requires that a man support himself and those who are rightly dependent on him, an economic order in *accord with reason* renders to

---

[72] *QA*, no. 69.
[73] *QA*, no. 53.
[74] *QA*, no. 53.
[75] *QA*, no. 53.
[76] *RN*, no. 20.
[77] *RN*, no. 20.
[78] *QA*, no. 71.

workers a wage sufficient to these dual-obligations. Very notably, in this regard, *Rerum novarum* attaches to the dual-obligations a duty – and right – that is manifestly prior to the state: regarding the individual, "There is no need to bring in the State. Man precedes the State, and possesses, prior to the formation of any State, *the right of providing for the substance of his body*"[79] [emphasis mine]. And regarding the family, "Hence we have the family, the 'society' of a man's house – a society very small, one must admit, but none the less a true society, and one older than any State. Consequently, it has rights and duties peculiar to itself which are quite independent of the State,"[80] and "*It is a most sacred law of nature that a father should provide food and all necessaries for those whom he has begotten*"[81] [emphasis mine].

For the sake of simplicity, let the "family wage" include the right to individual wage sufficiency, which is, after all, *a fortiori*. Then three ideas follow from the magisterial grounding of the family wage norm in a *natural right*: first, that the right to a wage of family sufficiency, which is an amount *above* the real lower bound, rests on a natural duty to work; recall that these doctrines fall under the principle of the twofold character of work. Second, that the family wage is not *in the first place* a product of the state, or of a managed economy, and not even of the employer, but rather in the first place a result of the industriousness of the father. This latter points to the idea that there is a "natural economy" – also prior to the state – that has its fullest and best expression in the combined efforts of fathers who mix their labor with natural resources (owned by themselves or others) to bring about an increase in the goods of the earth commensurate with their own duty to "Increase and multiply."[82] Hence Leo says: "For the soil which is tilled and cultivated with toil and skill utterly changes its condition; it was wild before, now it is fruitful; was barren, but now brings forth in abundance."[83] Third, and finally, the assistance provided to wage earners in cases of "extreme necessity,"[84] or when they are temporarily unable to meet family sufficiency, must be handled in a way that respects this natural economy and preserves the dependence of offspring upon the father. "The rules of the commonwealth must go no further; here, nature bids them stop. Paternal authority can be neither abolished nor absorbed by the State."[85] Taken together, these ideas support the

---

[79] *RN*, no. 7.
[80] *RN*, no. 12.
[81] *RN*, no. 13.
[82] *RN*, no. 12.
[83] *RN*, no. 10.
[84] *RN*, no. 14.
[85] *RN*, no. 14.

notion that the "family wage" norm is serious matter for the Leonine pontiffs;
but they also provide ample restraint upon naïve interpretations of the norm
that would make of it a singular "stick" by which to measure businesses or
economies. The "family wage" norm emerges from an intricate metaphysical
view of the economy, implicates several actors in its realization, and – at least
in the early development of the social magisterium – admits of no simple
formulation as a regulatory principle.

The second doctrinal proposition that emerges from the twofold character
of work is that wages should not be *unduly high*, as "the condition of a business
and of the one carrying it on must also be taken into account; for it would be
unjust to demand excessive wages which a business cannot stand without ruin
and consequent calamity to the workers."[86] Thus we have a norm that
describes an upper-boundedness of the just wage in which the common
good of the business enterprise is brought to bear. Where the "family wage"
norm acknowledged the individual character of work, this norm – say the
"business enterprise wage" norm – captures (though not fully) the social
character of work.[87] The norm states that to apprise wages correctly as just or
unjust, the health of the business enterprise – its survival, and the health of the
entrepreneur – the undertaker of the risky venture, ought to be included in the
appraisal. Pius XI qualifies this norm in two interesting ways: first, enterprises
are protected by the norm only insofar as they work hard, innovate, and aim
continually to remain competitive – in short, insofar as they are good businesses. If instead a business venture "makes too little money because of lack of
energy or lack of initiative or because of indifference to technical and economic progress,"[88] then if they reduce compensation they are very much to
blame. The second qualification is equally interesting: the pontiff points out
that like individuals, business ventures can also be "crushed by unjust burdens," say through being "forced to sell its product at less than a just price." In
this case, the enterprise is again excused from the lower-boundedness norm
and is morally blameless if it pays "wages less than fair" since it is "those who
are thus the cause of the injury [to the business who] are guilty of grave
wrong."[89] Thus, the "business enterprise wage" norm, like the "family wage"
norm, emerges from a sophisticated view of the economy, and implicates
many actors, ranging from the entrepreneur, to the civic entities that regulate

---

[86] *QA*, no. 72.
[87] I say "not fully" because the social character of work is not solely oriented to the health of the
       business enterprise, but also to the health of the entire economy, and the state, which rightly
       collects reasonable taxes on the value created by economic activity.
[88] *QA*, no. 72.
[89] *QA*, no. 72.

the venture, and including even other businesses and financial entities. Altogether, the lower- and upper-boundedness of the just wage implied by the twofold character of work leads to a third primary doctrine, which I formulate next and last.

This third primary doctrine concerning "just" wages is difficult to state correctly, and yet sits critically in the middle of *Quadragesimo anno* as a seemingly separate principle of right order that relates to fair wages. It may be rendered perhaps in this way: that there exists among economic realities, of which the wage is one expression, a "right proportion" between things – between, for instance, prices and quantities, as well as between prices and wages – and that this "right proportion" is subject to *natural inertia*, which might be, for lack of a better term, called an equilibrium. To see this, note that Pius XI says: "A right proportion among wages and salaries contributes directly" to the goal of offering work and a "suitable means of livelihood ... to the greatest possible number."[90] To support this, the pontiff describes a fact that bears superficial similarity to the principle of boundedness of just wages, but rests on a distinct metaphysical foundation. He says:

> the opportunity to work [ought to] be provided to those who are able and willing to work. This opportunity depends largely on the wage and salary rate, which can help as long as it is kept within proper limits, but which on the other hand can be an obstacle if it exceeds these limits. For everyone knows that an excessive lowering of wages, or their increase beyond due measure, causes unemployment.[91]

The idea that unemployment follows from both decreases *and* increases in the wage rate reflects an organic view of the economy, in which actors respond to changes in real variables according to natural incentives. The excessive lowering of wages leads to unemployment by diminishing the incentives for workers; on the other hand, the excessive raising of wages leads to unemployment by distorting the incentives for business to employ as many workers as can be naturally supported. Where the principle of boundedness depended upon a just division of the surplus value between laborers and owners, a matter of classical justice, or a rendering to each what is due, the principle of natural equilibrium, or right proportion, instead seems founded upon the part of justice that determines the right relation of things. Importantly, the Pontiff stops short of suggesting that there is any obvious way to size up the "right relation of things" in the economic order; but he does suggest that the "natural

[90]   *QA*, nos. 74–75.
[91]   *QA*, no. 74.

inertia" or equilibrium of economic realities augurs against swift and excessive adjustments. To my knowledge, *Quadragesimo anno*, no. 75 is the only papal articulation of economic equilibrium as a normative principle of social order.

Equilibrium is not, however, taken to suggest that long-run economic realities are static. The popes believe that, over time, especially through the virtues of industriousness and thrift, the condition of the working classes and all society improves when right relations are "properly maintained"[92] and the principles of sound philosophy (or right order) respected. Thus Pius closes his extensive treatment on property and wages with the following statement of long-run optimism – an optimism that expresses confidence based in an organic conception of the natural economy, prior to the state, ordained by the Creator to provide what is needed for a good and decent life:

> If all these relations are properly maintained, the various occupations will combine and coalesce into, as it were, a single body and like members of the body mutually aid and complete one another. For then only will the social economy be rightly established and attain its purposes when all and each are supplied with all the goods that the wealth and resources of nature, technical achievement, and the social organization of economic life can furnish. And these goods ought indeed to be enough both to meet the demands of necessity and decent comfort and to advance people to that happier and fuller condition of life which, when it is wisely cared for, is not only no hindrance to virtue but helps it greatly.[93]

D *Principles of Right Order*

It would be impossible to catalog every one of the principles of right order that emerge in *Rerum novarum* and *Quadragesimo anno*, principles by which capitalism is to be measured. Such an undertaking would constitute a book-length treatment, though certain principles have greater centrality and force, such as those related to property and natural difference. Nevertheless, it is worthwhile to make a few general remarks about how the principles are meant to operate in the context of a capitalist system.

First, the norms of right order should not be mistaken for a set of regulatory guidelines. Emphatically, this they are not. Rather, "the principles of right reason," says Pius XI, are "principles of Christian social philosophy."[94] These principles ought to guide actors at every level – in government, in private

---

[92] QA, no. 75.
[93] QA, no. 75.
[94] QA, no. 110.

enterprise, in charitable activity – to identify paths by which such principles might take hold. In some instances, legal or regulatory instruments may be wholly appropriate and in fact necessary; but in other instances, there may be no obvious legal or regulatory mode, as prudence might suggest that some principles are better spread through teaching, preaching, and evangelization. Take, for instance, a principle of right order already discussed here – the inviolability of private property – established firmly in *Rerum novarum* and defended at length in *Quadragesimo anno*. A closely related principle, always held by the Church but made more explicit in *Quadragesimo*, is that "the twofold character, that is individual and social, both of capital or ownership and of work or labor must be given due and rightful weight."[95] Now the first principle, the inviolability of private property, lends itself to a very clear legal institution, which, while admitting of historical differences between states, nonetheless requires in every instance, minimally, firm legal protections, in addition to the various cultural habits that assist in the development of sound property law. The second principle, however, that the "twofold character" of property, individual and social, be given proper emphasis, has a less obvious place in legal and regulatory frameworks. To begin, a close reading of the paragraphs devoted to property in *Quadragesimo anno* makes it clear that Pius XI does not mean to suggest – as some have suggested – that the state should limit private property rights in favor of distributive ends, or that the state should escalate tax and transfer schemes to meet social aims. Rather, it seems that Pius XI understands the individual character of property to have a primary expression in law, while the social character of property has a primary expression in the acute moral obligation of owners to use accumulated wealth for the good of others. To put it plainly, Pius XI is not envisioning an activist state that assists the poor chiefly through policy; rather he is envisioning a state that sits "on high like a queen and supreme arbitress, free from all partiality and intent upon the one common good and justice."[96] While he does not reject that public authorities may make prudent laws respecting ownership (or in relation to the rendering of taxes), Pius XI spends a great deal more time cautioning that "the State is not permitted to discharge its duty arbitrarily" and agreeing with Leo that "it is grossly unjust for a State to exhaust private wealth through the weight of imposts and taxes."[97] In the very next section, Pius XI articulates instead the stronger, *moral* claim: "Furthermore, a person's superfluous income, that is, income which he does

[95] *QA*, no. 110.
[96] *QA*, no. 109.
[97] *QA*, no. 49.

not need to sustain life fittingly and with dignity, is not left wholly to his own free determination. Rather the Sacred Scriptures and the Fathers of the Church constantly declare in the most explicit language that the rich are bound by a very grave precept to practice almsgiving, beneficence, and munificence."[98] Thus, Pius XI would not have agreed that a just or charitable social order could arise without making strong moral claims; less still could a good society arise without the *means by which to make strong moral claims* – hence Leo and Pius's insistence that "all the striving of men will be in vain if they leave out the Church, [as] it is the Church that insists, on the authority of the Gospel, upon those teachings whereby the [class] conflict can be brought to an end, or rendered, at least, far less bitter."[99] To conclude this point, the principles of right order as discerned by the social magisterium do not map into a neat correspondence to a regulatory framework. Even when they do point strongly in the direction of a special legal instrument – say the protection of private property, or fair and moderate taxation for the support of public goods – they are never fully captured by the regulatory policy. The principles themselves are metaphysical, and are meant to imbue not only law, but also customs and habits at the personal and social level. Finally, vis-à-vis capitalism, it should be clear that the principles of right order advanced by the Church will sometimes have the character of guiding, or restraining excessive tendencies in a market economy; but at other times, the same principles will have the character of shoring up a flagging market economy. It would be a mistake to see the principles as a set of constraints meant primarily to provide a balance to some real or imagined form of laissez-faire capitalism.

One further consideration follows from the first: where grace and virtue are lacking, the principles of right order alone – whether embodied in law or custom – fall short. As important as they are, the norms that the Church offers are necessary, but not sufficient, to bring about a good society. What is needed, in fact, is the full maternal care of the Church, through whose bosom moral claims are made and grace is provided to souls. Pius XI rendered it as follows, in a section that may be understood, according to Pius's own account, as summing up the whole argument of *Quadragesimo anno*:

> What We have thus far stated regarding an equitable distribution of property and regarding just wages concerns individual persons and only *indirectly touches social order*, to the restoration of which according to the principles of sound philosophy and to its perfection according to the sublime precepts of the law of the Gospel, Our Predecessor, Leo XIII, devoted all his thought and

[98] *QA*, no. 50.
[99] *RN*, no. 16.

care ... in order that what he so happily initiated may be solidly established, that what remains to be done may be accomplished, and that even more copious and richer benefits may accrue to the family of mankind, two things are especially necessary: *reform of institutions and correction of morals.*[100] [Emphasis mine.]

We see in this passage almost immediately a kind of dismissiveness toward the principles of right order, particularly as they touch upon matters related to economic life, that is property (capital), and wages (labor). Rather, Pius XI reads here as urgently wishing to impress upon his audience that these are insufficient. Strikingly, while the language of the English translation is somewhat outmoded, what Pius XI means by "reform of institutions and correction of morals" is precisely this: the renewal of Christian institutions in civil society, especially the family, education, and Christian societies of lay persons, and the strengthening of the life of grace among citizens. One can find dozens of similar expressions in *Rerum novarum*, but no. 32 comes to mind as especially apt:

Now a State chiefly prospers and thrives through moral rule, well-regulated family life, respect for religion and justice, the moderation and fair imposing of public taxes, the progress of the arts and of trade, the abundant yield of the land – through everything, in fact, which makes the citizens better and happier.

Note that Leo mentions first and foremost the place of moral goodness, and second, the role of Christian family life. Religion and the Church are third, and finally we have moderation of taxation, and other economic and cultural goods. Overall, a complete reading of the social magisterium of the Leonine and John Pauline eras would render the case that the popes *have never conceived* that a healthy capitalist economy could exist in the presence of weak family institutions, secularized educational programs, or wilting Church communities.

E *Naturally Ordered* Weak *Economic Liberty*

To complete the discussion of capitalism, some final distinctions are helpful. We have already distinguished between the term itself, capitalism, and what is in fact affirmed when socialism is rejected so forcefully. The affirmation takes place by way of principles of right order: therefore, capitalism *per se* is not affirmed by the Church, but rather capitalism *per se* is not rejected, and it is

---

[100] *QA*, nos. 76–77.

affirmed only contingently, as mentioned above. Is it possible, then, to give the principles of right order that relate most closely to capitalism – and by which capitalism is judged – any greater degree of coherence, keeping in mind that the Church "has no models"[101] of her own to present?

Note first that what unites these affirmative principles is a posture of reasoned discovery, enlightened by faith. The things that are affirmed, beginning very clearly with the language in *Rerum novarum*, are observations about the nature of man in society, akin to descriptions about the natural covering of the man, such as the skin or the hair; that is, these observations mean to document regularities that are inherent in the way the man is constituted and can no more be removed than any other organ of the body. Consider, for instance, this passage from *Rerum novarum*, no. 11:

> With reason, then, the common opinion of mankind, little affected by the few dissentients who have contended for the opposite view, *has found in the careful study of nature*, and in the laws of nature, the foundations of the division of property, and the practice of all ages has consecrated the principle of private ownership, as being pre-eminently in conformity with human nature, and as conducing in the most unmistakable manner to the peace and tranquility of human existence. The same principle is confirmed and enforced by the civil laws – laws which, so long as they are just, derive from the law of nature their binding force. [Emphasis mine.]

Overall, the term "nature" (and variations including "natural" and "naturally") are used forty-eight times alone in the English translation of *Rerum novarum* (the root "natura" appears fifty-four times in the original Latin), and one finds that many of its paragraphs read in a similar manner to no. 11, where Leo reasons from what is observed – a "careful study" – to what Nature and Nature's God must have intended for man. We might say, then, that what the Church has in mind to affirm is a set of conditions or principles that appear to characterize the right, or natural, ordering of social and economic life. By natural ordering is meant a correspondence to the "very Idea of the Government of things in God,"[102] the rational creature's participation in which is called the Natural Law, also referenced in *Rerum novarum*, no. 11. By right ordering is also meant that things are *real*, in contrast with what is fictitious; and by right ordering is also meant what is *just*. Leo frequently decries as unjust those things which depart from the natural (right) order. This too can be seen in the final sentence of *Rerum novarum*, no. 11.

---

[101]   CA, no. 43.
[102]   Thomas Aquinas, *Summa Theologiae*, I-II.91.1–2.

These discovered "natural" principles, it must be allowed, include at least a *weak* version of Economic Liberty as a basis for social flourishing, where "weak" is meant to denote that the derived principles consistent with the Liberty tradition arise in the social magisterium from *prior doctrines* about the nature of man, rather than from Liberty as a first principle.[103] These principles of "Weak" Economic Liberty include the inviolability of private property; the legal protection of contracts, property rights, and the just rights of workers; a preference for the free exchange of goods and services; defense of intellectual property and entrepreneurship; affirmation of the role of specialization and local information; subsidiarity in social, economic, and political life, and the realization of gift and talent through industry and hard work, savings and thrift.

Taken together, we might say that what is affirmed by the social magisterium, *in reference to capitalism*, is a set of norms that fall under the heading of "Naturally Ordered Weak Economic Liberty." Importantly, Naturally Ordered Weak Economic Liberty is not co-identical with capitalism, since it does not specify any system or model. This is true even though specific instantiations of capitalism may reflect some or all of the affirmative principles of Naturally Ordered Weak Economic Liberty. Also, importantly, note that what is affirmed under this heading is not affirmed as an "opposite" or "alternative" to socialism. Terms like "opposite" or "alternative" suggest the possibility of "adopting" or "putting on," in the way that a man might put on a suit of clothing, and might choose between this one or that one. Rather, the Church seems to see Naturally Ordered Weak Economic Liberty as a set of conditions for thriving that emerge somewhat naturally, according to tendencies in human nature, such as the tendency to "truck, barter and exchange,"[104] famously described by Smith in *Wealth of Nations*, and which – by the Providence of God – appear to be oriented to the flourishing of economic life.

One of the advantages of highlighting the distinction between capitalism *per se*, and the positive principles affirmed by the Church – what I have called Naturally Ordered Weak Economic Liberty – is that it allows for a further distinction between the term "system," as in "capitalist system" or "socialist

[103] Let "strong" Economic Liberty designate schools of thought in which principles or rules of economic flourishing identified with Liberty are advanced as the fundamental doctrines themselves.
[104] "This division of labour, from which so many advantages are derived, is not originally the effect of any human wisdom, which foresees and intends that general opulence to which it gives occasion. It is the necessary, though very slow and gradual, consequence of a certain propensity in human nature, which has in view no such extensive utility; the propensity to truck, barter, and exchange one thing for another," Smith, *Wealth of Nations*, chapter II.

system," and doctrine. This in turn helps to illuminate the earlier point made about the development of social doctrine. To begin, system tends to imply human design – as in a machine or a tool – or an economic technology. In contrast, the right ordering of social and economic life as conceived by the magisterium doesn't seem to have the character of a system, rather the character of a set of laws or rules discovered, understood, and refined over time – much like the way that doctrine is "discovered" over time, and yet affirmed as having been "always and everywhere" held as true.[105] Also, as with doctrine, there is no moment when the process of discovery and affirmation is obviously complete. Instead, truths are learned, refined, and clarified. New principles that do not strictly contradict old ones emerge in light of new social or economic realities, and in light of new errors or heresies. There are periods of rapid development (take, for instance, the Leonine era as one of these) and periods of synthesis and maturity (possibly the John Pauline era will be understood as such an era). This type of organic development might be marked as humble: it does not seek to build, rather it seeks to understand or see what is revealed now, and only what is revealed now. In short, authentic development of the social doctrine is not the construction of a theory; rather it is better likened to the progress of a science that depends upon both human and divine modes of learning about reality.

III CONCLUDING REMARKS: COLLECTIVISM AND INDIVIDUALISM

In this chapter, I have principally aimed to give an exposition of the development of Catholic social thought with respect to socialism and capitalism. I argued that socialism, furiously condemned by the Church, is the *founding heresy* of the formal tradition of the social magisterium. Socialism appears to be the principal error over and against which the Church defines and refines her own affirmative norms of right order, especially those which take pride of place in *Rerum novarum* and *Quadragesimo anno*. I also argued that capitalism, bearing no analogous treatment to the rejection of socialism, has a more nuanced position in the teachings of the social magisterium. In fact, it is understood to be able to *cooperate with nature* in setting the stage for the pursuit of the common good, facilitating the flourishing of individuals,

[105] "It belongs to the Church always and everywhere to announce moral principles, even about the social order, and to render judgment concerning any human affairs insofar as the fundamental rights of the human person or the salvation of souls requires it," *Code of Canon Law* (1983), 747, no. 2.

families, and communities, so long as it is adjusted to reflect the norms of right order.

While these conclusions may be drawn from a close reading of the magisterial texts, still it remains the case that interpreters of Catholic social thought often – mistakenly – propose that the magisterium offers a "third way," a middle ground between the errors of socialism and capitalism. For this reason, I spent a significant portion of this chapter providing what I take to be the bases for the claim that the magisterium does not view these systems as opposites to be, say, equally rejected. By way of concluding, I wish to propose a brief explanation for why the two are frequently considered opposites, by highlighting an important passage in *Quadragesimo anno* and providing some interpretation for the same.

From paragraphs 44 through 62, Pius XI undertakes a lengthy exposition on the right to private property, aiming to defend Leo XIII, "and the Church herself," from the charge that in *Rerum novarum* "she had taken . . . the part of the rich against the non-owning workers"[106] in her firm and absolute affirmation of the inviolability of private property. Pius XI presents and develops the traditional Catholic principle of the "twofold character of ownership" (already discussed previously) and, in this context, he warns against two ways of going awry regarding the principles of ownership. These errors, the "twin rocks of shipwreck," strike the reader at first glance as mistakes that are "opposite" to each other. The relevant text follows:

> First, then, let it be considered as certain and established that neither Leo nor those theologians who have taught under the guidance and authority of the Church have ever denied or questioned the twofold character of ownership, called usually individual or social according as it regards either separate persons or the common good. For they have always unanimously maintained that nature, rather the Creator Himself, has given man the right of private ownership not only that individuals may be able to provide for themselves and their families but also that the goods which the Creator destined for the entire family of mankind may through this institution truly serve this purpose. All this can be achieved in no wise except through the maintenance of a certain and definite order.
>
> *Accordingly, twin rocks of shipwreck must be carefully avoided.* For, as one is wrecked upon, or comes close to, what is known as "individualism" by denying or minimizing the social and public character of the right of property, so by rejecting or minimizing the private and individual character of this same right, one inevitably runs into "collectivism" or at least closely

---

[106]   *QA*, no. 44.

approaches its tenets. Unless this is kept in mind, one is swept from his course upon the shoals of that moral, juridical, and social modernism which We denounced in the Encyclical issued at the beginning of Our Pontificate.[107] [Emphasis mine]

Individualism and collectivism, as described here in relation to the nature of property, are philosophical mistakes that, on a superficial level, appear to stand as opposite to each other on a spectrum with a numeric of persons on the scale: one places undue emphasis on the single atomized individual in relation to his property; the other places undue emphasis on the collective – the additive sum of all the atomized individuals in relation to property. The trouble is, if these mistakes *do* sit at opposite extremes of a spectrum, then it is natural to think of the "virtue" as the mean, or the philosophical sweet spot, between the two ends. But this is clearly not so. In the first place, there is no natural "mean" between the numerical descriptors, one and all. We would be tempted to say "many," but this provides no moral or philosophical guidance, "many-but-not-all" occupying, logically, every place between individualism and collectivism. Second, when Pius XI says that property has a twofold character, he indicates that it must retain, as a metaphysical attribute, both character-istics fully. The correct view is not to say that property has a little bit of an individual character and a little bit of a social character. Rather, the principle of Christian social philosophy that Pius XI aims to explicate is that property has a *fully individual and a fully social character*, all of the time.

Building on the treatment in *Rerum novarum* (and following Aristotle's second book of the *Politics*), Pius XI argues:

> The right of property is distinct from its use. That justice called commutative commands sacred respect for the division of possessions and forbids invasion of others' rights through the exceeding of the limits of one's own property; but the duty of owners to use their property only in a right way does not come under this type of justice, but under other virtues, obligations of which 'cannot be enforced by legal action.'[108]

Pius therefore assigns to the political and legal sphere the duty to delineate and enforce the private, individual character of property, while he regards the duties of ownership arising from the social character of property as residing in a separate space, primarily moral and cultural – a space where the Church can and ought to wield a good deal of influence. Thus, the role of the Church is seen by Leo XIII and Pius XI as *vital* to the proper view and use of property in

[107] QA, nos. 45–46.
[108] QA, no. 47.

society. What we ought to conclude is that getting it right about the individual and social character of property – that is, avoiding the twin rocks of shipwreck – is not a matter of steering between two extremes. Instead, it is a matter of becoming facile with the dual nature of property, and thinking about how this dual nature can be reflected in the norms of social order.

In consequence, we see that individualism and collectivism, as here defined in relation to property, are not opposites in any coherent sense, but rather mistakes that are part of one philosophical blunder: failing to get the twofold character of property right. As an example, take the controversies related to the divinity and humanity of Jesus. Those who deny the divinity of Christ are not logically opposite to those who deny the humanity of Christ, since the truth about Christ does not lie in the middle between those two errors. In fact, the "median" position in this case – Jesus as partly God and partly man – is another heresy in itself: monophysitism. Therefore, we can say that these are two separate mistakes about the second person of the Trinity – twin rocks of shipwreck, even – but we should not think of them as opposites.

My final contention in this chapter is that two compounded faults based on the twin rocks treatment in *Quadragesimo anno* have helped to create the mistaken view – which I aimed to refute in this chapter – that socialism and capitalism are treated as "opposite errors" by the Church, leading to the equally mistaken view that the Church aims to offer or propose a "third way." The compounded faults are these: first, the logically convenient, but faulty, view that individualism and collectivism – as related to property rights – are opposite mistakes that admit of some median position; and second, the faulty assimilation of individualism and collectivism – as related to property rights – to capitalism and socialism. The first fault I have already treated at length. Of the second, I say merely that there is no attentive reading of the magisterial texts that can support the assimilation. Individualism and collectivism are philosophical mistakes relating to the true character of property according to the "Idea of the government of things in God."[109] Capitalism and socialism are specific arrangements of political economy, one of which, socialism, is completely vitiated and "fatally flawed from within," the other of which, capitalism, springs from intuitions that are consistent with the Natural Law, but which requires moral, cultural, and religious involvement to achieve the best possible results for the common good.

In what I have said by way of conclusion up to now, I have limited my remarks to the individualism and collectivism so defined by Pius XI, as related to the nature of property. But I want to suggest one remaining point that runs

[109]   Thomas Aquinas, *Summa Theologiae*, I-II.91.1.

TABLE 1 *Major and Minor Papal Encyclicals of the Leonine Era Referring to Socialism and/or Communism*

Year	Encyclical Title	Pope
1849	*Nostis et nobiscum* (On the Church in the Pontifical States)	Pius IX
1878	**Quod apostolici muneris (On Socialism)**	**Leo XIII**
1880	*Arcanum* (On Christian Marriage)	Leo XIII
1881	**Diuturnum (On the Origin of Civil Power)**	**Leo XIII**
1886	*Quod multum* (On the Liberty of the Church)	Leo XIII
1888	**Libertas (On the Nature of Human Liberty)**	**Leo XIII**
1888	*Exeunte iam anno* (On Right Order of Christian Life)	Leo XIII
1890	*Dall'alto dell'Apostolico Seggio* (On Freemasonry in Italy)	Leo XIII
1891	**Rerum novarum (On Capital and Labor)**	**Leo XIII**
1892	*Custodi di Quella Fede* (On Freemasonry)	Leo XIII
1901	**Graves de communi re (On Christian Democracy)**	**Leo XIII**
1902	*Fin dal Principio* (On the Education of the Clergy)	Leo XIII
1929	*Divini illius magistri* (On Christian Education)	Pius XI
1930	*Casti connubii* (On Christian Marriage)	Pius XI
1931	**Quadragesimo anno (On the Reconstruction of the Social Order)**	**Pius XI**
1937	**Divini redemptoris (On Atheistic Communism)**	**Pius XI**

Note: Encyclicals devoted to socialism, communism, or questions of social, political, and economic life bearing directly upon socialism or communism. Eight major encyclicals in bold type.

parallel to these distinctions. Earlier, in my treatment of socialism in the social magisterium, I made the point that by denying any special relations of right or duty between specific persons, socialism – which seems like a purely collecti-vist enterprise – tended to promote and embody at the same time a radical sort of individualism, and that this could be best observed through the obliteration of the natural family, though it extends to other natural associations and civic entities. I believe that this difficulty, inherent in socialism, has the same character as the other we have been considering: failing to apprehend the dual nature of persons who are fully individual but also fully familial or communal, never existing as independent beings in an idealized or imagined state of nature. Thus, while we can observe two ways of missing the mark about the dual nature – a modern liberalism, or individualism, which tends to locate all rights in the individual, over and against responsibilities owed to families and institutions, and a modern statism, or collectivism, which tends to locate all rights in the state over and against the claims of individuals and families – in reality, as with property, we might expect to see these two errors frequently occupy the same place in contemporary political economy, with the considerable apparatus of the modern state brought to support, alternatively, flawed individualist claims or flawed collectivist claims in the service of a rarely explicit social philosophy that is profoundly pagan and unnatural. Analogously, the way forward is not an intermediate space between contemporary liberalism and the modern atheistic state – a third way to balance out the extremes in each. Rather, the way forward, following Leo XIII and Pius XI, is to propose sound principles of Christian social philosophy by which those arrangements of political economy best suited to human flourishing may be fully and properly grounded. At the same time, the way forward includes marking out and defending the space in which the Church rightly operates, since her contribution rises above that of adjudicating between principles of social philosophy; she contributes additionally, most maternally, that life of grace which is life for society and the basis for all human thriving.

19

The Preferential Option for the Poor and Catholic Social Teaching

Martin Schlag

The preferential option for the poor (POP) has become an essential element of Catholic Social Teaching (CST). There are two major currents of interpretation of this preferential love of the poor.[1] One interpretation is that of Latin American theology of liberation, where the expression originated. Another is the position taken by the magisterium, especially by the papal magisterium,[2] that Pope Francis has developed and modified, nevertheless remaining in the range of the precedential magisterial texts, as I will try to show. In this chapter I will concentrate on the way the Catholic magisterium has presented the preferential option for the poor. The Second Vatican Council, papal social teaching, and the various General Assemblies of the Latin-American Bishops' Conference (CELAM) after their second gathering in Medellín in 1968 are of paramount importance to the development of the POP.

The Protestant theologian Helen Rhee has observed that while Catholic theologians opted for liberation theology and its understanding of the preferential option for the poor, "the poor themselves opted for the prosperity gospel (and Pentecostalism) in Latin America and elsewhere."[3] The streams of immigrants who are not heading for socialist countries that have implemented the dependence theory and other social programs based on Marxist analysis also confirm that liberation theology in its original philo-Marxist form is not the solution to poverty but possibly one of its causes. The magisterium, in

---

[1] See Rohan M. Curnow, "Which Preferential Option for the Poor? A History of the Doctrine's Bifurcation," *Modern Theology* 31, no. 1 (January 2015): 27–59.

[2] For the time up until nearly to the end of the pontificate of John Paul II see Gerald S. Twomey, *The "Preferential Option for the Poor" in Catholic Social Thought from John XXIII to John Paul II* (Lewiston: Edwin Mellen Press, 2004).

[3] Helen Rhee, *Loving the Poor, Saving the Rich. Wealth, Poverty, and Early Christian Formation* (Grand Rapids: Baker Academic, 2012), 217.

contrast, has opened the door for a better formulation of the POP in the Latin American context.

SETTING THE STAGE

The Second Vatican Council, particularly in its Pastoral Constitution on the Church in the Modern World, *Gaudium et spes*,[4] set the stage for a renewed comprehension of the Church's evangelizing mission in society. In his conclusive speech at the council, Paul VI characterized its spirit as that of the Good Samaritan who bows over humanity's needs with unending sympathy. The Church took an anthropological turn at the council, introducing a new humanism, centered on God and Christ.[5] This attitude also permeated Paul VI's encyclical on development, *Populorum progressio*, in which the pope specified that this new Christian humanism not only meant struggling for a better world in general but consisted in social concern for the poor, the disinherited, and developing countries.

In his Apostolic Exhortation *Evangelii nuntiandi*, a document dear to Pope Francis, Paul VI directly addressed the notions of liberation and development that had already been forcefully voiced in Latin America and at the two preceding bishops' synods in Rome. The pope made clear that spiritual and sacramental life had priority over any other aim in the church. However, he appealed to Christian conscience to realize, that salvation and social justice, human advancement, development, and liberation – though never identified – were linked.[6]

THE PONTIFICAL MAGISTERIUM AND THE PREFERENTIAL OPTION FOR THE POOR UP TO POPE FRANCIS

The first pontifical magisterial use of an expression similar to "the preferential option for the poor" is to be found in the document *Libertatis nuntius*,[7] that is, in a document aimed at critically purifying liberation theology. It gave love for the poor "highest priority" in the Church, which

---

[4] Vatican II, Pastoral Constitution *Gaudium et spes* (On the Church in the Modern World) (1965).

[5] See Paul VI, "Address During the Last General Meeting of the Second Vatican Council" (December 7, 1965).

[6] See Paul VI, Apostolic Exhortation *Evangelii nuntiandi* (On Evangelization in the Modern World) (1975), no. 25–38, esp. 28 and 35.

[7] Published in 1984 by the Congregation for the Doctrine of the Faith under the English title, "Instruction on Certain Aspects of the 'Theology of Liberation'" (1984).

"wants to be the Church of the poor."[8] The first time the expression "preferential option for the poor" appeared explicitly in a Roman document was in the Conclusions of the Extraordinary Bishops' Synod of 1985,[9] and then shortly afterwards in *Libertatis conscientia*. In this document of the Congregation for the Doctrine of the Faith, under the heading "love of preference for the poor," human misery was interpreted as a sign of our natural condition after sin. Christians give preferential love to those who suffer misery, and wish to bring them relief, defense, and liberation through works of charity, and also through structural changes, as taught by Catholic Social Doctrine. This special option for the poor manifests the universality of love and does not exclude anybody.[10]

From that point onwards Pope John Paul II consistently used the expression "option or love of preference for the poor" in many of his documents. He defined this attitude as "an option or a special form of primacy in the exercise of Christian charity."[11] This official formulation was the one that was received into the Compendium of the Social Doctrine of the Church, where it is situated as a subtitle in the chapter on the universal destination of goods, one of the principles of CST.[12]

Rohan Curnow has pointed out that John Paul II did not use the POP in the same sense that liberation theology does. The pope spoke of POP in terms of love, not in the sense of a necessary precondition for the possibility of reformulating the whole of theology. He thus did not "invoke the conversional and hermeneutical emphases" given to the POP by liberation theology.[13] In this

---

[8]   LN, nos. 2 and 5.

[9]   See The Final Report of the 1985 Extraordinary Synod (*relatio finalis*) December 8, 1985, available at www.ewtn.com/library/CURIA/SYNFINAL.HTM

[10] See Congregation for the Doctrine of the Faith, *Libertatis conscientia* (Instruction on Christian Freedom and Liberation) (1986), no. 68.

[11] See John Paul II, Encyclical Letter *Sollicitudo rei socialis* (On Social Concern) (1987), no. 42; John Paul II, Encyclical Letter *Centesimus annus* (On the 100th Anniversary of *Rerum novarum*) (1991), no. 11; but also in documents on topics that are not directly social in nature like: John Paul II, Encyclical Letter *Redemptoris mater* (On the Blessed Virgin Mary in the Life of the Pilgrim Church) (1987), no. 37; John Paul II, Apostolic Exhortation *Ecclesia in America* (On the Encounter with the Living Jesus Christ: The Way to Conversion, Communion and Solidarity in America) (1999), nos. 18 and 58; John Paul II, Apostolic Letter *Tertio millennio adveniente* (On Preparation for the Jubilee of the Year 2000) (1994), no. 51; John Paul II, Apostolic Letter *Novo millennio ineunte* (At the Close of the Great Jubilee of the Year 2000) (2001), no. 49f; John Paul II, Apostolic Exhortation *Vita consecrata* (On the Consecrated Life and its Mission in the Church and in the World) (1996), nos. 82 and 90.

[12] Pontifical Council for Justice and Peace, *Compendium of the Social Doctrine of the Church* (2004), no. 182. There is another mention of the preferential option for the poor in no. 449.

[13] See Curnow, "Which Preferential Option," 44.

sense, he positioned the POP among the other principles and elements of CST, not as its overarching and paramount foundation.[14]

Notwithstanding the above, the urgency with which John Paul II formulated his writings on the POP leave no doubts about the priority he gave to love for the poor and suffering, the oppressed and downtrodden, to those whose human rights have been denied. In his letter on the pastoral program for the new millennium that he left as a kind of spiritual testament he appealed to Christians to stake everything on charity. He reminded the Church that "there is a special presence of Christ in the poor, and this requires the Church to make a preferential option for them."[15] He deplores the "contradictions of an economic, cultural and technological progress which offers immense possibilities to a fortunate few, while leaving millions of others not only on the margins of progress but in living conditions far below the minimum demanded by human dignity."[16] Among these he mentioned the same concerns as those harbored by Latin American theologians and pastors, like hunger, illiteracy, lack of medical care, homelessness, drug addiction, abandonment in old age, marginalization, and so on. These appalling situations require an "act of faith in Christ by discerning his voice in the cry for help that rises from this world of poverty." Such formulations come near to those postulating the POP as an epistemological precondition for faith and theology. However, there is no rupture with the Catholic tradition; rather, it is a continuation of the "tradition of charity which has expressed itself in so many different ways in the past two millennia" and must be carried on with "greater resourcefulness" and new "'creativity' in charity."[17]

John Paul II's constructive vision of overcoming poverty and his positive program for developing a prosperous society was entrepreneurship or "the right of economic initiative"[18] and "good capitalism": "a 'business economy,' 'market economy,' or simply 'free economy.'"[19] This form of economic organization also attributes great importance to the legal (government) and moral (cultural) framework. It is the system others have called "democratic capitalism."[20]

---

[14]   Gustavo Gutiérrez does not make these distinctions but simply affirms that the popes have accepted the preferential option for the poor; see Gustavo Gutiérrez, *Teología de la Liberación* (Salamanca: Ediciones Sígueme, 2009), 28f. This is the 18th edition, with an important preface added in the 14th edition (1990). First edition 1971.

[15]   See *NMI*, no. 49.

[16]   See *NMI*, no. 50.

[17]   All quotations from *NMI*, 50.

[18]   See *SRS*, no. 15.

[19]   See *CA*, no. 42.

[20]   See Maciej Zięba, *Papal Economics* (Wilmington: ISI Books, 2016), 97–136; Michael Novak, *The Spirit of Democratic Capitalism* (New York: Touchstone, 1982), 315–360.

Benedict XVI continued this hermeneutical strand and treated the POP as a subordinate principle of CST and as a special kind of love.[21] It is noteworthy, however, that Benedict XVI did not use the expression at all in his social encyclicals,[22] even though he wrote a lot about the poor and the care that the Church had taken for them over the centuries. Nevertheless, he expressed great urgency, just as his predecessor did. Benedict XVI stated very clearly, "For the Church, charity is not a kind of welfare activity which could equally well be left to others, but is a part of her nature, an indispensable expression of her very being."[23] In other words, the option for the poor is not an optional but an essential and constitutive element of the Church as church. However, he separated charity very clearly from the Church hierarchy engaging in political affairs.

He did so too in the inaugural session of the Fifth General Assembly of CELAM in Aparecida where he directly addressed the POP and added new accents to it. His Christological affirmation of the POP as "implicit in the Christological faith in the God who became poor for us, so as to enrich us with his poverty (cf. 2 Cor 8:9)" was in line with statements by Latin American liberation theologians.

What is new and important for CST is Benedict XVI's rejection of a directly political application of the principle by the Church hierarchy:

> This political task is not the immediate competence of the Church. Respect for a healthy secularity – including the pluralism of political opinions – is essential in the Christian tradition. If the Church were to start transforming herself into a directly political subject, she would do less, not more, for the poor and for justice, because she would lose her independence and her moral authority, identifying herself with a single political path and with debatable partisan positions. The Church is the advocate of justice and of the poor, precisely because she does not identify with politicians nor with partisan interests. Only by remaining independent can she teach the great criteria and inalienable values, guide consciences and offer a life choice that goes beyond the political sphere. To form consciences, to be the advocate of justice and truth, to educate in individual and political virtues: that is the fundamental vocation of the Church in this area. And lay Catholics must be aware of their

---

21   See Benedict XVI, "Message for the World Day of Peace 2009" (Vatican City: LEV, 2008), no. 15; Benedict XVI, "Address during the Celebration of the First Vespers of the First Sunday of Advent 2010" (Vatican City: LEV, 2010); Benedict XVI, Apostolic Exhortation *Africae munus* (On the Church in Africa in Service to Reconciliation, Justice and Peace) (2011), no. 26f.

22   Benedict XVI, Encyclical Letter *Caritas in veritate* (On Integral Human Development in Charity and Truth) (2009), and the second part of his encyclical *Deus caritas est* (On Christian Love) (2005).

23   DCE, no. 25. Here he quotes Congregation for Bishops, Directory for the Pastoral Ministry of Bishops *Apostolorum successores* (2004), 194, 213.

responsibilities in public life; they must be present in the formation of the necessary consensus and in opposition to injustice.[24]

This position fits into his teaching on the political role of the Church as institution. In his first encyclical he declined any wish for political power, not even indirect power, and offered the Church's service in the process of purifying reason, without attempting to make this insight prevail politically.[25] In various other settings Benedict XVI repeated the same notions of dialogue and mutual need between Christian faith and society.[26] Needless to say, this is a further major modification of the concept of the POP as used by liberationists who advocate for the Church's active participation in the political struggle for the liberation of the oppressed.

However, before he became Pope Benedict XVI, Joseph Ratzinger appreciated the deep seriousness of, and recognized an important contribution of liberation theology to the Catholic faith: "The progress of the Church cannot consist in a belated embrace of the modern world – the theology of Latin America has made that all too clear to us and has demonstrated thereby the rightness of its cry for liberation."[27] Ratzinger was referring to the different modes of reception of *Gaudium et spes* in Europe and in Latin America. European theology embraced the Enlightenment, something that did not resonate or make sense in Latin America where the fruits of Enlightenment – liberalism and capitalism – had been implemented in a way that hurt and oppressed the population.

Pope Benedict XVI's constructive vision of overcoming poverty and his positive program for developing society was "civil economy," which takes up the challenge of inserting charity into the economy. Benedict XVI formulated this program as a challenge: its implementation requires including fraternity, gratuitousness, and the logic of gift into normal business dealings, not only into the nonprofit sectors of humanitarian commitment where their efficacy is obvious. All this is possible through an epistemological conversion in economics and business, and new concern for global social justice.[28]

---

[24] Benedict XVI, "Address at the Inaugural Session of the Fifth General Conference of CELAM" (May 13, 2007).

[25] See *DCE*, no. 28f.

[26] See Benedict XVI, "Address in Westminster Hall" (September 2010); Benedict XVI, "Address in the Reichstag Building" (September 2011).

[27] Joseph Cardinal Ratzinger, *Principles of Catholic Theology. Building Stones for a Fundamental Theology* (San Francisco: Ignatius Press, 1987), 390.

[28] See *CV*, nos. 34–42.

Benedict XVI placed the accent on the importance of civil society, not on governmental power. A similar stress can be found in the "theology of the people" that influenced Pope Francis.[29]

POPE FRANCIS AND THE THEOLOGY OF THE PEOPLE

With Pope Francis many things have changed, including the POP. From the outset, Pope Francis made it clear that he wanted a poor church for the poor. The choice of his name, his words and gestures characterized his whole pontificate as a great preferential option for the poor. Whether to categorize his interpretation of this principle as a moderate form of liberation theology or not depends entirely on how one defines liberation theology. For my part, I wish to distinguish Pope Francis's interpretation from the one given by liberation theology for reasons of clarity and intellectual honesty. Pope Francis has never called himself a theologian of liberation but a "son of the theology of the people."[30] The theology of the people is a variant of the theology of liberation that goes back to the work of Lucio Gera, Juan Carlos Scannone, and others like Alberto Methol Ferré.[31] It is true that in liberation theology itself there has been a shift from the first historical forms of liberation theology toward the contents and the methodology of the theology of the people. This shift put the emphasis on culture instead of the socioeconomic structures.[32] However, it is also true that the authors of the first phase have not changed their prose substantially and maintain the texts of their books unaltered in recent editions. That is why I prefer not to simply identify the theology of the people with liberation theology.[33] There are certainly many points in common but also differences.

In addition to the theology of the people, Pope Francis's notion of the POP was shaped by the general assemblies of the CELAM and by the Jesuit renewal after the Second Vatican Council. I will briefly sketch these three sources of influence before embarking on the analysis of Francis's statements as pope.

---

[29] See Juan Carlos Scannone, *Quando il Popolo Diventa Teologo* (Bologna: EMI, 2016), 35f.

[30] See Scannone, *Quando il Popolo*, 45. Scannone is careful to note that Bergoglio is not a "theologian" of the people but in his pastoral work he has been inspired by the theology of the people, in particular by the preferential option for the poor; see pages 47 and 54.

[31] See Alberto Methol Ferré and Alver Metalli, *Il Papa e il Filosofo* (Siena: Cantagalli, 2014).

[32] See Scannone, *Quando il Popolo*, 26f.

[33] I am aware of the fact that one of its founders does consider the theology of the people as part of liberation theology; see *Quando il Popolo*, 5.

THE JESUIT RENEWAL

"I feel a Jesuit in my spirituality . . . I have not changed spirituality, no. Francis, Franciscan, no. I feel a Jesuit and I think as a Jesuit."[34] These words show how deeply Francis is rooted in the tradition of his religious family, the Society of Jesus, and how strongly its spirituality influences him also as pope. As a young Jesuit, Fr. Jorge Mario Bergoglio was shaped by the renewal of the Society of Jesus under its energetic Superior General Fr. Pedro Arrupe. One of the capstones of this renewal was the intrinsic connection between faith and love for the poor. These convictions were notably formulated in the so-called Fourth Decree of the 32nd General Congregation: "The mission of the Society of Jesus today is the service of faith, of which the promotion of justice is an absolute requirement. For reconciliation with God demands the reconciliation of people with one another."[35]

The Bishops' Synod in Rome in 1971 and Pope Paul VI's Exhortation *Evangelii nuntiandi* had already expressed the intrinsic link between faith and social justice and charity. Its roots are not only to be found in Latin America, but Latin America had certainly begun to be a source of theological renewal.[36] One element of this spiritual leaven was the theology of the people.

TEOLOGÍA DEL PUEBLO

With liberation theology the theology of the people shares the tripartite analysis of "seeing–judging–acting" and the three mediations characteristic of liberation theology. However, the point of departure for the theology of people is not directly and immediately the poor but the people, in which the poor play a preeminent role. The people are the faithful, humble, and simple persons who possess an evangelical instinct,[37] or in the words of Pope Francis, *"el santo pueblo fiel de Dios"* (the holy faithful people of God), which is "a vaccine against the prevailing ideologies and political violence."[38] The people are the subject of a history (not of *the* history or of history in general) and of a culture. Culture is understood in the wide sense as the common life in

---

[34] Francis, "Press Conference During the Return Flight, Rio de Janeiro – Rome" (July 28, 2013).

[35] 32nd General Congregation of the Society of Jesus, *Decree 4* (December 2–March 7, 1975).

[36] Gustavo Gutiérrez speaks of *iglesia-reflejo* and *iglesia-fuente*, meaning that there are local churches that basically reflect what comes from outside, and others that contribute something of their own. Latin America has become an *iglesia-fuente*; see Gutiérrez, *Teología*, 183.

[37] See Juan Carlos Scannone, *Teologia de la Liberación y Doctrina Social de la Iglesia* (Madrid: Cristiandad and Buenos Aires: Guadalupe, 1987), 61.

[38] See Austen Ivereigh, *The Great Reformer. Francis and the Making of a Radical Pope* (New York: Holt, 2014), 116.

society, its ultimate meaning, its symbols and customs, its institutions and political structures. Culture and people are interrelated concepts in the theology of the people: a culture is constituted by its ethos and values, and when one becomes aware of them one feels part of a people. Awareness of a common culture and a common moral heritage and commitment constitute a people. Inevitably there is also a political dimension to it: belonging to a people or nation means sharing in the same culture by means of particular historical political decisions. Culture is a political and ethical concept because it stems from the human tendency to live together in society. Thus, the theology of the people is not apolitical. To the contrary, it awakens the Christian sense of responsibility for public affairs. However, in contrast to liberation theology, the theology of the people includes everyone in the notion of people, also the rich, unless they reject the common good by oppressing others. The poor have a preferential position among the people because they are more aware of their lack of power and thus of their need of commonality. "In a preferential way we call the multitude of the poor a people."[39] In a certain way the POP in this theological interpretation is mediated through the notion of the people.[40]

The methodological modification of liberation theology on the second and third analytical steps boils down to the rejection of Marxism by the theology of the people.[41] Pope Francis also rejects Marxism[42] and has opted for a model of social and economic organization that I will explain further on. In his development regarding the POP, Pope Francis is also influenced by the work of CELAM, of which he was a member for many years.

CELAM – CONSEJO EPISCOPAL LATINOAMERICANO

Relevant for the POP are the general assemblies of CELAM in Medellín (1968), Puebla (1979), Santo Domingo (1992), and Aparecida (2007).

[39] Lucio Gera, "Pueblo, religión del pueblo e iglesia," in *Escritos Teológico-Pastorales de Lucio Gera, vol 1: Del Preconcilio a la Conferencia de Puebla (1956–1981)*, eds. Virginia Raquel Azcuy et al. (Buenos Aires: Agape Libros–Facultad de Teología UCA, 2006), 717–744, 731.

[40] See Scannone, *Teologia*, 61–66; Lucio Gera, "Cultura y dependencia a luz de la reflexión teológica," in *Escritos Teológico-Pastorales de Lucio Gera, vol 1: Del Preconcilio a la Conferencia de Puebla (1956–1981)*, eds. Virginia Raquel Azcuy et al. (Buenos Aires: Agape Libros–Facultad de Teología UCA, 2006), 605–659; Gera, "Pueblo," 729.

[41] See Scannone, *Teología*, 41–44, 89.

[42] "The Marxist ideology is wrong. However, during my life I have known many Marxists who were good persons, that is why I don't feel offended" (for being called a Marxist), in Jorge Mario Bergoglio-Papa Francesco, *Interviste e conversazioni con i giornalisti. Due anni di Pontificato* (Vatican City: LEV, 2015), 119 (my translation).

It was Juan Carlos Scannone who summarized and characterized the particular position of the Latin American hierarchy and distinguished it from radical forms of liberation theology. Over the years, the hierarchy underscored the biblical and ecclesial dimension of liberation, insisting on the importance of evangelization and spirituality. Even though the bishops were aware of the importance of sociopolitical aspects and sometimes used socioeconomic data, they did not use the socioeconomic analysis as part of theological discourse. Instead they based their theological reflections on anthropological and ethical foundations. For this method, liberation of the oppressed was a topic of theology, but liberation and the option for the poor were not seen as the universal precondition for a new mode of theology.[43]

In this sense, at Medellín the Latin American bishops spoke of the effective preference of the Church for the poorest sectors.[44] They called on Christians to listen attentively to the imperative of their consciences and to live solidarity, and the bishops pledged to give a personal example of a poor church. "Preference" expressed nonexclusivity: the poor are the first but not the only ones who may expect love from us.

The long document of the assembly at Puebla contained a whole chapter with the title POP.[45] In it the bishops spoke of the need of the whole church to opt for the poor and to achieve their complete liberation (no. 1134). Prophetic denunciation and commitment to the cause of the poor had brought persecution and vexation to those who practiced them. Nevertheless, the bishops encouraged the poor themselves to make the option for the poor and struggle for the integrity of their faith, which includes claiming their civic rights (no. 1137f).

The assembly in Santo Domingo[46] reaffirmed the notion of the POP as used in the previous conferences without adding accents of its own. It drew the notion of the POP closer to that of the papal magisterium by underscoring its place among the principles of CST (see, e.g., *conclusión*, no. 50). At Aparecida, Archbishop Bergoglio, now Pope Francis, was entrusted with heading the commission drafting the concluding document. In a chapter dedicated entirely to the preferential option of the poor,[47] the bishops referred to it as one of "the distinguishing features of our Latin American and Caribbean church" (no. 391).

---

[43] See Scannone, *Teología*, 55.

[44] See the chapter, II Conferencia General, "Pobreza de la Iglesia," in *Documentos Finales de Medellin*, no. 9–15; see also Gutiérrez, *Teología*, 28.

[45] See Conferencia General del Episcopado Latinoamericano, "Documento de Puebla III" no. 1134–1165.

[46] Documento de Santo Domingo, "Mensaje a Los Pueblos de America Latina."

[47] See Benedict XVI, "Letter to the Bishops of Latina America and the Caribbean" (June 29, 2007), no. 391–398.

They therefore gave it a central function in pastoral care: "That it is preferential means that it should permeate all our pastoral structures and priorities" (no. 396). All pastors and the Church as a whole should continue to be "traveling companion(s) of our poorest brothers and sisters, even as far as martyrdom" (no. 396). The example of saints like St. Oscar Romero surely inspired these words. Another idea that brings the conclusions of the Fifth Assembly of CELAM in Aparecida close to the language of the theology of the people (and also of liberation theology) is the notion that the poor not only are the recipients of evangelization but they themselves evangelize and are subjects of historical change: "The option for the poor should lead us to friendship with the poor. Day by day the poor become agents of evangelization and of comprehensive human promotion" (no. 398).

However, there is no hint at class struggle; to the contrary, Aparecida included the world of business and finance in the POP: "The preferential option for the poor demands that we devote special attention to those Catholic professional people who are responsible for the finances of nations, those who promote employment, and politicians who must create conditions for the economic development of countries, so as to give them ethical guidelines consistent with their faith" (no. 395).

This brings us to the specific notion that Pope Francis has of the POP as it emerged from the various sources of influence.

THE SPECIFIC POP IN POPE FRANCIS'S TEACHING

Pope Francis has reinforced the church's message of inclusion of the poor, advocating for structural reforms that place the human person at the center of the economy and not money. Forcefully he has highlighted that Christian culture begins with the love of the poor:

> The proclamation of the Gospel is destined for the poor first of all, for all those who all too often lack what they need to live a dignified life. To them first are proclaimed the glad tidings that God loves them with a preferential love and comes to visit them through the charitable works that disciples of Christ do in his name. Go to the poor first of all: this is the priority. At the moment of the Last Judgment, as we can read in Matthew 25, we shall all be judged on this. Some, however, may think that Jesus' message is for those who have no cultural background. No! No! The Apostle affirms forcefully that the Gospel is for everyone, even the learned. The wisdom that comes from the resurrection is not in opposition to human wisdom but on the contrary purifies and uplifts it. The Church has always been present in places where culture is worked out. But the first step is always the priority for the poor.

Nevertheless we must also reach the frontiers of the intellect, of culture, of the loftiness of dialogue, of the dialogue that makes peace, the intellectual dialogue, the reasonable dialogue.

The Gospel is for everyone! This reaching out to the poor does not mean we must become champions of poverty or, as it were, 'spiritual tramps'! No, no this is not what it means! It means we must reach out to the flesh of Jesus that is suffering, but also suffering is the flesh of Jesus of those who do not know it with their study, with their intelligence, with their culture.[48]

Francis's version of the preferential option for the poor is clearly presented in these words: the POP is linked to charity and to evangelization without any form of exclusion. He also constantly repeats that all his teaching on society and the economy remains in the limits of Catholic social doctrine. The pope thus continues the theological line of the Assemblies of CELAM in Santo Domingo and Aparecida.

Pope Francis understands poverty in the wide sense of exclusion: "Moreover there is no worse material poverty, I am keen to stress, than the poverty which prevents people from earning their bread and deprives them of the dignity of work."[49]

Pope Francis understands love for the poor as an eminently theological and pastoral category. He himself said: "Poverty for us Christians is not a sociological, philosophical or cultural category, no. It is theological. I might say this is the first category, because our God, the Son of God, abased himself, he made himself poor to walk along the road with us."[50]

This formulation comes close to the use of the POP in liberation theology ("first theological category"); however, it is rather an expression of "theology of the people": the poor holy people of God are a source of religious experience, not passive receivers of beneficence. Francis is thus able to fully insert his love for the poor into the program of cultural transformation we call "the new evangelization," in continuity with his predecessor Benedict XVI:

> They (the poor) have much to teach us. Not only do they share in the *sensus fidei*, but in their difficulties they know the suffering Christ. We need to let ourselves be evangelized by them. The new evangelization is an invitation to acknowledge the saving power at work in their lives and to put them at the center of the Church's pilgrim way. We are called to find Christ in them, to lend our voice to their causes, but also to be their friends, to listen to them, to

---

[48] Francis, "Address to Participants in the Ecclesial Convention of the Diocese of Rome" (June 17, 2013).

[49] Francis, "Address to the Centesimus Annus Pro Pontifice Foundation" (May 25, 2013).

[50] Francis, "Address at the Vigil of Pentecost with Ecclesial Movements" (May 18, 2013). Similar words can be found in Francis, Apostolic Exhortation *Evangelii Gaudium* (2013), 198.

speak for them and to embrace the mysterious wisdom which God wishes to share with us through them.[51]

This is the reason, explains Pope Francis, why he wants a "poor Church for the poor." He does not advocate pauperism nor does he reduce his vision to a mere remedy of social evils: the poor for Francis are teachers of what Christ wants the Church to know here and now.

In his actions and words, Francis expresses what Benedict XVI had already taught in his encyclicals, two of which explicitly name charity in the title: *Deus caritas est* (2005), and *Caritas in veritate* (2009).[52] Charity is the central driving force, the most convincing argument, the aspect that draws people toward personal and cultural transformation. Charity is the heart and core of evangelization because only true and disinterested love is credible; only love opens minds and hearts to trust in God's and the Church's words. Christian faith by necessity turns into culture, and Christian culture begins with love for the poor. Christ himself taught as much: "For if you love those who love you, what recompense will you have? Do not the tax collectors do the same? And if you greet your brothers only, what is unusual about that? Do not the pagans do the same?"[53] We don't need Christ in order to love the rich or to return favors. We need Christ who has loved us unto the cross in order to love without reciprocity, with sacrifice and pain. We need Christ in order to love the poor.

Francis's Methodology

In most of his publications, Pope Francis starts with an analysis of socio-economic realities.[54] However, at the same time, he also states that he does not possess a monopoly regarding the interpretation of reality or the proposal of solutions.[55] There is no closure but an appeal to specialists to find the right solution.

Pope Francis is strong on denouncing situations of injustice and hardheartedness in our economic and social system. He also forcefully appeals to the individual operators' conscience, and asks them to live virtuous and

---

[51] *EG*, no. 198.
[52] Emeritus Pope Benedict XVI confirms this interpretation of continuity in Benedikt XVI, *Letzte Gespräche mit Peter Seewald* (München: Droemer, 2016), 245.
[53] Mt 5:46–47.
[54] See *EG*, no. 52–75; Francis, Encyclical Letter *Laudato si'* (On Care for Our Common Home) (2015) nos. 17–59.
[55] *EG*, no. 184: "Furthermore, neither the Pope nor the Church have a monopoly on the interpretation of social realities or the proposal of solutions to contemporary problems." See also *LS*, no. 60f.

responsible lives. He is less articulate on the institutional ethics that positively help to construct the economy and society. However, there are some hints in his speeches as to what his positive constructive vision is: social (market) economy and an economy of communion "that invests in persons by creating jobs and providing training."[56] Pope Francis wants the inclusion of the poor into the market economy, not government handouts:

> The need to resolve the structural causes of poverty cannot be delayed ... Welfare projects, which meet certain urgent needs, should be considered merely temporary responses. As long as the problems of the poor are not radically resolved by rejecting the absolute autonomy of markets and finan- cial speculation and by attacking the structural causes of inequality, no solution will be found for the world's problems or, for that matter, to any problems. Inequality (Spanish original: "*inequidad*") is the root of social ills.[57]

Francis accuses the existing form of capitalism of hypocrisy. In his vision, it generates wealth for a few big corporations that make philanthropic donations to patch up the negative consequences of their activities.[58] This judgment is ambiguous, because it refers only to that form of capitalism called "bad capitalism" by St. John Paul II and must not be understood as a wholesale condemnation of the Western economic system. The problem is more one of words than of concepts. Francis is aware of the good (capitalist) business does and has encouraged business people in their service to the common good. He does not call this form of business capitalist because capitalism in his Latin American experience means exploitation and cronyism. In any case, he wants a different cultural paradigm, a "bold cultural revolution,"[59] a "new lifestyle"[60] that places the human person, specifically the poor, at the center and sees everything else as an instrument; this requires overcoming what the pope calls the "technocratic paradigm" that excludes ethics.[61] He calls for integral development,[62] and another kind of progress that is "healthier, more human, more social, more integral."[63]

---

[56] Francis, "Address during the conferral of the Charlemagne prize" (May 2016).
[57] *EG*, no. 202.
[58] See Francis, "Address to Participants in the Meeting 'Economy of Communion'" (February 4, 2017).
[59] *LS*, no. 114.
[60] *LS*, no. 203.
[61] *LS*, nos. 108–110.
[62] *LS*, no. 102f.
[63] *LS*, no. 112.

It is sad and counterproductive that the POP for a long time has sailed under the flag of anticapitalism and antibusiness. The concentration on systemic and structural reform, which is undeniably important, has led to a neglect of what businesses and corporations can do to overcome poverty and improve the economic system.[64] Pope Francis to the contrary sees the potential of business and the role it must play for the POP:

> Business is a noble vocation, directed to producing wealth and improving our world. It can be a fruitful source of prosperity for the areas in which it operates, especially if it sees the creation of jobs as an essential part of its service to the common good.[65]

This is the way forward for the implementation of the preferential option for the poor that really creates and distributes wealth in a just and equitable manner.

---

[64]   See the insightful essay by Georges Enderle, "The Option for the Poor and Business Ethics," in *The Preferential Option for the Poor beyond Theology*, eds. Daniel G. Groody and Gustavo Gutiérrez (Notre Dame: University of Notre Dame Press, 2014), 28–46.

[65]   *LS*, no. 129.

20

Catholic Social Teaching and Living the Christian Life

Russell Shaw

I

The most important thing to say at the start is that many good people live by the tenets of Catholic Social Teaching without giving it much thought. They haven't read *Rerum novarum* or *Laudato si'*, and they would probably find it hard to explain the principle of subsidiarity or the universal destination of goods.[1] But they are kind and loving family members, thoughtful neighbors, conscientious citizens, and honest, reliable business owners, managers, and workers. Such people practice a modest lifestyle, their only extravagance, such as it is, being an occasional outing with the kids, and they are generous with their time and money in supporting good causes. Catholic Social Teaching is in good hands with them.

Things are more complicated with another sector of the Catholic populace. I mean middle- and upper-echelon professionals who find it necessary to wrestle with ethical issues more or less regularly in doing their work: for example, college admission officers and corporate personnel executives who must decide whether and how to apply race- and gender-based preferences in making decisions about admissions, hiring, and promotions; married professional couples who must pay the caterer's bill for costly elegance when entertaining clients and colleagues if they hope to preserve their social standing and get ahead professionally; legislators who are repeatedly called on to balance the competing claims of issues like economic inequality, free trade, the interests of the elderly and the poor, military needs, and public health when deciding how to allocate limited funds. What does Catholic Social

---

[1] One difficulty with the universal destination is that people naturally take a "universal destination" to be a place where everybody goes – a popular summer resort or something like that. Those responsible for framing the language in which the Church expresses itself need to pay more attention to the importance of communicating in intelligible speech.

Teaching have to say to people like these? And are they listening to what it says?

A friend of mine with a more than ordinary interest in Catholic Social Teaching asked me a while ago if I thought this body of doctrine had much impact in the United States. I thought for a moment, then said no – not directly anyway, although it was possible that it had more indirect impact than appears at first glance. (The "ordinary people" mentioned earlier may be a case in point.)

Nor is it likely, I might have added, that there was some kind of golden age in the past. Cardinal Gibbons of Baltimore had acted wisely and well in the nineteenth century by warding off an impending papal condemnation of an early organized labor group called the Knights of Labor,[2] but this was by no means the pattern with others in the Church. Writing of what she found after her conversion to Catholicism in 1927, Dorothy Day, the co-founder of the Catholic Worker movement, said this:

> I loved the Church for Christ made visible. Not for itself, because it was so often a scandal to me ... The scandal of businesslike priests, of collective wealth, lack of a sense of responsibility for the poor, the worker, the Negro, the Mexican, the Filipino, and even the oppression of these, and the consenting to the oppression of them by our industrialist-capitalist order – these made me feel often that the priests were more like Cain than Abel ... The worst enemies would be those of our own household, Christ had warned us.[3]

Day conceded that she later found many poor, self-sacrificing priests in the Church; but this, she said, was how it seemed to her at the time of her baptism.

Day's view was echoed and elaborated upon in the 1940s by Father John Hugo, her spiritual director, a priest of the Pittsburgh diocese who penned radical critiques of what he called the "watering down of Catholic identity" on the part of many American Catholics of that time. On birth control, for instance:

> Economic pressure ... does not explain the prevalence of this sin among the prosperous – worldliness does. Those who commit it balance the law of God over against the advantages to be gained through birth control – unrestrained pleasure, physical beauty, leisure, freedom from the responsibility of a family,

---

[2]   See John Tracy Ellis, *The Life of James Cardinal Gibbons, Archbishop of Baltimore, 1834–1921*, Vol. I (Milwaukee: The Bruce Publishing Company, 1952), 486–546.

[3]   Dorothy Day, *The Long Loneliness: The Autobiography of Dorothy Day* (Garden City, NY: Image Books, 1959), 145–146.

the opportunity to use all one's income on luxuries, and the satisfaction of earthly ambitions.[4]

One is not surprised to learn that Father Hugo suffered a form of silencing by his bishop until being rehabilitated by a later bishop.

And now? In an overview of recent surveys, the Pew Research Center found US Catholics to be generally supportive of government efforts to alleviate poverty, but no more supportive than the American public as a whole and rather less supportive than religiously unaffiliated Americans.[5] In 2011, the most recent (at the time this is written) in a series of surveys of Catholic attitudes conducted at six-year intervals found that 39 percent of those self-identified as "highly committed" to the Church believe one can be a good Catholic without giving time or money to help the poor. (Higher percentages believe the same concerning attendance at Sunday Mass, following Church teaching on birth control, divorce, and remarriage, and being married in the Church; 31 percent see no need to accept Church teaching on abortion.[6])

The state of affairs reflected in numbers like these undoubtedly is the product of a variety of different causes, but among them, surely, is simple ignorance of the Church's social doctrine. At the risk of offending everyone, I'd say this ignorance – which in at least some cases appears to some degree willful – lies on both sides of the liberal–conservative divide in American Catholicism. One has the impression that for many conservative Catholics the only two tenets of Catholic social teaching of which they are much aware are subsidiarity (interpreted as a principle of a priori opposition to big government) and the right to own private property. As for the liberals, they certainly talk more about social doctrine than their conservative coreligionists do; but it sometimes seems they do this as a prelude to endorsing elements of the Democratic party's socioeconomic platform said to express the teaching of the Church; this then allows them to claim that it is *they*, not the conservatives, who are the *real* Catholics despite their tolerance of abortion and their support for same-sex marriage.[7]

---

[4] David Scott and Mike Aquilina, eds., *Weapons of the Spirit: Selected Writings of Father John Hugo* (Huntington, IN: Our Sunday Visitor Publishing Division, 1997), 95.

[5] Tim Townsend, "U.S. Catholics mirror general public on views of inequality," Pew Research Center, March 27, 2014.

[6] William V. D'Antonio, "Persistence and Change," *National Catholic Reporter*, October 28– November 10, 2011. Other articles in the same issue of the newspaper also cover survey results.

[7] One of the less attractive features of the situation described here is the practice of some conservative and liberal Catholics of styling themselves respectively "John Paul II Catholics" and "Pope Francis Catholics," as if being a Catholic were similar to being a fan of a sports team.

An experience of mine illustrates the ignorance of Catholic social teaching as I have encountered it. Not long ago I spent an evening with some friends, a small group of Catholic professional men – doctors and university professors for the most part – who met occasionally for dinner and discussion of some designated topic. Our subject this evening was social doctrine. At one point in the conversation, I found myself intervening to say a word for the universal destination of goods, which I explained as simply and clearly as I could in words not unlike those used a few years later by Pope Francis: "The earth is essentially a shared inheritance, whose fruits are meant to benefit everyone."[8] This principle, I said, has been taught repeatedly by the magisterium in modern times and has ample grounding in Sacred Scripture.

My remarks were greeted with disbelief. Surely, my listeners replied, the Catholic Church had never said anything like *that*. Lacking immediate access to magisterial documents in order to make my case, I gave up. I suppose my companions went home later thinking I had made it all up. And these, I should add, were well-educated, practicing, serious American Catholics. One could say many things about an incident like this. I only repeat what I've already said: Catholic Social Teaching needs to be taught. On the evidence, it appears that today that simply is not happening.

To be educated in social doctrine is obviously no guarantee one will live it (and, as I remarked at the start, some ordinary people live it in an exemplary fashion with little or no formal education in it). But other things being equal, the absence of at least a working knowledge of social doctrine makes it more likely it will not be lived. Evidently, the first priority for those concerned that Catholic Social Teaching be lived by Catholic lay people is that it be *taught* much more widely than is apparently now the case.

II

An important part of that project must involve identifying areas where the efforts of lay Catholics schooled in social doctrine are particularly needed today. Pope St. John Paul II provided a useful, though by no means comprehensive, overview of eight of these in *Christifideles Laici*, the post-synodal apostolic exhortation on the vocation and mission of the laity, dated December 30, 1988, and published early in 1989.[9] It is important to note

8   Francis, Encyclical Letter *Laudato si'* (On Care for Our Common Home) (2015), no. 93.
9   John Paul II, Apostolic Exhortation *Christifideles laici* (On the Vocation and the Mission of the Lay Faithful in the Church and in the World) (1988), nos. 36–44. The material that follows is adapted from Russell Shaw, *Catholic Laity in the Mission of the Church* (Vancouver, BC:

these areas of lay involvement are areas for apostolate – the participation of the laity in the mission of the Church carried on in and to the world. Lay apostolate is not the same thing as lay ministry, which is the participation of the laity in roles of service within the structures of the Church – usually, the parish – and directed to building up the community of faith itself. Lay ministry is a meritorious form of activity by lay people; but the virtually exclusive emphasis in recent years on lay ministry and the virtually total neglect of formation for lay apostolate very likely help to explain why the principles of Catholic Social Doctrine do not have an impact on American society and the public policy debate at all proportionate to the size of the American Catholic population (officially said to number just under 70 million in 2014).

The eight areas of apostolate identified by St. John Paul II are promoting human dignity, respect for life, freedom of conscience and religious freedom, marriage and family life, works of charity, public life, placing the individual at the center of socio-economic life, and the evangelization of culture.

1 *Promoting the Dignity of the Person*

In his social encyclical *Laudato si'*, Pope Francis affirms "the immense dignity of each person," and then explains the Christian basis for commitment to human dignity in these words:

> Those who are committed to defending human dignity can find in the Christian faith the deepest reasons for this commitment. How wonderful is the certainty that each human life is not adrift in the midst of hopeless chaos ... We were conceived in the heart of God, and for this reason "each of us is the result of a thought of God. Each of us is willed, each of us is loved, each of us is necessary."[10]

In secular circles today, it is common for the affirmation of human dignity to be linked to, and indeed often virtually equated with, the affirmation of human rights. While this is not objectionable in principle, it often happens that some people claim their rights, or what they say are their rights, at the expense of the rights of others. This happens even in liberal democracies like

---

Chartwell Press, 2013), 144–175; originally published by Requiem Press of Bethune, SC, in 2005). See also my *Ministry or Apostolate: What Should the Catholic Laity Be Doing?* (Huntington, Ind.: Our Sunday Visitor Publishing, 2002) and *To Hunt, To Shoot, To Entertain: Clericalism and the Catholic Laity* (San Francisco: Ignatius Press, 1993).

[10] LS, no. 65. The internal quotation is from Pope Benedict XVI, "Homily for the Solemn Inauguration of the Petrine Ministry," April 24, 2005.

the United States – societies that pride themselves on their sensitivity to human rights. We shall see some examples of this happening in what follows.

Here, though, we need to consider another practical question: What can individuals do to promote the dignity and rights of the human person? That may be an easy question for political and social activists involved in human rights causes to answer, but most people aren't activists. What they can do on behalf of human dignity and rights normally takes more humble, everyday forms.

Forms like these: mothers who conscientiously teach their children to respect the rights and interests of siblings and playmates, and carefully correct them when they violate this norm; office managers who try consistently to deal with subordinates – even those whom they find irritating and troublesome – with fairness and charity; checkout clerks and sales personnel who give every customer, even the irritating ones, agreeable, courteous service delivered with a smile and a kind word; teachers who go out of their way to help students who are having trouble in school because of trouble at home (sickness in the family, an absent parent, etc.); people who are never brusque with elderly, garrulous neighbors even when they are in a rush themselves.

Little things like these are hardly world-changing, yet it is through such ordinary, everyday displays of respect for others that the world really does become a more truly human habitation. In the words of Pope St. John Paul II: "As an individual, a person is not a number nor simply a link in a chain, nor even less an impersonal element in some system."[11] Here is an approach to the promotion of human dignity (and human rights) that is immediately open to everyone in ordinary life.

2 *Fostering Respect for the Right to Life*

The right to life is the basis of other human rights. Declarations in defense of other rights – "the right to health, to home, to work, to family, to culture" – tend to be "false and illusory," says St. John Paul II, if this fundamental right is not upheld.[12] And that is how things often are in today's world, where what John Paul calls a Culture of Death is a powerful voice.

In 2003 the Congregation for the Doctrine of the Faith published an important doctrinal note concerning the duty of Catholic citizens and Catholics in public life to defend and promote ethical values pertaining to the common good of society. Among the "life" issues of particular concern

---

[11] CL, no. 37.
[12] CL, no. 38.

today are abortion, euthanasia and assisted suicide, experimentation on human embryos that involves their destruction, the cultivation of embryos in order to obtain their stem cells or other parts to be used for therapeutic purposes, capital punishment, nuclear deterrence, and other technological aspects of modern warfare. Many Catholic legislators and jurists in the United States and other countries support practices like these. Under the heading of "relativism," the CDF document said this:

> If Christians must "recognize the legitimacy of differing points of view about the organization of worldly affairs [reference to Vatican Council II, *Gaudium et spes*, 75],[13] they are also called to reject, as injurious to democratic life, a conception of pluralism that reflects moral relativism. Democracy must be based on the true and solid foundation of non-negotiable ethical principles, which are the underpinning of life in society.[14]

The moral imperatives of social doctrine in regard to human life extend beyond Catholic legislators and judges, however, to Catholic citizens, who have a duty to work for the right to life through their participation in public life, especially by informed, conscientious voting. Unfortunately, not all do. One recalls a remark by the newspaper columnist Michael Gerson, a political conservative with a sensitivity to issues of social justice, regarding the fact that voting by American Catholics so often mirrors the voting pattern of "their suburban neighbors": "There is something vaguely disturbing about the precise symmetry of any religious group with other voters of their same class and background. One would hope that an ancient, demanding faith would leave some distinctive mark."[15]

Back in 1968, five years before the Supreme Court's *Roe* v. *Wade* decision legalizing abortion throughout the United States, I published a book called *Abortion on Trial* warning that even then organized efforts were underway to bring about this result.[16] At the end of the book, I wrote this:

> The abortion controversy is, in any realistic view of things, likely to be prolonged and unpleasant. There will be ample opportunity for those who oppose abortion to become discouraged or simply to grow weary of the whole

[13] Vatican II, Pastoral Constitution *Gaudium et spes* (On the Church in the Modern World) (1965).
[14] *Doctrinal Note on Some Questions Regarding the Participation of Catholics in Political Life*, no. 3.
[15] "A Catholic Test for Politics," *Washington Post*, February 8, 2011.
[16] Like many people at the time, however, I supposed that if this were to come about, it would be by an incremental route involving the adoption of gradually more permissive state laws. A sweeping Supreme Court decision constitutionalizing a right to abortion did not then seem in the cards.

disagreeable subject. The stakes, however, are terribly high – as high as human life itself. There are very few better reasons for persevering in a fight than that.[17]

That remains as true today as it was then – except that now after "human life" one should add "from conception on."

3 Defending Freedom of Conscience and Religious Freedom

In the last century, and now in this one, many millions of people throughout the world have experienced religious persecution, and many of these have lost their lives. As this is written, the bloody persecution of Christians by Islamic extremists is spreading in the Middle East. Elsewhere, in countries from Saudi Arabia to China and North Korea, religious liberty is curtailed and persecution is taking place.

The problem even exists in nations of the supposedly tolerant liberal democratic West, although here it takes a different form. The objective of extreme secularizers is to drive the religious presence out of public life, allowing believers a limited liberty to worship privately as they wish but allowing them no voice either to evangelize or to take part in the policy debate. Thomas F. Farr, who teaches at Georgetown University and heads an institution called the Religious Freedom Institute, sums up the situation like this:

> In Europe religious freedom is no longer seen as intrinsic to human dignity and social flourishing. It is generally understood as merely an opinion, and, as a species, a dangerous opinion at that. While it is fine to practice your religion in churches, synagogues, mosques, and temples, democracy requires that you keep it there. To bring it into public life endangers democracy. This malevolent idea, which was most famously championed by the American political philosopher John Rawls, is gaining considerable purchase in our own country.[18]

In the United States at the present time, much of the reaction against the exercise of religious liberty described by Farr and others focuses on efforts to compel cooperation with the regime of same-sex marriage imposed by the Supreme Court's June 2015 decision in *Obergefell v. Hodges*. Two years earlier, in a majority opinion overturning relevant sections of the Defense of Marriage

[17]   Russell Shaw, *Abortion on Trial* (Dayton, OH: Pflaum Press, 1968), 198.
[18]   Thomas F. Farr, "Rescuing Religious Liberty," *Religious Liberty: Proceedings from the 35th Annual Convention of the Fellowship of Catholic Scholars* (2012), ed. Elizabeth C. Shaw (Fellowship of Catholic Scholars, 2014), 57–69.

Act (*United States v. Windsor*), Justice Anthony Kennedy, author of the majority opinion in *Obergefell*, had already expressed the view that bigotry was the only conceivable reason why anyone would object to granting same-sex unions legal recognition as marriages.

Lay people, individually and in organized groups, can and should do a great deal to forestall and resist coercive efforts that offend against the consciences of religious believers. Appropriate steps will include reaching out to other churches and religious groups to build coalitions, publicly stating their concerns in the media and other forums, and insisting that their elected representatives enact measures to protect against incursions on freedom of conscience and religious liberty.

4 Protecting and Encouraging Marriage and Family Life

Marriage and family life are under sustained assault today in many parts of the world, especially the secularized West. St. John Paul II, who made defending marriage and family life a central theme of his pontificate (for example, in the Post-Synodal Apostolic Exhortation *Familiaris consortio*,[19] as well as in a stream of other documents and talks), wrote:

> The family is the basic cell of society. It is the cradle of life and love, the place in which the individual is born and grows. Therefore a primary concern is reserved for this community, especially in those times when human egoism, the anti-birth campaign, totalitarian politics, situations of poverty, material, cultural and moral misery, threaten to make these very springs of life dry up.[20]

John Paul also expresses particular concern regarding "ideologies and … systems" that seek to usurp the family and parental role in education, and calls for a "vast extensive and systematic work" to resist threats to marriage and family life. In recent times, the campaign for the recognition of homosexual relationships as marriages has ushered in a new and more alarming stage in this assault on traditional marriage, with the US Supreme Court's *Obergefell* decision, which constitutionalizes same-sex marriage, an especially disturbing development.

Conscientious married couples are very aware of the secular culture's ongoing assault on marriage and family life via the media and other channels. Many feel isolated and in danger of being overwhelmed by the powerful forces

[19] John Paul II, Apostolic Exhortation *Familiaris consortio* (On the Christian Family in the Modern World) (1981).
[20] *CL*, no. 40.

lined up against them. In fact, the agencies of political and economic life often seem part of the antifamily campaign; and even religious bodies and institutions offer little help.

In these circumstances couples and families who wish to maintain traditional values need to come together in groups for mutual reinforcement and support. Where viable family organizations and movements do not exist, concerned couples should take the initiative by organizing gatherings of like-minded married friends, parishioners, and neighbors for the discussion of shared concerns and joint social action. This sort of grassroots effort to build up marriage and the family in the face of opposing forces is one of the most important forms of lay apostolate today – one at the service of individuals and the whole of society. As Pope John Paul II said, "the future of humanity passes by way of the family."[21]

5 *Engaging in Works of Charity*

The story of the Good Samaritan is one of the most cherished of Jesus' parables. Not surprisingly, works of charity performed out of love for God and neighbor have been a central element of Christian life and teaching from the start. "Charity towards one's neighbor, through contemporary forms of the traditional and corporal works of mercy, represent the most immediate, ordinary, and habitual ways that lead to the Christian animation of the temporal order, the specific duty of the lay faithful."[22]

Today, however, there are real obstacles to the personal practice of charity. Among these is the tendency to turn over responsibility for works of charity to government or organized private charities, or some combination of the two, while limiting the direct involvement of most individuals to paying taxes or making tax-deductible contributions. Of course there is nothing wrong in principle with government social services and large-scale organized charities. On the contrary – they are indispensable; government and the private sector have serious responsibilities to the poor and disabled; and well-planned, well-conducted programs of social service and charity by government and the private sector deserve generous citizen support. But there also are abuses, including waste, corruption, and the encouragement of immoral practices as elements of social policy. The latter is a growing problem for Catholic social welfare institutions and programs in the United States.

---

[21] CL, no. 86.
[22] CL, no. 41.

In any case, support for organized charities under government and private auspices does not exhaust the opportunities and obligations of individuals. Many Church leaders have made this point, including Pope John Paul II in a 1984 document called *Salvifici doloris*. While warmly commending government social services and large-scale private charities, he insisted on the continuing need for "voluntary 'Good Samaritan' work" by individuals and families in settings like hospitals and hospices, homes for the aged, soup kitchens and feeding programs, pregnancy counseling, blood banks, and others.

> Every individual must feel as if called personally to bear witness to love in suffering. The institutions are very important and indispensable; nevertheless, no institution can by itself replace the human heart, human compassion, human initiative, when it is a question of dealing with the suffering of another. This refers to physical sufferings, but it is even more true when it is a question of the many kinds of moral suffering, and when it is primarily the soul that is suffering.[23]

6 Participating in Public Life

Artemus Ward, an American humorist of the nineteenth century, got laughs by boasting, "I am not a politician, and my other habits are good." Joking aside, however, Ward's one-liner encapsulates a cynical, and apparently widely held, view of politics and participation in public life that has become deeply rooted in American life since his time. So much so that the "fed up" voter has now become a stock figure of our contemporary political discourse.

St. John Paul II addresses withdrawal from the political process in his overview of lay apostolic opportunities. He writes: "Charges of careerism, idolatry of power, egoism, and corruption that are sometimes directed at persons in government . . . as well as the common opinion that participating in politics is an absolute moral danger, does not in the least justify either skepticism or the absence of Christians from public life."[24] There is no little truth in the familiar saying that in a democracy citizens get the political leadership they deserve; if they don't like the result, they often have themselves to blame.

Considering the opportunities and obligations for apostolate in relation to the defense of life, we saw above that involvement in public life was one of

---

[23] John Paul II, Apostolic Letter *Salvifici doloris* (On the Christian Meaning of Human Suffering) (1984), no. 29.

[24] *CL*, no. 42.

these. What was said there about defending and promoting human life holds true across the board of the broad range of issues. Upright politics aims to promote the common good in respect to all the fundamental values and needs of the community; it is concerned with the full spectrum of public issues at any given time.

The most obvious way to participate in political life, open to all citizens of a democracy, is by voting. Low voter turnout usually means many people are neglecting their duty. But responsible voting must be conscientious and informed. People sometimes base their voting on frivolous or selfish considerations. Like serving in public office, voting should be based upon a sincere and generous calculation of what will serve the common good.

There are many other ways to participate in the political process at the grassroots level: taking part in meetings of public bodies (hearings, city council meetings, and the like), writing thoughtful, well-informed letters to public officials and the media, working for political parties in order to influence them for the better, working for candidates who meet the criteria of ethics and competence. Sitting on the sidelines and complaining about politics and politicians does not qualify as responsible participation.

As for seeking and holding office: Catholics in public life are not expected to take orders from the Church, but they do have a serious moral obligation to form their consciences and their policy positions in light of the Church's social teaching. The response of many Catholic politicians over the years that they are "personally opposed" to something like abortion but support it as a matter of public policy is a conspicuous instance of the "dichotomy between the faith which may profess and the practice of their daily lives" that the Second Vatican Council called "one of the gravest errors of our time."[25]

7 *Placing the Individual at the Center of Socioeconomic Life*

As a participant in a television discussion, I once heard the author of a book about corporate responsibility make the following remark: "The basic purpose of a corporation is to make money. No doubt a corporation which treats its employees well, doesn't pollute the environment, and deals fairly with consumers will generally be more successful than one which fails in these matters. Still, the fundamental reason why a corporation exists is to make money, not any or all of these good things." It seems likely that many people share that view.

---

[25]   GS, no. 43.

As a statement of how things are – profits come first – it is probably true in many cases if not most; but as a statement of how things ought to be, it conflicts with Catholic social teaching. Making money is a legitimate purpose for a commercial enterprise. Businesses that do not make money sooner or later fail, and many people are likely to suffer as a result. But when it comes to the *basic* purpose, Pope Francis's words are a clear and definitive statement of the Church's position.

> We are convinced that "man is the source and the aim of all economic and social life" . . . Work should be the setting for this rich personal growth, where many aspects of life enter into play: creativity, planning for the future, developing our talents, living out our values, relating to others, giving glory to God. It follows that, in the reality of today's global society, it is essential that "we continue to prioritize the goal of access to steady employment for everyone," no matter the limited interests of business and dubious economic reasoning.[26]

Earlier in the same document, Pope Francis rejects out of hand the view of those who believe the working of market mechanisms will solve problems of global hunger and poverty. Of them he writes:

> They are less concerned with certain economic theories which today scarcely anybody dares defend, than with their actual operation in the functioning of the economy . . . Their behavior shows that for them maximizing profits is enough. Yet by itself the market cannot guarantee integral human development and social inclusion.[27]

Although the market economy is an effective mechanism for generating wealth, the market mentality, left to its own devices, operates in an impersonal and sometimes brutal way, without concern for individuals and particular groups. This can be seen in practices like downsizing and outsourcing, where businesses eliminate jobs or shift operations to regions where workers come cheap, and in the assumption that dead-end, low-paid jobs are a necessary fact of economic life. Efficiency clearly is essential to the success of a business; it is impossible to shield all workers from unpleasant shocks; and not all jobs can be interesting and richly fulfilling. But shrugging and saying, "That's just the way a market-driven economy works" is an unacceptable obstacle to even looking for solutions to dehumanizing practices like these.

---

[26] LS, no. 127. The internal quotations are, respectively, from GS, no. 63; and Benedict XVI, Encyclical Letter *Caritas in veritate* (On Integral Human Development in Charity and Truth) (2009), no. 32.

[27] LS, no. 109. Citation to CV, no. 35.

Given the complexity of economic life, it would be foolish to suggest that these problems have easy answers. Catholic social teaching has no such answers to offer. But the search for solutions should be ongoing, and many different people and groups should be involved. Boards of directors, CEOs, executives and managers at all levels, union leaders and union members – these and others have a duty to shape and sustain a just socioeconomic order on the national and international levels where human dignity and human rights are central values.

8 *The Evangelization of Culture*

Few forms of lay apostolate are more important than the effort to infuse the intellectual, aesthetic, and moral environment with the vision and values of the gospel. Evangelizing the secular culture of the United States and other Western countries is particularly needed at a time when they are more and more becoming cut off from their religious roots.

Central to this is the evangelization of the media of communication. Pope St. John Paul II made this point in a passage of his 1990 encyclical on missionary work, *Redemptoris missio*:

> [S]ince the very evangelization of modern culture depends to a great extent on the influence of the media, it is not enough to use the media simply to spread the Church's authentic teaching. It is also necessary to integrate that message into the "new culture" created by modern communications. This is a complex issue, since the "new culture" originates not just from whatever content is eventually expressed, but from the very fact that there exist new ways of communicating, with new languages, new techniques and a new psychology.[28]

Three decades later, with the communication revolution still in full swing, this is a challenge to which the Church, like other institutions, is still seeking the best ways to respond.

There is a great need for committed lay Catholics and other religious believers to enter the field of secular communications and, in a manner entirely consistent with their professional responsibilities, seek to influence the media for the better. However, no one considering this work as a possible career should ignore the very real obstacles to doing that. Thorough

---

[28] John Paul II, Encyclical Letter *Redemptoris missio* (On the Permanent Validity of the Church's Missionary Mandate) (1990), no. 37.

preparation, including not only professional training but spiritual and religious formation, is imperative.

At the same time one must recognize that, occasional exceptions to the contrary notwithstanding, it is usually unrealistic to think of *using* secular media for direct evangelization. For the most part, the media are not available to be used for evangelization or to be evangelized themselves; they are more often obstacles to evangelization than vehicles for accomplishing it.

Thus, where media and evangelization are concerned, the Church must rely on its own media – Catholic books, the Catholic press, Catholic social media, church-sponsored television and radio. But religious media have their own limitations. They are divided – conservative versus liberal, traditional versus conservative, right versus left. And for the most part they reach only Catholics who are already convinced and practicing the faith. Thus the role of Catholic media is mainly to motivate and educate these potential evangelizers rather than to communicate directly with the larger number who are most in need of being evangelized.

The great exception to all this is found in the Internet and the social media, where many of the limitations present in traditional media do not exist. These new media have serious faults and weaknesses of their own, including the presence of pornography and rank consumerism. But the most worrisome aspect of the social media may also be their greatest strength in regard to evangelization – namely, the opportunity they provide for direct, immediate, unfiltered, uncensored communication of messages (in this case, the message of the gospel). Many committed Catholics already are active in this new media world, and many more are needed.

III

Several years ago, I taught an online course about the laity to a class of adult Catholics. Some weeks after the course ended, one of my students sent me an e-mail relating an experience she'd had. As a student, she had seemed to welcome what she heard in my course, and this is what she said now:

> Last week I gave a lecture to a group of women, and as an opening exercise I asked them to write on one side of a piece of paper all the everyday things they do in the course of a day or two. Then I asked them to write on the other side all the things they do in the same time frame that they consider to be holy.
>
> Without exception, they made up two entirely different lists – on one side, daily chores and activities, and on the other side things associated with what they consider to be "ministry" – serving as minister of communion or lector, attending Mass, things like that.

Many had only one or two items in that second column. No one simply drew an arrow from the daily activities to the list of "holy" things.

My lecture was about the apostolate of the laity. If nothing else, I wanted the women to come away with a sense of the dignity of our mission as lay people. That includes understanding that everyday activities really are holy when we do them as faithful Christians, and that in this context we aren't called only to *receive* the sacraments but, in a sense, to *be* sacrament and to live sacramental lives in which Christ's presence can be seen . . .

When the women took a second look at their lists and reflected on their everyday work as a vehicle for spreading the gospel and acting as Christ's missionaries and apostles, they began to personalize what apostolate meant for them.

This has an important bearing on Catholic Social Teaching. For if people do not live out the Church's social doctrine in their everyday lives, where exactly will they live it out? As we have seen, Vatican II declares "the dichotomy between the faith which many profess and the practice of their daily lives" to be "one of the gravest errors of our time."[29] Often this error is at the expense of the living out of Catholic social teaching.

Flannery O'Connor once pinpointed the difficulty with her customary acuity. Someone asked her why she, a Catholic, wrote about Protestants rather than her fellow Catholics. This was her reply:

To a lot of Protestants I know, monks and nuns are fanatics, none greater. And to a lot of the monks and nuns I know, my Protestant prophets are fanatics. For my part, I think the only difference between them is that if you are a Catholic and have this intensity of belief you join the convent and are heard from no more; whereas if you are a Protestant and have it, there is no convent for you to join and you go about in the world, getting into all sorts of trouble and drawing the wrath of people who don't believe in anything much at all down on your head . . . This is one reason why I can write about Protestant believers better than Catholic believers – because they express their belief in diverse kinds of dramatic action which is obvious enough for me to catch.[30]

Living according to Catholic Social Teaching is a large part of what it means to "go about in the world, getting into all sorts of trouble and drawing the wrath of people who don't believe in anything at all down on your head." Confused thinking about vocation is one of the principal reasons why more Catholics do not grasp that fact and accept the risk it entails.

---

[29]   GS, no. 43.
[30]   Letter to Sister Mariella Gable, May 4, 1963, in *Flannery O'Connor: Collected Works*, ed., Sally Fitzgerald (New York: The Library of America, n.d.), 1183.

It is customary to speak of four vocations: the clerical state (deacons, priests, bishops), consecrated life (for the most part, although not exclusively, religious women and men), matrimony, and the single lay state in the world. This way of understanding "vocation" equates it with state in life, with pride of place assigned to the vocations to the clerical state and the consecrated life. That has been common among Catholics for a long time, and even today it dominates the way many Catholics think and speak about vocations: To have a vocation means having a call from God to be a priest or a religious. But to think about vocation like that ignores the reality of personal vocation.[31]

Although the idea of personal vocation is sometimes regarded as a novelty, it can be found here and there in classical writers like St. Ignatius Loyola and St. Francis de Sales. John Henry Newman expresses it forcefully in one of his Anglican sermons:

> [T]hey who are living religiously, have from time to time truths they did not know before, or had no need to consider, brought before them forcibly; truths which involve duties, which are in fact precepts, and claim obedience. In this and such-like ways Christ calls us now. There is nothing miraculous or extraordinary in His dealings with us. He works through our natural faculties and circumstances of life. Still what happens to us in providence is in all essential respects what His voice was to those whom He addressed when on earth.[32]

In our day, the great expounder of personal vocation and its practical implications is Pope St. John Paul II. Especially notable is his apostolic exhortation *Christideles laici*, a document cited here several times already for the guidance it provides on the apostolic role of the laity in today's Church and world. A key passage deserves to be quoted at length.

> The fundamental objective of the formation of the lay faithful is an ever-clearer discovery of one's vocation and the ever-greater willingness to live it so as to fulfill one's mission.
>
> God calls me and sends me forth as a laborer in his vineyard. He calls me and sends me forth to work for the coming of his Kingdom in history. This personal vocation and mission defines the dignity and the responsibility of each member of the lay faithful and makes up the focal point of the whole

---

[31]   For a fuller explanation of personal vocation, see Germain Grisez and Russell Shaw, *Personal Vocation: God Calls Everyone by Name* (Huntington, IN: Our Sunday Visitor Publishing Division, 2003).

[32]   John Henry Newman, "Divine Calls," in *Parochial and Plain Sermons* (San Francisco: Ignatius Press, 1987), 1570.

work of formation, whose purpose is the joyous and grateful recognition of this dignity and the faithful living-out of this responsibility.

In fact, from eternity God has thought of us and has loved us as unique individuals. Every one of us he called by name, as the Good Shepherd "calls his sheep by name" (Jn 10:3). However, only in the unfolding of the history of our lives and its events is the eternal plan of God revealed to each of us. Therefore, it is a gradual process; in a certain sense, one that happens day by day.

To be able to discover the actual will of the Lord in our lives always involves the following: a receptive listening to the word of God and the Church, fervent and constant prayer, recourse to a wise and loving spiritual guide, and a faithful discernment of the gifts and talents given by God, as well as the diverse social and historic situations in which one lives.

Therefore, in the life of each member of the lay faithful there are particularly significant and decisive moments for discerning God's call and embracing the mission entrusted by him. Among these are the periods of adolescence and young adulthood. No one must forget that the Lord, as the master of the laborers in the vineyard, calls at every hour of life, so as to make his holy will more precisely and explicitly known. Therefore, the fundamental and continuous attitude of the disciple should be one of vigilance and a conscious attentiveness to the voice of God.[33]

This teaching by John Paul II, in a document about the laity, plainly applies to the integration of Catholic social teaching into their lives, including their lives in society and their participation in the political process, whether as public officials, candidates for public office, or citizens.

Alas, at the present time the picture is not very bright. As a new Congress was getting underway in 2011, columnist Michael Gerson, a former White House speechwriter who is an evangelical Protestant, observed that the number of Catholic Republicans in the House of Representatives was now sixty-four, almost equal to the Democratic Catholics' sixty-eight. But what difference would that make? "Not much," he concluded, explaining: "A century ago, many Catholics voted Democratic out of ethnic solidarity. Today, most Catholics vote almost exactly like their suburban neighbors. Catholics are often swing voters in elections precisely because they are so typical."

And Gerson's conclusion, cited above, deserves repeating here: "There is something vaguely disturbing about the precise symmetry of any religious group with other voters of the same class and background. One would hope that an ancient, demanding faith would leave some distinctive mark."[34]

---

[33] *CL*, no. 58.
[34] Michael Gerson, "A Catholic Test for Politics," *The Washington Post*, February 8, 2011.

Exit polls back to 2004 show a majority of Catholic voters not only supporting the winners of presidential elections but having done so by nearly the same
margin as the electorate as a whole. In 2004 Catholics went for George
W. Bush 52 percent to 47 percent (overall, 51–48); in 2008 they voted for
Barack Obama over John McCain, 53 percent to 46 percent (overall, 54–45); in
2012 Catholics supported Obama over Mitt Romney, 50 percent to 48 percent
(overall, an identical 50–48). The 2016 election was a slight – but only slight –
exception: Catholics once again backed the winner – 52 percent for Donald
Trump, 46 percent for Hillary Clinton, but the electorate as a whole actually
favored Clinton over Trump by a slim majority, 48.2 percent to 46.1 percent,
with Trump nevertheless emerging as victor in the all-important Electoral
College. Another observer of the general "symmetry" between Catholics and
American voters collectively, Stephen White, remarks: "Some people will tell
you the Catholic vote has become a national bellwether. But you could just as
easily say that the Catholic vote is, at least when it comes to electing
a president, meaningless."[35]

Someone might object that numbers like these ignore the notable difference, in voting and much else, between Catholics who attend Mass weekly
and Catholics who do that seldom or never, with Catholics of the first sort
generally, though not always, reflecting the values embodied in Catholic
Social Teaching to a significantly greater extent than Catholics in
the second group. No doubt that is so. But how much consolation is there in
the thought that the failure of many Catholics to make a distinctively Catholic
mark on public life reflects what appears to be a more general failure on their
part to practice the faith?

Part of the explanation for this state of affairs among a very large number of
Catholic laity is traceable to their assimilation into a secular culture in which
religious values as such no longer play a significant part.[36] Here is a brief
account of the results of this process as I described them in another book:

> How compatible with the values of the Catholic tradition, after all, are the
> values of secular America that so many assimilated Catholics more or less
> uncritically accept? ... On the evidence, many appear neither ready nor
> willing to provide a Christian critique of things like legalized abortion,
> a nuclear deterrence policy about which the public knows (and apparently
> cares) little or nothing, the contraceptionist–consumerist mentality that

[35] Stephen P. White, *Red, White, Blue, and Catholic* (Liguori, MO: Liguori Publications,
      2016), 11.
[36] It is often said that, from a historical perspective, today's secular values can be seen to have
      their origins in the religiously grounded values of earlier times. No doubt that is true. But only
      seldom are these religious origins recognized and acknowledged.

dominates the American dream of material success, the idol of American exceptionalism abroad, and much else in the world view of contemporary secular America in serious tension with their religious tradition.[37]

This is hardly a promising moral context for a distinctively Catholic view of a just social order to put down roots.

The second great cause of this state of affairs has to do with the impoverished idea of vocation still prevailing among many Catholics – in this case, the idea that, when all is said and done, responsibility for representing the Church's vision of a just society to the world rests with the clerical hierarchy rather than the laity. Underlying this way of thinking is the notion that clerics and religious have vocations in a full, robust sense but lay people do not. From this perspective, Vatican II's teaching that the "special vocation" of the laity is "to make the Church present and fruitful in those places and circumstances where it is only through them that she can become salt of the earth"[38] – that is, by applying the principles of Catholic social teaching to the secular order, including politics – is meaningless.[39]

In the first instance, what is involved in this living out of the Christian vocation is the effort to make this a more just and peaceful world. But – important to the matters under discussion here – the universal applicability of that duty to all members of the Church also has a fundamental eschatological dimension, as Vatican II teaches.

> For after we have promoted on earth, in the Spirit of the Lord and in accord with his command, the goods of human dignity, familial communion, and freedom – that is to say, all the good fruits of our nature and effort – then we shall find them once more, but cleansed of all dirt, lit up, and transformed, when Christ gives back to the Father an eternal and universal kingdom: "a kingdom of truth and life, a kingdom of holiness and grace, a kingdom of justice, love and peace."[40]

---

[37] Russell Shaw, *American Church: The Remarkable Rise, Meteoric Fall, and Uncertain Future of Catholicism in America* (San Francisco: Ignatius Press, 2013), 13.

[38] Vatican II, Dogmatic Constitution *Lumen gentium* (1964), no. 33.

[39] An anecdote illustrates the persistence of clericalism. In a parish I know, as in many others, the Prayer of the Faithful at Mass regularly includes a petition for "increased vocations to the priesthood and religious life." When a parishioner called to the pastor's attention something I had written suggesting it might be more helpful to say something like "That everyone will discern and accept the particular vocation to which God is calling him or her," that briefly became the version used in this particular parish. But soon it reverted to the old, clericalist form – more vocations to the priesthood and religious life. Clericalist thinking dies hard.

[40] GS, no. 39. Internal quotation from the Preface for the Feast of Christ the King. Authors' translation in Grisez and Shaw, *Personal Vocation*, 114.

Surely the "we" in that passage includes lay women and men as well as clerics and religious.

IV

Before concluding this overview of how to live the principles of Catholic Social Teaching, one other important matter needs to be considered. It is the question of lifestyle. Start with consumerism – the excess consumption of the world's goods. During the last several decades, it has been targeted repeatedly by Church leaders and writers on social justice. At the level of a society or a nation, it takes the form of what John Paul II called "superdevelopment" arising from "excessive availability of every kind of goods, for the benefit of certain social groups" and expressed in the obsessive quest to own and consume more and more.[41] On the individual level, too, consumerism has the same characteristics and finds expression in similar patterns of behavior. As a result of "compulsive consumerism," says Pope Francis, "people can easily get caught up in a whirlwind of needless buying and spending ... [They come] to believe that they are free as long as they have the supposed freedom to consume."[42]

Consumerism's cure lies in acquiring and practicing the virtue of temperance. One person living temperately gives good example. A multitude of people living temperately can change a nation or even the world for the better. Pope Francis makes much the same point in his environmental encyclical *Laudato si'*, where he uses the word "sobriety" to describe an attitude equivalent to temperance. Living in the manner required by sobriety, he writes, means "living life to the full ... learning familiarity with the simplest things and how to enjoy them."[43]

By long custom, temperance is commonly understood as the virtue of moderation in food, drink, and sex. And so it is. But temperance should also be seen in broader terms, an insight dating back to Aristotle, who calls it continence: "[T]he man who pursues excessive pleasures, or pursues necessary things to excess ... is intemperate and incontinent ... Opposed to incontinence is temperance ... preserving mastery."[44]

Temperance, along with allied virtues like detachment and chastity, is not just about avoiding this or that. Obviously it does involve self-restraint; but, as

---

[41] See John Paul II, Encyclical Letter *Sollicitudo rei socialis* (On Social Concern) (1987), no. 28.
[42] LS, no. 203.
[43] LS, no. 223.
[44] *Nicomachean Ethics*, bk. 7, in *The Ethics of Aristotle*, trans. J. A. K. Thomson (Baltimore, MD: Penguin Books, 1973), 210.

Pope Francis points out, it is at the same time a necessary path to "living life to the full." The practice of temperance in lifestyle is a way of growing in freedom: in acquiring and using temporal goods, a temperate person observes the criteria of social teaching while becoming increasingly accustomed to choose the right thing in the right way for the right reason.

Instances of intemperance and social irresponsibility are easily found all around us. In the city where I live, for instance, and in many others as well, it is common for developers to buy old houses in popular neighborhoods, tear them down, and in their place build new, oversized houses that are too large for the lots they occupy and in relation to the homes around them. These intemperately large edifices are then sold to apparently eager buyers for a much higher price than the old houses would have brought. A priest I know says his nephew, a practicing architect in a Southern city, calls these lavish structures "Redneck Versailles." Whatever you call them, they reflect intemperance in operation, driven by vanity and the profit motive.

Secular culture does much to create the pressure constantly brought to bear against the practice of temperance. Here, advertising plays a large role.

Some years ago, one of the Vatican dicasteries asked me to draft a statement on advertising. Determined to be as positive as possible, I concluded that advertising really does serve some very useful purposes – disseminating information, keeping the economy humming, even providing entertainment. (Not infrequently, the ads really are better than the shows.) I also found that the fundamental purpose of advertising is to get people to feel a need for something they didn't need before – a product, a service, a candidate for office. That is acceptable if the product or service or whatever it might be is truly beneficial. If not, though, the advertising that promotes it is inescapably exploitative and manipulative. Years ago, cigarette advertising did its best to get people to acquire an addictive and dangerous habit. There may be fewer cigarette ads these days, but much advertising still has the same ugly purpose – making people want something they should not want.

Considering all the obstacles, old and new, to the practice of temperance, how can people hope to acquire this virtue so important to a lifestyle congenial to living the principles of social doctrine?

The first step is introspection, getting to know oneself better – in this case, seeking a realistic picture of the form intemperance is most likely to take for oneself. Eating or drinking too much? At least those are fairly obvious faults. But if the problem is something more subtle – and there is a good chance it is – it may take time and effort to bring it out into the light. Here an experienced advisor, a spiritual director who knows us well, can be of much help.

Regular, repeated acts of voluntary self-denial also are classic means for acquiring the habit of temperance. Fasting is one. In recent times, of course, the Church has greatly relaxed its laws on fasting. That leaves it to individuals to take up the slack for themselves.

Some words of the philosopher Josef Pieper are relevant here. Pieper was writing before the Church relaxed its fasting laws, but what he says remains eminently sound. Although fasting is often thought to be "something extra-ordinary," something only for ascetics and saints, he remarks, St. Thomas Aquinas nevertheless declared it to be "a commandment of the natural law . . . intended for the average Christian." Pieper continues:

> Whoever has not reached the maturity of perfection – that is, all of us ordinary Christians – could not persevere, without recourse to the medicine, the discipline, of fasting, that inner order of virtue by virtue of which the turbulence of sensuality is kept in check and the spirit liberated ... Our natural duty obliges us to pay dearly so that we may become what we are by essence: the free moral person in full possession of himself.[45]

In the normal course of events, a life organized around principles like this is expressed in a lifestyle congenial to the living out of social doctrine. Pope Francis, linking it to the environmental sensitivity he so strongly advocates as a key part of the contemporary practice of social justice, calls it a "prophetic and contemplative lifestyle," and describes it like this:

> Christian spirituality proposes a growth marked by moderation and the capacity to be happy with little. It is a return to that simplicity which allows us to stop and appreciate the small things, to be grateful for the opportunities which life affords to be spiritually detached from what we possess, and not to succumb to sadness for what we lack. This implies avoiding the dynamic of dominion and the mere accumulation of pleasures ... Such sobriety, when lived freely and consciously, is liberating. It is not a lesser life or one lived with less intensity. On the contrary, it is a way of living life to the full.[46]

An obvious objection to what I've been saying is that it implies the integration of social teaching with ascesis and spirituality, to the point that one's life becomes an integral life of faith. The reply is equally obvious: Exactly. Now let's get on with it.

---

[45] Josef Pieper, *The Four Cardinal Virtues* (New York: Pantheon Books, 1959), 181–182.
[46] *LS*, nos. 222–223.

PART IV

EVALUATIVE AND CRITICAL REFLECTIONS

21

Catholic Social Teaching *Is* Catholic Moral Teaching

E. Christian Brugger

DEFINITION OF CATHOLIC SOCIAL TEACHING

Catholic Social Teaching (CST)[1] is an exercise of Christian practical reasoning in relation to social realities.[2]

By calling it *teaching* we mean firstly normative – *moral* – reflection and instruction: the questions CST addresses are above all moral questions.[3] CST is therefore considered a branch of moral theology.[4] Its normative content is expressed in two forms: a set of general and universal principles that guide reflection, establish criteria for judgment, and yield directives for action; and

---

[1] The term "Catholic Social Teaching" here refers to the authoritative documentary tradition on social questions set forward (principally) by the popes beginning with Pope Leo XIII's encyclical *Rerum novarum* (On the Condition of the Working Classes) (1891). Some refer to it as *Modern* Catholic Social Teaching.

[2] "The Church's social doctrine is ... [the] formulation of the results of a careful reflection on the complex realities of human existence, in society and in the international order, in the light of faith and of the Church's tradition." John Paul II, Encyclical Letter *Sollicitudo rei socialis* (On Social Concern) (1987), no. 41. "The Church's social teaching is ... essentially orientated toward action"; Congregation for the Doctrine of the Faith, *Libertatis conscientia* (Instruction on Christian Freedom and Liberation) (1986), no. 72.

[3] "This social teaching ... concerns the ethical aspect of this life. It takes into account the technical aspects of problems but always in order to judge them from the moral point of view." *LC*, no. 72. "It will thus be seen at once that the questions facing us are above all moral questions; and that neither the analysis of the problem of development as such nor the means to overcome the present difficulties can ignore this essential dimension." *SRS*, no. 41.

[4] "Its aim is thus to guide Christian behavior. It therefore belongs to the field, not of ideology, but of theology and particularly of moral theology." *SRS*, no. 41.

"The Church's social doctrine, by its concern for man and by its interest in him and in the way he conducts himself in the world, 'belongs to the field ... of theology and particularly of moral theology.'" John Paul II, Encyclical Letter *Centesimus annus* (On the 100th Anniversary of *Rerum novarum*) (1991), no. 55.2.

the contingent judgments drawn from those principles applicable to particular situations.[5]

By *social* we mean CST's normative instruction bears upon the complex reality of moral life in society. Although its scope extends to all spheres of social life, it gives special attention to the economic and political realms.

By *Catholic* we mean that its normative content is theologically Christian. Its principles are contained in or are implications of the teaching of divine revelation: specifications of the commandment to love God and neighbor.[6] This does not deny their universal relevance since charity includes natural justice and (as we shall see later) the normative principles of CST are all, in various forms, principles of justice.[7] Through the articulation, defense, and application of these principles, CST concerns itself with both the temporal and eternal welfare of all.[8] It is therefore part of the Church's mission *ad gentes*.

The definition is meant to show (inter alia) that CST *is just* Catholic moral teaching with emphasis upon the political and economic realms. This has not always been so clear. A harmful and indeed nonsensical bifurcation exists in the minds of many between the Church's commitment to "social justice" on the one hand and her teachings on the Fifth and Sixth Commandments of the

---

[5] "Being essentially orientated toward action, this teaching develops in accordance with the changing circumstances of history. This is why, together with principles that are always valid, it also involves contingent judgments." *LC*, no. 72.

[6] "Social doctrine is built on the foundation handed on by the Apostles to the Fathers of the Church, and then received and further explored by the great Christian doctors." Benedict XVI, Encyclical Letter *Caritas in veritate* (On Integral Human Development in Charity and Truth) (2009), no. 12. " The Church's social teaching is born of the encounter of the Gospel message and of its demands summarized in the supreme commandment of love of God and neighbour in justice with the problems emanating from the life of society." *LC*, no. 72. "In this search for the changes which should be promoted, Christians must first of all renew their confidence in the forcefulness and special character of the demands made by the Gospel. The Gospel is not out-of-date because it was proclaimed, written and lived in a different sociocultural context." Paul VI, Apostolic Letter *Octogesima adveniens* (On the 80th Anniversary of *Rerum novarum*) (1971), no. 4. "The Church's social teaching is born of the encounter of the Gospel message and of its demands summarized in the supreme commandment of love of God and neighbor in justice with the problems emanating from the life of society." *LC*, no. 72. "The Church's social doctrine is ... the accurate formulation of the results of a careful reflection on the complex realities of human existence, in society and in the international order, in the light of faith and of the Church's tradition. Its main aim is to interpret these realities, determining their conformity with or divergence from the lines of the Gospel teaching on man and his vocation, a vocation which is at once earthly and transcendent." *SRS*, no. 41.

[7] "'*Caritas in veritate*' is the principle around which the Church's social doctrine turns, a principle that takes on practical form in the criteria that govern moral action. I would like to consider two of these in particular, of special relevance to the commitment to development in an increasingly globalized society: *justice and the common good*." *CV*, no. 60.

[8] *OA*, no. 4.

Decalogue on the other. Academic reflection on CST has been dominated by those inclined to disregard authoritative teaching on a range of moral issues, mainly pertaining to sex. CST is rarely appealed to in defense of the absolute negative norms taught by the Church protecting marriage and life. The authoritative heavy lifting in this regard is done by what this essay refers to as "moral documents," texts not ordinarily associated with the CST corpus. Why did this bifurcation arise and how can it be overcome? This is the subject of this chapter.

After a brief elaboration of the nature and purposes of CST and its dominant "principles," the essay reflects on why the disassociation between CST and Catholic moral teaching has come about. It argues that as a body of ethical instruction CST would be much more coherent and pastorally effective by explicitly incorporating the exceptionless moral norms taught and defended by the Church. The final section contains suggestions on how this incorporation might take place.

JUSTICE AND THE "PRINCIPLES" OF CST

Every social unit from the family to the community of mankind has a common good. CST addresses all these communities. It especially concerns itself with so-called perfect communities, viz., nations and states. Since justice is the norm that directs activity consistent with the common good, justice is the governing norm for CST.[9]

Justice has many expressions. CST articulates norms governing these expressions in the form of its "principles."[10] Generally speaking, its principles are norms of justice. Because their articulation in the documents of CST is ad hoc, they are nowhere set down in the form of a systematic philosophy. Nor are they all formulated as normative propositions specifying a clear "ought," even though all have normative implications. Rather, together they comprise a set of enduring truths on the nature of and requirements for a just social order.

Different lists and formulations can be found in the literature, and this chapter makes no pretense of being definitive. The purpose of the more numerous itemization of principles here – sixteen – is to identify the most

---

[9]　There is no antinomy between this and Benedict XVI's assertion that "'*Caritas in veritate*' is the principle around which the Church's social doctrine turns" (CV, no. 6; cf. no. 7). For Benedict's aim in CV for proposing charity, not only as a Gospel requirement but a social norm for all, especially in the economic realm – entailing the "logic of giving and forgiving" and "relationships of gratuitousness, mercy and communion" – is to ensure justice. In other words, when we shoot for charity, we have a better chance of attaining justice.

[10]　"The permanent principles of the Church's social doctrine constitute the very heart of Catholic social teaching" (Pontifical Council for Justice and Peace, *Compendium of the Social Doctrine of the Church* (2004), no. 160).

prominent demands of justice singled out, and conspicuously so, in the social documents of the past 125 years. The first two occupy an architectonic position in relation to the rest. The remaining fourteen are normative specifications of justice directed to the common good.

    1. Master Principle: **Primacy of the Human Person**[11]
    2. Guiding Norm: **Justice and the Common Good**[12]
    3. **Conformity of the Social Order to the Moral Order**[13]
    4. **Human Solidarity**[14]
  5/6. **Private Ownership vs. Universal Purpose of the World's Resources**[15]
    7. **Subsidiarity**[16]
    8. **Importance of Marriage and the Family**[17]
    9. **Importance of Religion**[18]
  10. **Dignity of Work & Dignity of Workers** (Primacy of *Labor* over *Capital*)[19]
  11. **Morally Responsible Openness to Life**[20]
  12. **Preferential Option for the Poor**[21]
  13. **Fair Wage**[22]
  14. **Right of Labor to Organize**[23]
  15. **Right to Participate**[24]
  16. **Stewardship for Creation**[25]

[11]   John XXIII, Encyclical Letter *Mater et magistra* (On Christianity and Social Progress) (1961), nos. 219–220; John XXIII, Encyclical Letter *Pacem in terris* (On Establishing Universal Peace in Truth, Justice, Charity, and Liberty) (1963), no. 26.

[12]   E.g., Vatican II, Pastoral Constitution *Gaudium et spes* (On the Church in the Modern World) (1965), no. 26; *PT*, nos. 54, 55, 60; *Catechism of the Catholic Church*, 1907–1909.

[13]   E.g., *CV*, nos. 67, 25, 34, 36, 46. I thank Dr. Christopher Wolfe for suggesting this be added to the list of principles.

[14]   *As a virtue*: SRS, nos. 38.6, 39; as *friendship and social charity*: CA, no. 10.

[15]   E.g., *CA*, no. 31; *GS*, no. 69; Paul VI, Encyclical Letter *Populorum progressio* (On the Development of Peoples), no. 23.

[16]   E.g., *QA*, no. 79; *CA*, no. 48.4–5; early formulation, *RN*, no. 51.

[17]   E.g., *PP*, no. 36; *CA*, no. 39; *CV*, no. 44.

[18]   E.g., *RN*, no. 27, 62; *QA*, no. 136; *MM*, no. 208; *CV*, no. 78.

[19]   E.g., the whole of John Paul II's, Encyclical Letter *Laborem exercens* (On Human Work) (1981), but especially nos. 4 and 6; also nos. 9.3, 12.1, 12.6, 15.1; *QA*, nos. 61, 83.

[20]   E.g., *CV*, no. 44; John Paul II, Encyclical Letter *Familiaris consortio* (On the Role of the Christian Family in the Modern World), no. 30; Paul VI, Encyclical Letter *Humanae vitae* (On the Regulation of Birth) (1968), no. 1; *SRS*, no. 25; *CA*, no. 47.

[21]   E.g., *RN*, no. 37; *SRS*, no. 42; *CSDC*, no. 182.

[22]   E.g., *RN*, no. 44; *QA*, nos. 71–72; *LE*, nos. 19.2–3; *CV*, no. 63.

[23]   E.g., *QA*, no. 83; *GS*, no. 68.

[24]   E.g., *PT*, no. 73; US Bishops' Pastoral Letter, *Economic Justice for All* (1986), no. 78; *CCC*, 1913.

[25]   E.g., *PT*, no. 22; *LE*, no. 25; *CV*, no. 48, 51; *LS*, no. 160.

Numbers three through ten assert descriptive truths about the nature of civil society and the state with normative implications. The principle of solidarity, for example, affirms the common humanity of all members of the human community, implying all share common human dignity and should be treated accordingly; as a *habitus*, it is the virtue of general justice, an orientation of the mind and will (and affect) to the common good. Subsidiarity affirms that all civil and political communities are constituted by smaller intermediate communities where the members are bound together by countless elements from the bond of marriage and the blood of families to deep commitments such as shared religion, to location, ethnicity, and other common interests and tasks. Although interdependent on larger communities for their wider flourishing, these smaller communities have their own authorities, principles of action, legitimate rights, and so common goods. This yields the prescriptive conclusion that political society *should* affirm their existence, protect their goods, and reasonably facilitate their shared purposes. It should also leave to these smaller communities those functions and responsibilities which they can reasonably fulfill on their own. The universal purpose of the world's resources affirms that prior to its division into private property, the earth and its resources are *for* everyone, for the sustenance of the whole human race; nobody – no race, class, ethnicity, nationality, or individual – has a prior claim to the resources of the earth, implying that personal possessions should not be regarded as private in any absolute sense, but always also as common in the sense that they should be available to benefit all, especially those with serious needs (e.g., CA, 48). And so on.

Numbers eleven through fifteen are more straightforwardly norms of justice, several formulated in the language of rights.

POSITIVE VS. NEGATIVE NORMS

The sixteen principles are ordinarily rendered as positive norms of justice. By norm here I mean precept of the natural law. All moral norms are prescriptive inasmuch as they impose obligation. But the nature of the obligation differs according to whether it is an affirmative law (a positive norm) or a prohibitive law (a negative norm). Positive norms oblige the performance of an action, while negative norms oblige the omission of an action. Though both types oblige always, positive norms do not bind absolutely; they do not oblige people at every moment to perform the kind of action they prescribe, only under certain circumstances. For example, the norm prescribing that we should pay our workers a fair wage binds only those who have workers to pay and when those workers have performed some kind of remunerable labor. Negative norms, on the other hand, bind absolutely – always and in every instance (*semper et pro semper*); they require that we always refrain from – *not* perform – the kind of action they proscribe (see *VS*, 52, 82).

The distinction is important for assessing the harmful bifurcation spoken about above. Assessing what a norm of justice positively enjoins can be much more complicated than assessing what it prohibits. For example, assessing the prohibitory implications of the norm, "one ought always to act in accord with economic justice" (or "ought never to act unjustly") can be straightforward: don't defraud your neighbor; don't cheat him, lie to him, or steal from him. But what does acting with economic justice positively enjoin? Giving money to the poor? Whose money? Only to the poor? How much? To which poor? Money for food only or also education? What about travel opportunities? Even money that's earmarked for my own children's education? And so on. "Don't defraud the poor" is more straightforward. "Help them overcome their poverty" is not.

NEGATIVE NORMS IN CST

CST has been concerned primarily with the teaching and elaboration of positive norms of justice. These norms imply moral prohibitions, which the documents of CST do not entirely ignore. But the teaching of the prohibitory part is often terse and lacking in specification. For example, *RN* condemns "rapacious usury,"[26] *QA* the actions of those who fail to address social conditions that incite the poor to violence,[27] *Mater et magistra* and *Rerum novarum* the unjust exercise of the wage system to the disadvantage of the poor,[28] *Populorum progressio* (no. 26) "unbridled liberalism" and the "international imperialism of money," *Octogesima adveniens* the "economic domination" of multinational enterprises,[29] *Centesimus annus* the concentration of the power

---

[26] "The mischief has been increased by rapacious usury, which, although more than once condemned by the Church, is nevertheless, under a different guise, but with like injustice, still practiced by covetous and grasping men." *RN*, no. 3.

[27] "All the more gravely to be condemned is the folly of those who neglect to remove or change the conditions that inflame the minds of peoples, and pave the way for the overthrow and destruction of society." *QA*, no. 112.

[28] "To exercise pressure upon the indigent and the destitute for the sake of gain, and to gather one's profit out of the need of another, is condemned by all laws, human and divine" (*RN*, no. 20); "As for the wage system, while rejecting the view that it is unjust of its very nature, he [Pius XI] condemned the inhuman and unjust way in which it is so often implemented, and specified the terms and conditions to be observed if justice and equity are not to be violated." *MM*, no. 31.

[29] "By extending their activities, these private organizations can lead to a new and abusive form of economic domination on the social, cultural and even political level. The excessive concentration of means and powers that Pope Pius XI already condemned on the fortieth anniversary of *Rerum Novarum* is taking on a new and very real image." *OA*, no. 44.

to hire and conduct trade in the hands of the few,[30] *Sollicitudo rei socialis* acts of terrorism, racism, eugenics, and systematic campaigns against birth,[31] and *Centesimus annus* abortion and systematic antichildbearing campaigns.[32] The condemnations are passing remarks and not carefully formulated. What constitutes instances of the condemned acts in question is not specified. In fact, some of CST's most prominent examples of prohibitory instruction are confusing mixtures of moral absolutes, ideals, and prudential teaching. Consider, for example, the famous catalogue of "infamies" (*proba*) taught by Vatican II:

> whatever is hostile to life itself, such as any kind of homicide (*cuiusvis generis homicidia*), genocide, abortion, euthanasia and voluntary suicide; whatever violates the integrity of the human person, such as mutilation, physical and mental torture and attempts to coerce the spirit; whatever is offensive to human dignity, such as subhuman living conditions, arbitrary imprisonment, deportation, slavery, prostitution and trafficking in women and children; degrading conditions of work which treat laborers as mere instruments of profit and not as free responsible persons: all these and the like are *probra*, and so long as they infect human civilization they contaminate those who inflict them more than those who suffer injustice, and they are a negation of the honour due to the creator. (GS, no. 27)[33]

The usually precise *Veritatis splendor* refers carelessly to the offenses listed here as "examples" of intrinsically evil acts.[34] But "degrading work conditions" and "subhuman living conditions" are not acts at all, but rather sad states of

---

[30] "To this must be added that the hiring of labor and the conduct of trade are concentrated in the hands of comparatively few; so that a small number of very rich men have been able to lay upon the teeming masses of the laboring poor a yoke little better than that of slavery itself." *RN*, no. 3; cf. *CA*, no. 61.

[31] "[A]cts of terrorism are never justifiable." *SRS*, no. 24; "systematic campaigns against birth," *SRS*, no. 25; "[R]acism, or the promotion of certain equally racist forms of eugenics ... deserves the most forceful condemnation." *SRS*, no. 25; cf. *CA*, no. 39.

[32] "Human ingenuity seems to be directed more towards limiting, suppressing or destroying the sources of life – including recourse to abortion" *CA*, no. 39.

[33] Quaecumque insuper ipsi vitae adversantur, ut cuiusvis generis homicidia, genocidia, abortus, euthanasia et ipsum voluntarium suicidium; quaecumque humanae personae integritatem violant, ut mutilationes, tormenta corpori mentive inflicta, conatus ipsos animos coërcendi; quaecumque humanam dignitatem offendunt, ut infrahumanae vivendi condiciones, arbitrariae incarcerationes, deportationes, servitus, prostitutio, mercatus mulierum et iuvenum; condiciones quoque laboris ignominiosae, quibus operarii ut mera quaestus instrumenta, non ut liberae et responsabiles personae tractantur: haec omnia et alia huiusmodi probra quidem sunt, ac dum civilizationem humanam inficiunt, magis eos inquinant qui sic se gerunt, quam eos qui iniuriam patiuntur et creatori honori maxime contradicunt.

Latin and English from *Decrees of the Ecumenical Councils*, vol. 2, ed. Normal Tanner, SJ (London: Sheed and Ward, 1990), 1085–1086.

[34] John Paul II, Encyclical Letter *Veritatis splendor* (1993), no. 80; Vatican English translation.

affairs, which may or may not imply those who suffer or have suffered them have had evil – intrinsic or otherwise – done to them as a result. Moreover, the phrase "any kind of homicide" leaves open the questions of capital punishment, and killing in war and private self-defense. And treating laborers "as free responsible persons" teaches a positive norm.

All these negative teachings of CST are not entirely without value. They are rhetorically powerful and may serve to tutor the moral sentiments; and they stake out the broad outlines of the ethical terrain the Catholic Church means to defend in its wider moral teaching. But most of it has little or no value in the formation of mature consciences inasmuch as it offers almost no precise guidance on specified *kinds* of choices: what precisely constitutes rapacious usury, an unjust exercise of the wage system, economic imperialism, or an unreasonable concentration of power to conduct trade, or for that matter physical and mental torture?[35]

REASONS WHY POSITIVE NORMS ARE PREEMINENT IN CST

Given the issues with which the early authors of the documents of CST were concerned, it is not difficult to see why the tradition began as a medium for the proclamation of positive norms of justice. The "social situation" in Europe under the lengthy pontificate of Pope Leo XIII's predecessor, Pius IX (r. 1846–1878), must have appeared from Rome like an ever-expanding circle of anti-Catholicism, with *Kulturkampfs* and other nationalist movements, closures and seizures of Church properties, and the rise of lethal anticlericalism proliferating across the continent. By the time Pope Pius assumed the Chair of Peter in 1846, Christendom was only a memory. With its disappearance went the privileged role of the papacy in European affairs. Pope Pius was forced to come to terms with the dawning of a heretofore nonexistent phenomenon – a secularized Europe. Consequently, his social policies increasingly focused around defending the rights of the Church and securing the free exercise of religion for Catholics.

By the time Leo XIII became pope in 1878, the Church's marginalization from its ancient role as administrator of secular justice was practically

---

[35] Compare this to the precision and specificity of the following two formulations from John Paul II's Encyclical Letter *Evangelium vitae* (On the Value and Inviolability of Human Life) (1995) and Paul VI's Encyclical Letter *Humanae vitae* (On Regulation of Birth) (1968), respectively: "the direct and voluntary killing of an innocent human being is always gravely immoral" (*EV*, no. 57). "Similarly excluded is every action, which, either in anticipation of the conjugal act, or in its accomplishment, or in the development of its natural consequences, intends, whether as an end or a means, to render procreation impossible" (*HV*, no. 14).

complete. The pope thankfully was no longer a monarch or commander in chief; he no longer needed to administrate or defend the vast Papal States. In consequence he was freer to exercise his Christ-appointed duties of feeding the Lord's flock with spiritual food. Leo saw that the most dangerous and enduring enemies of the Church were not anticlerical rulers but anti-Christian philosophies. Their fathers – particularly Nietzsche, Darwin, and Marx – spoke powerful social messages. Marx especially addressed the rapidly changing and appalling conditions of the growing class of wageworkers caused by the new industrialism. His formidable writings on capital, wage labor, and class struggle gained the high ground on the social question. Europe awaited a reply from her older moral authorities.

Leo XIII had written on anti-Christian social philosophies before 1891.[36] And he continued after *Rerum novarum* to address social issues.[37] But none of his writings had the impact and enduring influence of *Rerum*. This is because it turned a muscular spotlight on a population that was greatly in need of effective Christian advocacy. *Rerum* was the Church's reply to Marx's doctrine of class struggle.

Many of *Rerum's* ideas were first articulated in the writings of the influential Thomist social philosopher and theologian, Aloysius Taparelli, SJ (1793–1862).[38] Taparelli had taught the young Gioacchino Pecci (Leo XIII) at the Collegium Romanum (later the Gregorian), and the two had collaborated closely while he was editor of the journal *Civiltà Cattolica* (referred to by one commentator as "the Jesuit incubator of neoscholasticism" in the nineteenth century[39]). A resolute defender of property rights and critic of the contractarian and laissez-faire theories of John Locke and Adam Smith, Taparelli's ambitious goal was to set out a Catholic theory of society grounded in Thomistic theology and what he called the "facts of history" (he thought the "state-of-nature" accounts of the social contract theorists were laughingly counterfactual).[40]

---

[36] In 1878 he published a polemical encyclical, *Quod apostolici muneris* (On the Problem of Socialism) (1878).

[37] See, for example, his 1901 encyclical, *Graves de communi re* (On Christian Democracy) (1901).

[38] Thomas Patrick Burke, "The Origins of Social Justice: Taparelli d'Azeglio," *First Principles* (January 2008): www.firstprinciplesjournal.com/print.aspx?article=1760&loc=b&type=cbbp.

[39] Michael J. Schuck, "Early Modern Roman Catholic Social Thought, 1740–1890" in *Modern Catholic Social Teaching: Commentaries & Interpretations*, ed. Kenneth Himes (Washington, DC: Georgetown University Press, 2005), 99–124, quote on 113.

[40] He published his most influential work in five volumes between 1841 and 1843, *Saggio teoretico di dritto naturale appoggiato sul fatto* (A Theoretical Treatise on Natural Law Resting on Fact). Speaking about Taparelli's concept of a "Catholic economy," Burke writes: "It is founded on belief in God, submits to divine revelation, maintains respect for the human person and for

When Pope Leo resolved to address an encyclical specifically to the "social question" he turned to one of Taparelli's students and confreres, neo-Thomist Matteo Liberatore, SJ, who wrote the first draft of what became *Rerum novarum*. Although Leo left behind some of Taparelli's more extreme conservative ideas, the Jesuit's influence is felt throughout the document; as it is in *Rerum's* successor, *Quadragesimo anno*.[41] *Rerum* must be seen as a lasting first fruit of Leo's own admonition to the universal Church – and so to himself – twelve years earlier in *Aeterni patris* "to restore the golden wisdom of St. Thomas, and to spread it far and wide for the defense and beauty of the Catholic faith, for the good of society, and for the advantage of all the sciences."[42]

From the beginning, then, modern CST was concerned with economic questions and social conditions arising from the phenomenon of an increasingly secular and anti-Catholic Europe. The three concerns that shaped – and still shape – its discourse were the rights and duties of workers (broadened later to include the "poor" more generally), un-Christian capitalism, and atheist socialism. What the concerns elicited as a body of material can hardly be equated with a coherent Christian social philosophy. The chronological texts on the "social question" are rather, as stated above, a series of principled ethical reflections on the unfolding concrete social situations in the West and later in the world.

The early pastoral protagonists of the Catholic social movement in Europe were also concerned with these problems.[43] The formidable

---

the Christian ideals of charity and self-sacrifice, and is alone capable of explaining what actually happens in economic life. As against the 'iron law of wages,' for example, Taparelli argues that in practice an employer must pay wages sufficient to support not only the individual worker but his family, and furthermore that this is the right and Catholic thing to do – an argument that was to become a founding doctrine of official Catholic social teaching."

[41] Pius XI was also an admirer of Taparelli's social writings. He asked one of Liberatore's students and confreres to draft his encyclical on the fortieth anniversary of *Rerum novarum*, the German theologian Oswald von Nell-Breuning, SJ (see Edward Cahill, SJ, "The Catholic Social Movement: Historical Aspects" (1932), reprinted in *Official Catholic Social Teaching*, eds. Charles E. Curran and Richard A. McCormick, SJ (New York: Paulist Press, 1986), 3–31, esp. 7; Oswald von Nell-Breuning, "The Drafting of *Quadragesimo Anno*" (1971), reprinted in *Official Catholic Social Teaching*, 60–68). Nell-Breuning was a member of the influential German Catholic School of Sociology (the so-called "Konigswinterer Kreis") (see Oswald von Nell-Breuning, SJ, "Der Konigswinterer Kreis und sein Anteil an *Quadragesimo Anno Soziale Verantwortung*," *Festschrift fur Goetz Briefs* (Berlin, 1968), 571–585). Other members of the circle included Gustav Gundlach, SJ and Heinrich Pesch, SJ.

[42] Leo XIII, Encyclical Letter *Aeterni patris* (On the Restoration of Christian Philosophy) (1879), no. 31.

[43] See Edward Cahill, SJ, "The Catholic Social Movement: Historical Aspects," 9–17.

Bishop Von Ketteler (1811–1877) of Mainz, in an address to a Catholic Congress in 1848, two years before his episcopal consecration, stated: "The task of religion, the task of the Catholic societies in the immediate future, has to do with social conditions. The most difficult question – one which no legislation, no form of government has been able to solve – is the social question."[44] (Marx and Engels had published their *Communist Manifesto* one year earlier.) Count Albert de Mun (1841–1914) in France, facing the ruthless tit-for-tat between the Communists and nobles in the 1870s, worked to spread the idea of Christian fraternal organizations ("Catholic Workingman's Clubs"). Cardinal Mercier (1851–1926) in Belgium at the end of his life founded "The International Union for Social Studies" (the "Union of Malines"), which exercised considerable influence over Catholic social thought in Europe and the United States in the reconstruction years after World War I. And the great English Cardinal Manning (1808–1892) successfully advocated on behalf of striking workers during the volatile London Dock Strike in 1889.

Given the concerns of the first generation of theorists and activists, the penchant in CST for elaborating positive norms of justice was fixed within two decades.

BIPOLARITY AND CST

It is common to say that Pope Pius XII never published a social encyclical.[45] This is a narrow reading indeed of the meaning of "social." The pope's impassioned appeal to the principle of solidarity in October 1939 on the outbreak of the "dread tempest of war";[46] his plea for abandoned children after the war's conclusion;[47] his extraordinary succession of short encyclicals on prayers for world peace,[48] including those directed to particular regions

---

[44] Cahill, "The Catholic Social Movement," 9.

[45] "Pius XII, unlike his predecessor Pius XI and his successor John XXIII, did not in the nineteen years of his pontificate issue a single social encyclical." John P. Langan, SJ, "The Christmas Messages of Pius XII (1939–1945): Catholic Social Teaching in a Time of Extreme Crisis," in *Modern Catholic Social Teaching: Commentaries and Interpretations*, ed. Kenneth R. Himes OFM (Washington, DC: Georgetown University Press, 2005), 175–190, quote on 176.

[46] Pius XII, Encyclical Letter *Summi pontificatus* (On the Unity of Human Society) (1939); see especially nos. 11, 12, 15, and 35.

[47] Pius XII, Encyclical Letter *Quemadmodum* (Pleading for the Care of the World's Destitute Children) (1946).

[48] Pius XII, Encyclical Letter *Communium interpretes dolorum* (Appealing for Prayers for Peace During May) (1945); Pius XII, Encyclical Letter *Optatissima pax* (On Prescribing Public Prayers for Social and World Peace) (1947); Pius XII, Encyclical Letter *In multiplicibus curis* (On Prayers for Peace in Palestine) (1948); Pius XII, Encyclical Letter *Summi maeroris* (On

(e.g., Palestine[49] and Hungary[50]); and his addresses on national atrocities;[51] these all deserve, at least to some degree, the title of "social encyclicals." And his letters and discourses to members of international and national social movements were certainly social documents.[52] But it is true that he did not write any encyclical commemorating the publication of *Rerum*,[53] the tradition of which became a kind of gold standard for the designation of social encyclicals.

Pius XII chose the medium of his Christmas radio addresses, especially after 1939, to disseminate his most forceful social teachings.[54] These, as well as his literally hundreds of ad hoc addresses on social questions, have generally fallen beneath the radar of CST. But they did not escape his successor's attention. John XXIII's *Pacem in terris* (1963) references Pius's social addresses over thirty times.

Yet when Pope Paul VI opened his social encyclical, *Populorum progressio* (1967), the only "noteworthy messages ... on contemporary social questions" he mentions of his predecessors are RN, QA, MM, and PT.[55] His choice a year later not to link his important encyclical *Humanae vitae* to the seventy-five-year-old succession of social encyclicals turned out to be very significant for segregating the new generation of "moral documents" from the corpus of CST. He had no intention of introducing a bifurcation, and could hardly have been expected to foresee that he was initiating a new generation of documents with relevance to the social order equivalent to RN's successor

Public Prayers for Peace) (1950); Pius XII, Encyclical Letter *Mirabile illud* (On the Crusade of Prayer for Peace) (1950).

[49] Pius XII, Encyclical Letter *Auspicia quaedam* (On Public Prayers for World Peace and Solution of the Problem of Palestine) (1948); Pius XII, Encyclical Letter *Laetamur admodum* (Renewing Exhortation for Prayers for Peace for Poland, Hungary, and the Middle East) (1956).

[50] Pius XII, Encyclical Letter *Luctuosissimi eventus* (Urging Public Prayers for Peace and Freedom for the People of Hungary) (1956).

[51] Pius XII, Encyclical Letter *Datis nuperrime* (Lamenting the Sorrowful Events in Hungary and Condemning the Ruthless Use of Force) (1956) addresses the use of force in Hungary by the Soviets when the latter invaded Hungary to suppress the Hungarian revolution of 1956.

[52] For example, his *Discourse to the Representatives of the International Union of Catholic Employers Association* (May 7, 1949); *Discourse to the International Congress of Social Studies* (June 3, 1950); and *Address to Italian Catholic Association of Owner-Managers* (January 31, 1952).

[53] He did offer an address on the fiftieth anniversary of *Rerum*; see Pius XII, "The Anniversary of *Rerum Novarum*" on the Solemnity of Pentecost (June 1, 1941), in *Major Addresses of Pope Pius XII*, vol. 1, ed. Vincent Yzermans (St. Paul, MN: North Central, 1961), 28.

[54] One example was his *Message Calling on Mankind to Aid the Poor and Showing the Road to True Salvation* (1952).

[55] *PP*, no. 2.

documents. But it will not do to say the content of Paul's document was fundamentally different from documents of CST and therefore could not have been published in succession to *Rerum*. Like *Rerum*, *HV* addresses a grave worldwide social issue, answers political and economic questions related to it, addresses itself to the duties of civil authority, and proposes solutions from Catholic moral principles. He might have explicitly linked *HV*'s teaching to *RN*'s insistence on the rights and duties of the family (nos. 13–14) or to Leo's admonition to public authority to work to ensure "that all things should be carried on in accordance with God's laws and those of nature; that the discipline of family life should be observed and that religion should be obeyed; that a high standard of morality should prevail, both in public and private life" (no. 36). The only real difference with *HV* is that the moral norm that does the most work in it takes the specification of a *lex negativa*. The obstinate rejection of that norm – and later of almost all exceptionless negative norms – by many progressive Catholics effectively ensured the solidification of the division between the two types of documents.

Over the last forty-five years, many papal[56] and Vatican[57] documents have been published in response to pressing social/ethical questions. They address issues of sexual ethics, healthcare ethics and moral methodology, and questions of public policy in the light of those issues. This tradition of what I have called moral documents has done the heavy lifting in regard to the Church's modern teaching on exceptionless negative norms. Since each addresses problems intimately bound up with the common good, each might – indeed should – be considered in its own right a document of CST or at least explicitly related to CST. But none is ordinarily included in compendiums of CST.[58]

---

[56] John Paul II, *Veritatis splendor* (1993), *Evangelium vitae* (1995).

[57] Congregation for the Doctrine of the Faith, Instruction *Dignitas Personae* on Certain Bioethical Questions (2008); Responses to Certain Questions of the United States Conference of Catholic Bishops Concerning Artificial Nutrition and Hydration (2007); Considerations regarding proposals to give legal recognition to unions between homosexual persons (2003); Responses to questions proposed concerning uterine isolation and related matters (1993); Some considerations concerning the response to legislative proposals on the non-discrimination of homosexual persons (1992); Instruction on the ecclesial vocation of the theologian (*Donum veritatis*) (1990); Instruction on respect for human life in its origin and on the dignity of procreation (*Donum vitae*) (1987); Letter to the Bishops of the Catholic Church on the Pastoral Care of Homosexual Persons (1986); Declaration on Euthanasia (*Iura et bona*) (1980); Declaration on Certain Questions Concerning Sexual Ethics (*Persona humana*) (1975); Declaration on Procured Abortion (*Quaestio de abortu*) (1974).

[58] The two CDF documents on "Liberation Theology" are sometimes associated with CST: Instruction on Christian freedom and liberation (*Libertatis conscientia*) (1986); Instruction on certain aspects of the "Theology of Liberation" (*Libertatis nuntius*) (1984).

The liberal–conservative bifurcation that widened during this period is familiar. Socially active progressive Catholics self-consciously aligned themselves with what they called the social teaching of the Church, referring to their project broadly as seeking "social justice"; they tended to ignore, criticize, or outright dissent from the Church's teaching on negative norms related to the Fifth and Sixth Commandments; and they dominated academic and pastoral discourse in the field of CST. Socially active conservative Catholics took the rump-roast duties on pro-life and later pro-family issues and were superciliously dismissed by progressives as single-issue voters.

During the pontificate of John Paul II (r. 1978–2005) the illogical and destructive polarity hardened into distinct factions in the Catholic community. The saintly pope unwittingly contributed to the bifurcation by explicitly linking his great encyclicals *Laborem exercens*, *Sollicitudo rei socialis*, and *Centesimus annus* to the *Rerum novarum* succession, while publishing *Veritatis splendor* and *Evangelium vitae* as standalone encyclicals on the cultures of dissent and death.

INCORPORATING NEGATIVE NORMS EXPLICITLY INTO CST

Catholic Social Teaching would be greatly strengthened and this harmful division in part addressed if it were broadened to include other parts of Catholic moral doctrine relegated until now to what I have called moral documents.[59] In particular, it should explicitly incorporate exceptionless negative norms concerning sex, marriage and the transmission of human life, killing and wounding, enslaving and trafficking, and lying. It should specify them with the precision that can be found in other moral documents of the magisterium. And the Church should make clear – indeed crystal clear – that the teachings *are doctrines of CST*.

Exceptionless negative norms belong to the Church's social doctrine inasmuch as their respect is an absolutely minimal demand of social justice and an essential first step on the way to that perfection in Christian charity called for by the Gospel. It is true that justice and the common good require far more than conformity to negative norms. But a community in which these primordial requirements of human good and social harmony are ignored and attacked is suffering from a debilitating cancer. As the saintly pope forcefully taught, there are "no privileges or exceptions" whatsoever to the moral norms prohibiting intrinsically evil acts: "It makes no difference whether one is the master of the

[59] The *CSDC* does this to some extent.

world or the 'poorest of the poor' on the face of the earth. Before the demands of morality we are all absolutely equal" (VS, 96). Since such acts always "radically contradict" human good, the norms excluding their commission follow most directly and forcefully from CST's master principle of the inherent dignity of the human person (see VS, 80). Finally, their connections to the three classical concerns of CST – the welfare of the poor (and of all), un-Christian capitalism, and atheist statism – are hardly obscure and need only to be elaborated.

Since the publication of *Humanae vitae* the bitterest disputes within Catholic theology have surrounded these norms, and against them have arisen histori-cally unprecedented levels of dissent within the Church.[60] No teachings on Catholic morality demand more clarity and repetition from the magisterium and no area of pastoral concern demands more solicitude than supporting and accompanying the faithful in living them out. Widening CST by explicitly linking nonabsolute positive norms and exceptionless negative norms as two sides, as it were, of the same moral coin, namely, the field of rational guidance toward integral human fulfillment, will help to overcome the appalling con-ceptual bifurcation that presently exists in Catholic moral thinking.

GOING FORWARD

Because the term Catholic Social Teaching has come to be associated with this ambiguous dissociation, we would do better to refer as often as possible to *Catholic moral teaching* on … the family, economy, government, race, poverty, demographics, immigration, development, intermediate commu-nities, sex, gender, science and technology, education, and so on. The tradi-tion of linking magisterial documents on social questions to the legacy of *Rerum* (or one of its successors) is pedagogically useful as it permits the Church's living ecclesial memory to act as a sort of lens through which to look at the present. Yet the living ethical memory of the Church on social questions long predates *Rerum*, which, although an important period piece, is itself merely a successor document. Making this clear in all CST by reaching far beyond the late nineteenth century to the apostolic tradition elaborated, specified, and handed on by the fathers, doctors, and councils, and, yes, contextualized and applied in contemporary times in modern CST, would be much more pedagogically powerful than referencing only the latter phase

---

60   In 1993, John Paul II wrote: "A new situation has come about *within the Christian community itself* … with regard to the Church's moral teachings. It is no longer a matter of limited and occasional dissent, but of an overall and systematic calling into question of traditional moral doctrine, on the basis of certain anthropological and ethical presuppositions" (VS, no. 4).

of that tradition. Moreover, not only should negative norms be incorporated into the texts of CST, but generous reference to *Rerum* and its successors should be made wherever possible in all documents of Catholic moral teaching. This would help dispel the incoherent bifurcation in Catholic thinking between social justice and pro-life/pro-family commitments. We might also consider using the clearer term "principles (or norms) of justice" to refer to the principles of CST.

NEGATIVE AND POSITIVE IMPLICATIONS OF JUSTICE DEMANDS

In future documents, the authors should make every effort to articulate *both* the negative (exclusionary) implications as well as the positive implications of the justice issues under consideration. So, for example, in addressing the rights of workers, the presumptive moral minimum is that neither they, nor their children, including unborn and embryonic children, ought ever be intentionally killed. No griping about single-issue centeredness can change the fact that without a commitment to the absolute respect for the inviolability of every innocent human life there can be no respect for workers, indeed no coherent social teaching.

The documents should be careful to communicate the differences in the ways that negative norms and nonabsolute positive norms bind (*semper et pro semper* vs. *semper sed non pro semper*), and they should solicitously avoid the common mistake of formulating their teachings of positive norms in overly absolutist ways, implying conclusions that are neither justified by Divine Revelation nor sound moral reasoning. Moreover, before they set forward a normative teaching, they should make distinctions between the normative requirements of justice for the civil community and requisites of charity that bind members of the Christian community. And to obviate that malignant error of ethical legalism that infects so much popular Catholic thinking – the idea that moral norms are merely rules to conform to in order to stay right with the rule-makers rather than moral truths connected to humanity's flourishing – the constitutive connection between fidelity to justice norms and human happiness should be made often and evident in every document.

RESPECTING THE COMPETENCY OF THE MAGISTERIUM TO SPEAK

When treating the positive implications of norms of justice, concrete models for community action and recommendations for public policy are best avoided, recognizing that the task of prudentially applying moral principles to the needs of particular communities is the proper sphere of the laity and, in particular, of the authorities over those communities. The words of John Paul II should be kept in mind:

> The Church has no models to present; models that are real and truly effective can only arise within the framework of different historical situations, through the efforts of all those who responsibly confront concrete problems in all their social, economic, political and cultural aspects, as these interact with one another. [note deleted] (CA, no. 43)

If documents do criticize social models, address policy questions, or propose concrete social solutions, they should ordinarily use hypotheticals such as "if *such and such* is the case, then *x*, *y*, *z* ought to be done," or "where *conditions a, b, c* prevail, public authority should guarantee *rights x, y, z*," etc., or they should raise questions about existing sociological or technical conditions without asserting that *x, y, z* is the case.[61] The competency of the magisterium to authoritatively teach extends not only to matters of faith, but also to what pertains to good morals. This means that the magisterium rightly addresses social issues bearing upon human good. But Church leaders should be mindful to remain within their proper competencies while doing so. If, for example, some behavior is rightly identified as an instance of the kind singled out by an exceptionless negative norm, Church leaders rightly oppose every social initiative aimed at shielding that behavior or securing liberties to carry it out. But a concrete positive application of some justice norms can require specialized knowledge of scientific, historical, or cultural states of affairs, the ability to foresee economic or political consequences of the adoption of one alternative over another, or access to information not readily available. Since the magisterium has *no* special competency in the physical and social sciences or mandate from Christ to exercise authority in the secular sphere, it should be very careful when addressing these matters. Whether deforestation or "fracking" are necessarily instances of unjust exploitation of the earth's resources, whether the UN should adopt a global resolution restricting carbon emissions,

---

[61] So rather than saying that advanced societies "can and must lower their domestic energy consumption," and that what is needed "is a worldwide redistribution of energy resources" (CV, no. 49), the document should say: "if members of advanced societies can reasonably alter their energy consumption so as to benefit energy-poor nations, they ought to do it." John Paul II provides an example of the kind of moderation proposed here. In addressing the need for "Sunday rest" and the duty of public authority to guarantee the right to religious liberty, he says: "In this regard, one may ask whether existing laws and the practice of industrialized societies effectively ensure in our own day the exercise of this basic right to Sunday rest" (CA, no. 9).

whether particular forms of wealth redistribution are advisable in the developed world – these and questions like them are matters involving the prudential application of moral norms to concrete situations. The Church has no more authority to teach concrete conclusions on these questions than she has to teach about what medications are most efficacious for helping migraines. Members of the hierarchy as individuals may, of course, express what opinions they have, but they should ensure that the faithful do not take those opinions as the teaching of the Catholic Church.

This certainly does *not* mean muting the powerful voice of the Church in its proper domain, or turning the magisterium into an enabler of social injustices. It means respecting the proper domains of sacred and secular authority. Jesus authorized the successors of the apostles to govern everything pertaining to the sacraments; to preach the kingdom, instruct the faithful, safeguard divine revelation, preserve the unity of the faith and life of God's people; to convince, rebuke, and exhort in season and out; and to cast out demons and nurture Christian growth. When the hierarchy does these things faithfully, the lay faithful are empowered by sacramental grace and inspired by good example. But experience shows that the purposes of the Gospel and the Church's credibility as teacher can be frustrated, sometimes for centuries, when ecclesiastical leaders attempt authoritatively to intervene into matters over which they have no divine mandate and hence about which they have no ecclesial competency to speak.

CONCLUSION

Justice norms are directives for action and conditions for pursuing human fullness and social well-being. Some things radically contradict that fullness. These are singled out and prohibited by exceptionless justice norms. Others are consistent with it according to circumstances of time and place. These are addressed by positive justice norms, also called principles of CST.

The Church's social teaching would be strengthened and the harmful bifurcation in the Catholic community between social justice thinking and pro-life/pro-family thinking mitigated if both types of norms were explicitly incorporated into all social documents.

POSTSCRIPT: ON THE VIRTUES OF SHORTER DOCUMENTS

If the magisterium wants its documents to be read by the faithful, authors should consider shortening the length of documents to between 5,000 and 10,000 words, never more than 15,000. *Humanae vitae* is a model in this respect, coming in at just below 8,000 words.[62] In that relatively brief space, the pope contextualized the social problem, set forth morally relevant principles, applied them to action, and offered pastoral directives. Attempting more than this, in my opinion, is a mistake in a social document, especially a papal encyclical. Shorter documents mean fewer issues can be addressed. That is good: the documents can more easily be read and discussed and their contents assimilated.[63] Overly long texts are unwieldy and many of their teachings get ignored. There is a point of diminishing return in our ability to assimilate long messages and *megadocuments breach that point.*[64]

---

[62] *AL* on the other hand is just under 60,000 words! Others include: *LS*, 41,000; *EV*, 50,000; *RN*, 14,000; *QA*, 20,000; *MM*, 21,000; *PT*, 16,000; *PP*, 13,000; *SRS*, 23,000; *CA*, 27,000; *VS*, 45,000; *FR*, 36,000; *CV*, 30,000.

[63] It is true that shorter, more specified documents on fewer issues may tempt the authors to tread into territory over which they have no special competency. They must resist this temptation.

[64] One pitfall I see with this proposal is the possibility of underarticulating the distinction between negative and positive applications of norms of justice. This could lead some people to read into a discussion of the prudential application of positive norms the kind of absoluteness that's only proper to negative norms. But this can be obviated by lucid moral explication.

22

How Bishops Should Teach Catholic Social Doctrine

Gerard V. Bradley

The first twenty-three chapters of this volume identify a ribbon of thought running all the way through Catholic Social Teaching (CST). This chapter identifies the trunk (if you will) that steadies and unites all the branches of CST, just as it critically regulates CST's scope and, to some extent, its content. Pope Paul VI identified this core in *Populorum progressio*, where he wrote that "the Church was founded to establish the Kingdom of Heaven" and "not to acquire earthly power."[1] Nonetheless, Paul VI added, because "the Church is situated in the midst of men," and because she "desires to assist [men] to attain to their greatest fulfillment," the Church "offers to them what she alone possesses, that is, a view of man and of human affairs in their totality" (*PP*, no. 13). Pope Saint John Paul II described the same foundation in *Centesimus annus*: the Church's "contribution to the political order is precisely her vision of the dignity of the person revealed in all its fullness in the mystery of the Incarnate Word."[2] There too the Pontiff echoed the episcopal disclaimer, repeated countless times since the pontificate of Leo XIII, that the Church does not prescribe forms of government or take sides in partisan contests. "The Church has no models to present ... The Church ... is not entitled to express preferences for this or that institutional or constitutional solution" (*CA*, nos. 43, 47).

The Church does not, in other words, have a political doctrine at all. Its social teaching is (as Christian Brugger showed in his chapter) really applied moral teaching, the preaching of which is central to the Church's divine mission. The heart of CST is the Church's religious purpose, namely, to

---

[1]   Paul VI, Encyclical Letter *Populorum progressio* (On the Development of Peoples) (1967).
[2]   John Paul II, Encyclical Letter *Centesimus annus* (On the 110th Anniversary of *Rerum novarum*) (1991), no. 47.

"spread the Kingdom of Christ throughout the earth for the glory of God the Father, to enable all men to share in His saving redemption."[3]

Bishops are obliged to teach and to preach, in season and out, the integral gospel (2 Tim. 4:2), so that they might discharge their divine responsibility to evangelize everyone, including nonbelieving public officials. They must teach the whole moral truth, including those truths bearing upon social life and political affairs. This is the commission that Jesus gave to the apostles and the Apostles' successors. When they teach CST bishops are, and should always be conscious that they are, teaching *in persona Christi*.

Describing the bishops as "speaking truth to power" is cliché and mistaken: CST is addressed to everyone, including the powerless, for even the lowliest citizen has important social justice duties. There is no need to call CST "prophetic," for it pertains to the here and now; it is not otherworldly, strictly a religious construction, or utopian. It is distorting to describe CST as "trans-formative" or "revolutionary," or any other adjective with principally political connotations. It is enough to say that CST is that part of the Good News that is about justice and genuine human flourishing in society, and that bishops teach it as part of their sacred responsibility to help people get to heaven.

This deep theological root of CST does not justify every expression of it by popes and bishops through the years. It does, however, unify and ground the vast bulk of those expressions. It also supplies the criteria according to which one can judge the rest as excrescences. Here too lies the source of the bishops' limited competence to teach authoritatively about social and political affairs – and of the norms for *how* they should teach CST, which I describe in Part III of this chapter. Those norms need to be first situated, however, within two epochal recent developments, not exactly in CST itself, but in its status as a set of moral truths addressed to the consciences of everyone. I consider (in Part I) the apostolate of the laity as taught authoritatively by the Fathers at Vatican II, and (in Part II) the unicity of morality, taught with force and clarity by John Paul II in *Veritatis splendor*.

I consider in Part IV an important but neglected element of CST, namely, the great intransitive (if you will) good that the Church does for political society when its pastors respect the limits of their competence and thus preserve proper separation of church and state, *but then fearlessly teach Catholic social doctrine*. For the Church's greatest contribution to any political society consists in just being the Church.

---

[3] Paul VI, Decree on the Apostolate of the Laity *Apostolicam Actuositatem* (Apostolic Activity) (1965), no. 2.

In the conclusion I advance some prudential proposals for how bishops should teach CST – what they should emphasize and how they might best engage the hearts and minds of Catholic laypersons – both now and in the future.

I

Bishops teach the Church's social doctrine as part of their obligation to spread the Good News. Prominently included in that responsibility are the tasks of instructing and supporting the laity in *their* vocation to redeem the temporal order. This truth about the laity's calling emerged clearly, in authoritative form, only at the Second Vatican Council. Pope John Paul II wrote in *Christifideles laici* that the Council wrote "as never before on the nature, dignity, spirituality, mission, and responsibility of the lay faithful."[4] This development of the Church's understanding of the lay apostolate greatly affected the tone of episcopal teaching, shifting its predominant form of address from the *imperative* – a superior's directive to a subordinate – to that of *exposition*, or the statement of conscientious obligations rooted in moral truth. But the emergence of a clear and certain understanding of the lay apostolate did more than that. A sound understanding of the lay apostolate permeates the whole of CST. How bishops should teach CST is now conceptually intertwined with the laity's proper vocation, and cannot be understood save in dialectical relation to it. A firmer grasp upon the lay apostolate has also caused (and was, perhaps, itself caused by) a much sharper understanding of the relationships among moral principle, positive law, local tradition, and other contingencies in any full-orbed account of what CST means for those who would bring it to bear on contemporary problems.

The Council Fathers' development of doctrine about the *munus* of lay men and women is remarkable, even in light of the progressive vision of the laity that emerged in the mid-twentieth century. At that time, beginning with Pope Pius XI's *Quadragesimo anno*, the Church's pastors recognized that if faith were to effectively shape the temporal order, the laity would have to play a larger role in making it happen.[5] But even these teachings envisioned the laity's newfound activism as an unprecedented participation in the *hierarchy's* apostolate – as if the laity were deputies of the bishops, who alone had received the relevant charge from the Lord. The almost universal understanding within

---

[4] John Paul II, Apostolic Exhortation *Christifideles laici* (On the Vocation and the Mission of the Lay Faithful in the Church and in the World) (1988), no. 2.
[5] Pius XI, Encyclical Letter *Quadragesimo anno* (On Reconstruction of the Social Order) (1931).

the American Church before World War II, for example, was that the laity acted *as Catholics* in the political sphere only at the direction of the bishops. American bishops commonly asserted, without a trace of irony or apology, that the laity were foot soldiers in armies they commanded. This vision unfortunately suggested that Catholic activity for the common good of political society was *either* at the bishops' direction, *or* simply "political" or "partisan," not meaningfully related to the Church's social teaching and thus fair game for lay activity. This vision was not good for the bishops, for the laity, for the temporal order, or for CST.

The reasons for encouraging greater lay initiative were cogent. Altar and throne arrangements were almost extinct by the time of the Council. Christendom as a cultural force was waning. In some countries Catholic bishops could still pressure political leaders to do the right thing. But by 1960 this happened in only a few countries, and there less frequently, and then all too often because on other occasions the bishops collaborated (if only by their silences) with powerful people when those people did bad things. Lingering examples of episcopal strong-arming were often subject to considerable backlash in less clubbable settings, as the conviction that political economy should be emancipated from clerical control and even religious influence spread among elites and common folks alike. International affairs, mass culture, popular education, the arts, and literature were all increasingly secularized. That laypersons would be the primary instruments whereby Gospel values could be insinuated into social and political life, through their example and by their daily choices, became an undeniable fact of modern life.

Apostolicam actuositatem makes it abundantly clear that the laity receive their distinctive call to be "leaven" in the temporal order directly from Christ. It is not a share or participation in the hierarchy's apostolate. "The laity derive the right and duty to the apostolate from their union with Christ the head; incorporated into Christ's Mystical Body through Baptism and strengthened by the power of the Holy Spirit through Confirmation, they are assigned to the apostolate by the Lord himself."

There are countless descriptions of this apostolate in the papal corpus. Lay men and women reside "in the midst of the world and [are] in charge of the most varied temporal tasks."[6] "The *apostolate* in the social milieu, that is, the effort to infuse a Christian spirit into the mentality, customs, laws, and structures of the community in which one lives, is so much the duty and

---

[6] Paul VI, Encyclical Letter *Evangelii nuntiandi* (On Evangelization in the Modern World) (1975), no. 70.

responsibility of the laity that it can never be performed properly by others. In this area the laity can exercise the *apostolate* of like toward like. It is here that they complement the testimony of life with the testimony of the word" (AA, no. 13, emphasis added). The laity's field of activity "is the vast and complicated world of politics, society and economics, but also the world of culture, of the sciences and the arts, of international life, of the mass media"; their range of operations also extends to "other realities which are open to evangelization, such as human love, the family, the education of children and adolescents, professional work, suffering" (*EN*, no. 70).

The importance of the lay apostolate reverberates through the Council's descriptions of the bishops' role in CST. That role is both overarching and subsidiary, both directive and supportive. "Pastors must clearly state the principles concerning the purpose of creation and the use of temporal things, and must offer the moral and spiritual aids by which the temporal order may be renewed in Christ by the laity" (AA, no. 7). "The hierarchy should promote the *apostolate* of the laity, provide it with moral guidance and spiritual support, direct the conduct of the *apostolate* to the common good of the Church, and attend to the preservation of doctrine and order" (AA, no. 24, emphasis added). After the Council, Paul VI wrote in *Evangelii nuntiandi* that, while it is the "specific role of the pastors" to establish and develop the ecclesial community, the laity's "primary and immediate task" is "to put to use every Christian and evangelical possibility latent but already present and active in the affairs of the world" (*EN*, no. 70). Pope John Paul II wrote about solving political problems in that "models that are real and truly effective can arise only within the framework of different historical situations, through the efforts of all those who responsibly confront concrete problems in all their social, economic, political and cultural aspects, as those interact with one another" (CA, no. 43). He wrote in *Christifideles laici* that the laity's distinctive mission required that they be "animated by a real participation in the life of the Church and enlightened by her social doctrine," as well as "supported by the nearness of the Christian community and their pastors" (CL, no. 42).

According to a sound understanding of the laity's apostolate, one can critically judge a particular pastoral intervention as inappropriate, for it might impose obligations of assent and deference upon the laity that in truth they should not be made to bear, or invade the proper autonomy of the laity to judge for themselves contingent matters of fact, to balance certain moral considerations, to weigh prudential considerations, and to decide in the particular case what constitutes fair (or unfair) material cooperation with evil and whether and to what extent moral norms about giving scandal and providing false witness should be applied. Respecting this lay competence is not simply desirable or generally advisable for bishops. It is a strict moral duty, supported by the truth that laity and bishops are partners in the effort to redeem the world, and that they all labor as humble servants of the Lord Jesus.[7]

Recognition of the divine constitution of the laity as co-redeemers of the temporal order was enabled, or at least accompanied, by the emergence just before and after the Council of a genuine "Christian humanism." By this term I mean most simply the sense that living the Christian moral life is *intrinsically* good and worthwhile, and not just *extrinsically* recommended as the means by which one can get to heaven (itself popularly conceived to be so exclusively contemplative as to be radically discontinuous with many forms of earthly flourishing). In a more humanistic (one could even say "Incarnational") moral theology, true human goods figure crucially in human well-being as anchoring points of moral norms. Norms such as "do not kill" or "do not commit adultery" or "do not bear false witness" should not be understood, then, mainly as commands from God (even though there is a God, the norms are His will for us, and He issues them as commands), or as rules put into place by ecclesial authorities to keep us on track for heaven (even though abiding by the norms tends to that end). It is, rather, imperative to see that basic moral norms correspond to genuine goods constitutive of true human flourishing. Doing good is living well, even if doing good leads to suffering in this life.

The Second Vatican Council's decree on the laity states: "All these things which make up the temporal order, namely, the good things of life and the prosperity of the family, culture, economic matters, the arts and professions, the laws of the political community, international relations, and other matters of this kind, as well as their development and progress, not only aid in the attainment of man's ultimate goal but also possess their own intrinsic value. *This value has been established in them by God*" (AA, no. 7, emphasis added). The lay apostolate is therefore a much richer – even, a more *religious* – undertaking than just seeing to the grimy business of the City of Man.

And it is Kingdom building. The Council Fathers proclaimed that not only did God infuse mundane things with intrinsic value; He also endowed them

[7] This is why the factual detail and the contingent judgments authoritatively taught by the American bishops in their 1983 Pastoral Letter on War and Peace provoked an invitation to the Vatican for consultation. The bishops refused to limit themselves to general theological observations, as they were asked to do by the Prefect of the Congregation for the Doctrine of the Faith, Joseph Cardinal Ratzinger. Archbishop John Roach, then-President of the national bishops' conference, replied that "Our position in the United States is that if we were to issue a document that outlines only the moral principles, not the application, no one would listen." A sound grasp of pastoral competence and lay responsibility would show that reply to be deeply mistaken notwithstanding the arguable accuracy of Roach's assessment.

with eternal worth. Jesus "calls some to give clear witness to the desire for a heavenly home and to keep that desire fresh among the human family. He summons others to dedicate themselves to the earthly service of men and to *make ready the material of the celestial realm this ministry of* theirs."[8] This preparation is "a foretaste of the heavenly banquet" (GS, no. 38).

The Council Fathers proclaimed that *all* the good works we do on earth last forever. In this connection the sublime statement in *Gaudium et spes* is worth extensive quotation:

> We do not know the moment of the consummation of the earth and of humanity nor the way the universe will be transformed. The form of this world, distorted by sin, is passing away and we are taught that God is preparing a new dwelling and a new earth in which righteousness dwells, whose happiness will fill and surpass all the desires of peace arising in human hearts. Then death will have been conquered, the daughters and sons of God will be raised in Christ and what was sown in weakness and dishonor will become incorruptible; charity and its works will remain and all of creation, which God made for humanity, will be set free from its bondage to decay.
>
> We have been warned, of course, that it profits us nothing if we gain the whole world and lose or forfeit ourselves. Far from diminishing our concern to develop this earth, the expectation of a new earth should spur us on, for it is here that the body of a new human family grows, foreshadowing in some way the age which is to come. That is why, although we must be careful to distinguish earthly progress clearly from the increase of the kingdom of Christ, such progress is of vital concern to the kingdom of God, insofar as it can contribute to the better ordering of human society.
>
> When we have spread on earth the fruits of our nature and our enterprise – human dignity, sisterly and brotherly communion, and freedom – according to the command of the Lord and in his Spirit, we will find them once again, cleansed this time from the stain of sin, illuminated and transfigured, when Christ presents to his Father an eternal and universal kingdom "of truth and life, a kingdom of holiness and grace, a kingdom of justice, love and peace." Here on earth the kingdom is mysteriously present; when the Lord comes it will enter into its perfection. (GS, no. 39, internal notes omitted)

This interpenetration of the two Kingdoms is a truth knowable only by dint of revelation. Its authoritative clarification by the Council consummates (if you will) the development of doctrine about the laity. The divine constitution of their work as independent of the hierarchy (in the manner previously described), and as inchoate Kingdom building, makes any episcopal incursion

---

[8]   Vatican II, Pastoral Constitution *Gaudium et spes* (On the Church in the Modern World) (1965).

upon their competence a serious moral error. It would also be a usurpation of a work assigned by God to others. It is imperative that the Church's pastors continually bring the lastingness of good works to the laity's attention. For the vicissitudes of mundane affairs and the stubbornness of evil in the world portend no more than modest success in redeeming the temporal order. The laity need regular encouragement to stay their course with courage and integrity. Pastors should do so, not as they have, legalistically, in the past by holding out heaven as the extrinsic reward for finishing the race without mortal mishap, or by preaching that (or at least, *as if*) all the faithful will no doubt arrive in heaven one day, but rather by teaching the faithful that they are to strive for the Kingdom of God first of all (see Mt 6:33) and that they are cooperating with Jesus by assembling materials which, transformed by divine power, will be part of that Kingdom.

This whole development of doctrine (concerning the laity, in morality, about the Kingdom) affects in other ways how bishops should teach CST. Such an approach is a fatal blow to *legalism* – the view that morality consists of playing within the (more or less stipulated) rules. It also demolishes (or should demolish) the ambient *clericalism* that suffused the now-superseded vision of lay subordination to the hierarchy. The demise of clericalism and legalism in turn fortifies the distinctive, complementary competences of pastors and laity in making CST effective in the world. The whole complex of truths and insights supporting these developments also powerfully warrants (if they do not quite establish) the *unicity of morality*, to which I now turn.

II

One arc of CST's development, traced through the preceding chapters, is compactly indicated by papal declarations that social doctrine is rooted in the dignity of the human person. This line of thought reached a denouement in 1993 when John Paul II wrote in *Veritatis splendor*, "*When it is a matter of the moral norms prohibiting intrinsic evil, there are no privileges or exceptions for anyone. It makes no difference whether one is the master of the world or the 'poorest of the poor' on the face of the earth. Before the demands of morality we are all absolutely equal.*"[9]

The Holy Father also observed that the "commandments of the second table of the Decalogue in particular – those which Jesus quoted to the young man of the Gospel (cf. Mt 19:19) – constitute the *indispensable* rules of *all*

---

[9] John Paul II, Encyclical Letter *Veritatis splendor* (On Fundamental Questions on Church's Moral Teaching) (1993), no. 96; emphasis in original.

social life" (VS, no. 97, emphasis original). "The negative precepts of the natural moral law are universally valid. They oblige each and every individual, always and in every circumstance . . . It is prohibited – to everyone and in every case – to violate these precepts. They oblige everyone, regardless of the cost" (VS, no. 52). Recognizing that absolute negative moral norms apply without exception to all public officials also makes fully intelligible the concept of absolute human rights; that is, unconditional immunities of *everyone* against certain harmful acts performed by *anyone*, even by the "master of the world."

This proper unity of what might otherwise be described as "public" and "private" morality – call it the *unicity* of morality – shapes CST and how bishops should teach it. It undermines one reading of Romans 13 (about the obligation of Christians to obey "governing authorities"). On this now unsustainable view, public officials would enjoy a moral prerogative that, it is supposed, God Himself possesses (because "the authorities that exist have been established by God"). The Prince may and sometimes must do things – kill an innocent or torture a terrorist – which are invariably forbidden to ordinary people, because he is God's vice-regent on earth. Leaving aside the prospect that God would will the death of anyone, the claim that public authorities operate according to a special morality above and beyond the common morality where exceptionless moral norms are concerned is now authoritatively rejected in CST. Whether and to what extent an earthly ruler is acting as God would have him act is determined at a foundational level by his action's conformity to the unvarying requirements of morality. Bishops can no longer condone government actions that violate the common morality by citing either a vague government license to do whatever it takes to preserve order or combat wrongs, or by simply calling upon the laity to obey the civil authorities.

Bishops teaching CST must instead hold public authorities to account, in the first instance by stating clearly their moral duties. Then bishops should educate the laity about *their* responsibilities to hold government to account, to promote the election of morally sound public officials, to recognize the moral limits upon their own cooperation with unjust laws and government policies, and in limited cases to conscientiously refuse to comply with unjust laws.

III

How then should bishops express themselves when authoritatively teaching CST? What manner(s) of expression best complies with their complex obligations to instruct and fortify the laity, while fully respecting the autonomy of the lay apostolate? How should bishops both forcefully exhort the laity to obey the exceptionless norms of justice in the midst of everyday affairs, and yet leave the myriad contingencies of social life to lay persons to sift, analyze, and evaluate?

In this Part I offer four general rules of composition for episcopal teaching of CST. Each of the first three could be labeled a *genre*.

A *The Exhortatory Genre*

This first genre includes the task of identifying the moral norms at stake in particular contingent circumstances. Popes and bishops through the ages have emphasized with vigor and clarity, for example, perennial norms protecting innocent life from direct attack as the technologies of armed conflict have created challenges to the cogency, or even the apparent relevance, of those norms. The Church has consistently rejected any concept of "total war" in which the distinction between combatant and noncombatant would be oblit- erated, or at least rendered inoperative. Starting with the advent of aerial bombing during the Spanish Civil War and extending to the present day, bishops have at least fitfully warned against the moral hazards of killing from great heights, or over long distances. The Church has also repeatedly warned that the employment of nuclear weapons poses an acute danger of violating moral norms protecting noncombatants. In all these instances, pastors do not derive new moral norms or themselves apply them to novel situations. They perform the necessary if more humble task of calling everyone's attention to the perennial liveliness of the common morality.

This genre also includes the clarification, development, and occasional application of unvarying norms. One example of sound episcopal guidance of this sort has involved new reproductive technologies. In the face of new technological challenges the bishops have rightly (and creatively) applied moral norms about not treating persons as things or as property to be used by others. They have rightly taught that all human cloning and all *in vitro* fertilization procedures are immoral as two different ways of manufacturing persons. And they have taught that manufacturing persons violates the human right to be born of the sexual intercourse of a mother and father.

This mode of teaching may also be executed in less clear-cut circumstances. But here the episcopal expression must be hypothetical. The guiding principle is the bishops' limited competence when it comes to temporal matters, and their incompetence when it comes to settling the facts of the matter. Matters of sociological, economic, demographic, and scientific fact – including the patterns of earth's temperatures and the human responsibility for any sharp deviations from expected patterns – are not within the bishops' distinctive competence.

But even the healthiest respect for the laity's competence need not lead bishops to present themselves as altogether innocent of these realities. Rather, they should incorporate into their prescriptive declarations facts that are, to all fair minds, practically certain, or they should rely upon hypothetical factual scenarios. In either case there is no realistic possibility of usurping the proper freedom and competence of the laity to investigate factual matters for themselves and to determine for themselves what is the real story. In the first case the relevant facts are undeniable. In the second, the laity remain free to judge for themselves what the relevant facts are.

The bishops might therefore rightly take to be true the reliably reported and uncontested blast radius of certain munitions, and the demographic characteristics of frequently targeted areas in enemy territory. In light of these (and other) certain facts, the bishops might teach authoritatively about the manner in which military pilots and those collaborating with them must think about proposed bombing missions. The bishops could helpfully offer a few realistic hypothetical cases in which the collateral destruction of noncombatant persons would be disproportionate to any military advantage anticipated by the bombing, rightfully concluding that such missions should not be undertaken. The bishops should emphasize that pilots might be ordered to carry out raids that they must, in conscience, refuse to perform no matter what the professional and personal consequences might be for those pilots. The bishops might also authoritatively teach that some recently completed bombing raid could not have been rightly chosen by anyone who knew, or who had strong reasons to believe, that the facts were as they turned out to be. The bishops should teach too that persons faced with such momentous choices are under a strong moral duty to do all that they reasonably can to get the relevant facts *right*.

B *The Incompatibility Genre*

The second mode of expression has a broader scope; it does not only pertain to moral norms or to specific acts. It extends to the whole range of metaphysical, scientific, historical, and other realities, correct belief about which can pertain to Catholic faith. The central pastoral concern here is that the faithful *not* deny (even if only implicitly or as a matter of presupposition) some proposition upon which the faith relies or which is strictly entailed by the faith. The episcopal tasks here include those of identifying the anthropological, metaphysical, and ethical presuppositions of a particular proposal, practice, institution, or body of political or social thought; next, identifying the implications of these presuppositions and the proposals they support for the moral and spiritual welfare of persons; then, describing the morality of actions required of persons in order to maintain the system or activity under consideration; and, finally, evaluating all of this as it pertains to persons' salvation. The Congregation for the Doctrine of the Faith (CDF)'s two *Instructions* concerning liberation theology (1984 and 1986) are good examples of this genre.

There is a great deal of this genre in the CST corpus. Pius XI wrote: "[T]he whole scheme of social and economic life is now such as to put in the way of vast numbers of mankind *serious obstacles* which prevent them from caring for the one thing necessary, namely, their eternal salvation" (QA, no. 130, emphasis added). Pius XII marked the fiftieth anniversary of *Rerum novarum* with a radio broadcast in which he affirmed "the indisputable competence" of the Church to "decide whether the bases of a given social order are in accord with the unchangeable order which God ... has shown us through the Natural Law."

This mode of expression is a corollary of what Cardinal Ratzinger described, in the CDF's 2002 *Doctrinal Note* on Catholics' participation in political life, as the "legitimate freedom" of Catholics to "choose among the various political opinions that are *compatible* with faith and the natural moral law, and to select, according to their own criteria, what best corresponds to the needs of the common good."[10] This freedom arises from the nature of political life itself. "[P]olitics are concerned with very concrete realizations of the true human and social good in given historical, geographic, economic, technological and cultural contexts."[11] The *Doctrinal Note* concluded that a "plurality" of morally acceptable options is bound to be present.

Saint Paul sternly admonished those who read and heard his letter to Timothy that the "time will come when people will ... follow their own desired and insatiable curiosity, [and] will accumulate teachers and will stop listening to the truth and will be diverted to myths" (2 Tim 4:3). For this reason Christian pastors must "persistent[ly]" (as Paul wrote) "proclaim the word," whether "it is convenient or inconvenient," and "convince, reprimand, encourage through all patience and teaching." An essential part of bishops' responsibility to teach the laity is, then, to be prepared to rebuke, at times publicly, those who abandon the truth for myths. This duty is especially keen when the miscreant is a public official, because the consequences and the scandal are liable to be greater.

---

[10]   Congregation for the Doctrine of the Faith, *Doctrinal Note* (On Some Questions Regarding the Participation of Catholics in Political Life), no. 3; emphasis added.

[11]   CDF, *Doctrinal Note*, no. 3.

One important field for incompatibility-type directives remains seriously underdeveloped. This field is populated by false conceptions of the human person embedded in so many cultural and legal norms about abortion, euthanasia, embryo-destructive research, and sexual behavior. The bishops have been forceful in teaching the wrongness of abortion, euthanasia, and so forth, proposed by so many sectors of our culture and promulgated or pre-supposed by so many civil laws. But they could do more, in my judgment, to identify and to criticize in the strongest terms possible the body–self dualism that is (in turn) assumed or presupposed in such acts. This dualism is not only false, but is a barrier to making sound moral judgments: perhaps most obviously, it promotes false moral judgments in favor of nonmarital sexual acts because it leads the choosing person to identify himself with the pleasure-experiencing psyche ("self") and thus to treat the body (and its production of sensations) as merely an instrument of the conscious self. Body–self dualism is also dangerous to faith, as it threatens to undermine the faithful's belief in the dignity of bodiliness, and in the presence of Jesus in the Eucharist, the virginal conception and birth of the Lord, the resurrection of the body, and even original sin.

It is very important that when the bishops teach in this second mode, they resist the temptation to rank or to otherwise handicap the competition among options that pass muster as compatible with the relevant norms and proposi-tions of faith. Once again, the basic objective is to warn the faithful away from practices or acts that inescapably, if only implicitly, involve them in false views of the human person or creation, or some other truth of, or pertaining to, the faith. This genre would also include bishops' current teaching about crema-tion, which is permissive but full of caveats and limitations. While the practice of cremation is not incompatible with the faith or sound morality, it is so liable to be chosen for the wrong reasons (or in reliance upon false beliefs) that it is prudent and appropriate for bishops to reiterate here the truth about the human body.

C *The Discernment Genre*

The third genre is the more speculative project of identifying and interpreting the signs of the times, or what Paul VI called in *Octogesima adveniens* "the new needs of the changing world."[12] The purest description of this genre is likely found in *Gaudium et spes*: "[T]he Church has always had the duty of

---

[12] Paul VI, Encyclical Letter *Octogesima adveniens* (On the Occasion of the Eightieth Anniversary of the Encyclical *Rerum novarum*) (1971), no. 1.

scrutinizing the signs of the times and of interpreting them in the light of the Gospel ... We must therefore recognize and understand the world in which we live, its expectations, its longings, and its often dramatic characteristics" (GS, no. 4).[13] Pope John Paul II wrote of "keep[ing] a watchful eye on the world," "the field in which the faithful are called to fulfill their mission." What, he asked, is the *"actual state of affairs* of the 'earth' and the 'world', for which Christians ought to be 'salt' and 'light'?" (CL, no. 3, emphasis original).

This might as well be called the *discernment* genre. John Paul II in *Sollicitudo rei socialis* gave it fuller expression: "The Church's social doctrine is ... the accurate formulation of the results of a careful reflection on the complex realities of human existence, in society and in the international order, in the light of faith and of the Church's tradition. Its main aim is to interpret these realities, determining their conformity with or divergence from the lines of the Gospel teaching on man and his vocation" (SRS, no. 41).

Identifying the signs of the times is not a matter of producing a newsreel or of collating statistics, as if the telling signs were a long encyclopedic loop of uninterpreted events and occurrences. It is rather evaluative work focused upon certain descriptive information, but also upon cultures, institutions, customs, and practices – in short, the world made by men. It is, as these excerpts from papal teachings state or imply, a highly interpretive undertaking.

There is an appreciable risk of misinterpretation and of overinterpretation in this third genre. This risk includes the possibility that, in describing the signs of the times, the Church's pastors will either settle some matter of fact that truly lies beyond their competence, invade the laity's province by selecting from among eligible options, implicitly ranking them, or disfavoring at least some. Pastors should be very cautious about seeking and declaring these signs, for we are here quite distant from the Gospel and thus perched near the outer edge of pastors' competence. These risks are somewhat ameliorated by the fact that teachings on

---

[13] The fuller text: "To carry out such a task, the Church has always had the duty of scrutinizing the signs of the times and of interpreting them in the light of the Gospel. Thus, in language intelligible to each generation, she can respond to the perennial questions which men ask about this present life and the life to come, and about the relationship of the one to the other. We must therefore recognize and understand the world in which we live, its explanations, its longings, and its often dramatic characteristics. Some of the main features of the modern world can be sketched as follows." The "task" referred to is found in the preceding paragraph of GS: "Therefore, this sacred synod, proclaiming the noble destiny of man and championing the Godlike seed which has been sown in him, offers to mankind the honest assistance of the Church in fostering that brotherhood of all men which corresponds to this destiny of theirs. Inspired by no earthly ambition, the Church seeks but a solitary goal: to carry forward the work of Christ under the lead of the befriending Spirit. And Christ entered this world to give witness to the truth, to rescue and not to sit in judgment, to serve and not to be served" (GS, no. 3).

signs typically steer away from clear-cut judgments about what the faithful are obliged to do, or what they must never do. Signs discourses are typically reflective and speculative rather than practical, and unlikely to unintentionally lead readers into taking on a burden not meant to be imposed. But because the laity – particularly those who are most loyal to the magisterium – are liable to take a sign of discourse as more authoritative than it is, it is unsurpassably important that bishops and even the pope make clear that Catholics are free to reject episcopal descriptions of complex social phenomena or diagnoses of what ails society if they conscientiously judge them to be flawed.

Even so, the discernment genre can be and often is a legitimate pastoral help to the laity's performance of their temporal duties. In the words of Paul VI, what I am calling this genre of discourse helps "Christian communities to analyze with objectivity the situation which is proper to their own country, to shed on it the light of the Gospel's unalterable words and to draw principles of reflection, norms of judgment and directives for action from the social teaching of the Church" (OA, no. 4). It is, however, the laity's task to devise answers. Local Christian communities, Paul wrote, are "to discern the options and commitments which are called for in order to bring about the social, political and economic changes seen in many cases to be urgently needed" (OA, no. 4).

Popes and bishops often bring to the laity's urgent attention underreported, if not obscure, injustices to be addressed. They often describe persistent social conditions of need and want that, without predications of injustice, might alert lay men and women to a fruitful path for their personal vocations. For this reason, substantial nondidactic and nonmoral analyses of prevailing social conditions, and likely future courses, are a proper complement to teaching material in a CST document. So too are diagnoses of certain political movements or ideologies. Substantial efforts to derive the more strictly moral content of such documents from Scripture, tradition, and prior teaching instruments are, moreover, important to clarify the teaching, promote confidence in its authoritativeness (and sometimes to establish its special status as infallibly taught by the ordinary magisterium), and for the edification of the lay reader who seeks to see how his or her apostolic work really contributes to assembling material for the Kingdom. Indeed, CST documents rightly and commonly include exhortatory material meant to steel the laity for the sacrifices that all too often are required to bear faithful witness to the Gospel.

D Nonauthoritative Material

There is no realistic likelihood that an episcopal teaching document would be limited to a series of expressions, each falling into one of three preceding genres. Nor should there be, for treatments of various additional subjects are not only to be expected in authoritative episcopal teaching, but are needed and welcome. Popes and bishops rightly seek to situate their didactic messages within a tradition of thought; sometimes lengthy pedigrees in Scripture, prior magisterial statements, and other documents in the tradition are in order. Addressing the consciences of the faithful with a view to spurring their initiative, popes and bishops rightly provide spiritual inspiration along with the teaching material. Equipping the laity to be leaven in an increasingly pagan world calls for more apologetics than it did in recent decades. All of these matters (and more) are proper parts of how bishops should teach CST.

Entirely nonauthoritative episcopal lectures and writings about political and social matters are a different matter. These should generally be welcomed, so long as the following caveats are heeded. Foremost among these cautions is that the bishop-author make unmistakably clear that he is not teaching as a shepherd of souls. The fact is most readily apparent when the author possesses no pastoral responsibility. In the case of a bishop-scholar or retired prelate, for example, even moral/theological speculation pertaining to the political common good presents only a modest risk that faithful Catholics will mistakenly judge themselves to be under a religious obligation to assent.

Nonauthoritative publications and speeches about matters within the ambit of Catholic social doctrine by pastors, and especially by Ordinaries, present a greater risk of being misunderstood by the faithful. In case where these publications treat matters that no well-formed layperson could mistake as subjects of morally binding instruction (such as, say, the American founders' understanding of religious liberty or the history of anti-Catholicism in America), well-placed caveats about the nonauthoritative character of the piece should suffice. But where an Ordinary writes about a topic within the scope of CST (say, emerging technologies of gene editing and the moral constraints most likely appropriate to them), but intends to do so in an exploratory and nonauthoritative manner, the burden is upon him to make sure that no reader mistakes his speculations for binding instruction.

It is morally incumbent upon the bishops to express themselves perspicuously. Their duty to convey what the faith requires, their moral duty to treat the laity fairly and to respect their rightful freedom of conscience, and their obligations to the American people to contribute to the common good according to their special but limited competence – all these duties impose an overriding moral obligation on the bishops to speak so that any competent reader of their utterances can know with practical certainty whether the bishops speak as pastors, or in some other capacity.[14]

Bishops have an overriding obligation to head off avoidable contributions to the perception that they are partisans (like other think tanks or political organizations) or lobbyists (like other interest groups or institutional players). It is easy to see why this obligation is paramount. One reason is that the bishops are *not* partisans or lobbyists. Another reason is that the prestige and influence of their nonauthoritative interventions depend upon the perception that the bishops stand outside normal political channels. If these interventions were neutered by perceptions that the bishops were partisans or rent-seekers, the loss would not be that great. But the damage could not be so restricted: any perception that the bishops were partisan, regardless of its cause, would undermine the proper receipt of the bishops' truly pastoral, authoritative teachings.

IV

Some might lament an emphasis (like mine) upon the limited competence of the Church's pastors as a brake upon the forthright expression of enlightened views about social justice. Even if the bishops are more often than not "enlightened," however, it is important to recognize that respecting the limits upon their competence is a powerful (and enlightened, if you wish) way to teach CST. The separation of church and state is original to Christianity: Jesus' proclamation to "render therefore to Caesar the things that are Caesar's, and to God the things that are God's" (Mt 22:21) was delivered to an ancient world very differently minded. It entered a world that treated the state as sacred

---

[14] The American bishops intervened in the 2009–2010 debate about universal health insurance ("Obamacare") speaking as *"we,"* and as stating *"our"* position, saying that the bishops themselves could never support certain versions of the healthcare reform act, but that they could support others. This whole manner of speaking indicates a confused understanding of their competence. The bishops did not overtly instruct the laity or evangelize the wider culture. They did not speak forthrightly as pastors. They announced a collective stance. To my knowledge their interventions *never* included an assertion of the sort one would expect, namely and in so many words: *Catholic faith requires*, or *No one may*, or *The Church holds*, or *All Catholic legislators must*. It might well be that all things considered precluded any such judgments about a two-thousand-page bill overhauling the nation's healthcare system. No doubt in the course of recounting for public consumption their own thoughts about what to do, the bishops managed to educate the laity about relevant moral norms and their possible application to the reform bill. But they went well beyond that project.

By announcing their evolving stances *as the USCCB* the bishops seem to have been trying to get the laity to adopt positions that moral truth did not compel and which the laity were free to conscientiously reject, trafficking in authority without invoking it and (it would seem) knowing that they should not invoke it.

and God as a wizard to be flattered into vouchsafing earthly victories for the city. The novel Christian distinction between this world and the heavenly Kingdom, and the presence in a well-ordered society of the two "swords" or competent authorities – the spiritual and the temporal – exploded the accustomed manner of thinking about the relationship between earthly affairs and divine reality.[15]

The Council Fathers wrote, in the second half of *Dignitatis humanae* that "[a]mong the things that concern the good of the Church and indeed the welfare of society here on earth . . . this certainly is preeminent, namely, that the Church should enjoy that full measure of freedom which her care for the salvation of men requires."[16] (*DH*, no. 13). The Fathers concluded that "the freedom of the Church is the fundamental principle in what concerns the relations between the Church and governments and the whole civil order" (*DH*, no. 13).

The teaching of *Dignitatis humanae* has been the unvarying message of the magisterium at least since *Immortale dei* (1885).[17] In that encyclical letter Leo XIII endorsed the language of Gregory XVI in *Mirari vos* (1832) by which Gregory criticized "those who desire that the Church be separated from the State."[18] But what Gregory (and Leo) understood by that phrase is then made immediately clear in *Immortale dei*: the "dissolution" of the "concord between the secular and ecclesiastical authority" (*ID*, no. 34). In the very next paragraph Leo *affirms* the separation of jurisdictions – the "two swords" – and, in questions of what he called "mixed jurisdiction," he called for "complete harmony" between them, "such as suited to the end for which each power exists" (*ID*, no. 35).

Joseph Ratzinger wrote in his "Theology and the Church's Political Stance": "the *fundamental* task of the Church's political stance . . . must be to maintain this balance of a dual system as the foundation of freedom" [emphasis added]. "[T]he Church must make claims and demands on public law and cannot simply retreat into the private sphere . . . [I]t must also take care on the other hand that Church and state remain separated and that belonging to the Church retains its voluntary character." During his

---

[15]   Pope Gelasius famously wrote in the late fifth century: "two there are, august Emperor, by which this world is ruled on title of original and sovereign right – the consecrated authority of the priests and the royal power."

[16]   Vatican II, Declaration on Religious Freedom *Dignitas humanae* (On the Right of the Person and of Communities to Social and Civil Freedom in Matters Religious) (1965), no. 13.

[17]   Leo XIII, Encyclical Letter *Immortale dei* (On the Christian Constitution of States) (1885).

[18]   Gregory XVI, Encyclical Letter *Mirari vos* (On Liberalism and Religious Indifferentism) (1832).

pontificate Pope Benedict XVI spoke often (perhaps most forcefully on his 2008 trip to France, there especially upon his welcome on September 12 by President Sarkozy) of what he calls a healthy secularity, which the pope sharply distinguished from secularism. Benedict nonetheless repeatedly affirmed the separation of church and state, for the benefit of both. By jealously guarding itself against close identification with any particular culture or political, economic, or social system, the Church promotes its universal commission. It also "can be a close bond between the various communities of peoples and nations, provided they trust the Church and guarantee it true freedom" (GS, no. 42).

The "two swords" concept (or "separation," as it is most often called in the United States) has not been neglected by our pastors, or by the laity for that matter. But it is rarely seen as the vital part of CST that it is. In other words, maintaining a *proper* understanding of the relationship between the Church and any state, as well as (by extension) between religion and public life, is itself an invaluable contribution to any society's genuine common good. The bishops contribute to this great good when they soundly teach CST, both in the transitive effects of the message they convey, and by the example they set in saying it.

CONCLUSION

Since what is typically dated as the commencement of CST in 1891 with Pope Leo XIII's inauguration promulgation of *Rerum novarum,* the Church's pastors have very often said too *little* about CST. Bishops have often been unwilling to state clearly what morality requires of both statesman and citizen alike. Sometimes the Church's teachers have condoned injustice, as with the American hierarchy's failure to challenge the United States' indiscriminate conventional bombing and its use of nuclear weapons against Japan, all the while calling upon American Catholics to give their all to the war effort. Much more often, pastors have let down the laity and their own political communities by being silent. Their reticence failed the laity, so many of whom surely faced crises of conscience at twenty thousand feet, or in a foxhole contemplating whether to execute a wounded enemy prisoner.

In some instances the bishops have also said too *much*. They have often, in the name of the Church, advanced or supported detailed legislative proposals and policy initiatives that were predominantly, if not almost wholly, within the province of the laity. The American bishops' 1919 "Plan for Social Reconstruction" is a leading example, as was the bishops' 1986 economics pastoral, "Economic Justice for All."

No doubt there are manifold reasons why the Church's pastors have said too little and too much. These reasons would range from the psychological to the political. But these reasons would surely include a profound misunderstanding of what their responsibilities and competence with CST truly are (as John Finnis compellingly shows in this volume's concluding chapter).

The importance of bringing up these shortcomings now is not to criticize or to lament. It is rather to consider how they might be overcome, for the need for the bishops to fearlessly preach and teach sound social doctrine is likely to grow, not recede.

The suggestion supported by the analysis of this chapter is that they should say less and more than they have been saying. "Less" in a quantifiable sense; that is, they should say less about detailed political and economic plans. They should abandon interventions grounded in attempts to simply say something that people might actually want to hear (the example of Bishop Roach), and which amount to semiauthoritative lobbying of the laity for proposals the bishops judge better rather than worse (the Obamacare debacle). By saying less the bishops would be doing their jobs, and helping the laity to do theirs.

Bishops ought also to say more, in a more qualitative sense: They should teach incessantly the integral Gospel, fearlessly taking their preaching where the care of souls requires them to go. No doubt this will very often require bishops to say much about the moral truths at the heart of a social, economic, or political problem. Many bishops will blanch at the prospect of getting a fair hearing for the norms and insights of CST. Thinking of them, though, not as a set of political (or economic or legal or sociological) recommendations competing for acceptance with those of the Democrats or Republicans, but as the Good News that saves and which lasts, would be an encouraging thought.

23

A Radical Critique of Catholic Social Teaching

John Finnis

The magisterial teachings described (along with associated scholarly and popular discourse) as *Catholic Social Teaching(s)* [or *Doctrine*] are flawed – by ambiguity about their scope or subject matter; by insufficient attention to the teachings' dependence upon (a) judgments concerning empirical facts and likelihoods, and/or (b) the other contingent (subrational) factors (preferences) inherent in any assessment of how the Golden Rule applies; and by inappropriate assumptions or even assertions about who it is that has primary responsibility for making such judgments and assessments, and for deciding and choosing how to act in line with them.

These three flaws are interconnected and mutually reinforcing, but will here be explored more or less in sequence. The conclusion will be that the form, the delivery, and, in a sense, the content of Catholic Social Teaching need substantial reforms, if the Church is not to remain hobbled in its primary mission.

Form: Much of the teaching should be formulated hypothetically, and most if not all efforts by pastors to apply it – in preaching to or otherwise guiding the faithful – should be framed in hypothetical/contingent form, roughly summarizable as: if you judge that such and such facts obtain, or are likely, then (unless you judge that certain other facts do not obtain or are unlikely), true moral principles and norms, confirmed by divine revelation, direct that you should choose thus-and-thus.

Delivery: Popes, bishops, and other pastors should not address CST in documents or preaching any more often than they address home-making, dating, discipline of children, contraception and other antimarital practices, dishonesty in work and provision of services, gossip, surliness between family members, or pornography.

Content: CST is partly moral doctrine, but in larger part is theology not doctrine. As interiorized and deployed in practical life, it is necessarily, in still larger part, a matter of making scientific, historical, and political judgments and predictions. Popes and other bishops therefore should be involved in it very little, and only when solid doctrine is at stake – as in matters of Christological or ecclesiological theology. Their task as teachers is to preach the Gospel to unbelievers, the Gospel of the Kingdom that is largely not of this world; and to instruct, exhort, and encourage believers in living, in love of God, self, and neighbor, the truths that come to them from the Apostles, as understood in the tradition that extends to this very day. As against this critique there stands the *praxis* of the popes and bishops for a century and a half (and more), but *much of that directive praxis has already been rightly abandoned*, and still more should be abandoned as soon as possible – remitted to the laity – retaining clarity and authoritativeness of magisterial teaching in the appropriate, limited, but supremely important domain of unchanging principles and moral norms.

I

CST as Part of Catholic Moral Teaching

What is CST about? As a matter of words, "social teaching/doctrine" means, of course, teaching or doctrine concerning social matters, identifying principles and norms of social justice. But justice is the virtue concerned with any and every choice and act or omission that affects the wellbeing of other persons, who are therefore entitled to my respect and care in deliberating and choosing. So all justice is social and the meaning of "social justice" therefore needs basic clarification. Likewise, all moral teaching that bears on one's relations with other persons is inherently social teaching. So why did the Church of the late nineteenth century begin announcing a "social teaching"?

Leo XIII and his draftsmen wrote *Rerum novarum* to deal with "the social question." It was a time-bound idiomatic phrase – a jargon of the day. As the drafts show,[1] and the eventual full title confirms, "the social question" meant for Leo (as it did later for Pius X)[2] the question how to think rightly about *the condition of the workers*. That was "the" social issue of most concern, in the late nineteenth century, especially for European leaders rightly fearful of the growing and substantially justified discontent. If left without reasonable responses, more just and loving than offered by Marxist and other socialist revolutionaries, such discontent would generate ruin for their political

---

[1] For the drafts, see Giovanni Antonazzi and Gabriele de Rosa, eds., *L'Enciclica Rerum Novarum e il Suo Tempore* (Rome: Edizioni di Storia e Letteratura, 1991), 88.
[2] Pius X, Encyclical Letter *Il fermo proposito* (On Catholic Actions in Italy) (1905), nos. 13, 16, 20; Pius X, Encyclical Letter *Singulari quadam* (On Labor Organizations) (1912), no. 3.

communities (states), their families, and other associations within them, and
the Church. The fears were made vivid by the Commune, the socialist
revolutionary regime controlling the Paris district in April and May 1871,
and were to be fully verified by the International Socialist destruction of
Russian society in and after 1917 and by many lesser events in the period to
which *Rerum novarum* spoke with immediacy. "The social question" thus
meant something like "the socialism question" – itself a sprawling, partly
accidental cluster of questions. Is private property, including property rights
over "means of production," justifiable? Are organizations of employees criminal conspiracies to violate contracts of employment, or can they be justifiable
coordination of stance in negotiating the ongoing terms of those contracts?
Should proposals to abolish or radically limit rights of property and freedom of
contract (proposals characteristically associated with proposals to abolish or
radically modify marriage and family relationships, and religion) be actively
resisted, not only by argument but by organized action in schools, churches,
workplaces, and the whole domain of political action)? Should resistance offer
something specifiable and more just and benevolent than sheer continuance
of existing patterns branded by their opponents as dehumanizing, immoral, or
amorally "traditional," "capitalist," "clerical," "oppressive," and so forth?

A body of teaching or doctrine needs a more stable and principled set of
unifying issues and principles than those picked out by "social" in the context in
which "Catholic social teaching" became a term of art. The instability of "social"
is shown by chapter headings in Vatican II's *Gaudium et spes* (1965), and by the
introductory explanations of them: "Christ … gave His Church no proper
mission in the *political, economic or social* order";[3] "worthy elements are found
in today's social movements, especially an evolution toward unity, a process of
wholesome *socialization* and of association in *civic and economic* realms"(GS,
no. 42); "Christians … are free to give proper exercise to all their earthly activities
and to their humane, domestic, professional, social and technical enterprises"
(GS, no. 43); "Part II. Some problems of special urgency" (GS, no. 46) …
"Chapter I … *Marriage and the Family* … " (GS, no. 47); "the family … is
the foundation of society. All … who exercise influence over communities and
social groups should work efficiently for the welfare of marriage and the family"
(GS, no. 52); "Chapter II. The Proper Development of *Culture*" … "When man
develops the earth by … his hands or … technology, in order that it may bear
fruit and become a dwelling worthy of the whole human family and when he
consciously takes part in the life of social groups, he carries out the design of

[3] Vatican II, Pastoral Constitution *Gaudium et spes* (On the Church in the Modern World)
(1965), no. 42.

God ... that he should subdue the earth, perfect creation and develop himself [and] obeys the commandment of Christ that he place himself at the service of his brethren." (GS, no. 57) ... "Chapter III. *Economic and Social Life.* In the *economic and social realms* too the dignity and complete vocation of the human person and the welfare of *society as a whole* are to be respected and promoted ... " (GS, no. 63); "Section 1. *Economic* Development ... Section 2. Certain Principles governing *Socio-Economic Life* as a Whole" (GS, no. 67; in nos. 68–69 and 71 the principles enunciated in *Rerum novarum* about property and labor unions are rearticulated; GS, no. 70 interposes some remarks about investment and development of poor countries) ... "Chapter IV. The Life of the *Political Community.* In our day, profound changes are apparent also in the structure and institutions of peoples ... [changes] result[ing] from their *cultural, economic and social* evolution [and having] a great influence on the life of the *political* community ... " (GS, no. 73) ... "The Church ... by reason of her role and competence, is not identified in any way with the political community nor bound to any political system ... The Church and the political community in their own fields are autonomous and independent from each other. Yet both, under different titles, are devoted to the *personal and social vocation* of the same men." (GS, no. 76) ... "Chapter V. The Fostering of Peace and the Promotion of a *Community of Nations*" (GS, no. 77) ... "The Council, considering the immensity of the hardships which still afflict the greater part of mankind today, regards it as most opportune that an organism of the universal Church be set up in order that both justice and the love of Christ toward the poor might be developed everywhere. The role of such an organism would be to stimulate the community of Catholics to promote progress in needy regions and international social justice" (GS, nos. 90, 91).

The "organism" thus projected by the Council was the dicastery of the Roman curia that was responsible between 1967 and 2016 for informing the papal magisterium in its articulation and development of Catholic Social Teaching: the Pontifical Commission [later Council] for Justice and Peace. More will be said below about that body.[4] The point of the foregoing selection of passages from Vatican II's primary document on CST – in many respects a fine articulation of CST – is to illustrate the vagueness of the term "social" as intended to pick out a domain or subject-matter for teaching. The real subject is justice (and peace understood in its Augustinian amplitude as good order) considered as the whole set of moral obligations and responsibilities that should guide the way in which one relates to other human persons who may be affected by one's choices to act (or refrain from acting).

---

[4] See text and n. 49 below.

But Leo XIII and his neoscholastic advisers were inhibited from delimiting the territory of their concern by reference to "justice," because they held to a mistaken academic theory of classification according to which one's duties to redistribute one's *superflua* (property one does not need for one's authentic vocation) are duties not of justice but of charity.[5] This theory had no better basis than that they thought it was St. Thomas Aquinas's view. But it was not, and Aquinas's rejection of the contrast helps confirm that it was and is mistaken, as is confirmed also by its abandonment[6] in subsequent magisterial articulations of CST.

The interpersonal concern of Christians properly extends as far as the demands of justice extend. And this is the proper scope of CST. So it integrally includes the availability of euthanasia and assisted suicide; the maintaining of means of mass destruction of innocents for deterrence; pornography of lust and violence; artificial and other nonmarital generation of children; irresponsibility in marrying, generating children, and dissolving marital life; excess and deficiency in patriotism; and many other ways of damaging or neglecting the wellbeing of others. Within this vast domain, the responsibilities of different individuals and groups will differ widely and intricately – but are capable in principle of a *coherent* articulation worthy of being called Catholic social teaching: what the Church teaches us about our duties of justice and about ways in which we can have a vocation to promote harmony with and among our neighbors near or far.

Example (1): The "Family Wage"

To illustrate the ambiguities in the idea and phrase "social teaching" – and to indicate how what is at stake is the whole of justice, and *every* virtue insofar as unvirtuous conduct may impact on other persons and thereby engage justice – consider the *family wage*.

---

[5]   See Finnis, "Aquinas as a Primary Source of Catholic Social Teaching" (Chapter 1 in this volume) at p. 23, nn. 20–21.

[6]   Without ratifying or repeating *RN*'s mistake, John XXII, Encyclical Letter *Mater et magistra* (On Christianity and Social Progress) (1961), nos. 120–121 points out that *charitable* giving is often appropriate and suggested by Christian faith. *Quadragesimo anno* (1931) does not repeat *RN*'s claim about the duty to distribute *superflua* being one of charity, but does assert that

> Loftier and nobler principles – social justice and social charity – must, therefore, be sought whereby [the economic dictatorship which has recently displaced free competition] may be governed firmly and fully. Hence, the institutions themselves of peoples and, particularly those of all social life, ought to be penetrated with this justice, and it is most necessary that it be truly effective, that is, establish a juridical and social order which will, as it were, give form and shape to all economic life. Social charity, moreover, ought to be as the soul of this order. (*QA*, no. 88)

Quadragesimo anno said:

71. . . . *the worker must be paid a wage sufficient to support him and his family* [citation to encyclical *Casti Connubii* (1930)].[7] That the rest of the family should also contribute to the common support, according to the capacity of each, is certainly right, as can be observed especially in the families of farmers, but also in the families of many craftsmen and small shopkeepers. But to abuse the years of childhood and the limited strength of women is grossly wrong. Mothers, concentrating on household duties, should work primarily in the home or in its immediate vicinity. It is an intolerable abuse, and to be abolished at all cost, for mothers on account of the father's low wage to be forced to engage in gainful occupations outside the home to the neglect of their proper cares and duties, especially the training of children. *Every effort must therefore be made that fathers of families receive a wage large enough to meet ordinary family needs adequately.* But if this cannot always be done under existing circumstances, social justice demands that changes be introduced as soon as possible whereby such a wage will be assured to every adult workingman. It will not be out of place here to render merited praise to all, who with a wise and useful purpose, have tried and tested various ways of adjusting the pay for work to family burdens in such

---

7   Presumably nos. 117–124. For example:

> 117. . . . every effort must be made to bring about that which . . . Leo XIII has already insisted upon [citation to *RN*] namely, that in the State such economic and social methods should be adopted as will enable every head of a family to earn as much as, according to his station in life, is necessary for himself, his wife, and for the rearing of his children . . . To deny this, or to make light of what is equitable, is a grave injustice and is placed among the greatest sins . . . nor is it lawful to fix such a scanty wage as will be insufficient for the upkeep of the family in the circumstances in which it is placed.
> 119 . . . Christian charity . . .
> 120. If, however, for this purpose, private resources do not suffice, it is the duty of the public authority to supply for the insufficient forces of individual effort, particularly in a matter which is of such importance to the common weal, touching as it does the maintenance of the family and married people . . . [where] families, particularly those in which there are many children, have not suitable dwellings; if the husband cannot find employment and means of livelihood; if the necessities of life cannot be purchased except at exorbitant prices; if even the mother of the family, to the great harm of the home, is compelled to go forth and seek a living by her own labor; if she, too, in the ordinary or even extraordinary labors of childbirth, is deprived of proper food, medicine, and the assistance of a skilled physician . . .
> 122. We are sorry to note that not infrequently nowadays it happens that through a certain inversion of the true order of things, ready and bountiful assistance is provided for the unmarried mother and her illegitimate offspring (who, of course must be helped in order to avoid a greater evil) which is denied to legitimate mothers or given sparingly or almost grudgingly.

a way that, as these [burdens] increase, the former may be raised and indeed, if the contingency arises, there may be enough to meet extraordinary needs.

This thought is cited, but stated in only a compressed and muted form, in Vatican II's *Gaudium et spes*, no. 67. It is revived and clarified considerably in *Laborem exercens* (written for the 90th anniversary of RN) no. 19:

[I]n every case, a just wage is the concrete means of *verifying the justice* of the whole socioeconomic system and, in any case, of checking that it is functioning justly. It is not the only means of checking, but it is a particularly important one and, in a sense, the key means.

This means of checking concerns above all the family. Just remuneration for the work of an adult who is responsible for a family means remuneration which will suffice for establishing and properly maintaining a family and for providing security for its future. Such remuneration can be given either through what is called a *family wage* – that is, a single salary given to the head of the family for his work, sufficient for the needs of the family without the other spouse having to take up gainful employment outside the home – or through *other social measures* such as family allowances or grants to mothers devoting themselves exclusively to their families. These grants should correspond to the actual needs, that is, to the number of dependents for as long as they are not in a position to assume proper responsibility for their own lives.

Experience confirms that there must be a *social re-evaluation of the mother's role*, of the toil connected with it, and of the need that children have for care, love and affection in order that they may develop into responsible, morally and religiously mature and psychologically stable persons. It will redound to the credit of society to make it possible for a mother – without inhibiting her freedom, without psychological or practical discrimination, and without penalizing her as compared with other women – to devote herself to taking care of her children and educating them in accordance with their needs, which vary with age. Having to abandon these tasks in order to take up paid work outside the home is wrong from the point of view of the good of society and of the family when it contradicts or hinders these primary goals of the mission of a mother. [Emphases in the original][8]

The superiority of *LE*'s treatment should not obscure the fact that several key issues are left aside, as if unnoticed. Suppose that many women choose to "take up paid work outside the home," because their formation by their families, their schools, and the media has led them to think that doing so is required for their equality, freedom, and self-worth; or has led them to look askance at hands-on child-rearing, housework, and homemaking, and to care

---

[8] John Paul II, Encyclical Letter *Laborem exercens* (On Human Work) (1981), no. 19.

little that such preferences when widely shared can and do result in a demographically unsustainable population whose problems of sustainability will be resolved willy-nilly by euthanasia and population-replacing immigration (often lawless). The consequence (verified all over the western world) will be a diminution (on average) of individuals' wages (especially but not exclusively for men) such that, together with the increase in the price of accommodation (driven up by the buying power of two-earner households), it will be increasingly difficult to provide a family wage – even with the help of the welfare payments ("other social measures") envisaged by *LE*, no. 19 – to men whose wives do *not* take paid work outside the home. This downward spiral has helped radically change the demographics of all Western countries. And it makes ever more imperative the Church's need to catechize its own teachers and members about the truth that all Christian moral teaching about sex not only is a teaching about the requirements of a true marriage and the preconditions of justice to children, but is *entirely integral* to Christian teaching about human flourishing, including justice, *and* to "Catholic Social Teaching."[9]

The National Conference of Catholic Bishops (US), in their 58,000-word statement *Economic Justice for All* (1986), showed, unwittingly, how far an understanding of justice depends on an adequate account of human flourishing. For what *LE*, no. 19 had rightly called "the key means" of checking the justice of the socioeconomic system as a whole, a means that "above all" concerns the family, has in the US statement shriveled away to a passing allusion to one among half a dozen ways of exploiting "workers":

---

[9]   A part, but far too small a part, of the necessary clarifications can be found in the treatment of the family wage in the *Compendium of Catholic Social Teaching*, nos. 250–254. For example:

> 253. Society's service of the family becomes concrete in recognizing, respecting and promoting the rights of the family. This means that authentic and effective family policies must be brought about with specific interventions that are able to meet the needs arising from the rights of the family as such. In this sense, there is a necessary prerequisite, one that is essential and indispensable: the recognition – which entails protecting, appreciating and promoting – the identity of the family, the natural society founded on marriage. This recognition represents a clear line of demarcation between the family, understood correctly, and all other forms of cohabitation which, by their very nature, deserve neither the name nor the status of family. [Emphases in original]

Since the CSDC (a work of the Pontifical Council for Justice & Peace offered to the magisterium, not by the magisterium, but subsequently treated as if magisterial) was issued in 2004, it has become necessary to clarify further that "founded on marriage" of course means founded on genuine marriage, not state-recognized imitations such as "same-sex marriage" or "civil union."

103. Because work is this important, people have a right to employment. In return for their labor, workers have a right to wages and other benefits sufficient to sustain life in dignity ... justice, not charity, demands certain minimum guarantees. The provision of wages and other benefits sufficient to support a family in dignity is a basic necessity *to prevent this exploitation of workers*. The dignity of workers also requires adequate health care, security for old age or disability, unemployment compensation, healthful working conditions, weekly rest, periodic holidays for recreation and leisure, and reasonable security against arbitrary dismissal. (citation to *LE*, no. 19)[10]

As for *LE*'s rearticulation (in the third paragraph of no. 19 just quoted) of the centrality of maternal home care and education when considering the justice of wages and of the whole socioeconomic system, it finds no echo at all in the thoroughly de-Catholicized paragraphs[11] where the US bishops speak of women, their underemployment, poverty, discrimination against them in employment, salary inequity, need for alimony, and so on. The US document is a signal witness to the moral wreckage, and mission failure, caused by taking Catholic Social Teaching as narrower in scope (and shallower in depth) than it truly is.

In sum, CST is a part of Catholic moral teaching and cannot be well studied or taught without a clear grasp of its dependence upon, and integration within, that moral teaching as a whole. It is not so much a plan for "making a better world" as a reminder of individuals', groups', and communities' duties of justice.[12]

II

Negative and Affirmative Moral Norms

All moral teaching means to inform and guide practical reasoning, that is, one's deliberations about which of two or more proposals for action it would be both permissible and preferable to choose. All practical reasoning includes premises of two kinds: one (or more) *evaluative* premise(s), about what is desirable, good, appropriate, permissible, and so forth; and at least one *factual* premise about what behavior would be involved in the proposed action, and

---

[10]   United States Conference of Catholic Bishops, "*Economic Justice for All*: Pastoral Letter on Catholic Social Teaching and the U.S. Economy," (November 13, 1986), no. 103, in Hugh J. Nolan, ed., *Pastoral Letters of the United States Catholic Bishops* V (1983–88) (Washington DC: National Conference of Catholic Bishops and United States Catholic Conference, 1989), 411.

[11]   *Economic Justice for All*, nos. 140, 178–180, 199, 353; cf. nos. 2, 3, and the last-minute *pro forma* generalities inserted artificially in 346.

[12]   See Grisez, *The Way of the Lord Jesus*, vol. 2 (1992), ch 6.G.1; see n. 51 below.

what good and bad effects can or are likely to result from that behavior in the circumstances as they actually are or are likely to be. Moral norms (whether general or specific precepts or rules) are articulated to serve as more or less general premises of the first kind – as the (or an) evaluative premise in deliberation (that is, in practical reasoning toward choice and action).

Some ("negative") moral norms identify kinds of acts that should never be chosen, and some of these norms do so in terms that do not depend for their applicability on other moral judgments.[13] Other ("affirmative") moral norms identify responsibilities to act. As Aquinas rightly teaches, in line with a tradition found in Scripture and theologically elaborated by St Augustine:[14] negative moral norms bind always and in relation to every instance of the kind of act they pick out; affirmative moral norms, however, although always to be borne in mind as general guidance, do not bind *specifically* except in appropriate circumstances. The application of affirmative moral norms of justice is always dependent, therefore, on an assessment of the circumstances, an assessment that, though morally guided, always involves some judgment about facts and likelihoods, especially about unintended effects of one's action or inaction.

It is true that even the application of exceptionless *negative* moral norms, such as the norm excluding the intent to kill a person or persons, can sometimes involve difficult assessments of complex facts. What is the object (the structure of intentions) of a threat to kill where the threat is intended to make unlikely the occurrence of circumstances of the kind in relation to which the threat is made? In morally assessing the acts and intentions of those involved in making the threat, and/or in maintaining its real potency and credibility, and/or in carrying it out if it failed to achieve its principal purpose, does it matter that the threat is made on behalf of a group (political community) by one group of persons (legislators and/or executive officials) but would be carried out (if ever) by a distinct group (military personnel in silos or submarines)? But it remains that the application of affirmative moral norms is inherently even more – much more – relative to assessments of circumstances, many of which are or concern the future consequences of action and inaction: a matter about which reasonable people often reasonably disagree.

---

13 Such norms can be called exceptionless moral norms, identifying kinds of acts that are intrinsically wrongful. These are a primary subject of John Paul II, Encyclical Letter *Veritatis splendor* (On Fundamental Questions on Church's Moral Teaching) (1993), nos. 74–83. These norms identify the relevant kinds of act by reference to the act's "object," that is, its immediate intention – what it intends to bring about as a means to some purpose that in itself is or may well be legitimate or good.

14 John Finnis, *Moral Absolutes* (Washington, DC: Catholic University of America Press, 1991); VS, nos. 52, 82.

The mission and therefore the authority of the apostles has always been to teach to the nations all that the Lord commanded,[15] commands that certainly include the whole of morality as it can be known (albeit with less certainty and clarity) independently of those revealed commandments. But this apostolic authority does not extend to the making of judgments about the factual premises of practical reasoning, except where those premises concern facts that, even if complex, are transparent to reason – as facts about *kinds of intention* are, at least in principle.

So, in relation to *affirmative* responsibilities – that is, to most of the whole domain of Catholic Social Teaching – the form of the guidance and direction given by or on behalf of bishops should in most cases be *hypothetical/conditional*: if you judge (A) that the circumstances (present situation, relevant causalities, likely risks and consequences …) are in fact thus-and-thus (or likely to be thus and thus), *and* (B) that on that factual assumption the golden rule of justice requires such and such, *then* (C) you should act to promote such and such so far as your responsibilities permit. In some kinds of cases the general principles and institutions of justice as approved by revelation and established Church doctrine permit the Church's teachers to declare condition (B) certainly satisfied in the prevailing circumstances. But in most if not all circumstances it would be beyond their competence, and outside their mandate to teach *on matters of faith and morals*, for them to declare and teach that condition (A), concerning facts, likelihoods, and circumstances, is satisfied. Much of the teaching since *Rerum novarum* has not respected this entailment of the logic of practical reasoning and of the divine mandate to teach what reason confirmed by revelation establishes are moral truths.

Before illustrating that failure to respect the proper boundaries of CST, a word should be said about the teaching of *negative* responsibilities and norms. In this domain, stable and specific teaching can rightly be proposed as certain on a good many matters where the chosen acts (or omissions) in question can be identified by their objects (their close-in intentions) with sufficient clarity, and securely condemned as wrongful. But the intentional structure of the kind of act in question has to be sufficiently describable, whether the Church's public judgment be permissive or condemnatory. Here are two examples of insufficiently clarified judgments, in the domain of CST.

Example (2): Nuclear Deterrence

The Holy See on June 11, 1982 delivered to the UN Second Special Session on Disarmament a Message stating that "In current conditions 'deterrence' based on balance, not as an end in itself but as a stage on the way toward a progressive

---

[15] *Matthew* 28:20.

disarmament, may still be judged morally acceptable." This statement effectively set aside the position argued by some (including the present author) that the principles of Catholic moral doctrine entail that policies and systems for nuclear deterrence of any of the distinct kinds publicly maintained by the United States, the UK, and France include a real present intent (on the part of at least some of the persons involved) to kill noncombatants (precisely as noncombatants) if certain contingencies arise, and are therefore policies and systems that it is certainly gravely wrong to support. But neither in the Holy See's statement, nor in the US Bishops Pastoral Letter *The Challenge of Peace* (1983), which (taken with the Pastoral's 1988 follow-up documents) relies upon it to declare the US policy and systems morally tolerable, is any *reason* offered on the basis of which it would be compatible with the Catholic faith to set aside the position that holds these deterrent systems to be gravely immoral and against the Lord's commandment. The Holy See's position could be interpreted as a suspension of judgment pending clarification the Church's thought. The US bishops' position amounts to a judgment favorable to nuclear deterrence but without reasons compatible with the Catholic moral principles and norms taught in their own documents. That the suspension and the inexplicable and erroneous judgment are both in place over 30 years later is (to say the least) very corrosive of CST.[16]

Example (3): Usury

Corrosion like that can be illustrated by the history of the Church's teaching on usury. A dominant element in the Church's social teaching through the Middle Ages was the condemnation of usury, that is, of making a charge *for lending* money.[17] The key moral norm was negative,[18] and was treated as

---

[16] For further discussion and references, see Finnis, *Religion and Public Reasons* (Oxford: Oxford University Press, 2011), 200; with John Finnis, Joseph Boyle, and Germain Grisez, *Nuclear Deterrence, Morality and Realism* (Oxford: Oxford University Press, 1987), 97–98, passim.

[17] For an unusually lucid history of this teaching, see Marjorie Grice-Hutchinson, *Early Economic Thought in Spain 1177–1740* ([London, 1978] Indianapolis: Liberty Fund, 2015), 20–30. Uncharacteristically, her explanation of the word "interest," *interesse*, is blurred; better to say, with Aquinas, that *interesse* denotes an indemnity or compensation for loss incurred; we could say: it is what is needed to fill the gap "between," *inter*, what the lender had or would have had and the lesser amount he now has or will have unless compensated.

[18] It was and is a condemnation of a kind of extortion, of a distinct inequality in exchange, of charging for what has "value" only because of the borrower's need (rather than because the person imposing the charge has created value or has undergone compensable loss in preparing to make and making the transaction). It is found also where monopolists or a controlling "ring" charge prices for goods or services in excess of reasonable compensation for the costs (actual or contingent) of supplying the good or services. Modern antitrust legislation is an attempt to obviate usurious pricing. More directly aimed at usurious pricing are laws against price-gouging (raising of prices during times of emergency), and such laws often, rightly, make allowance for price rises to offset increased costs of maintaining supply during the relevant period.

exceptionless in relation to those charges to which it applied. The prohibited charges did not, however, include all kinds of charges associated with a money-loan; there were kinds of charges identified as morally permissible, notably charges levied to cover the genuine expenses or costs that the making of the loan imposed upon the lender: for example, the costs of transporting the money from the lender to the borrower, including the costs of guarding it and of insuring against its loss in transit; and charges for insurance premiums payable under contracts insuring the lender against such loss as would arise if the borrower were to default and the security (if any) – taken by the lender from the borrower to protect the former against possible default by the latter – were to prove unavailable, unmarketable, or otherwise unrealizable. These "titles" (grounds of moral entitlement to make a charge in connection with a loan) all had the feature that each of them authorized lenders to be compensated for a species of loss incurred by or on occasion of making the loan. Eventually it was recognized (A) that *where there is a sufficiently liquid and free capital market in both equities* (shares in productive or in some other way profitable joint commercial ventures) *and bonds* (marketable contracts of loan), the opportunity cost to lenders of making loans of monies that they could (but for the loan) have invested in joint commercial ventures as such or by way of purchases of shares/stocks is a cost that can be more or less objectively and fairly measured as the average rate of *dividends* in the share/stock market – and (B) that in the medium term that rate will approximate, when discounted for risk of loss through failure of the venture, to the market rate of return on *bonds*: call that the going "interest rate." Once a fair charge by way of interest could thus be identified as a genuine compensation for a calculable cost of lending as opposed to investing, that charge could be seen to fall outside the kind of charge that the Church had rightly identified as usury and had rightly condemned as a kind of theft from the borrower, a theft made possible by the borrower's *need*.[19]

The historic moral condemnation of usury should be regarded as true, and therefore still "in force." But most Catholics, including prelates, do not understand the basis on which that condemnation was made, still less the reasons why the condemnation became inapplicable to many kinds of interest on many kinds of loan. Many, outside and inside the Church, have the impression that the Church was for centuries mistaken in its teaching of a moral absolute – one that dominated Catholic social teaching for centuries – but later saw the light and (silently) revoked its teaching. That corrosive impression is erroneous, albeit near impossible to overcome.

[19] For all this, see Finnis, *Aquinas: Moral, Political, and Legal Thought* (Oxford: Oxford University Press, 1998), ch. VI.3.

What is the moral of the story? The Church's pastors were too slow to grasp the complex social facts that constitute a capital market; the Church's own scholarly experts had great difficulty sorting out the ways in which already complex facts are complexified further by exchange dealings between one capital market and another in the meta-market constituted by foreign trade and foreign exchange.[20] Both scholars and pastors were too slow in making a clear analysis of the morally relevant intentions involved in making loans and interest charges in a multilayered and linguistically shifting social context.[21] The understanding, analysis, and assessment of social facts is inherently liable to be difficult, not least when indispensable to the correct application of a true moral norm. In the case of the moral norm against usury – but not only that moral norm! – all such understanding and assessment is doubly complexified by the availability and practice of ways and schemes of feigning some legitimate kind of intentions and transaction while actually pursuing a more convenient and immediately useful but illegitimate kind (often conventionally and widely redescribed with the name of the legitimate kind: say, "sale and repurchase," "insurance," "foreign exchange," "loss," or "discount," or, to take another kind of issue, "refugee").

Affirmative moral principles and norms, all of them, always, are *only* decisive, and settle one's obligations in making a concrete individual or group choice, *if and when* that choice – that "application" of the relevant affirmative norm(s) – is appropriate in the circumstances of the proposed conduct. (*Most* of the general responsibilities articulated in CST are affirmative.) Affirmative norms hold *semper sed non ad* [or: *pro*] *semper*: literally, "always but not for always," i.e., not in all situations. That is to say, their concrete applicability always requires an awareness and understanding of facts, causalities, and likelihoods, and a consideration of other, competing moral responsibilities arising under the same or other affirmative moral norms (not to mention any relevant negative moral norms and obligations). So too does the identification of relatively *specific* affirmative moral norms, on the basis of more general affirmative moral principles. That is what is properly meant in the common but murky saying that the specification and application of affirmative moral

---

20 For an introduction to these complexities and the response to them of scholars in the sixteenth century, see Marjorie Grice-Hutchinson, *The School of Salamanca: Readings in Spanish Monetary Theory, 1544–1605* (Oxford: Oxford University Press, 1952).

21 The analysis needed was one that could display – to the practical reason, and thus to the forming of intentions, of the relevant acting persons – the way(s) in which charges for money can be just because really correlated (whether directly or indirectly) to the prevailing average return on investments in goods and services in that market, since that (prospective) return (when discounted for the greater risk of equities) is what is forgone by (lost to) the lender by making the money loan (that is, by buying a bond rather than a share in a productive enterprise).

principles and norms calls for the exercise of prudence – "prudential judgments."

The implications of this can conveniently be considered in tandem with CST's third flaw: inappropriate assumptions or assertions of teaching authority; clerical overreach.

III

There are very many facts and probabilities about present or foreseeable conduct (and its effects) which are not within the deposit of faith, that is, the set of truths identified in Scripture as it has been handed down and read in the Church's tradition and doctrine. The mandate of bishops is to hand on that deposit, and to guide and admonish the faithful (and others) by recalling and drawing on that whole set of truths. The truth of episcopal (including papal and conciliar) teachings is certain to the extent that the propositions taught are included explicitly or implicitly in the deposit of faith. That deposit certainly includes many negative moral norms, and many affirmative moral principles at least as important for shaping moral life. But it does not include propositions articulating or presupposing judgments about the likely causes, context, and/or effects of present or future facts and probabilities. Such judgments, therefore, are – broadly speaking – outside the episcopal mandate and jurisdiction to teach truths (including moral truths) with the reliability of Christ.

Paul VI's Apostolic Letter, *Octogesima adveniens* (On the 80th anniversary of *Rerum novarum*) (1971), addressed the issue in a way that has affected all subsequent statements attempting to describe the nature or status of CST, and has enveloped those attempts in obscurity:

> 4. In the face of such widely varying situations it is difficult for us [Paul VI; or any pope] to utter a unified message and to put forward a solution which has universal validity. Such is not our ambition, nor is it our mission. It is *up to the Christian communities* to analyze with objectivity the situation which is proper to their own country, to shed on it the light of the Gospel's unalterable words and to *draw principles of reflection, norms of judgment and directives for action from the social teaching of the Church.* [Emphasis added]

This passage rightly, though unclearly, indicated the limits of universal CST. The distinction between "principles of reflection," "norms of judgment," and "directives for action" was made in a context hinting that at least the directives for action would be found, not so much in the Church's CST, but rather in or by contingent, fact- and situation-dependent judgments, judgments attentive to the high-level teaching but made at a lower, more local ecclesiastical (perhaps the laity's) level, the level of "the Christian communities" that, attentive to "the situation . . . in their own country," can make the concrete decisions and choices from each of which follows an *imperium*, a (self)-directive to action.[22]

But that is not how things remained. The trilogy was taken up again in the 1986 Instruction on liberation theology, *Libertatis conscientia*:

> As an "expert in humanity," the Church offers by her social doctrine a set of *principles for reflection* and *criteria for judgment* [fn OA, no. 4] and also directives for action [fn. *Mater et magistra*, no. 235) so that the profound changes demanded by situations of poverty and injustice may be brought about, and this in a way which serves the true good of humanity.[23]

Here the "directives for action" are unambiguously located in the high level, of teaching by "the Church." And the citation to *Mater et magistra* takes us back to something like *Quadragesimo anno*'s call for Catholic Action directed by the orders of popes and bishops:

> Needless to say, when the Hierarchy has made a decision on any point Catholics are bound to obey their *directives*. The Church has the right and obligation not merely to guard ethical and religious principles, but also to declare its authoritative judgment in the matter of putting these principles into practice.[24]

---

[22] See also, e.g., *Octogesima adveniens* no. 42:

> [T]he social teaching of the Church accompanies men in their search. If it does not intervene to authenticate a given structure or to propose a ready-made model, it does not thereby limit itself to recalling general principles. It develops through reflection applied to the changing situations of this world.

[23] Congregation for the Doctrine of the Faith, *Libertatis conscientia* (On Christian Freedom and Liberation) (1986), no. 72.

[24] MM, no. 239 (emphasis added). This is evidently the passage cited in *Libertatis conscientia*, no. 72 as "235." It is prefaced in 238 [234] by recognition that "Differences of opinion in the application of principles can sometimes arise even among sincere Catholics." Consider Pius X's nineteen "fundamental regulations" for Popular Catholic Action, in his Motu Proprio, *Fin dalla Prima*, December 18, 1903, which a twentieth regulation required to be sent to all "Catholic committees, societies and unions of every kind" and to be "exposed in their rooms and read frequently at their meetings": "**I.** Human society, as established by God, is composed of unequal elements, just as the different parts of the human body are unequal; to be make them all equal is impossible, and would mean the destruction of human society. (Encyclical *Quod apostolici muneris*.) **II.** The equality existing among the various social members consists only in this: that all men have their origin in God the Creator, have been redeemed by Jesus Christ, and are to be judged and rewarded or punished by God exactly according to their merits or demerits . . . **III.** Hence it follows that there are, according to the ordinance of God, in human society princes and subjects, masters and proletariat, rich and poor, learned and ignorant, nobles and plebeians, all of whom, united in bonds of love, are to help one another to attain their last end in heaven, earth . . . **V.** The right of private property,

The issue was taken up again in *Sollicitudo rei socialis*:

> [Continuity and newness are] typical of her teaching in the social sphere. On the one hand it is constant, for it remains identical in its fundamental inspiration, in its "principles of reflection," in its "criteria of judgment," in its *basic* "directives for action," and above all in its vital link with the Gospel of the Lord. On the other hand, it is ever new, because it is subject to the necessary and opportune adaptations *suggested* by the changes in historical conditions and by the unceasing flow of the events which are the setting of the life of people and society.[25]

Here "directives for action" have retreated toward the level of principles: they are "basic" directives, rather than marching orders to all the laity by popes or to more local sets of lay people by their bishop(s). Finally, dropping both "basic" and "directives," the *Catechism* reformulates the trilogy:

> The Church's social teaching proposes principles for reflection; it provides criteria for judgment; it gives guidelines for action.[26]

As we can see, the trilogy, "principles, criteria and guidelines/basic directives," is irredeemably hazy: the three elements can scarcely be distinguished from each other. But in the end this failure of staff-work does not matter. For it all leaves intact the basic structure of practical reasoning (two kinds of premise) and the basic division between the two kinds of moral norm (affirmative and negative) that the Church, like common morality, teaches.

So we can return to the problems raised by the contingency and reasonable disputability of premises about facts as they bear on the application of affirmative moral norms and responsibilities. A good many statements have been made by popes since 1891 that were in this domain of facts, probabilities, causalities, and circumstances, and were more or less seriously mistaken or of

---

the fruit of labor or industry, or of concession or donation by others, is an incontrovertible natural right; and everybody can dispose reasonably of such property as he thinks fit. (Encyclical *Rerum novarum*) ... **XIII.** Moreover, Christian Democracy must have nothing to do with politics, and never be able to serve political ends or parties; this is not its field; but it must be a beneficent movement for the people, and founded on the law of nature and the precepts of the Gospel ... **XIV.** In performing its functions, Christian Democracy is bound most strictly to depend upon ecclesiastical authority, and to offer full submission and obedience to the Bishops and those who represent them. There is no meritorious zeal or sincere piety in enterprises, however beautiful and good in themselves, when they are not approved by the pastor ... " etc.

[25] John Paul II, Encyclical Letter *Sollicitudo rei socialis* (On Social Concern) (1987), no. 3. Emphasis added.

[26] CCC, no. 2423. CSDC, no. 85 opts for the *SRS*, no. 3 statement of the constancy of all the elements of the trilogy.

very questionable truth, and should not have been proposed to the faithful with apparent magisterial authority.

Example (4)

Quadragesimo anno contains some striking diagnoses and prescriptions. Before considering a couple of them, consider that encyclical's teaching about CST itself:

> [T]hat principle which Leo XIII so clearly established must be laid down at the outset here, namely, that there resides in Us the right and duty to pronounce with supreme authority upon social and economic matters [fn. *Rerum novarum*, nos. 24–25]. Certainly the Church was not given the commission to guide men to an only fleeting and perishable happiness but to that which is eternal. Indeed "the Church holds that it is unlawful for her to mix without cause in these temporal concerns" [fn. Pius XI, encyclical *Ubi arcano* (1922)]; however, she can in no way renounce the duty God entrusted to her to interpose her authority, **not of course in matters of technique[,] for which she is neither suitably equipped nor endowed by office, but in all things that are connected with the moral law.** For as to these, the deposit of truth that God committed to Us and the grave duty of disseminating and interpreting the whole moral law, and of urging it in season and out of season, bring under and subject to Our supreme jurisdiction not only social order but economic activities themselves.[27]

This is all true, but only when disambiguated. Matters of "technique" (of *ars* or *technē*) are outside the Church's competence just insofar as they are, by definition, the deploying of means effective for some defined purpose. The *purposes* of techniques are not outside the domain of moral judgment, but the effectiveness of means (not to mention the extent and likelihood of their side-effects) is a matter of fact, causalities, and probabilities – and so is outside the Church's competence. Morality's principles, norms, and judgments are all within the Church's authority to teach, *except* insofar as moral judgment about the responsibilities defined by *affirmative* principles and norms *depends upon* a further judgment – call it an *aestimatio*, an assessment – about the circumstances, an *aestimatio* that is or will include judgments about facts, causalities, and probabilities, concerning certain, likely, or possible effectiveness and certain, likely, or possible side-effects, including likely or possible responses and reactions by human persons.[28] All such

---

[27] *QA*, no. 41, emphasis added. The Latin for "in matters of technique" is *iis quae artis sunt* [Italian: *cose tecniche*] and for "connected with the moral law" is *quae ad regulam morum referuntur* [Italian: *che ha attinenza con la morale*]. The Latin and Italian make clear that the comma should be inserted after "technique" – all matters of technique are being stated to be (precisely as such) outside the Church's competence.

[28] Some simple analogies or examples: Christian parents have a strong affirmative moral responsibility to provide for their children a Christian education, but need to make specific

aestimationes are outside the Church's competence for the same general reason as the workability of techniques is. So "all things connected with the moral law" are within the Church's jurisdiction and competence insofar as there is no kind of human choice that is not subject to moral principles and norms, and there are no moral principles or general norms that are outside the Church's jurisdiction and competence. But, especially in relation to the much more numerous class of principles and norms, namely *affirmative* ones, there are *many questions* concerning the morally right application of moral principles and general norms to particular circumstances (and indeed to many specific kinds of circumstance) that are questions which the Church is *not* equipped to answer authoritatively – except in hypothetical form.[29]

QA made a number of strategic diagnoses – and offered a number of more or less corresponding prescriptions[30] – that (a) included and depended upon judgments about social causalities and likely effects, and (b) were substantially mistaken then, did substantial harm to the repute of the Church with unbelievers and to the confidence of the faithful in the Church's teachings, and have been quietly but thoroughly abandoned by the magisterium. To demonstrate this would overburden this chapter. Suffice it to point to a number of them.

(i) Pervading the encyclical was a high-level analysis of society (at the level of the nation-state) asserting that it should be understood as an organism, in which cells and organs (individuals and groups) can and should cooperate for the common good, with a prospect of unity of judgment and action comparable to the unity of cells and organs in a healthy

judgments about whether the schools held out to them by their local bishop as Christian are in fact morally safe and suitable for promoting rather than undermining their children's education and faith. Nations have an affirmative responsibility to disarm and devote the costs of armaments to just and peaceful development of peoples, but need to make specific judgments about whether doing so would, in the contingent circumstances, result in them being conquered and enslaved or subjected to an inhuman ideology. And so forth.

[29] As already indicated (see at p. 558 above, on hypotheticals/conditionals), a sketch of the form would be: "If the causes operative or likely to operate in this situation are such and such, and the likely effects of choice X are so and so, and the likely effects of choice Y (or not-X) are such and such, then subject to any other similarly contingent responsibilities, you have the responsibility to choose X."

[30] The full title of QA in English, Italian, etc. as stated on the Vatican website in September 2017 says the encyclical is for "reconstruction of the social order," but the Latin says (in line with no. 76) that it is *also* for "perfecting it [that social order] conformably to the precepts of the Gospel," as was stated in the English translation issued by the Holy See simultaneously with the Latin, German, Italian, and French in May 1931: *et ad evangelicae legis normam perficiendo.* Unfortunately, "reconstruction" savors too much of technique, and determining or assessing just how to "perfect" social order necessarily involves many fact-dependent judgments of changing circumstances, including countless assessments of the recalcitrance and pushback from persons with different ideas and competing wills.

body. The whole analogy overlooks the disanalogies between political community and (say) military operations or a one-ship, one-voyage business venture, where in each case there is a single overriding objective that can be achieved and finished off. Political communities, like individual and family life, are schemes of cooperation in the open horizon of "human life as a whole" (as Aquinas puts it), in which there are many legitimately competing goods (not to mention conceptions of good), including process goods (such as fair trial, at the expense of past and future victims of crime; and free elections, at the cost of sophisticated lying and bribery and short-termism).

(ii) *QA* assumed that unsound "organism" analogy, and presupposed also some grave misjudgments, not only about the causes of social and economic breakdown in the 1930s (ascribing too much to the effects of alleged "individualism" and "monopoly power"), but also about the workability and likely working of establishing and empowering "vocational groups." On these defective bases, *QA* strenuously called for such establishment and empowering: call it corporatism, for short. This call extended so far as to offer an account of Italian fascist "syndicalism and corporative organization" (91), an account in which the system's beneficial features and their beneficial effects are crisply stated and firmly approved, before sec. 95 mentions some "fears" and "risks," which are all, however, described as the opinions of "some" and stated, not ratified.

In 1972, Oswald Nell-Breuning, SJ published reflections[31] on the drafting of *QA*, which he ascribed very largely to himself. But nos. 91–95 he ascribed wholly to Pius XI who, he said, drafted them precisely as they now stand in *QA*. About those paragraphs, Fr. Nell-Breuning said (forty years on):

> I read it and was convinced that here the Holy Spirit really was guiding the Pope's pen. I was enthusiastic and . . . found the place where the note fitted in smoothly. It needed only to be translated into Latin (the Italian translation of *QA* contains the original draft of the note – one of the few cases where the text of an encyclical was edited by the Pope himself). This my first opinion did not last very long. What Pius XI wrote to Cardinal Schuster (Milan) about fascism[32] aroused doubts in me as to whether Pius XI really understood the phenomenon

---

[31] Oswald von Nell-Breuning, *Wie sozial ist die Kirch?* (Dusseldorf: Patmos, 1972), 103–120; see note 35 for an English translation of those pages.

[32] This will be a reference to Pius XI, Chirograph Letter to Cardinal Alfredo Ildefonso Schuster (On Italian Catholic Action) (April 26, 1931) (three weeks before *QA*), rejecting (on the basis of an overoptimistic analysis of the actual character of the actual fascist state) fears that the Concordat between Italy and the Holy See was a trap for the Church.

of fascism. Today I am firmly convinced that he did not understand it, that he was not acquainted with the social and political character of fascism ...

It is clear to me today that the insertion of Pius XI's comments on fascism bears the chief blame for the total misunderstanding of the picture of order, or rather outline of a social order, developed in *QA*, which in the German translation is called by the unhappy word "occupational" and in French by "corporatism." This is no excuse for the inadequate delineation that was my responsibility exclusively. On the contrary, I blame myself. I became confident because the Pope did not complain in any way about my exposition; and I blame myself far more because I approved the supplement to it written by him. I lulled myself into a false sense of security and undertook no further reflections.[33]

More broadly, the Fr. Nell-Breuning of 1972 opined that Pius XI, in entrusting to him drafting responsibilities as extensive and single-handed as (according to his 40-year retrospect) he had, was "frighteningly irresponsible."[34] He added: "What is distressing for me now is the thought that even today, apparently, if the occasion arose, they would proceed in a manner similar to that for *QA*."

Nell-Breuning had published a prompt and extensive commentary on *QA* in Germany in 1932, in English translation in 1936.[35] This showed in depth how far the encyclical was committed, not just in nos. 91–95, but in nos. 76 through 110, to analyses and prescriptions that overlook significant realities of the actual (and any foreseeable) social situation. To mention just one: attempts to create vocational groups (he called them vocational corporations) would interpose between functioning enterprises and their working members

[33] Fr. Oswald von Nell-Breuning, "Documentation: The Drafting of Quadragesimo Anno", *Crisis Magazine*, February 1, 1985, www.crisismagazine.com/1985/documentation-the-drafting-of-quadragesimo-anno.
[34] His 1972/1985 statement says:

> Formally, the whole responsibility lay with Fr. Ledochowski [the General of the Society of Jesus], though in fact he depended on me in technical questions. When I think back on it today, it seems to me that such a procedure, that allowed the whole bearing of an official document to be determined by a consultant ... without establishing any counter check worth mentioning, seems frighteningly irresponsible.

It is possible that Nell-Breuning in 1972 oversimplified (and gilded the lily) a bit, but the archive-based account by Johannes Schasching SJ, *Zeitgerecht–zeitbericht: Nell-Breuning und die Sozialenzyklika Quadragesimo anno nach dem Vatikanischen Geheimarchiv* (Bornheim: Ketteler Verlag, 1994) substantially confirms Nell-Breuning's centrality, and supplies (91–148) his first draft to manifest it. (QA's fulsome praise of RN actually moderated Nell-Breuning's draft's, which begins "Licht vom Himmel ... [Leo XIII brought light from heaven ...]".)

[35] Oswald von Nell-Breuning SJ, *Die Soziale Enzyklika* (Cologne: Katholische Tat-Verlag, 1st and 2nd ed. 1932); Bernard W. Dempsey SJ, trans., *Reorganization and Social Economy: The Social Encyclical Developed and Explained* (New York: Bruce, 1936) (451 pages, including the Holy See's English translation of QA).

(not to mention stakeholders such as their suppliers, competitors, and consumers) a layer of power-holders whose existence would present – for what good end is never made apparent – a remarkably easy opportunity for ensuring that each enterprise (with its members), as included in the relevant vocational group (or groups?), would become disruptively entangled willy-nilly in *national* (and international) political movements and struggles, immediately supplying these problematic national phenomena (in the limiting case, Nazi and Communist parties) with a whole new arena to *politicize* in all the pejorative senses of that word. For this disruptiveness the only remedy would be the open authoritarianism of (if not Italian fascism) those "corporative" states that, thinking to be loyal Catholics, took *QA* to heart: Austria (March 1934 until its destruction by Hitler four years later), Portugal (1933–1968), and falteringly Vichy France (1940–1944); in the first two countries very adverse political circumstances rendered scarcely available desirable alternatives to this method of avoiding or surmounting the destructive and futile politicization of vocational groups (groups thus rendered futile or worse) by the device of closing down national political controversy and competition.

Since the death of Pius XII, by whose views (as expressed in 1930 as papal nuncio in Germany) Fr. Nell-Breuning claimed to have been inspired,[36] the

---

[36] He refers to:

> the expression used by Nuncio Pacelli [later Pius XII] at the Freiburg Catholic Convention of 1929, "From the confrontation between classes to the harmonious cooperation of professions" (*QA*, no. 81), on which this whole section of the encyclical is "suspended." Fr. Ledochowski was not prepared, without further consideration, to introduce these thoughts into the encyclical. I had to intercede strongly for it. I recall chiefly his doubting question, "How long do you think it will take to achieve this?" and my disarming reply, "It will never be achieved; it is much too sensible for people ever to do it. "When I consider today, that this heart of the encyclical (for that it is, without any doubt) has brought about misunderstandings and has been disparaged in the widest circles of Catholic social teaching as "statist" or "restorative" [restorationist] or "reactionary." etc. – quite apart from the political decisions referring to it and their consequences (Austria, Portugal) – then the thought is for me oppressive that without my insistence this section would surely not have been included in the encyclical. What I wanted to say in it and what I am convinced it does say unambiguously, I considered afterwards as before to be progressive, liberal, definitely democratic, against individualism and against statism; in short, correct.

> But the quoted words of no. 81 are followed immediately by "82. The social policy of the State, therefore, must devote itself to the re-establishment of the Industries and Professions." If Nell-Breuning really believed that the "heart of the Encyclical" was, as he said to his superior, an actually unattainable ideal goal (something he expressly denies in his 1932 commentary, 6; Dempsey ed. 6), he should not have written the document as what it is, a call to immediate politico-social action by Catholic activists addressed like soldiers "undertaking with Us the solution of the social problems" (no. 138; likewise 141, 143) and all who might be persuaded by its teaching.

magisterium has marginalized and covered over the corporatism of *QA*.[37] But has it responded to its mistakes with the clarity and resolution needed?

One can hardly say so. Obscuring the limits of the Church's teaching competence – a competence that does not extend to secure its categorical (nonhypothetical) judgments about contingent facts, causalities, and probabilities – the magisterium has taken to saying that "the Church is an expert in humanity."[38] This is true, so far as it means only that:

> As an expert in humanity, she is able to understand man in his vocation and aspirations, in his limits and misgivings, in his rights and duties, and to *speak a word of life* that reverberates in the historical and social circumstances of human existence.[39]

But it is not true, so far as it means that popes or bishops are expert in diagnosing the causes, let alone the probable further consequences, of political, economic, and other social realities such as the French Revolution; the Italian fascist movement; the creation of statewide vocational groups; the collapse of Italian Christian Democratic and associated parties; the teachings[40] and psychology of the dominant religion of today's immigrants to Europe; the wide availability of smartphones but not air conditioning in Africa; the socioeconomic, political, and moral effects of mass migration in general and of mass migration into Europe; the long-term effects of nuclear deterrence; the likely effects of unilaterally abandoning it; and countless other matters likely to affect decisively, one way or another, the social contexts in which affirmative moral responsibilities of individuals and

---

[37]   *MM*, no. 37 briefly recalls it as an idea of Pius XI, while Vatican II makes no reference to it. John F. Cronin SS, "Forty Years Later: Reflections and Reminiscences," *American Ecclesiastical Review* 164 (1971): 310–318, describes how Catholic activists in the United States, under his leadership, promoted *QA* vocational groups under the name "industry councils"; how he was chided in the 1950s by the Jesuit Frs. Nell-Breuning and Gundlach for taking the encyclical's teachings on family wage and on vocational groups too "like biblical fundamentalists" (313) if not for misinterpreting them totally (by seeking to apply them outside Germany and Italy?; see 313–314); and how the whole matter, like Catholic Social Teaching at large, had faded away by 1971.

[38]   Paul VI, Encyclical Letter *Populorum progressio* (On the Development of Peoples) (1967), no. 13; Paul VI, "Address to the United Nations" (October 5, 1965); SRS, nos. 7 and 41; Benedict XVI, "Angelus Message" (July 12, 2009): "The Church does not have technical solutions to present, but, as an expert in humanity, she offers to everyone the teaching of the sacred Scripture on the truth about man and proclaims the Gospel of Love and justice."

[39]   *CSDC*, no. 61 (emphasis added).

[40]   How could it be a function of bishops to teach what propositions do or do not belong to another religion? A Catholic who has carefully investigated the facts is consequently free to judge that the statement in Francis, Apostolic Exhortation *Evangelii gaudium* (2013), no. 253, that "authentic Islam and the proper reading of the Koran are opposed to every form of violence" is erroneous; and may rightly reflect: error about facts of this kind is liable to be very dangerous for peace and justice, for the faithful, and for evangelization.

groups have to be discharged with faith, hope, and love and in accordance with *all* moral principles and norms, both negative and affirmative.

Increasingly, the magisterium says that its social teachings, right down to fact-dependent particulars, "read the signs of the times"[41] and are "guided by the Holy Spirit."[42] For the reasons explained in this section, statements such as these do not require faithful Roman Catholics to set aside this section's conclusions[43] (or the proposals set out in the next section). They are conclusions founded on the very structure of all practical reasoning, and on the established meaning[44] of the Church's doctrine about what kinds of propositions its true doctrine includes.

---

[41]   GS, no. 4; *PP*, no. 13; *SRS*, no. 7.

[42]   *SRS*, no. 1:

> The Popes have not failed to throw fresh light by means of those messages upon new aspects of the social doctrine of the Church. As a result, this doctrine, beginning with the outstanding contribution of Leo XIII and enriched by the successive contributions of the Magisterium, has now become an updated doctrinal "corpus." It builds up gradually, as the Church, in the fullness of the word revealed by Christ Jesus and *with the assistance of the Holy Spirit* (cf. Jn 14:16, 26; 16:13, 15), *reads events as they unfold* in the course of history. She thus seeks to lead people to respond, with the support also of rational reflection and of the human sciences, to their vocation as responsible builders of earthly society. [Emphasis added]

> CCC, no. 2422: "The Church's social teaching comprises a body of doctrine, which is articulated as the Church interprets events in the course of history, *with the assistance of the Holy Spirit*, in the light of what has been revealed by Jesus Christ" [*Sollicitudo rei socialis*, nos. 1, 41]. *SRS*, no. 41 is perhaps the most extended effort of the papal magisterium to say what CST is. Neither it, nor *SRS* 1's reference to the assistance of the Holy Spirit promised "in all things" by Christ to the apostles (*John* 12 and 16), can supersede the Church's sober doctrine about the reality and limits of its infallibility and about the graduated authority (presumptive reliability) of its teachers' pronouncements: see note 44 below.

[43]   E.g., Francis, "Message of His Holiness Pope Francis for the 104th World Day of Migrants and Refugees" (August 15, 2017): "the lamentable situation of many migrants and refugees fleeing from war, persecution, natural disasters *and poverty* ... is undoubtedly a 'sign of the times' which I have tried to interpret, with the help of the Holy Spirit, ever since my visit to Lampedusa on 8 July 2013." There follow many injunctions, such as: "the principle of the centrality of the human person ... obliges us to always prioritize personal safety over national security." These injunctions all need limitation and interpretation to be made compatible with Christian moral teaching and common sense, and need to be supplemented by teaching, here (unlike in analogous teachings by or under John Paul II and Benedict XVI) entirely absent, about the responsibilities of would-be fleers from poverty toward their own people and toward the law and common good of the countries they plan to live in or off by stealth or *fait accompli*. (It is integral to the duty of a bishop that he "advocate obedience to just laws and reverence for legitimately constituted authorities," Vatican II, Decree *Christus Dominus* (On the Pastoral Office of Bishops) (1965), no. 19.)

[44]   See Vatican II, Dogmatic Constitution *Lumen gentium* (Light of the Nations) (1964), no. 25. The aspect of concern here is summarized accurately enough in the CSDC, no. 80 (which in turn is summarizing the Congregation for the Doctrine of the Faith, Instruction *Donum*

IV

What, then, should pastors and lay people think and do about CST? Here are seven proposals.

1. *Popes and other pastors should generally state only its timeless moral norms and general moral principles; if they teach anything beyond these as CST, it should always be in **hypothetical** form. Pastors should generally not propose even hypothetical CST teachings without first having every disputable question of economic causality, other social consequences, or natural–scientific facts, carefully and even-handedly **debated** in their presence by competent lay Catholics who hold opposing opinions about those matters.*

Pastors should treat CST as a part, and scarcely a distinct part, of the body of moral truths that, as both inherent requirements of reason and[45] revealed commandments of God, the Church's pastors must to the end of time teach to the faithful and unbelievers alike. The Church's pastors should more or less completely abandon attempts to *teach* diagnoses of the current causes of the evils that afflict their societies and humanity as a whole, and attempts to teach that the Church has "solutions"[46] to those supposed causes.

Veritatis on the Ecclesial Vocation of the Theologian (1990), nos. 16–17, 23): *"Insofar as it is part of the Church's moral teaching, the Church's social doctrine has the same dignity and authority* ... The doctrinal weight of the different teachings and the assent required are determined by the nature of the particular teachings, *by their level of independence from contingent and variable elements"* (second emphasis added). Anyone who concludes from (or who intends to imply in) statements such as the Message of August 15, 2017 (see preceding footnote) that Catholics must hold the proposition that it would be wrong to institute policies intended to reduce migration from Africa and Asia to Europe to negligible numbers, using only means compatible with the negative exceptionless moral norms taught by the Church, is certainly mistaken about what Catholics must hold, since the proposition cannot be affirmed without reliance on premises about circumstances and consequences that are almost as entirely dependent on "contingent and variable elements" as, for example, Pius XI's mistaken affirmations about Italian Fascism and its variety of corporatism. All that is certain is that the Holy Spirit always helps the magisterium to avoid teaching *definitively* (see *Lumen gentium*, no. 25) any proposition contrary to Catholic faith and morals.

45 *Romans* 2:12–15.

46 Cf. (among numerous examples) MM, nos. 220, 223, 225:

> [T]he Church ... has formulated, particularly over the past hundred years ... a social doctrine which points out with clarity the sure way to social reconstruction. The principles she gives are of universal application, for they take human nature into account, and the varying conditions in which man's life is lived. They also take into account the principal characteristics of contemporary society, and are thus acceptable to all ... 223 ... it should be taught as part of the daily curriculum in Catholic schools of every kind, particularly seminaries ... 225 ... the best way of demonstrating the truth and efficacy of this teaching is to show that it can provide the solution to present day difficulties.

Instead, pastors should encourage lay believers to undertake such diagnoses and pursue remedies that are fully compatible with their negative and affirmative moral duties, carefully taught by pastors precisely as true moral norms and principles. Pastors and laity alike should constantly remind themselves (and, where appropriate, others) that, *because* the diagnosing of causalities, effects and side-effects, risks and probabilities is an inherently difficult and often uncertain matter, it is entirely possible for informed and well-catechized Catholics in good faith to hold *diametrically opposed views on, say, climate change, migration policy, sentencing policy, healthcare policy, the organization of employment, laws of inheritance and taxation*, and so on, while respecting all relevant moral principles and norms.

The urgent duty to be informed by and genuinely respectful of these principles and norms – a duty scandalously neglected by many Catholics in public life – can be reinforced by pastors who carefully and even-handedly formulate their teaching of affirmative moral norms and responsibilities in hypothetical form. For example:

> *If* you believe that there is a significant probability that humanly caused emissions of CO_2 will so raise the Earth's temperatures that a decision to accept the probable bad effects of that occurring, considered in relation to (i) other means of alleviating those effects, (ii) the good effects of increased temperature, and (iii) the bad effects of restricting or counteracting CO_2 (especially bad and certain effects on the vulnerable and impoverished here and now) would be disrespectful of human dignity and justice, and of the subhuman natural world, **then** you should be prepared to support efforts to restrict or counteract emissions *provided* you are satisfied that the efforts you support are not being adapted to the collateral purpose of instituting a universal religion to replace Christian faith and/or a world government disrespectful of the rights of parents and children and other aspects of the moral law and less amenable to correction than national governments are . . .

and so forth, or similarly.

2. *Teach the true perennial rights and responsibilities of the faithful (and of other persons).*

By the 1980s the NCCB and US Catholic Conference of Bishops had taken to issuing every year over 160 pages about social matters, and the flood has not receded. This sort of practice should come to be regarded as an abuse, or at least as a well-intentioned practice that proved most inopportune and obstructive of the Church's primary mission, evangelization. Ten pages a year would more than suffice, if at the same time the clergy and laity were being insistently catechized about the whole of the Church's moral doctrine.

Thus pastoral teaching should be relatively little concerned with formulating fact-dependent contingent policy recommendations, even in the
contingent form just sketched about supposed dangerous levels of anthropogenic global warming. In the field of CST, pastors' primary concern
should be to *inform* and *animate* the consciences of the faithful by
preaching and teaching (1) the simple fundamentals of vocation, and
the vocational responsibilities of those who earn or inherit resources of
the kind needed to discharge their vocational responsibilities as parents,
children, neighbors, village, town or city dwellers and voters, and as
citizens, and then, too, as members of a worldwide humanity now able
to observe, at a distance, the struggles and dangers of many and to assist
concretely only at most a few (though many more by coordination with
other holders of resources); and (2) straightforward, perennially valid
teaching about the right to hold property (resources held with the right
to exclude others from it) for one's legitimate vocational purposes and
responsibilities, a right of exclusion overridden only in circumstances of
extreme necessity, but permanently qualified by a strict duty to distribute
(via taxation and/or charitable giving) *all* one's *superflua*, all holdings
beyond what one needs to discharge one's vocation.

Without such clear, sober teaching about obligation and entitlement,
pastoral presentation of CST brings the faithful to thinking that *whatever*
they do, they have deeply sinfully neglected the poor and will be goats
at the Last Judgment – so that for them the Gospel is depressing news,
too burdensomely demanding, morally too fanatical to be really
believable.[47]

---

[47] This adds to their temptation to believe (often reassured in this by misguided pastors) that
there will be no such last judgment, since *whatever* they do, everybody is going to heaven,
since "all creatures are moving forward with us and through us to a common point of arrival,
which is God, in that transcendent fullness where the risen Christ embraces and illumines *all
things*," in "the universe which *with us will share* in unending plenitude … in which *each
creature*, resplendently transfigured, will take its rightful place." Francis, Encyclical Letter
Laudato si' (On Care for Our Common Home) (2015), nos. 86, 243 (emphasis added).
Contrast the final verses of the real *Laudato si'*, St Francis of Assisi's "Canticle of the
Creatures" (partially quoted in sec. 1 of the encyclical, more fully in *CCC*, no. 344), verses
added by the saint on his deathbed (and quoted in *CCC*, no. 1014): "Praised be You, my Lord,
through our Sister Bodily Death, from whom no one living can escape. Woe to those who die
in mortal sin. Blessed are those whom death shall find in Your most holy will." Contrast also
Leo XIII, *RN*, no. 21: "God has not created us for the perishable and transitory things of earth,
but for things heavenly and everlasting; He has given us this world as a place of exile, and not as
our abiding place."

3. *Teach CST integrally with the Church's moral teachings on sex, marriage, and family, and all other aspects of living a Christian life, and leave the applicability and implementation of the teaching to those concerned.*

There is of course a distinction between individual life, living in the marital society of the family, and living in civil society with its wider range of economic, associational, political, and international relationships. But there are many profound interconnections between these levels on which persons – who, after all, are (under God) the essential sources of all action including social actions – deliberate, choose, and act. It is artificial and hazardous to separate the Church's teachings in the way that has become institutionalized in the Roman Curia's separate organs for marriage (and family), and for justice (and peace and development).[48]

And that institutionalization is itself very questionable.[49] The mission of the Church and of the successor of Peter is essentially to evangelize. It is daily more obvious that that mission is faltering, and that the energies

---

[48] As from January 1, 2017 the organ established after Vatican II to deal with Justice and Peace is replaced with the Dicastery for Promoting Integral Human Development, which:

> expresses the Holy See's concern for issues of justice and peace, including those related to migration, health, charitable works and the care of creation,

and whose constitution says it may be constituted entirely of lay people and:

> studies the social teaching of the Church and works to make it widely known and implemented, and so that social, economic and political relations are increasingly imbued with the spirit of the Gospel;

and:

> collects information and research in the areas of justice and peace, the development of peoples, the promotion and defense of human dignity and human rights, such as rights pertaining to work, including that of minors; the phenomenon of migration and the exploitation of migrants; human trafficking and enslavement; imprisonment, torture and capital punishment; disarmament and arms control as well as armed conflicts and their effects on the civilian population and the natural environment (humanitarian law).

As from the same date the former Council for the Laity and the Council for the Family are replaced by a Dicastery for the Laity, Family, and Life, which:

> is competent in matters that pertain to the Apostolic See regarding the promotion of life, the apostolate of the lay faithful, the pastoral care of the family and its mission according to God's plan and for the safeguard and support of human life.

[49] The author of these proposals was for about forty years a part of this institutional framework, as Consultor to and then Member of the Pontifical Commission *Iustitia et Pax*, a Member of the International Theological Commission, a Member of the Pontifical Academy *Pro Vita*, and involved some of that time also with comparable organs of the Conference of Bishops of England and Wales.

of pastors are misdirected when directed toward matters that should be the concern of lay associations that act on their own responsibility, are animated by CST and by saintly exemplars, and are resolved to adhere to the negative principles and norms of Catholic moral teaching and the affirmative responsibilities appropriate to their various specific missions. Such undertakings need plenty of information about needs, causalities both natural and social, and circumstances. But why should this be being collected and studied by or on behalf of clerical bureaucrats or even (save in exceptional, limited instances) by or on behalf of bishops and their staff? Bishops do indeed need to attend constantly to, and clearly teach, the moral implications of the Gospel, and need the competent assistance of clerics in that responsibility. But since moral teaching on most of the matters in CST should be in hypothetical form, bishops need not and therefore should not attempt to replicate the information-gathering and reflective and deliberative engagements of lay people and associations in their role of making categorical (and then actual!) what was hypothetical. The recently established Roman dicasteries, like their predecessors, should be abolished, along with the Pontifical Academies of Science, of Social Science, and for Life. As the wealth of experience since *Rerum novarum* has convincingly shown, all are (very expensive) distractions from the saving mission of the successors of the apostles, including that mission's particular involvement with the poor.

CST is a part of the doctrine of the faith. The only dicastery needed for unfolding Catholic teaching is a perhaps somewhat enhanced Congregation for the Doctrine of the Faith.[50] *All the essentials of CST*

---

[50] The Holy See needs other dicasteries to assist the Roman Pontiff in governing the Church as (in the spiritual domain) a complete society. In these reflections and proposals it is *teaching*'s content and dissemination that is addressed. But it seems right to add this: just as the papacy's extremely unwilling surrender (*de facto* in 1870) of its secular power over the Papal States of Italy is now welcomed by the Church as freeing up the popes for teaching, including CST, so too the Church and its essential spiritual mission would be freed of significant burdens and abuses by the abolition of the Secretariat of State and the cessation of the Holy See's dealings with states and international organizations as a state or quasi-state, the abolition of the Diplomatic Service of the Holy See, and the withdrawal of diplomatic functions from any prelates or other clerics sent to countries or regions to represent and inform the Holy See about ecclesiastical matters in that country or region. The entanglement of the Holy See in secular affairs is one among other causes of its ever-increasing overreach in propagating fact-dependent CST as if it were within its spiritual power to make nonhypothetical judgments about the application of affirmative moral norms to contingent circumstances; its withdrawal from secular affairs would markedly limit the temptation to continue (let alone exacerbate) this overreach.

can be set out in less than a dozen pages, and should be.[51] And then these should be preached and insisted upon, keeping priestly and episcopal preaching free from all usurpation of the lay role of forming reasonable judgments about the facts, causalities, trends, and consequences at stake in applications of all the affirmative responsibilities commanded by the Lord and taught by the Church.

4. *Teach moral obligations evenhandedly.*

Removed from the unsustainable (because theologically only questionably legitimate) context of Church campaigns predicated on disputable judgments about facts, causalities, and probabilities, magisterial teaching will again have to include clear reference to the duties of the poor as well as the rich – to the crimes and sins that can be committed by the poor in stealing goods, or states, or social welfare and its underlying taxes from the rich – as CST used to do (see *Rerum novarum*[52]) before it was hollowed out into the big-vision campaigning and politicking (prime examples: *Quadragesimo anno*, *Populorum progressio*, and *Laudato sí*) for "construction" of a "better world."

And it cannot be said that such evenhandedness contradicts the "preferential option for the poor." The *Catechism of the Catholic Church*, which

---

[51] See, e.g., Lawler, Wuerl, and Lawler, *The Teaching of Christ: A Catholic Catechism for Adults* (1975; 5th ed. 2005), ch. 21. That chapter was largely written by the author in collaboration with Germain Grisez, who went on to expound theologically the whole of Catholic moral teaching, with CST integrated into vol. 2: *The Way of the Lord Jesus*, 2. *Living a Christian Life* (Quincy: Franciscan Press, 1993), now conveniently online http://twotlj.org/G-2-V-2.html; supplemented by vol. 3 *Difficult Moral Questions* (Quincy: Franciscan Press, 1997), http://twotlj.org/G-3-V-3.html. These two volumes, especially *Living a Christian Life*, should be a first resort for anyone seriously interested in understanding CST in depth. Much in the present essay is there anticipated, if only in some respects rather implicitly: see especially vol. 2 chs. 5C, 6G, and 11C.

[52] RN, no. 2 ("the relative rights and mutual duties of the rich and the poor"); fundamental regulations (1903) of Pius X (n. 25 above):

VII. The following are obligations of justice binding on the proletariat and the working-man: To perform fully and faithfully the work which has been freely and, according to equity, agreed upon; not to injure the property or outrage the person of masters; even in the defense of their own rights to abstain from acts of violence, and never to make mutiny of their defense.

VIII. The following are obligations of justice binding on capitalists: To pay just wages to their workingmen; not to injure their just savings by violence or fraud, or by overt or covert usuries; not to expose them to corrupting seductions and danger of scandal; not to alienate them from the spirit of family life and from love of economy; not to impose on them labor beyond their strength, or unsuitable for their age or sex.

nowhere speaks of such an "option," speaks of the "preferential love" that all of us must have for God, for the Lord, and for the sick, and for those oppressed by poverty.[53] The "preferential option for the poor" spoken of in CST[54] is an extension or application of this same *imitatio Christi*; it includes among the poor for this purpose many of the rich: those, for example, who are poor in culture or religion.[55] It was part of the Church's tradition and catechetics, e.g., as corporal works of mercy,[56] long before the emergence of CST as such, which in this matter has truly added little or nothing to the tradition.

5. *Theologians: Show how CST in each part and development is founded in Catholic doctrine and harmonious with prior magisterial teaching.*

The faithful being catechized with CST are entitled to know how it is rooted in prior magisterial teaching. How can they be expected to treat as authoritative for their own lives and commitments a teaching that is promulgated in documents that, though hundreds of paragraphs long, display no interest in showing how they are connected with – and not at odds with – prior conciliar, papal, or episcopal pronouncements about the same modern world?

So the invocations of CST in *Laudato sí* are seriously deficient in neglecting to mention – let alone to show how the new encyclical can be reconciled with – the particular teaching of Vatican II (and behind it the whole Catholic tradition) that John Paul II made central to his teaching on that foundational element in CST, the dignity that *human* beings each have because man is "the only creature on earth that God has willed for its own sake."[57] More generally, this encyclical fails to indicate how far the Church

---

[53] See *CCC*, nos. 311, 1503, 1586, 2589.
[54] *SRS*, no. 42; *CSDC*, no. 182.
[55] *CCC*, no. 2444; *CSDC*, no. 184.
[56] *Baltimore Catechism* (1885) "221. ... The chief means by which we satisfy God for the temporal punishment due to sin are: Prayer, Fasting, Almsgiving, all spiritual and corporal works of mercy, and the patient suffering of the ills of life. 222. ... The chief spiritual works of mercy are seven: To admonish the sinner, to instruct the ignorant, to counsel the doubtful, to comfort the sorrowful, to bear wrongs patiently, to forgive all injuries, and to pray for the living and the dead. 223. The chief corporal works of mercy are seven: To feed the hungry, to give drink to the thirsty, to clothe the naked, to ransom the captive, to harbor the harborless, to visit the sick, and to bury the dead." See also *CCC*, no. 2447 (in which the list of "essentials" omits prayer and ransom).
[57] *GS*, no. 24.3; John Paul II, Encyclical Letter *Centesimus annus* (On the 110th Anniversary of *Rerum novarum*) (1991), no. 53; *CCC*, nos. 356, 358, 1703, 2258; *CSDC*, nos. 34, 96. *LS*, no. 65 cites *CCC*, no. 357, but not 356 or 358; this unexplained omission weakens no. 65's account of human dignity, as if the Church cannot have an ecological concern for subhuman creatures while at the same time recognizing the profoundly greater dignity of human beings.

had always acknowledged manifold human responsibilities in respect of the rest of creation,[58] even while it maintained and proclaimed the teaching of its Scripture and Tradition that the earth was made to be *subjected* by human persons to their *use*, they being the only earthly creatures that God willed for their own sakes.

6. *Pastors: Teach the fundamentals of the faith.*

A. *Do not suspend CST from a vision of earthly progress.* Whatever the sources of such a vision – and there are various sources, old and new-fangled, in the marketplace of ideas and dreams – they all, along with a simple optimism, are contradicted by the words of the Lord, integrated into the Church's doctrine as summarized in CCC, no. 675:

> Before Christ's second coming the Church must pass through a final trial that will shake the faith of many believers. [*Luke* 18.8: "when the Son of Man comes, will he find faith on earth?"; *Matt.*24.12: "And because wickedness is multiplied, most men's love will grow cold."] ... 676. The Antichrist's deception already begins to take shape in the world every time the claim is made to realize within history that messianic hope which can only be realized beyond history through the eschatological judgment. The Church has rejected even modified forms of this falsification of the kingdom ... especially the "intrinsically perverse" political form of a secular messianism. [Pius XI, *Divini redemptoris* (1937),[59] condemning [no. 8] the "false mysticism" of this "counterfeit of the redemption of the lowly"; cf. GS, nos. 20–21].

The basis of CST is love (of neighbor as oneself, in the last analysis for love of God). It is not any kind of worldly hope that things will come right in the long run. For even if, as is most probable, they will not go well, we each must do what we can to avert injustice, first of all our own. For the measure of justice is, again, that supreme principle of earthly practical reason: love of neighbor as oneself, and so doing to and for others as you would have them do to and for you, for the sake of your common and mutual flourishing: "the common good."

B. *Christianity is divine revelation rather than an "experience" of "faith."* There is an even deeper consideration. Since Vatican II's close in 1965, pastors have neglected their overriding duty to teach that the Gospel is true, that Christ did, for example, really feed the 5,000 and again the

---

[58]   See, e.g., the assemblage in CCC, nos. 226, 339, 344, 2415–2418.

[59]   Pius XI, Encyclical Letter *Divini redemptoris* (On Atheistic Communism) (1937).

4,000[60] and thereby foreshadow his institution of the Eucharist as a permanent extension of his vocational choice: to be faithful to his mission; and for that fidelity to suffer and die the most humiliating of deaths; but rise bodily from the grave on the third day, show himself to disciples, converse with them, be touched by them, eat fish and bread with them; and in all these ways and more, open before us the prospect of a Kingdom (beginning here but by miraculous divine power and grace extending to eternity in the divine presence) in which good works will be found to have been fruitful.

But priests who as Scripture scholars openly deny much, most, or all of this (and who contemptuously disdain those who question the reasoning behind those denials) have again and again been promoted, notwithstanding, to very high positions of responsibility for teaching the Church's Scriptures and representing to the faithful the Catholic attitude to the Scriptures and to the Church as their guardian. *Unsurprisingly, the faithful whom Leo XIII, Pius XI, and John XXIII could summon – indeed in increasing numbers – to Catholic Action and the promotion of CST have, in large majority (especially in Europe[61]), simply walked away from the promotion, the practice and indeed the holding of the faith.* The response of high pastors has been to multiply calls to the self- and family-sacrificial application of CST, while preserving a chilled silence about the very public revolt

---

[60]   *MM*, no. 5:

> When He said "I am the way, and the truth, and the life," ... it was doubtless man's eternal salvation that was uppermost in His mind, but He showed His concern for the material welfare of His people when, seeing the hungry crowd of His followers, He was moved to exclaim: "I have compassion on the multitude" [Mark 8:2]. And these were no empty words of our divine Redeemer. Time and again He proved them by his actions, as when he miraculously multiplied bread to alleviate the hunger of the crowds. Bread it was for the body but it was intended also to foreshadow that other bread, that heavenly food for the soul, which he was to give them on the night before he suffered.

See Mark 6:35–44 (5,000); Mark 8:1–9 (4,000); Mark 8:18–20 (two miracles, not one).

[61]   Especially in German-speaking countries, where since 1979 *Das Neue Testament* signed and circulated by their main bishops states that we know Matthew and Luke were written c. AD 80–90 *because* they prophesy (or adjusted Mark in prophesying) the fall of Jerusalem in AD 70 – leaving readers to understand that gospel writers made up events and sayings to fit the situation when they were writing, and that to an indeterminate extent Christianity is made up, make-believe – happy-talk for the poor and the simple-minded.

of their Scripture scholars (most of the teachers of Scripture to priests and bishops) against the foundation of the faith.[62]

CST cannot flourish if proposal A is set aside. It cannot long survive if the facts recalled in B are neglected.[63] Whatever the appearances, CST is likely to be a dead letter in any diocese where there are few priests and lay men and women who hold as really true what is declared in *Dei verbum*, nos. 18 and 19 about the simple historical truth of what the Gospels (while preaching the Lord's theology as apostolically appropriated) actually tell us, eye to eye, was said and done – a truth not because inspired, nor because taught by the Church, but because conveying directly or at one remove the testimony of informed and sincere eyewitnesses.

7. *Keep CST pure of philosophy (and pseudo-philosophy) not solidly confirmed in Scripture and Tradition.*

The articulation of the principle of subsidiarity in QA was legitimate because it had been worked up in scholarly writing and discourse among thinkers strongly rooted in the Church's whole doctrinal tradition. Illegitimate is the introduction into the magisterium of the "four principles" announced in *Evangelii gaudium*, no. 221:

---

[62] Vatican II, *Dei verbum* (On Divine Revelation) (1965), no. 18 (with no. 19: on the apostolic authorship and historicity of all parts of the Gospels). Benedict XVI, having declared to the Synod his dismay at the revolt of "priests" against the truth of the Gospels, issued a Post-Synodal Apostolic Exhortation *Verbum Domini* (2010) making no reference to anything like this, or to Vatican II's long-meditated and authoritative teaching in *DVe*, nos. 18–19.

[63] They are everywhere neglected by bishops, who indeed avert their eyes from the obvious facts. Thus in the Post-Synodal Apostolic Exhortation *Ecclesia in Europa* (2003), John Paul II, in line with the Synod, states the reasons for the collapse of Christianity in Europe as follows:

> The great certainties of the faith are being undermined in many people by a vague religiosity lacking real commitment; various forms of agnosticism and practical atheism are spreading and serve to widen the division between faith and life; some people have been affected by the spirit of an immanentist humanism, which has weakened the faith and often, tragically, led to its complete abandonment; one encounters a sort of secularist interpretation of Christian faith which is corrosive and accompanied by a deep crisis of conscience and of Christian moral practice. (no. 47)

This evades the obvious primary causes: the interpretation of the Gospels as anything other than honest eyewitness or eyewitness-derived accounts of real events; and the interpretation of Jesus' information about heaven and hell as myth or symbol. Since 1965, most Catholic writings have one way or another promoted these interpretations. The efforts of Leo XIII, Pius X, and popes before Paul VI to encourage scholars and pastors to show their falsity have been abandoned without explanation.

Progress in building a people in peace, justice and fraternity depends on four principles related to constant tensions present in every social reality. These derive from the pillars of the Church's social doctrine, which serve as "primary and fundamental parameters of reference for interpreting and evaluating social phenomena." (*Compendium*, no. 161)

The citation is misleading, since *Compendium*, no. 161 concerns "the permanent principles of the Church's social doctrine" which are "principles of a general and fundamental character, since they concern the reality of society in its entirety" and are presented by the Church "as the primary and fundamental parameters of reference for interpreting and evaluating social phenomena." They were identified in *Compendium*, no. 160 as "the principles of the dignity of the human person ... the common good; subsidiarity; and solidarity."[64] The *Compendium*'s articulation (which has no magisterial authority as such) is no triumph of clear thinking; but it is recognizably grounded in the magisterial documents of CST since 1891. The "four principles" announced in *Evangelii gaudium*, nos. 221–237 are, however, rooted in nothing but the private quasi-philosophical speculations of Jorge Bergoglio, and are not principles of practical reason, but "postulates"[65] that hover between the status of (questionable and ambiguous) generalizations about human affairs and articulations of simplistic practical-rational priorities among options. In 2010, in an address as Archbishop of Buenos Aires, he said:[66]

To grow as citizens it is necessary to elaborate, at the confluence of the logical categories of society and popular "myths" (?) [*mitiche di popolo*], these four principles: time is superior to space,[67] unity is superior to

---

[64]   *CSDC*, nos. 162–196 gives a slightly different list: (i) the responsibility of everyone for the common good," (ii) the "universal destination" of the goods of the earth (essentially: the duty to distribute one's *superflua*), (iii) the principle of subsidiarity and participation, and (iv) the principle of solidarity.

[65]   See the Italian and Spanish versions of *EG*, nos. 228, 231, which speak of the need to "postulate" the second and third "principles."

[66]   Jorge Mario Bergoglio, *Noi come cittadini. Noi come popolo* (Milan: LEV-Jaca Book, 2013), 68 (my translation). In *EG* "superior to" in the second and third is replaced by "prevails over" and "is more important than." Ambiguity and overreach replaced by ambiguity and overreach. Fr. Juan Carlos Scannone, SJ (a main seminary teacher of his) stated in 2016 that he recalls Fr. Bergoglio using these four principles while they were working together on Jesuit affairs over 40 years ago, in 1974, www.terredamerica.com /2016/03/07/dedicato-bergoglio-anche-se-lui-non-lo-sa-un-nuovo-libro-del-teologo-argentino-juan -carlos-scannone-alla-vigilia-del-terzo-anno-di-pontificato/.

[67]   See now Francis, Encyclical Letter *Lumen fidei* (On Faith) (2013), no. 57; *EG*, nos. 222–225; *LS*, no. 178; Francis, Apostolic Exhortation *Amoris laetitia* (On Love in the Family) (2016), nos. 3, 261.

conflict,[68] reality is superior to the idea,[69] and the whole is superior to the part.[70]

Much could be said; suffice it here to say that the Christian people primarily addressed by CST are entitled not to have imposed upon them propositions so half-baked, statements so obviously open to interpretations orthogonal to the true (and valuable!) principles of Catholic moral teaching, among them the principles of CST. The explanations of them offered cloudily in *EG* only exacerbate the impropriety.

If it was "frighteningly irresponsible" of Pius XI to entrust the drafting of *QA* largely to a 40-year old Jesuit, except for the sections drafted by the pope himself on a fascism poorly understood by him,[71] how much more irresponsible must it be to give over the magisterium to the speculations of a 38-year-old[72] Jesuit, speculations so untested by discourse that only future biographers will be able to unearth their roots in readings but very likely to include, or consist in, Hegelian,[73] Marxist, and other gnoses of the Enlightenment, antipathetic both to authentic revelation and to the philosophies (Plato, Aristotle, etc.) that proved open to that revelation. If, in the meantime, disciplined theological investigation unearths some meaning of the four "postulates" that is fit to be included in CST, then we can conclude that it is that meaning that ought to have been included articulately in these magisterial documents, not the pretended "principles" we actually read there.

8. *Keep in any teaching's foreground Christ's warnings, and promises – his information – about God's new creation, the Kingdom that is beginning in this one irrevocable, unrepeatable lifetime, but is completed only in the world to come, after his Judgment on that lifetime.*

Gaudium et spes, nos. 38–39 made better sense than Pius XI[74] about the relation between this perishable world and the world to come. But it in no

---

[68] See now *LF*, no. 55; *EG*, nos. 226–320; *LS*, no. 198.

[69] See now *EG*, nos. 231–233; *LS*, no. 201.

[70] See now *EG*, nos. 234–237; *LS*, no. 141.

[71] See text and nn. 33–35 earlier in this chapter.

[72] Pope Francis was born in 1936; see n. 66 on his reported appeal to the "principles" in 1974.

[73] Another dubious Hegelian artifact scarcely needed in magisterial documents is "the other," as deployed for example in the address of September 22, 2017 to National Directors of Pastoral Care for Migrants of the Catholic Bishops' Conferences of Europe (see chapter on Globalisation at no. 51): http://w2.vatican.va/content/francesco/en/speeches/2017/september/documents/papa-francesco_20170922_direttori-pastoralimigranti.html. As Comte's neologism "altruism" subtracts from (and adds nothing worthwhile to) the Christian concepts of friendship, charity, and love of neighbor, so "the other" subtracts from ideas of neighbor and person left to us by Christ and the Fathers.

[74] See at n. 27 above.

way obscured the reality and (all things considered) the priority of the latter. Nor did it cover over or even (all things considered) soften the Lord's information about the conditionality of sharing in the Kingdom, and warnings about the fact that, as many have and will, so I too may well be found to have condemned myself to be forever outside it. CST is animated by the enlightened desire, and resolve, to act as the sheep in Jesus' final "parable" act, and not to act or fail to act as the goats do.[75] Pastors who do not really believe that he said it and meant it, or that he worked miracles to show his privileged knowledge of the matter, cannot properly teach CST.

---

[75]   The Church should with prompt clarity repudiate the propositions suggested if not entailed by statements in *LS* (see n. 47 earlier) retailing a pan-Christic Teilhardian universalism; and repudiate equally the complementary proposition asserted more clearly though not magisterially by interview in the Casa Santa Marta that if any fail to reach heaven it is only because they have ceased to exist at all.

Bibliography

32nd General Congregation of the Society of Jesus. "Decree 4." December 2–March 7, 1975.

Acta Synodalia Sacrosancti Concilii Oecumenici Vaticani II. Vol. V, pt. 1. Vatican City: Typis Polyglotis Vaticanis, 1989.

Acta Synodalia Sacrosancti Concilii Oecumenici Vaticani II. Vol. III, pt. 5. Vatican City: Typis Polyglotis Vaticanis, 1975.

Altholz, Josef L. *The Liberal Catholic Movement in England: The "Rambler" and Its Contributors, 1848–1864.* London: Burns & Oates, 1962.

Ambrose of Milan. *De officiis.* Edited by Maurith Testard. Turnhout: Brepols, 2000.

Anderson, David E. "The Religious Sources for Modern Human Rights." *Religion and Ethics Newsweekly.* PBS.org. (January 3, 2017).

Angelini, Fiorenzo Cardinal. "The Pope most quoted by Vatican Council II." In *30 Days* 9. 2008, at www.30giorni.it/articoli_id_19268_l3.htm

Antione, Charles. *Cours d'Économie Sociale.* 6th Edition. Paris: Alca, 1921.

Antonazzi, Giovanni, ed. *L'Enciclica Rerum Novarum: Testo Autentico e Redazioni Preparatorie dai Documenti Originali.* Rome: Edizioni di Storia e Letteratura, 1991.

Antonazzi, Giovanni. *L'Encyclica "Rerum Novarum" e il suo tempo.* Roma: Edizioni di Storia e Letteratura, 1991.

Aquinas, Thomas. *De Regimine Principum.* Leonine Edition, *Opera Omnia* vol. 42, Rome: Editori di San Tommaso, 1979.

Aquinas, Thomas. *Sententia libri Ethicorum.* Leonine Edition, *Opera Omnia* vol. 47, Rome: Editori di San Tommaso, 1969.

Aquinas, Thomas. *Sententia libri Politicorum.* Leonine Edition, *Opera Omnia* vol. 48, Rome: Editori di San Tommaso, 1971.

Aquinas, Thomas. *Summa contra Gentiles.* Leonine Edition, *Opera Omnia* vol. 13–15, Rome: Editori di San Tommaso, 1882.

Aquinas, Thomas. *Summa Theologiae.* Leonine Edition, *Opera Omnia* vol. 5, Rome: Editori di San Tommaso, 1882.

Aradi, Zsolt. *Pius XI: The Pope and the Man.* Literary Licensing, LLC, 2012.

Aristotle. *Metaphysics.* Translated by W. D. Ross. In *The Complete Works of Aristotle: The Revised Oxford Translation.* Edited by Jonathan Barnes. Princeton, NJ: Princeton University Press, 1984.

Aristotle. *Nichomachean Ethics*. Translated by W. D. Ross. In *The Complete Works of Aristotle: The Revised Oxford Translation*. Edited by Jonathan Barnes. Princeton, NJ: Princeton University Press, 1984.

Aristotle. *Physics*. Translated by R. P. Hardie and R. K. Gaye. In *The Complete Works of Aristotle: The Revised Oxford Translation*. Edited by Jonathan Barnes. Princeton, NJ: Princeton University Press, 1984.

Aristotle. *Politics*. Translated by B. Jowett. In *The Complete Works of Aristotle: The Revised Oxford Translation*. Edited by Jonathan Barnes. Princeton, NJ: Princeton University Press, 1984.

Aroney, Nicholas. "Subsidiarity, Federalism and the Best Constitution: Thomas Aquinas on City, Province and Empire." *Law and Philosophy* 26 (2007): 161–228.

Aubert, Roger. *Aspects divers du néo-thomisme sous le pontificat de Léon XIII*. Roma: Ed. 1961.

Aubert, Roger. *Catholic Social Teaching: A Historical Perspective*. Milwaukee, WI: Marquette University Press, 2003.

Aubert, Roger. *Le Pontificat de Pie IX (1846–1878)*. Paris: Bloud et Gay, 1952.

Aubert, Roger. *The Church in an Age of Liberalism*. Translated by Peter Becker. New York: Crossroad, 1981.

Augustine. *The Catholic and Manichaean Ways of Life*. Translated by Donald A. and Idella J. Gallagher (The Fathers of the Church, vol. 56). Washington, DC: The Catholic University of America Press, 1966, xx–128.

Augustine. *The City of God*. Translated by George E. McCracken (Loeb Classical Library Nos. 411–413). Cambridge, MA: Harvard University Press, 1957.

Augustine. *Quaestiones in Heptateuchum*. Corpus Christianorum Series, *Latina Aurelii Augustini Opera*, Pars V. Turnholt: Brepols, 1958.

Ball, Deborah. "Hundreds of migrants believed dead in shipwreck off Libya." *Wall Street Journal*. April 19, 2015, at www.wsj.com/articles/about-700-believed-dead-in-shipwreck-off-libya-says-unhcr-1429432174

Banerjee, Abhijit and Esther Duflo. *Poor Economics*. New York: Public Affairs, 2011.

Barnes, Jonathan. "The just war." In *The Cambridge History of Later Medieval Philosophy: From the Rediscovery of Aristotle to the Disintegration of Scholasticism, 1100–1600*. Edited by Norman Kretzmann, Anthony Kenny, and Jan Pinborg. Cambridge: Cambridge University Press, 1982.

Behr, Thomas C. "Luigi Taparelli D'Azeglio, SJ (1793–1862) and the Development of Scholastic Natural-Law Thought as a Science of Society and Politics." *Journal of Markets and Morality* 6 (2003): 99–115.

Behr, Thomas C. *Social Justice and Subsidiarity. Luigi Taparelli and the Origins of Modern Catholic Social Teaching*. Washington, DC: Catholic University of America Press, 2018.

Bellarmine, Robert. *Opera omnia*. Edited by Justinus Févre. Paris: Vivès, 1870–74.

Benedict XV. *Pacem, Dei munus pulcherrimum*. Vatican City: Vatican Press, 1920.

Benedict XV. *Quod iam diu*. Encyclical Letter. Vatican City: Vatican Press, 1918.

Benedict XVI. "Address at the Inaugural Session of the Fifth General Conference of CELAM." May 13, 2007.

Benedict XVI. "Address during the Celebration of the First Vespers of the First Sunday of Advent 2010." Vatican City: LEV, 2010.

Benedict XVI. "Address in the Reichstag Building." September 2011.

Benedict XVI. "Address in Westminster Hall." September 2010.

Benedict XVI. "Address to the Pontifical Council for Pastoral Care of Migrants and Itinerant People." May 15, 2006.

Benedict XVI. "Address to the Roman Curia." December 22, 2005.

Benedict XVI. *Africae munus*. Apostolic Exhortation.Vatican City: Vatican Press, 2011.

Benedict XVI. *A Reason Open to God*. Edited by John Garvey and J. Steven Brown. Washington, DC: The Catholic University of America Press, 2013.

Benedict XVI. *Caritas in veritate*. Vatican City: Vatican Press, 2009.

Benedict XVI. *Deus caritas est*. Vatican City: Vatican Press, 2005.

Benedict XVI. "Homily for the Solemn Inauguration of the Petrine Ministry." April 24, 2005.

Benedict XVI. *Jesus of Nazareth*. New York: Doubleday, 2007.

Benedict XVI. Letter to the Bishops of Latin America and the Caribbean. June 29, 2007.

Benedict XVI. *Letzte Gespräche mit Peter Seewald*. München: Droemer, 2016.

Benedict XVI. *Light of the World: A Conversation with Peter Seewald*. San Francisco: Ignatius Press, 2010.

Benedict XVI. "Message for the World Day of Peace 2009." Vatican City: LEV, 2008.

Benedict XVI. "Peace and Justice in Crisis." In *Joseph Ratzinger in Communio, vol. I: The Unity of the Church*. Grand Rapids, MI: W. B. Eerdmans Publishing Company, 2010.

Benedict XVI. *Spe salvi*. Vatican City: Vatican Press, 2007.

Benestad, Brian J. *Church, State, and Society. An Introduction to Catholic Social Doctrine*. Washington, DC: Catholic University of America Press, 2011.

Beretta, Simona. "Ordering Global Finance: Back to Basics." In *Catholic Social Thought: Twilight or Renaissance?* Edited by J. S. Boswell, F. P. McHugh, and J. Verstraten. Leuven: University Press, 2000.

Bergoglio, Jorge Mario. *Interviste e conversazioni con i giornalista. Due anni di Pontificato*. Vatican City: LEV, 2015.

Bergoglio, Jorge Mario. *Noi come cittadini. Noi come popolo*. Milan: LEV-Jaca Boo, 2013.

Bhagwati, Jagdish. *In Defense of Globalization*. Oxford: Oxford University Press, 2004.

Bishops Conference of England and Wales. *Choosing the Common Good*. Stokes on Trent: Alive Publishing, 2010.

Bokenkotter, Thomas. *A Concise History of the Catholic Church*. Crown Publishing Group, 2007.

Boudinhon, A. "Laity." In *The Catholic Encyclopedia*. New York: Robert Appleton Company, 2010.

Boyle, Joseph. "Fairness in Holdings: A Natural Law Account of Property and Welfare Rights." In *Natural Law and Modern Moral Philosophy*. Edited by Ellen Frankel Paul, Fred D. Miller, Jr., and Jeffrey Paul. Cambridge: Cambridge University Press, 2001.

Boyle, Joseph. "Natural Law, Ownership and the World's Natural Resources." In *The Journal of Value Inquiry*. 1989.

Boyle, Joseph. "Fairness in Holdings: A Natural Law Account of Property and Welfare Rights." In *Social Philosophy and Policy*. 2001.

Brennan, Patrick McKinley. "Subsidiarity in the Tradition of Catholic Social Doctrine." *Global Perspectives on Subsidiarity*. Edited by Michelle Evans and Augusto Zimmermann. 2014.

Búrca, Gráinne. "The Principle of Subsidiarity and the Court of Justice as an Institutional Actor." *Journal of Common Market Studies* 36 (1998): 214.

Burigana, Riccardo and Giovanni Turbanti. "The Intersession: Preparing the Conclusion of the Council." In *History of Vatican II*, vol. 4, *Church as a Communion: Third Period and Intersession, September 1964–September 1965*. Eds. Giuseppe Alberigo and Joseph A. Komonchak. Maryknoll, NY: Orbis, 2003.

Burke, Thomas Patrick. "The Origins of Social Justice: Taparelli d'Azeglio." *Modern Age* 52 (Spring 2010): 97.

Cahill, Maria. "The Origin of Anti-Subsidiarity Trends in the Regulation of the Family." *International Journal of the Jurisprudence of the Family* 4 (2013): 85.

Cahill, Maria. "Sovereignty, Liberalism and the Intelligibility of Attraction to Subsidiarity." *American Journal of Jurisprudence* 61 (2016): 109.

Cahill, Maria. "Theorizing Subsidiarity: Towards an Ontology-Sensitive Approach." *International Journal of Constitutional Law* 15(1) (2017).

Cajetan, Thomas de Vio. *Commentaria in Secundum Secundae Divi Thomae ad Aquino*. 1518.

Calvez, Jean-Yves, SJ *The Social Thought of John XXIII*: Mater et magistra. Translated by George J. M. McKenzie. Chicago: Henry Regnery, 1964.

Calvez, Yves, SJ and Jacques Perrin, SJ. *The Church and Social Justice: The Social Teaching of the Popes from Leo XIII to Pius XII (1878–1958)*. London: Burns and Oates, 1961.

Calvez, Yves SJ and Jacques Perrin, SJ. *The Church and Social Justice: The Social Teaching of the Popes from Leo XIII to Pius XII (1878–1958)*. Translated by J. R. Kirwan. Chicago: Henry Regnery Co., 1961.

Candeloro, Giogio. *Il Movimento Cattolico in Italia*. Roma: Edizioni Rinascita, 1953.

Carozza, Paolo. "The Problematic Applicability of Subsidiarity to International Law." *American Journal of Jurisprudence* 61 (2016): 51.

Carozza, Paolo. "Subsidiarity as a Structural Principle of International Human Rights Law." *American Journal of International Law* 97 (2003): 38.

Carroll, Michael O. *Pius XII: Greatness Dishonored*. Dublin: Laetare Press, 1980.

Cass, Deborah. "The Word That Saves Maastricht? The Principle of Subsidiarity and the Division of Powers within the European Community." *Common Market Law Review* 29, no. 6 (1992): 1170.

Catechism of the Catholic Church. Libreria Editrice Vaticana. 1997.

Cathrein, Victor, SJ. *Philosophia Moralis in Usum Scholarum*. 5th Edition. Freiburg im Breisgau: Herder, 1950.

CELAM III, Puebla, 1979 (Third Conference of the Latin American Episcopal Council: Conferencia General del Episcopado Latinoamericano). Final Document. 1979.

CELAM IV, Santo Domingo, 1992. Final Document: "Mensaje a Los Pueblos de America Latina," 1992.

Chadwick, Owen. *A History of the Popes 1830–1914*. Oxford: Clarendon Press, 1998.

Chafuen, Alejandro Antonio. *Faith and Liberty: The Economic Thought of the Late Scholastics*, 2nd Edition. Lanham, MD: Lexington Books, 2003.

Chaplin, Jonathan. "Subsidiarity and Social Pluralism." In *Global Perspectives on Subsidiarity*. Springer, 2014. Edited by Michelle Evans and Augusto Zimmermann. 2014.

Chélini, Jean and Joël-Benoît d'Onorio, eds. *Pie XII et la Cité: Actes du Colloque de la Faculté de Droit d'Aix-en-Provence*. Marseille: Presses Universitaires d'Aix, 1988.

Churchill, Winston S. "Zurich Speech." In Blood, Toil, Tears and Sweat: The Great Speeches. Edited by David Canndine. London: Penguin Books, 2007.

Cicero. *Republic*. Translated by Clinton W. Keyes (Loeb Classical Library No. 213). Cambridge, MA: Harvard University Press, 1928.

Clark, Charles M. A. and David A. Zalewski. "Rethinking Finance in Light of Catholic Social Thought." *Journal of Catholic Social Thought* 12 (2015): 19–44.

Clum, Cyrill C., ed. *The Social Teachings of Pope Pius XII: 1956*. Oxford: The Catholic Social Guild, 1958.

Coase, Ronald. "The Regulated Industries: Discussion." *American Economic Review* 54, no. 2 (March 1964): 195.

Code of Canon Law. 1983.

Collins, Ross William. *Catholicism and the Second French Republic, 1848–52*. New York: Columbia University, 1923.

Congar, Yves M. J., OP. *Lay People in the Church*. Translated by Donald Attwater. Westminster, MD: Newman Press, 1962.

Congregation for the Doctrine of the Faith. Considerations regarding proposals to give legal recognition to unions between homosexual persons, 2003.

Congregation for the Doctrine of the Faith. *Iura et bona*. Declaration of Euthanasia, 1980.

Congregation for the Doctrine of the Faith. *Persona humana*. Declaration on Certain Questions Concerning Sexual Ethics, 1975.

Congregation for the Doctrine of the Faith. *Quaestio de abortu*. Declaration on Procured Abortion, 1974.

Congregation for the Doctrine of the Faith. *Dignitas Personae*. Instruction on Certain Bioethical Questions. Vatican City, Vatican Press, 2008.

Congregation for the Doctrine of the Faith. Doctrinal Note on Some Questions Regarding the Participation of Catholics in Political Life, 2002.

Congregation for the Doctrine of the Faith. *Donum Vitae*. Instruction on respect for human life in its origin and on the dignity of procreation, 1987.

Congregation for the Doctrine of the Faith. *Donum veritatis*. Instruction on the ecclesial vocation of the theologian, 1990.

Congregation for the Doctrine of the Faith. *Homosexualitatis problema*. Letter to the Bishops of the Catholic Church on the Pastoral Care of Homosexual Persons, 1986.

Congregation for the Doctrine of the Faith. *Libertatis conscientia*. Instruction on Christian Freedom and Liberation. Vatican City: Vatican Press, 1986.

Congregation for the Doctrine of the Faith. *Libertatis nuntius* Instruction on certain aspects of the "Theology of Liberation". Vatican City: Vatican Press, 1984.

Congregation for the Doctrine of the Faith. Responses to certain questions of the United States Conference of Catholic Bishops concerning artificial nutrition and hydration, 2007.

Congregation for the Doctrine of the Faith. Responses to questions proposed concerning uterine isolation and related matters, 1993.

Congregation for the Doctrine of the Faith. Some considerations concerning the response to legislative proposals on the non-discrimination of homosexual persons, 1992.

Congregation for Bishops. *Apostolorum Successores*. Directory for the Pastoral Ministry of Bishops, 2004.

Coppa, Frank J. *The Modern Papacy since 1789*. London and New York: Longman, 1998.

Coppa, Frank J. *Origins of the Italian Wars of Independence.* New York: Routledge, 1992.

Coulson, John. "Introduction." In *On Consulting the Faithful in Matters of Doctrine.* New York: Sheed and Ward, 1961.

Cronin, John F., SS. "Forty Years Later: Reflections and Reminiscences." *American Ecclesiastical Review* 164 (1971): 310–318.

"Crony Capitalism." *Business Dictionary.com.* www.businessdictionary.com/definition/crony-capitalism.html.

Curci, Carlo Maria. "Il giornalismo modern ed il nostro programma." In *Civiltà Cattolica.* 1850.

Curci, Carlo Maria. "Il Socialismo plebeo ed il volterianismo Borghese." In *Civiltà Cattolica.* 1850.

Curnow, Rohan M. "Which Preferential Option for the Poor? A History of the Doctrine's Bifurcation." *Modern Theology* 31, no. 1 (January 2015): 27–59.

Daniel-Rops, H. *The Church in an Age of Revolution, 1789–1870.* Translated by J. Warrington. London: J. M. Dent & Sons, 1965.

D'Antonio, William V. "Persistence and Change." *National Catholic Reporter.* October 28–November 10, 2011.

Darring, Gerald. "Pope Pius XII, 1939–1958." www.shc.edu/theolibrary/resources/popes_pius12.htm.

Davies, Gareth. "Subsidiarity as a Method of Policy Centralisation." *Hebrew University International Law Research Paper* 11/06 (2006).

Davies, Gareth. "Subsidiarity: The Wrong Idea, in the Wrong Place, at the Wrong Time." *Common Market Law Review* 43 (2006): 63.

Day, Dorothy. *The Long Loneliness: The Autobiography of Dorothy Day.* Garden City, NY: Image Books, 1959.

Delors, Jacques. Address to mark the opening of the 40th academic year of the College of Europe in Bruges, Belgium. October 17, 1989. Available at www.cvce.eu/en/obj/address_given_by_jacques_delors_bruges_17_october_1989-en-5bbb1452-92c7-474b-a7cf-a2d281898295.html

Delos, Joseph-Thomas, OP. "La fin proper de la politique: le bien commun temporal." In *Semaines sociale de France, 25th session, Reims, 1933, La société politique et la pensée chrétienne.* Paris: J. Cabalda, 1933.

Delos, Joseph-Thomas O.P. *La société international et les Principes du Droit public.* Paris: A Pedone, 1929.

Delsol, Chatal. *Le principe de subsidiarité.* Vendôme: Presses Universitaires de France. 1993.

Dempsey, Bernard W., SJ, trans. *Reorganization and Social Economy: The Social Encyclical Developed and Explained.* New York: Bruce, 1936.

Dezza, Paolo. *Alle origini del neo-tomismo.* Milano: Fratelli Bocca, 1940.

Diamond, Martin. "Ethics and Politics: The American Way." In *The Moral Foundations of the American Republic.* Edited by R. Horwitz. Charlottesville: University Press of Virginia, 1997.

Dognin, Paul-Dominique, OP. "La notion thomiste de justice face aux exigences modernes." In *Revue des Sciences Philosophiques et Théologiques.* 1961.

Doino, William. "A Civil Rights Hero Remembers a Pope." In *First Things.* July 30, 2012.

Donagan, Alan. *The Theory of Morality*. Chicago: Chicago University Press, 1977.

Dorr, Donal. *Option for the Poor and for the Earth: Catholic Social Teaching*. Maryknoll, NY: Orbis Books, 2012.

Droulers, Paul, SJ. *Cattolicesimo sociale nei secoli XIX e XX. Saggi di storia e sociologica*. Rome: Edizioni di Storia e Letteratura, 1982.

Droulers, Paul, SJ. "Des éveques parlent de la question ouvrière en France avant 1840." *Revue de l'action populaire* (1961), 442–460.

Droulers, Paul, SJ. "La presse et les mandements sociaux d'éveques français avant 1849." In *Cahiers d'histoire* (1964), 385–397.

Droulers, Paul, SJ. "L'episcopat devant la question ouvrière en France sous la Monarchie de Julliet." *Revue Historique* (1963), 335–362.

Droulers, Paul, SJ. "Un Anglican associationniste-chrétien chez Pie IX en 1847." In *Cattolicesimo sociale nei secoli xix e xx*. Rome: Edizioni di Storia E Letteratura. 1982.

Duroselle, Jean Baptiste. *Les Débuts du Catholicisme Social en France*. Paris: Presses Universitaires de France, 1951.

Easterly, William. *The White Man's Burden*. New York: Penguin, 2006.

Ederer, Rupert J. *Pope Pius XII on the Economic Order*. Scarecrow Press, 2011.

Eissrich, Daniel. "An Economist's View of the Work of Wilhelm Emmanuel von Ketteler and Its Influence on the Encyclical *Rerum novarum*." In *On the Economic Significance of the Catholic Social Doctrine*. Edited by J. Backhaus. Cham, Switzerland: Springer International Publishing, 2017.

Ellis, John Tracy. *The Life of James Cardinal Gibbons, Archbishop of Baltimore, 1834–1921*, Vol. I. Milwaukee: The Bruce Publishing Company, 1952.

Enderle, Georges. "The Option for the Poor and Business Ethics." In *The Preferential Option for the Poor beyond Theology*. Edited by Daniel G. Groody and Gustavo Gutiérrez. Notre Dame: University of Notre Dame Press, 2014.

Estrella, Antonio. *The EU Principle of Subsidiarity and Its Critique*. 2003.

Evans, Andrew. *Whatever Happened to Human Rights?* The Washington Free Beacon. October 11, 2015.

"European Convention on Human Rights." Protocol No. 15. Signed November 4, 1950.

Extraordinary Synod of 1985. *Relatio finalis*. December 8, 1985. www.ewtn.com/library/CURIA/SYNFINAL.HTM.

Farr, Thomas F. "Rescuing Religious Liberty." *Religious Liberty: Proceedings from the 35th Annual Convention of the Fellowship of Catholic Scholars*. Edited by Elizabeth C. Shaw. Fellowship of Catholic Scholars, 2014.

Ferré, Alberto Methol and Alver Metalli. *Il Papa e il Filosofo*. Siena: Cantagalli, 2014.

Finn, Daniel. "Commentary on *Centesimus Annus*." In *Modern Social Teaching, Commentaries and Interpretations*. Edited by Kenneth Himes, OFM. Washington, DC: Georgetown University Press, 2004.

Finn, Daniel. "John Paul II and the Moral Ecology of Markets." *Theological Studies* 59 (1998): 669–670.

Finnis, John. "Absolute Rights: Some problems illustrated." *American Journal of Jurisprudence* 61, no. 2 (2016): 195–215.

Finnis, John. *Aquinas: Moral, Political and Legal Theory*. Oxford: Oxford University Press, 1998.

Finnis, John. "Boundaries." In *Collected Essays of John Finnis vol. III: Human Rights and Common Good*. Oxford: Oxford University Press, 2011.

Finnis, John. "Cosmopolis, Nation States, and Families." In *Intention and Identity*. Oxford: Oxford University Press, 2011.

Finnis, John. "Discrimination between Faiths: A Case of Extreme Speech." In *Extreme Speech and Democracy*. Edited by Ivan Hare and James Weinstein.Oxford: Oxford University Press, 2010.

Finnis, John. "Is Natural Law Theory Compatible with Limited Government?" In *Natural Law, Liberalism, and Morality*. Edited by R. George. New York: Oxford University Press, 1996.

Finnis, John. "Limited Government." In *Human Rights and Common Good, Collected Essays: Volume III*. Oxford: Oxford University Press, 2011.

Finnis, John. "Migration rights." In *Human Rights and Common Good: Collected Essays, Volume III*. Oxford: Oxford University Press, 2011.

Finnis, John. *Moral Absolutes*. Washington, DC: Catholic University of America Press, 1991.

Finnis, John. *Natural Law & Natural Rights*. Oxford: Oxford University Press, 1980, 2011.

Finnis, John. "The Priority of Persons." In *Collected Essays of John Finnis*. Oxford: Oxford University Press, 2011.

Finnis, John. *Religion and Public Reasons*. Oxford: Oxford University Press, 2011.

Finnis, John. "Social Virtues and the Common Good." In *The Truth about God and Its Relevance for a Good Life in Society, Proceedings of the XI Plenary Session of the Pontifical Academy of St. Thomas Aquinas*. Vatican City: Pontifical Academy of St. Thomas Aquinas, 2012.

Finnis, John, Joseph Boyle, and Germain Grisez. *Nuclear Deterrence, Morality and Realism*. Oxford: Oxford University Press, 1987.

Flannery, Kevin L., SJ, and Thomas V. Berg. "Amoris Laetitia, Pastoral Discernment, and Thomas Aquinas." In *Nova et Vetera* 16 (2018): 81–111.

Føllesdal, Andreas. "Survey Article: Subsidiarity." *Journal of Political Philosophy* 6 (1998): 190–218.

Fortin, Ernest. "From *Rerum Novarum* to *Centesimus Annus*: Continuity or Discontinuity." In *Human Rights, Virtue and the Common Good. Untimely Meditations on Religion and Politics, Ernest L. Fortin: Collected Essays*. Edited by Brian Benestad. Lanham: Rowman & Littlefield, 1996.

Fortin, Ernest. "'Sacred and Inviolable': *Rerum Novarum* and Natural Rights." *In Human Rights, Virtue and the Common Good. Untimely Meditations on Religion and Politics, Ernest L. Fortin: Collected Essays*. Edited by Brian Benestad. Lanham: Rowman & Littlefield, 1996.

Fortin, Ernest. "The Trouble with Catholic Social Thought." In *Human Rights, Virtue and the Common Good. Untimely Meditations on Religion and Politics, Ernest L. Fortin: Collected Essays*. Edited by Brian Benestad. Lanham: Rowman & Littlefield, 1996.

Francis. "Address at the Vigil of Pentecost with Ecclesial Movements." May 18, 2013.

Francis. "Address during the conferral of the Charlemagne prize." May 2016.

Francis. "Address to National Directors of Pastoral Care for Migrants of the Catholic Bishops' Conferences of Europe." September 22, 2017.

Francis. "Address to Participants in the Meeting 'Economy of Communion.'" February 4, 2017.

Francis. "Address to the Centesimus Annus Pro Pontifice Foundation." May 25, 2013.

Francis. "Address to the European Parliament." November 25, 2014.

Francis. "Address to the Participants in the Ecclesial Convention of the Diocese of Rome." June 17, 2013.

Francis. *Amoris laetitia.* Apostolic Exhortation.Vatican City: Vatican Press, 2016.

Francis. "Cuba: Point of Encounter." In *Pope Francis Speaks to the United States and Cuba: Speeches, Homilies, and Interviews.* Huntington, IN: Our Sunday Visitor Press, 2015.

Francis. *Evangelii gaudium.* Apostolic Exhortation. Vatican City: Vatican Press, 2013.

Francis. *Laudato si'.* Encyclical Letter. Vatican City: Vatican Press, 2015.

Francis. *Lumen fidei.* Encyclical Letter. Vatican City: Vatican Press, 2013.

Francis. "Message of His Holiness Pope Francis for the 104th World Day of Migrants and Refugees." August 15, 2017.

Francis. *The Name of God Is Mercy: A Conversation with Andrea Tornielli.* New York: Random House, 2016.

Francis. *Open to God, Open to the World.* With Antonio Spadaro. Bloomsbury Continuum, 2018.

Francis. "Press Conference During the Return Flight, Rio de Janeiro-Rome." July 28, 2013.

Franz, Georg. *Kulturkampf. Staat und Katholische Kirke in Mitteleuropa von der Säkularisation bis zum Abschluss des Preussischen Kulturkampfes.* Translated by Ernst and Louise Helmreich. Georg D. W. Callwey, 1954.

Friedman, Milton and Rose Friedman. *Free to choose, A Personal Statement.* New York: Harcourt, 1980.

Gaius. *Institutes.*

Gehring, John. *The Francis Effect: A Radical Pope's Challenge to the American Church.* Rowman & Littlefield, 2015.

Gera, Lucio. "Cultura y dependencia a luz de la reflexión teológica." In *Escritos Teológico-Pastorales de Luio Gera, vol 1: Del Preconcilio a la Conferencia de Puebla (1956–1981).* Edited by Virginia Raquel Azcuy et el. Buenos Aires: Agape Libros-Facultad de Teología UCA, 2006.

Gera, Lucio. "Pueblo, religion del pueblo e iglesia." In *Escritos Teológico-Pastorales de Lucio Gera, vol 1: Del Preconcilio a la Conferencia de Puebla (1956–1981).* Edited by Virginia Racquel Azcuy et al. Buenos Aires: Agape Libros-Facultad de Teología UCA, 2006.

Gerken, John D., SJ. *Toward a Theology of the Layman.* New York: Herder and Herder, 1962.

Gerson, Michael. "A Catholic Test for Politics." *The Washington Post.* February 8, 2011. Available as *Catholic Republicans' Political Beliefs, Challenged by Their Faith* at www.washingtonpost.com/opinions/a-catholic-test-for-politics/2011/02/07/ABXYjZF_story.html?noredirect=on&utm_term=.aa1e58499e7c

Gerwan, Jef Van, SJ. "Global Markets and Global Justice? Catholic Social Teaching and Finance Ethics." In *Catholic Social Thought: Twilight or Renaissance?* Edited by J. S. Boswell, F. P. McHugh, and J. Verstraeten. Leuven: University Press, 2000.

Gillet, M. S., OP. Translator of *Somme Théologique, La Justice.* Volume 1. With notes and appendices by Joseph-Thomas Delos, OP. Paris: Desclée & Cie, 1932.

Gladstone, W. E. "The Vatican Decrees in Their Bearing on Civil Allegiance." In *A Free Church in a Free State? The Catholic Church, Italy, Germany, France, 1864–1914*. Edited by Helmreich. Boston: D. C. Heath and Co., 1964.

Glendon, Mary Ann. *Rights Talk: The Impoverishment of Political Discourse*. New York: Free Press, 1991.

Gregg, Samuel. *Becoming Europe*. New York: Encounter Books, 2013.

Gregg, Samuel. *Challenging the Modern World, Karol Kojtyla/Pope John Paul II and the Development of Catholic Social Teaching*. New York: Lexington Books, 1999.

Gregory XVI. *Mirari vos*. Encyclical Letter. Vatican City: Vatican Press, 1832.

Grice-Hutchinson, Marjorie. *Early Economic Thought in Spain 1177–1740*. London: George Allen & Unwin, 1978.

Grice-Hutchinson, Marjorie. *The School of Salamanca: Readings in Spanish Monetary Theory, 1544–1605*. Oxford: Oxford University Press, 1952.

Grice-Hutchinson, Marjorie. *The School of Salamanca*. Oxford: Clarendon Press, 1952.

Grisez, Germain. *The Way of the Lord Jesus, Vol. 1, Christian Moral Principles*. Chicago: Franciscan Herald Press, 1983.

Grisez, Germain. *The Way of the Lord Jesus, Vol. 2, Living a Christian Life*. Quincy: Franciscan Press, 1993.

Grisez, Germain. *The Way of the Lord Jesus, Vol. 3, Difficult Moral Questions*. Quincy: Franciscan Press, 1997.

Grisez, Germain and Russell Shaw. *Personal Vocation: God Calls Everyone by Name*. Huntington, IN: Our Sunday Visitor, 2003.

Grootaers, Jan. "The Drama Continues Between the Acts: The 'Second Preparation' and Its Opponents." In *History of Vatican II*. Edited by Giuseppe Alberigo and Joseph Komonchak. Maryknoll, NY: Orbis/Leuven: Peters, 1995–2006.

Gudorf, Christine E. *Catholic Social Teaching on Liberation Themes*. Lanham: University Press of America, 1981.

Guerra, Marc. *Liberating Logos: Pope Benedict XVI's September Speeches*. South Bend, IN: St. Augustine's Press, 2014.

Gutiérrez, Gustavo. *Teología de la liberación* (1971).

Habermas, Jurgen and Joseph Ratzinger. *The Dialects of Secularization, On Reason and Religion*. San Francisco: Ignatius, 2006.

Hayek, F. A. *The Road to Serfdom*. Chicago: Chicago University Press, 1944.

Hayek, Frederick. "The Use of Knowledge in Society." In *Individualism and the Economic Order*. Chicago: Chicago University Press, 1948.

Hearder, Harry. *Italy in the Age of the Risorgimento, 1790–1870*. London: Longman, 1983.

Henkel, Christoph. "The Allocation of Powers in the European Union: A Closer Look at the Principle of Subsidiarity." *Berkeley Journal of International Law* 20 (2002): 359–386.

Hirschfeld, Mary L. "Reflection on the Financial Crisis: Aquinas on the Proper Role of Finance." *Journal of the Society of Christian Ethics*, vol. 35.1 (2015): 73–74.

Hittinger, Russell. "The Coherence of the Four Basic Principles of Catholic Social Doctrine: An Interpretation." In *Pursuing the Common Good: How Solidarity and Subsidiarity Can Work Together*. Edited by Margaret S. Archer and Pierpaolo Donati. 2008.

Hittinger, Russell. "Introduction to Modern Catholicism." In *The Teachings of Modern Roman Catholicism on Law, Politics, & Human Nature*. Edited by John Witte, Jr. and Frank S. Alexander. New York: Columbia University Press, 2007.

Hittinger, Russell. "Pope Leo XIII (1810–1903)." In *The Teachings of Modern Roman Catholicism on Law, Politics, and Human Nature*. Edited by John Witte, Jr. and Frank S. Alexander. New York: Columbia University Press, 2007.

Hittinger, Russell. "*Quinquagesimo Ante*: Reflections on *Pacem in Terris* Fifty Years Later." In *The Global Quest for Tranquilitas Ordinis: "Pacem in Terris" Fifty Years Later*. Edited by Mary Ann Glendon, Russell Hittinger, and Marcelo Sánchez Sorondo. Vatican City: Pontifical Academy of Social Sciences, 2013.

Holland, Joe. *Modern Catholic Social Teaching: The Popes Confront the Industrial Age, 1740–1958*. Paulist Press, 2003.

Hollenbach, David, SJ. "The Pope and Capitalism." *America* 1 (June 1991): 591.

Howard, Thomas Albert. *The Pope and the Professor: Pius IX, Ignaz von Döllinger and the Quandary of the Modern Age*. Oxford: Oxford University Press, 2017.

Hünermann, Peter. "The Final Weeks of the Council." In *History of Vatican II*, vol. V, *The Council and the Transition: The Fourth Period and the End of the Council, September 1965–December 1965*. Edited by Giuseppe Alberigo and Joseph Komonchak. Maryknoll, NY and Leuven: Orbis and Peters, 2006.

Hyde, Lewis. *The Gift: Imagination and the Erotic Life of Property*. New York: Vintage Books, 1979.

International Monetary Fund. "Fact Sheet." Available at www.imf.org/About/Factshe ets/Sheets/2016/08/01/16/11/Debt-Relief-Under-the-Heavily-Indebted-Poor-Countries-Initiative?pdf=1.

International Theological Commission. "In Search of a Universal Ethic: A New Look at the Natural Law." (2009). Available at www.vatican.va/roman_curia/congregations/cfaith/cti_documents/rc_con_cfaith_doc_20090520_legge-naturale_en.html.

Irwin, Terence. "The good of political activity." *Aristoteles "Politik" Akten Des XI Symposium Aristotelicum*. Edited by Günther Patzig. Göttingen: Vandenhoeck & Ruprecht, 1990.

Ivereigh, Austen. *The Great Reformer. Francis and the Making of a Radical Pope*. New York: Holt, 2014.

Jacquin, Robert. *Taparelli*. Paris: Lethielleux, 1943.

Jalilian, J., C. Kirkpatrick, and D. Parker. "The Impact of Regulation on Economic Growth in Development Countries: A Cross Country Analysis." In *Regulating Development: Evidence from Africa and Latin America*. Edited by E. Armann. Edward Elgar Publishing, 2006.

Jalilian, H., C. Kirkpatrick, and D. Parker. "The Impact of Regulation on Economic Growth in Developing Countries: A Cross-Country Analysis." *World Development* 35, no. 1 (January 2007): 87–103.

John Paul II. *The Acting Person: Karol Wojtyla*. Translated by Andrzej Potocki. Dorcrecht: D. Reidel, 1979.

John Paul II. "Address to Catholic Jurists, Rome." November 25, 1978.

John Paul II. "Address at the Opening of the Third General Conference of the Latin-American Bishops." 1979.

John Paul II. Ad Limina Address to Polish Bishops. Rome: L'Osservatore Romano, 1987.

John Paul II. *Centesimus annus*. Encyclical Letter. Vatican City: Vatican Press, 1991.

John Paul II. *Christifideles Iaici*. Apostolic Exhortation.Vatican City: Vatican Press, 1988.

John Paul II. *Dominicae cenae*. Encyclical Letter. Vatican City: Vatican Press, 1980.

John Paul II. *Ecclesia in America*. Apostolic Exhortation. Vatican City: Vatican Press, 1999.

John Paul II. *Evangelium vitae*. Encyclical Letter. Vatican City: Vatican Press, 1995.

John Paul II. *Familiaris consortio*. Apostolic Exhortation. Vatican City: Vatican Press, 1981.

John Paul II. *Fides et ratio*. Encyclical Letter. Vatican City: Vatican Press, 1998.

John Paul II. *Laborem exercens*. Encyclical Letter. Vatican City: Vatican Press, 1981.

John Paul II. *Letter to Italian Bishops*. 1994.

John Paul II. *Letter to Nafis Sadik, Executive Director of the United Nations Population Fund, on Preparations for the 1994 Cairo Conference on Population and Development*. Vatican City: Vatican Press, 1994.

John Paul II. *Man and Woman He Created Them, A Theology of the Body*. Translated by Michael Waldstein. Boston: Pauline Books and Media, 2006.

John Paul II. *Memory & Identity*. London: Weidenfeld, 2005.

John Paul II. "Message of John Paul II to the General Assembly of the United Nations," August 22, 1980.

John Paul II. *Novo millennio ineunte*. Encyclical Letter. Vatican City: Vatican Press, 2001.

John Paul II. *Reconciliatio et paenitentia*. Encyclical Letter. Vatican City: Vatican Press, 1984.

John Paul II. *Redemptoris missio*. Encyclical Letter.Vatican City: Vatican Press, 1990.

John Paul II. *Salvifici doloris*. Apostolic Letter. Encyclical Letter.Vatican City: Vatican Press, 1984.

John Paul II. *Sollicitudo rei socialis*. Encyclical Letter. Vatican City: Vatican Press, 1987.

John Paul II. *Tertio millennio adveniente*. Apostolic Letter.Vatican City: Vatican Press, 1994.

John Paul II. *Undocumented Migrants*. Message of Pope John Paul II. July 25, 1995.

John Paul II. *Veritatis splendor*. Encyclical Letter. Vatican City: Vatican Press, 1993.

John Paul II. *Vita consecrata*. Apostolic Exhortation. Vatican City: Vatican Press, 1996.

John XXIII. *Mater et magistra*. Encyclical Letter. Vatican City: Vatican Press, 1961.

John XXIII. *Pacem in terris*. Encyclical Letter.Vatican City: Vatican Press, 1963.

Juncker, Jean-Claude. "Speech before the European Parliament," July 15, 2014. Available at http://europa.eu/rapid/press-release_SPEECH-14-567_en.htm

Kay, John. *Other People's Money: The Real Business of Finance*. New York: Public Affairs, 2015.

Kennedy, Robert G. "The Practice of Just Compensation." *Journal of Religion and Business Ethics* 1 (2010). Available at http://via.library.depaul.edu/jrbe/vol1/iss1/1.

Kennedy, Robert G. "Social Justice, Charity, and Catholic Social Doctrine." In *The Concept of Social Justice*. Edited by C. Wolfe. Forthcoming, St. Augustine's Press.

Kempshall, M. S. *The Common Good in Late Medieval Political Thought*. Oxford: Clarendon Press, 1999.

Kersbergen, Kees van and Bertjan Verdeek. "The Politics of Subsidiarity in the European Union." *Journal of Common Market Studies* 332 (1994): 215.

Kirchoff, Timothy. "Is Pope Francis Right about Traditionalists Who Love the Latin Mass? *America*, September 13, 2017. Available at www.americamagazine.org/faith/2017/09/13/pope-francis-right-about-traditionalists-who-love-latin-mass

Kristol, Irving. "About Equality." In *Commentary*. November 1, 1972. Available at www.commentarymagazine.com/articles/about-equality/

Krueger, Paulus and Theodorus Mommsen, eds. *Corpus Iuris Civilis*. Berlin: Weidmann, 1990–1905.

Kullman, Wolfgang. "Man as a Political Animal in Aristotle." In *A Companion to Aristotle's "Politics."* Edited by David Keyt and Fred D. Miller Jr. Oxford/Cambridge, MA: Blackwell, 1991.

Langan, John P., SJ. "The Christmas Message of Pius XII (1939–1945): Catholic Social Teaching in a Time of Extreme Crisis." In *Modern Catholic Social Teaching: Commentaries and Interpretations*. Edited by Kenneth R. Himes OFM. Washington, DC: Georgetown University Press, 2005.

Latourette, Kenneth Scott. *Christianity in a Revolutionary Age: A History of Christianity in the Nineteenth and Twentieth Centuries. Volume I, The Nineteenth Century in Europe: Background and the Roman Catholic Phase.* New York: Harper & Brothers, 1958.

Lawler, Michael G., Todd A. Salzman, and Eileen Burke-Sullivan. *The Church in the Modern World: "Gaudium et Spes" Then and Now.* Collegeville, MN: The Liturgical Press, 2014.

Lawler, Ronald, Donald W. Wuerl, and Thomas C. Lawler. *The Teaching of Christ: A Catholic Catechism for Adults.* Huntington, IN: Our Sunday Visitor, 1975, 5th ed. 2005.

Lee, Timothy B. "Entangling the Web." *New York Times*, August 3, 2006.

Leiber, Robert. "Pius XII." In *Stimmen der Zeit*. November 1958.

Pius XII Sagt. Frankfurt, 1959.

Leo XIII. *Aeterni patris*. Encyclical Letter. Vatican City: Vatican Press, 1879.

Leo XIII. *Amantissima voluntatis*. Apostolic Letter. Vatican City: Vatican Press, 1895.

Leo XIII. *Arcanum divinae*. Encyclical Letter. Vatican City: Vatican Press, 1880.

Leo XIII. *Diuturnum*. Encyclical Letter. Vatican City: Vatican Press, 1881.

Leo XIII. *Graves de communi re*. Encyclical Letter. Vatican City: Vatican Press, 1901.

Leo XIII. *Humanum genus*. Encyclical Letter. Vatican City: Vatican Press, 1884.

Leo XIII. *Immortale dei*. Encyclical Letter.Vatican City: Vatican Press, 1885.

Leo XIII. *Inscrutabili dei consilio*. Encyclical Letter.Vatican City: Vatican Press, 1878.

Leo XIII. *Libertas*. Encyclical Letter. Vatican City: Vatican Press, 1888.

Leo XIII. *Longinqua*. Encyclical Letter. Vatican City: Vatican Press, 1895.

Leo XIII. *Nihil nobis optatus*. Letter to Gaspar Decurtins. *Acta Sanctae Sedis* 26 (1893–1894): 74–76.

Leo XIII. *Praeclara gratulationis publicae*. Apostolic Letter. Vatican City: Vatican Press, 1894.

Leo XIII. *Quarto abrupto saeculo*. Encyclical Letter. Vatican City: Vatican Press, 1892.

Leo XIII. *Quod apostolici muneris*. Encyclical Letter. Vatican City: Vatican Press, 1878.

Leo XIII. *Quod multum*. Encyclical Letter. Vatican City: Vatican Press, 1886.

Leo XIII. *Rerum novarum*. Encyclical Letter. Vatican City: Vatican Press, 1891.

Leo XIII. *Sapientiae christianae*. Encyclical Letter. Vatican City: Vatican Press, 1890.

Leo XIII. *Testem benevolentiae nostrae*. Encyclical Letter.Vatican City: Vatican Press, 1899.

Lewis, V. B. "Aristotle, the Common Good, and Us." *Proceedings of the American Catholic Philosophical Association* 87 (2014): 69–88.

Lewis, V. B. "Democracy and Catholic Social Teaching: Continuity, Development, and Challenge." In *Studia Gilsoniana* 3 (2014): 167–190.

Liberatore, Matteo. *Institutiones Ethicae et Iuris Naturae*. 9th Edition. Prati: Ex officiana Giachetti filii et soc., 1887.

Liberatore, Matteo. "Razionalismo politico della rivoluzione italiana." In *Civiltà Cattolica*. 1850.

Llanos, Christopher. "Refugees or economic migrants: Catholic thought on the moral roots of distinction." In *Driven from Home: Protecting the Rights of Forced Migrants*. Edited by David Hollenback. Washington, DC: Georgetown University Press, 2010.

Lottin, Dom Odon. *Morale Fondamentale*. Paris: Desclée & Cie., 1954.

Madison, James. "The Structure of Government Must Furnish the Proper Checks and Balances Between the Different Departments." *New York Packet*, February 8, 1788, *Federalist*, no. 51.

Madison, James. "The Total Number of the House of Representatives." *New York Packet*, February 15, 1788. *Federalist*, No. 55.

Malcolm, Teresa. "The Lay Apostolate in a Clerical Church." *National Catholic Reporter*, September 17, 2004.

Malgeri, Francesco. "Leone XIII." In *Enciclopedia dei Papi*. Roma: Treccani, 2000.

Mandle, Jay R. *Globalization and the Poor*. Cambridge: Cambridge University Press, 2003.

Mannet, Pierre. *Beyond Radical Secularism*. Translated by Ralph C. Hancock. Introduction by Daniel J. Mahoney. South Bend, IN: St. Augustine's Press, 2016.

Manning, Cardinal. "To the Editor of the Times, 7th November 1874." In *A Free Church in a Free State? The Catholic Church, Italy, Germany, France 1864–1914*. Edited by Helmreich. Boston: D. C. Heath and Co., 1864.

Marquardt, Paul. "Subsidiarity and Sovereignty in the European Union." *Fordham International Law Journal* 18 (1994): 616.

Martin, Inés San. "Pope Francis Denies that Islam Is Violent." *Crux*, July 31, 2016.

Martin, Inés San. "Vatican Judge Says Cardinal-Critics of Pope Could Lose Red Hats." *Crux*, July 31, 2016.

Martina, Giancomo. "Curci, Carlo Maria." In *Dizionario Biografico delgi Italiani*. Roma: Treccani, 1985.

Martina, Giancomo. "Pius IX." In *Enciclopedia dei Papi*. Roma: Treccani, 2000.

Masnovo, Amato. *Il neo-tomismo in Italia*. Milano: Vita e Pensiero, 1923.

Mayo, Dambisa. *Dead Aid: Why Aid Is Not Working and How there Is a Better Way for Africa*. New York: Farrar, Straus and Giroux, 2009.

McAdams, John. *The New Class in Post-Industrial Society*. New York: Palgrave and Macmillan, 2015.

McCool, Gerald. *Nineteenth-Century Scholasticism*. New York: Fordham University Press, 1989.

Messner, Johannes. *Social Ethics: Natural Law in the Modern World*. St. Louis, MO: B. Herder Book Co., 1949.

Meuller, Franz H. "The Principle of Subsidiarity in the Christian Tradition." *The American Catholic Sociological Review* 4 (1943): 144.

Mich, Marvin L. "Commentary on *Mater et Magistra*." In *Modern Catholic Social Teaching*. Edited by Kenneth R. Himes, OFM. Washington, DC: Georgetown University Press, 2004.

Misner, Paul. *Social Catholicism in Europe: From the Onset of Industrialization to the First World War*. London: Darton, Longman and Todd, 1991.

Molony, John. *The Worker Question: A New Historical Perspective on "Rerum Novarum."* Dublin: Gill and Macmillan, 1991.

Montalembert, Comte. *L'Église libre dans l'état libre, discours prononcés au Congrès Catholique de Malines*. Paris: Ch. Douniol et Didier et Cie, 1863.

Moody, Joseph N. *Church and Society. Catholic Social and Political Thought and Movements, 1789–1950*. New York: Arts, Inc., 1953.

Mucci, Giandomenico. *Carlo Maria Curci. Fondatore della Civiltà Cattolica*. Rome: Edizioni Studium, 1988.

Murphy, Charles M. "Action for Justice as Constitutive of the Preaching of the Gospel: What Did the 1971 Synod Mean?" *Theological Studies* 44 (1983): 298–311.

Neuhaus, Richard. *Doing Well and Doing Good, the Challenge to the Christian Capitalist*. New York: Doubleday, 1992.

Neuhaus, Richard John. "The Pope, Liberty, and Capitalism: Essays on *Centesimus Annus*." *National Review* 34, no. 11 (June 24, 1991): 8–9.

Newman, John Henry. *An Essay on the Development of Christian Doctrine*. South Bend, IN: University of Notre Dame Press, 1994.

Newman, John Henry. "Divine Calls." In *Parochial and Plain Sermons*. San Francisco, Ignatius Press, 1987.

Norman, Edward. *The English Catholic Church in the Nineteenth Century*. Oxford: Clarendon Press, 1984.

Novak, Michael. *The Catholic Ethic and the Spirit of Capitalism*. New York: Free Press, 1993.

Novak, Michael. *The Spirit of Democratic Capitalism*. New York: Touchstone, 1982.

O'Brien, David J. and Thomas A. Shannon, eds. *Catholic Social Thought: The Documentary Heritage*. Maryknoll, NY: Orbis Books, 2010.

O'Connor, Flannery. Letter to Sister Mariella Gable, May 4, 1963. In *Flannery O'Connor: Collected Works*. Edited by Sally Fitzgerald. New York: The Library of America, n.d.

O'Connor, Flannery. *The Habit of Being*. New York: Farrar, Straus and Giroux, 1979.

Oliveira, Plinio Corrêa. *Nobility and Analogous Traditional Elites in the Allocutions of Pius XII*. Hamilton Press, 1993.

O'Neill, William R. and William C. Spohn. "Rights of Passage: The Ethics of Immigration and Refugee Policy." *Theological Studies* 59, no. 1 (1998): 84–106.

Pacepa, Ion M. and Ronald J. Rychlak. *Disinformation: Former Spy Chief Reveals Secret Strategies for Undermining Freedom, Attacking Religion and Promoting Terrorism*. WND Books, 2013.

Pagden, Anthony. *The Fall of Natural Man: The American Indian and the Origins of Comparative Ethnology*. Cambridge: Cambridge University Press, 1982.

Pakaluk, Catherine Ruth. "Dependence on God and Man: Toward a Catholic Constitution of Liberty." *Journal of Markets and Morality* 19, no. 2 (Fall 2016): 227–252.

Pakaluk, Catherine Ruth, Joseph Anthony Burke, and Andreas Widmer. "Solidarity and Job Creation: Substitutes or Compliments?" In *The Challenge of Charity: Freedom and Charity Working Together.* Edited by M. Schlag, J. A. Mercado, and J. E. Miller. Rome, Italy: MCE Books, 2015.

Pakaluk, Michael. "Is the Common Good of Political Society Limited and Instrumental?" *The Review of Metaphysics* 55 (September 2001): 57–94.

Partisi, Refah. *European Human Rights Report* 1, section 123 (2003).

Paul VI. "Address During the Last General Meeting of the Second Vatican Council." December 7, 1965.

Paul VI. "Address to the General Assembly of the United Nations." AAS 57 (1965).

Paul VI. "Address to the United Nations." October 5, 1965.

Paul VI. *Ecclesiam suam.* Encyclical Letter. Vatican City: Vatican Press, 1964.

Paul VI. *Evangelii nuntiandi.* Apostolic Exhortation. Vatican City: Vatican Press, 1975.

Paul VI. *Humanae vitae.* Encyclical Letter.Vatican City: Vatican Press, 1968.

Paul VI. *Letter to the 52nd Social Week at Brest.* In *L'homme et la révolution urbaine.* Lyon: *Chronique sociale,* 1965.

Paul VI. *Octogesima adveniens.* Encyclical Letter. Vatican City: Vatican Press, 1971.

Paul VI. *Populorum progressio.* Encyclical Letter.Vatican City: Vatican Press, 1967.

Pavan, Pietro. *The Place of Mater et Magistra in the Papal Social Teaching.* 1962. Quoted in Gerald Darring, *Pope Pius XII, 1939–1958.*

Percy, Anthony G. "Private Initiative, Entrepreneurship, and Business in the Teachings of Pius XII." In *Journal of Markets & Morality* 7 (2004): 7–25.

Pernice, Ingolf. "The Framework Revisited: Constitutional, Federal and Subsidiarity Issues." *Columbia Journal of European Law* 2 (1996): 403.

"The Peronist Pope." *The Economist,* July 9, 2015.

Pieper, Josef. *The Four Cardinal Virtues.* New York: Pantheon Books, 1959.

Pieper, Josef. *Justice.* New York: Pantheon Books, 1955.

Pius IX. *Nostis et nobiscum.* Encyclical Letter.Vatican City: Vatican Press, 1849.

Pius IX. *Quanta cura.* Encyclical Letter. Vatican City: Vatican Press, 1864.

Pius IX. *Qui pluribus.* Encyclical Letter. Vatican City: Vatican Press, 1864.

Pius X. *Il Fermo proposito.* Encyclical Letter. Vatican City: Vatican Press, 1905.

Pius X. *Notre charge apostolique.* AAS 2 (1910): 607–633.

Pius X. *Singulari quadam.* Encyclical Letter. Vatican City: Vatican Press, 1912.

Pius XI. *Acerba animi.* Encyclical Letter. Vatican City: Vatican Press, 1932.

Pius XI. *Casti connubii.* Encyclical Letter. Vatican City: Vatican Press, 1930.

Pius XI. Chirograph Letter to Cardinal Alfredo Ildefonso Schuster. April 26, 1931.

Pius XI. *Divini illius magistri.* Encyclical Letter.Vatican City: Vatican Press, 1929.

Pius XI. *Divini redemptoris.* Encyclical Letter.Vatican City: Vatican Press, 1937.

Pius XI. *Mit brennender sorge.* Encyclical Letter.Vatican City: Vatican Press, 1937.

Pius XI. *Nova impendet.* Encyclical Letter.Vatican City: Vatican Press, 1931.

Pius XI. *Quadragesimo anno.* Encyclical Letter.Vatican City: Vatican Press, 1931.

Pius XI. *Quas primas.* Encyclical Letter.Vatican City: Vatican Press, 1925.

Pius XI. *Studiorum ducem.* Encyclical Letter.Vatican City: Vatican Press, 1923.

Pius XI. *Ubi arcano dei consilio*. Encyclical Letter.Vatican City: Vatican Press, 1922.

Pius XII. "Address of His Holiness prepared for the delegates to the Catholic International Congress for Social Study (Fribourg Union) and Social Action (Saint Gall Union)" (June 3, 1950).

Pius XII. "Address on Guiding Principles of the Lay Apostolate to the Second World Congress of the Law Apostolate" (October 5, 1957).

Pius XII. "Address to 400 delegates to the Ninth International Congress of the International Union of Catholic Employers, assembled at the Vatican" (May 7, 1949).

Pius XII. "Address to the College of Cardinals on the Feast of St. Eugene" (June 2, 1947).

Pius XII. "Address to the Directors of the Associations for Large Families of Rome and Italy" (1958).

Pius XII. "Address to the Employees of the Bank of Naples" (June 20, 1948).

Pius XII. "Address of His Holiness to the delegates of the World Congress of Chambers of Commerce" (April 27, 1950).

Pius XII. "Address to Italian Catholic Association of Owner-Managers" (January 31, 1952).

Pius XII. "Address to the Members of the International Office of Work" (March 25, 1949).

Pius XII. "Address to the Personnel of the Bank of Italy" (April 25, 1950).

Pius XII. "Address to the Personnel of the Roman Electrical Society" (July 2, 1950).

Pius XII. "Address to World Congress" (April 27, 1950).

Pius XII. "Address to Young Members of Italian Catholic Action." *AAS* 40 (1948): 412.

Pius XII. "Allocution at the Beatification of Pius X." *AAS* 43 (1951): 475–476.

Pius XII. "The Anniversary of Rerum Novarum (June 1, 1941)." In *Major Addresses of Pope Pius XII*, vol. 1. Edited by Vincent Yzermans. St. Paul, MN: North Central, 1961.

Pius XII. *Auspicia quaedam*. Encyclical Letter. Vatican City: Vatican Press, 1948.

Pius XII. "Christmas Message (December 24, 1942)." *AAS* 35 (1942).

Pius XII. "Christmas Message." *AAS* 35 (1943).

Pius XII. *Communium interpretes dolorum*. Encyclical Letter. Vatican City: Vatican Press, 1945.

Pius XII. "Easter Sunday Homily (April 9, 1939)." In Reginald F. Walker. *Pius of Peace*. M. H. Hill and Son, 1946.

Pius XII. *Exsul familia nazarethana*. Apostolic Constitution.Vatican City: Vatican Press, 1952.

Pius XII. *Datis nuperrime*. Encyclical Letter. Vatican City: Vatican Press, 1956.

Pius XII. "Directive to the 18th Spanish Social Week at Seville." (May 14–20, 1956). In *The Social Teachings of Pope Pius XII: 1956*. Ed. Cyrill C. Clum. Oxford: The Catholic Social Guild, 1958.

Pius XII. "Discourse of His Holiness Pope Pius XII given at the Solemn Audience Granted to the Plenary Session of the Academy." In *Discourses of the Pope from Pius XI to John Paul II to the Pontifical Academy of the Sciences 1939–1986*. Vatican City: Pontifical Academy of Sciences, 1986.

Pius XII. "Discourse of His Holiness Pope Pius XII Given on 3 December 1939 at the Solemn Audience Granted to the Plenary Session of the Academy." In *Discourses of the Popes from Pius XI to John Paul II to the Pontifical Academy of the Sciences 1939–1986*. Vatican City: Vatican Press.

Pius XII. "Discourse to the International Congress of Social Studies" (June 3, 1950).

Pius XII. "Discourse to the Participants of the World Health Organization" (June 27, 1949).

Pius XII. "Discourse to the Representatives of the International Union of Catholic Employers Association" (May 7, 1949).

Pius XII. *Humani generis*. Encyclical Letter. Vatican City: Vatican Press, 1950.

Pius XII. *In multiplicibus curis*. Encyclical Letter. Vatican City: Vatican Press, 1948.

Pius XII. *Laetamur admodum*. Encyclical Letter. Vatican City: Vatican Press, 1956.

Pius XII. "*Radio Message La Solennità della Pentecoste*." (1941).

Pius XII. "Letter to Charles Flory." *AAS* 39, 1947.

Pius XII. *Luctuosissimi eventus*. Encyclical Letter. Vatican City: Vatican Press, 1956.

Pius XII. *Message Calling on Mankind to Aid the Poor and Showing the Road to True Salvation*. 1952.

Pius XII. "Message of 1 September 1944." In *AAS* 36, 1944.

Pius XII. *Mirabile illud*. Encyclical Letter. Vatican City: Vatican Press, 1950.

Pius XII. *Miranda prorsus*. Encyclical Letter. Vatican City: Vatican Press, 1957.

Pius XII. *Mystic corporis Christi*. Encyclical Letter. Vatican City: Vatican Press, 1957.

Pius XII. *Optatissima pax*. Encyclical Letter. Vatican City: Vatican Press, 1947.

Pius XII. *Quemadmodum*. Encyclical Letter. Vatican City: Vatican Press, 1946.

Pius XII. "Radio address to the German Catholic Congress, Bochum" (September 4, 1949).

Pius XII. "Radio Message for Pentecost." *AAS* 33 (1941).

Pius XII. "Radio Message *La Solennità della Pentecoste*." (1969).

Pius XII. *Sertum laetitiae*. Encyclical Letter. Vatican City: Vatican Press, 1939.

Pius XII. "Speech to ACLI." In *AAS* 37, 1945.

Pius XII. "Speech to Italian Workers." In *AAS* 35, 1943.

Pius XII. *Summi maeroris*. Encyclical Letter. Vatican City: Vatican Press, 1950.

Pius XII. *Summi pontificatus*. Encyclical Letter. Vatican City: Vatican Press, 1939.

Pius XII. "To Members of the Vatican Diplomatic Corps." In *The Social Teachings of Pope Pius XII: 1956*. Ed. Cyrill C. Clum. Oxford: The Catholic Social Guild, 1958.

Pius XII. "To Members of the Italian Water Works Society." In *The Social Teachings of Pope Pius XII: 1956*. Ed. Cyrill C. Clum. Oxford: The Catholic Social Guild, 1958.

Pius XII. "To Domestic Workers of Rome and Italy." In *The Social Teachings of Pope Pius XII: 1956*. Ed. Cyrill C. Clum. Oxford: The Catholic Social Guild, 1958.

Pius XII. "To the 77th Congress of German Catholics at Cologne." In *The Social Teachings of Pope Pius XII: 1956*. Ed. Cyrill C. Clum. Oxford: The Catholic Social Guild, 1958.

Pius XII, "To those in Power and Their Peoples" (August 24, 1939).

Plato. *Gorgias*. In *Platonis Opera, Vol. 3: Tetralogiam V–VII Continens*. Ed. Ioannes Burnet. Oxford: Oxford University Press, 1974.

Plato. *Laws*. In *Platonis Opera, Vol. 5: Tetralogiam IX Continens*. Ed. Ioannes Burnet. Oxford: Oxford University Press, 1922.

Plato. *Republic*. In *Platonis Opera, Vol. 4: Tetralogiam VIII Continens*. Ed. Ioannes Burnet. Oxford: Oxford University Press, 1922.

Pollard, John. *The Papacy in the Age of Totalitarianism, 1914–1958.* Oxford: Oxford University Press, 2014.

The Pontifical Academy of Sciences. Servant of God Pius XII (1939–1958). www .casinapioiv.va/content/accademia/en/magisterium/piusxii.html.

Pontifical Commission "Iustitia et Pax." "At the Service of the Human Community: An Ethical Approach to the International Debt Question." Vatican City: Vatican Polyglot Press, 1986.

Pontifical Council "Cor Unum." "Welcoming Christ in Refugees and Forcibly Displaced Persons: Pastoral Guidelines." Vatican City: Vatican Press, 2013.

Pontifical Council for Justice and Peace. *Compendium of the Social Doctrine of the Church.* Libreria Editrice Vaticana, 2004.

Pontifical Council for Justice and Peace. "Towards Reforming the International Financial and Monetary Systems in the Context of Global Public Authority" (2011).

Pontifical Council for the Pastoral Care of Migrants and Itinerant People. *Erga migrantes caritas Christi. AAS* 96 (2004): 772.

Poulat, Emile. *Eglise contre bourgeoisie. Introduction au devinir du catholicisme actuel.* Paris: Casterman, 1977.

Prümmer, Dominicus M., OP. *Manuale Theologiae Moralis.* Barcinone: Herder, 1961.

Pullman, Bernard. *The Atom in the History of Human Thought.* Oxford: Oxford University Press, 1998.

Ratzinger, Joseph Cardinal. *Church, Ecumenism and Politics.* New York: Crossroad, 1988.

Ratzinger, Joseph Cardinal. *God and the World: A Conversation with Peter Seewald.* San Francisco: Ignatius, 2002.

Ratzinger, Joseph Cardinal. *God is Near Us: The Eucharist, The Heart of Life.* San Francisco: Ignatius Press, 2003.

Ratzinger, Joseph Cardinal. *Principles of Catholic Theology. Building Stones for a Fundamental Theology.* San Francisco: Ignatius Press, 1987.

Ratzinger, Joseph Cardinal with Vittorio Messori. *The Ratzinger Report.* San Francisco: Ignatius Press, 1985.

Ratzinger, Joseph Cardinal. *Salt of the Earth: The Church at the End of the Millennium, An Interview with Peter Seewald.* San Francisco: Ignatius Press, 1997.

Ratzinger, Joseph Cardinal. *Truth and Tolerance: Christian Belief and World Religions.* San Francisco: Ignatius, 2004.

Ratzinger, Joseph Cardinal. *Values in a Time of Upheaval.* San Francisco, Ignatius Press, 2006.

Reid Jr., William Au. C. J., ed. *Peace in a Nuclear Age.* 1986.

Rhee, Helen. *Loving the Poor, Saving the Rich. Wealth, Poverty, and Early Christian Formation.* Grand Rapids: Baker Academic, 2012.

Richter, Aemilius Ludovicus and Aemilius Friedberg, eds. *Decretum Magistri Gratiani,* vol. 1, *Corpus Iuris Canonici.* Leipzig: B. Tauchnitz, 1879.

Riebling, Mark. *Church of Spies: The Pope's Secret War Against Hitler.* Basic Books, 2015.

Rommen, Heinrich. *The Natural Law.* Indianapolis: Liberty Fund, 1998.

Rommen, Heinrich. *The State in Catholic Thought.* St. Louis, MO: Herder, 1945.

Rosa, Gabriele. "L'Enciclica nella Corrispondenza del Vescovi con il Papa." In *L'Enciclica Rerum Novarum e il Suo Tempore.* Edited by Giovanni Antonazzi and Gabriele de Rosa. Rome: Edizioni di Storia e Letteratura, 1991.

Rosa, Gabriele. "L'orizzonte e il contest di un'enciclica." In *I tempi della Rerum Novarum*. Edited by Gabriele de Rosa. Roma: Instituto Luigi Sturzo, Rubbettino Editore, 2002.

Rosa, Gabriele. *Il movimento cattolico in Italia. Dalla restaurazione all'etá giolittiana*. Bari: Laterza, 1996.

Rosa, Gabriele. "Le Origini della 'Civiltà Cattolica.'" In *Civiltà Cattolica (1850–1945)*. Napoli: Landi, 1971.

Routhier, Gilles. "Finishing the Work Begun: The Trying Experience of the Third Period." In *History of Vatican II*, Vol. 5. Eds., Giuseppe Alberigo and Joseph Komonchak. Maryknoll, NY: Orbis/Leuven: Peters, 1995–2006.

Rychlak, Ronald J. *Hitler, the War, and the Pope*. Huntington, IN: Our Sunday Visitor Publishing Division, 2010.

Rychlak, Ronald J. *Righteous Gentiles: How Pius XII and the Catholic Church Saved Half a Million Jews From the Nazis*. Spence Publishing, 2005.

Rychlak, Ronald J. "Pius XII, John XXIII, and the Newly-Opened Archives." *Catalyst*. March 2007.

Safire, William. "On Language; Crony Capitalism." *New York Times*, February 1, 1998.

Scannone, Juan Carlos. *Quando il Popolo Diventa Teologo*. Bologna: EMI, 2016.

Scannone, Juan Carlos. *Teología de Liberación y Doctrina Social de la Iglesia*. Madrid: Cristiandad and Buenos Aires: Guadalupe, 1987.

Schall, James V. "Concerning the Ecological Path to Salvation." *Catholic World Report* (June 21, 2015).

Schasching, Johannes SJ. *Zeitgerecht-zeitberict: Nell-Breuning und die Sozialenzyklika Quadragesimo anno nach dem Vatikanischen Geheimarchiv*. Bornheim: Ketteler Verlag, 1994.

Schilling, Theodor. "Subsidiarity as a Rule and a Principle, or: Taking Subsidiarity Seriously." *Harvard Jean Monnet Working Paper* 10/95 (1995).

Schindler, David. *Heart of the World, Center of the Church*. Grand Rapids, MI: Wm. B. Eerdmans, 1996.

Schuck, Michael J. "Early Modern Roman Catholic Social Thought, 1740–1890." In *Modern Catholic Social Teaching: Commentaries & Interpretations*. Edited by Kenneth Himes. Washington, DC: Georgetown University Press, 2005.

Schumpeter, Joseph A. *History of Economic Analysis*. London: Allen & Unwin, 1954.

Scott, David and Mike Aquilina, eds. *Weapons of the Spirit: Selected Writings of Father John Hugo*. Huntington, IN: Our Sunday Visitor Publishing Division, 1997.

Schwalm, R. P. *Leçons de Philosophie sociale*. 2 volumes. Paris: Bloud & Cie., 1910.

Shadle, Matthew. "Twenty Years of Interpreting *Centesimus Annus* on the Economy." *Journal of Catholic Social Thought* 9 (2012): 171–191.

Shakespeare, William and Thomas Middleton. *The Life of Timon of Athens*. Edited by John Jowett. The Oxford Shakespeare. Oxford: Oxford University Press, 2004.

Shaw, Russell. *Abortion on Trial*. Dayton, OH: Pflaum Press, 1968.

Shaw, Russell. *American Church: The Remarkable Rise, Meteoric Fall, and Uncertain Future of Catholicism in America*. San Francisco: Ignatius Press, 2013.

Shaw, Russell. "Americanism: Then and Now." In *The Catholic World Report*. May 1995.

Shaw, Russell. *Catholic Laity in the Mission of the Church*. Vancouver, BC: Chartwell Press, 2013.

Shaw, Russell. "Laity in the Mission of the Church." *The Newman Rambler* 7 (2003): 3.

Shaw, Russell. *Ministry or Apostolate: What Should the Catholic Laity Be Doing?* Huntington, IN: Our Sunday Visitor Publishing, 2002.

Shaw, Russell. "On Clericalism." *Catholicity*, May 6, 2008.

Shaw, Russell. *To Hunt, To Shoot, To Entertain: Clericalism and the Catholic Laity*. San Francisco: Ignatius Press, 1993.

Shiller, Robert J. "Traders and Markey Makers." In *Finance and the Good Society*. Princeton, NJ: Princeton University Press, 2012.

Simon, Yves R. *Philosophy of Democratic Government*. Notre Dame, IN: University of Notre Dame Press, 1993.

Simon, Yves. "General Theory of Government." In *The Philosophy of Democratic Government*. Chicago: University of Chicago Press, 1951.

Skinner, Quentin. *The Foundations of Modern Political Thought*. Cambridge; New York: Cambridge University Press, 1978.

Skojec, Steve. "Pope: It Is the Communists Who Think Like Christians." *One Peter 5* (November 11, 2016).

Smit, Jan Olav. *Angelic Shepherd: The Life of Pope Pius XII*. New York: Dodd & Mead, 1950.

Smith, Adam. "Of the Principle Which Gives Occasion to the Division of Labour." In *An Inquiry into the Nature and Causes of the Wealth of Nations*. 1776.

Sniegocki, John. "The Social Ethics of John Paul II: A Critique of Neo Conservative Interpretations." *Horizons* 33 (2006): 24.

Spaemann, Robert. "Interview about Amoris Laetitia." *Catholic News Agency*, April 29, 2016.

Spahn, Martin and Thomas Meehan. "Catholic Congresses." In *The Catholic Encyclopedia*. New York: Robert Appleton Company, 1908.

Speiker, Manfred. "The Universal Destination of Goods: The Ethics of Property in the Theory of a Christian Society." *Journal of Markets & Morality* 8 (Fall 2005): 333–354.

Spencer, Philip. *Politics of Belief in Nineteenth-Century France: Lacordaire, Michon, Veuillot*. New York: Grove Press, 1954.

Stigler, George. "The Theory of Economic Regulation." *The Bell Journal of Economics and Management Science* 2, no. 1 (Spring 1971): 3–21.

Stiglitz, Joseph. "The Private Uses of Public Interests: Incentives and Institutions." *Journal of Economic and Management Science* 12, no. 2 (Spring 1998): 3–22.

Stiglitz, Joseph. *Globalization and Its Discontents*. New York: Norton, 2003.

Synod of Bishops. *De Iustitia in Mundo*. AAS 73 (1971): 924.

Tanner, Norman. "The Church in the World (Ecclesia ad Extra)." In *History of Vatican II*, vol. IV. Eds. Giuseppe Alberigo and Joseph A. Komonchak. Maryknoll, NJ: Orbis, 2003: 269–386.

Taparelli, Luigi. "Abbozzo del Progetto d'Ordinazione intorno agli Studii Supp." Archivio della *Civiltà Cattolica*.

Taparelli, Luigi. "Ordine sociale e commando diretto." In *Civiltà Cattolica*. 1850.

Taparelli, Luigi. "Osservazioni sugli Studii del Collegio Romano." 1827. Folder number 20 "Difesa della Scolastica." Archivio della *Civiltà Cattolica* (ACC).

Taparelli, Luigi. *Saggio theoretic di dritto natural appoggiato sul fatto*. 2 vols. Roma: Edizioni La Civiltà Cattolica, 1949.

Taparelli, Luigi. "Sulla Libertà di Associazione. Ai Siciliani." In De Rosa, *I Gesuiti in Sicilia e la rivoluzione del'48*. Rome: Edizioni di Storia et Letteratura, 1963.

Taparelli, Luigi. "Teorie sociali sull'insegnamento." In *Civiltà Cattolica*. 1850.

Tassello, Graziano and Luigi Favero, eds. *Chiesa e Mobilità Umana: Documenti della Santa Sede dal 1883 al 1983*. Rome: Centro Studi Emigrazione, 1985.

Taylor, A. J. P. *Bismarck: The Man and the Statesman*. New York: Knopf, 1955.

Taylor, Charles. "Irreducibly Social Goods." In *Philosophical Arguments*. Cambridge: Harvard University Press, 1995.

Thornton, John F. and Susan B. Varenne, eds. *The Essential Pope Benedict XVI: His Central Writings and Speeches*. San Francisco: Harper, 2007.

Tocqueville, Alexis. *Democracy in America*. Translated by Harvey C. Mansfield and Delbra Winthrop. Chicago: Chicago University Press, 2002.

Townsend, Tim. "U.S. Catholics mirror general public on views of inequality." Pew Research Center. March 27, 2014.

"Treaty on European Union (as amended by the Treaty of Lisbon)." Signed February 7, 1992.

Truman, Tom. *Catholic Action and Politics*. Melbourne: The Merlin Press, 1959.

Tucci, Roberto, SJ. "Introduction historique et doctrinale a la Constitution pastorale." In *L'Église dans le monde de ce temps: Constitution pastorale "Gaudium et spes."* Edited by Y. M. J. Congar, OP and M. Peuchmaurd, OP. Paris: Cerf, 1967.

Tucci, Roberto, SJ. "La vie de la communauté politique." In *L'Église dans le monde de ce temps: Constitution pastorale "Gaudium et spes."* Edited by Y. M. J. Congar, OP and M. Peuchmard, OP. Paris: Cerf, 1967.

Turkson, Peter Cardinal. "Subsidiarity in a Company." Speech, Venite Roundtable of Entrepreneurs, Bratislava, December 1, 2014.

Twomey, Gerald S. *The "Preferential Option for the Poor" in Catholic Social Thought from John XXIII to John Paul II*. Lewiston: Edwin Mellen Press, 2004.

United States Conference of Catholic Bishops. *Compendium of the Catechism of the Catholic Church*. Washington, DC: Libreria Editrice Vaticana, 2006.

United States Conference of Catholic Bishops. "Economic Justice for All: Pastoral Letter on Catholic Social Teaching and the U.S. Economy." In *Pastoral Letters of the United States Catholic Bishops*. Edited by Hugh J. Nolan. Washington, DC: National Conference of Catholic Bishops and United States Catholic Conference, 1989.

United States Conference of Catholic Bishops. *Forming Consciences for Faithful Citizenship: A Call to Political Responsibility from the Catholic Bishops of the United States*. Revised edition. Washington, DC: United States Conference of Catholic Bishops, 2015.

Vatican I. *Dei filius*. Dogmatic Constitution. 1870.

Vatican II. *Apostolicam actuositatem*. Decree on the Apostolate of the Laity. Vatican City: Vatican Press, 1965.

Vatican II. *Christus Dominus*. Decree on the Pastoral Office of Bishops. Vatican City: Vatican Press, 1965.

Vatican II. *Dei verbum*. Dogmatic Constitution on Divine Revelation. Vatican City: Vatican Press, 1965.

Vatican II. *Dignitatis humanae*. Declaration on Religious Freedom. Vatican City: Vatican Press, 1965.

Vatican II. *Gaudium et spes*. Pastoral Constitution on the Church in the Modern World. Vatican City: Vatican Press: 1965.

Vatican II. *Gravissimum educationis*. Declaration. Vatican City: Vatican Press, 1965.

Vatican II. *Lumen gentium*. Dogmatic Constitution on the Church. Vatican City: Vatican Press, 1964.

Vatican II. "Decree of the Apostolate of the Laity of Vatican II, with Commentary by John B. Sheerin, C.S.P." Glenn Rock, NJ: Paulist Press, 1966.

Vidler, Alec R. *A Century of Social Catholicism, 1820–1920*. London: S.P.C.K., 1964.

Viganò, Carlo Maria. "Letter from August 25, 2018." www.lifesitenews.com/news/for mer-us-nuncio-pope-francis-knew-of-mccarricks-misdeeds-repealed-sanction.

Viganò, Carlo Maria. "Letter from September 27, 2018." www.lifesitenews.com/news/ breaking-vigano-releases-new-testimony-responding-to-popes-silence-on-mccar.

Vilanova, Evangelista. "The Intersession (1963–1964)." In *History of Vatican II*, vol. 3: *The Mature Council Second Period and Intersession. September 1963–September 1964*. Ed. Giuseppe Alberigo and Joseph A. Komonchak. Maryknoll, NY: Orbis, 2000.

Villeneuve-Bargemont, Alban. *Economie politique chétienne ou recherches sur la nature et les causes du pauperisme en France et en Europe et sur les moyens de le soulager et de le prévenir*. Paris: Paulin, Libraire-Éditeur, 1834.

Vischer, Robert K. "Subsidiarity as a Principle of Governance: Beyond Devolution." *Indiana Law Review* 35 (2001): 103.

Vitoria, Francisco. *Obras de Francisco de Vitoria: Relecciones teologicas*. Edited and translated by Teogilo Urdanoz. Madrid: Biblioteca de Autores Cristianos, 1960.

Vitoria, Francisco. *"De indis et De iure belli relectiones: Being parts of the 'relectiones theologicae XII.'"* Edited by Ernest Nys. Washington: The Carnegie Institution of Washington, 1917.

Vitoria, Francisco. *Relecciones de Indis: o Libertad de los Indios*. Madrid: Espasa-Calpe, 1975.

Vitoria, Francisco. *Vitoria: Political Writings*. Edited and translated by Antony Pagden and Jeremy Lawrance. Cambridge: Cambridge University Press, 1991.

Von Nell-Breuning, Oswald, SJ. "The Catholic Social Movement: Historical Aspects." In *Official Catholic Social Teaching*. Edited by Charles E. Curran and Richard A. McCormick, SJ. New York: Paulist Press, 1968.

Von Nell-Breuning, Oswald, SJ. *Commentary on the Documents of Vatican II, vol. 5: Pastoral Constitution of the Church in the Modern World*. Edited by Herbert Vorgrimler. New York: Herder and Herder, 1969.

Von Nell-Breuning, Oswald, SJ. "Der Konigswinterer Kreis und sein Anteil an *Quadragesimo Anno Soziale Verantwortung*." *Festschrift fur Goetz Briefs*. Berlin, 1968.

Von Nell-Breuning, Oswald, SJ. *Die Soziale Enzyklika*. Cologne: Katholische Tat-Verlag, 1932.

Von Nell-Breuning, Oswald, SJ. "Documentation: The Drafting of Quadragesimo Anno." *Crisis Magazine*, February 1, 1985. www.crisismagazine.com/1985/docu mentation-the-drafting-of-quadragesimo-anno.

Von Nell-Breuning, Oswald, SJ. "The Drafting of *Quadragesimo Anno*." In *Readings in Moral Theology, No. 5: Official Catholic Social Teaching*. Edited by Charles E. Curran and Richard A. McCormick, SJ. New York: Paulist Press, 1986.

Von Nell-Breuning, Oswald, SJ. *Reorganization of the Social Economy: The Social Encyclical Developed and Explained*. English edition prepared by Bernard W. Dempsey, SJ. New York: The Bruce Publishing Company, 1936.

Von Nell-Breuning, Oswald, SJ. "Some Reflections on Mater et Magistra." *Review of Social Economy* 20 (Fall 1962).

Von Nell-Breuning, Oswald, SJ. *Wie sozial ist die Kirch?* Dusseldorf: Patmos, 1972.

Walker, Reginald F. *Pius of Peace: A Study of the Pacific Work of His Holiness Pope Pius XII in the World War 1939–1945*. M. H. Gill and Son, Limited, 1946.

Weddell, Sherry A. *Forming Intentional Disciples: The Path to Knowing and Following Jesus Christ*. Huntington, IN: Our Sunday Visitor, 2012.

White, Stephen P. *Red, White, Blue and Catholic*. Liguori, MO: Liguori Publications, 2016.

Wiarda, Howard J. *Corporatism and Comparative Politics*. New York: W. E. Sharpe, 1997.

Will, George F. "Pope Francis's Fact-free Flamboyance." *Washington Post*, September 18, 2015.

Wright, John J. *National Patriotism in Papal Teaching*. Westminster, MD: Newman Bookshop, 1943.

Wright, Terence C. *Dorothy Day: An Introduction to Her Life and Thought*. San Francisco: Ignatius Press, 2018.

Zieba, Maciej. *Papal Economics*. Wilmington, DE: ISI Books, 2016.

Index of Names and Subjects

Financial Crisis of 2008, 339, 340, 343
Finnis, John, 7, 11–33, 77, 94, 95, 96, 101, 245,
   246, 257, 259, 261, 262, 270, 271, 273, 274,
   275, 279, 288, 316–344, 348, 368, 384,
   423, 547, 548–584
First Council of Nicaea, 444
First Principle
   Inviolability of private property as a, 269, 274,
      438, 457, 461, 463
   Liberty as a, 461
   Non-absolute first principles, 269
   of the whole ethical and social order,
      268, 297
   Universal Destination as a, 269
Fitzpatrick, John Bernard (Bishop), 45
Flannery, Kevin L., SJ, 365–386
France, 1, 33, 35–40, 44, 48, 106, 193, 224, 230,
   327, 519, 546, 559
Francis of Assisi, Saint, 220
Francis, Pope, i, 106, 217, 341, 343, 383, 388,
   469, 486, 487, 495, 503, 504, 571, 583
French Social Week, 143, 251, 254
Friedman, Milton, 180, 181
Friedman, Rose, 180, 181
Friendship
   as a basic good, 244, 246, 440, 478
   Civic, 393
   with God, 306, 393
   with the poor, 298, 478
Fulfillment, 2, 12, 61, 75, 79, 146, 184, 237, 238,
   309, 391, 392, 394, 359, 402, 523, 528
   of God's plan, 167
   of Groups, 180
   heavenly, 306
Fundamentalism, 222, 227

Galileo, 127
General Assembly of Catholic Societies, 39
Gerken, John D., 302
German Catholic Conference, 116
German Catholic Congress, 40
Germany, 1, 35, 90, 108–109, 112, 139, 193, 224, 253
Gerson, Michael, 489, 500
The logic of gift, 394–396, 397, 399, 403, 404,
   407, 410, 411, 413
Gioberti, Vincenzo, 40, 41
Glendon, Mary Ann, 138, 368
Globalization, 144, 316–344, 414
Goering, Hermann, 192
Government
   Abuse of power, 360–364

Action, 345
Corruption, 41, 43, 60, 297, 365, 405, 408,
   422, 492, 493
Failure, 358, 359
Intervention, 107, 345, 348, 359
Limits on, 154, 349, 350, 351–360
Limits on (Limited), 350
Role of, 405–406, 421, 425
Trust in, 345–364
Great Depression, 90
Greed, 70, 80, 82–84, 88, 159, 219, 356, 384, 389,
   398, 411, 438
Gregg, Samuel, 90–107, 175
Gregory I, Pope, 387
Gregory the Great, Saint, 275
Gregory XVI, 40, 42, 545
Grisez, Germain, 12, 300, 301, 310, 314, 499,
   502, 559, 577
Gundlach, Gustav, 143, 250, 518
Guild, 16, 37, 72, 86–88, 100, 102, 103

Hammel, Jacques Father, 230
Handmaid Metaphor, 19
Hannon, Phillip Archbishop, 150
Haubtmann, Pierre, 149, 150
Hayek, F. A., 173, 434
Healthcare, 194, 201, 521, 544, 573
Hegel, G. W. F., 50, 106, 583
Heisenberg, Werner, 127
Hellenization, 213–214
Henry VIII, King, 207, 208
Hierarchy of the Catholic Church
   Apostolate of the, 303
   Cooperation between laity and, 301
Historicism, 200, 213–214
Hitler, Adolf, 111, 113, 191, 192, 193
Hittinger, Russell, 56, 138, 235, 423, 426
Homosexuality, 218, 227, 229, 491, 521
Hugo, Father John, 484, 485
Human
   Action, 59, 123, 170, 177, 386
   Capital, 363, 446
   Development, 154, 156, 160, 251, 395,
      399–403, 410, 411, 575. *see also* integral
      human development
   Dignity, 4, 13, 77–80, 133, 149, 171, 190, 204,
      205, 207, 211, 223, 236, 239, 307, 321, 348,
      355, 419, 420, 422, 428, 471, 478,
      487–488, 490, 496, 502, 513, 515, 534,
      573, 575, 578
Ecology, 176, 212

Index of Ecclesiastical Texts

Lightning Source UK Ltd.
Milton Keynes UK
UKHW020006280821
389610UK00002B/356